DATE DUE			

URBAN LIFE

URBAN LIFE

THE SOCIOLOGY OF CITIES AND URBAN SOCIETY

Albert N. Cousins
Cleveland State University

Hans Nagpaul
Cleveland State University

John Wiley & Sons
New York   Chichester   Brisbane   Toronto

Text and Cover Design by Laura C. Ierardi

Library of Congress Cataloging in Publication Data

Cousins, Albert N   1919–
  Urban life.

  Includes bibliographies and index.
  1. Sociology, Urban. 2. Urbanization. 3. Urbanization—United States. 4. City and town life.
5. City and town life—United States. I. Nagpaul,
Hans, joint author. II. Title.
HT151.C65   301.36′3′0973   78-14427
ISBN 0-471-03026-0

Printed in the United States of America

10 9 8 7 6 5 4 3 2 1

FOR ROSE D. COUSINS

PREFACE

Urban Life originated from our years of experience attempting to teach college students how to understand their social surroundings. Although most of these students have been residents of greater Cleveland, they have varied a good deal as to their place in that populous community. They have been the grandchildren of European immigrants; inner-city blacks newly arrived from the south or mobile blacks from the suburbs; young men and women opting for careers in law, medicine, nursing, social work, engineering, education, and business; political activists angry with the establishment; fledgling politicos on the verge of elective office; some Puerto Rican Americans; a few Junior Leaguers; many Vietnam veterans; and occasionally a central European freedom fighter, a repatriate Israeli, or a Cuban refugee. Our students have been the inhabitants of Cleveland's urban villages, of neighborhoods split by expressways or razed for urban renewal, of racial ghettoes, sequestered suburbs, industrial satellites, the polymorphous fringe, and the exurbia of Portage, Medina, and Geauga counties. Not in spite of but precisely because of their differences, they have all been participants in urban America no less than in metropolitan Cleveland.

The thousands of young men and women we have taught have been concerned with comprehending the often perplexing and always changing circumstances of their lives. The more articulate of them have repeatedly asked the questions that their urban society poses:

Is the governmentally fragmented metropolis an anachronism?

Does urbanization necessarily produce more crime?

Can a nation of big industrial cities prevent the destruction of the environment?

What population shifts accompany the growth of cities in the underdeveloped agrarian regions as compared to our own country?

After declining so sharply in one city after another at least in many parts of the United States, has the central business district any further promise?

How may the racial tensions which have rocked our largest metropolitan areas in recent years best be eased?

Such questions pertain to the social problems that college students are aware of from their own background as well as from their expectations of leadership in public affairs in the future.

Aside from voicing pragmatic concerns, many students have also convinced us of their theoretical, philosophical, and aesthetic interest in urban life. The questions that arise on these scores have a different ring to them:

Does suburbanization invariably lead to a stodgy, uniform materialism?

Must the modern city foresake the natural beauty of the countryside as well as the created beauty of the pre-industrial religious and cultural center?

Is urban man simply an atom devoid of deep personal ties and energized only by the mass around him?

In fact, despite the surface brilliance of science, technology, and public administration, has not urbanization been a regrettable choice from the very beginning, and was not Jefferson right in condemning cities for cunning crassness always, and terroristic mobs in the end?

It would be claiming too much to say that this text satisfactorily answers all of these questions. Many are unanswerable at present, or at best invite rumination. Yet it would be misleading to say that *Urban Life* contains only inconclusive, speculative material. Far from that.

Urban Life was designed to provide a relatively synoptic but thorough coverage of the field of urban sociology today, with reference to the contemporary American city and to modern American urban society in particular. In the successive sections of the text, we present: (1) an overview of world urbanization at the present time; (2) the 6000-year history of cities; (3) the various types of analysis applied to urban phenomena; (4) the exercise of political and economic power in the city; (5) urban institutions; (6) the city's social problems; and (7) urban planning for cities, regions, and whole nations. Chapter 1 furnishes a more detailed introduction to the book's contents than we think appropriate here in the preface. At this point, we wish to say merely that our overriding intention in developing *Urban Life* was to communicate the vast literature on the subject in a manner that would serve the interests of the student and the needs of the instructor.

In writing this book we have relied on a variety of disciplines although the writings of sociologists have been most prominent. Moreover, we have attempted to include fitting references to the old masters of urban sociology such as Simmel, Marx, Weber, Wirth, the Lynds, and Burgess and Park, no less than the new masters like Firey, Gans, Hauser, Sjoberg, Davis, and Hawley. We hope we have not inadvertently neglected ideas and points of view which instructors deem necessary to a full and balanced treatment. Errors of fact as well as of interpretation are of course our own.

For patient clerical work we thank Patricia Natale, the twins Patsy and Peggy Congdon, Patti Martin, and Annie Wade. The library staff of Cleveland State University could not have been more cooperative. The expert judgment and skills of Richard Baker, Laura Ierardi, Stella Kupferberg, and Rosie Hirsch, representing John Wiley & Sons, were indispensable to this volume. The senior author wishes to acknowledge a sabbatical year at the London School of Economics and extensive professional travel in Europe in conjunction with that as most stimulating, and the junior author his three years of service with the Indian National Planning Commission in Delhi. We have labored to keep our international perspective properly subordinated to the American urban experience.

Albert N. Cousins
Hans Nagpaul

CONTENTS

PART ONE
INTRODUCTION TO THE STUDY OF URBAN LIFE
1

CHAPTER 1
THE STUDY OF URBAN LIFE
The Plan of the Text   The Urban Trend   The Great City   The
Urban Concept   The Urban Way of Life   Inadequacies of
Urban Life   Constructive Urbanism   The Social Sciences and the Study
of Urban Life   Conclusion   For Further Reading
3

PART TWO
THE HISTORICAL DEVELOPMENT OF CITIES
23

CHAPTER 2
URBANISM AND CIVILIZATION
The Urban Revolution   The Rise of Cities   Cities of the Classical
World   Conclusion   For Further Reading
25

CHAPTER 3
PREINDUSTRIAL URBANIZATION
The Preindustrial City   The Renewal of European Cities   Preindustrial Cities
Outside Europe   Preindustrial Cities as Cultural Centers   From Preindustrial
to Industrial Urbanism   Conclusion   For Further Reading
45

CHAPTER 4
INDUSTRIAL URBANIZATION
The Transition from the Preindustrial City in England   English Industrial-
Urban Society   The Growth of Cities in America   Metropolitan Regionalism
in the United States   Megalopolitan America   Conclusion
For Further Reading
61

PART THREE
THEORETICAL APPROACHES
89

CHAPTER 5
THE RURAL AND URBAN AS CONTRASTING TYPES

The Rural-Urban Typological Dichotomy   Urban Life as a Unique Social Type   Validity of the Distinction between "Rural" and "Urban"   Informal Interaction and Voluntary Associations as Tests of Urban Typology   The Suburban Style of Life   Modernization and Urban Development   Conclusion   For Further Reading
91

CHAPTER 6
URBAN ECOLOGY

The Ecological Approach   Spatial Theories   Ecological Processes and Structures   Conclusion   For Further Reading
113

CHAPTER 7
THE DEMOGRAPHIC PERSPECTIVE

Population Distribution   Composition   Growth   The Vital Processes of Fertility and Mortality   Migration   Sociocultural Characteristics   A Note on Social-Area Analysis   Conclusion   For Further Reading
139

PART FOUR
THE ORGANIZATION OF POWER
167

CHAPTER 8
URBAN GOVERNMENT AND POLITICS

Urban Government   The Background of American Local Government   Types of Urban Government in the United States   The Merits and Shortcomings of American Local Government   Governmental Fragmentation in the Metropolitan Area   Reform and Reorganization   Relations with State and Local Government   Interest Groups and Political Parties   Urban Power Structures   Conclusion   For Further Reading
169

CHAPTER 9
THE URBAN ECONOMY
The City and the Larger Economy   The Metropolitan Economy   Business and
Industry   The Protection of Labor and the Consumer   Municipal
Finance   Conclusion   For Further Reading
203

CHAPTER 10
SOCIAL STRATIFICATION
Stratification in Principle   Urbanization and Stratification   Stratification in
Cities at Present   The Elements of Modern Urban Stratification   Social
Mobility   Class Consciousness and Conflict   Conclusion   For Further
Reading
233

CHAPTER 11
THE MASS MEDIA
The Organization of the Media   Media Impact   Advertising and Public
Relations   The Public Interest   Conclusion   For Further Reading
259

PART FIVE
URBAN SOCIAL AND CULTURAL SYSTEMS
281

CHAPTER 12
THE SUBURBAN COMMUNITY
The Growth of Suburbia   The Residential Suburb and Its Demographic
Characteristics   The Ecology of Suburbia: Residential Suburbs and Industrial
Satellites   The Suburban Way of Life   Suburbia—Still Further
Differentiation   America's Suburbs: A Look Ahead   Conclusion   For
Further Reading
283

CHAPTER 13
KINSHIP IN THE CITY
Urbanization and the Atomization of the Family   The Family in Transition:
Atomization in the Developing Countries   The Atomistic Urban Family and Its
Other Correlates   The Kin Network   Urban Youth   Urban Kinship and

CONTENTS

xiii

Aging   Women in the Urban Family   The Conjugal Family and Its
Psychosocial Implications   Other Family Forms   Conclusion   For Further
Reading
297

CHAPTER 14
RELIGION AS AN INSTITUTIONAL SYSTEM
Religion in the Urban Milieu   Urbanization and Secularism   The Protestant
Background of the Industrial City   Social Change and the Church   The Urban
Church Today   Conclusion   For Further Reading
323

CHAPTER 15
URBAN EDUCATION
The Purposes of Education   The Schools and Cleavages in the Urban
Community   Educating the Economically Disadvantaged   The Urban
University   Other Trends and Problems   Conclusion   For Further
Reading
343

CHAPTER 16
ART AND LEISURE
Architectural Beauty   Museums and Theatres   Patronage and the Higher
Arts   Recreation and Entertainment   Leisure in Postindustrial
Society   Mass Culture   Conclusion   For Further Reading
365

PART SIX
URBAN SOCIAL PROBLEMS
389

CHAPTER 17
DEVIANCE AND LAW ENFORCEMENT
Urbanization and Deviance   Urban Sources of Deviance   Crime in
the City   Coping with Crime in Urban America   Conclusion   For Further
Reading
391

CHAPTER 18
URBAN MINORITIES AND POVERTY
The Ethnic Factor in Urban Life   The Urban Poor   Poverty in American
Cities   Combatting Poverty   Civil Rights and the
Disadvantaged   Conclusion   For Further Reading
421

CHAPTER 19
SOCIAL WELFARE AND THE ADMINISTRATION OF HEALTH
The Development of Welfare   The Welfare Ideal   Social Security Health
Services   Family Planning   The Future of Welfare in
America   Conclusion   For Further Reading
451

CHAPTER 20
HOUSING, TRANSPORTATION, AND THE ENVIRONMENT
Housing, Slums, and Urban Renewal   Transportation   Ecological
Impairment   Conclusion   For Further Reading
477

PART SEVEN
TOWARD TOMORROW'S CITY
513

CHAPTER 21
URBAN DESIGN AND PLANNING
Planning the Preindustrial City   The Industrial City and the Urban
Planner   Contemporary Urban Design and Planning   Conclusion   For
Further Reading
515

CHAPTER 22
URBANIZATION AND URBAN PLANNING IN
UNDERDEVELOPED AREAS
Urbanization in the Newly Developing Countries   The Effects of Urbanization in
Underdeveloped Areas   Urban Planning in the Newly Developing
Countries   Urban Planning in Communist Countries   International
Organization and Urban Planning   Conclusion   For Further Reading
451

CONTENTS

XV

CHAPTER 23
NATIONAL PLANNING AND THE FUTURE OF URBAN SOCIETY

National Urban Planning in the United States   Antiurban Bias   A New
Prourbanism in America?   The Future of National Planning   University,
Private, and Public Urban Research   Urban Philosophers: The Contemporary
Utopians   Conclusion   For Further Reading

561

PHOTO CREDITS
589

NAME INDEX
593

SUBJECT INDEX
603

PART ONE

INTRODUCTION TO THE STUDY OF URBAN LIFE

Crowded Martin Place, heart of Sydney, Australia's central business district.
Source: Australian News and Information Bureau, *Australia: A Portfolio* (Adelaide, Griffin Press, 1966), p. 4.

CHAPTER 1

THE STUDY OF URBAN LIFE

The importance of studying urban life lies not only in the many cities and urban societies that exist today, but also in their increasing significance for the future.

Never before have so many people lived in cities: more than 25 percent of the entire human race! Never before have cities been as large as they are today: at least three cities have more than 10 million inhabitants each! And never before has the trend toward more urbanization been as strong as it is now: not just in North America and Europe, but in Asia, Latin America, Africa, and in the Middle East too!

The urban age that is now at hand virtually all around the world may be said to signify the spread of a type of society different from what preceded it. Urban society differs from rural society, and urban man is of a different order from the kinds of personality associated with the communities and cultures of the past. As a matter of fact, so rapidly and decisively has the modern urban age materialized that knowledge of it has failed to keep up with events. The result is that in many ways we fail to understand our social system, or ourselves as participants in it.

Also, the city and urban society as a whole reveal serious weaknesses. These include social problems like crime, poverty, and racial tensions; environmental damage; governmental shortcomings; and even the insolvency of some of our largest metropolitan communities. Unless these weaknesses are overcome, they will probably intensify. Capably dealt with though, the challenge of the "urban problem"—or "urban crisis" as some insist on calling it—can lead to a level of living possibly superior to any in the past.

For all these reasons, the study of urban life has unusual value today.

THE PLAN OF THE TEXT

This book attempts to present the basic sociology of modern urban life, particularly in the United States. Some comparative material from other societies and other periods is used in certain places, but writing this volume with the American college student in mind, we have paid attention principally to the contemporary American scene.

This introductory chapter, which presents the major themes of the text, makes up *Part One*.

Part Two reviews the history of cities from their origins 6000 years ago to our present-day Boston-to-Washington megalopolis ("Bowash"), which epitomizes the urbanism of the postindustrial variety. Such historical study clearly reveals both the progressive and the destructive forces of urbanization.

What interpretations have been developed to explain urban life? How are cities and their inhabitants to be understood? *Part Three* is devoted to the outstanding perspectives, namely, the typological, ecological, and demographic, used by sociologists and kindred scholars to describe and analyze urban phenomena.[1] This material is meant to inform the reader of the various schools of thought embodied in the vast literature on the sociology of urban experience.

The *Fourth* and *Fifth Parts* of the text are closely related to each other. Both pertain to the urban social structure. These two sections of the text differ though in that the first deals with the power elements in urban government, the urban economy, social stratification, and the media of mass communication. The other concentrates on social and cultural systems,

[1] A comparable schema is to be found in Paul Wheatley, "The Concept of Urbanism," in Peter J. Ucko, Ruth Tringham, and G. W. Dimbleby, eds., *Man, Settlement and Urbanism* (London: Gerald Duckworth, 1972), pp. 601–37. Wheatley proposes five approaches, none of them mutually exclusive of the others: (1) ideal-type constructs (rural-urban); (2) ecological theories; (3) trait-complexes (psychosocial characteristics); (4) cities as centers of dominance (functional types); and (5) the expedential (demographic) approach.

specifically kinship, religion, education, and the aesthetic institutions of the urban world as well as the suburban type of community so characteristic today.

In his book *The Sociological Tradition,* Robert Nisbet recently reminded us that "the city . . . forms the context of most sociological propositions relating to disorganization, alienation, and mental isolation—all stigmata of loss of community and membership."[2] Certain exceptions aside, the fact remains that various social pathologies—crime, relative deprivation, emotional illness, and environmental damage—are all thought to be definitely associated with the urban milieu. The scope of these unfortunate conditions, their causes, and also the current efforts being made to remedy them comprise the focus of *Part Six.*

Finally at the end of the text in *Part Seven,* we develop the outlines of city planning and urban policy taking shape in the United States and other countries today. Urbanization is one of the fundamental processes of society at the present time everywhere, and planning for its further outcome is also going on practically all around the globe, including the underdeveloped regions of the Eastern and Western hemispheres.

THE URBAN TREND

The concentration of people in urban settlements is greater today than at any previous time in the history of the world. In 1800, scarcely 22 million persons lived in cities of at least 20,000 in size. But in 1950, fully half a billion did, and they made up one-fifth of the world's entire population. By 1970, the comparable figure had risen to 800 million and now included upwards of a fourth of the total population of the planet. (The reader should observe that United Nations demographers use 20,000 as their base line, while the nearest U.S. Census Bureau figure is 25,000. This prevents strict comparability but does not greatly obscure historical trends toward urbanization affecting the United States and the rest of the world.)

The rapidity of urbanization, which accelerated sharply after 1800, will continue to be swift "for some time to come," as one authoritative United Nations report recently phrased it.[3] Table 1-1 conveys that progression very graphically. In the period from 1800 to 1850, the number of people in communities of at least 20,000 rose by more than 80 percent. That pace was outstripped in the half century from 1850 to 1900, when the rate climbed to 114 percent. It was exceeded again in the period from 1900 to 1950, when the world's rate of urbanization reached 116 percent. The increase in urban pop-

[2] (New York: Basic Books, 1966), p. 28.

[3] Bureau of Social Affairs, *Report on the World Social Situation* (New York: United Nations, 1957), p. 114.

TABLE 1-1 Approximate Urban Population (20,000 and over) as a Percentage of Total World Population: 1800–1960 and as Estimated to 2000

YEAR	PERCENTAGE WORLD POPULATION URBAN
2000	38
1980	31
1960	25
1950	21
1940	19
1930	16
1920	14
1900	9
1850	4
1800	2

Sources: "Growth of the World's Urban and Rural Population, 1920–2000" *International Social Development Review,* No. 1 (New York: United Nations, 1969), p. 12. See also W. Parker Frisbie, "The Scale and Growth of World Urbanization," in John Walton and Donald E. Carns, eds., *Cities in Change* (Boston: Allyn & Bacon, 1977), 2nd ed., pp. 44–58.

ulation anticipated by the year 2000 means a rate of 81 percent during the second half of the twentieth century, but even this will be greater than the figure for the 50 years from 1800 to 1850.[4] By 1980, the number of persons living in communities of at least 20,000 is expected to rise to 1.3 billion, and to exceed even that in the year 2000, when one person out of every three on earth will be the inhabitant of a place having no fewer than 20,000 residents.

In line with this general trend, the more urbanized nations at present will go on to achieve still higher levels of urbanization. As one of the most heavily urbanized countries, the United States is expected to give leadership to the overall movement that is going on. According to Table 1-2, the urban trend has been fairly steady in the United States since 1920 with regard to: (1) the percentage of the total population in dense areas; (2) the number of places of unusual size; and (3) the aggregate number of persons in urban places. By the end of the twentieth century, considerably more than the three-fourths of the American population residing in places of at least 25,000 in 1970 will be so situated. In addition, a still larger part of America's future urban population will live in metropolitan communities although the growth of these super-concentrations will not be the same from one region to the

[4] These percentages are calculated from data derived from several sources: Kingsley Davis and Hilda Hertz, "Patterns of World Urbanization for 1800–1950," ibid., Table 1, p. 114; Homer Hoyt, *World Urbanization* (Washington, D.C.: Urban Land Institute, 1962), Table 3, p. 31; and International Social Development Review, *Growth of the World's Urban and Rural Population: 1920–2000* (New York: United Nations, 1969), Table 32, p. 59.

TABLE 1-2 Urbanization in the United States: 1910–1970, by Percentage of Population; Places of 100,000 or More and 25,000 or More; and Total Population

	1910	1920	1930	1940	1950 [a]	1960	1970
Percentage of Population:							
urban	45.7	51.2	56.2	56.5	64.0	69.9	73.5
rural	54.3	48.8	43.8	43.5	36.0	30.1	26.5
Number of Places of:							
100,000 or more	50	68	93	91	106	132	156
25,000 or more	228	287	376	411	484	765	916
Population (1000):							
urban	41,999	54,158	68,955	74,424	96,468	125,269	149,325
rural	49,973	51,553	53,820	57,246	54,230	54,054	53,887

Source: U.S. Bureau of the Census, *Statistical Abstract of the United States: 1971* (92nd edition), (Washington, D.C.: Government Printing Office, 1971), Table 17, p.17.

[a] Current urban definition used for data beginning in 1950.

next, and the very largest of them will probably not grow as fast as will the more moderate-size metropolitan areas.[5]

As for the regions of the world that are less urban at present, notably Africa and South Asia, the expansion of their urban population will proceed at an even more rapid rate than that of the already extensively urbanized areas of North America and Western Europe. Still, the final level of popula-

TABLE 1-3 Approximate Urban Population (20,000 and over) as a Percengage of Total Population in Major Areas of the World, 1920–1960; 1980 and 2000 (rough estimates)

MAJOR AREA	1920	1930	1940	1950	1960	1980	2000
Europe (ex USSR)	32	35	37	38	41	49	55
Northern America	38	43	45	50	57	67	71
East Asia	7	10	13	15	20	26	33
South Asia	6	7	8	11	14	19	26
Soviet Union	10	13	24	28	36	51	63
Latin America	14	17	19	25	32	43	53
Africa	5	6	7	10	13	20	28
Oceania	34	35	38	42	50	56	60

Source: "Growth of the World's Urban and Rural Population: 1920–2000," *International Social Development Review* No. 1 (New York: United Nations, 1969), p. 52.

[5] See Norman B. Ryder, "The Future Growth of the American Population," in Charles F. Westoff, ed., *Toward the End of Growth* (Englewood Cliffs, N.J.: Prentice-Hall, 1973).

tion concentration in the period under review here—to the end of the twentieth century—will remain higher for North America and Western Europe than it will finally be for Africa and Asia. As Table 1-3 reveals, by the beginning of the twenty-first century, somewhat more than one-half of the people of Europe and Latin America and two-thirds of those in the Soviet Union and Oceania (Australia and New Zealand) will be concentrated in cities of at least 20,000 in size. Furthermore, no region of the globe will probably fail to advance, and substantially too, toward greater urbanization during the balance of the present century.

THE GREAT CITY

Besides the general trend toward greater urbanization, modern society also reveals the existence of increasing numbers of cities of unusually large size. In 1900, only 11 cities of one million or more persons are believed to have been present in the world. By 1960, the world's 14 largest cities (enumerated only within their political boundaries and not including the population of their impacted fringe, that is, the total agglomeration) had no fewer than 3 million inhabitants each. And, according to United Nations estimates, there may be as many as 273 in the super-city size, in other words, of at least a

Heavy vehicle and pedestrian traffic in Tokyo, one of the world's super cities, and the largest in Asia.

million, by 1985, and many more than this by the beginning of the twenty-first century.

Table 1-4 gives the world's 50 largest cities (or, in some cases, urban agglomerations) none of them of less than 2.3 million in size as of approximately 1970. Scores of other giant cities in the one million-plus range could easily be added. China's Harbin had an estimated 1.6 million inhabitants in 1968. Dacca, in Bangladesh, possessed a population, in 1973, of about a million. Other little known Asian metropolises include Bangalore, 1.6 million (1971); Surabaja, 1.6 million (1971); Nagoya, 1.4 million (1970); Pyongyang, 1.5 million (1970); Lahore, 1.7 million (1973); and Ubon-Katchatani, 1.5 million (1970).

Despite its relatively low level of urbanization, Africa too has centers of population of a size of one million or more: Kinshasa (formerly Leopoldville), 1.2 million and Constantine, 1.5 million (1966). So also does Latin America: for example, Belo Horizonte, 1.3 million (1972); Porto Alegre, 1 million (1972); Coli, 1.1 million (1972); Guadalajara, 1.2 million (1970); and Recife, 1.2 million (1972).

THE URBAN CONCEPT

Both the proportion of a nation's people in concentrated communities and the presence of very large population centers within a country signify what is basically meant by the "urban concept." Thus, in the 1970 U.S. Census, four major categories were employed to classify the nation's urban population. These were: (1) Urban Place; (2) Urbanized Area; (3) Standard Metropolitan Statistical Area; and (4) Standard Consolidated Area. It should be observed that these classifications are built around the concept of the "city," which is a populated but also legally incorporated place having governmental jurisdiction over a specified territory. From the standpoint of population composition, growth, and functional interdependence, however, "city" is a somewhat artificial entity, and therefore the various other definitions used for census purposes.

1 An Urban Place was defined as either having 2500 inhabitants or more and incorporated as a city, borough, village, or town; the densely settled urban fringe, either incorporated or unincorporated, of an Urbanized Area; or an unincorporated territory having at least 2500 inhabitants.

2 An Urbanized Area contained at least one city of no fewer than 50,000 inhabitants as well as the fringe area surrounding it.

3 The idea of the Standard Metropolitan Statistical Area (SMSA) was developed in order to get at not only demographic statistics but socioeconomic characteristics as well. Each SMSA had to be a county containing a city of

TABLE 1-4 Population and Rank Order of the World's 50 Largest Cities or Urban Agglomerations

NAME	RANK	POPULATION SIZE
New York, U. S. A. (1970)	1	11,571,899
Tokyo, Japan (1970)	2	11,454,000
Shanghai, China (1970)	3	10,820,000
Buenos Aires, Argentina (1970)	4	8,352,900
Paris, France (1968)	5	8,196,746
Peking, China (1970)	6	7,570,000
London, U. K. (1971)	7	7,379,014
Mexico City, Mexico (1970)	8	7,314,900
Moscow, U. S. S. R. (1971)	9	7,172,000
Los Angeles, U. S. A. (1970)	10	7,032,075
Calcutta, India (1971)	11	7,005,362
Chicago, U. S. A. (1970)	12	6,978,947
São Paulo, Brazil (1972)	13	6,339,000
Bombay, India (1971)	14	5,968,546
Seoul, Korea (1970)	15	5,536,377
Cairo, Egypt (1970)	16	4,961,000
Philadelphia, U. S. A. (1970)	17	4,817,914
Djakarta, Indonesia (1971)	18	4,576,009
Tientsin, China (1970)	19	4,280,000
Rio de Janeiro, Brazil (1970)	20	4,252,009
Detroit, U. S. A. (1970)	21	4,199,931
Leningrad, U. S. S. R. (1971)	22	4,002,000
Santiago, Chile (1972)	23	4,000,000
Shenyang, China (1965)	24	4,000,000
Lima, Peru (1972)	25	3,800,000
Delhi, India (1971)	26	3,629,842
Luta, China (1965)	27	3,600,000
Karachi, Pakistan (1971)	28	3,441,000
Berlin, (East & West) (1969 & 1970)	29	3,218,028
Rangoon, Burma (1970)	30	3,186,886
Teheran, Iran (1970)	31	3,150,000
Madrid, Spain (1970)	32	3,146,071
San Francisco, U. S. A. (1970)	33	3,109,519
Osaka, Japan (1970)	34	3,100,000
Canton, China (1965)	35	3,000,000
Washington, D. C., U. S. A. (1970)	36	2,861,123
Sydney, Australia (1972)	37	2,850,630
Bogotá, Columbia (1972)	38	2,800,000
Rome, Italy (1970)	39	2,755,135

NAME	RANK	POPULATION SIZE
Boston, U. S. A. (1970)	40	2,753,700
Montreal, Canada (1972)	41	2,720,413
Baghdad, Iraq (1970)	42	2,696,000
Athens, Greece (1972)	43	2,540,000
Bangkok, Thailand (1972)	44	2,500,000
Saigon, South Vietnam (1968)	45	2,500,000
Madras, India (1971)	46	2,470,280
Toronto, Canada (1972)	47	2,425,000
Pittsburgh, U. S. A. (1970)	48	2,401,245
Melbourne, Australia (1971)	49	2,394,117
Birmingham, U. K. (1971)	50	2,369,205

Note: Among other cities or urban agglomerations which are reported to have reached or exceeded the two million mark by 1973 are Baltimore, St. Louis, Cleveland, and Houston in the United States; also Hamburg in Germany; Budapest, Hungary; Caracas, Venezuela; Singapore, Yokohama and Nagoya, Japan; Wuhan and Chungking, China; Taipei, Taiwan; Alexandria, Egypt; Lahore, Pakistan; Pusan, South Korea; Ahmedalead and Hyderalead, India; and Phnom Penh, Cambodia.

Sources: United Nations, *Demographic Yearbook, 1971* (New York: United Nations, 1972), pp. 353–81; *The Official Associated Press Almanac, 1974* (Maplewood, N.J.: Hammond Almanac, 1973); and *Whitaker's Almanak, 1974* (London: William Clowes, 1973), p. 204.

50,000 or more in population. Contiguous counties were included in such a SMSA if they were both metropolitan in character (their labor force being predominantly nonagricultural) and socioeconomically integrated with the central city. As of 1973, the United States contained 265 SMSAs.

4 In view of the very special importance of the enormous metropolitan complexes around the nation's two largest cities—New York and Chicago—several contiguous SMSAs and additional counties having close interrelationships with them were combined into Standard Consolidated Areas (SCAs). These were designated as the New York-Northeastern New Jersey SCA and the Chicago-Northwestern Indiana SCA, the two unparalleled urbanized agglomerations of present-day America.

"Urban" refers basically to the size and density of a population, hence to a *state* of things. In one well known definition of urbanization, that is, the *process* by which such communities take form, the demographer Hope Tisdale has referred to it simply as population concentration. Tisdale does, however, recognize two other distinct demographic aspects of urbanization, "the multiplication of points of concentration and the increase in the size of individual concentrations."[6] We ourselves have begun with these two considerations regarding urbanization, first, the proportion of people inhabiting places of 20,000 or more and, second, the increasing numbers of cities of very large size.

THE URBAN WAY OF LIFE

At the same time that sociologists have been singling out demographic size and density as, more than anything else, indicative of the urban mode of human existence, many have also insisted that an urban society denotes a unique type of community organization and a special form of individual membership in it.[7] In spite of this, scholars do have some difficulty in identifying the precise qualitative characteristics which typify urban society. Still, they attribute systematic differences to urbanism involving the economy, the social structure, and the general way of life among people living in cities. Thus we have the hypothesis of urbanism as a singular form of social organization and culture, and of urban man as a unique type of personality.

Urbanism certainly characterizes not only the settlement pattern but also the sociocultural configuration of the so-called *advanced* nations of the world today. These countries, such as the United States and the Scandinavian nations among others, have three major elements in common: (1) an unusual degree of economic development; (2) pronounced tendencies toward rational organization; and (3) a good deal of individual enhancement and mobility. The description "advanced" ought not to be thought a condition of absolute moral significance, but only as an expression of these three particular sociocultural and socioeconomic circumstances.

In addition, it should be recognized that the advanced nations themselves may be divided into two subtypes: the industrial and the postindustrial.[8] No entirely satisfactory definition of the differences between the two can be given. Yet, it is probably correct to say that in all three respects—of economic development, rational organization, and individual advancement—the postindustrial state represents a progression from the industrial type and is a further extension of industrial urbanism. For example, an industrial economy derives its energy from fossil fuels (coal, natural gas, and oil), a postindustrial one from fossil fuels and solar sources as well. Again, an industrial nation is organized with less total efficiency than a postindustrial

[6] "The Process of Urbanization," *Social Forces, 20* (March 1942), pp. 311–16.

[7] Consult Albert J. Reiss, Jr., "Urbanism," in Julius Gould and William L. Kolb, eds., *Dictionary of the Social Sciences* (New York: Free Press, 1969), pp. 738–39.

[8] Two leading monographs on the subject are Colin Clark, *Conditions of Economic Progress* (London: Macmillan, 1940), which differentiates the primary (agricultural), secondary (manufacturing), and tertiary (service) stages of economic growth; and Daniel Bell, *The Coming of Post-Industrial Society* (New York: Basic Books, 1973).

EXHIBIT 1-1   Standard Metropolitan Statistical Areas: U.S.A., 1972

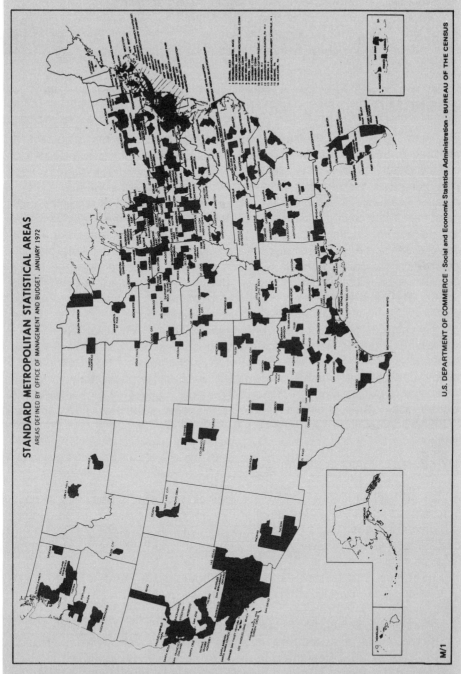

The Standard Metropolitan Statistical Areas (SMSAs) of the United States evidence some regional patterning, but the fact that we have become a nation of big cities from coast to coast is quite obvious.

Source: Bureau of the Census, *Census of Governments: 1972* (Washington, D.C.: Government Printing Office, 1975), "Graphic Summary," No. 5, p. 35.

one, for overall planning and coordination play a major role in the latter. And, finally, postindustrial society impinges on individuals, both as producers and consumers, more than an industrial society does. This last item refers not merely to the regulatory nature of government but also to the tremendous expansion of the service sector that takes place under postindustrialism.

ECONOMIC DEVELOPMENT

First and most obviously, modern urbanization equates with a network of productive, transit, and communication facilities that results in a degree of material development never previously reached by any large body of people. Along with certain other countries, notably Britain, West Germany, Scandinavia, Belgium, Holland, Denmark, France, Japan, and Australia-New Zealand, the United States is in this stage of development at the present time. In the United States, air, land, and water routes connect numerous population centers into a single, vast transportation system. Our mass media of communication also make up a truly nationwide grid. Together with the highly productive echelons of industry (including mechanized agriculture), these urban-based and urban-serving systems contribute to a level of productive efficiency and general wealth that is historically unique.

By virtue of the size of their populations, large cities make intense specialization possible, thereby boosting productive capacity. Large cities also generate emergent wants that stimulate consumption. As a result, urban concentrations have a creative influence on industry because they foster efficiency in production and demand in the marketplace. Combined, these two factors make up a dynamic techno-organizational system in which production and consumption keep reinforcing each other.

RATIONAL ORGANIZATION

Advanced society is organizationally distinct too. Being industrial and postindustrial, modern cities deviate sharply from earlier types of urban centers with respect to their social structure. The outstanding values of the modern city are technical proficiency, on the one hand, and the administrative coordination of many specialists, on the other. This contrasts sharply with the state of affairs that existed earlier when individual artisans followed traditional standards of work and operated in a personal and relatively inefficient manner.

Power, defined as the ability to control others, is exercised in modern urban society by a centralized decision-making process working through large, impersonal, bureaucratic agencies. Moreover, these bureaucracies typically justify themselves and their leadership as instruments serving the

Modern urban society requires extensive administrative organization, as shown in these new Department of Transportation buildings in Washington, D.C.

expanding expectations of the public in general. Note, for instance, that the postindustrial nations subscribe by and large to policies of full employment, decent housing for all, and a full array of welfare guarantees. These nations also try to regulate if not control public utilities and even the basic industries of the economy in a public-service capacity.

Such an exercise of responsibility by managerial and technical experts leads to a mixed system of elitist and populist components. The exact degree to which power is both centralized and diffused in modern urban society remains a matter of no little controversy. Scholars differ in their assessments of the situation. Yet they do agree that modern urbanism does necessitate a very complex administrative setup commensurate with the multiplicity of industry, business, and professional services, and also responsive to a legitimately rising galaxy of socioeconomic aspirations voiced by the public as a whole.

The cities of the advanced industrial and postindustrial nations tend to be built around commercial and industrial focal points rather than the religious and governmental centers of the past. The church and the palace no longer dominate the city as they did prior to the Industrial Revolution. Of late though and as a result of the assumption of a broader service role by public agencies, governmental institutions have taken on added significance. For one thing, city, state, and federal office buildings and tax-supported colleges and universities as well as government-operated health facilities have come to be situated at the core of the city, giving that area a civic character added to its commercial one. Though these centralizing tendencies, which are also locating high-rise banks and corporate office buildings in the city's once-dominant central business district, can be definitely observed, other currents of change continue to disperse the general population and much of its economic life into a widening sprawl of shopping centers, industrial parks, and commercial developments all interconnected by a burgeoning network of highways and super-highways.

Contrasting currents of change also affect the cultural and social systems of the modern city. On the one side and owing to the prominence of productive values, a city's commercial, industrial, and professional elites participate very actively in the community's formal organization. That enables them not only to run things efficiently but also to be known and rewarded as successful competitors in the productive system. On the other side and concurrently with these values of production, occupational achievement, and managerial control, a trend toward the values of consumption also materializes in advanced urban society. Consequently, stratification on the basis of cultivated life-styles, including the humanistic values of art and the hedonistic values of leisure, also gains ground. Thus, differing and even antagonistic ways of life arise to challenge each other.

INDIVIDUAL ENHANCEMENT AND MOBILITY

Cities in the advanced societies make possible a great deal of occupational mobility for individuals and of technological and economic innovation for organizations. Change becomes incessant. For example, changes occur that affect whole occupational groups, like the rise of the automotive industry and, more recently, of television and electronic data-processing. Such changes modify the availability of opportunity and, with it, the allocation of power and prestige.

Because individual competence tends to be enhanced in urban society, individual rights are correspondingly sanctioned. In the urban social system, the freedom of the citizen under impartial law becomes an important principle of social life. Desire for personal development gains greater recognition. The need for education, entertainment, and sheer amusement grows, while for people at work, values such as security, equity, individuation, and demo-

[9] For principles on redesigning the job system to fit the worker's character structure today, see Neal Q. Herrick and Michael Maccoby, "Humanizing Work," in *Hearings on the Worker Alien-*

The migration of rural populations into cities indicates the benefits that urban life offers, or appears to offer, in most regions of the world today.

cratic decision-making take on added importance.[9] Because the nuclear family permits greater individual freedom, it supplants extended kinship in the urban milieu, although to some extent kin networks continue as informal, backup systems. In addition, a youth culture arises in accordance with the lengthening period of adolescence and the mushrooming of age-segregated activities. Similarly, the segregation of the aged—people now anachronistic to the economy—also develops. The elderly are systematically removed from positions of power and influence where they might arrest the tendencies toward greater efficiency, economy of production, and organizational growth.

In sum, it may be said that the sociocultural life of modern industrial and postindustrial urban nations have distinctive, if not unique, features.

INADEQUACIES OF URBAN LIFE

While material and social benefits accrue from advanced urbanism, the inadequacies of urban life rise to trouble the very people who otherwise prosper from it. As city planner Constantine Doxiadis declares, "The dynamic city which we have created today does not function properly."[10] As if to sus-

ation Act, U.S. Senate Subcommittee on Employment, Manpower, and Poverty (Washington, D.C.: Government Printing Office, July 1972).

[10] "The Coming World-City: Ecumenopolis," in Arnold Toynbee, (ed.), Cities of Destiny (New York: McGraw-Hill, 1967), pp. 345–58.

tain this scholarly judgment, a 1972 Gallup poll of the American public asked, "If you could live anywhere in the United States you wanted to, would you prefer a city, suburban area, small town, or farm?" Only 13 percent favored city residence. Furthermore, fully 80 percent of the inhabitants of our largest cities said they would prefer to leave![11]

The specifics of the "case" against the city are well known.

First, environmental damage takes on major proportions. Air and water are polluted. Congestion intensifies. Open land is consumed at a dismaying rate. Though more efficient vehicles become available, there is little if any improvement in the speed of transportation.

Second, social disorganization grows. The central business district loses much of its economic vitality. The inner-city community, more and more populated by rural in-migrants and the hard-core disadvantaged, succumbs to social decay.

Third, because it is devoted to individual specialization and economic betterment, the urban community as a whole loses solidarity. Weak social controls and a sense of relative deprivation (the disparity between what one has and what he believes he rightfully should have) combine to lead many to resort to unlawful means to gratify their wants. Both individual and organized crime multiplies.

Fourth, not only widespread criminal conduct but a confused, dispirited mood also arises. Part of this malaise is born out of a feeling of unlimited potentialities, which gives people a sense of great power. But when their lofty ambitions are not realized, as indeed they cannot fully be, people experience frustration and self-doubt. Another part of the malaise is a feeling of aimlessness or satiety, that since in the multiplex urban setting everything is possible, nothing in particular is either very important or exceptionally worthwhile. Consequently, urbanites may fall victim to a numbing disorientation and corrosive purposelessness.

Fifth, still another aspect of the urban problem is present in the conduct of local government: the so-called metropolitan problem. In the typical metropolitan area, public affairs proliferate and become very costly to administer. At the very same time that the expenditures of the central city rise, its tax base melts away, owing to the relocation of business and industry out on the periphery. Also, the central city and its suburbs come to feel mutually estranged and to blame each other for the administrative problems that they suffer from. As historian Zane L. Miller understands it, "the mania for local self-government in the suburbs block[s] annexation and perpetuate[s] deep social, economic, cultural, and racial cleavage within metropolises."[12]

---

[11] As cited by Jeffrey K. Hadden and Josef J. Barton, "An Image That Will Not Die: Thoughts on the History of Anti-Urban Ideology," in Louis H. Masotti and Jeffrey K. Hadden, eds., *The Urbanization of the Suburbs* (Beverly Hills, Calif.: Sage Publications, 1974), p. 109.

[12] Zane L. Miller, *The Urbanization of Modern America* (New York: Harcourt Brace Jovanovich, 1973), p. 226.

To some critics, then, the only prospect for metropolitan life in the United States in particular and in the other advanced nations in general is, in more than one prognosticator's words, "political, financial, and administrative disaster!"

CONSTRUCTIVE URBANISM

Manifest as these undesirable conditions may be, strengthening counterforces are also at work ameliorating the plight of the modern city and of urban society today. They include: government of great scope and power; highly developed sciences and technologies; effective voluntary associations; and the proliferation of professional and service occupations. Brought together in a spirit of enlightened social planning, these instrumentalities can succeed in turning the city, according to anthropologist Conrad Arensberg's felicitous phrase, into a "crazy quilt of discontinuities," but a viable one, nonetheless.

Perceived in this light, the metropolitan problem, for one, takes on a somewhat different character. The specific difficulties it pertains to, as phrased by Robert Wood, once Undersecretary of Housing and Urban Development, become "questions of value and judgment, of what we should and should not do, and how much."[13] If so, the present difficulties are serious but not overwhelming and they may, in fact, yield to solution by means of a large variety of measures, among them the transfer of municipal responsibilities to the county, federated arrangements between neighboring communities to take care of particular functions, and special districts with jurisdiction over designated services and facilities.

Constructive urbanism is not without its weaknesses, for it denotes a need for systematic planning, for the collective determination of long-term common goals. How should industry be regulated so as to improve the quality of the environment? What should public funds be invested in: jetports or low-cost housing, for example? On whom should educational resources be allocated: the gifted or the poor? How should poverty be dealt with? Whose interests should receive priority?

Planning of this sort threatens vested interests. More than this, it runs counter to the individualistic urban mentality resistant to the thought of concentrating power in government.[14] Planning also disagrees with the positivistic character of social science. Traditionally, the social scientist has taken the goals of the community as given rather than as something for the scien-

[13] Robert C. Wood, "Metropolitan Government, 1975: An Extrapolation of Trends," *American Political Science Review,* 52 (March 1958), pp. 102–22.

[14] See John W. Dyckman, "Societal Goals and Planned Societies," *Journal of the American Institute of Planners,* 32 (March 1966), pp. 66–76, for an exposition on the perils attributed to planning.

tist himself to participate in determining, except perhaps to demonstrate the probable outcome of a proposed course of action.

Regardless of such misgivings, no little progress in coping with urban problems may be observed in what sociologist Alvin Boskoff calls corrective planning and creative design.[15] Corrective planning deals with the symptoms of urban distress and malfunctioning through renewal and relocation, mass transit, zoning and building codes, and expanded social services. Corrective planning has relatively limited objectives. Creative design is much more visionary. It aspires to entirely new dimensions in urban life: intense social solidarity, greatly improved governmental services, a wider distribution of wealth, and a higher level of civic grandeur. For intimations of innovative, creative urbanism one is directed to the civil-rights legislation and Model Cities program of the United States; the New Towns program of the United Kingdom; and Brasilia, the recently built, dazzling capital of Brazil. These experiments in social adminstration and large-scale urban planning may point the way to new and gratifying emergents in the continuing process of urbanization.

THE SOCIAL SCIENCES AND THE STUDY OF URBAN LIFE

As the present chapter has revealed through its references to cultural, political, and economic phenomena, *all* of the social sciences are relevant to an understanding of urban life. Geographers attempt to explain the spatial location of population centers. Demographers measure the size and composition of the inhabitants of these populated places; historians chronicle the political and cultural evolution of the city; economists examine a city as a resource-allocation entity and also as a unit in various larger regional, national, and international economic systems; and social psychologists probe the phenomena of communication, opinion formation, leadership, and even the irrational, emotional currents that ebb and flow among the people of cities.

Similarly, anthropologists, sociologists, and other types of social scientists are also capable of throwing light on given cities as cultural carriers, communities, and additional kinds of social phenomena as well. All of the social sciences are germane to the study of urban life in general, apart from particular cities as individual entities.

Necessarily, then, some attempt has been made to employ the full range of the social sciences in this book's coverage. Depending on the given subject, for example, the corporate organization of business or the structure of

---

[15] Alvin Boskoff, *The Sociology of Urban Regions* (New York: Appleton-Century-Crofts, 1962), Chs. 17–18.

city government, insights from economics or political science are employed as appropriate. Overall though, our study of urban life is primarily *sociological,* that is, *the treatment of the city and urban society as social systems associated with large, dense populations characterized by distinctive patterns of culture.* The other disciplines are subordinated to this general perspective.

CONCLUSION

We have in this initial chapter sought to introduce the student to the study of urban life and to the text as an educational instrument. We have pointed out the massive urban trend today as justifying greater familiarity with the subjects dealt with in subsequent chapters, that is, the history, theoretical interpretations, social structure, pathologies, and types of urban planning characteristic of urban society. This chapter has also presented the urban concept and the major features of the urban way of life. In addition, it has contrasted the inadequacies of cities and urban society with the constructive forces that are present in them. It has also expressed the sociological perspective as its primary point of view toward urban life, while recognizing the contributions of other disciplines toward an understanding of urban phenomena. In brief, this first chapter has taken up the range of subject matter to which the rest of the book will devote itself in greater detail.

FOR FURTHER READING

H. Wentworth Eldredge, ed., *World Capitals: Toward Guided Urbanization* (Garden City, N.Y.: Anchor Press/Doubleday, 1975). Describes the growth of 11 major cities and the thinking now going on to accommodate their expansion in an orderly manner.

Sylvia Fava, ed., *Urbanism in World Perspective* (New York: Thomas Y. Crowell, 1968). Articles that offer much insight into urban society around the globe.

Eli Ginzberg, ed., *The Future of the Metropolis* (Salt Lake City: Olympus, 1974). Eight scholars project present urban trends in the United States into the future.

International Social Development Review, *Growth of the World's Urban and Rural Population: 1920–2000* (New York: United Nations, 1969). Data gathered on the widest possible scale and projected ahead.

National Research Council, *Toward an Understanding of Metropolitan America* (San Francisco, Calif.: Canfield, 1974). Develops 34 generalizations on urbanism in the United States today.

William A. Robson and D. E. Regan, eds., *Great Cities of the World* (Beverly Hills, Calif.: Sage Publications, 1972). The world's premier cities with no attention though to those of the Communist lands.

Michael P. Weber and Anne Lloyd, eds., *The American City* (New York: West Publishing Co., 1975). The history of cities in the United States and their current problems and opportunities.

PART TWO

THE HISTORICAL DEVELOPMENT OF CITIES

A print (by Cavallieri) of Renaissance Rome, showing Pope Gregory XIII opening the Holy Year of 1575. At the rear, St. Peter's dome, designed by Michelangelo, is still under construction.

Source: Aubrey Menen, *Rome for Ourselves* (New York: McGraw-Hill, 1960), p. 151; © Aubrey Menen and Thomas & Hudson, T. Ltd., 1960.

CHAPTER 2

URBANISM AND CIVILIZATION

The history of the city is short but momentous. Of the vast number of years that man, the toolmaking hominid, has spent on earth, all but the last 6000 preceded the dawn of urbanization. Yet all of the characteristics of civilized existence—literacy, art, trade, complex technology, and social control exercised over a large population—are directly traceable to the very first urban centers.

Beginning in the fourth millennium B.C., cities originated among people independent of one another in four different places around the world: in the valley of the Tigris-Euphrates Rivers, the Indus valley, in North China, and among the Meso-American Mayas.[1] Neither the preexisting conditions nor

[1] Egyptian evolution was of longer duration, and its urbanization less distinct. The political unification of Egypt occurred very early but on a household basis. Thus until 1000 B.C., Egypt was

the specific outcomes were alike in every instance where the first cities arose, but the general consequences of the urban revolution were to prove highly significant.

THE URBAN REVOLUTION

The prehistorian V. Gordon Childe has identified ten essential characteristics of the urban revolution.[2] In doing so he has informed us of the particular ways in which the earliest cities differed from what preceded them and also how they came to affect their surrounding societies.

1 The prototypic city had a larger and denser population than any settlement before it. Mohenjo-Daro, Erech, and Harappa, none of which probably ever exceeded 20,000 in size, were quite small by comparison with modern cities. Still, contrasted with the villages that preceded them or were their contemporaries, these original cities reached unparalleled magnitude.

2 Though the countryside was peopled by peasants all engaged in much the same work, the city contained many specialists practicing a variety of occupations. There were brickmakers, stevedores, potters, cooks and bakers, gold- and silversmiths, clerks, diviners, priests, soldiers, and administrators. Since the ancient city did not produce its own subsistence, it had to exchange valued goods and services with the rural hinterland. For this, specialization was necessary.

3 The first urban communities provided security by means of a walled citadel within which the whole countryside could escape marauders. A city might also construct a granary to safeguard the community's harvested grain from flood waters, or levees and canals to assure proper irrigation.

4 The city could furnish the entire region with a temple and other religious structures for communicating with the deities believed capable of either protecting and promoting its welfare or destroying it. The monumental religious buildings, oftentimes awesome in size and ornamentation, were staffed by functionaries who not only conducted sacred rites but also administered the community's economic and technical and military affairs from them.

5 The officials of the temple and the court made up a ruling class that was socially superior to the rank and file because it engaged in nonmanual tasks,

agrarian in contrast to the "industrial" Mesopotamians, who concentrated workshops and fortifications amid their dense populations.

The oldest known town in the world is Jericho, on the Dead Sea. For a brief but factual treatment of Jericho, consult James Mellaart, "Roots in the Soil: The Beginning of Village and Urban Life," in Stuart Piggott, ed., *The Dawn of Civilization*. (New York: McGraw-Hill, 1961), pp. 41–64.

[2] See his "The Urban Revolution," *The Town Planning Review*, 21 (April 1950), pp. 3–17.

EXHIBIT 2-1 Where the World's Earliest Cities Arose

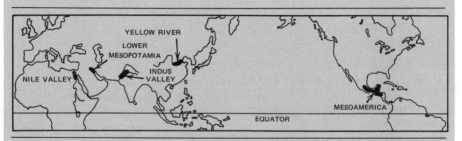

These maps give the regional locations of the ancient "urban revolution" in the Fertile Crescent of Mesopotamia, the Indus Valley, China's Yellow River lands, MesoAmerica—and also Egypt, where urbanization appeared eventually but less decisively than elsewhere.

*Source:*Gideon Sjoberg, "The Origin and Evolution of Cities," in *Scientific American, Cities: Their Origin, Growth, and Human Impact* (San Francisco: W. H. Freeman, 1971), pp. 20–21. © 1973 by Scientific American.

such as planning how to escape drought, flood, and human enemies. This, in fact, clearly entitled the priesthood and the members of the royal entourage to claim a rank for themselves superior to that of their dependent population.

6 It was incumbent on the administrative urban elite to create a system of notation in order to adequately control the revenues and public works entrusted to them. Required for practical purposes, these records were the original impetus to the invention of both a written language and mathematics.

7 Given the capacity to write and compute, the clerks and scribes were then in a position to develop the sciences of astronomy and chronometry. Obviously, these disciplines had enormous practical application. By predicting periodic inundations and by guiding sowing and reaping, they could greatly increase agricultural output.

8 Pictorial art was stimulated, both of the plastic and graphic varieties, on pottery, in the form of seals or figurines, and at times on a very large scale. Although the type of art differed from one to another of the original urban settlements, it is noteworthy that art of this kind is not encountered in neolithic remains until cities become a reality.

9 The dawn of urbanization was followed by an expansion of trade to what today would properly be described as interregional and even intercontinental. Raw materials were eventually sought at great distances, for example, between the cities of the Indus valley and the settlements of Egypt, and between Mesopotamia and the eastern Mediterranean.

10 The persons who made up the urban population were not kinsmen but citizens who belonged to the community politically as well as religiously. To be sure, in these earliest cities reliance on intense ideological devices and brute force to maintain discipline was commonly the case. However, the concept of citizenship—of moral rights derived from mutual interdependence—was not wholly absent.

URBANISM AND CULTURAL GROWTH

Although the first cities were established gradually, with improvement in technology and the production of an agricultural surplus going on over a long period of time, the fact remains that urbanization proved to be historically disjunctive.[3] Urbanization changed the scale on which social organization could be carried on. This, in turn, resulted in far-reaching, permanent alterations in the character and quality of human life.

Preurban man had been essentially traditional. Whatever was old and long established deserved to be followed. Certainly individual desire was not sufficient justification for doing anything new. The neolithic preliterate was deeply emotional too. Nature, he believed, was infused with human feelings. The universe was thought to harbor innumerable spirits that in some vast and complex manner took man's life and ultimate destiny beyond human determination, and even beyond comprehension. Mundane existence might, in fact, be only an accident in the passage of one's own spirit from its mysterious origin to its unfathomable end. Prehistoric man was by no means a stranger to physical sanctions. He was indeed accustomed to their frequent use. However, just as there were good and bad spirits who had their counterparts in moral and immoral behavior, the good was whatever the tribe or clan approved of. In this social setting then, the individual was clearly subordinated to the community, held there, as it were, in the mechanical grip of the whole.

The new social outlook that characterized the ancient urban communities when they appeared centered on the new division of labor which had developed. Accordingly, urban men sensed an added efficacy in themselves and also the need to respect the wishes of the numerous productive specialists who made up the new order of things. These became embodied in contractual rights. In addition, having achieved feats of engineering, defense, and material production, the populations of the ancient cities were more inclined to be objective toward nature and to confront the future with greater confidence and, indeed, to welcome change as the forebearer of still greater benefits in store.

---

[3] Compare Lewis Mumford, *The City in History* (New York: Harcourt Brace and World, 1961), which describes "the urban drama" in terms of new technology, enhanced creativity, the productive division of labor, and property rights, all of which ensued in a "rhythm of development."

Reconstruction of the Ishtar Gate in ancient Baylon on the Euphrates River.

EXPANDED PRODUCTION

The coming of cities did not entirely sweep away what already existed. However, by actualizing things that had been impossible to realize earlier, they drastically augmented the preexisting mode of life. Of signal importance was the expansion of the means of production. As the economic historian Shepard Clough has carefully observed, the early cities concentrated capital, which their elites employed in making loans of seeds and implements, maintaining drainage and irrigation ditches, and hiring craftsmen to turn out goods in workshops.[4] In Mesopotamia the temple priests were the entrepreneurs, while in India an honorable, ceremonial class of bourgeois merchants served in that capacity.

The institution of contract (found as early as 1750 B.C. in the code of Hammurabi), the use of money (beginning in 600 B.C.), specialization, and increased trade combined to raise the level of living. The presence of parasitic social classes did restrict the allocation of wealth and frequently entailed the waste of materials and labor for honorific purposes, such as massive tombs, memorials, and pyramids. All of this diminished what was available for consumption. Nonetheless, more substantial housing now appeared. Public sanitation became a reality, just as did storehouses that eased the severity of famines. In fact, the increase of population, which occurred as a concomitant of early urbanization, is itself possibly the best indication of the widespread economic benefits of the original urban revolution.

GREAT CULTURE

The invention of writing and mathematics together with the consequent development of the predictive sciences was a vital expansion of knowledge and art. The results included more systematic learning, the encouragement of the skills and techniques of painting, sculpture, and other forms of artistic expression.

Above all, urbanization meant the creation of a great culture. The intellectual achievement contrasted sharply with the local, peasant conditions of life that were capable of being sustained by an agricultural, essentially village, society. In the hands of specialized urban literati, the preexisting religious conceptions became more complex, so much so that they were soon beyond the grasp of the rural mind. Architects invented unusual ways of making use of building materials. Officials worked out intricate forms of courtly protocol. Pedagogues discovered the rules of inference and, as philosophers, combined their reflections into sophisticated systems of thought that would long interest, if not fascinate, countless people.

[4] Shepard B. Clough, *The Rise and Fall of Civilization* (New York: Columbia University Press, 1951), p. 35.

THE DETRIMENTAL EFFECTS OF URBANISM

Recent experience with cities has undoubtedly brought about a critical sensitivity toward urban society. Certainly it has impaired the complacency with which many writers long regarded urbanism in general and the triumph of industrial urbanism in particular. From its beginnings thousands of years ago, in fact, definite shortcomings were present in urban life. While cities were producing civilization they were also deepening a wide variety of serious human problems.

Four factors responsible for the presence of largely undesirable conditions in urban centers from the very outset need to be recognized.

First, by giving rise both to occupational specialization and political citizenship, urbanization engendered frail social relationships that were continuously in danger of breaking down. Thus the obligations of specialists to one another could be evaded and, similarly, claims of self-interest and personal rights be selfishly pressed to the point of endangering the community.

Second, the cultivation of wealth that urbanization made possible was capable of not merely doing injustice to the poor but also of demoralizing the rich. Cities drew people to them, and their increased population density led to epidemics and high death rates. Often the predatory tax policies of despotic urban elites impoverished the surrounding countryside, and at times cities were abandoned by royal whim.

Third, the city's complex social organization together with its ability to command resources had dreadful as well as beneficial consequences. An urban society could mobilize far greater powers of destruction than its agrarian counterpart and practice more terrible forms of aggression.

And finally, because they were engaged in concentrated enterprise, cities had a heavy impact on their surroundings. They consumed large quantities of materials and before long even upset the balance of nature.

It is surely correct though to say that, overall, the positive influence of our earliest cities on society, economic life, and culture far outweighed their detrimental effects. The history of original urbanization in the several regions where it occurred bears this out.

THE RISE OF CITIES

THE FERTILE CRESCENT

Until the Sumerians of ancient Mesopotamia brought the Tigris and the Euphrates Rivers under control by means of dikes and canals, the land of the Lower Valley, the so-called Fertile Crescent, was an expanse of "mud-flats, reed marshes, shallow lagoons, and stretches of dry soil where life, though precarious, was more richly sustained than in less watered areas."[5] The cities of Kish, Ur, Lagesh, Eridu, and Nippur that the Sumerians eventually established were made possible by rivertine engineering, including irrigation.

Temples, Irrigation, and Civic Life

The protoliterate period of Mesopotamian history witnessed the emergence of civic life from an antecedent communal existence in a territory the size of Denmark. Unquestionably, a key factor was the need for cooperation to deal with the floods brought about by tides on the Persian Gulf, unusually heavy snow in the Armenian highlands where the rivers have their source, and also rock slides in the gorges of the Zabs that could temporarily impound and then suddenly release the volume of water that had accumulated.

Apart from greater population density, the first evidence of urbanization in the Fertile Crescent was the appearance of monumental temple architecture. The first temples built there, such as those in the south at Eridu and in the north at Tepe Gawra, established the Mesopotamian pattern of conceiving of a "mountain god." He owned the city and its people, and they erected a ziggurat, or tower mound, to communicate with him. It was thus a focus of community endeavor, this building of the ziggurat temple.[6]

Industry and Construction

The impetus that the Mesopotamian cities gave technology and human organization is evident in the fact that these settlements became centers of industry. Wheel-turned pottery supplanted the handmade type. By 2500 B.C. copper tools were in wide use. Knives, saws, chisels, hammers, drills, bellows, and the adze began to be crafted. Then when tin (a soft metallic element malleable at ordinary temperatures) began arriving in large quantities from the Danube valley around 2500 B.C., bronze implements also came to be manufactured. An alloy of copper and tin, bronze takes a better edge than copper alone, and can cut better.

It was in construction, however, that the Sumerian cities achieved unusual success. Sometime during the third millennium, cake-shaped bricks yielded to the sharp-edged oblong block, although due to the scarcity of fuel these were seldom fired. Urban construction in Mesopotamia was so good that as early as the year 4000 B.C., the city of Eridu had a population of several thousands.

[5] Ralph Turner, *The Great Cultural Traditions* (New York: McGraw-Hill, 1941), Vol. I, p. 133.

[6] See Henri Frankfort, *The Birth of Civilization in the Near East* (Bloomington, Ind.: Indiana University Press, 1959), pp. 54–55.

Social Organization

As people concentrated in the Mesopotamian cities, the extended kinship relations that tied persons together in the villages gave way to social-class differentiation based on specialization. Thus a kind of feudal organization of manorial groupings arose in which priests and warriors dominated serflike retainers, including craftsmen and agriculturists as well as simple slaves. The sumptuous private residences, the "palaces," and the opulently equipped tombs, containing the skeletons of subordinates killed to accompany their masters into death, testify to the wealth and class differences of these ancient Sumerian urbanites.

Warfare

The dozen or so cities that the Sumerians built were all in a territory only 100 miles square. Despite their cultural unity, they frequently went to war with one another in struggles over land and water rights. The theocratic social organization of the temple manors made it relatively easy to mobilize forces for aggression, particularly since the shifting rivers often confused boundaries. In addition, economic exploitation within the city itself, of which there are records inscribed on clay tablets, created stresses that lent themselves to being discharged outward against an external enemy and to justify aggrandizement at the expense of others.

The Sumerian cities were attacked, pillaged, destroyed, and rebuilt time and again. In fact, as war became chronic it encouraged the further establishment of cities, for cities could shelter tens of thousands at a time. Trade grew to support military effort, to expend the profits of conquest—rich stores of goods, war captives, precious metals, and arms—and also to supply the needs of the corps of artisans whose skills required large amounts of raw materials. Therefore, commerce in timber, textiles, mineral ores, and foodstuffs sustained the urban revolution in the Fertile Crescent.

CITIES OF THE INDUS VALLEY

At the time of the late Sumerian cities, from 3000 to 2500 B.C., strong and affluent settlements already existed along the Indus River and its tributaries in present-day Pakistan. These communities were established by bronze-age people who may some five centuries earlier, at least through the Baluch (Iranian) borderland, have already been in contact with the advanced settlements beside the Tigris and Euphrates, possibly through the city of Tepe Yahyā in the Soghun valley of what is today Iran.[7]

[7] C. C. and Martha Lamberg-Karlovsky, "An Early City in Iran," in *Scientific American, Cities: Their Origin, Growth, and Human Impact* (San Francisco, Calif. W. H. Freeman, 1973), pp. 28–37.

The Indus valley civilization arose from a neolithic farming society that existed in an area which was very fertile. It was also a region infested with wild animals, subject to disease, and liable to terrible flooding.

Mohenjo-Daro and Harappa

Fully seven different layers of buildings have been uncovered at the site of Mohenjo-Daro, most prominent of the Indus valley urban centers. These superimposed cities had been founded on the River Indus in the Pakistan province of Sind toward the end of the fourth millennium before the Christian era.[8] Like Harappa, nearly 400 miles upstream on the Hindus, and Chandhu-Daro 80 miles downstream, Mohenjo-Daro had a gridiron arrangement of streets quite different from the typical rabbit warren of the ancient Eastern village. Owing to the systematic placement of its roads, notably the main thoroughfare, 30 feet wide and at least one-half mile long, Mohenjo-Daro may be regarded as an early example of city planning.

It was of the utmost importance in the cities of the Indus valley to safeguard grain both from human attack and from flood waters when the rivers burst their banks following torrential rains. At Mohenjo-Daro, an artificial mound 50 feet high was encircled by a brick wall punctuated by sentry towers and surmounted by the public bath and the huge granary. Its dimensions 135 by 169 feet, the granary had a massive brick base constructed with vents to insure proper air circulation, and walls and roofs made of timber. Sheaves of grain, including wheat and barley, were delivered by ox-drawn, solid-wheel, single-shaft carts and were then hoisted for storage to the upper levels of the structure.

Plundered for materials by railway engineers in the nineteenth century, Harappa has been excavated to the extent that although its street plan has not yet been made entirely clear, the citadel of the city has been unearthed. The granaries there had a total floor space of some 9000 square feet, approximately the same size as the granary at Mohenjo-Daro.

Mercantilism

The merchants of Mohenjo-Daro carried on trade with other places at great distances from themselves. They dealt in foodstuffs, cotton, timber, and domesticated animals and, of course, the excellent crafts turned out by jewelers, potters, sculptors, and ornamentalists. Metals and precious stones were imported from southern India and silver from Afghanistan. Contact was also long sustained between Mohenjo-Daro and the Sumerians, Egyptians, and Cretans, probably by means of ocean vessels. With an upturned prow

[8] Cf. A. D. Pusalker, "The Indus Valley Civilization," in R. C. Mahumdar, ed., *The Vedic Age* (Bombay: Bharatiya Vidya Bhavan, 1951), pp. 195–96.

and a steersman at the rudder, these resembled the ships of the ancient Mediterranean nations.

The Decline of the Indus Civilization

After the period of early progress in which urbanization occurred at Mohenjo-Daro, Harappa, and Chandhu-Daro, construction deteriorated sharply and, in fact, the whole Indus civilization declined. Then about the middle of the second millennium before Christ, even though its final destruction by flood has not been entirely ruled out, Mohenjo-Daro was apparently sacked by invaders. These were possibly Indo-European Aryans worshipping the war god Indra. The invaders massacred the city's inhabitants and left their bodies to rot in the streets. Except for a handful of Buddhist monks who took up residence there almost 2000 years later, what had once been a city teeming with life remained only a deserted ruin.

Eastern India

Meanwhile at the opposite (eastern) edge of the Indian subcontinent, in the valley basins of the Ganges and Jumna Rivers, town life was taking root around 1000 B.C. The Indus civilization may have had only a remote influence here, but not a great deal is yet known about it. However, it is extremely doubtful that diffusion from the west played a major role. In the five centuries following 1000 B.C., the cities of India's classical writings appeared in fertile clearings along the eastern streams making up the trunk route from the head of the Bay of Bengal to the Arabian Sea. These included Hastinapura on the upper Ganges; Ahichhatra in Uttar Pradesh; Kaushambi along the Jumna; and Vaisati, home of the tribe into which Buddha was born. From that time on India was to remain a major civilization without ever again lapsing into non-urban localism.

ANCIENT CHINA

Geographically comparable to Mesopotamia, China's great central plain formed by the Yellow River in Honan province was the cradle of the ancient cities of the Far East. Now only a small fraction of the land area of China, the central plain consisted in 2200 B.C., as it still does now, of an expanse of finely compacted earth (*loess*) subject to flooding. Naturally arable and capable of retaining water, *loess* enabled the neolithic Chinese to grow millet and barley and to domesticate animals. Thus they were able to accumulate the agricultural surplus that together with social factors made possible an urban mode of life on the Asian mainland before it did anywhere else except for the Tigris, Euphrates, and Indus River civilizations.[9]

The First Capital

Great Shang, the earliest of the known ancient capitals of China, measured half a mile in one direction and a quarter of a mile in the other. Situated on a promontory, the city was held in the grip of the northward loop of the river Huan. Archaeological excavations at Hsiao T'un, the village presently at that site, have revealed that Great Shang was walled and that around the "palace quarter" clustered the dwellings and workshops of craftsmen. We know that the people of Great Shang were organized into clans, because some provision was made to segregate kinsmen into different residential sectors. Their nearness to the palace of the ruler, however, showed how much royal favor they had.

Chinese Urban Culture

From the time of their first appearance through their advancement under successive dynasties, China's cities produced a great culture of rivertine engineering, military science, the architectural and decorative arts, and the ethical philosophy of Confucius and Lao-tze.

The early Shang monarchs made up a priesthood. Frequent ceremonies, some on a surprisingly large scale, were called for in revering ancestors, divining spiritual powers, and conducting human sacrifices. The emperor himself officiated at the springtime "opening of the soil" at the capital, and lesser dignitaries led similar services in the subordinate towns. Dragon dances taking the participants right into the waters of the river were executed in order to insure proper inundation of the soil. One of the emperor's most solemn responsibilities was to lead the summer sacrifice for rain.

Upon the creation of the feudal empire, which took a thousand years to crystallize, civil service occupations became available to the classically trained scholars. These literati were conversant with Chinese philosophy, the hallmark of the civilized gentleman. This facilitated cultural integration as well as social and geographic mobility. The subordination of trade to handicrafts and farming in the Chinese scale of values, implicit in the very first of that nation's cities and made manifest in the status of the literati, was to last until modern times when Western technology, warfare, and economic imperialism would finally undermine it.

[9] See Wolfram Eberhard, "Data on the Structure of the Chinese City in the Pre-Industrial Period," *Economic Development and Cultural Change, 4* (1955–1956), pp. 253–68. Also Herrlee Blessner Creel, *The Birth of China* (New York: Frederick Ungar, 1937).

THE MAYAS

An agrarian civilization with a 3000-year history in a wooded, tropical setting in present-day Central America, the Mayas are still a challenge to analysis. As early as 1500 B.C., these people were producing pottery and cultivating the Petén forests. They lacked not only the wheel but also draft animals, yet they became successful agriculturists and builders. Their tools were of flint, obsidian, and granite, but with these they were able to shape heavy stones with which to raise numerous buildings at times reaching a height of more than 200 feet, as in the case of Temple IV at Tikal.

Although the Mayas never entirely freed themselves of their rural settlement pattern and never committed a sizable portion of their people to permanent residence in their impressive religious and mercantile cities, it is clear, as Redfield has phrased it, that from their precivilized folk condition they had indeed developed "the beginnings of an urban dimension of living."[10] The Mayan cities of Copán, Chichén Itzá, Tikal, and Uxmal—some of them at their height 1000 years before Columbus—were unlike present-day urban centers, for their dwellings and other structures were not compact. Rather, they were made up of "quarters," in which each household was a farm. The whole sprawling community was organized into religious and administrative subunits, each centering on a group of public buildings around large, landscaped squares. The buildings adjoining the squares consisted of the temple, an astronomical observatory, some pyramids, the palace, and even a platform for dancing. These gave the appearance of complete urban life, but as the sixteenth-century Bishop Diego de Landa observed, the Mayan population actually resided in the countryside surrounding the civic centers.[11]

The Ceremonial Center

Eric Thompson has drawn a parallel between the Mayan communities of the pre-Columbian era and those in the Guatemalan highlands today. Hence, he asserts, the Mayan city was less a residential than a ceremonial center. Civic functions and marketing were carried out in the ancient Mayan cities, but these places were mainly the sites of religious observances. The stone buildings forbade permanent use, for they lacked chimneys and windows though some had small vents. In fact, they were damp and, lacking illumination, resembled caves, certainly in their inner recesses that seem suitable

[10] Robert Redfield, *The Primitive World and Its Transformations* (Ithaca, N.Y. Cornell University Press, 1953). See also Thomas Gann, *Glories of the Maya* (New York: Scribner's, 1939), pp. 235ff.

[11] Consult Paul Rivet, *Mayan Cities,* trans. by Miriam and Lionel Kochan (New York: G. P. Putnam, 1960).

Temple of the Giant Jaguar, Maya ruins at Tikal, Guatemala.

only for storing ceremonial artifacts and ritual dress. Many of the rooms even enclosed earthen daises like stages for seating deity figures or rulers. And, finally, many skeletons have been found buried beneath these "houses," probably sacrificial victims, indicating still further the unlikeliness of their continued residential use.[12]

Between celebrations the Mayan city would lie vacant except for the resident priests and the sweeps making repairs to the temple accoutrements. Periodically, as at market times every fifth day and on the occasion of the communal rituals, the surrounding "suburbs" would pour into the civic cen-

[12] Eric S. Thompson, *The Rise and Fall of Mayan Civilization* (Norman, Okla.: Oklahoma University Press, 1954), pp. 61ff.

ter, build the necessary fires, draw blood for the eerie rites, burn incense, make offerings, view the sacred processions, attend ballgames (using springy rubber balls) and, bemasked, participate in the mystical dances to the accompaniment of fife and drum.

CITIES OF THE CLASSICAL WORLD

The urban revolution in Mesopotamia was most important for ancient "classical" Western society because cities never completely disappeared from the Mediterranean area thereafter. In fact, in the civilizations of Greece and Rome urbanization loomed large.

GREEK CIVILIZATION

A thousand years before urban Greece matured on the European mainland, the Minoan cities of Crete had already arisen. Each included a palace and an open central place, the *agora,* suitable for both festivals and political gatherings alike. A dozen Minoan centers, most notably that of Knossos, achieved a level of writing, craftsmanship, and architecture comparable to that of Mesopotamia.

The Hellenic Centers

On the continent, the Hellenic city-states grew slowly from the start of the first millennium before Christ. United in patriarchal clans each known as a *genos,* the people lived in scattered communities lying in valleys separated by mountains. In time, the clans formed associated brotherhoods (*phratries*) and, in warfare, recognized the authority of a supreme king (the *basileus*).[13]

The primary nucleus of the older Greek cities was the acropolis, a defensible promontory overlooking the community's farming land. Believed to be descended from the clan's god, the king was responsible for the local military forces. He made the acropolis his seat. Around this eminence or only on one side of its slopes were clustered the houses of the people. Here in the lower town (the *asty*) was to be found the *agora,* for which, R. E. Wycherley has written, " 'market place' is a very inadequate translation, and the rather frigid term 'civic centre' even worse."[14] In time this was to prove decisive, for the participation of the polis in government paved the way for the transition from monarchy to democratic rule.

The visible embodiment of the community's spirit in the Greek city was the beautiful temple structures atop the acropolis. They were severely or-

---

[13] G. Glob, *The Greek City and Its Institutions* (New York: Alfred A. Knopf, 1930).

[14] R. E. Wycherley, *How the Greeks Built Cities* (London: Macmillan, 1962).

The acropolis of Athens topped by the Parthenon as it appears today.

dered marble buildings featuring Doric, Ionic, and later—especially favored by the Romans—Corinthian columns. The Parthenon (447 **B.C.**) is the most celebrated of all and, sadly, the historical culmination of the Hellenic urban world.

Commerce eventually brought wealth into Greece, it is true, but the polyglot people it also produced lacked the loyalty that their cities needed in times of adversity. By the beginning of the fourth century **B.C.**, there were 25,000 to 50,000 mercenaries in the military service of the Greeks. Recruited by the various cities, the mercenaries were symptomatic of the expediency of the cosmopolitan polis in coping with its problems of colonizing abroad while seeking political stability at home. Despite wealth, fidelity to the Greek city-state diminished, as did public sacrifice and civic service. It was at this time that in the *Republic,* Plato vainly urged social reform in the Greek community through eugenics and a dedicated class of guardians.

ROMAN URBANISM

Originally, the Etruscan cities of present-day Italy from which Roman civilization eventually developed were built on hilltops ditched for defense. They were without paved streets, landscaping, systematic drainage, or any open spaces except for a marketplace. A shrine or temple was common though. Otherwise, houses were placed wherever it suited their owners. These had timber superstructures resting on stone or mud-brick foundations. The mansions of the rich might have gabled roofs with brightly painted ridge-poles.[15]

Roman urbanism grew out of this earlier Etruscan concern for fortifying strongholds. But as they pacified the countryside and accumulated wealth, the Romans began to display the strong sense of civic consciousness they had absorbed from the early Greeks. In the process, the many phenomena we associate with Roman cities materialized: public buildings, plazas, capacious avenues, and heroic monuments. Eventually a tenth of the whole population of the Empire was to live in cities, perhaps as many as 400,000 in Rome itself.

From City-State to Empire

Typically, Roman cities were urban nuclei surrounded by the productive country estates of the local patricians who dominated the city's affairs. The cultivation of the land had the stature of a quasisacred act among the Romans. This rivaled the values of urbanism. Accordingly, the Roman patricians managed large plantations in the country and also in-town workshops turning out a variety of manufactured commodities.[16]

Foreign conquest over Greece, Carthage, and Asia Minor gave the Roman aristocracy any number of excellent port cities. Maritime trade and banking made this equestrian order a moneyed class that in the end literally dominated the Mediterranean world.

The cities of the Roman Empire performed important public services as district communities within a wider community of interests.[17] The cities built the roads. They collected taxes. They maintained local safety. But as the military-commercial system grew, the centralization of political authority followed, and the confederation of autonomous city-states eventually gave way to the Empire ruled from the capital itself.

Decline and Decay

Owing to the expansion of the centralized national bureaucracy, by the third century A.D. local government in the Empire had lost its vigor. Corruption among officials could not be averted, and public safety could not be guaran-

---

[15] An excellent source is H. H. Scullard, *The Etruscan Cities and Rome* (London: Thames and Hudson, 1967).

[16] See F. Poland, E. Reisinger, and R. Wagner, *The Culture of Ancient Greece and Rome,* trans. by John H. Freese (Boston: Little, Brown, 1926), pp. 249–50.

[17] Cf. H. Stuart Jones, "Administration," in Cyril Bailey, ed., *The Legacy of Rome* (Oxford: Clarendon Press, 1923), pp. 91–131.

teed. Responsibilities to the central government, especially the remission of taxes, went unfulfilled. In response, the emperors sought by various means to preserve municipal integrity and to reinstill loyalty among local populations. The emperors lent their names to cities, or they founded new ones. They conferred citizenship on segments formerly consigned to the "depressed classes." Another measure was to take people still living at the tribal level and organize them into civic communities, like the Oresti of Macedonia by Diocletian.

Centralization alone did not account for the disorganization of Roman society in its later stages. Gordon Childe identifies two specific economic trends that contributed to the decline.[18] First, instead of increasing production as new dominions were secured, Roman industry simply exported itself to the provinces. This made each region relatively self-sufficient. In addition, the farms of the landed aristocracy grew into Oriental manors where the need for manufactured products tended to be met on the spot. "The inevitable result," writes Childe, "was a decline of urban industries and the impoverishment of the once-flourishing cities."[19]

The Christian ethic of poverty, brotherhood, and otherworldliness proved appealing to many persons who were demoralized by the social changes thus going on. This contributed still further to the growing alienation. The despotic centralization attempted during the Byzantine period in order to stem the tide of decay was the last futility.

The "fall" of Rome had neither a single cause nor a single form of expression. Yet the decline of Roman society together with its ability to administer a large territory on a plane of relative affluence and great military power was especially the eclipse of urban life. To the east, in Byzantium, a Hellenized urbanism did linger on, but in the West urban culture disappeared. It was not to be renewed until the tenth century.

CONCLUSION

The origin of cities 6000 years ago ushered in the social and cultural achievements of civilization and provided the foundation for human progress thereafter. The first cities arose from sources independently of one another in the Middle East, present-day Pakistan, North China, and Central America. Not only did these communities represent a new stage of specialized social organization capable of previously unknown economic productivity. They were also responsible for the invention of writing and mathematics as well as the development of a "high culture" in religion, philosophy, and the arts.

[18] V. Gordon Childe, *What Happened in History* (Baltimore: Penguin Books, 1954), pp. 283ff.
[19] Ibid.

Although our urban settlements were historically disjunctive in this respect, reaching a new level of sociocultural evolution, not everything connected with city building was of positive significance. In fact, from its beginning urbanization also had detrimental consequences, such as unstable institutions, great disparities of wealth and poverty, military power capable of being used for aggressive purposes, and an oftentimes unfortunate impact on the natural environment. The early history of urbanism in Mesopotamia, the Indus valley, Honan Province, and the Yucatan peninsula testifies to both of these connotations of urban life.

Once discovered, urbanism was by no means always continuous either. The cities of the Indus River and Mayan civilization ended in exhaustion. Yet in China and Mesopotamia, the first cities did give rise to urban societies that despite periods of conflict, decline, and disorganization went on for thousands of years. The city-states of classical Greece and the municipalities of the Roman Empire were the culmination of the original urban revolution among the Sumerians on the Tigris, and also the historical bridge to the preindustrial cities of medieval Europe.

FOR FURTHER READING

Shepard Clough, *The Rise and Fall of Civilization* (New York: Columbia University Press, 1951). A review of early Western urban cultures, bringing out their fundamental values.

V. Gordon Childe, *New Light on the Most Ancient East* (London: Routledge & Kegan Paul, 1964). The assertion that urbanization emerged when a technological complex created an economic surplus.

Rushton Coulborn, *The Origin of Civilized Societies* (Princeton, N.J.: Princeton University Press, 1959). The role of religion in the formation of the early civilizations.

Mason Hammond, *The City in the Ancient World* (Cambridge, Mass.: Harvard University Press, 1972). City design and planning in the Greco-Roman era.

Jorge E. Hardoy, *Pre-Columbian Cities* (New York: Walker, 1973). Claims the rise of a Central American ruling class made cities necessary here in the Western Hemisphere.

Karl Polanyi, *The Great Transformation* (Boston: Beacon Press, 1944). The social implications of the market economy which, though ancient, grew to its full stature only in the nineteenth century.

Ralph Turner, *The Great Cultural Traditions* (New York: McGraw-Hill, 1941). Covers several ancient cultures and the growth of their cities.

Mortimer Wheeler, *The Indus Civilization* (Cambridge, Eng.: Cambridge University Press, 1960). Describes the rise of India's first cities.

R. E. Wycherley, *How the Greeks Built Cities* (London: Macmillan, 1962), 2nd ed. The Greek settlements and their artifacts.

CHAPTER 3

PREINDUSTRIAL URBANIZATION

The history of urbanization from the revival of city life in Europe during the tenth century to the advent of the Industrial Revolution in the eighteenth is the story of the preindustrial community. The ancient cities from those of Mesopotamia to Rome had of course been preindustrial too. Yet the distinction between preindustrial and industrial urbanism allows us to distinguish between the two major eras in the entire history of cities: first, what cities were from the time they first arose in antiquity, and then the form they took at the beginning of the Industrial Revolution only 200 years ago—and which they continue to have in the advanced nations of the world today. For this reason, the conception of the preindustrial city must be regarded as an unusually important sociological tool.

THE PREINDUSTRIAL CITY

The preindustrial city was a commercial, governmental, religious, or educational center rather than the manufacturing and technological entity that the modern city typically is. In the preindustrial urban community, dynastic, theological, caste, and aesthetic values overshadowed economic interests in the style of life pursued by the decision-making elites. Such an urban settlement leaned toward the virtues of feudalism and was tightly bound to its immediate geographic vicinity. Much effort was expended to embellish local glories and to build a small kingdom centered on the city itself.

The designation of the preindustrial city must be credited primarily to the sociologist Gideon Sjoberg.[1] For 10 years, beginning in 1950, Sjoberg sought to arrive at an understanding of the urban community prior to the time it was transformed through industrialization. As Chapter 2 indicated, Sjoberg's quest meant covering almost 6000 years of human history, to the dawn of civilization itself. A sociologist and not a historian, however, Sjoberg directed his attention toward uncovering the so-called "structural universals" of the preindustrial city, in other words, toward generalizing the common patterns of such communities wherever encountered, in Eurasia, Africa, Meso-America, or the Far East, and whatever their particular cultures. Thus Sjoberg considered many diverse cities like Seoul, Peking, Lhasa, Mecca, Cairo, Fez, Florence, and Bukhara. Despite the fact that many preindustrial cities, possibly most of them, have completely disappeared, some have continued into the present though not without great changes resulting from industrialization. The heyday of the preindustrial city is long gone, however.

Sjoberg's depiction of the preindustrial city encompasses no fewer than seven variables. These include (1) demography and ecology; (2) social stratification; (3) the family; (4) economic structure; (5) the political system; (6) religious institutions; and (7) education. Although according to Sjoberg, preindustrial communities can vary profoundly among themselves, they make up one, single distinct type, and as such they differ drastically from the modern city that has come into existence since the beginning of the Age of Steam toward the close of the eighteenth century. Almost a thousand years before that time, the characteristics of the preindustrial city emerged in medieval Europe. And that took place centuries after Roman preindustrial urbanism had been extinguished by agrarian localism in what are today Italy, France, Germany, and Spain. The renewal of European cities eventually paved the way for the modern city as we know it.

---

[1] Sjoberg's fullest analysis of preindustrial urbanism is contained in his *The Pre-Industrial City: Past and Present* (New York: Free Press, 1960).

THE RENEWAL OF EUROPEAN CITIES

With Roman rule gone, Europe's cities shrank to towns, usually only the residence of the diocesan bishop and a miniscule marketplace.[2] These ecclesiastical centers subsisted on their immediate farming vicinities and provided their people religious services and occasional festivals and fairs. Otherwise, the farming communities that made up feudal Europe were oriented to the manor houses from which the local lords governed and protected them.

BOURGS AND BOURGEOISIE

After the decline of the Carolingians, a Frankish dynasty that had somehow administered Europe following the end of Roman rule, mounting pressure from the Saracens to the south and from the Normans to the north led to the stronger fortification of the manorial houses. Often called bourgs and ruled by local aristocrats, the strong castles that arose were built by commandeered labor. These structures domiciled a garrison of knights and included storehouses, workshops, stables, and a chapel.

The revival of substantial commerce, something that was first perceptible in the latter half of the tenth century, began to upset this manorial pattern which had long now settled over Western Europe. Itinerant tradesmen, often Jews and Syrians, found the perils of extended travel prohibitive. They acquired the habit of stopping for long sojourns in the fortified bourgs. Here their merchandise brought in from Scandinavia and Venice as well as other eastern ports benefiting from the stability of the Byzantine Empire was safe from seizure.

At the bourgs the merchants eventually applied themselves to processing locally produced raw materials and trafficking in the handicrafts turned out in the neighborhood. As their scope widened they found it necessary to construct buildings for themselves directly against the walls of the castle, and to put up another encircling wall to protect themselves. Hence these merchants and artisans made up a second bourg, in which they were the bourgeoisie.

The merchants and their craftsmen, originally runaway serfs or sailors, were under the authority of the lord of the manor. He could tax their merchandise, curtail their movement, or even confiscate their property altogether. Since it brought in useful commodities and was a source of wealth, the feudal aristocracy profited from this business. It was here that the bourgeoisie possessed the means of putting themselves on a more secure footing. Mainly by purchase made by their merchant associations (the guilds) and

---

[2] In medieval usage the term *city* was reserved for the cathedral seat of the bishop regardless of how tiny a settlement it might be. If they were without a cathedral, even the largest communities when they did develop were referred to only as towns.

aided by the financial needs of the nobility that had grown out of the Crusades, the mercantile communities began to obtain charters for themselves. These charters called for self-rule within the commercial commune. The charters also confirmed the right of the townspeople to own property, in itself a signal departure from the feudal principle of the integrity of property under the stewardship of the lord.

The conferment of charter liberties had far-reaching consequences. Now the inhabitants of the bourgs could work and travel pretty much at their own discretion. As a result, the towns grew because they attracted outsiders, fugitives usually, who if they resided without challenge for a year and a day in the commune, gained freedom for themselves. Therefore, the old German proverb "City air makes a man free."

URBAN DIFFUSION

Medieval European urbanism lacked the size and massive impact of the modern metropolis. Nonetheless, urbanization persisted, with two forces in particular sustaining urban life following its reappearance in Europe during the tenth century: technology and social control.

Technology

More a matter of the reintroduction of Roman machinery than new invention, technology became increasingly apparent as time went by. Most of the engineering equipment used in the European preindustrial city—the crane, pulley, treadmill, hoisting tackles, and such—had been known to the Romans. However, medieval Europe did add to the world's stock of productive machines. Textile apparatus appeared before 1300. The saw was converted from an exclusively hand tool to a mechanical device utilizing water power for propulsion. But the single most important technological advancement made by medieval Europe was unquestionably Guttenberg's invention of printing by means of movable type. More than anything else printing accelerated the spread of knowledge and the pace of sociocultural change.

During these centuries agriculture was also improved in Europe. Forests were cleared and swamps drained. This increased the population, many of whom migrated to the cities where a still more affluent mode of life could be achieved. The interplay between urbanism and agrarian progress proved so stimulating that as early as 1350 there were already more people in Europe than there had been at the time of the Caesars.

Social Control

The second factor that was especially productive of urbanization in medieval Europe was stronger social control. Contributing to the increased ability to command the loyalty and services of people were skillful banking that furthered the circulation of money; the growth of learning; legal procedures and agencies to safeguard persons and property; and the rise of voluntary associations, notably the guilds, to produce and distribute goods and human services. All of these played a part in rooting urban life deeply in Europe beginning 500 years after the Roman Empire had disappeared as a cohesive entity.

THE MEDIEVAL CITY

The cities that came to be established during the Middle Ages consisted of jumbled structures clustered together under the shelter of a protecting wall and encircling moat. The only premeditated design that was apparent in them lay in the central or near-central location of the marketplace and the relatively straight streets leading to it from the guarded portals in the surrounding wall. Occasionally religious considerations were decisive, as in dividing a city into 12 districts representing the Apostles of Christ.

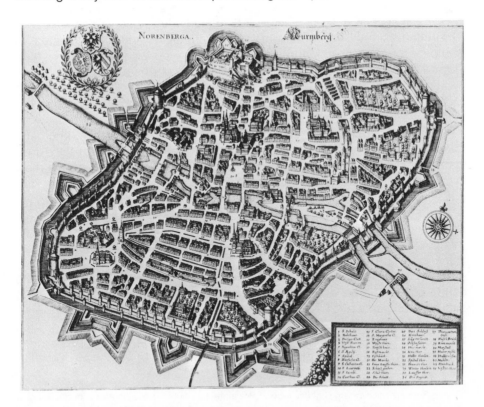

The walled city of medieval Nurenburg centering on the cathedral and open-air market.

Not atypically, the European city of the Middle Ages had the seat of princely and ecclesiastical authority at its very heart. Around the palace and the cathedral in roughly concentric rings according to diminishing status stood the homes of the several social strata. The most spacious and well built, the city residences of the local nobility and the most prosperous burghers, were nearest to the center. Prominent too, adjacent to either the marketplace or the civic core, were to be found the guildhalls, community baths, warehouses, and other public buildings. Toward the periphery one came to a hodgepodge of hovels housing the poor.

Space was socially segregated in the preindustrial city, there being "quarters," or "wards," even walled off from one another, for each of the ethnic, castelike minorities making up the population. Little specialized use was made of land, since homes served also as workshops, churches as schools, and civic centers, such as the guildhalls, also as places of religious observance.

The preindustrial city of medieval Europe had its own form of social organization. The governmental elite was made up of the few aristocrats who possessed the countryside as vassals to the higher, regional lord. For him they commandeered labor, performed military duty, and collected taxes, more often than not in the form of farm commodities and crafted wares. In service to both the church and the nobility were the local clergy. They legitimized feudal rule as the secular expression of God's heavenly ways.

Engaged in turning out handmade goods, the townspeople subsisted in a condition of marked subordination. Between them and the top governing elite of the aristocracy and the clergy, however, came to stand the increasingly affluent merchants. Their wealth enabled them gradually to encroach upon the prerogatives of the landed gentry at the same time that they drew themselves apart from the rank-and-file. Outcast groups performing the most menial and despised tasks, butchering cattle, working as porters, and digging graves, rounded out the status system.

The extended family, the subordination of women and their confinement to domesticity, age grading with those of advanced age accorded greatest recognition, a respect for theology, and the permeation of religion in economic and political affairs were other pronounced tendencies in the medieval city of Europe. National and regional government was at first in the hands of the landed elite, but in time these wider ruling circles came to include merchants already prominent in local urban administration.

Reviewing all this, Sjoberg concludes that for the most part preindustrial cities were "integral parts of broader social structures."[3] European cities usually grew up in some opposition to the ideology of feudalism. Yet their

[3] Svend Riemer, *The Modern City* (New York: Prentice-Hall, 1952), pp. 22ff, and Gideon Sjoberg, "The Pre-Industrial City," *American Journal of Sociology, 60* (March 1955), are instructive in this regard.

sociocultural separation from the larger society that existed during the medieval era has been greatly overstated.

PREINDUSTRIAL CITIES OUTSIDE EUROPE

The preindustrial city was, of course, not confined to medieval Western Europe. In Russia (at Novgorod and Kiev), in Asia, the Middle East, and Africa, too, trade was carried on at urban centers.[4] For example, Ibn Yasin, pan-Islamist of the 11th century, took Sudanese Aoudaghast on his march southward from Maghreb in 1055. Aoudaghast was situated at the southern terminous of the trans-Saharan caravan trail from Sijilmassa. Now gone, Aoudaghast was "a very large city with several markets, many date palms and henna trees as big as olives." It was "filled with fine homes and solid buildings."[5]

The territory of Ghana lay between the northern salt deposits and the gold-bearing soil of Wangara. The Ghanans tried to monopolize the resources of both by imposing tribute on the caravans passing through. The capital of Ghana consisted of two cities six miles apart. One contained the King's seat and domed huts encircled by a wall. The other was the site of a dozen mosques and was a merchant city of Muslims who had migrated south to trade. Excavations 205 miles north of Bamako on the Niger have confirmed a built-up area of one square mile suggestive of a population that may have numbered 30,000.

When commerce was revived in Europe during the Middle Ages it was not long before it crossed the Mediterranean and penetrated the sub-Sahara. Of this Basil Davidson writes:

> *Timbuktu and Djenne, Walata, Gao, Agades—these were the Milans and Nuremburgs of the medieval Sudan: much less magnificent, indeed, yet rich and powerful and imposing in their time and place. Trading cities first and foremost, they welcomed the caravans which came in stumbling thirst out of the northern desert with loads of copper and salt, Venetian beads, the sword blades of Europe and Damascus. They assembled and dispatched the caravans which embarked again northward on that fearful journey, often with slaves, and the merchants with their even more precious purseloads of gold. Their reputation spread across the world.[6]*

---

[4] For a review of early Arabic preindustrial urbanism, see L. Carl Brown, ed., *From Madina to Metropolis* (Princeton, N.J.: Darwin Press, 1973).

[5] Basil Davidson, *The Lost Cities of Africa* (Boston: Little, Brown, 1959), p. 84.

[6] Ibid., p. 90.

In Asia, preindustrial centers flourished in present-day China, Korea, and Indo-China for literally thousands of years. These cities were administrative capitals, centers of trade, military citadels, religious shrines, and places where aristocrats could enjoy ease and luxury. Like their European counterparts, Asia's cities waxed and waned over the centuries according to the shifting fortunes of dynasties, military conquest, and economic changes. Like their European analogues too, the population centers of Asia were inseparable from their regional localities. The cities of Asia evidenced regional influence in their architecture, language, handicrafts, ethnic composition, and municipal government.

PREINDUSTRIAL CITIES AS CULTURAL CENTERS

Among Europe's great commercial cities during the Middle Ages were Florence, Milan, Upsala, Stockholm, Genoa, Rouen, Paris, York, London, Winchester (the old capital of England), Toledo, Nuremburg, Cologne, and Hamburg. They were the product of the revival of trade. Yet the European preindustrial city always remained an integral part of the whole agrarian feudal social order. This was most conspicuous in the cities which served as cultural centers during the Middle Ages, namely, the cathedral cities and university towns.

CATHEDRAL CITIES

Religion and government were both of importance in establishing the European preindustrial city. According to the Oxford historian F. M. Powicke, the acceptance of Christianity in Western Europe was less a matter of individual conversion than "an affair of state."[7] Successful missionaries like St. Boniface in Germany during the eighth century and the Cistercian monk Christian of Oliva in the thirteenth century made certain that secular and ecclesiastical authority were joined together. Thus a cultural tradition adapting Christianity to paganism came to be established.

With the passing of time, the Christian Church became the institutionalized expression of European society. Clearly, the Church legitimized the State. But above all, the Church afforded the masses supernatural sanctions for the vicissitudes of their lives and held out the prospect of eternal salvation beyond the grave.

No doubt the most tangible form taken by medieval Christianity was church and monastic architecture. The structures of this tradition were crowned by the Romanesque and the Renaissance Gothic cathedrals that

[7] "The Christian Life," in C. G. Crump and E. F. Jacob, eds., *The Legacy of the Middle Ages* (Oxford: Clarenson Press, 1962), p. 22.

were as much a part of the European preindustrial city as were the handicraft economy and the communal political organization. The cathedral should not be thought of as simply a monument apart from the daily life of the medieval city. Far from it. Each cathedral was constructed under spiritual and secular administration and with the close cooperation of the merchant and craft guilds. As the center of worship the cathedral involved all of the different orders of the local society.

The mature Gothic phase of medieval church architecture embodied traceried windows, ribbed vaults, and flying buttresses. Stone-cutting, stained glass, sculpture, altar-carving, gilding, carpentry, heraldic flags and shields, glazed tiles, tapestries, murals, sarcophagi, furniture, and enamel work—all of which went into the cathedral—were the contributions of engineers, craftsmen, artisans, and artists forged into cooperative endeavor by the guilds and the economic institutions of the commune. Municipal pride motivated gifts of labor and money in order to make the local cathedral not only a place of worship but the cynosure of all eyes.

CENTERS OF EDUCATION

Except in Italy, the coming of the Dark Ages to Europe had been accompanied by the disappearance of the old imperial and municipal schools and their replacement by either cathedral or monastic schools run by the Church. Novitiates were trained to their future duties within the Church, while clerks and men at arms were schooled at their masters' castles.

Schools continued to be maintained under municipal auspices throughout the Middle Ages only in Italy. Such schools were eventually to be very valuable to the merchant burgesses because it was to the schools and their cultivation of law and the arts of expression that the nascent Third Estate—the urban commune—frequently turned in their struggle for home rule against the feudal aristocracy.[8] Town authorities in Italy were the first to capitalize on their own academic resources in their struggle for autonomy. Later in Britain, France, and Germany other urban leaders applied themselves to the problem of gaining control over the schools in their midst, which were administered by the Church. Often a compromise solution had to be worked out in which authority was shared between the Church and the municipality, perhaps by having a monk employed as the teacher and the commune responsible for paying his salary. Thus greater educational opportunity became available to the merchants and artisans of the European preindustrial city.

[8] R. Freeman Butts, *A Cultural History of Western Education* (New York: McGraw-Hill, 1955), p. 126.

Colleges and Universities

Beginning in the thirteenth century, university growth was very rapid in Western Europe. Bologna, which had had two faculties in 1200 and which was recognized by Pope Innocent the Sixth as a seat of general studies in 1360, was joined by academic centers at Padua, Rome, Perugia, Pisa, Florence, and Turin. Besides Paris, French universities were located in Toulouse, Avignon, Grenoble, Poitiers, Caen, and Montpellier. In central Europe were found the universities of Prague, Cracow, Vienna, Heidelberg, Leipzig, Freiburg, Budapest, and others as well. England possessed only Oxford and Cambridge, both of them modeled after the University of Paris, though Scotland had three universities established before the Reformation: St. Andrew, Glasgow, and Aberdeen.[9]

Conflicts between town and gown were not uncommon in medieval Europe. These often involved students and professors charged with crimes and the question of who had legal jurisdiction over them. Another reason for friction lay in the opportunity for merchants and money lenders to profiteer at the expense of the academic community. It was actually a dispute of this sort that led to the migration from Oxford to Northampton in 1261 or thereabouts and the establishment of a permanent university at Cambridge. Indeed, declares Hastings Rashdall, "half the universities in Europe owed their origin to such migrations."[10]

Humanism

Medieval European cities brought about the recovery of ancient culture with its stress on human development. One notable instance would be fifteenth-century Florence, described by Harold Acton as "the centre of human culture, second only to Athens in its influence on European civilization."[11] So influential was Florence in the advancement of humanism that the Italian language long came to be spoken of as merely the "Florentine vernacular."

Business success for several generations of Florentine merchants, bankers, lawyers, and the like predisposed the entire class to value leisure, intellectual activity, and urbanity. They sought out scholars and artists who might commemorate their lives in biographies or grace their palaces with aesthetic creations. The quintessence of these mercantile princes was to be found in the Medici and the syndicate who ruled the principality of central Italy. Cosimo de' Medici furthered the study of Platonism in the Platonic

[9] A chronology is contained in "Medieval Universities," *Encyclopedia Britannica* (Chicago: Encyclopedia Britannica, 1967), Vol. 22, pp. 745–49.

[10] Hastings Rashdall, *The Universities of Europe in the Middle Ages*, ed. by F. M. Powicke and A. B. Emden (London: Oxford University Press, 1964), Vol. III, pp. 86ff.

[11] In his "Medicean Florence" in Sir Maurice Bowra et al., eds., *Golden Ages of the Great Cities* (London: Thomas and Hudson, 1952).

Florence, Italy, in 1470.

Academy at Florence. Fra Angelico decorated the walls of the Convent of San Marco that Cosimo had had rebuilt and which was also used as a library for treasured manuscripts.

Lorenzo, grandson of Cosimo, continued in the latter half of the century to build up Florence as a cultural center although he also restored the University of Pisa to a position of eminence in the field of legal studies. Lorenzo maintained an art collection in the gardens of San Marco and patronized the sculptor Verrocchio. Michelangelo was only one, albeit the greatest, of the students who studied at San Marco. Botticelli also made his studio in Florence. These achievements in secular and sensuous art suffered a temporary setback after Lorenzo's death when Savonarola succeeded in restoring ecclesiastical puritanism, though Savonarola was himself condemned, hanged, and burned in 1498 in the Piazza Della Signoria of Florence.

The Growth of Science

Humanistic philosophy meant not simply the recovery of antiquity but also a freer conception of man in society. One element in that more liberal attitude which the European centers of higher education were fashioning in the later Middle Ages was the pursuit of science.

Two Oxford scholars of the thirteenth century proved unusually significant in this regard. Robert Grosseteste fathered an interest in Aristotelian logic and also wrote on mathematics and physical science, especially agriculture and medicine. By far the more influential of the two, the Franciscan monk Roger Bacon deplored excessive dependence on formal logic, metaphysics, and intellectual authority. Instead, Bacon asserted the merits of observation, experimentation, and inductive reasoning to the point where, as Rashdall says, "All the characteristic ideas of the sixteenth century were held in solution, as it were, in the writings of Roger Bacon."[12] It was Bacon who anticipated the enormous strides in mathematics that the Enlightenment would take in facilitating the measurement of physical force in a harmonious system subject to general laws, and which would accelerate the movement toward industrial urbanism.

FROM PREINDUSTRIAL TO INDUSTRIAL URBANISM

European urban society of the late Middle Ages laid down the habits of mind, human relationships, and social structures that made possible the Industrial Revolution and, furthermore, our own modern social order.

INNOVATIONS IN BUSINESS PRACTICES

Among the sociocultural innovations that had momentous consequences were the belief in a fair and customary price; the guaranteeing of the quality of goods; marketing as a dignified and honorable occupation; and the prompt payment of debts. Coined money safe from arbitrary debasement was yet another concept pioneered for modern times by the medieval commerical city in its struggles with princes determined to pursue their own interests without hindrance. Bills of exchange, banking, and single and double entry bookkeeping added still more to systematic business enterprise.

Of special significance were the types of commercial organizations that the medieval city fostered. Coming out of twelfth-century Genoese shipping, the partnership was the forerunner of stockholding. Eventually the joint-stock company, so vital an element of sixteenth-century commercial expansion in England's Muscovy, East India, and Massachusetts Bay Companies, proved a most applicable device for large-scale business.

Together with these arrangements for encouraging capital formation, investment, and entrepreneurship went the mercantilist regulation of the region or the entire nation. This was largely an extension of the protectionist spirit of the earlier economic policies within the towns. So too were the national tariffs elaborated out of the municipal practice of taxing imports. The intense

[12] Rashdall, op. cit., Vol. III, p. 245.

A late sixteenth-century Flemish market place enlivened by the new spirit of business activity in Europe's urban centers of the time.

rivalries of the Italian cities—Palermo, Venice, Naples, Genoa, Salerno, and Amalfi—kept them from banding together for mutual advantage. Others, however, around the North and Baltic Seas, succeeded in establishing cartels that enacted reciprocal tariffs, cooperated in protecting their liberties, maintained navies against pirates, and even engaged in colonization.

A SECULAR SPIRIT

Behind these undertakings stood an awakened consciousness, a new and strong secular spirit relative to the cultivation of material enterprise in sharp contrast to the ideational Catholicism of liturgy, monasticism, static canon law, contemplation, and commitment to a belief in life after death—all of them consistent with a stable rural economy. Although Protestantism was derived from Lutheran and Calvinist theology, it was the spiritual ally of the ambitious and industrious class of men already brought to high levels of prosperity by the medieval commercial city. That city had often stood against the Church and the landed gentry. The aspiring men of the commune were thus eager to extend their businesses beyond the narrow, separate political units represented by the merely local communities. Toward this end they sought improved security for life and property; more widely standardized weights, measures, and money; and the free ownership, individually, of land rather than the patrimonialism of the old manorial economy.

When Columbus discovered America and Vasco da Gama discovered the sea route to India by way of the Cape of Good Hope within 10 years of each other at the close of the fifteenth century, exploration gave still further impetus to the commercialization of Europe. The maritime transportation that this made possible reoriented Europe to the West and away from the Mediterranean. Amsterdam, Cadiz, Antwerp, St. Malo, Bordeau, and Bristol supplanted Venice, Genoa, Alexandria, and Constantinople. Half a millennium of urban growth, however, had already turned the face of Europe toward the prospect of a new age, one of an aggressive, individualistic, and national order.[13]

Eventually that new "modern" spirit was to be embodied in the industrial city, a phenomenon in the history of urbanization that first appeared in England in the latter part of the eighteenth century but soon diffused throughout Europe, the United States, and many other regions of the world as well.

CONCLUSION

Preindustrial urbanization, which is the record of cities in Europe from the tenth century onward to the Industrial Revolution, developed principally as the commercial aspect of feudal agrarianism. The first cities that arose on the continent long after the collapse of Roman rule did so as mercantile adjuncts to the fortified manor houses of the lords of the local countryside. In these bourgs, where handicrafts were turned out and trade carried on, the new freemen gradually won a greater share of autonomy for themselves and their own guilds of merchants and craftsmen.

Though often chartered as self-governing communes, medieval cities did not stand entirely apart from the prevailing agrarian, feudal system. In fact, as religious and administrative centers they made up an important element in the whole social fabric of the Middle Ages, and exemplified the cultural values of Catholic Christendom as well as the dynastic rivalries of local princes.

Yet in pursuing a life of commerce, the preindustrial cities of medieval Europe increased production and fashioned a set of social institutions, including business practices, that led eventually to the emergence of the modern industrial metropolis. The sequence of events was, of course, convoluted and indirect, involving as it did agricultural progress, religious conflict, innovations in education, the discovery and exploration of the New World, and the appearance of a philosophy of secular humanism and enterprise which

[13] A concise account of the socioeconomic background of the Reformation is James W. Thompson, *Economic and Social History of Europe in the Later Middle Ages: 1300–1530* (New York: Frederick Ungar, 1960).

helped not only to create modern science but also usher in steam technology, beginning in the eighteenth century.

FOR FURTHER READING

Edwin Benson, *Life in a Medieval City* (New York: Macmillan, 1920). Surveys medieval Europe with special reference to urbanization.

Jacob Burckhart, *The Civilization of the Renaissance in Italy* (New York: Harper & Row, 1958). On the refinement of life that accompanied the acquisition of wealth in Italy's cities.

T. A. W. Buckley, *The Great Cities of the Middle Ages* (London: Routledge and Kegal Paul, 1971). Detailed and comprehensive.

Robert Dickinson, *The West European City* (London: Routledge and Kegan Paul, 1951). Interprets urbanization geographically.

Michael Maclaglen, *The City of Constantinople* (New York: Frederick A. Praeger, 1968). Urbanism under Christianity outside Western Europe.

Lewis Mumford, *The City in History* (New York: Harcourt Brace, 1961). Cities in the West and the changes they have undergone in time.

John H. Mundy and Peter Riesenberg, *Medieval Town* (New York: Van Nostrand, 1958). Town life in the Middle Ages.

Henri Pirenne, *Economic and Social History of Medieval Europe* (London: Kegan Paul, Trench, Trubner, 1936). On the renewal of urbanism following its Roman decline.

Josiah C. Russell, *Medieval Regions and Their Cities* (Bloomington, Ind.: Indiana University Press, 1972). Medieval cities in Western Europe, with some attention also to the Near East.

Gideon Sjoberg, *The Pre-Industrial City: Past and Present* (New York: Free Press, 1960). The nature of cities in preindustrial societies and the various facets of their organization.

Max Weber, *The City,* trans. by Don Martindale and Gertrude Neuwirth (New York: Free Press, 1958). The place and function of the city in Western civilization.

CHAPTER 4

INDUSTRIAL URBANIZATION

Industrial urbanization, often referred to as modernization, denotes a distinct pattern of settlement and social organization. Chief among its characteristics are inanimate power for manufacturing, transportation, and communication; a diversified division of labor; a high material standard of living made possible by mass production; large population size accompanied by its concentration in organizationally very complex communities; the decline of the family and the rise of the individual as the unit of production in the economy; a predilection for science, natural philosophy, and a secular outlook on life; formal education; communication by means of mass-media dissemination; and, finally, the possession of political power by a financial-industrial-governmental elite shared, in varying degrees, with a large hierarchy of professional and technological functionaries.[1]

[1] The latter should not be taken to refer exclusively to Western pluralism, for industrial urbanism also characterizes Communist society. Under Communism, a patrimonial political leadership exercises

Incident to the original development of industrial urbanization in Europe was the preindustrial stage of urban history. In fact, the industrialization of Europe following 1750 would probably not have occurred at all had it not been for the socioeconomic transition that the commercial city of feudalism brought about prior to the Industrial Revolution itself. Preindustrial urbanism was responsible for advances in social organization, business practices, humanistic philosophy, and scientific method. All of these, as we learned in Chapter 3, contributed to the quickening of social change in the direction of modernization.

The last links in the chain of events by which urbanism materialized out of the feudal preindustrial system fell into place originally in England. There the industrial-urban mode of life arose first.

THE TRANSITION FROM THE PREINDUSTRIAL CITY IN ENGLAND

The preindustrial city of medieval Europe was essentially the fortified center of an agrarian region governed in feudal fashion. In certain cases the preindustrial city was also a scene of artistic and intellectual culture.

In most instances, too, the preindustrial community of Europe existed as a nucleus of economic production. It processed local raw materials like wool, cotton, clay, flax, copper, iron, lumber, silk, and food, all of these activities closely controlled by associations of merchants and artisans. These cities served only the immediate rural area. Depending on the skill of their craftsmen, the enterprise of their merchants, and the means of transportation available to them, they might also produce for a wider market. The commercial cities of England were particularly enterprising, and for this reason they were better able than those of other nations to facilitate industrialization.

The industrial city of England came about as a result of a combination of forces, material and nonmaterial, manifesting themselves in the 100 to 150 years before the invention of the steam engine by James Watt in 1769, and not simply as the outgrowth of preindustrial urbanism. Specifically, the factors that prepared the ground for English urban industrialization included new inventions, both agricultural and manufacturing; new types of social roles and relationships; demographic changes; and emergent ideological and intellectual currents justifying the institution of innovative urban patterns. These elements can scarcely be separated from one another although they have to be described individually.

power in conjunction with the uppermost technologists of the industrial and military segments of the social structure in a manner not wholly unlike the state of affairs in non-Communist nations.

A meeting of a merchants guild, probably during the mid-sixteenth century.

AGRICULTURAL CHANGE AND PROGRESS

Much technical progress took place in English agriculture during the six-teenth century in the design and introduction of farm implements.[2] Con-sequently, English agriculture was caught up in a rising tide of activity, as

[2] An excellent review is to be found in Louis W. Moffit, *England on the Eve of the Industrial Revolution* (London: Frank Case, 1963), first published in 1925.

can be seen from the introduction at that time of the "new husbandry," as historians call it. In brief, what transpired was that the feudal manorial economy in which strips of land had been sown to wheat, barley, and oats augmented by sections set aside for fuel, fodder, and unproductive rotation was replaced by the enclosure of fields and their intensive tillage by individual proprietors producing for the commercial market. This proved to be a system that greatly increased farm yields. The vast improvement in English farming that took place on the eve of the Industrial Revolution is made evident by the fact that in the 56 years following 1700, the export of wheat increased 416 percent; the export of barley 281 percent; and that of malt, 317 percent.[3]

As might be expected of so expanded a farm technology, important changes took place in the manner of marketing agricultural commodities. A network of specialized middlemen dealing in farm products grew up following the Restoration. The widening benefits of improved agriculture created a market for more crafted goods, while the division of labor in the agricultural-related trades served as a model for specialization in industry.

Accompanying and facilitating the demise of the manorial economy were, of course, manifold changes in the laws of land tenure. Hundreds of thousands of luckless former serfs now found themselves freemen but without subsistence and literally forced off the land, with the result that the English countryside became stripped of a good deal of its population. In 1688, some 90 percent of all Englishmen were engaged in agriculture. By 1769, the comparable figure was closer to 80 percent.[4] A landless populace was thus readied for manufacturing and, in fact, had already migrated to the towns as potential industrial labor.

TECHNOLOGICAL INNOVATION

The greatest number of these landless Englishmen went into the Midlands, particularly into the towns situated among the rich mineral deposits of Lancashire County. Mineral resources were plentiful in Lancashire in the strip from Blackburn through Burnley and up to Colne, and also in the neighborhood of Wigan, Rochdale, Bolton, and Bury. A relatively large amount of mechanical production had come into operation in England prior to the use of steam, and most of it was in the Midlands, owing to a relative freedom from guilds and medieval municipal regulations in the communities of that district, which had grown up late in the feudal age and had not had time to become encrusted with vested interests.

Whatever the original causes, however, English industrialization was most strongly felt in Lancashire. In the interval between 1685 and 1760, and *before* mechanization, it should be noted, Liverpool grew tenfold, Manches-

[3] *Ibid.*, p. 112.
[4] *Ibid.*, Ch. 5.

ter and Birmingham perhaps sevenfold, and Sheffield sixfold. In the half century following 1700, Lancashire County's population increased nearly 80 percent, rising from 166,200 in 1700 to 297,400 in 1750, 19 years prior to the first appearance of Watt's steam turbine.

With the coming of the Industrial Revolution, English manufacturing grew still further in scale. The steam engine gave industry unprecedented power with which to turn out products in unheard of volume. Since English industry was already highly advanced from the standpoint of technology and economic organization, the change from the domestic system of the early eighteenth century to factory production under steam 50 years later was as much transitional as it was abrupt.

LEGAL CHANGES

The evolutionary process by which the new economic order emerged from the preindustrial English commercial system can be observed in the legal changes that had been going on for more than a century before the Industrial Revolution.

The growth of water-driven factories in England overcame many legal obstacles before industrialization. Elizabethan legislation had given a monopoly over the crafts to duly trained persons, so that the ownership, say, of looms was forbidden to those engaged in finishing operations. Also, in the interest of preventing harm to the masters and journeymen, the number of apprentices in any given line of work was severely limited. All such regulatory measures had the intent of strengthening occupational and commercial security, but they obviously did block the employment of large numbers of unskilled workers in factories when the presence of many landless people and the availability of new machinery made their employment potentially profitable. Such workers had to be defined as apprentices despite their noncraft relationship to the employer, and it was therefore necessary time and again to get the restrictions temporarily removed, even against the representations of the guilds.

The civil wars of the mid-seventeenth century reduced the number of artisans. This also helped ease resistance to the employment of unskilled labor in the mechanized but water-powered factories. After the Restoration an attempt was made to enforce the work laws, but legal fictions frustrated the intent of the policy. For instance, a workman was declared a master after seven years of illicit service during which time he had paid token fines to avoid indictment. Thus the Elizabethan statutes gradually passed into disuse.

PERSONAL FREEDOM AND LAISSEZ-FAIRE IDEOLOGY

Both technological and social change stemming mainly from the preindustrial commercial city preceded the appearance of the industrial city. So too did a new conception of personal freedom and a laissez-faire ideology.[5]

Even prior to the French Revolution, England had already attained the substantial degree of personal liberty necessary to sever people's ties to the soil and to allow them to settle in new places, work in factories and mines, and operate railroads. In addition, the new economic order which could exist only in an urban milieu was given secure intellectual legitimization by Adam Smith's *Wealth of Nations,* published in 1776. The mercantilist theory current from the fourteenth century on, held that a people's wealth consisted of the gold they were able to accumulate. This thinking was embodied in the sumptuary laws against extravagent expenditure beyond one's proper station in life, and in the regulatory policies designed to keep specie and bullion out of international trade. In contradistinction to the theory of mercantilism, Smith advanced the principle that nations trading their surplus goods with one another would all benefit accordingly. His laissez-faire doctrine against the protection of domestic industry only furthered the already existing tendencies toward the factory system. The French Revolution, of course, gave powerful momentum to free trade everywhere, but the English industrial city had already appeared by 1789.

ENGLISH INDUSTRIAL-URBAN SOCIETY

The first industrial cities of England also differed greatly from the preindustrial cities that were in existence when they arose. Earlier, factories driven by water were found adjacent to the towns in England, because the towns were the markets for their products. These work places were not concentrated in tight clusters, however. All of this was decisively changed by the introduction of steam.

MANCHESTER: A PROTOTYPE

Consider Manchester as the typical case of industrial urbanization in England. Manchester had merely 8000 inhabitants as late as 1717, though it always seemed larger perhaps because it served as the trading point for the entire district to a depth of some ten miles. The cutting of the Worsley Canal brought cheap coal to Manchester, and afterwards the completion of the

[5] *Economic Development in the Nineteenth Century* (New York: Augustus M. Kelley, 1967), originally published in 1932 as No. 109 in *Studies in Economics and Political Science* of the London School of Economics.

Mersey Canal gave Manchester an easier route to Liverpool. As a result, Manchester's population began to increase even during its watermill days, the enclosures to the south having brought thousands there. The presence of this large labor force, then, in turn, became a stimulus to the location of machine industry in the already growing city.

In 1786, Arkwright's spinning mill began to change Manchester, although at that time it pierced the Manchester sky with the only chimney around.[6] Fifteen years later, in a Manchester now having 100,000 people, 50 such mills, most of them powered by steam, had been established. Alongside them now were rows of working-class dwellings on damp, dark streets, overhung by a pall of smoke. Other additions were the large houses on landscaped tracts some distance southeast from the city which the so-called "cotton lords" had built for themselves.

Though large—with a quarter of a million people by 1850—Manchester lacked municipal beauty. True, Manchester's main streets were now broader than they had been earlier, and the center of the city had been improved, with many new shops there and high brick houses for the retail merchants. But there was not a single garden in the entire municipality! The industrialists of Manchester simply devoted themselves to production and profit, not the endowment of either civic facilities or the high culture of the church, the landed gentry, and the preindustrial merchant guilds. Illuminating gas and iron pipes for carrying water were now available. Yet these improvements were slow in being introduced into Manchester or the other new industrial cities of Britain, governed as they were by cost-conscious oligarchies little mindful of the public weal.[7]

The spirit of the times was one of individual initiative and personal development, "of substituting science for custom," as Jeremy Bentham wrote. As a result, public welfare suffered in urban Britain. Only by the middle of the nineteenth century when agitation by the Chartists had made itself felt and numerous commissions had reported grave problems of public health, sanitation, congestion, and services, were legislative reforms even drawn up. No town-planning measure, however, was enacted in England until the beginning of the twentieth century.

THE INDUSTRIAL URBAN BOOM

Manchester, Leeds, Liverpool, indeed the scores of industrial cities that had arisen in England, particularly in the Midlands, possessed a uniform ugliness and indifference to public amenities. But they also had an underlying

[6] For Manchester see Paul Mantoux, *The Industrial Revolution in the Eighteenth Century,* trans. by Marjorie Vernon (New York: Harcourt Brace, 1927).

[7] L. Hammond and Barbara Hammond, *The Rise of Modern Industry* (New York: Harcourt Brace, 1937), pp. 224–28.

vitality. From these industrial cities poured a stream of manufactured wealth that went out into the country, across Europe, and even beyond the seas. Though the large mass of obscure factory workers might exist in ignominious fashion, the newly rich industrial aristocracy, the founders and managers of the steam-driven "satanic mills," were not only enjoying their immense profits but plowing them back into the further expansion of their plants.

Certain signal inventions that had made mechanical production possible in the first place were everywhere installed in greater and greater numbers. In the cotton industry there were Arkwright's water-frame patented in 1769; Hargreaves' spinning-jenny, in 1770; and Crompton's mule, in 1779. These technical improvements created a manufacturing and consequently, an urban boom in England. Everywhere in old barns and renovated outbuildings, loom-shoops arose. There was work for all hands, men, women, and children alike, although often at mere subsistence levels and always under the threat of a collapse of the market or technological unemployment as the result of the introduction of a more efficient machine or work process.

The power-loom illustrates the labor-saving consequences of machine production in the first decades of the Industrial Revolution. Just as the spinning-jenny had affected the manufacture of thread, the power-loom made weaving a factory process and took it out of the home where it had been the mainstay of the cottage industry superintended by the putting-out merchants of the commercial towns. The power-loom cut greatly into the demand of weavers, intensifying competition for jobs in industry. By 1829, the wage rate for weaving calico in the new factories had dropped to one-sixth of what it had been in 1814.

It was this type of pauperism that led Thomas Malthus to write his *Essay on Population,* first published in 1798, in which he warned against the inevitability of population pressing on the means of subsistence in conformity to a universal law of nature. Later, when it had been voluminously documented by the investigations of royal commissions, the dolorous condition of England's working class became the basis of Karl Marx's indictment of capitalism as a predatory system that would have to be overthrown by force.

THE RAILROADS

As has been indicated, the enlargement of the market was conducive to the concentration of population in cities. Indeed the use of power on a large scale, beginning in the middle of the eighteenth century, necessitated great demographic density. But it was the development of the new means of transportation and communication in the nineteenth century that assured the final triumph of industrial urbanism.[8]

[8] The thesis set forth in Adna Weber, *The Growth of Cities in the Nineteenth Century* (Ithaca, N.Y.: Cornell University Press, 1965), originally published in 1899.

The colliers of the Newcastle district first took the lead in exploiting railroad transportation, with George Stephenson in charge of engineering at the Killingworth Colliery in 1813. The first passenger and freight line, the one between Liverpool and Manchester, was opened in 1830. It immediately dispelled all fears about its success, and trunk lines soon followed.

A parallel combination of business interests became rapidly apparent as a result of this improved transportation. The railroads made raw materials cheaper and diminished the importance of local natural resources. This enabled manufacturers to locate their plants close to their customers, therefore in the large cities, which then grew larger still.

INDUSTRIAL CAPITALISM

The new industry of Britain's cities affected not only individual population centers. It also modified English social structure as a whole.

At the middle of the eighteenth century, the British economy and consequently, the nation's institutional life was headed by two classes: country landlords, by virtue of their monopoly of land, and urban merchants with their control over trade. These elites came to be successfully challenged as an aftermath of the Industrial Revolution by the new manufacturers now possessed of the competitive advantages of steam and mechanical production.[9] Among the most notable of the early English industrialists were Josiah Wedgewood of the Staffordshire potteries, and James Watt and his partner, Mathew Boulton, with their Birmingham engineering works.

Basic to the rise of this new class of industrialists was their participation as businessmen from the purchase of raw materials through their manufacturing and, finally, to the disposal of their products on the market. Since the rise of towns in medieval Europe, these functions had been carried on by the well-to-do, socially superior merchants jobbing out the processing operations to lowly cottagers working at jennies and mules, and to journeymen artisans doing the finishing work in town. Now industrial capital was put directly into commercial relations. In other words, whether pottery, iron, or textiles, the new industry called for much capital, but its profitability allowed the manufacturers to engage in marketing their products too. As a result, they set up warehouses, business offices, and even banks. This not only strengthened their financial position and political power, it also contributed even more to urban concentration.

If the new manufacturing gentry had little concern for the welfare of the urban communities in which they conducted their enterprises, they did exhibit great interest in national and international affairs. Britain's cities were not represented in Parliament, but interest in electoral reform lagged far

[9] Cf. Witt Bowden, *Industrial Society in England Towards the End of the Eighteenth Century* (New York: Barnes & Noble, 1965), Ch. 3.

The Cyclops steel works at Sheffield, England, in 1853.

behind the organization of manufacturers to further their own ends through concerted action. Following tentative local activities that had been going on in Britain for no less than 50 years, the General Chamber of Manufacturers was organized in 1785. This industrial group voiced the concerns of the textile, pottery, and iron manufacturers with respect to government policy. In such a manner were the new urban industrialists consolidating their power.[10]

THE RISE OF THE MIDDLE CLASS AND LABOR

Although economic and political power was progressively centralized in the hands of the industrial capitalists, it was not long before a counter-trend toward the sharing of power with other segments of the industrial-urban population began to manifest itself. This became evident in the rising affluence of the new classes of retailers, clerks, property managers, factory supervisors, and purveyors of services that the industrial city had created. It also showed itself in the pressures toward democracy and equality that were increasingly felt by the great mass of English city dwellers as a whole. The 1832 Electoral Reform Bill enfranchised the middle class, not only by giving cities an elective form of government but also by establishing retail business on a freer legal footing than before.

[10] W. Cunningham, *The Growth of English Industry and Commerce in Modern Times* (Cambridge, Eng.: Cambridge University Press, 1907), Vol. I, pp. 602ff.

Industrial labor soon joined in the agitation for greater socioeconomic equity that the middle class had pioneered. The London Workingmen's Association published its "People's Charter" in 1838 claiming universal suffrage and voting by secret ballot as the means of ultimately attaining "social equality." Workers threatened a general strike if the Chartist demands remained unmet, and in the long run they were all complied with by the British government. Factory legislation ameliorated many of the unwholesome conditions in Britain's industrial plants, while a stream of enactments relieved much of the physical and social distress of Britain's lower-class urban population: sanitary facilities mandated in the home, a network of underground sewers, improved zoning and housing codes, paved streets, outdoor lighting, food inspection, the administration of public health, parks, improved police and fire departments, and an adequate system of mass transit to supply the needs of an urban population grown to unforeseen proportions.

THE GROWTH OF CITIES IN AMERICA

In principle, the 350-year history of American urbanization resembles that of England's, which of course covered a far longer period of time. Here on this side of the Atlantic, city building was preindustrial first. Later, American urbanization turned to industrialization. In the course of further develop-

---

EXHIBIT 4-1 The Great Towns of America: 1790, 1870, and 1970

	1790	1870	1970
The Great Towns of America	1. New York, N.Y.	New York, N.Y.	New York, N.Y.
	2. Philadelphia, Pa.	Philadelphia, Pa.	Chicago, Ill.
	3. Boston, Mass.	Brooklyn, N.Y.	Los Angeles, Ca.
	4. Charleston, S.C.	St. Louis, Mo.	Philadelphia, Pa.
	5. Baltimore, Md.	Chicago, Ill.	Detroit, Mich.
	6. Salem, Mass.	Baltimore, Md.	Houston, Texas
	7. Newport, R.I.	Boston, Mass.	Baltimore, Md.
	8. Providence, R.I.	Cincinnati, Ohio	Dallas, Texas
	9. Gloucester, Mass.	New Orleans, La.	Washington, D.C.
	10. Newburyport, Mass.	San Francisco, Ca.	Cleveland, Ohio

Both the Westward movement and American urbanization from 1790 to 1970 are revealed by this exhibit as well as two other features of our national history: the growth of the federal establishment at the nation's capital and the recent surge to prominence of the sun belt, stretching across our southern and southwestern states.

Source: Population Education Newsletter (Washington, D.C.: Population Reference Bureau, March 1976). Derived from James E. Vance, Jr., "Cities in the Shaping of the American Nation," *Journal of Geography*, (January 1976), pp. 41–52.

---

ment, metropolitan centers dominating whole regions appeared and then coalesced into a single national urban system topped by an "impacted" east coast of megalopolitan dimensions.

In certain respects, though, the course of urban progress, first in colonial America and then in the United States, diverged from the British prototype. Among the most significant differences were the establishment of towns as part of the British mercantile-imperialist policy; the presence of an idealistic spirit of social reform that influenced city planning; and aggressive economic expansion especially westward toward the frontier. These factors gave American urban development a character which set it apart from the urbanization of England.

THE PREINDUSTRIAL PERIOD

In 1640, New Amsterdam had a population of 400; Boston, 1200; and Newport, only 96. Such towns were encouraged by the British government as trade centers for its transatlantic empire. Not only these towns, but also Charleston and Savannah came into being as entrepôts from which to import British goods and to ship vital raw materials home, and where vessels of the Royal Navy could be berthed against the king's enemies in the Western Hemisphere, principally France and Spain.

At the same time, individual proprietors like Maryland's Lord Baltimore, Georgia's James Oglethorpe, and Pennsylvania's William Penn looked on the New World as the virgin soil in which to root a social order superior to that of the Old. So, in 1681, Penn instructed his commissioners on laying out Philadelphia to see to it that in the placing of every house "there be ground on each side for gardens or orchards or fields, that [Philadelphia] may be a green country town, which will never be burnt, and always be wholesome."[11]

Though urbanization went on in colonial America in the seventeenth and eighteenth centuries, the country remained a rural society. By 1730 New York had grown to only 8000, Boston to 13,000, and Philadelphia had reached slightly more than 11,000. In 1820, almost half a century after independence, the United States contained just 12 cities with a population of at least 10,000.

Apart from mercantile and philanthropic interest in city building on this side of the Atlantic, another type of motivation contributed to urbanization in America. This was as an adjunct to the agrarian conquest of the great heartland of the continent. Norfolk, Baltimore, Wilmington—the coastal cities generally—became suppliers of the vigorous westward movement, which was animated by the presence of unlimited land and which became so con-

---

[11] Quoted from Samuel Hazzard, *Annals of Pennsylvania* (Philadelphia: 1850), pp. 527–31, as cited by Charles N. Glaab, ed., *The American City: A Documentary History* (Homewood, Ill.: Dorsey Press, 1963), p. 36.

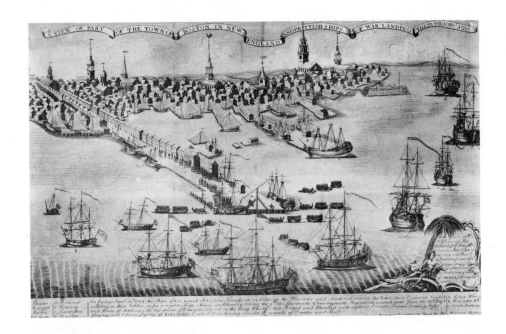

The harbor at Boston, Massachusetts, in 1768, as engraved by Paul Revere.

ducive to political autonomy later on. Soon Pittsburgh, Marietta, and Cincinnati were the western counterparts of these Atlantic ports "from which the farmers could move out and begin to subdue the new land to their purpose."[12]

In the preindustrial United States, each city had a markedly different character from the others.[13] Charleston was gracious, Baltimore uniform and genteel, New Orleans Creole, and St. Louis a hive of activity. Each tended to be a relatively independent center expressive of the local culture and functionally integrated into its natural environment. In this manner, in 1800 Boston was Yankee, Congregational, and abolitionist; and Charleston, patrician, Episcopal, and proslave. The former had small farms surrounding it producing grain and livestock for its inhabitants and the market outside; the latter, plantations sown to cotton and rice. Similarly, the river and canal cities of the nineteenth century—Cincinnati, Buffalo, St. Louis, Louisville, and Pittsburgh—shared the flatboat and frontier civilization of the early West. They varied ethnically, depending on the presence within them of immigrant

[12] Charles N. Glaab and Theodore Brown, *A History of Urban America* (New York: Macmillan, 1967), p. 29.

[13] Carl Bridenbaugh, *Cities in the Wilderness* (New York: Ronald Press, 1938), pp. 160–61.

groups, and economically according to the fur trade, distilling, and the processing of regional commodities such as timber, leather, bricks, and food. In fact, the strong interest which American merchants of the time had in developing the regional potentialities of their cities has led historian Blake McKelvey to think of these communities as transitional between the preindustrial and the industrial types.[14]

At any rate, the pristine environment was still at hand almost everywhere in America's cities, at least up to the middle of the nineteenth century. In 1826, Washington was graced not only by the Capitol and the White House but also by the War Office, Navy Office, the Department of State, the Post Office, and other structures as well, all in the stately if derived neoclassical style. At the time, the city was very small, merely a village in fact, where the natural delights of the Potomac led at least one visitor to exclaim that "it is not in the power of imagination to conceive a scene so replete with every species of beauty."

THE INDUSTRIAL PERIOD

The Civil War was the watershed that separated preindustrial from industrial urban America. One manifestation that a turn of events had taken place was that the scale of growth changed drastically. In the half century from 1860 to 1910, the number of our cities boasting a population of over 100,000 leaped from 9 to 50. In 1860, only 100 places in America had had a population in excess of 10,000. Fifty years later that number had increased to 600, with no fewer than 228 of them over 25,000 in size. Indeed, in 1910, 8 of our cities exceeded half a million in population, and fully 45 percent of all Americans were urban at that time.

Significant technological advances like the railroad, the telegraph, the rotary press, and Cyrus McCormick's reaper had received strong impetus from the legislative policies of the victorious Union over the agrarian Confederacy. Western cities either arose from nothing or expanded enormously as a result of the land booms fostered by the construction of the transcontinental railways. In 1873, the arbitrary choice of Duluth, Minnesota, and Tacoma, Washington, as terminals for the Northern Pacific Railroad made them important centers of population overnight. Cities were clearly instrumental in the settlement of the West and its development of mining, cattle raising, and farming. The railroads not only created these boomtowns in the first place—Denver, Wichita, Omaha, and Dodge City—they also bound them together into a far-flung network that served national and international markets.

Not all communities prospered by any means, though any number did. There were hundreds of ambitious towns encouraged by the railroads. Those

[14] Blake McKelvey, *American Urbanization: A Comparative History* (Glenview, Ill.: Scott, Foresman, 1973), pp. 39ff.

with the most aggressive businessmen and financiers, or manipulators, managed to dominate the surrounding territory and eclipse their local rivals through options, investments, speculation, and sheer chicanery. In some places the discovery of minerals, special inventions, or the pull of ethnic groups to other immigrants, gave some mushrooming cities advantages over their competing neighbors.

The urbanization of the United States was also a process in which millions of farming folk were lured away from the soil. Many novelists have written evocatively of the diminution of the American village and the depopulation of the countryside between the Civil War and World War I—Hamlin Garland, Ellen Glasgow, Theodore Dreiser, Edward Eggleston, Sherwood Anderson, Willa Cather, and Ole Rolvaag. Isolation and loneliness, always present on the farm, became more frustrating than ever in the context of the amenities of the city, such as morning mail deliveries and the daily penny press.

The pleasures of rural life continued, of course, "its picnics and its gatherings at the swimming hole in summer, its nutting and hunting expeditions in fall, its annual county fair and horse races, its family reunions at Thanksgiving, its bob-sled parties of merrymakers in winter, its country dances in all seasons of the year."[15] But these diversions could not long compare with the city's theaters, amusement parks, museums, plazas, restaurants, and above all, the freedom and stimulation of its crowds of people. Fed by the rise of higher education in the form of the high school, technical institute, and municipal college, urban career opportunities cast into the shade the neolithic labor of the farm. Even sweatshop conditions, because they were thought to offer a foothold to the young and aspiring, outweighed the rural perils of drought, flood, winged pests, high interest rates, and piratical freight agents.

The Census of 1890 had first disclosed how widespread the rural exodus was becoming. While Philadelphia reached a million in 1890, two-fifths of Pennsylvania's counties had lost population. In Ohio more than one-half of the 1316 townships were declining in numbers, although the state as a whole was increasing its population by a seventh. Thirty-three hundred farms had been abandoned for agricultural purposes in Maine alone. In 1890, the average wealth of the American farm family was $3250, that of city families in excess of $9000!

Another major portion of the population of urban America at the turn of the century came from European immigration. In the decade of the 1880s, 5.2 million newcomers arrived in the United States, and in the 10 years following 1900, 8.2 million more. By far the majority settled in our cities. Nearly 10 million persons were to be found in America's cities in 1910 who were foreign born. In particular, immigrants formed a significant part of the na-

[15] Arthur Meir Schlesinger, *The Rise of the City: 1878–1898* (New York: Macmillan, 1933), p. 59.

tion's industrial labor force. Approximately half of the residents of Fall River and Duluth were of immigrant origin in 1890, and 40 percent in both Chicago and San Francisco. Even Southern industrial centers like Wheeling, West Virginia, and San Antonio and Galveston, in Texas, attracted large numbers of foreign-born working men and women.[16]

METROPOLITAN REGIONALISM IN THE UNITED STATES

As mentioned earlier in this chapter, the superior economic power of the industrial cities of England had eclipsed that nation's weaker communities of small and moderate size. The functions which the latter centers had been serving, trade, the processing of goods, finance, communications, and the like, passed to the centralizing metropolis because it possessed superior resources and because it constantly opened up added opportunities. A like process of regional dominance unfolded here in the United States at the start of the twentieth century.[17]

The rapid growth of American cities following the Civil War culminated on the eve of World War I in the domination of entire regions by their metropolitan centers, defined for the first time by the 1910 Census as an area of settlement centering on a city of at least 200,000 persons. True, Chicago, Salt Lake City, Denver, Omaha, Minneapolis, Kansas City, and the like, matured first as transportation hubs. Again, certain cities such as Pittsburgh, Cleveland, Detroit, Birmingham, Indianapolis, and Youngstown originally became manufacturing complexes turning out machine tools, steel, and durable goods. In the final analysis though, whether transport or production were basic to its economy, the particular city also developed a set of sustaining institutions and organizations, that is, banks, professional facilities and services, retail trade, and suppliers of subassemblies and components. This process of internal growth, when added to their impact on the region surrounding them, gave many cities the impetus to metropolitan growth. As a result, the emergent metropolis drew into its orbit numerous smaller cities in its section of the country, which it then served economically and culturally, if it did not entirely subjugate or destroy.

The Census of 1910 showed the presence of the United States of 25 metropolitan centers. Nineteen others had a nuclei of cities of 100,000 in size. More important perhaps was the added revelation that these 44 very large communities were dispersed over no fewer than 23 states. These demographic facts confirmed the materialization of what N. S. B. Gras called "a met-

[16] Blake McKelvey, *The Emergency of Metropolitan America: 1915–1966* (New Brunswick, N.J.: Rutgers University Press, 1968), pp. 63–65.

[17] Don J. Bogue, *The Structure of the Metropolitan Community* (Ann Arbor, Mich.: University of Michigan Horace H. Rackham School of Graduate Studies, 1949), states the process very ably.

Urbanization of the Midwest: Omaha, Nebraska, in 1916, after the invention of the automobile.

ropolitan economy," that is, a coordinated national system in which big cities were the focal points.

ECONOMIC CONCENTRATION

Economic concentration was primarily responsible for the appearance of this constellation of super-cities now spanning the continent. This same factor also gave the metropolis its distinctive ecological pattern within its own indistinct periphery.

At the center of each metropolis stood a dense commercial district offering a multitude of retail, entertainment, and professional services to its own inhabitants and those of its hinterland. The skyscraper, economizing on land and making use of steel framing and the cable-hung Otis elevator for vertical transportation, gave the business hub a distinctive architecture. First horse-drawn and then electric street railways supplementing the steam-powered railroads afforded the swelling population access both to the downtown district and the many manufacturing establishments in the metropolitan area. The telephone provided instantaneous communication.

In fact, a host of mechanical inventions and social innovations contributed to the rapid growth of metropolitan America in the first years of the twentieth century: the typewriter; the Westinghouse air-brake; ready-to-wear clothing; precast concrete blocks and reinforced concrete; aggressive advertising; the septic tank; well-drilling machines; improvements in central heating and ventilation; new mortgage practices; the installment plan; home appliances like refrigerators, washing machines, and vacuum sweepers; and others truly too numerous to mention. Their adoption gave the metropolitan population its livelihood, and their use, its character as an urban society.

It was the coming of the automobile that most decisively permitted the great city to extend its radius—and also the intensity—of its influence over a large area. Rail transportation had brought America's cities into a single nationwide web of hauling bulk commodities economically even between distant regions. This drew cities into a national economy of accelerating enterprise. The automobile, bus, and truck, however, freed the large city from the constraints of the railroad without losing its benefits, and made possible the flexible kind of transportation necessary for this new, metropolitan type of community. The fact is clearly apparent in the suburbanization of the city.

In another sense automotive transportation contributed to metropolitan regional dominance, by making the great city more fully accessible to a wider area.[18] The rapid growth of trucking bears this out. In 1910, there were virtually no trucks on the road at all. By 1920, they numbered 1.1 million, and at the end of the decade 3.4 million.

SUBURBANIZATION

According to the 1930 Census, nearly one-half of all Americans lived either in or less than 50 miles from cities of 100,000 or more. Fully three-fourths of the nation's population growth in the decade following 1920 had been absorbed by its nearly 100 metropolitan areas, but while the population of the central cities had increased 22 percent, that of their suburban rings had grown twice as much.

Distant tracts of new housing appeared in all directions permitted by the terrain and within commuting distance, preferably by auto, from the heavily invested and economically indispensable center. These bedroom communities, the dormitories of the offices and factories of the central city, possessed little if any industry of their own. In fact, their chief attraction lay in offering a greater measure of space and solitude than the dense metropolitan core. However, our metropolitan suburbs were being increasingly supplied with all the amenities of life: incipient shopping plazas (to grow immensely after World War II), doctors' and dentists' offices, restaurants, office buildings, and repair shops to service the stream of household appliances pouring out of the nation's factories.[19]

[18] See R. D. McKenzie, *The Metropolitan Community* (New York: Russell and Russell, 1967), first published in 1933.

[19] An account is to be found in Howard P. Chudacoff, *The Evolution of American Urban Society* (Englewood Cliffs, N.J.: Prentice-Hall, 1975), pp. 187–95.

SOCIOCULTURAL URBANISM

The impact of the metropolis upon a wide expanse of territory and increasing numbers of people was not only economic. It was sociocultural as well. Newspapers emanating from the metropolis blanketed an army of readers for scores of miles around, as Robert E. Park showed in his pioneering studies of the great Windy City surrounding the University of Chicago.[20] The city's other resources for the communication of ideas—its libraries, book stores, magazines, galleries, lyceums, colleges, and radio stations—combined to give it intellectual hegemony over an entire region. Furthermore, the areas of cultural rule were coterminous with those of traffic and trade as well, indicating still more clearly the comprehensiveness of metropolitan dominance. Some cities, notably Boston, Chicago, and New York, exercised cultural influence not only regionally but nationwide.

The urbanite, now in the majority of America's population, was more mobile and probably freer of traditions than people in the past. Social groupings were more transitory. The urban American was also perhaps more rational and calculating, with loyalties less dependable, a sense of interpersonal solidarity weaker, but a tolerance for differences in others more highly developed. Being in a milieu primarily oriented to achievement and innovation, the urbanite could more easily accept change. As a further consequence of this evolution, the urbanite might perhaps yield to feelings of mastery and power on the one hand, and helplessness and hopelessness on the other.

URBAN PROBLEMS

The suburbanization of the city which accompanied metropolitan growth in the United States redistributed our urban population as an expression of rising affluence. But that was not all. That movement, as one national committee of inquiry declared in the 1930s, was also a response to "the urge to escape the obnoxious aspects of urban life."[21] These were severe indeed, despite the economic power of the emergent metropolis. As historian Arthur Schlesinger lamented, the new Jerusalem was also ancient Babylon.

For example, Pittsburgh had at the beginning of the twentieth century disclosed shortcomings and problems no less severe than Charles Booth's dismal revelations about London 15 years earlier.[22] The Steel City, spurred on by the reformist zeal of the progressives, surveyed itself at length between 1909 and 1914, only to uncover a host of infirmities like the "shame of

[20] Robert E. Park, "Urbanization and Newspaper Circulation," *American Journal of Sociology*, 35 (July 1929), pp. 60–79.

[21] National Resources Committee, *Our Cities: Their Role in the National Economy* (Washington, D.C.: Government Printing Office, 1937), p. 35.

[22] See Charles Booth, *Life and Labour of the People of London* (London: Macmillan, 1903).

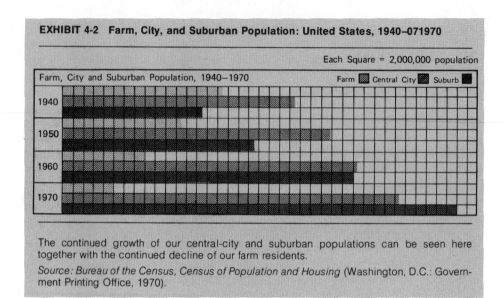

EXHIBIT 4-2   Farm, City, and Suburban Population: United States, 1940–071970

Each Square = 2,000,000 population

Farm, City and Suburban Population, 1940–1970

Farm ▨   Central City ▨   Suburb ■

1940	
1950	
1960	
1970	

The continued growth of our central-city and suburban populations can be seen here together with the continued decline of our farm residents.

Source: Bureau of the Census, Census of Population and Housing (Washington, D.C.: Government Printing Office, 1970).

the cities" decried by Lincoln Steffens generally in the United States at that time.

Although Greater Pittsburgh functioned as an economic unit with its market and office center in the inner city, the total metropolitan area included a combination of "groups of outlying mill towns and half-agricultural districts between." Pittsburgh's public schools were administered in fragmented fashion. Each ward levied a property tax for school buildings. The resulting disparity of income showed that while the 31st ward had school buildings valued at $41 per child, those of the 2nd ward were worth $1033 for each. Declared the Pittsburgh survey: "There was abundant evidence of overcrowding, inadequate heat, poor or nonexistent ventilation, schools unconnected with the sewer, and buildings without fire escapes, all in contrast to those in the better wards possessed of first-rate equipment, small classes, good plumbing, and adequate heat."[23]

Pittsburgh's hospitals were being built and operated without coordination or compassion. Although seven new ones were going up at the time of the survey, not one was situated in the low-income wards where disease was most prevalent. Despite the large—and dangerous—iron-and-steel industry in the city, the Pennsylvania Department of Industrial Inspection had yet to locate a single office in Pittsburgh. In fact, 500 lives were being lost in industrial accidents in the city every year.

Sanitary deficiencies were obvious in the Pittsburgh area, where 129

[23] As cited in Glaab, op. cit., p. 420.

towns and boroughs mindlessly cast their sewage into the very Allegheny and Monongahela rivers from which the metropolis drew its drinking water. The neglect of public sanitation and health boosted morbidity and mortality rates for typhoid, diarrhea, enteritis, pneumonia, and bronchitis, as well as other diseases of the respiratory system. Decent housing was in short supply, the census of the first 20 wards alone showed 6000 units supplied with only outdoor privies. In the adjacent mill towns of Braddock, Duquesne, McKeesport, Homestead, and Sharpsburgh, the survey stated, building codes were notoriously obsolete. Many "foreigners" lived there amid conditions so adverse that in Homestead's 2nd ward, a third of the children died before reaching the age of two!

URBAN REFORM

So glaring did the social problems of urban America become that an energetic Progressive Movement, of which the Pittsburgh survey was itself an expression, eventually succeeded in remedying any number of ills. Building codes were adopted to provide better public health and safety. Public parks materialized. Andrew Carnegie endowed numerous municipal libraries. The Progressives also gave a good deal of attention to municipal reform. "Muckrakers" like Steffens had for years publicized inequities in local government. As a result finally, many changes were introduced to bring about

Mullen's Alley, a New York City slum, around 1888.

more efficiency in municipal affairs. The city-manager and commission forms of government were designed to eliminate sordid politics from city administration. To an extent these steps were productive, but not always. Sometimes all they did was show that a politically leaderless city was weaker than before. Where mayors succeeded in gaining the support of the new ethnic minorities, as Hazen S. Pingree did in Detroit in battling the City Railway Company's demand for a self-serving franchise, they discovered untapped strength in the traditional political institutions at the local level.[24]

Later, the New Deal undertook an urban program in the 1930s. The Federal Housing Act of 1937 offered loans and grants to demolish slums and rebuild in their place. Subsequent housing acts authorized funds to buy up blighted areas and transfer cleared land to developers. Both slum clearance and the support of property values in the waning business districts were thus envisioned, and the latter did benefit. Yet preexisting problems like ghettoization and social distress continued.

MEGALOPOLITAN AMERICA

The Depression temporarily retarded urbanization in the United States. World War II and its aftermath, however, intensified the metropolitan trend that had already become prominent. At midcentury not only was America a land of cities with a way of life singularly different from its agrarian tradition. It had also developed a national system functionally subordinate to an East Coast megalopolis. In fact, twentieth-century urbanism was unlike any previous period in history. As the geographer Jean Gottmann put it, the megalopolitan East Coast was "the cradle of a new order in the organization of inhabited space."[25]

A NEW PATTERN

By 1960, the 53,000-square-mile cluster of metropolitan areas stretching for 400 miles from Boston to Washington and west to the Appalachians had a population of 37 million. As Gottmann observed, the megalopolis constituted a revolution in land use in terms both of scale and purpose. It also signified new patterns of intense living that called for the constant succession of practices. Finally, the megalopolis meant infinite—and fragile—interdependence, including public-utility services, education, local government, and of course the economy.

[24] Melvin G. Hall, *Reform in Detroit: Hazen S. Pingee and Urban Politics* (New York: Oxford University Press, 1969).

[25] Jean Gottmann, *Megalopolis: The Urbanized Northeastern Seaboard of the United States* (New York: The Twentieth Century Fund, 1961), pp. 774–75.

Gottmann persuasively contended that the megalopolis had itself been a creative element in history. The northeast seaboard was more than a national focus. By virtue of its efficiency and its legitimation of abundance, the urban east coast had been the catalyst for the new affluent society. The immense natural endowment of America, the technological progress that enabled these resources to be developed, the large common market established by the Constitution, the isolation of the nation and hence its safety from invasion, the presence of millions of immigrant workers, and the secular philosophy of our culture—all these doubtlessly contributed to the attainment of abundance. The megalopolis, however, was also responsible, since organizationally it was indispensable to the realization of such widespread prosperity. Gottmann wrote:

> *The United States may well claim to be the first large nation to have achieved a high degree of general abundance well distributed among the population, and there can be little doubt that this abundance was due not so much to the extent and fecundity of the land as to the dynamism of the urban economy developed in megalopolis and founded on the management of redistribution.*[26]

NEW YORK CITY: THE CENTER OF MEGALOPOLIS

At the heart of the high-density development making up the American megalopolis was the New York area, centering on the five boroughs of the city itself. As defined by the Census Bureau in 1970, the New York metropolitan area covered nine counties with a population of nearly 10 million. New York's impacted mode of life, density, and complexity of organization clearly conveyed the city's role in the megalopolitan complex. In 1970, there were 26,404 people per square mile in the New York central-city core. The overall density of the entire Standard Metropolitan Statistical Area was 7206 per square mile.

The rationale for New York's concentration lay in the fact that metropolitan New York provided a considerable part of the services essential to the national economy. With only nine percent of the nation's population, the New York region employed 40 percent of all Americans in national wholesaling, more than 33 percent of everyone in finance, and 25 percent of those in business and professional service occupations.

In the Boston-Washington megalopolis, one found a score of large cities oriented to New York. Concord, Manchester, Boston, Worcester, Fall River, Providence, Hartford, New Haven, and Bridgeport represented New England. Farther south were located Newark, Jersey City, Elizabeth, Trenton, Camden, and Wilmington, and to the west Scranton, Allentown, Reading, Philadelphia,

---

[26] Ibid.

Hub of the twentieth century Boston-to-Washington megalopolis: New York City seen from the air.

and Harrisburg. Baltimore and Washington completed the corridor-like aggregation. In addition to these cities and thousands of local governments, there were more than 100 counties in the megalopolis. All or part of 10 states was blanketed by it.

The cities making up the east coast megalopolis were nodes in a web of production, transportation, and communication that formed the economic hinge of the whole country. The megalopolis was the nation's money market. It also provided the bridge of rail, water, and air transportation between the United States and Europe as well as the telephone, telegraph, cable, photocopying, and television grids for the voluminous communication that sustained the massive movement of the nation's goods and its people.

Similarly, but on a smaller scale and subordinate to the Boston-Washington complex, the Chicago-Pittsburgh megalopolitan buildup at the heart of the continent, the San Francisco-Los Angeles concentration on the Pacific coast, and the rapidly expanding Florida population centers were exercising a dynamic centralization in their respective regional empires.

EXHIBIT 4-3   The Urban Regions (or Megalopolitan Complexes) of the United States: As Anticipated in the Year 2000

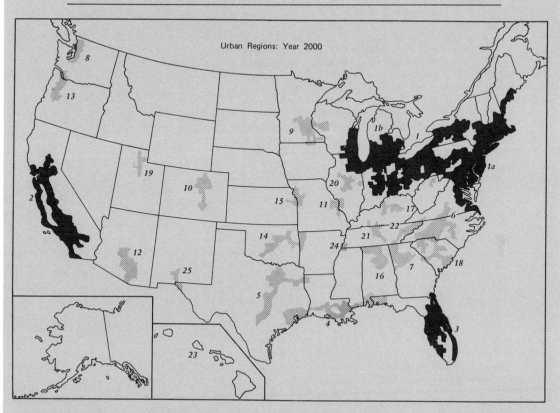

Urban Regions: Year 2000

1. Metropolitan belt
   1a. Atlantic Seaboard
   1b. Lower Great Lakes
2. California region
3. Florida peninsula
4. Gulf Coast
5. East–central Texas–Red River

6. Southern piedmont
7. North Georgia–Southeast Tennessee
8. Puget Sound
9. Twin Cities region
10. Colorado piedmont
11. St. Louis
12. Metropolitan Arizona

13. Willamette Valley
14. Central Oklahoma–Arkansas Valley
15. Missouri–Kau Valley
16. North Alabama
17. Blue grass
18. Southern coastal plain
19. Salt Lake Valley

20. Central Illinois
21. Nashville region
22. East Tennessee
23. Oahu island
24. Memphis
25. El Paso–Ciudad Juarez

Three megalopolitan complexes are shown here as existing in the United States at the beginning of the twenty-first century: the Boston-Washington area linked with Chicago-Pittsburgh (which some scholars believe ought to be thought separate); San-Francisco-Los Angeles-San Diego; and Florida. These appear as the dark areas. The other 22, shown in light shading, are anticipated as super-metropolitan developments, if not outright megalopolises, by 2000 A.D.

Source: Presidential Commission on Population Growth and the American Future (Washington, D.C.: Government Printing Office, 1972).

SERIOUS WEAKNESSES

Although vital as a whole, the component cities not only of the megalopolis but of the country's metropolitan areas generally were beset by serious weaknesses that cast a shadow on our entire urban system. These included financial problems verging on municipal insolvency; the vehicular congestion of the downtown business districts impairing their ability to absorb the expanding office industry; air and water pollution; and indigency and crime. Finally, conflict over poverty and race added a new depth to our urban life, now defined by many as a crisis. Whether this might threaten not only individual metropolitan centers but the nation as a whole remained an unanswered question in the 1970s.

CONTINUED METROPOLITANIZATION

Despite its not insubstantial shortcomings, America's urban society continued to evidence more metropolitanization as the country moved through the second half of the twentieth century.[27] From 1960 to 1970, more than 80 percent of our national growth occurred in our 243 metropolitan communities. These now contained 140 million persons, or two out of every three Americans. In fact, so swift was the country's metropolitan growth that in January 1972, 21 newly designated SMSAs were added to the national census, bringing the new total to 264.

Demographers projected that America's metropolitan population would increase another 58 percent in the quarter of a century ending in 1985. This would mean that out of a total United States population of 252 million, 178 million of them would reside in metropolitan communities. Most of the growth up to 1985 was anticipated in the suburban and exurban rings of the SMSAs, with central-city growth, if present at all, far less than that of our nonmetropolitan communities.

Subject to uncertain forces, urban America of the 1970s found itself in a situation where urbanization was both promise and peril almost everywhere.

CONCLUSION

The most recent stage of the history of urbanization is that of the industrial city. That type of community possesses distinct characteristics, notably the use of inanimate power for production, a complex division of labor, a high plane of material well-being, bureaucratic organization, and a secular-scientific ethos.

[27] Patricia L. Hodge and Philip M. Hauser, *The Challenge of America's Metropolitan Population Outlook: 1960 to 1985* (Washington, D.C.: National Commission on Urban Problems, 1968).

As the successor to preindustrialism, the industrial city arose first in England during the late eighteenth century. The path to its realization had been paved earlier by the development of business and nonsteam technology in the English commercial cities. When steam power became a reality, the new industry took root there and made the nation the strongest power on earth. The transition to industrial urbanism, however, thoroughly altered British society and its culture though not without controversy and conflict.

The growth of cities in America paralleled the British experience. Colonial cities and those of the newly established United States served first as preindustrial centers. Following the Civil War, industrial urbanism went forward very rapidly in the United States. Subsequent to 1865, in a process of opportunity as well as struggle, America's cities grew, developed regional networks, and finally coalesced into a single nationwide system capped by the megalopolitan east coast. That course of events, it could be claimed, had added an entirely new postindustrial dimension, one of socioeconomic intensity and general abundance, to the social order.

Yet, despite the achievements of this latest stage in the history of urbanization, America's cities were not without serious shortcomings in the 1970s. Problems of environmental damage, organizational deficiencies, and social disorganization were proving to be chronic regardless of the continued metropolitanization that forecasts anticipated would go on steadily in the foreseeable future.

FOR FURTHER READING

Nels Anderson, *The Industrial Urban Community* (New York: Appleton-Century-Crofts, 1971). The features of urban life, the internal structure of cities, urban problems.

T. S. Ashton, *The Industrial Revolution* (London: Oxford University Press, 1962), revised edition. A review of the achievements as well as the baneful effects of early industrialization.

Alexander B. Callow, ed., *American Urban History* (New York: Oxford University Press, 1969). Articles on the course of American urban life by different specialists.

Howard P. Chudacoff, *The Evolution of American Urban Society* (Englewood Cliffs, N.J.: Prentice-Hall, 1975). The social side of the urbanization of the United States.

Charles Glaab and Theodore Brown, *A History of Urban America* (New York: Macmillan, 1967). City building in America up to World War I.

Blake McKelvey, *The Urbanization of America: 1880–1915* (New Brunswick, N.J.: Rutgers University Press, 1963); *The Emergence of Metropolitan*

America: 1915–1966 (New Brunswick, N.J.: Rutgers University Press, 1968); and *American Urbanization: A Comparative History* (Glenview, Ill.: Scott, Foresman, 1973). The development of the United States leading up to today's massive urbanism.

Zane L. Miller, *The Urbanization of Modern America* (New York: Harcourt Brace Jovanovich, 1973). The rise of American cities and the role they have played in our history.

Janet Roebuck, *The Shaping of Urban Society* (New York: Charles Scribner's Sons, 1974). The effects of industrialization upon the modern city.

Stephan Thernstrom and Richard Sennett, eds., *Nineteenth-Century Cities: Essays in the New Urban History* (New Haven, Conn.: Yale University Press, 1969). Various articles seeking to remove misconceptions about earlier urbanization.

PART THREE

THEORETICAL APPROACHES

A settlement of 2.5 million here around a natural harbor suggests the ecological approach to urban society: human beings in conjunction with their environment.

Source: Australian News and Information Bureau, *Australia: A Portfolio* (Adelaide: Griffin Press, 1966), p. 40.

CHAPTER 5

THE
RURAL AND URBAN
AS CONTRASTING TYPES

In their voluminous research, urban sociologists have made use of three different theoretical approaches, that is, points of view from which to describe and explain urban phenomena. These are the (1) typological, (2) ecological, and (3) demographic. Of course, many scholars have combined them in one way or another. Nonetheless, as principles for both organizing and interpreting knowledge about the city and urban society, they remain logically separate and distinct. These three perspectives make up the content of the following three chapters, beginning with this one.

The typological tradition in urban sociology attempts systematically to distinguish between rural and urban communities as fundamentally different social phenomena.[1] In addition, typologists also strive to account for the be-

[1] The history of typological thought on urbanization is summarized in Jean B. Quant, *From the Small Town to the Great Community* (New Brunswick, N.J.: Rutgers University Press, 1970).

havior of urban populations on the basis of the characters which are attributed to cities as representative of a generic type of community.

THE RURAL-URBAN TYPOLOGICAL DICHOTOMY

There is scarcely a major social theorist who has not identified the rural and urban genuses as opposites.[2]

They have reviewed the concrete characteristics, in other words, the ideas, relationships, and modes of social organization, of people living in cities and then compared them with life in rural communities. These scholars have reduced myriads of observations to tendencies. They have then linked these together into logically consistent patterns. By such a process of abstraction they have finally arrived at coherent "ideal" types that may, as generalizations, be compared point by point as diametrically, mutually exclusive, polar entities.

Of special importance among typologists are Ferdinand Tönnies, Emile Durkheim, Robert Redfield, Pitirim A. Sorokin and his collaborator Carle C. Zimmerman, Georg Simmel, and Louis Wirth. Their conceptual antitheses do differ, but as has been observed, they also have much in common, in that they all seek the attributes distinguishing the urban from the rural as fundamentally different modes of social life.

TÖNNIES: GEMEINSCHAFT AND GESELLSCHAFT

The German sociologist Ferdinand Tönnies conceived of nineteenth-century European history as a process of movement from the type of social structure, which he designated as *Gemeinschaft,* to that of its antithesis, the *Gesellschaft.* That was the period of industrial city-building in Europe, which greatly affected the quality of life of the people of that continent generally and perhaps mainly so in Tönnies' own Germany.

According to Tönnies, *Gemeinschaft* refers to the association of people habituated to one another by virtue of their close kinship, long-term residence together, and ties of deep sentiment. *Gemeinschaft* also signifies a spirit of cooperation, social goals possessed by people in common with one another, and a communal friendliness that blankets everyone alike.

Although the *Gemeinschaft* type of social body is not entirely precluded by a complex, industrial-urban civilization, its clearest expression is to be found in the prototypic rural community that has grown out of primal tribalism. Tönnies writes of the meaning of *Gemeinschaft* in the following words:

[2] For an analytical review see John C. McKinney and Charles P. Loomis, "The Typological Tradition," in Joseph S. Roucek, ed., *Contemporary Sociology* (New York: Philosophical Library, 1958), pp. 557–82.

Folk society, the Platte River Indians of Nebraska photographed at a tribal ceremony in 1871.

[We] *find a common state of mind which in its higher forms—common custom and common belief—penetrates to the members of a people (Volk) . . . It is found in the most perfect development in the related families of the early and important formation of organic life, the clan or tribe which may be said to be the family before the family.*

. . . Partly from the village, partly independent of it, develops the town, which, in its perfection, is held together as by common spirit. . . . In the next stage a town will dominate a surrounding territory, thereby representing a new organization of the district within the larger unit of the country, and thus changing or reforming the structure of a tribe or a people. . . . [This is] the last and highest expression of which the idea of Gemeinschaft is capable.[3]

Stopping at this point, Tönnies implies that the communal spirit of *Gemeinschaft,* its "unity of will," simply cannot continue to exist in the heterogeneous industrial-urban metropolis. In Tönnies' analysis, *Gesellschaft* clearly indicates the complete urban condition: behavior motivated by self-interest, specific rather than diffuse social obligations, expectations of a contractual instead of a traditional nature, and the presence of a deliberately instituted rather than a simply spontaneous social order handed down from the past. This image of the city as a *Gesellschaft* makes it the exact antithesis of the rural community.

[3] Ferdinand Tönnies, *Community and Society: Gemeinschaft und Gesellschaft,* trans. and ed. by Charles P. Loomis (East Lansing, Mich.: Michigan State University Press, 1957), pp. 49–50.

DURKHEIM: MECHANICAL AND ORGANIC SOLIDARITY

In a manner similar to Tönnies, though employing a somewhat different vantage point, more than half a century ago Emile Durkheim also observed that a historical transition was enveloping the Western world.

Durkheim's *Division of Labor in Society* makes two considerations fundamental to this process.[4] These are mechanical solidarity and organic solidarity. According to Durkheim, people are in a state of mechanical solidarity when their actions represent conformity to a homogeneous, coercive value system. Persons infringing on the revered values of a mechanically ordered society are necessarily dealt with harshly, because their breaches of the law offend the deeply rooted sentiments of everyone. Contrariwise, people are in a state of organic solidarity when their behavior reflects the individualized interests of numbers of persons related to each other not as virtually identical members of a unitary collectivity, but as rational and functionally interdependent specialists. When such individuals violate the rules, little opprobrium attaches to their behavior. No sense of outrage grips them. The reason is that the public in an organically organized community have a pragmatic attitude and simply want whatever damage has been done repaired or whatever loss has been incurred remedied.

Durkheim was obviously describing, roughly speaking, the differences between traditional and modern society, in short, between rural and urban modes of social organization. Certainly in modern Western urban society, restitutive law has replaced punitive law. Witness the widespread trend toward rehabilitation as the goal of legal sanctions. Durkheim's distinction between the mechanically ordered rural community and the organically based complex metropolitan system remains a penetrating insight into differing social realities.

SOROKIN AND ZIMMERMAN: RURAL AND URBAN "WORLDS"

In contrast to Durkheim's basic dichotomy between the mechanical and the organic kinds of social cohesion, Sorokin and Zimmerman, Harvard sociologists during the 1930s and 1940s, carefully formulated a detailed concept of urbanism made up of eight separate variables.[5]

The urban "world" that Sorokin and Zimmerman define evidences (1) the proliferation of nonagricultural occupations. In it (2) the man-made environment takes on great saliency. (3) The size, (4) heterogeneity, and (5) density of the population are all on a scale significantly different from that of the rural

[4] Trans. by George Simpson (Glencoe, Ill.: Free Press, 1947).

[5] Pitirim A. Sorokin and Carle C. Zimmerman, *Principles of Rural-Urban Sociology* (New York: Henry Holt, 1929), Ch. 2.

community. (6) Social stratification and (7) mobility are more pronounced in urban than rural society and finally (8) the system of interaction in the city is predominantly secondary and, hence, segmental and instrumental rather than diffuse and expressive.

REDFIELD: FOLK SOCIETY AND URBAN SOCIETY

Robert Redfield, a University of Chicago anthropologist, derived the idea of the folk society as the direct opposite of urban society from the constructs fashioned earlier by many scholars. Among them were sociologists and anthropolgists like William Graham Sumner, Henry Sumner Maine, Tönnies, Durkheim, A. R. Radcliffe-Brown, and Alfred Kroeber.[6]

Redfield elucidates on folk society and leaves the characteristics of urban society as merely implicit antitheses. The social system of the *folk,* says Redfield, consists of "the characters which are logically opposite to those which are to be found in modern society."[7] A folk society is small, isolated, and nonliterate. Its members exhibit the somatic homogeneity of a local, inbred population. Very intimate with one another, they possess a sense of belonging together. Their technology is simple in the sense that their tools are not devices for making still other implements. In a folk society the division of labor is rudimentary. The folk collectivity is economically self-sufficient, with its culture largely static but containing the conventionalized solutions for meeting all of the recurring problems of existence.

Thus a folk society has a subsistence economy with goods and services exchanged, usually ceremonially, in accordance with the accepted statuses of persons rather than the anticipation of commercial gain. Although in a folk community there is knowledge, even much knowledge, as abstract and systematic thought, science is conspicuously absent. Religion, however, being woven into practically all relationships and activities is very prominent. Kinship is equally prominent. In fact, writes Redfield, "folk society may be thought of as composed of families rather than of individuals." Redfield's conception of folk society is, in his own words, poles apart from the "vast, complicated, and rapidly changing world in which the urbanite and even the urbanized country-dweller live today."[8]

[6] Robert Redfield, "The Folk Society," *American Journal of Sociology, 52* (January 1947), pp. 293–308.

[7] Ibid.

[8] Ibid.

URBAN LIFE AS A UNIQUE SOCIAL TYPE

The work of two other exponents of urban study by typological means have had great impact on sociological theory. They are the German philosopher and sociologist Georg Simmel, a contemporary of Durkheim, and the University of Chicago urbanist Louis Wirth. Their analysis of the "urban way of life" and of the personality characteristics unique to it have unusual perceptive depth.

SIMMEL'S "THE METROPOLIS AND MENTAL LIFE"

In "The Metropolis and Mental Life," published for the first time at the turn of the century, Simmel observed that both the tempo of interaction and the multiplicity or urban existence are stimulating.[9] Being so innervated, the urbanite becomes a more sophisticated person, cognitively and evaluatively, and with greater awareness than the rural inhabitant possesses. Simmel also emphasizes the importance of the money economy as well as the domination of intellect as major urban phenomena. These two conditions critically influence social relationships and modes of thought in the city. They create a matter-of-fact atmosphere and inhibit the emotional expression of sentiment. These conditions are conducive to logical, rational arrangements in which people are regarded with impersonal objectivity. As Simmel states:

> The modern metropolis . . . is supplied almost entirely by production for the market, that is, for entirely unknown purchasers who never personally enter the producer's actual field of vision. Through this anonymity the interests of each party acquire an unmerciful matter-of-factness; and the intellectually calculating economic egoism of both parties need not fear any deflection because of the imponderables of personal relationships.[10]

The extent of individual freedom in the metropolitan area, Simmel continues, "has no analogy whatsoever under other conditions." Except in the city, people generally conduct themselves within very strict behavioral boundaries that are conducive to the solidarity of the family, the church, or other collectivity. Occupational specialization, style-of-life preference, and mobility all contribute to greater subjective and behavioral liberty in the city than in the country. Even today, Simmel noted at the time, a metropolitan man placed in a small town, where the social circle is much narrower, experiences discomfort.

[9] See Kurt H. Wolff, ed. and trans., *The Sociology of Georg Simmel* (New York: Free Press, 1950), pp. 409–24.

[10] Ibid., p. 412.

The mass character of the metropolis is readily apparent in this aerial photo of a San Francisco residential district.

The urban community is a dynamic system that exerts great control over the environment. Its increasing affluence multiplies opportunities, provided that the citizens possess the necessary knowledge and skills requisite for renumerative specialization within the total structure. Such intense individual development has its counterpart in the efflorescence of personal mannerism, modes of dress, and psychic traits designed to attract attention to oneself. "For many character types," Simmel declares, "ultimately the only means of saving for themselves some modicum of self-esteem and the sense of filling a position is indirect, through the awareness of others."[11] In the city, much weight is placed on function, on activity, on performance, and the individual strives defensively to identify himself within the vast, impersonal system,

[11] Ibid., p. 421.

"this culture which outgrows all personal life." Nevertheless, in its capacity to enable people to distinguish themselves from one another, even though only antagonistically, the big city represents a great historical transformation. The sociologist, Simmel concludes, should neither excuse nor condemn the city but simply try to understand it.

WIRTH'S "URBANISM AS A WAY OF LIFE"

Louis Wirth called Simmel's "The Metropolis and Mental Life" the most important single article on the city from the sociological standpoint."[12] This is high praise, for Wirth himself wrote perhaps an equally respected analysis in his celebrated paper "Urbanism as a Way of Life."[13] In that essay Wirth summed up the theoretical import of 20 years of urban research at the University of Chicago. In it, in fact, he viewed modern society as a whole mainly from the standpoint of urban culture. More and more, Wirth wrote, the city was drawing "the most remote parts of the world into its orbit and [weaving] diverse areas, people, and activities into a cosmos."[14]

Wirth proceeded to his analysis of the unique characteristics of the urban mode of life by first defining a city sociologically as "a relatively large, dense, and permanent settlement of socially heterogeneous individuals." From this starting point he went on logically to deduce the essential properties of urban existence as "compendent hypotheses."

Given a large, diverse population, one would on the basis of probability expect that the potential for still greater differentiation would be present. Accordingly, says Wirth, that "such variations should give rise to the spatial segregation of individuals according to color, ethnic heritage, economic and social status, tastes and preferences, may readily be inferred." Competition and formal controls alone suffice to achieve sufficient solidarity to move things along. In an incisive passage Wirth observes:

> *The contacts of the city may indeed be face to face, but they are nevertheless impersonal, superficial, transitory and segmental. The reserve, the indifference, and the blase outlook which urbanites manifest in their relationships may thus be regarded as devices for immunizing themselves against the personal claims and expectations of others.*[15]

[12] Compare "Introduction" by Albert J. Reiss, Jr., to his edited volume of Louis Wirth, *On Cities and Social Life* (Chicago, Ill.: University of Chicago Press, 1964), pp. ix–xxx.

[13] "Urbanism as a Way of Life," *American Journal of Sociology, 44* (July 1933), pp. 1–24.

[14] Ibid.

[15] Ibid.

Having gone this far, Wirth is compelled to take note of the distemper of urbanism, in other words, its disharmony. He does so in the following manner. If social relationships in the city are utilitarian, then one may infer that they are also predatory. In fact, the impersonal corporation is the ideal instrument of urban cooperation, for it affords efficiency together with limited liability. Moreover, lacking a "soul," the corporation can engage in whatever unconscionable activities may be required in order to make money.

Wirth next turns to the sociocultural effects of population density. He presents them as greater differentiation and contact, proximity and yet social insulation, "glaring contrasts between splendor and squalor . . . order and chaos," the economic utilization of space, functional segregation, and the like. Indeed, the concomitants of density are identical with those resulting from sheer numbers.

Wirth's third premise, urban heterogeneity, leads to a more complex social structure. That structure is one in which the system of stratification becomes extremely differentiated, and with fateful consequences too, for the plural hierarchies contribute to the further disorientation of the city dweller. Wirth gives us to understand that:

> There is little opportunity for the individual to obtain a conception of the city as a whole or to survey his place in the total scheme. Consequently, he finds it difficult to determine what is to his own 'best interest' and to decide between the issues and leaders presented to him by the agencies of mass suggestion.[16]

Yet despite the more intensive stratification of any given city, in it all people are leveled to a homogeneous, passive "average" for the purpose of participating in urban services, such as education, recreation, and communication. Likewise, if they actively seek to influence policy making, they must immerse themselves in "mass movements."

Although Wirth recognized the demographic and ecological aspects of urbanism, he treated the city principally in terms of the attitudes and ideas of its modal personality. Wirth considered this personality to be vitally dependent and interdependent, but psychically related to others by only the most "fragile," "tenuous," and "volatile" ties. The total population is divided into innumerable voluntary associations each seeking the realization of its own peculiar set of interests. Individuals are atomized in the city. Kinship is a fiction, and "personal disorganization, mental breakdown, suicide, delinquency, crime, corruption, and disorder might be expected under these circumstances to be more prevalent in the urban than in the rural community."[17]

[16] Ibid.

[17] Ibid.

EXHIBIT 5-1 Reading and Science Achievement by Rural and Urban Residence and by Urban Location

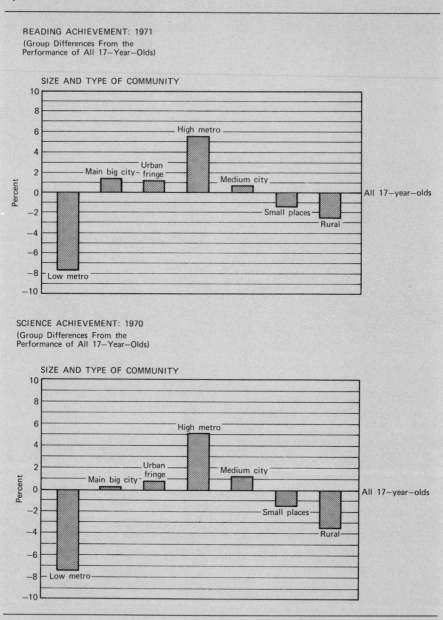

READING ACHIEVEMENT: 1971
(Group Differences From the
Performance of All 17—Year—Olds)

SIZE AND TYPE OF COMMUNITY

SCIENCE ACHIEVEMENT: 1970
(Group Differences From the
Performance of All 17—Year—Olds)

SIZE AND TYPE OF COMMUNITY

A common pattern exists in reading and science achievement scores of 17-year old students and the size and type of their communities. In general, positive achievement correlates with urbanization and above-average socio-economic status of the children's parents. In the fig-

VALIDITY OF THE DISTINCTION BETWEEN "RURAL" AND "URBAN"

However axiomatic the antithetical modes of rural and urban life may appear to be in the conceptions drawn up by the typologists who have been reviewed, they arouse serious misgivings, and a variety of objections.

For simplicity, Horace Miner has attempted to group the many criticisms of the folk-urban constructs under three headings.[18]

1 A lack of agreement exists between the actual evidence that can be marshalled and the general states of affairs inferred from the concepts themselves.

2 The traits that make up these ideal-type polarities are deficient in clarity. Consequently, they fail to facilitate observation.

3 These constructs are not processual. That is, being simply descriptive, they lack predictive power. As concepts, Miner declares, neither folk nor urban denotes any specific causation, because in the final analysis all either one does is represent configurations of correlative elements. With the help of historical, psychological, or other theoretical principles, they may achieve explanatory power, but standing alone they have no such value.

Quite a few scholars agree with these strictures. The anthropologist Oscar Lewis has disputed the folk-urban continuum very vigorously on grounds similar to Miner's. Lewis declares the folk-urban types comprise "an inadequate theoretical model for the study of cultural change."[19] Richard Dewey has gone so far as to show (1) that as many 40 different variables have been used by writers in defining urbanity, thereby only creating confu-

---

[18] Horace Miner, "The Folk-Urban Continuum," *American Sociological Review, 17* (October 1952), pp. 529–37.

[19] Compare "The Folk-Urban Ideal Types," in Philip M. Hauser and Leo F. Schnore, eds., *The Study of Urbanization* (New York: John Wiley, 1965), pp. 491–503.

sion; and also, unfortunately (2) that temporocentric biases are present in most typological thinking on supposed rural-urban cultural differences.[20] In other words, what exists today in industrial-urban structures the typologists are assuming is necessarily characteristic of urban communities universally. It need not be. Nor do rural communities act in the static manner that typologists think either. Manuel Avila recently studied four supposedly "traditional" Mexican villages, two of them even the same ones that Redfield had investigated. Avila found that these communities were not stagnant or uninterested in going into modern commercial farming. In general, they favored active economic development.[21]

Wirth's, and indirectly Simmel's, propositions on the sociology of the city have been subjected to critical examination by R. N. Morris, and with notable effect too.[22] Morris feels that the image of the city Wirth projected does not completely accord with the historical record in either the preindustrial city or in modern urban society. Although they are valid to some extent, Morris judges that Wirth's generalizations apply more to contemporary Western cities than they do to earlier cities or to those in the developing countries today. Morris says of Wirth's basically correct but incomplete cultural perspective:

> Progress in theoretical understanding is more likely to come through a closer identification than Wirth made between the city and the society in which it is found; a classification of cities and societies together; and separate analyses for different types of cities, based on the recognition that the city as a type of social organization may arise for quite different reasons and be subject to quite different sets of conditions for survival in different societies.[23]

INFORMAL INTERACTION AND VOLUNTARY ASSOCIATIONS AS TESTS OF URBAN TYPOLOGY

Social atomism has been repeatedly emphasized as basic to urban communities. According to Wirth, "Distinctive features of the urban mode of life have often been described sociologically as consisting of the substitution of secondary for primary contacts, the weakening of bonds of kinship, and the declining social significance of the family, the disappearance of the neigh-

---

[20] In "The Rural-Urban Continuum: Real but Relatively Unimportant," *American Journal of Sociology, 66* (July 1960), pp. 60–66.

[21] Manuel Avila, *Tradition and Growth* (Chicago, Ill.: University of Chicago Press, 1969), p. 165.

[22] R. N. Morris, *Urban Sociology* (New York: Frederick A. Praeger, 1968).

[23] Ibid., p. 172.

Continued neighborly association even in large cities argues against the atomistic theory of urban typology.

borhood, and the undermining of the traditional basis of social solidarity."[24]

This assertion, so important to the typological conception of urban life, has, understandably, been the subject of considerable investigation seeking to examine the actual patterns of social relationship and group formation that do obtain in the city generally and also among selected elements within the urban population. This research has thus been a continuing test of the postulated atomistic urban type.

NEW YORK CITY

In one research project, Mirra Komarovsky surveyed 2223 adult residents of New York City and showed that the stereotype of the urban dweller as "a man who no longer identifies himself with the primary groups such as the neighborhood or the larger kinship unit" must be revised.[25] In Komarovsky's study, the unaffiliated make up the bulk of New York's inhabitants. Yet in the

[24] "Urbanism as a Way of Life," op. cit., p. 21.

[25] Mirra Komarovsky, "The Voluntary Associations of Urban Dwellers," *American Sociological Review*, 11 (December 1946), pp. 686–98.

middle and upper classes, membership in purposeful voluntary associations was found to be common, so much so as a matter of fact that among the most affluent fully 98 percent of the men and 100 percent of the women were so affiliated.

SAN FRANCISCO

Studying San Francisco, Bell and Boat sought to determine the persistence of local community life in the metropolis.[26] Interviewing a sample of adult males, these investigators discovered little evidence of complete social detachment. Even in the Mission district where rooming-houses are prevalent, a mere 2.9 percent of the men studied reported no informal contacts at all. Although the different neighborhoods covered did vary in their frequencies of neighborhood relations among coresidents, the observed differences did not prove statistically significant. Bell and Boat concluded that despite the prevalence of formal association in the city, social relationships there are not typically impersonal and anonymous. Furthermore, economic and family factors affect both the incidence and the quality of the informal contacts that are established.

LANSING AND DETROIT, MICHIGAN

Other studies have also confirmed the survival of the local community under urban conditions. Attacking the postulate that the rural-urban fringe areas are "institutional deserts, lacking in organization, inhabited only by unintegrated isolates and disgruntled old-timers," Kurtz and Smith surveyed a random sample of farmers and nonfarmers in the unincorporated territory surrounding Lansing, Michigan.[27] "Minimal social bonds" were declared to exist, the theory of urban atomism notwithstanding. Similarly, in 1971, a survey of a cross section of the population of metropolitan Detroit revealed that only 15 percent of the men and 34 percent of the women belonged to no clubs or associations at all (other than churches). In fact, 50 percent of the men and 40 percent of the women had membership in two or more voluntary associations.[28]

[26] Wendell Bell and Marion D. Boat, "Urban Neighborhoods and Informal Social Relations," *American Journal of Sociology, 62* (January 1957), pp. 391–98.

[27] Richard A. Kurtz and Joel Smith, "Social Life in the Rural-Urban Fringe," *Rural Sociology, 26* (March 1961), pp. 24–38.

[28] Otis D. Duncan, Howard Schuman, and Beverly Duncan, *Social Change in a Metropolitan Community* (New York: Russell Sage Foundation, 1973), Table 18, p. 49.

George A. Hillery, Jr., reviewed the rural-to-urban change theories of Tönnies, Durkheim, Redfield, Wirth, and others, and hypothesized that the shift to urbanism is one toward increasing heterogeneity, a more pronounced division of labor, greater social segmentalism, and more prevalent contractual relationships.[29] As a test of the general proposition that a large city approximates this generic urban type, Hillery examined five cities for the presence, modification, and absence of community organization, defined as "heavily institutionalized systems which lack defining goals." The cities selected were quite varied. They included Ch'u, located in the Yangtze plain and almost 1000 years old; Timbuctoo, between the Niger and the Sahara and in existence for almost a millennium; Mérida on the Yucatan Peninsula; and our own New Orleans and "Middletown" (Muncie, Indiana). Assembling historical, anthropological, and sociological materials, Hillery tested for interaction, sentiment, and institutional, attachment.

Hillery concluded first that the stranger is an integral part of each city. Even in religious ceremonies, interpersonal relationships tended to be segmented, impersonal, and superficial. Nevertheless, there were normative considerations that ameliorated human exploitation in the urban community. In Ch'u, for example, the sentiment of *kan-ch'ing* operated between strangers and restricted their conduct, keeping them from taking full advantage of one another.

A diffuse universalism (respect for human rights) rather than sheer individualism permitted stable interaction among the members of the large urban population, although clearly enough it did not prevent class and ethnic conflict from occurring. Besides economic integration, that is, the fact that everyone tried to satisfy his interests in the economic market, another factor helped knit people together. That was the residential segregation of status groups, a condition which afforded both gratification for achievement and shared expectations regarding behavior.

DRAGOR, DENMARK

Historical studies of the evolution of rural communities into urban concentrations are also helpful in discerning the role of voluntary associations in the urban community. The study of Dragor, a Danish fishing village on the southeast coast of Amager Island, which in less than half a century became an urban complex, shows that:

[29] *Communal Organization: A Study of Local Societies* (Chicago, Ill.: University of Chicago Press, 1968).

One finds a mounting dependency of the community as well as the individual on voluntary associations which appears particularly in records of family and kin, class, age grades, neighborhood, and church. It is a pre-eminence, however, which voluntary associations must share with another institution—the government. The growth of governmental agencies matches that of associations in increased complexity and range of influence.[30]

In Dragor, the Andersons found that neighborliness persisted as an ideal despite the multiplication of tract-homes and community-apartment divisions and an influx of urban summer residents. The residents of multiple dwellings disdained this ideal of neighborliness. Yet, often limited to the residents of a single block or even a single household-complex unit, voluntary association did exist in Dragor to resolve common problems.

CHICAGO, ILLINOIS

Sociologist Gerald D. Suttles painstakingly surveyed a residential section of Chicago's Near West Side, the Addams area around Hull House populated by 30,000 people. There Suttles came to realize that a complicated system of what he called "ordered segmentation" existed. In other words, the diverse ethnic groups inhabiting the Addams region—Italians, Blacks, Puerto Ricans, and Mexicans—expressed hostility toward one another across the street boundaries that separated their enclaves. Frequently teenage gangs fought over the territory they claimed as exclusively theirs. Such contests could also erupt, and at times did, into confrontations involving adult members of the disparate ethnic populations. However, when antagonisms broke out between an ethnic group living in the Addams territory and a dissimilar group outside it, the diverse Addams population tended to join in to defend their neighbors, so to speak, as the lesser of the two evils, their propinquitous Addams inhabitants distrusted though they may be preferred over their more distant Chicagoans, so that a sense of territorial solidarity pervaded the otherwise divided population.[31]

Findings of this kind underscore the limited validity of urban typology and the need for its revision to more nearly correspond with objective reality. In fact, recent and more refined quantitative studies, which take size of community and hence supposedly the degree of "atomism" into account, fail to

[30] Quoted from Robert T. Anderson and Gallatin Anderson, "Voluntary Associations and Urbanization: A Diachronic Analysis," *American Journal of Sociology,* 65 (November 1959), pp. 265–73.

[31] Gerald D. Suttles, *The Social Order of the Slum: Ethnicity and Territory in the Inner City* (Chicago: University of Chicago Press, 1968), Ch. 2.

demonstrate that group-membership rates correlate with community size at all.[32]

THE SUBURBAN STYLE OF LIFE

Still another critical approach has been taken toward typological theory, particularly of the sort formulated by Simmel and Wirth. That is the recognition of suburbanism as indicative of cultural, social, and psychological states at variance with the typological conception of urban life.

Stated very briefly, the suburbanist critique of typology calls attention to the fact that analyses like Wirth's fail to recognize the varying and contrasting life-styles pursued within the city itself and between the inner city and its surrounding suburbs. For example, the trapped and desperately, downwardly mobile inner-city elderly differ sharply from the semicommunal mode of life characteristic of the garden-type suburban tracts populated by middle-class families with young children. Also, the semitribalism of much of suburbia contradicts the atomistic hypothesis of the typologists. These and similar findings expose glaring weaknesses in typological theory when it is applied to the urban community in an empirical, fact-oriented fashion. For a fuller treatment of the suburban community refer to Chapter 12.

MODERNIZATION AND URBAN DEVELOPMENT

One further test of the rural-urban dichotomy differentiates between premodern and modern states of sociocultural organization.

The concept of modernization is, of course, broader and more inclusive than urbanization alone. Modernization denotes industrialization too. However, the modernizing process does generally refer to the concentration of population in cities and possibly also the realization of advanced, that is, Western urban styles of life.

This alleged correlation between urbanism and modernity has been put to a good deal of observation of late, with the result, unfortunately, that perhaps as many questions have been raised about it as have been answered.

---

[32] James Curtis, "Voluntary Association Joining: A Cross-Cultural Comparative Note," *American Sociological Review, 36* (October 1971), pp. 872–80. See also Nicholas Babchuk and Alan Booth, "Voluntary Association Membership: A Longitudinal Analysis," *American Sociological Review, 34* (February 1969), pp. 31–45.

One prominent scholar who has been concerned about the objective nature of modernization is Gideon Sjoberg.[33] Taking the point of view that rural-urban patterns may be profitably examined separately "in preindustrial civilized societies, in developing (or modernizing) ones, and in industrial orders," Sjoberg has made an important contribution to the refinement of typological and developmental urban theory. From his work one gains the impression that though cities in the developing countries may eventually take on the Western pattern, to date in their present transitional form any number of them simply have not done so.

At present, in the underdeveloped lands, says Sjoberg, rural-urban patterns are undergoing great modification. Substantial migration into the city occurs, but it does not prevent the rural population out in the country from increasing. New social arrangements and serious tensions arise too. Circular patterns of migration are set up, with urban in-migrants returning to the land and then repeating the process over and over. A culture of poverty binds the rural and urban masses together and indiscriminately imposes the same restrictions on both. When a measure of affluence is realized, however, it only enables the successful people of the hinterland to finally achieve the feudal values that they have long respected. This may end in a polarization against the "progressive" Western views of the urban intelligentsia, but it may also motivate many in the city to try to join the older rural governing class themselves. In short, the urban transition now unfolding in the developing regions of the world is something about which not a great deal is yet systematically known.

VILLAGE ENCLAVES IN THE CITY

Conversely, one of the possible consequences of the urban transition is the ruralization of the city, for agriculture often tends to be carried on at the very edges of the city in a newly developing region. Urban ruralization has actually been observed when large numbers of people from the countryside suddenly take up residence in an urban area in a country undergoing modernization and make up village enclaves in the city.

Janet Abu-Lughod has documented this process going on in Cairo, Egypt.[34] At the time of her study, in 1960, more than one-third of Cairo's per-

---

[33] In his "The Rural-Urban Dimension in Preindustrial, Transitional, and Industrial Societies," in Robert E. L. Faris, ed., *Handbook of Modern Sociology* (Chicago: Rand McNally, 1964), pp. 127–60.

[34] See her article "Migrant Adjustments to City Life: The Egyptian Case," *American Journal of Sociology*, 67 (July 1961), pp. 22–32.

manent residents had been born outside the city, most of them coming from rural areas. These formed two groups: one—aspiring, mobile, youthful, seeking education and opportunity; the other, and incidentally far more numerous, disadvantaged rural inhabitants turning to the city because of the dearth of land in the country. It is the latter who cluster in segregated village-like communities within Cairo.

A United Nations report that saw urbanization of the underdeveloped nations of Asia and the Far East as contributing to the emergence of "a new way of life" also saw fit to emphasize the persistence of rural society and culture in the very confines of the emerging metropolis. The survey said:

> Many cities in Asia and the Far East in contrast with Western cities, often retain strong village characteristics or those of an agglomeration of villages. In general they tend to be characterized by two distinct areas: (i) the Western type area, and (ii) the indigenous type area consisting of an agglomeration of villages. In consequence, although a rather small elite indigenous population appears in Asian cities with the same characteristics as those possessed by urban residents in the West, the mass population of many Asian cities are resident in village agglomerations and tend to retain 'folk' characteristics. The characteristics of the urban resident, identified with such dichotomies of continua as the 'folk-urban,' 'rural-urban' or 'community-society' categories, do not hold for the mass of residents in many Asian cities.[35]

THE POSSIBLY CULTURAL UNIQUENESS OF WESTERN URBANIZATION AND NEW FORMS ELSEWHERE

The study of modernization, which calls the rural-urban distinction into question, has occasioned the reexamination of the very premises of typological sociology. As a result, the assumed differences between rural and urban modes of life have come, more and more, to be seen as adherence to particular cultural values rather than as generically contrasting universal categories.

The correspondence between the economic system incorporating the Western ethos on the one hand and the urban complex on the other may have given earlier scholars of urban phenomena a false impression. They may have concluded that what was indigenous to the Western value system and was institutionalized in urban modes of social organization in the United States and Europe was universal. If so, then projecting Western history onto Far Eastern society is unwarranted. Preliminary observations such as those

---

[35] Reprinted from Bureau of Social Affairs, *Report on the World Social Situation* (New York: United Nations, 1957), p. 193.

presented here support the cautious conclusion of Philip Hauser regarding the general validity of rural-urban typology: namely, that it is a debatable assumption to think "that urbanization . . . in Asia must necessarily follow the same pattern as that described for the West in respect to value orientations."[36] It may not. As Bert Hoselitz, another specialist in cross-cultural sociology, has written, in the final analysis the economic structures of Asian society may come to incorporate the prototypic values of universalism, achievement, and functional specificity, and yet the political system of Asia "display the principles of ascription, particularism, and functional diffuseness."[37]

The cultural mix that Hoselitz postulates may turn out to be an impossibility. But the divergence of many Far Eastern cities from the ideal type derived from Western experience suggests perhaps hitherto unrealized urban phenomena that the typological tradition has not prepared us to anticipate.

CONCLUSION

Much scholarship has hypothesized urban society as a unique form of social organization, and the urban person as a singular type of personality. Typologists have thus applied to the urban community the terms *Gesellschaft* and organic solidarity, and have described it as comprising a distinct urban world. In addition, they have imputed a secular ethos to urbanism different from that of the traditional folk type of society. Furthermore, typologists have also viewed the behavior of urban residents as manifesting a specific range of conduct and a spectrum of values peculiar to urban life.

No doubt the urban type does possess some validity. Its postulated attributes correspond to many phenomena, such as atomistic trends and formal organization, and they do enable us to comprehend them. Yet both logic and empirical research raise serious questions about the adequacy of typological analysis. As a type, urbanism is held to be incongruent with sociocultural reality, if only because it was formulated at an earlier and now largely surpassed period. Field studies of informal interaction and voluntary associations reveal that to some extent the solidary community continues to persist even in the metropolis. Research into suburbanism reaches a similar conconclusion. (This is covered extensively in Chapter 12.) Similarly, studies of rural people undergoing modernization at present have produced findings that do not strongly confirm the assumption of the urban mode of existence

---

[36] In Philip M. Hauser, ed., *Urbanization in Asia and the Far East* (Calcutta: UNESCO, 1957), p. 92.

[37] "Generative and Parasitic Cities," *Economic Development and Cultural Change,* 3 (April, 1955), pp. 278–94, as cited in Hauser, ibid.

which the typologists have identified. In all, these lend added support to the conclusion that however valuable, the postulated urban model is possibly only a rough, "primitive" concept.

FOR FURTHER READING

J. N. Edwards and Alan Booth, *Social Participation in Urban Society* (Cambridge, Mass.: Schenkman, 1973). Articles on social interaction and association in the city, with implications for research.

Herbert J. Gans, *The Urban Villagers* (New York: Free Press, 1962). An ethnographic study of an Italian blue-collar neighborhood in Boston showing the persistence of primary ties under urban conditions.

David A. Karp, Gregory P. Stone, and William C. Yoels, *Being Urban* (Lexington, Mass.: D. C. Heath, 1977). On the perfection of methods by which the individual copes with urban congestion, such as anonymity and privacy.

Oscar Lewis and Philip M. Hauser, "The Folk-Urban Ideal Types," in Philip M. Hauser and Leo F. Schnore, eds., *The Study of Urbanization* (New York: Wiley, 1965). On the typological tradition in urban study that seeks to advance our understanding of social change.

Paul Meadows and Ephraim H. Mizruchi, eds., *Urbanism, Urbanization, and Change* (Reading, Mass.: Addison-Wesley, 1969). Comparative perspectives in the study of urbanization.

Dennis E. Poplin, *Communities* (New York: Macmillan, 1972). Theories of communities and constructed types are reviewed.

Miller Lee Taylor and A. R. Jones, *Rural Life in Urbanized Society* (New York: Oxford University Press, 1964). A text on rural sociology in the contemporary United States.

CHAPTER 6

URBAN ECOLOGY

The ecological outlook on urban phenomena differs sharply from that employed by typologists. Ecologists conceive of cities and urban society generally as social organizations occupying geographic locations. They contend that urban life may best be examined as a mosaic of areas in which natural forces operate to produce an orderly, but also continually changing, distribution of people, facilities, and activities.

Social ecologists treat cities in a manner that bears the influence of the Darwinian conception of life. In showing the interplay between urban populations and their natural habitat, ecologists make use of concepts such as nuclei, sectors, and zones; processes like concentration, centralization, and succession; regional and national dominance patterns; and functional types of cities. By and large, social ecologists allow us to understand a good deal about urbanism and urbanization, and to do so quite systematically. It may be said in summary though that the ecological interpretation, as many ecologists themselves recognize, gives us only inconclusive insight into the totality of urban phenomena.

THE ECOLOGICAL APPROACH

Social ecologists borrowed their environmental rationale from plant ecologists and carried it over into their ecological studies. Like plant ecologists, human ecologists reasoned that specific ecological processes operate in the community, and that human organization could be successfully analyzed as subject to the operation of those processes.

THE CHICAGO SCHOOL AND CLASSICAL URBAN ECOLOGY

The ecological interpretation of urban life assumed its so-called classical form at the University of Chicago beginning at the time of World War I. The first step in this development was taken in 1916 with the publication of Robert E. Park's article "The City: Suggestions for the Investigation of Human Behavior in the Urban Environment."[1] Park referred to the city as a natural phenomenon brought about by spontaneous forces. These forces were evident in the undesigned concentration of activities and facilities into clearly demarcated areas of business, industry, transportation, and residential habitation. Moreover, Park pointed out that residentially the people themselves clustered in well-defined though unplanned locations according to ethnic, social, and cultural differences.

Park's collaboration with Ernest W. Burgess and other scholars who joined them in a long program of urban research made the University of Chicago the leading American center of social ecology for decades. From 1923 on, Park and Burgess investigated the "natural areas" of the city, principally Chicago itself, from two aspects—the ecological and the cultural. But primarily it was the first of these, the "spatial pattern," as they called it, that was stressed and that, in Burgess' words, "gave rise to ecological studies." The spatial pattern, said Burgess, included "everything that could be mapped." That was the city's topography together with the buildings and other facilities which its inhabitants had put up and in which they showed their behavioral responses to the everpresent, inexorable environment.[2]

The "classical" ecological position that Park and Burgess took is that the city may be described and analyzed in terms of subsocial, impersonal competition. In their *Introduction to the Science of Sociology* in 1921, and in *The City,* which they wrote together with Roderick McKenzie and Louis Wirth in 1925, Park and Burgess gave formal expression to their theory of human ecology. They distinguished between the community as "that natural resultant of the competitive process" and society as the product of the "cultural process." The community denoted human groupings organized at the biotic

---

[1] *American Journal of Sociology,* 20 (March 1916), pp. 577–612.

[2] Cf. Ernest W. Burgess and Donald J. Bogue, "Research in Urban Society: A Long View," in their edited volume *Urban Sociology* (Chicago: University of Chicago Press, 1967), p. 7.

The ecological impact on urban society: the Mississippi River at Vicksburg, with the Yazoo Diversion Channel, center, entering the river.

level, and corresponded to the naturally adaptive, nonpurposive structuring of plant and animal life within specific environments.[3] Thus classical urban ecology separated the physical and economic aspects of human life from its purely social components. And even though the Chicago ecologists were neither consistent nor entirely clear, the fact remains that their thinking gave primacy to deterministic factors in urban life such as a city's geographic environment, the division of labor in its population, and its dominance or subordination with respect to other communities in its locale.

Within 10 years after the principles of classical urban ecology were formulated by Park and Burgess, they had inspired a large number of widely read monographs, among them Frederick M. Thrasher's *The Gang* (1927); Louis Wirth's *The Ghetto* (1928); Nels Anderson's *The Hobo: The Sociology of the Homeless Man* (1923); Roderick D. McKenzie's *The Neighborhood: A Study of Columbus, Ohio* (1923); Ernest R. Mowrer's *Family Disorganization* (1927); Clifford R. Shaw's *Delinquency Areas* (1929); and Harvey W. Zorbaugh's *The Gold Coast and the Slum* (1929).[4] These books contained much descriptive material, often strikingly ethnographic, about urban distributions.

[3] Robert E. Park, "Succession, an Ecological Concept," *American Sociological Review, 1* (April, 1936), p. 178.

[4] All published by the University of Chicago Press.

Almost from the beginning, however, classical urban ecology had its detractors. They divided chiefly into two groups.

One group of dissidents simply wanted to strengthen urban ecology by improving its research design and also to refine it by subjecting it to strict empirical verification. James A. Quinn of the University of Cincinnati was a social ecologist who thought so.[5] For example, Quinn advanced the hypothesis of median location, stating that unless prevented, an ecological unit will occupy a middle location with respect to the environment whose resources it utilizes, the units it serves, and the units upon which it depends. This formulation, Quinn held, was applicable to the location of schools, stores, factories, homes and, in the context of a particular region, even entire cities. However, Quinn's insistence on exact substantiation cast doubt on the principle of environmental determination so vital to classical urban ecology.[6]

Amos Hawley, who esteemed classical ecology highly, typified the second group of critics, the sociologists who shared some outright reservations about the basic adequacy of ecological theory.[7] In Hawley's mind, assigning the key role in urban life to the subsocial process of competition was unwarranted monism. To the extent that mutual aid and, in fact, culture in general were neglected, he said, the ecological approach was an oversimplification of the social process. The moral components of the urban system, Hawley reasoned, must be studied in their own right as determining variables, not in isolation, to be sure, but as interdependent with the sustenance (biotic) aspects of the urban order as Park and Burgess had originally envisaged them.

According to Hawley, community structure was not a property of individuals but of the social order. Community structure consisted of "corporate" units like families and business firms, and also of "categoric" groupings. The latter were large, scattered publics made up of homogeneous individuals like entrepreneurs and professionals evidencing collective but not corporate forms of behavior. Hawley considered community structure as the major legitimate focus of ecological study, because it was community structure that gave expression to human competition for scarce resources in any given habitat. Hence, concluded Hawley, studying community structure offered a way of overcoming the unfortunate, false dichotomy between the bio-

---

[5] See his "The Nature of Human Ecology: Reexamination and Redefinition," *Social Forces, 28* (December 1939), pp. 161–68, and *Human Ecology* (New York: Prentice-Hall, 1950), especially Ch. 12.

[6] Cf. George A. Theodorson, ed., *Studies in Human Ecology* (Evanston, Ill.: Harper & Row, 1961), pp. 135ff.

[7] Amos H. Hawley, *Human Ecology* (New York: Ronald Press, 1950), pp. 73–74.

tic and the cultural aspects of urban life.[8] Hawley advocated research into the urban community according to the extent to which it is, in fact, either economically dependent on its habitat or independent of it by acting as an autonomous modifying force. In this manner of conceptualizing the community at the social level, although still allowing it to be examined in terms of its settlement patterns, Hawley believed that the ecological study of urban phenomena could be reasonably delimited.

Despite its many supporters besides Quinn and Hawley, additional research continued to call classical ecology into question. For example, Maurice Davie reviewed the way in which land was used in 20 American and Canadian cities only to conclude that despite some similarities, there was no single, universal pattern of urban settlement.[9] Again, Milla Alihan's searching analysis of natural areas showed a lack of both consistency and precision on the part of the research ecologists.[10]

CULTURE AND ECOLOGICAL PATTERNING

Eventually, the status of culture as an independent variable in shaping even the spatial configuration of the city was given telling expression not only in theory but also in empirical research.

In *Land Use in Central Boston,* Walter Firey forcefully advanced a counterargument to the employment of land in strictly economic fashion, an idea fundamental to the ecological approach.[11] Firey's doctoral dissertation called systematic attention to the role of ideological orientations in determining the utilization of land in Boston, especially the honorific space of the Common, Beacon Hill, and the sites made sacred by the War for Independence. Similarly, Firey demonstrated that regardless of the objective blight there, Boston's North End attracted Italians for communal reasons. This was still another instance of noneconomic motivation regarding land use.

In a subsequent book, *Man, Mind, and Land,* Firey extended his cultural reservations concerning ecological theory into considerations regarding some possible formal system of thought that would combine ecological, ethnological, and economic principles into one coherent scheme useful for

[8] In a more recent publication, Hawley has in ecological fashion systematically pursued the idea that "the form and content of man's collective life is a function of the efficiency of his means of transportation and communication." Cf. *Urban Society: An Ecological Approach* (New York: Ronald Press, 1971).

[9] Maurice R. Davie, "The Pattern of Urban Growth," in George Peter Murdock, ed., *Studies in the Science of Society* (New Haven, Conn.: Yale University Press, 1937), pp. 131–62.

[10] Milla Aissa Alihan, *Social Ecology: A Critical Analysis* (New York: Cooper Square, 1964).

[11] (Cambridge, Mass.: Harvard University Press, 1947).

Louisburg Square, a focal point of Boston's exclusive downtown residential district, Beacon Hill.

public-planning purposes.[12] In a rather complex manner differentiating economic from purely normative action, Firey believes that due regard can be given to both volitional and deterministic aspects.

Earlier, A. B. Hollingshead had taken note of the dissonance between the then existing ecological theory and Firey's work.[13] Hollingshead had also declared the concept of "abstract ecological man" a fallacy. Culture might be a difficult variable to reduce to research design, he had said, but it was

[12] (Glencoe, Ill.: Free Press, 1960).

[13] In "A Re-Examination of Ecological Theory," *Sociology and Social Research, 31* (January/February 1947), pp. 194–204.

imperative to do so, that is, to take ethnicity, usages and values, kinship structures, and the like into proper account so as to bring generalization and research into line with each other. Hollingshead did not deny the achievements of ecology. He sought only to circumscribe it properly.

SPATIAL THEORIES

One of the outstanding successes of the ecological study of urban life has been the formulation of descriptive theories concerning the spatial patterning of cities. True, a considerable degree of variation has come to exist among social ecologists regarding the spatial arrangement of urban communities.[14] Nevertheless, the spatial theories that urban ecologists have developed do possess distinct merit. Among them, three theories have been most prominent. They are the (1) concentric-zone, (2) sector, and (3) multiple-nuclei conceptions of urban location and spatial distribution.

THE CONCENTRIC-ZONE THEORY

As shown in Figure 6-1, the concentric-zone theory, originally developed by Park and Burgess, refers to the description of any given large city in terms of six circular belts having a common center.[15] Each belt, or zone, represents the tendency of the metropolitan population to expand outward from the core. Thus the center exercises dominance over the surrounding community, and one may expect particular variables like home ownership and transportation facilities to be differentially distributed with respect to the center, and also to exhibit different but related rates of change.

Zone I, the central business district, contains the major concentration of financial, commercial, civic, and transportation activities in the entire metropolitan area. Here are located the principal banks, department stores, offices, theaters, restaurants, government offices, law courts, libraries, auditoriums, and museums. The tallest buildings and most frequented places are to be found in this innermost territory.

Surrounding the central business district at the city's heart is a deteriorated belt, Zone II, the zone in transition. Encroachment by the expanding center, the presence of transportation service facilities, such as railroad

[14] Cf. Ralph Thomlinson, *Social Structure: The Social and Spatial Characteristics of Cities* (New York: Random House, 1969).

[15] First presented in 1923 in Ernest W. Burgess, "The Growth of the City," in Robert E. Park, Ernest W. Burgess, and Roderick D. McKenzie, eds., *The City* (Chicago: University of Chicago Press, 1925), pp. 47–62. A predecessor may be found in Richard M. Hurd, *Principles of City Land Values* (Chicago: University of Chicago Press, 1903), which suggested that growth patterns in European and American cities tended to fall into concentric circles and radial paths along major routes of transportation.

FIGURE 6-1 The Concentric Zone Hypothesis

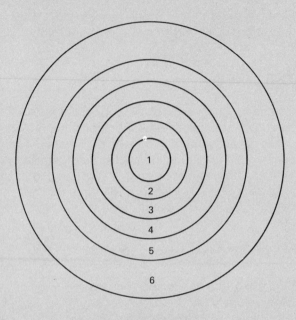

1 Central business district
2 Wholesale light manufacturing
3 Low—class residential
4 Medium—class residential
5 High—class residential
6 Commuters' zone

Source: Chauncey D. Harris and Edward L. Ullman, "The Nature of Cities," *The Annals of the American Association of Political and Social Science,* 242 (November, 1945), pp. 7–17. Adapted.

yards, and the location here of light manufacturing immediately adjacent to the major stores and offices all cast a blight on the residential utilization of the area. Dilapidated houses, partitioned mansions surviving from an earlier era, and other types of substandard housing accommodate the economically deprived and culturally disadvantaged, principally migrants from nonurban localities. Poverty and crime are generally more prevalent here than anywhere else in the whole city, since the zone in transition affords the various forms of vice a location accessible to a clientele from the entire urban area. Disease and degradation also have their highest incidence in the zone in transition.

On the outermost fringe of Zone II live the more prosperous of the sub-

The central business district of Houston, Texas.

merged social classes. They seek escape into Zone III, which Park and Burgess called "the zone of independent workingmen's homes," where are to be found second-generation immigrants, people desirous, out of necessity, of living near the factories and shops where they work.

Still farther out, Zone IV encloses the better residences, including single-family houses and the more generally sought after apartment buildings. The residents of Zone V are likely to be people of higher-class status with technical, clerical, and business occupations.

Finally, beyond the corporate limits of the municipality lie the affluent suburbs of spacious homes and elegant apartment structures and residential hotels dotting the major corridors. This is Zone VI, "the commuters' zone," the area inhabited by those of highest socioeconomic status.

As Quinn concludes, Park and Burgess' depiction of a symmetrical pattern does give us a good general picture that can be definitely recognized in most cities.[16] But despite the favorable reception given the concentric-zone theory, its proponents have been criticized in two ways.

First, they have been reproached for asserting an ideal-type arrange-

[16] James A. Quinn, "The Burgess Zonal Hypothesis and Its Critics," *American Sociological Review, 5* (April 1940), pp. 210–18.

ment that does not closely conform to actuality. Thus the hypothesis does not allow for affluent enclaves, like New York's Park Avenue and Chicago's Gold Coast, inside the deteriorated zone in transition adjacent to the commercial and civic core. The concentric-zone theory also fails to recognize that there are dispersal factors in the urban community constantly working against business concentration at the heart. The automobile, which has made a great difference in urban land use since the 1920s when the concentric-zone hypothesis was first formulated, is a compelling illustration of this. In addition, modifications from the symmetrical ideal-type are clearly attributable to topographical features like waterways and ravines capable of accommodating transit lines. Modifications also stem from previous land use depending on social factors, such as the settlement patterns of racial minorities carrying over from preindustrialism,[17] and the distribution of population groups, among them young families with children.[18]

Second, the proponents of the concentric-zone hypothesis have recognized that the zones are not rigidly demarcated, that, in fact, where they meet each blends imperceptibly into the ring inside it or the one surrounding it. For this reason, then, the Park and Burgess hypothesis has been held to lack precise specification and discrimination.

To meet these objections, other conceptions of the urban pattern have also been advanced.

THE SECTOR THEORY

Homer Hoyt's sector theory has many adherents, although it is much more restricted in scope than the concentric-zone hypothesis.[19] Figure 6-2 represents the sector theory graphically. The sector theory deals mainly with the structuring of residential areas, although it can be applied to other land uses as well. Sectors are described as growing in wedge-shape fashion from the core toward the periphery. The resulting sectors are each homogeneous for particular values. That is, low-rent, middle-rent, and high-rent housing clearly evidence separation from one another.

Hoyt reviewed high-rent areas in 142 American cities for 1900, 1915, and 1936. His general findings may be seen in Figure 6-3. Hoyt learned that high-rent usage tends toward high ground and also along bodies of water unencumbered by industry, particularly where there is open land for still further expansion outward.

[17] Cf. Leo F. Schnore, *Class and Race in Cities and Suburbs* (Chicago: Markham, 1972), especially Ch. 3.

[18] Avery M. Guest, "Retesting the Burgess Zonal Hypothesis: The Location of White-Collar Workers," *American Journal of Sociology*, 76 (May 1971), pp. 1094–1108.

[19] See his *The Structure and Growth of Residential Neighborhoods in American Cities* (Washington, D.C.: Federal Housing Administration, 1939).

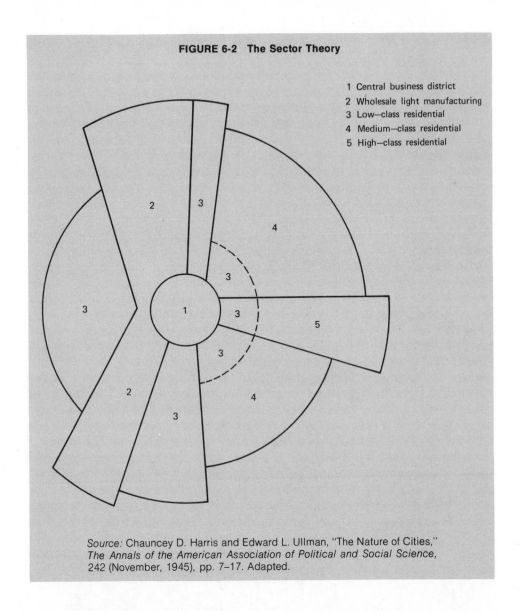

FIGURE 6-2 The Sector Theory

1 Central business district
2 Wholesale light manufacturing
3 Low—class residential
4 Medium—class residential
5 High—class residential

Source: Chauncey D. Harris and Edward L. Ullman, "The Nature of Cities,"
The Annals of the American Association of Political and Social Science,
242 (November, 1945), pp. 7–17. Adapted.

Therefore, one may conclude, urban growth proceeds axially along transit routes or, in a sense, along the line of least resistance, making for a star-shaped urban configuration in general. But once in motion, sector development goes on persistently. In Boston, for example, the fashionable residential area moved northwestward; in Seattle, due east; in Minneapolis, southwestward; and in Richmond, Virginia, directly west. (See Figure 6-3.)

Hoyt's sector theory is not so much a replacement for the Park and Burgess concentricity hypothesis as it is a modification of it: though expand-

FIGURE 6-3 Shifts in the Location of Fashionable Residential Areas in Six American Cities: 1900–1936 (fashionable residential areas indicated by shading)

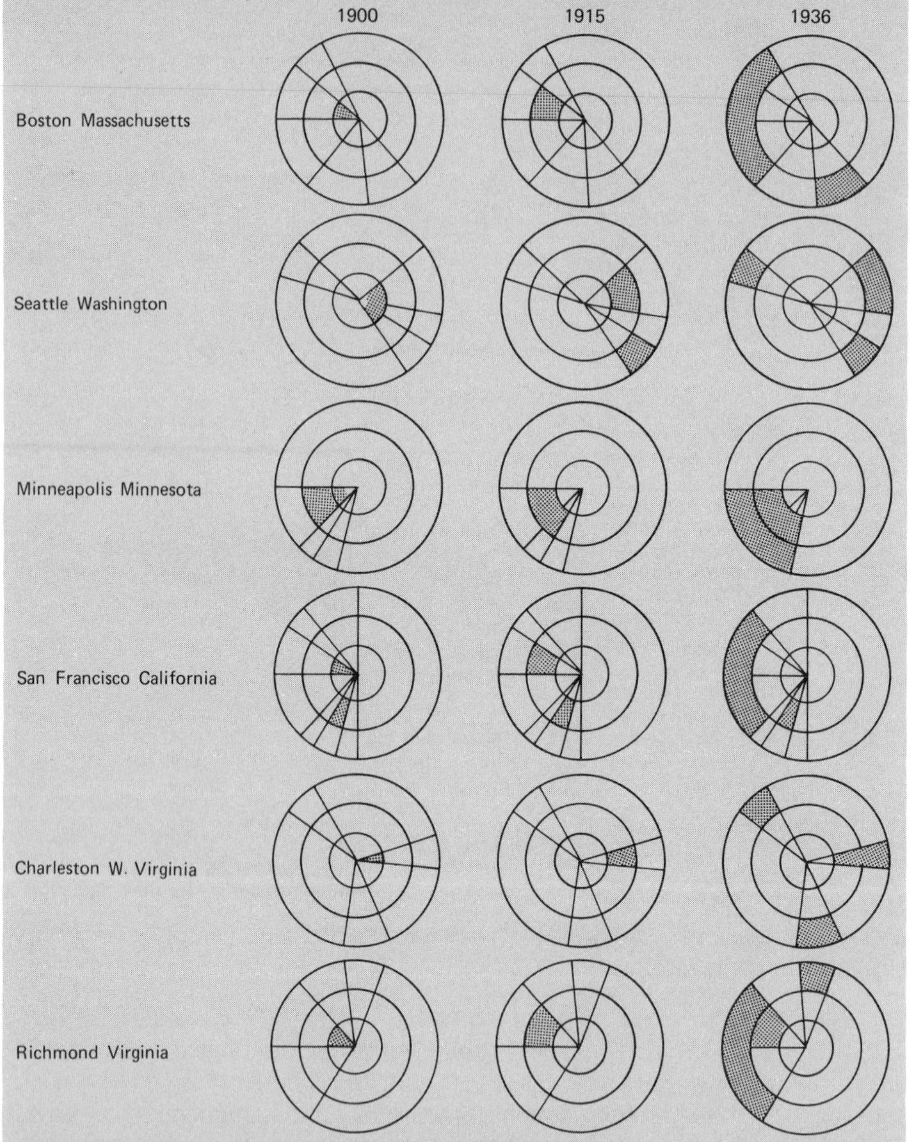

Source: Homer Hoyt, *The Structure and Growth of Residential Neighborhoods in American Cities* (Washington, D.C.: Federal Housing Administration, 1939), Figure 40, p. 115. Adapted.

ing from a single center, land use tends to be concentrated in segments instead of circular belts.

Probably because of the extensive data Hoyt used in originally presenting his theory, not much research has been done to test his conclusions further. Twenty-five years after his original work, Hoyt himself observed that sector patterns of residential land use continued to be found in American cities, but that the automobile and the expressway had introduced unusual flexibility in the distribution of rental values.[20] In the intervening period, manufacturing and retailing had decentralized in most of our large cities, while a massive downtown office boom, reflecting the need for greater commercial and governmental administration, had taken place.[21] Some recent research, however, has confirmed Hoyt's sector hypothesis, one study being that made by Peter W. Amato of Bogotá, Colombia. Amato ascertained that "the direction of the growth of upper-income residential areas in Bogotá was of a sector nature."[22]

THE MULTIPLE-NUCLEI THEORY

That a more appropriate conception of urban location was needed than both the zonation idea and the sectoring scheme led the University of Chicago geographers Chauncey D. Harris and Edward L. Ullman to formulate another theory of city growth, one recognizing multiple nuclei.[23] Figure 6-4 gives a conventionalized treatment of a city in terms of multiple nuclei. Harris and Ullman observed that cities are often built around more than a single center. For example, London has two nuclei: the city, which is its financial core, and Westminster, which makes up its political hub.

Accordingly, Harris and Ullman hypothesized that whatever a city's original nucleus, perhaps the waterfront of a port, say, four factors combine to produce separate nuclei thereafter. These are (1) activities requiring specialized facilities, such as retailing, which calls for maximum accessibility; (2) activities benefiting from clustering, like insurance underwriters and financial institutions; (3) activities that are detrimental to one another and which benefit from separation, for example, the unloading of vehicles at commission houses separated from the smooth distribution of pedestrians among re-

[20] Homer Hoyt, "Recent Distortions of the Classical Models of Urban Structure," *Land Economics, 40* (May 1964), pp. 199–212.

[21] Brian Berry and Yehoshua S. Cohen, "Decentralization of Commerce and Industry: The Restructuring of Metropolitan America," in Louis H. Masotti and Jeffrey K. Hadden, eds., *The Urbanization of the Suburbs* (Beverly Hills, Calif.: Sage, 1973), pp. 431–55.

[22] Peter W. Amato, "Environmental Quality and Locational Behavior in a Latin American City," *Urban Affairs Quarterly, 5* (September 1969), pp. 83–101.

[23] Chauncey D. Harris and Edward L. Ullman, "The Nature of Cities," *The Annals of the American Academy of Political and Social Science, 242* (November 1945), pp. 7–17.

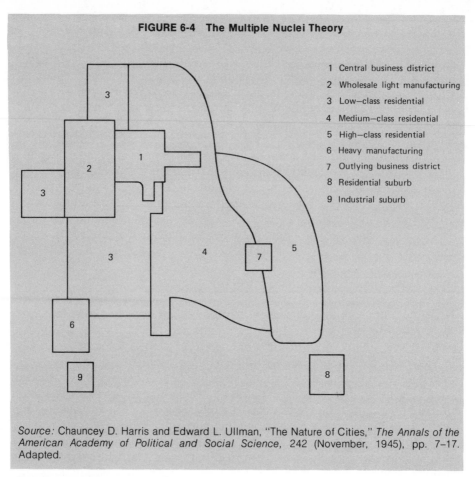

FIGURE 6-4 The Multiple Nuclei Theory

1 Central business district
2 Wholesale light manufacturing
3 Low—class residential
4 Medium—class residential
5 High—class residential
6 Heavy manufacturing
7 Outlying business district
8 Residential suburb
9 Industrial suburb

Source: Chauncey D. Harris and Edward L. Ullman, "The Nature of Cities," *The Annals of the American Academy of Political and Social Science,* 242 (November, 1945), pp. 7–17. Adapted.

tail establishments; and (4) activities unable to afford sites of high value, such as storage warehouses.

The larger the city, Harris and Ullman generalized, the more numerous its nuclei. In the very largest cities, the financial district stands at some distance from the business core, although in the medium-size communities the two are not clearly separated.

Manufacturing facilities divide into the light and heavy varieties. Light manufacturing plants tend to be located not far from the central business district but adjacent to interurban transportation. By contrast, heavy industry requires much land and therefore its installations are at the earlier or present edge of the city away from the subdivided tracts but accessible to transportation, either water or rail.

Harris and Ullman also identify two other types of nuclei: the residential district and what they call "minor phenomena." High-value residential areas occupy elevated, well drained land comfortably removed from the nuisance of industry. Among the "minor" districts are to be found unusual entities, such as universities. Harvard and Berkeley are examples of institutions of higher learning situated in metropolitan centers and forming the core for land-use activities clustering around them.

Finally, Harris and Ullman recognize the presence around most large American cities of both residential and industrial suburbs and satellites.

In 1962, Ullman updated the earlier multiple-nuclei theory by adverting to the centrifugal distribution of retail trade and specialized entertainment and cultural facilities made possible by the automobile and the expressway. He confirmed the decline of the central business district. He also reviewed the growing importance of scattered centers and concluded that in the future a large city would probably be a composite of general and special centers rather than a single cohesive entity.[24]

THE THREE THEORIES IN COMBINATION

Most urbanists agree that all three of the graphic propositions, concentricity, sectoring, and multiple nuclei, do have validity. They also accept the idea that the three are supplementary, that together they provide considerable understanding of the complexities of urban distribution and growth.[25]

In addition, it has been found that the three theories may have sequential significance, in other words, to refer to successive phases of a city's development. Breese, who has studied cities in the newly emerging countries, accepts the applicability of the Burgess and Park, Hoyt, and Harris and Ullman theories to the urban centers of non-Western cities as well as those of the United States from which they were originally derived. However, Breese generalizes that a zonal pattern may be most characteristic of cities in their early stages of development, and that the sector pattern of growth may represent their later history, "although the multiple nuclei growth patterns in these urban areas cannot be overlooked either."[26]

The zonal, sectoral, and nuclear approaches have descriptive value, to be sure. Yet the need remains for them to be reconciled with one another. The economic and institutional viewpoints that they embody should be synthesized. But, unfortunately, this problem persists stubbornly. Wearily, Thomlinson has concluded that the combination of rings, sectors, and gradients yields a result that is likely, he says, "to be so perplexing as to discourage generalization."[27]

[24] Edward L. Ullman, "Presidential Address: The Nature of Cities Reconsidered," *Regional Science Association: Papers and Proceedings, 9* (1962), pp. 7–23.

[25] Harris and Ullman, op. cit., p. 17.

[26] Gerald Breese, *Urbanization in Newly Developing Countries* (Englewood Cliffs, N.J.: Prentice-Hall, 1966), p. 106.

[27] Op. cit., p. 150.

Recently, however, Frank Sweetser has been seeking to bring the three ecological models together by means of factor analysis. Sweetser recognizes serious methodological problems, but believes that analyzing given factors in the various sectors and zones, and then ascertaining which are unique to locational pattern can lead to the fruitful comparison of different types of cities according to their underlying ecological design.[28] One suggestive lead contributing to such an effort at synthesis has possibly been supplied by Kent Schwirian and Marc Matre. Examining the ecological configuration of 11 Canadian cities, these sociologists learned that while social status evidences a sector arrangement, the degree of familism shows a zonal distribution.[29]

ECOLOGICAL PROCESSES AND STRUCTURES

Still another contribution of urban ecologists has been the identification of particular processes operating within cities, urban regions, and even entire urban nations. Perhaps most significant of these are (1) concentration, (2) centralization, (3) dispersion, (4) segregation, (5) invasion, and (6) succession. They have been systematically observed primarily in connection with land use, intergroup relations, and regional economic dominance and subordination.

CONCENTRATION

Concentration refers to the arrangement of populous places in a hierarchy of economic influence according to the power that each exercises over those subordinate to itself. Concentration thus denotes the aggregation of services and facilities in such a way as to create an interdependent system of communities functioning within a given natural environment.

Concentration has long been a subject of interest for economists and geographers who inquire into what determines site selection. These scholars have concluded that two considerations are most vital. First, cities are regional service centers concentrating within their own boundaries the facilities on which the surrounding territory depends and can most efficiently utilize by virtue of their location. Second, according to the break-in-transportation theory formulated by an early American sociologist, Charles Horton Cooley, cities grow up where transfers of goods between modes of carriage

[28] Frank L. Sweetser, "Ecological Factors in Metropolitan Zones and Sectors," in Mattei Dogan and Stein Rokkan, eds., *Quantitative Ecological Analysis in the Social Sciences* (Cambridge, Mass.: M.I.T. Press, 1969).

[29] Kent P. Schwirian and Marc Matre, *The Ecological Structure of Canadian Cities* (Columbus, Ohio: Sociology Department, Ohio State University, 1969).

are necessary, for instance, at water's edge in the case of maritime gateways like San Francisco and Marseilles.[30]

A number of urban sociologists, notably Donald Bogue, Otis D. Duncan, and Alvin Boskoff, and to a lesser extent rural and regional sociologists like Howard W. Odum, Harry E. Moore, Rupert B. Vance, Edgar T. Thompson, and Carle C. Zimmerman have emphasized the regional significance of the urban metropolis. Of these possibly Bogue's research on metropolitan regionalism, Boskoff's work on regional dominance, and Duncan's study of cities within the national economy are more representative of successful research on the importance of concentration in modern industrial societies.

Metropolitan Regionalism

Bogue infers that "dominance is a status that every community possesses in some degree with respect to other communities with which it interacts."[31] Therefore, in the exercise of their influence upon one another, communities fall into four categories.

The first are the metropolitan centers of the premier order, like New York, Los Angeles, and, most recently, Dallas. They virtually control many of the conditions of life of the cities located in their vicinity. Thus, in 1965, four-fifths of all Texas banks were correspondents (clients) of financial institutions located in Dallas.[32]

Second are the "subdominants," the hinterland cities like Erie, Pennsylvania, and Worcester, Massachusetts, that are specialized intermediaries between the metropolis and the outlying areas in the economic activities of a sizable territory, perhaps a section within a state.

"Influents" are Bogue's third type. These smaller cities have still more modest areas of dominance in the overall urban region, although in some few particulars, such as local education, they may actually be compelling.

Finally, there are the "subinfluents," the small town and rural-farm populations that in true ecological fashion simply "accept the conditions imposed by the dominants."

Altogether then, dominants, subdominants, influents, and subinfluents constitute a regional ecosystem distributed into a single, stable territorial pattern. Such stability, however, depends in the final analysis on the slowness with which major socioeconomic change takes place, for example, a shift from control exercised by the extractive-manufacturing segment of the

---

[30] See his "The Theory of Transportation," in R. C. Angell, ed., *Sociological Theory and Social Research* (New York: Holt, Rinehart & Winston, 1930), pp. 75–83.

[31] Donald Bogue, *The Structure of the Metropolitan Community* (Ann Arbor, Mich.: Horace H. Rackham School of Graduate Studies, University of Michigan, 1949).

[32] Beverly Duncan and Stanley Lieberson, *Metropolis and Region in Transition* (Beverly Hills, Calif.: Sage, 1970), p. 254.

economy to that of the financial-service-governmental sector. For this reason, alterations in the ecological equilibrium are continually taking place.

Urban Regionalism

Together with Bogue, Boskoff also views the large city as a regional dominant. Its influence is strongest on those communities that are nearest and weakest on those that are farthest away. The impact of a major city is discernible in the degree to which neighboring cities specialize their activities within the coordinating order directed from the core.[33]

In Boskoff's thinking, the urban region is a "continuously evolving entity" that exports functions to peripheral areas. By doing so, it establishes networks of interdependence between service organizations and their clients. The nodal city thus exerts political as well as economic influence over a geographic region.

Boskoff also emphasizes status distinctions and style-of-life differentials in the urban region's entire pattern of settlement. Consider the so-called urban fringe, an ecological area beyond the suburban zone and one to which Boskoff assigns a long list of unique attributes.

First, the fringe is easily accessible, since it lies along major lines of transportation. Second, although there is much vacant land inside the fringe, what land is under use exhibits different kinds of largely uncoordinated utilization. Third, the fringe tends toward the lower end of the rental spectrum, for its inhabitants are socioeconomically inferior to the suburban population. Also, the fringe lacks well developed public utilities, community services, and social organization so that, fourth, Boskoff refers to it as "an institutional desert." In the absence of effective social controls, the fringe is thus a place of expansion in ways that are objectionable to the more orderly processes of the metropolis in general. Hence, nuisance activities—trash dumps, racetracks, junk yards, and vice—may be relegated to the fringe.

Besides the suburban zone and the urban fringe, Boskoff's ecological concept of the urban region also includes two other entities: exurbia and satellite cities. Exurbanites, such as successful professionals and executives, live in places like Bucks County, about 50 miles from Philadelphia, where they can have an affluent rural environment without impairing their enjoyment of the indispensable city. Satellite cities are usually located on the border between two contiguous metropolitan regions, like Toledo, which ships its output of automobile glass to Detroit and receives machine tools from Cleveland.

---

[33] Alvin Boskoff, *The Sociology of Urban Regions* (New York: Appleton-Century-Crofts, 1962), pp. 130–50.

Cities in the National Economy

Comparative urban and metropolitan dominance research was undertaken at midcentury by Otis Duncan and his collaborators, at least partially to survey the significance of America's largest cities at the time.[34] The Duncan research team attempted to arrive at a classification of cities that would do justice to the hierarchy concept, the criteria of metropolitanism, and to center-regional relationships as well. Fifty cities were classified, the ultimate objective "not to produce a classification for its own sake, but to suggest some principles determining the structure of a system of cities."[35]

The Duncan team relied on selected indicators to sort out Standard Metropolitan Statistical Areas, namely, value added by manufacturing, wholesale sales, business service receipts, nonlocal commercial loans, and demand deposits. Accordingly, they identified seven types of cities, for example, New York and Chicago as national metropolises, and others as regional dominants.

The Duncan group concluded that in the distribution of manufacturing activities the cities of the United States did form a single hierarchy. In other respects, however, they had only regional significance. Wrote Duncan, "In regard to service . . . it may be meaningful to think of broad regions as having more or less self-contained hierarchies of cities, although some kinds of service industries clearly are organized on a national basis."[36] Owing to the overlapping that exists between regions, however, the Duncan group had to concede that the geometry of city-region relationships was most complex, and that the central-place theme could satisfactorily account for only some kinds of industrial variation by city size.

In summary, the Duncan group's research, published as *Metropolis and Region,* is an example of the refined treatment of the regional importance of urbanism, but also an example of the ecologist's limited success in recognizing different functional types of cities.

CENTRALIZATION

The process of centralization refers to the congregation of people in dense clusters for the purpose of satisfying specific interests.

Centralization may be said to express economic behavior in spatial terms. That is, the production and exchange of goods and services require human activity. That involves time-cost considerations. Thus centralization with respect to the territory served permits the realization of maximum benefits. Both the concentric-zone and multiple-nuclei theories of urban pattern-

---

[34] Otis D. Duncan et al., *Metropolis and Region* (Baltimore, Md.: The Johns Hopkins Press, 1960).

[35] *Ibid.,* p. 266.

[36] *Ibid.,* p. 7.

ing presented earlier definitely reflect this process of centralization.

In the large city, two areas of centralization typically exist.

The first of these is the commercial hub consisting of the city's principal banks, office buildings, hotels, and department stores. They function in a tight cluster of high-rise structures that take as full advantage as possible of their central location and also reduce ground costs by building up into the overlying space. These facilities are interspersed with any number of adjunct specialists that also occupy quarters in the densely inhabited central business district: accountants, data processors, tax consultants, designers, brokers, lawyers, engineers, agents, and the like. Altogether, they staff the commercial and administrative network that pertains to the urban community as an economic enterprise and, depending on the size and location of the particular city, possibly an entire geographic region.

The second area of centralization is the city's primary industries. They too tend to cluster into relatively distinct but none too compact a precinct. Here will be found the iron and steel mills, oil refineries, paint factories, machine shops, and other processing plants. Typically, a city's heavy industries are located adjacent to railroads and waterways, and as a result may be strung out rather than close together. The determining factors are the availability of transportation and competition from other land users for particular sites. Since heavy industry needs a considerable amount of land and since it creates noxious conditions—noise, fumes, and unsightliness—its facilities get to be established in otherwise unwanted locations. Although sheer economic calculation determines the location of a city's industries, the historical stage of its development will affect their siting too. For example, as the city grows, the use of land for business purposes may well encroach on industrial sites. This will result in factory use giving way to office buildings, with industry moving to a new location some distance from the core.

DISPERSION

The opposite of centralization, dispersion means the movement of people, facilities, and functions away from the center and towards the fringe of the urban community. Although an urban settlement displays the process of centralization very conspicuously, given growth, dispersion occurs from the very beginning of the community's existence and continues throughout its history.

Dispersion results from two general causes. On the one hand, outward movement goes on as a consequence of factors on the periphery that pull people away from the center. Here may be mentioned new means of transportation, lower land values, greater freedom from regulation, and the presence of natural resources. On the other hand, dispersion also occurs in response to deleterious factors present at the center that, consequently, "push" people and facilities outward. Business firms are often driven out by taxes and high labor costs, the first resulting from a higher level of municipal

A corporate headquarters on the metropolitan fringe conveniently located alongside the expressway cloverleaf.

services provided by the more mature type of community and the latter by advanced unionization. Added reasons for forced dispersion are obsolete structures, congestion, and inimical social conditions, notably crime, poverty, and blight.

The forces of attraction and expulsion indicate why centralization and dispersion are actually reciprocal, and not merely contrary, processes. For instance, the attraction of higher-income residents to a city's outlying areas, and consequently their dispersion, will almost inevitably lead to concentration of low-income families and individuals in the dwellings that have been vacated. Similarly, as social ecologist Avery Guest has recently shown, the location of types of families in the city (young families, old families, and the like) varies rather systematically according to distance from the dense central business district and age of the residential area.[37]

SEGREGATION

In Quinn's definition, segregation "consists of a sequence of change whereby units of contrasting types are sifted and sorted into different subparts of an area."[38] Segregation may occur consciously and voluntarily for

[37] Avery M. Guest, "Patterns of Family Location," *Demography, 9* (February 1972), pp. 159–172.
[38] James A. Quinn, *Human Ecology* (New York: Prentice-Hall, 1950), p. 352.

the sake of convenience or protection, or it may take place involuntarily, that is, by imposition. It may also be brought about without deliberate effort, as for instance the separation of people into different areas of the city according to style of life.

Studies of spatial segregation in the urban community have highlighted, above all, the operation of ethnicity and race. Thus, Jahn, Schmid, and Schrag developed four mathematical indices to measure the spatial distribution of the races.[39] The presence of blacks in the inner cities of the metropolitan areas of the United States and their virtual absence from the suburbs was documented by Schnore and Sharp.[40] Further research has been conducted under the impetus of the civil rights movement.[41] Recent inquiry shows the dispersion of blacks from the central city into the suburbs though generally not without the reappearance of segregation in the areas newly inhabited.[42] In fact, some predominantly black suburbs have resulted from the recent migration, such as Maywood, adjoining Chicago, and East Cleveland, Ohio.[43]

INVASION

Invasion refers to the encroachment in an area by one activity upon another activity and by one population upon another. Industry or business may encroach upon a residential district, and as a result a circular process of physical deterioration and obsolescence be set into motion. On the other hand, penetration by a subordinate social group represents a lower-order type of residential land use which may produce congestion and hence affect property use accordingly.

Detailing the several aspects of succession is important in studying invasion. Burgess recognized this in the following statement:

> Succession as a process has been studied and its main course charted as (1) invasion, beginning often as an unnoticed or gradual

---

[39] Julius Jahn, Calvin F. Schmid, and Clarence Schrag, "The Measurement of Ecological Segregation," *American Sociological Review, 17* (June 1947), pp. 293–303.

[40] Leo F. Schnore and Harry Sharp, "Racial Changes in Metropolitan Areas, 1950–1960," *Social Forces, 41* (March 1963), pp. 247–52.

[41] See Morton Grodzins, "Metropolitan Segregation," *Scientific American, 197* (October 1957), pp. 33–41; Donald O. Cowgill, "Trends in Residential Segregation of Nonwhites in American Cities, 1940–1950," *American Sociological Review, 21* (February 1956); and also Karl Taeuber, "Negro Residential Segregation: Trends and Measurement," *Social Problems, 12* (Summer 1964), pp. 42–50.

[42] Howard X. Connolly, "Black Movement into the Suburbs: Suburbs Doubling Their Black Population During the 1960s," *Urban Affairs Quarterly, 9* (September 1973), pp. 91–112.

[43] See Reynolds Farley, "The Changing Distribution of Negroes Within Metropolitan Areas: The Emergence of Black Suburbs," *American Journal of Sociology, 75* (January 1970), pp. 512–29.

penetration, followed by (2) reaction, or the resistance mild or violent of the inhabitants of the community, ultimately resulting in (3) the influx of newcomers and the rapid abandonment of the area by its old-time residents, and (4) climax, or the achievement of a new equilibrium of communal stability.[44]

In a comprehensive "race relations cycle" theory, Park asserted that as the presence of interethnic or interracial contact unfolded in a city, several distinct stages could be identified.[45] First, once proximity had been established between the two populations, competition between them soon ensued. This might even carry over into outright conflict. This conflict could continue for a longer or shorter period of time. Eventually, however, with better appreciation of one another across the barriers of custom, language, and kinship differences, and especially on realization of the benefits to be secured from the reduction of both competition and conflict, various kinds of accommodation could be expected. For example, mutual aid institutions could be merged. Community improvement programs might be similarly combined. Ultimately, reasoned Park, even total fusion might ensue. Another possibility, of course, is simply succession.

SUCCESSION

Paul F. Cressey's Chicago study of ethnic succession, defined succinctly as displacement, is an early example of the long-term examination of ecological succession.[46] Cressey assumed that the median distance of an ethnic group from the center of the city was a good index of the degree to which its members were assimilated into American society. He found that in 1898 the rank order of nine ethnic populations in distance from the center of Chicago were Old White American Stock (farthest), then Swedes, Irish and Germans, Poles, Czechoslovaks, blacks, Russians, and finally Italians (closest). In 1930, the sequence was different, with Swedes farthest out and followed in turn toward the city's center by the Old Americans, Irish, Germans, Czechs, Russians, Poles, blacks, and Italians. As an indication of displacement, or succession, Cressey's study is valuable, although only in connection with other types of research.

More recently, Laurenti summarized the factors that usually interact

[44] Ernest W. Burgess, "Residential Segregation in American Cities," *The Annals of the American Academy of Political and Social Science,* Pub. No. 2180 (November 1928), as cited by Alihan, op. cit., p. 172.

[45] Robert E. Park, *Race and Culture* (New York: Free Press, 1950).

[46] Paul F. Cressey, "Population Succession in Chicago: 1898–1930," *American Journal of Sociology, 44* (July 1938), pp. 59–69.

when nonwhites enter a neighborhood populated by whites.[47] The most important are the socioeconomic status of the two groups, the community leadership that emerges, and the long-run trend of both property and social values. Eleanor Wolf has emphasized the influence of lending institutions, realtors, and political officials in determining the course taken by racial incursion and the type of reaction that occurs toward it.[48] The concept of succession constitutes a frame of reference for such research.

In addition to understanding the racial composition of the urban neighborhood, the ideas of invasion and succession together are also useful in interpreting various innovating elements such as changes in transportation, industry, and marketing.[49]

CONCLUSION

The ecological investigation of urban places regards them basically as settlements within a determining environment. Though this outlook has merit, as the several theories of the spatial patterning of cities show, it also reveals serious weaknesses. The principal shortcoming is the uncertainty regarding the sociocultural aspects of urban populations and what produces them as well as what they affect in turn. Many scholars believe that the ecological approach has proved disappointing, especially in view of the great promise it was originally thought to have. But the various processes that social ecologists have identified probably do offer a potentially valuable way of understanding a wide range of urban phenomena. So also do the concepts and principles of urban dominance.

Finally, urban ecology implies that a city is an organized population, a point of view central to the demographic perspective on cities and urban society. The demographic mode of analysis is related to ecology, but it is also sufficiently distinct to be considered independent of it, as we shall learn in the next chapter.

FOR FURTHER READING

James M. Beshers, *Urban Social Structure* (New York: Free Press, 1962). Investigates the social relationships among urban inhabitants as an overall network.

[47] Luigi Laurenti, *Property Values and Race* (Berkeley, Calif.: University of California Press, 1960).

[48] Eleanor P. Wolf, "The Invasion-Succession Sequence as a Self-Fulfilling Prophecy," *Journal of Social Issues, 13* (1957), pp. 7–20.

[49] Roderick D. McKenzie, "The Ecological Approach to the Study of the Human Community," in Park, Burgess, McKenzie, op. cit., p. 75.

Amos Hawley, *Urban Society: An Ecological Approach* (New York: Ronald Press, 1971). Communication and transportation as the basic condition of urban settlement.

Leo F. Schnore, *Class and Race in Cities and Suburbs* (Chicago, Ill.: Markham, 1972). A critical test of the concentric-zone hypothesis, showing lower strata residents inhabiting valuable locations at the center of the metropolis.

Kent P. Schwirian, ed., *Comparative Urban Structure* (Lexington, Mass.: D. C. Health, 1974). Advanced material on the ecology of cities in the United States and elsewhere.

George Theodorson, ed., *Studies in Human Ecology* (New York: Harper and Row, 1961). The major schools of social ecology examined systematically and critically.

Ralph Thomlinson, *Urban Structure: The Social and Spatial Characteristics of Cities* (New York: Random House, 1969). Applies the ecological rationale to urbanization generally.

Sidney M. Willhelm, *Urban Zoning and Land-Use Theory* (New York: Free Press, 1962). Reviews classical and neoclassical ecological theory and its evaluation.

CHAPTER 7

THE DEMOGRAPHIC PERSPECTIVE

Alongside the typological and ecological points of view, the demographic conception of cities and urban societies occupies a prominent place in sociology. Population concentration is of course basic to all things urban, for in the absence of a sizable and compact population urbanization cannot take place nor urbanism exist.[1] Accordingly, the demographic outlook on the urban scene singles out population, including its size, composition, movement, and vital processes, for systematic examination as *the* route to an understanding of urban phenomena.

Specifically, the demographic approach focuses on six relatively dis-

[1] Cf. Hope Tisdale Eldridge, "The Process of Urbanization," *Social Forces, 20* (March 1942), pp. 311–16.

tinct aspects of urban populations: (1) distribution; (2) composition; (3) growth; (4) vital processes; (5) movement; and (6) sociocultural characteristics. Though interrelated, these can and need to be treated separately and in sequence.

POPULATION DISTRIBUTION

Studies of population distribution have been made relative to the level of urbanization of different nations, regions, and continents and also with respect to the size of cities. Four outstanding conclusions illustrate the importance of this research.

The first generalization is that in the world at present the rate of urbanization varies with the recency with which an area has been urbanized. More precisely, countries urbanized early as well as those sustaining only incipient urbanization today have lower rates of urban growth than do those whose urbanization was achieved less recently, though not earliest.

Examining the globe in terms of these three groups reveals clear-cut demographic differences. The first group consists of five regions that were at least 25 percent urbanized by 1920: Western Europe, Northern Europe, North America, Temperate South America, and Australia-New Zealand.[2] In the 40-year span from 1920 to 1960, their total population increased 52 percent, and their urban population doubled as a whole. The second group, the regions whose population was at least 25 percent urban by 1960 but not before 1920, included Southern and Eastern Europe, Japan and East Asia but not the mainland, the U. S. S. R., Tropical South and Central America, and Northern and Southern Africa. Here, during the same period, population growth amounted to 61 percent, although the proportion urbanized multiplied fully 36 times! The third category was occupied by the east Asian mainland; the middle-south, southeast, and southwest regions of Asia; the Caribbean, Tropical Africa, and Oceania, excluding Australia and New Zealand. In these regions where urbanization had not yet reached 25 percent (as of 1960), although total population rose in the same 1920 to 1960 period by 63 percent, urban population increased by a factor of only 4.5. Admittedly, this was a considerable jump but far from the rate of growth of the middle group. Rural population grew in these three sets of regions, respectively, by 17, 22, and 48 percent.

The second principal conclusion on distribution reached by urban demographers concerns the distribution of urban localities by size, for this has undergone much change in recent years.

The UN has used a multiplier of five in classifying urban aggregations, that is, 20,000 and over as "urban population;" 100,000 and over as "city

[2] At the 20,000 population level.

TABLE 7-1 Growth of Population in Urban Localities, by Size: 1920–1970 (percentages of population)

SIZE OF URBAN LOCALITY	DECADE BEGINNING					
	1920	1930	1940	1950	1960[1]	1970[1]
20,000 and over	30	30	25	42	—	—
100,000 and over	35	33	25	46	37	39
500,000 and over	41	32	28	57	37	39
2,500,000 and over	61	36	27	65	40[2]	34[2]

[1]Kingsley Davis, *World Urbanization: 1950–1970* (Berkeley, Calif.: Institute of International Studies, 1972), Vol. II, Table 25.

[2]Based on two million and over in size of urban locality.

Source: Adapted from Department of Economics and Social Affairs, "Urbanization: Development Policies and Planning," *International Social Development Review,* No. 1 (New York: United Nations, 1968), p. 11.

population;" 500,000 and over as "big-city population;" and 2.5 million and over as "metropolitan region." As seen in Table 7-1, the largest communities have also generally shown the greatest growth. Whereas in 50 years the urban population of the globe has tripled, the world's big-city population has quadrupled. As a result then, an increase in "top-heaviness" has been taking place in the world. This trend reveals the broad movement now going on toward metropolitanization, that is, the further implosion of population into dense agglomerations of service-oriented communities.

A third significant finding on urban demographic distribution applies to the recency of urbanization and big-city growth taken together. When these two factors are observed in combination, both the date of urbanization and the expansion of metropolitan areas, a striking reversal is noted. Thus, the 1940–1960 gain in big-city population was greater by 52 percent to 34 percent in the early urbanized regions of the world, namely, Europe and North America, as compared with the more recently urbanized areas like the U.S.S.R. and Japan. The fact is striking confirmation of postindustrial metropolitanization.

Finally, a fourth principle notable in the area of urban population distribution is embodied in the work of the famed Swiss-Italian economist and sociologist Vilfredo Pareto. It is the Pareto curve of size-of-place distribution which stipulates that any substantially urbanized country will have a curvilinear pattern of cities, their number varying inversely by size according to the total population.[3] Not a few writers have interpreted the Pareto curve as cor-

[3] For Pareto's work, see Raymond Aron, *Main Currents in Sociological Thought* (New York: Basic Books, 1967), Vol. II, pp. 99–176.

responding to the functional hierarchy of service centers that run the gamut from the many small market centers to the fewer but larger regional cities, and ultimately to the handful of gigantic national hubs. Duncan judges that "recognition of this connection is probably one of the most promising leads to an empirically based theory of population distribution." Similarly, the size of any given city apparently depends on the size and location of all other cities, since the particular city functions within the total urban milieu.[4] That stands as a further corollary of the size-of-place distribution principle.

COMPOSITION

Once one goes beyond the mere enumeration of population relative to location and begins to specify the characteristics of a population apart from its territorial incidence, he is dealing with population composition.

In treating the composition of urban population, age and sex are the two basic attributes, so much so in fact that their distribution within a particular aggregate may be referred to as its population structure. To amplify this, age and sex are exceedingly significant because they greatly determine the incidence of births, deaths, and migration.[5]

Population structure differs systematically not only between rural and urban areas and among countries and regions according to the level of urbanization, but also by size of urban community and between the central city and its suburbs.[6]

AGE

By and large, an urban population has a higher average or median age than a rural population does. First, rural communities usually have higher fertility rates. And, second, the out-migration of young adults from agricultural to urban areas lowers the age level of the rural population while, conversely, it raises that of the urban community. In addition, the concentration of the elderly in the towns and cities, where medical care and the amenities of life suitable to the retired and infirm are available, tends to reinforce the age disparity.

It follows then that in any given country, the greater the percentage of its urban population, the higher will its median age be. In our own society, with the growing pace of urbanization the median age of the population in-

[4] Harry W. Richardson, *The Economics of Urban Size* (Westmead, Eng.: Saxon House, 1973), pp. 139–71.

[5] William Peterson, *Population* 2nd ed., (London: Macmillan, 1969), p. 59.

[6] Otis D. Duncan and Albert J. Reiss, Jr., *Social Characteristics of Urban and Rural Communities* (New York: John Wiley & Sons, 1956), pp. 119–21.

creased consistently from 16.7 years in 1820 to 22.9 years in 1900 and 30.2 in 1950. There was a slight decline in 1960 to 29.5 and in 1970 it was around 28.1.[7]

Increasing age, which is thus characteristic of urban society, entails a number of specific occupational and economic consequences. Among them are possible declines in output per capita, impairment of the regularity or continuity of employment, and occupational imbalance resulting from the preemption of jobs by older incumbents. Increasing age has still other socio-economic concomitants, such as changes in the demand for goods and services (health, for example, instead of education) and stronger emphasis on security.

Dependency Ratio

Median age, however, is not as useful a measure of age distribution as is the dependency ratio, because median age does not reveal as clearly the relative presence of either nonproducers or the economically valuable part of the population. The dependency ratio expresses the number of persons outside the labor force that every 100 persons in the productive years must support. It is computed by dividing the population 20 to 64 years of age into the total population under 20 and over 65, and then multiplying by 100. Hence, as Table 7-2 informs us, in the world in 1960 every 100 persons age 20–64 supported 103 others, 94 of them youthful and 9 elderly. Table 7-2 shows that except for Latin America, the areas that are above the world average in urbanization are far below the world average for dependency ratio.

With an increased proportion of its population in the older age group, an urban society need not necessarily expect that its labor force will have to support an increasingly larger nonproductive segment, however. In fact, the relative number of productive workers may actually rise despite a higher average age for the population as a whole. It will do so if an offsetting decrease occurs in the proportion of young nonworkers in the population. Table 7-2 reveals, for example, that although Europe had 17 and Oceania had 16 persons 65 years of age or older for every 100 persons in the productive years, Europe had a ratio of youth to the productive-age group that was 22 percent smaller. It may be added that when a country's population under 15 years of age is about 40 percent or over, the greater part of the nation's resources will usually be devoted to current consumption of food, clothing, housing, and education. Correspondingly, fewer resources will be available for capital investment devoted to industrialization.

[7] See Warren S. Thompson and David T. Lewis, *Population Problems* (New York: McGraw-Hill, 1965), Table 5–9, p. 90, and Table 6–3, pp. 124–25. Also Bureau of the Census, *Statistical Abstract of the United States, 1972* (Washington, D.C.: Government Printing Office, 1972), Table 23, p. 24.

TABLE 7-2 Urban population (20,000 and over) as a Percentage of Total Population in Major Areas of the World, and Population by Estimated Dependency Ratios: 1960

CONTINENT	URBAN POPULATION	DEPENDENCY RATIO		
		TOTAL	YOUTH	OLD AGE
Northern America	57	86	68	18
United States	69	91	73	18
Oceania	50	92	76	16
Europe (ex USSR)	41	76	59	17
USSR	36	85	74	11
Latin America	32	118	110	8
East Asia	20			
		114	108	6
South Asia	14			
Africa	13	117	111	6
World Total	25	103	94	9

Source: Adapted from Department of Economic and Social Affairs, "Urbanization: Development Policies and Planning," *International Social Development Review,* No. 1 (New York: United Nations, 1968), Table 4, p. 12; and Donald J. Bogue, *Principles of Demography* (New York: John Wiley & Sons, 1969), Table 7-3, p. 156.

SEX

The sex ratio of the population, that is, the number of males for every 100 females, tends to be lower for industrial urban societies, regions, nations, and communities than it is for their rural counterparts. This is generally true although a particular sex ratio may be affected, and even drastically at that, by wars, economic circumstances, and short-term migration. For instance, even though few countries have a sex ration as high as 105, that for oil-rich Kuwait, a masculine habitat, has been reported as standing at 158. Expressive of the general correlation between urbanism and the sex ratio is the fact that in the United Kingdom, Sweden, The Netherlands, France, Denmark, and Japan, where levels of urbanization are fairly high (80 percent for the UK and 63 percent for France, to give two particulars), the overall sex distribution has been around 94 to 95 males per 100 females in recent years. In comparison, in the less well developed and less urbanized lands, such as Nigeria, the United Arab Republic, Brazil, India, Iran, Pakistan, and the Philippines, the sex ratio has stood between 102 and 106.

A number of considerations typically combine to give urban areas, particularly in industrial countries, a low sex ratio. Employment opportunities attract females to industry, commerce, and the professions in the city. These are simply unavailable in rural districts. Again, low fertility results in less ma-

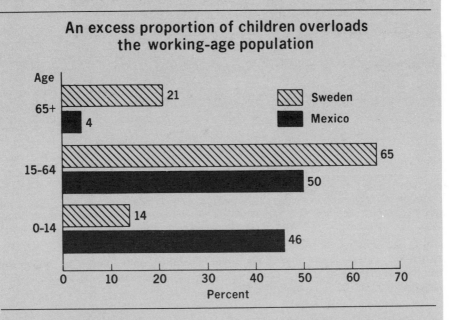

An excess proportion of children overloads the working-age population

The heavy child dependency of an underdeveloped nation such as Mexico contrasts with the relatively low proportion of children under 14 years of age and the high percentage of the elderly typical of a developed, industrial-urban country like Sweden. Altogether, the labor force of Mexico, making up 50 percent of the population, has to support the remaining 50 percent, while in Sweden the working 65 percent of the population is responsible for the remaining 35 percent dependent by virtue of either youth or age.

Source: Public Health Service, *A Response to a National and International Problem (Washington, D.C.: Health, Education, and Welfare Department, 1975), Figure 4, p. 5.*

ternal mortality and, with good medical care, the tendency of females to outlive males is augmented further, thereby reducing the sex ratio in urban communities still more.[8]

The typically lower sex ratio of urban areas shows up very clearly in historical and regional data for the United States. Table 7-3 conveys the historical trend during the period from 1910 to 1970 toward a reduction in the American sex ratio generally, and the correlation of our urbanism with a relatively low sex ratio.

Table 7-4 pertains to the sex ratio by regional divisions, for which urbanization data are also given. It will be seen that the overall Middle Atlantic states have the highest level of urbanization and the lowest sex ratio. The

---

[8] Typically, 105–106 boys are born for every 100 girls, but differential mortality helps bring about adult parity.

TABLE 7-3 Sex Ratios, United States, by Rural-Urban Distribution: 1910–1970

YEAR	URBAN	NONFARM	RURAL	FARM
1970	94.4		100.0	
1960*	94.0	103.3		107.2
1950	94.6	103.6		110.1
1940	95.5	103.7		111.7
1930	98.1	105.0		111.0
1920	100.4	106.5		109.1
1910	101.7		109.8	

*Excludes Alaska and Hawaii.

Sources: Warren S. Thompson and David T. Lewis, *Population Problems* (New York: McGraw-Hill, 1965), Table 5-4, p. 79. Originally U.S. Bureau of the Census, *U.S. Census of Population: 1960,* General Social and Economic Characteristics, United States Summary, pp. 1–200; other years from earlier censuses. Also, U.S. Bureau of the Census, *Statistical Abstract of the United States, 1972* (Washington, D.C.: Government Printing Office, 1972), Table 31, p. 29.

TABLE 7-4 Percent Distribution of the Urban Population, United States, by Regions and Sex Ratios: 1960–1970

REGION	1960		1970	
	PERCENTAGE OF POPULATION URBAN	SEX RATIO	PERCENTAGE OF POPULATION URBAN	SEX RATIO
Northeast				
New England	76.4	95.0	76.4	93.3
Middle Atlantic	81.4	94.5	81.7	92.2
Northcentral				
East North Central	73.0	97.3	74.8	94.9
West North Central	58.8	97.7	63.7	95.2
South				
South Atlantic	57.2	97.1	63.7	95.0
East South Central	48.4	96.2	54.6	94.3
West South Central	67.7	97.4	72.6	95.4
West				
Mountain	67.1	101.2	73.1	98.1
Pacific	81.1	100.4	86.0	97.5
U.S.A.				
Total (1970)	69.9	97.1	73.5	94.8

Sources: Adapted from Warren S. Thompson and David T. Lewis, *Population Problems* (New York: McGraw-Hill, 1965), Table 5–2, p. 76, and Table 6–8, p. 139. And from U.S. Bureau of the Census, *U.S. Census of Population: 1970,* Number of Inhabitants, Final Report, Pc(1) A-1 U.S. Summary, Table 18; and *U.S. Census of Population Characteristics,* Pc(1)-B1 Final Report, U.S. Summary (Washington, D.C.: Government Printing Office, 1971).

other regions exhibit rather ambiguous data. A striking anomaly is the Far West. The Pacific division has a relatively high sex ratio, which can be explained by the presence there of economic circumstances conducive to the concentration of men: lumbering, large-tract dry farming, intensive irrigated agriculture, and rapid expansion in manufacturing. All of these are industries affording opportunities to young, single males. The historical background of this interesting. In 1850, at the time of the California gold rush, the sex ratio of the Pacific West reached an astronomical 778.5!

Women in the Labor Force

Of major significance regarding the rural-urban sex ratio differential is the greater participation of women in the urban labor force. As a case in point, in 1960 about one-fifth of the rural farm women 14 years of age and older in the United States were classified as being in the labor force. The corresponding proportion for urban women was approximately one-third.

Labor-force participation by women relates inversely to marital status and motherhood. Race is an added factor. Bogue has ably summarized the several implications of this generalization for the population of the United States by concluding that "the women with the lowest labor force participation rate are currently married, white, with four or more children under 18, with the youngest under 3 years of age."[9]

Elderly Women

In mature industrial-urban countries, particularly in the postindustrial ones, the higher median age of the urban population and its lower sex ratio also find expression in a city's tendency to have a disproportionate number of elderly women. Thus in comparison with our urban population (as of 1960), American farm communities had a far larger percentage of males in the age group 45 and older than did the nation's cities.

Furthermore, the sexual imbalance among the elderly has the tendency of growing with continued modernization into metropolitan postindustrialism. Accordingly, it is estimated that between 1960 and 1990 there will be a 78 percent increase in the number of males aged 70 and older in the American population, but that the growth of the elderly female population will be greater still. By 1990, the female population of the United States 70 and older will probably have shown a 105 percent rise over 1960.[10] Some possible socioeconomic implications of this trend include conservative investment and political policies.

[9] Donald J. Bogue, *The Population of the United States* (Glencoe, Ill.: Free Press, 1959), p. 228.
[10] Ibid., p. 468.

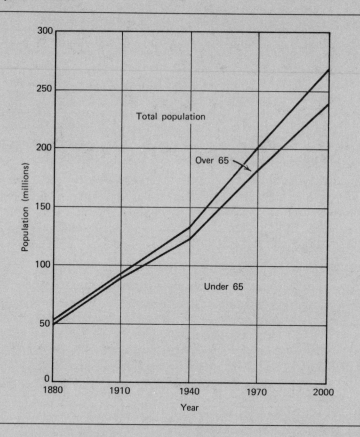

EXHIBIT 7-2 Population in the United States Older and Younger than 65: 1880–1970 and Projected to 2000

Total population

Over 65

Under 65

Population (millions)

Year

The expected growth in both the total population of the United States and in that of persons over 65 is shown in these census figures and projections.

Source: Commission on Population Growth and the American Future, *Demographic and Social Aspects of Population Growth* (Washington, D.C.: Government Printing Office, 1972), pp. 52–53.

GROWTH

The rapid increase of the world's population during the past 300 years corresponds roughly to the period in history in which industrial urbanization and now postindustrialization have occurred.

Growth took place before the Industrial Revolution but at a rate considerably lower than that which ensued later. During the century prior to 1750

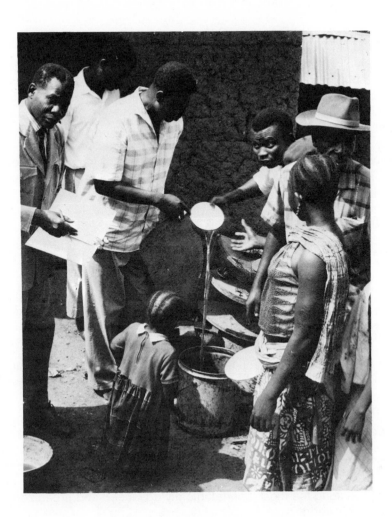

Population growth resulting from death rates lowered by better sanitation. An African health worker taking action against water-borne diseases.

the population of the globe rose at an estimated annual rate of 0.34 percent, from 507 million to 711 million persons. With the advent of steam, however, the rate of population growth increased sharply: 0.50 percent annually in the half-century following 1750; 0.43 percent in the period 1800–1850; and 0.68 percent from 1850 to 1900. Since 1920 the rate has exceeded 1.7 percent per year.[11]

[11] Ibid., Table 3–2, p. 48.

The particular type of population growth since 1750—to a world total of around 3.3 billion in 1970— is commonly referred to as the process of demographic transition.[12] In theory, the unique expansion of numbers has occurred as a result of greater productivity, improved medicine, public sanitation, and superior means of transportation, four conditions that have reduced mortality without a commensurate decline in natality taking place.

Demographers generally recognize five stages of transitional development.

In the first of these, actually the pretransitional one, high birthrates are balanced by high death rates, as in Nigeria today.

The second, or early transitional, is marked by high birthrates together with reduced death rates resulting from technological and sociocultural improvements. China, India, and Egypt are current examples.

In the third stage, birthrates are still higher than death rates although both are declining. At the present time, Cuba and Mexico are in this category.

The fourth stage may be said to be reached when death rates are low and the birthrates are declining even further, because fertility has been brought under exercisable control. Argentina, Japan and the Soviet Union probably exemplify this late transitional stage nowadays.

Finally, the fifth, and actually the posttransitional period, is reached when low death rates are matched by low birthrates and, except after a considerable span of time, the population does not grow at all. In this category we have Australia, Canada, France, Germany, Italy, the United Kingdom, and possibly the United States at present. These are, of course, among the most technologically advanced and urbanized countries in the world.

In short, although inconsistencies with this overall pattern show up with uncomfortable frequency, population growth bears an exponential relationship to industrial urbanization, that is, varying by historical stages in an S-shaped curve.

THE VITAL PROCESSES OF FERTILITY AND MORTALITY

The vital processes of fertility and mortality underlie population growth and decline. Fertility refers to reproduction, and mortality to population depletion

[12] Consult Population Division, *The Determinants and Consequences of Population Trends* (New York: United Nations, 1953), pp. 21–44.

resulting from death. As the demographic transition indicates, urbanization has a distinct influence over both of these phenomena.

FERTILITY

Fertility differentials commonly relate to the distribution of population between urban and rural areas and also to community size.

Rural-Urban Differentials

Typically, birthrates are lower for urban than they are for rural populations, as the systematic examination of international demographic data shows. Crude fertility rates have been observed to be higher in rural than in urban areas in recent years in Southern Rhodesia, Canada, Panama, Israel, the United States, Taiwan, the U. S. S. R., the Philippines, Pakistan, Puerto Rico, Cuba, Brazil, Mexico, Hungary, and Australia.[13] Conversely, these rates have also been observed higher for urban than rural communities in the Congo, Gabon, Mali, Sierra Leone, El Salvador, and Hungary.[14] Yet for the world as a whole, fertility rates tend to be lower in urban areas than they are in rural regions, even though as urbanization continues to diffuse around the globe, rural-urban fertility differentials continue to decline.

In its impact on fertility, urbanization includes a number of distinct though interacting causal factors.

First, the society's policies, laws, institutional practices, religion, and styles of living influence natality. Thus the proper age at which marriage can take place is significant for birthrates. For example, the extended family, which one may encounter in rural areas, permits youths to enter marriage early, because economic responsibility for their offspring can be shared by the total kinship group. Again, as the level of living rises, it physiologically induces a decline in the average age at menarche.

Second, the age and sex characteristics of the population, its demographic structure, affect fertility so that, other things being equal, a decline in the sex ratio will have a depressing effect on fertility.

Third, economic considerations constitute an important variable. They encourage a decline in the birthrate when, in conjunction with cultural values such as consumer norms, they consign children in the urban milieu to the category of consumer durables in which they are economic liabilities instead of the producers that they are in an agrarian society.

It must, of course, be understood that the variables affecting fertility

[13] For the survey literature consult Stephen Boyden, "Ecology in Relation to Urban Population Structure," in G. A. Harrison and A. J. Boyce, eds., *The Structure of Human Populations* (Oxford: Clarendon Press, 1972), pp. 425–26.

[14] Ibid.

TABLE 7-5   Children Ever Born per 1,000 Women 35–44 Years Old, Ever Married, for Urbanized Areas by Size, Central Cities, and Urban Fringe: United States, 1960

SIZE OF URBAN AREA	TOTAL URBAN AREA	CENTRAL CITIES	URBAN FRINGE INCORPORATED PLACES OF 2,500 OR MORE	OTHER URBAN
ALL URBANIZED AREAS	2374	2346	2392	2441
3,000,000 or more	2256	2167	2332	2408
1,000,000 to 3,000,000	2391	2345	2438	2409
250,000 to 1,000,000	2430	2418	2443	2445
Less than 250,000	2515	2520	2472	2519

Source: U.S. Bureau of the Census, 1960 Census of Population, *Size of Place,* Pc(3)-1B, Tables 1-5, and Vol. I, *Characteristics of the Population,* Part 1, U.S. Summary, Table 100, as found in Clyde V. Kiser, Wilson H. Grabil, and Arthur A. Campbell, *Trends and Variations in Fertility in the United States* (Cambridge: Harvard University Press, 1968), Table 5-8, p. 92.

operate selectively and differentially for the various segments of a population rather than totally and uniformly. Factors such as education, occupation, and socioeconomic status bear this out in their correlations with fertility. Yet the negative association between urbanism and fertility is quite typical. In 1971, for the United States as a whole, the number of children born per 1000 women 35 to 44 years old totaled 3272 for our farm population, and 2917 for our metropolitan population.[15]

Fertility and Community Size

Yet another aspect of the relationship between rural-urban residence, with its many implications for mode of life on the one hand and fertility on the other, is the differential observed according to community size. Table 7-5 gives data for the generally progressive decline of natality in urbanized areas in the United States, beginning with those having fewer than 250,000 population and ending with areas of 3 million or more, and also for the satellite communities in the urban fringe.

[15] *The 1975 U.S. Factbook* (New York: Grosset & Dunlap, 1975), Table 74, p. 55.

Although urbanization is inclined to correlate with reduction of the mortality rate, it is commonly agreed that the question of mortality in its relation to rural-urban residence is anything but clear-cut. Continuous inroads have been made into death rates in modern times. The lengthening expectation of life that we have witnessed in the world for several hundred years now, particularly in the advanced countries, has coincided with increased urbanization. As shown in Table 7-6, for the nations given expectation of life at birth has risen progressively in line with their urbanization.

Disentangling the specific "urban factor," however, which is necessary for the precise assignment of cause, does not provide complete clarification. Basically, as scholars insist, urban residence complicates the mortality question on account of two things. The hazards of city life, including congestion, pollution, infectious disease, and the like, tend to terminate life. Yet the better health care that the urban community and the urban level of living can provide promotes longevity. In addition, migration introduces other complications. The result then is a situation about which one may generalize only with cautious qualification.

David Glass studied rural-urban mortality in the United Kingdom for a period of over a century.[16] He found that during the early days of industrialization, the average expectation of life was shorter in the large English population centers than it was in the nation as a whole. By the middle of the twentieth century conditions had changed, however. The expectation of life for Londoners was now 67.4 years, almost a whole year more than for the nation generally.

Although the mortality state of affairs, as Glass reported, has now reversed itself, the rural-urban differential is pronounced but not constant. Mortality rates may, in fact, be higher for persons in middle and old age in the city than in the country. Reviewing international statistics, Thompson and Lewis have concluded that "it would appear probable that city populations now possess certain advantages over rural populations in controlling deaths up to about 30–35 years of age, while at older ages living conditions in rural communities are better suited to retarding the onset of the chronic and organic diseases which develop later in life."[17] These demographers speculate that space, cleaner air, a slower social tempo, and even perhaps better and fresher foods may be responsible.

Still, in the long run, as urbanization permits the average expectation of life to press upon the upper limits of the life-span, death rates may be expected to rise. Depending on the forces governing fertility, the result would

---

[16] David V. Glass, "Some Indicators of Differences between Urban and Rural Mortality in England and Wales and Scotland," *Population Studies,* 17 (March 1964), pp. 263–67.

[17] Thompson and Lewis, op. cit., p. 364.

TABLE 7-6 Life Expectation at Birth, in Selected Countries and Periods, by Sex

COUNTRY	PERIOD	LIFE EXPECTANCY AT BIRTH (YEARS)	
		MALE	FEMALE
England and Wales	1841	40.2	42.2
	1881–1890	43.7	47.2
	1920–1922	55.6	62.9
	1961–1963	68.0	73.9
	1968–1970	68.6	74.9
France	1795	23.4	27.3
	1877–1881	40.8	43.4
	1920–1923	52.2	56.1
	1963	67.2	74.1
	1969	67.6	75.3
	1972	68.6	74.4
India	1891–1901	23.6	24.0
	1921–1931	26.9	26.6
	1951–1960	41.9	40.5
Japan	1899–1903	44.0	44.8
	1926–1930	44.8	46.5
	1963	67.2	74.1
	1968	69.05	74.3
	1972	70.5	75.9
Netherlands	1900–1909	51.0	53.4
	1953–1955	71.0	73.9
	1970	70.7	76.5
	1973	71.2	77.2
United States	1929–1931	57.7	61.0
	1949–1951	65.5	70.1
	1963	66.6	73.4
	1969	66.8	74.3
	1972	67.4	75.2

Sources: Adapted from Dennis Wrong, *Population and Society* (N.Y.: Random House, 1963), Third Edition, Table 4, p. 34. Original source: Woytinsky, W. S., and Woytinsky, E. S., *World Population and Production: Trends and Outlook.* © 1953 by The Twentieth Century Fund, New York. Also *Life Tables*, Vol. II, Sec. 5, *Vital Statistics of the U.S.A., 1969,* U.S. Department of Health, Education, and Welfare (Washington, D.C.: Government Printing Office, 1970). Also United Nations, *Demographic Yearbook: 1974* (N.Y.: United Nations, 1975).

be zero population growth or even population decline. Some of the nations of Western Europe already evidence these ultimate tendencies of the demographic transition.

Infant Mortality

Dramatic reductions in infant-mortality rates have added substantially to the long-term decline that has taken place in overall mortality as a concomitant of industrial urbanization. Moreover, these reductions have been considerably responsible for the lengthening of life in almost every region of the world. In the United States, where in the period from 1915 to 1919 it was 95.7 per 1000 live births, the infant mortality rate dropped to 55.7 by 1935. In 1970 it stood at 20.0.[18]

Infant death rates vary with the provision made for health care, which ordinarily is greater in urban than in rural communities. Rates are also influenced by a range of other factors, such as education (which can optimize medical services), cultural standards governing diet, psychological stress, and others as well, including the concentration of poor people in the inner cities of metropolitan aggregations. Thus, as the U. S. Children's Bureau informs us, as of 1960, 9 of America's 10 largest cities revealed death rates greater than the average for the country as a whole, owing to the presence in these urban areas of considerable economic deprivation and cultural disadvantage. Only Los Angeles, of these 10 cities, had a lower rate than that of the nation generally.[19]

MIGRATION

Migration, people moving from one geographic location to another, a phenomenon that is basic to demographic study although it is difficult to measure, need not be related to urbanization. Oftentimes though it is, owing to the socieconomic attractiveness of urban life in comparison with the rigors of rural society. In fact, in recent years virtually all around the globe, in-migration into the cities has occurred in substantial volume.

URBAN MIGRATION IN THE UNITED STATES

The cityward migration of persons in the United States from abroad and from the rural countryside permits us to recognize the factors that are generally

[18] Bureau of the Census, *Statistical Abstract of the United States: 1975* (Washington, D.C.: Government Printing Office, 1975), Table 84, p. 80.

[19] Children's Bureau, "Geography of Infant Mortality in the United States," *Public Health Reports,* 78 (March 1963), pp. 270–71.

associated with such movement, and also to identify those which are unique to our own society.

United States migrants, Donald Bogue has concluded, are "highly urban-oriented."[20] In 1960, out of every 100 migrants, 70 moved to urban areas, 26 to rural-nonfarm areas, and only 4 migrated to farms. The annual average net migration from farms, already 4.4 percent in the 1940's, rose to 6.3 percent in the first years of the decade of the 1960s. The energy crisis of the mid-1970s may, however, be modifying this trend somewhat by attracting people to small coal-mining towns, just as the strong market for agricultural commodities may currently be enticing population into the rural areas. Whether such counter-trends will be sustained cannot be definitely anticipated.

Typically, young, single persons predominate among our migrants, with slightly more males than females among them. Yet given a complex, specialized, and stable economy, the tendency grows for families to migrate. Correspondingly, the participation rate of the married increases. That is why, then, that the frequency curve of migrants by age shows two peaks, one for young adults and the other for very young children, who are present in the movement of whole families.

Recognition of the large volume of cityward migration in the United States should not obscure the fact that it contributes only a relatively small part to urban growth in the nation today, perhaps no more than one-third. This contrasts sharply with the historic role of rural-urban migration in the growth of European cities prior to the Industrial Revolution. As Thompson and Lewis remind us, it used to be that the rural areas "produced" population and the cities "consumed" it.[21] Today by comparison, the metropolitan areas of the United States receive about 65 percent of their growth from natural increase and only about 35 percent from net migration into them.

Three Recent Trends

The characteristic extent of urban migration in the United States ought not to exclude three other trends in the movement of the American population which have occurred recently or which are observable at present. They consist of the concentration of blacks in many metropolitan areas outside the South; a shift of America's urban concentrations to the so-called *Sun Belt* stretching across the lower half of the country; and a decanting of population from our metropolitan to our nonmetropolitan communities.

A massive shift of blacks from rural areas of the South to metropolitan centers in our Northeast and North-Central states took place in the 1950s and early 1960s. In the decade beginning 1950, except for Florida, Dela-

[20] Bogue, op. cit., p. 766.

[21] Thompson and Lewis, op. cit., p. 149.

ware, and Maryland, every southern state sustained a net out-migration of blacks; and except for the Dakotas, every northern state had a black net in-migration. Moreover, the greatest rates of black population growth occurred in our northern, and to some extent also western, cities.[22] It should not be thought, however, that black migrants avoided southern cities. They did not. By 1960, 6.5 million blacks lived in cities in our southern states as compared with 7 million in northern cities. Yet the northward movement of black Americans, particularly into the metropolises of the northeast region—from Chicago to Boston—remained the major migratory phenomenon of the United States during the years following 1950. It would continue to have weighty consequences too.

Although the black south-to-north urban in-migration has been momentous, it appears now to have run its course. From 1970 to 1975, the South had a net migration gain of 1.8 million persons five and older, whereas the Northeast and North-Central regions experienced net migration losses during that period.[23] The extent to which blacks were moving southward may be gauged from the fact that in 1970 to 1973, whereas 124,000 blacks migrated from the Northeast to the South, only 54,000 made the opposite move.[24]

The southward migratory pattern of black Americans in the first years of the 1970s corresponded to a more general regional redistribution of population taking place at that time. While the big cities of the North, East, and North-Central states were showing population declines (New York, Philadelphia, Chicago, and Detroit all being expected to have fewer residents in 1980 than in 1970), the population centers of the Sun Belt could look forward to substantial gains on top of the growth they had already experienced since midcentury. By 1980, Houston would probably displace Detroit as America's fifth largest SMSA, with Phoenix taking twelfth place.[25] Why the drift of Americans to the Sun Belt? A whole complex of factors was responsible: improved transportation and communication, new forms of agriculture and food processing (notably, irrigation and light-weight frozen foods), investments drawn by cheaper unorganized labor, growth in the ranks of our elderly, more secure retirement financing, and others as well. Together they added up to the benefit or at least the growth of the newer cities of the Sun Belt.

If the expansion of the urban Sun Belt in the 1970s surprised few demographers, the accelerating shift of population out of our metropolitan and into our nonmetropolitan communities perhaps did. From 1970 to 1974,

[22] Karl E. Tauber and Alma F. Tauber, *Negroes in Cities* (New York: Atheneum, 1969), p. 13.

[23] Bureau of the Census, *Mobility of the Population of the United States: March 1970–March 1975* (Washington, D.C.: Government Printing Office, 1976), Series P-20, No. 285.

[24] Bureau of the Census, *Current Population Reports* (Washington, D.C.: Government Printing Office, November, 1973), P-20, No. 256.

[25] *Intercom* (Washington, D.C.: Population Reference Bureau, January, 1976), pp. 2–3.

THE DEMOGRAPHIC PERSPECTIVE

U.S. nonmetropolitan areas gained 5.0 percent in population, whereas the nation's metropolitan areas recorded an expansion of only 3.8 percent.[26] Two reasons lay behind this nonmetropolitan growth. One was industrial and institutional decentralization, for example, companies preferring lower population densities, and state university systems establishing regional and branch campuses away from the most congested places. Another factor also probably contributed, and that was the attractiveness to homeowner and retail merchant alike, of the less heavily settled open areas beyond even the suburban ring around the metropolis. In short, the manifold physical, social, and fiscal problems of the great cities were deterring in-migrants and encouraging the resettlement of those already living or doing business there.

Adjustment of the Urban In-Migrant

The three trends examined above indicate that the adjustment of migrants to urban conditions cannot be described as a single process in the United States at present. Because of the varieties of our rural-to-urban and urban-to-urban migration today, accommodation to the new social settings and structures confronting the migrant must be viewed as multiplex. Certain occurrences appear very frequently, however.

Migrants from farms are typically younger and have less education than either nonfarm migrants or the population of the cities they enter. If nonwhite, they often face the added difficulties of inner-city ghettoization and discrimination. Generally these farm-to-city migrants avail themselves of kin-network ties to ease their transition. Of late, more liberal public-assistance policies, federal civil-rights intervention, and affirmative action have contributed toward probably easier adjustment on the part of migrants in this category though the evidence here is less than conclusive. Nonwhite diffusion into the suburbs, improved inner-city housing, and higher educational achievement indicate improvement. Very high teenage unemployment and the heavy incidence of violent crime in the ghetto argue otherwise. Spanish-speaking migrants confront a language problem, especially those from Puerto Rico.

Persons moving from one urban area to another ordinarily have little difficulty adjusting. True, the previous sentence is a value judgment, but the reader must consider that such migrants usually have adequate educational backgrounds and oftentimes move with assured jobs waiting for them. At times, structural unemployment, like the government's cutback on the space program, creates joblessness among well educated professionals whose migration may represent gross hardship. In addition, even affluent migrants have to reckon on frustrations: being disfranchised by residence laws; facing

---

[26] Bureau of the Census, *Population Profile of the United States: 1974* (Washington, D.C.: Government Printing Office, March, 1975), P-20, No. 279, Table 15.

unique subcultures; and reestablishing their multiple ties to voluntary associations.

MIGRATION IN THE DEVELOPING NATIONS

In the developing countries, unlike the United States, as one summary given
at the 1965 World Population Conference concluded, the increase of the
urban population is due mainly to the in-migration of persons from rural
areas.[27]

Rural-to-urban migrants outside the United States are not markedly different in selected characteristics from mobile Americans. Characteristically,
they too are males and youthful too. Their motivation to migrate to urban
areas includes economic and social factors, though these are often complex
and difficult to disentangle. Consider the following judgment:

> *Among these complications is the fact that the migrant usually re-*
> *sponds not to the reality of the city but to his conception or image of*
> *it; his motives are multiple rather than single, frequently unclear to*
> *himself, or at least diffuse ('seeking a better life') and not articulated*
> *in clear-cut categories; if certain amenities that he is seeking, such*
> *as better education, are brought to him in the village, his migratory*
> *tendency may paradoxically increase—a small taste of moderniza-*
> *tion creating a demand for more.*[28]

Among the economic causes may be found surplus population in the
rural areas resulting from both the modernization of agricultural practices
and natural increase brought about by declining mortality. Educational opportunities, medical and social services, leisure and recreation, public housing, and even welfare payments all play a role in drawing migrants to the cities in the underdeveloped lands. At the same time, the relative absence of
these benefits in the rural areas serves to push people in these nations
toward the cities. The difficult living conditions in many of the urban centers
in the developing regions seldom deter further in-migration.

SOCIOCULTURAL CHARACTERISTICS

Significant sociocultural variables differentiate the rural and urban segments
of a population. Most notably they include literacy, education, and the socioeconomic level of living.

[27] Toshio Kuroda, "Internal Migration: An Overview of Problems and Studies," in Charles B. Nam,
ed., *Population and Society* (Boston: Houghton Mifflin, 1968), pp. 336–39.

[28] Department of Social and Economic Affairs, *Urbanization: Development Policies and Planning*
(New York: United Nations, 1968), p. 91.

An urban population tends to have a higher average degree of literacy than its rural counterpart, and also to participate more in the media of mass communication. In countries undergoing modernization, as Daniel Lerner has verified, not only are these differential levels observable, they actually constitute several related aspects of the total urban phenomenon.[29] A United Nations study of 36 countries showed high correlation values between the percentage of the population urban and selected social indicators: literacy rate (0.65); school enrollment (0.70); letter mail (0.57); cinema attendance (0.62); and newspaper circulation (0.69).[30] Such findings definitely indicate that urbanization includes a better educated population and one that is more enmeshed in a network of communications.

The causes of this state of affairs are not difficult to identify, although in given cases they are intertwined in a complex way and presumably operate with considerable circularity. Some of the more prominent demographic factors are (1) population density, which tends to multiply interpersonal contacts and the diffusion of ideas; (2) population size, whose control necessitates more intensive and broader communication; and (3) population heterogeneity, which calls forth educational efforts designed to achieve the performance of specialized functions as well as coordination through a deliberately cultivated consensus.

At each age in the United States, the typical level of educational attainment is considerably greater in urban than in rural areas. The same trend is also evident in comparing the per capita educational achievement of our rural-farm population with that of America's rural nonfarm population. Here, too, the differences are large and favor the people of the rural-nonfarm communities. According to the U. S. Census of 1970, the median school years completed by the nation's urban population 25 years old and over was 12.2 (male, 12.2; female 12.2); rural-nonfarm population, 11.2 (male, 10.9; female, 11.5); and rural-farm, 10.7 (male, 9.9; female, 11.5).

The level of education and communication that is associated with any urban population depends of course on the existence of the facilities necessary to provide the appropriate services. Schools, newspapers, television and radio broadcasting stations, printing plants, sales outlets, the post office, and other delivery systems are usually concentrated in the larger centers of population where they are more accessible to the urban community as a whole.

---

[29] Daniel Lerner, "Communications Systems and Social Systems; A Statistical Exploration in History and Policy," *Behavioral Science, 2* (October 1957), pp. 266–75.

[30] Department of Social and Economic Affairs, op. cit., Table 4, p. 30.

The greater productivity of urban populations is reflected in higher levels of living. New Yorkers using the new banking technology.

LEVELS OF LIVING

Correlative with literacy and education are the typically higher levels of living that are enjoyed by urban populations and by urbanized countries in comparison with nations less extensively urbanized. These include diet, clothing, shelter, and public-utility services. They reflect the productivity resulting from the advanced state of technology and human organization in the urban milieu. The same UN study cited above that found educational and communication differentials favoring the more highly urbanized countries also reported significant differences in the vital areas of income and consumption. Thus, for 36 countries surveyed around 1960, the correlations between the percentage of the population that was urban and (1) protein consumption was 0.65; energy consumption, 0.62; and (3) income per capita, 0.56.[31] Correlations from 0.40 to 0.60 indicate a "moderate" degree of association, and from 0.60 to 0.80 a "marked" degree.

Measurement in terms of socioeconomic achievement, an index that combines the factors of income and education, throws added light on the concentration in cities of populations possessing relatively superior eco-

[31] Ibid.

TABLE 7-7 Distribution of Occupational Categories, Employed Male Population, by Urban and Rural Residence, United States: 1970

OCCUPATIONAL CATEGORY	URBAN	RURAL NONFARM	RURAL FARM	TOTAL
	PERCENTAGE DISTRIBUTION			
Professional and kindred workers	16.15	10.25	3.22	14.28
Farmers and farm managers	0.26	2.08	47.09	2.83
Managers, officials, and proprietors	11.96	9.97	3.98	11.16
Clerical and kindred	8.72	5.09	2.44	7.65
Sales workers	7.84	4.88	2.04	6.94
Craftsmen and foremen	20.58	25.36	11.36	21.18
Operatives	12.90	17.16	8.66	13.61
Transport equipment operatives	5.71	7.09	4.09	5.93
Private household workers	0.08	0.07	0.03	0.08
Service workers, except household	8.94	6.21	2.67	8.06
Farm workers	0.52	3.78	10.16	1.67
Laborers, except farm	6.33	8.08	4.24	6.61
Total	100.00	100.00	100.00	100.00

Source: Bureau of The Census, Census of Population: 1970 (Washington, D.C.: Government Printing Office, 1973), Vol. I, Table 222, p. 735.

nomic resources. Table 7-7 presents the association in the United States between socioeconomic position and occupational distribution, on the one hand, and rural-urban residence, on the other. Those categories that command the greatest income, principally the professional, managerial, and sales occupations, are represented most heavily among the urban population. These indications underscore the greater prevalence of higher levels of living in urban places.

A NOTE ON SOCIAL-AREA ANALYSIS

The demographic approach to urban phenomena can assume very complex proportions. One example is social-area analysis. The more technically minded student, particularly if he is preparing for a career in urban research, may find this method of interest.

Social-area analysis was developed by Eshref Shevky, Marilyn Williams, and Wendell Bell, and was first applied on the West Coast. It is a method of study "proceeding on the assumption that the urban phenomena of Los Angeles were regional manifestations of changes in the total society, and the further assumption that, in urban analysis, facts of economic differentiation and of status and power had a significance transcending in importance the significance of relations occurring within the boundaries of the local community."[32]

Social-area analysis takes its point of departure from the conviction that industrial society exhibits three phenomena in particular: (1) increasing social rank (as evidenced by the greater prevalence of managerial in contrast to manual occupations); (2) increasing functional differentiation; and (3) increasing complexity of social organization. These postulates are expressed succinctly as (I) social rank, that is, economic level; (II) urbanization, or familism; and (III) segregation, or in other words, ethnicity. The three variables are given concrete expression in observations such as the growth of clerical occupations, the declining importance of the household, and in the increasing heterogeneity of the population in employment and education. From census-tract data on schooling, fertility, the residential separation of ethnic groups, and rental values, the Shevky procedure enables one to derive territorial index scores. These then permit the designation of social areas each of which "contains persons having the same level of living, the same way of life, and the same ethnic background." The final inference is that these clusters of factors differentiate the people so designated both attitudinally and behaviorally from the people of other areas.

An inquiry by Van Arsdol, Camilleri, and Schmid of 10 representative American cities, among them Atlanta, Minneapolis, and Seattle, confirmed the Shevy system as a "limited model of urban society."[33] Further interpretation, however, revealed variation in the internal structure of the tested factors and the conclusion that "ecologists should look to other theoretical and empirical systems for describing the differentiation of census tract populations."[34]

Criticism of the Shevky social-area method also emphasizes that it is only a correlational classification, in short, a method without causal significance. Hence, urbanization may well be indicated by a high proportion of women gainfully employed, a low percentage of the population living in one-family dwellings, and a low fertility ratio, but the critics of social-area analysis contend that this is finally simply a definition. Leonard Reissman declares, "Aside from the usual, and by now, familiar, correlations between the

[32] Eshref Shevky and Wendell Bell, *Social Area Analysis* (Palo Alto, Calif.: Stanford University Press, 1955), p. 1. Consult also Eshref Shevky and Marilyn Williams, *The Social Areas of Los Angeles: Analysis and Typology* (Berkeley and Los Angeles, Calif.: University of California Press, 1949).

[33] Maurice D. Van Arsdol, Santo F. Camilleri, and Calvin F. Schmid, "An Application of the Shevky Social Area Indexes to a Model of Urban Society," *Social Forces, 37* (October 1958), pp. 26–32; "The Generality of Urban Social Area Indexes," *American Sociological Review, 33* (June 1958), pp. 277–84; and "An Investigation of the Utility of Urban Typology," *Pacific Sociological Review, 4* (Spring 1961), pp. 26–32.

[34] Ibid.

index and other measures, there are no bases for the suggestion of theory."[35]

In defense of social-area analysis, Bell and Greer have conceded that additional elaboration and formulation are necessary, but that in view of the present reather primitive type of urban theory, "social-area analysis constitutes a unifying, general, powerful, and *sociologically-meaningful* approach to the study of urban phenomena."[36]

CONCLUSION

The demographic study of urban phenomena features the various aspects of population as shaped by other factors and as these factors themselves determine future development. In this regard, distribution, composition, growth, the vital processes of fertility and mortality, movement, and sociocultural characteristics are of special importance.

Studies of population distribution reveal that urbanization today is most rapid in regions whose initial urbanization was sustained neither earliest nor most recently, and that the largest cities of the world, especially those in areas that were first to urbanize, that is, in the present-day postindustrial sector, are experiencing the greatest rate of growth currently.

The composition of urban populations differs from that of rural populations. Typically, urban residents have a higher median age and lower dependency as well as lower sex ratios. Also, among urban people there is a tendency toward more labor-force participation by women and a larger proportion of elderly females.

Historically, in the period since 1750, owing to industrial, technological, and scientific progress, urbanization has been responsible for rapid population growth. Eventually, however, as the nations of the world reach the postindustrial stage, many believe that population growth will come to an end.

Migration also has discernible relationships with urbanization. In recent years, both in the United States and in other regions of the world, the movement of people has been in the direction of population centers and away from rural areas. Despite the large numbers of migrants coming into America's cities in recent years, natural increase accounts for the greater part of our metropolitan growth.

Finally, the demographic study of rural-urban contrasts shows that urban populations evidence higher levels of literacy, education, and socioeconomic standards of living as a whole. These findings only underscore still further the value, even though it is perhaps more descriptive than explana-

[35] Leonard Reissman, *The Urban Process* (New York: Free Press, 1964), p. 88.

[36] Wendell Bell and Scott Greer, "Social Area Analysis and Its Critics," *Pacific Sociological Review*, 5 (Spring 1962), pp. 3–9.

tory, of the demographic approach to urban life as a general method of study.

FOR FURTHER READING

Eugene B. Brody (ed.), *Behavior in New Environments: Adaptation of Migrant Populations* (Beverly Hills, Calif.: Sage, 1970). The determinants and consequences of migration, chiefly in the United States.

Kingsley Davis, *World Urbanization* (Berkeley, Calif.: University of California Institute for International Studies, 1969). In two volumes, the first containing basic demographic data, and the second analyses.

Thomas R. Ford and Gordon F. De Jong, ed., *Social Demography* (Englewood Cliffs, N.J.: Prentice-Hall, 1970). The manner in which population composition interacts with social structure.

G. A. Harrison and A. J. Boyce, eds., *The Structure of Human Populations* (Oxford: Oxford University Press, 1972). On the multi-dimensional study of population.

Judah Matras, *Population and Societies* (Englewood Cliffs, N.J.: Prentice-Hall, 1973). An advanced text useful for theory and method.

Quentin H. Stanford, ed., *The World's Population* (New York: Oxford University Press, 1972). Readings representative of the field of demography at present.

Report of the Commission on Population Growth and the American Future (Washington, D.C.: Government Printing Office, 1972). Besides the main report seven volumes containing research papers completed for the Commission are also available.

United Nations, *Demographic Year Book: 1970* (New York: United Nations, 1971). Official data on many countries; highly statistical with extensive footnotes showing further sources of information.

PART FOUR

THE ORGANIZATION OF POWER

Freeway and ramps at Houston, Texas, one expression of power in urban life.
Source: Charles E. Rotkin, *The U.S.A.—An Aerial Close-Up* (New York: Crown Publishers, 1968), frontispiece.

CHAPTER 8

URBAN GOVERNMENT AND POLITICS

A city functions as an entity in which power, that is, the capacity for both control and collective achievement, is crystallized chiefly in four institutions: government, the economy, social stratification, and the media of mass communication. To some degree, all of these are independent of one another. To a larger extent, they are interwoven, especially in today's dynamic urban societies.

The present chapter deals with government at the local level. This involves the maintenance of order; the provision of municipal services like water and street lighting; and also the promotion of the residents' economic, social, and cultural interests. Consequently, this chapter reviews the various forms that municipal government takes; relations between local, state, and national government; and the activities of interest groups and political parties on the local scene.

The subsequent three chapters of this section are devoted to the other three centers of power in the urban community.

URBAN GOVERNMENT

Urban government consists of the authoritative arrangements by which the security of the local community is maintained, its common needs served, and expression given to the concerns of its constituent groups.

THREE TYPES OF LOCAL GOVERNMENT

Three general types of local government exist at present in Western society. These are the English, French, and Soviet.[1] Each of the three has a distinct character that not only differentiates it from the others but also from indigenous forms of nonurban local rule as well as non-Western municipal government.[2]

The English Model

The English type of urban government allows a great deal of local autonomy, in other words, home rule. Conceived of as an independent corporation, the local community is invested, according to the English tradition, with virtually all the powers of government. Policy decisions are made locally by a representative council whose committees work in coordination with professional administrators. In addition, voluntary citizen participation is also a strong feature of the English pattern of municipal government. English institutions of city government have been adopted not only in the United States (as the next section of this chapter shows), but also in British-settled Africa, India, and Latin America, and in the Commonwealth nations.

The French Form

Local government of the French variety contrasts sharply with its English counterpart. The French model reveals "centralization, chain of command, hierarchical structure, executive domination, and legislative subordination."[3] The French pattern of local government is quite widespread in Western

---

[1] Harold F. Alderfer, *Local Government in Developing Countries* (New York: McGraw-Hill, 1964).

[2] Tokyo offers an illustration of non-Western municipal government, also cities in some of the underdeveloped nations. See Charles Abrams, *Man's Struggle for Shelter in an Urbanizing World* (Cambridge, Mass.: MIT Press, 1964).

[3] Alderfer, op. cit., p. 7.

Europe, the Middle East, and Latin America. Centralized administration is the key to French political institutions. In France itself, from the time of Napoleon to the present, a hierarchical system connecting the national government to the local communes has been in operation. Elected councils and mayors are present, to be sure, but they have very limited powers subject to the executive authority of the central regime.

The Soviet Variety

City government along the lines of the Soviet model calls for national centralization together with large-scale local participation. The scope of government in the U. S. S. R. is of course much broader than Americans have been accustomed to think of, at least until recently, since it includes responsibility for the day-to-day conduct of industrial and agricultural enterprise. Local elections of city soviets from hand-picked candidates presented by the official political party in uncontested races result in large government bodies being selected at the local level. These in turn choose executive committees responsible to their own parent body and, under "democratic centralism," to the next higher executive committee as well. Subordinate to central authority, the Soviet type of city government is expected to provide necessary services and to participate in local, regional, and even national administration and planning. Soviet influence over other nations has expressed itself in the adoption of its pattern of urban government, with different degrees of fidelity, in Vietnam, Yugoslavia, and the countries of Central Europe.

THE BACKGROUND OF AMERICAN LOCAL GOVERNMENT

The American city can be traced as a governing body to the English model in general and to the English boroughs of the seventeenth century in particular.

HOME RULE

English borough government provided for local home rule consistent with national law. A charter thus meant that the affairs of the borough were entrusted by the crown to a "close" corporation, in other words, to a self-perpetuating body of aldermen chosen by the corporation of citizen-freeholders for life. The public were generally satisfied because their local officeholders protected them from the potentially oppressive demands of the central authorities in the colonial capital and London itself.

PROMOTING INDUSTRY AND TRADE

Muncipal government originated in colonial America not, as one might think, in the need to furnish local services. It was the spirit of colonization that more than anything else fostered the municipal movement in the English New World. As Ernest Griffith notes, Governor Culpepper of Virginia in 1680 announced that the king was determined that there should be towns, "as no nation has ever begun a colony without them and none thrived without their development."[4]

Municipal incorporations were expected to promote industry and trade in America, because home rule carried with it the right of merchants and artisans to establish guild monopolies and also to benefit from immunities to special taxation. In addition, it was anticipated that the establishment of towns would improve the quality of goods, since they too would be subject to corporate control. Finally, concentrating economic activity at ports of entry would facilitate the collection of revenues.

POPULISM AND GENERAL GOVERNMENT

The seed of local self-government contained in the English municipal charter germinated under the impact of urban growth in America. Not fearful of the distant colonials on this side of the Atlantic—since they had no voice in Parliament—the British authorities came to permit the election of some officials in the chartered municipalities in the New World. The intellectual ferment at the time of the Revolution also affected municipal government, with the issuance of local charters passing from the governors to the new state legislatures. Generally, too, the mayor came to be elected by the public rather than by the aldermen.

The state governments, however, resisted municipal populism as much as they could. They made each municipal charter a separate legislative enactment, which resulted in much interference in local affairs. Yet state opposition to popular local government could not go on indefinitely. Short terms of office together with the Jacksonian attitude that a public office is a prize led to the spoils system at the municipal level and the greater concentration of power there. In the final analysis, it was the growth of population and of economic enterprise in nineteenth-century America that compelled the change from a municipality with limited duties to one having the general powers of government to occur.

---

[4] Ernest S. Griffith, *History of American City Government: The Colonial Period* (New York: Oxford University Press, 1938), p. 52.

TYPES OF URBAN GOVERNMENT
IN THE UNITED STATES

The period from 1890 to 1915 was an innovative one in American local government. The three forms of municipal policymaking and administration now prevailing took shape at that time. With some modification they have been present in the cities of the United States ever since. The (1) mayoral, (2) manager-council, (3) commission systems were responses to inefficiency and corruption, it is true, but also to new needs and aspirations of the period.

Richard T. Ely, at various times professor of economics at Johns Hopkins and the University of Wisconsin, was a prophet of change in American local government late in the nineteenth century. In a speech before the Evangelical Alliance in Boston in 1890, Ely listed what he believed were the needs of the American city and then summed them up as "municipalism," which he then equated with "local nationalism."[5] Abetted by natural disasters like floods, which brought the inadequacies of local government to a head, pronouncements such as Ely's resulted in the adoption of new systems of municipal rule in many cities of the United States in the 50 years following 1900.

By 1974, of a total of 3612 American cities with populations exceeding 5000, 1805 were being served by the mayor-council form of government. The council-manager type was to be found in 1641 cities. Only 166 municipalities were governed under the commission pattern. The three forms were not equally divided among cities by size. In general, the mayor form served the largest population centers: in fact, 81 percent of all cities over 500,000. The manager type predominated in cities of modest size: 47 percent of all with a population between 50,000 and 100,000. Government by commission was most prevalent in the smallest municipalities and was found in only 6 percent of all cities in the United States over 50,000 in size.[6]

THE MAYORAL SYSTEM

The mayor-council form of local government clearly separates the executive from the legislative branch. A "strong" mayor is thus elected independently of the city council and is entrusted with many powers, including the appointment, supervision, and removal of staff, the management of the budget, and responsibility for recommending policy. The "strong" mayor also possesses the power to veto council legislation. Most of the major cities of the United States have such a system of government today, among them New York, Chicago, Philadelphia, and Detroit.

[5] "Richard T. Ely on the Needs of the City," in Charles N. Glaab, ed., *The American City* (Homewood, Ill.: Dorsey Press, 1963), pp. 391–98.

[6] *The Municipal Year Book* (Washington, D.C.: International City Management Association, 1974), Table 3.

The mayoral system also makes possible the "weak" type of mayor. This kind of local chief executive has little authority. For example, he may need council concurrence to remove department heads. Or his control over the city's budget may be so slight that it will be incumbent on him to recognize budget decisions worked out between his own subordinates and the council. Except for being elected, the weak mayor resembles a city manager. At present in the United States only two of our largest cities operate under the weak mayor plan: Los Angeles and Minneapolis.

THE CITY-MANAGER TYPE

The manager principle calls for the selection of the city's chief executive by the council instead of by popular election. In theory, this plan derives from the way in which private corporations are organized and also some public agencies, like school boards assisted by superintendents of their own choice. The city manager is expected to concentrate administrative functions under the authority of the city council. Typically, the manager has supervisory authority over his staff, but only such tenure himself as the council sees fit. At present five of America's principal cities are governed under the managerial form: Kansas City, Dallas, Cincinnati, San Antonio, and San Diego.

LOCAL GOVERNMENT BY COMMISSION

If the council-manager pattern dispenses with an independent chief executive, the commission form of government eliminates centralized administration altogether. Introduced first in Galveston, Texas, in 1901, after a hurricane and flood had taken 6000 lives and discredited the conduct of municipal affairs in that city, the commission form calls for the election of a small number of policymakers (five on the average). Election is usually at large on a nonpartisan basis. Each of these commissioners is also required to head one of the municipal departments—safety, health, and so on. In addition, one commissioner may be chosen by the commission itself to serve ceremonially as mayor, and even to exercise some veto and appointive powers. The commission pattern is being employed now perhaps most notably in St. Paul, Memphis, and Jersey City.

THE MERITS AND SHORTCOMINGS OF AMERICAN LOCAL GOVERNMENT

Experience with the three forms of American municipal government has been subjected to much analysis by political scientists. As a result, both their strengths and weaknesses are well known.

THE MAYORAL SYSTEM

New York's Fiorello LaGuardia, Cleveland's Tom Johnson, and Philadephia's Richardson Dilworth, famous mayors all, illustrate the cardinal value of the mayor-council form of local government: leadership. As one authority has phrased it, "Concentration, simplicity, and confidence, principles of good government, are all embodied in the strong mayor plan." The mayor makes policy decisions and, therefore, is essentially political rather than administrative. For this very reason, though, the mayoral plan has often been denounced. "Bossism," that is, behind-the-scenes manipulation in favor of special interests, has been frequently associated with the mayor-council arrangement. Especially is this apt to be charged when conflict arises between the mayor and the city council.

THE MANAGERIAL PLAN

The constant need to actively cope with a city's problems and not be satisfied with procedural performance is apparent in the vicissitudes of the council-manager plan where it has been adopted. Don K. Price has observed that "in city after city where the manager plan was studied, it was clear that the manager was less likely to get fired for advocating a policy than for administering one; less for proposing a bond issue or a health program than for firing somebody's cousin, or collecting somebody's taxes, or refusing someone a building permit."[7] The successful city managers, Price concludes, were precisely those who exercised community leadership as well as achieved "operating efficiency." As cities grow in size and as they acquire responsibility for more complex functions, the need for policy leadership increases. That is no doubt why the city-manager plan has proved unappealing to our largest urban communities.

In spite of its handicaps the council-manager plan has demonstrated a good deal of merit in actual practice. Policymaking can be concentrated, and a qualified, professionally trained specialist can be selected as manager. With executive responsibility placed in his office, he can avoid administrative confusion and inaction. In short, the manager can reduce political factionalism, provide better services, and achieve important unit economies.

Yet, the combination of an administratively-oriented city manager and a policymaking council, even a competent one, may not be able to carry the community on major issues. In this light it is understandable why manager-council local government appears to be most successful where the community is socially homogeneous and, hence, where a strong consensus already

[7]"The Promotion of the City Manager Plan," *Public Opinion Quarterly*, 5 (Winter 1941), pp. 563–78.

Metropolitan Chicago (as of 1973–74): 1172 local governments!

exists. Adrian's study of three middle-sized council-manager cities in Michigan showed little discord among their inhabitants. Adrian states: "Judged on the basis of the amount of controversy engendered, the time required to achieve a policy decision by the council, and the amount of space devoted to the issue by the local press, the number of important issues coming before the councils of the three cities averaged about two a year."[8]

The large cities that have voted to abandon the manager plan after having some experience with it include Cleveland, Santa Barbara, and Madison. On the othar hand, its continued presence in a few of our large population centers argues for its viability even where dissensus and factionalism are strong. As of the late 1960s, some 600 city-manager governments were serving in our metropolitan areas, nearly all in the suburbs, communities that tend to be relatively homogeneous within themselves.

THE COMMISSION FORM OF GOVERNMENT

Like the mayor and manager patterns, the commission form is also of mixed value. Although in theory the commission should achieve superior service, in

[8] Charles R. Adrian, "Leadership and Decision-Making in Manager Cities," *Public Administration Review, 18* (Summer 1958), pp. 208–13.

operation it tends to backfire, for the joint policymakers-administrators find it difficult to agree on priorities save by expedient compromise. Leadership is weak. Each commissioner becomes loath to inquire critically into the affairs of his colleagues. That is why friction decreases and decisions can be implemented promptly. Still, the likelihood of a given individual being administratively very proficient and at the same time also capable of broad, general political judgment appears small. According to MacDonald, experience with commission government shows possibly improved service but a higher-than-average tax rise.[9] Because of its weaknesses, the commission type of local government has been steadily losing favor in the United States. In 1940, 16 percent of our cities were being governed by commissions. Thirty-five years later that figure was less than half.

GOVERNMENTAL FRAGMENTATION IN THE METROPOLITAN AREA

Few social generalizations can be put forth categorically. That is not the case in regard to the fragmentation of American local government in the nation's metropolitan areas. Nowhere in the United States today, it can be said, does the entire social and economic metropolitan area coincide with a single governmental unit that includes the whole territory.

Metropolitan Los Angeles may be the typical situation: 10 other cities within a radius of 10 miles of the center of the core city, each with no fewer than 25,000 inhabitants; in all, 45 cities within the county; 33 county "islands" surrounded by incorporated jurisdictions; and, to complete the picture, 7 "city islands," 14 "shoestrings" of annexed territory, and other irregularities of the "peninsula" and "isthmus" type! The 1962 Census showed that the 212 SMSA's of the United States had a total of 18,442 separate governmental units. The average was 87. Metropolitan fragmentation has not lessened much since. In 1967, the Chicago SMSA had 1113 local government units; New York had 551; and Philadelphia had 876.[10]

THE SOURCES OF FRAGMENTATION

The multiplicity of governments in the metropolitan community is attributable, as Edward Banfield, for one, asserts, to several basic factors combined in a peculiar way in each particular instance.[11]

[9] Austin F. MacDonald, *American City Government and Administration* (New York: Thomas Y. Crowell, 1966), 6th ed., pp. 201–03.

[10] Bureau of the Census, *Statistical Abstract of the United States: 1972* (Washington, D.C.: Government Printing Office, 1972), pp. 851, 871, and 891.

[11] Edward C. Banfield, *The Unheavenly City* (Boston: Little, Brown, 1970), Chs. 2–4.

Exhibit 8-1 Population and number of local governments in 74 selected SMSA's of the United States: 1973–74

AREA	POPULA-TION[1]	LOCAL GOVERN-MENTS[2]	AREA	POPULA-TION[1]	LOCAL GOVERN-MENTS[2]
Total	113,468,960	14,482			
Birmingham, Ala.	787,292	109	Louisville, Ky.–Ind.	885,826	202
Phoenix, Ariz.	1,126,620	112	New Orleans, La.	1,082,600	42
Anaheim–Santa Ana–					
Garden Grove, Calif.	1,596,920	111	Baltimore, Md.	2,128,161	29
Los Angeles–Long			Boston, Mass.[6]	3,392,612	231
Beach, Calif.	6,923,813	232	Springfield–Chicopee–		
Riverside–San Bernar-			Holyoke, Mass.[7]	596,021	76
dino–Ontario, Calif.	1,196,691	233	Worcester, Mass.[8]	649,397	124
Sacramento, Calif.	864,374	210	Detroit, Mich.	4,445,758	352
San Diego, Calif.	1,469,822	151	Flint, Mich.	516,915	91
			Grand Rapids, Mich.	552,918	93
San Francisco–Oakland,			Minneapolis–St. Paul,		
Calif.	3,143,300	302	Minn.–Wis.	1,999,753	396
San Jose, Calif.	1,156,734	75	Kansas City, Mo.–Kan.	1,298,849	292
Denver–Boulder, Colo.	1,365,243	277			
Bridgeport, Conn.[3]	792,555	61	St. Louis, Mo.–Ill.	2,391,384	572
Hartford, Conn.[4]	822,164	67	Omaha, Nebr.–Iowa	575,436	234
New Haven, Conn.[5]	756,734	69	Jersey City, N.J.	598,164	33
Wilmington, Del.–N.J.–			Newark, N.J.	915,431	260
Md.	515,894	77	New Brunswick–Perth		
Washington, D.C.–Md.–			Amboy–Sayreville,		
Va.	3,019,513	96	N.J.	594,372	76
Fort Lauderdale–			Albany–Schenectady–		
Hollywood, Fla.	756,139	46	Troy, N.Y.	800,229	253
Jacksonville, Fla.	660,630	43	Buffalo, N.Y.	1,344,757	142
Miami, Fla.	1,369,917	33	Nassau–Suffolk, N.Y.	2,630,044	366
Orlando, Fla.	549,498	52	New York, N.Y.–N.J.	9,739,066	349
Tampa–St. Petersburg,			Rochester, N.Y.	971,522	242
Fla.	1,275,673	55	Syracuse, N.Y.	642,715	182
Atlanta, Ga.	1,747,987	163	Charlotte–Gastonia, N.C.	588,202	37
Honolulu, Hawaii	685,717	4	Greensboro–Winston–		
Chicago, Ill.	7,002,458	1,172	Salem–High Point,		
Gary–Hammond–East			N.C.	756,607	51
Chicago, Ind.	640,774	129	Akron, Ohio	677,133	98
Indianapolis, Ind.	1,136,598	296			

AREA	POPULA-TION[1]	LOCAL GOVERN-MENTS[2]	AREA	POPULA-TION[1]	LOCAL GOVERN-MENTS[2]
Cincinnati, Ohio–Ky.–Ind.	1,382,984	260	Providence–Warwick–Pawtucket, R.I.[9]	776,184	76
Cleveland, Ohio	2,006,371	210	Memphis, Tenn.–Ark.–Miss.	863,431	74
Columbus, Ohio	1,057,267	195	Nashville–Davidson, Tenn.	732,015	95
Dayton, Ohio	848,371	161			
Toledo, Ohio–Mich.	782,479	196			
Youngstown–Warren, Ohio	543,366	107	Dallas–Ft. Worth, Tex.	2,464,090	341
Oklahoma City, Okla.	750,076	129	Houston, Tex.	2,168,474	315
Tulsa, Okla.	572,324	198	San Antonio, Tex.	960,109	76
			Salt Lake City–Ogden, Utah	753,289	111
Portland, Oreg.–Wash.	1,062,451	298			
Allentown–Bethlehem–Easton, Pa.–N.J.	610,762	256	Norfolk–Virginia Beach–Portsmouth, Va.–N.C.	697,673	11
Northeast Pennsylvania	629,405	397	Richmond, Va.	563,357	10
Philadelphia, Pa.	4,805,746	852	Seattle–Everett, Wash.	1,383,069	269
Pittsburgh, Pa.	2,364,637	698	Milwaukee, Wis.	1,416,773	149

[1]Estimated for July 1, 1973. [2]Based on the 1972 Census of Governments. [3]Connecticut State Economic Area A. [4]Connecticut State Economic Area C. [5]Connecticut State Economic Area B. [6]Massachusetts State Economic Area C. [7]Massachusetts State Economic Area A. [8]Massachusetts State Economic Area B. [9]Rhode Island State Economic Area A.

The population aggregates range from New York-New Jersey's 9.7 million to 0.5 million for Wilmington, Del.-N. J./Md. The number of local governments show a high of 1172 for Chicago and a low of only four for Honolulu.

Source: Bureau of the Census, *Local Government Finances in Selected Metropolitan Areas and Large Counties: 1973–1974* (Washington, D.C.: Government Printing Office, 1976), p. 4.

First, demographic growth has meant an expanding population occupying a growing area.

Second, technological facilities, especially improved transportation and communication, have supported the rapid dispersion of population beyond the already established legal boundaries.

Third, economic imperatives have also been at work, the free-enterprise system attracting cheap labor to the metropolitan center and at the same time providing varying degrees of affluence to the whole population, thereby widening their options. Hence, the dispersion of commercial establishments and residences in a broadening sprawl.

Fourth, we have witnessed the differentiation of social classes into subcultures and the territorial expression of such interests in the form of separate local governments.

Finally, fifth, the last major variable is race. It obviously has economic and social-class and, therefore, territorial implications too.

Altogether these five elements are responsible for the typical metropolitan mosaic. It follows then that political atomization receives support from industrial, commerical, social-class, and ethnic forces. Indeed, the many legal components of an area are to be understood as serving special interests. Consider the political rationale of suburbs given by Scott Greer, that "incorporation protects the residential community from annexation and governmental control by a larger unit." As a result, Greer goes on to add, suburbs are "governmental game preserves whose citizens are immune to municipal law" whether as manufacturing sites, tax-exempt enclaves, autonomous bedroom communities, or even shelters for illicit activities.[12]

THE CONSEQUENCES OF FRAGMENTATION

Political separateness and functional unity are the paradox of the metropolitan area, with two major problems stemming from this.

First, the multiplicity of governments in the metropolis leaves service needs unmet in specific localities. Some suburbs are unable to provide their citizens with sidewalks, sewers, or a professional fire department. The rising tide of expectations only adds to the limitations present in governmental fragmentation.[13]

Second, fragmentation not only leaves certain local needs unfulfilled, but it also prevents the service needs of the entire metropolitan area from being dealt with satisfactorily. In fact, the regional inadequacies resulting from fragmentation are the more striking of the two main problems precipitated by it. Many observers agree on "the failure in virtually every city, and in all metropolitan areas, to work out any *comprehensive community program for general development* and for tackling the major social and economic problems of the foreseeable future."[14]

Fragmentation and the Los Angeles Water System

That fragmentation is of massive importance for the American metropolitan area can hardly be denied. Yet it cannot be thought of as heralding disaster for local government either. The management of water in greater Los

[12] Scott Greer, *Governing the Metropolis* (New York: John Wiley & Sons, 1962), pp. 53–54.

[13] Cf. Robert C. Wood, *1400 Governments* (Garden City, N.Y.: Doubleday, 1964) and a much earlier statement, Committee on Metropolitan Government, *The Government of Metropolitan Areas in the United States* (New York: National Municipal League, 1930).

[14] Luther H. Gulick, *The Metropolitan Problem and American Ideas* (New York: Alfred A. Knopf, 1962), p. 121.

Angeles illustrates the complex coordination generally achieved in our metropolitan communities, in spite of their governmental divisiveness.[15]

The Los Angeles area is supplied with water by a system consisting of no fewer than 1 metropolitan water district, 3 irrigation districts, 5 municipal water districts, 8 county waterworks districts, 10 county water districts, 33 municipal water departments, and 283 mutual water companies! Water is naturally available in Los Angeles only from underground basins because there are neither usable rivers nor much rainfall in the area. Shortly after 1900 when large-scale inhabitation of Los Angeles began, the separate cities there quickly become involved in a fierce struggle to control the ground water. Cities condemned or purchased privately owned water companies, or they acquired additional land overlying water resources. Thus the cities of metropolitan Los Angeles established their competitive positions in a contest for leadership in industry and investment in southern California.

The autonomous governments in metropolitan Los Angeles also turned to the importation of water from the distant Colorado River to supplement local supplies. Two instrumentalities were devised for this purpose: the Los Angeles Municipal Water System and the Metropolitan Water District of Southern California. The Metropolitan District is the organization of a number of cities and municipal water districts capable of sufficient taxation to carry out so large an engineering enterprise. The joint effort that the Metropolitan District represents, however, is offset by the continuing litigation over water priorities and allocation rights that has been carried on by the cities of metropolitan Los Angeles in the face of lowered water basins. The pattern of water supply in Los Angeles indicates the interplay of private interests utilizing municipal corporations as vehicles of competition in the metropolis.[16] It also exemplifies the organizational ingenuity which metropolitan fragmentation has engendered in our large cities.

EFFECTIVE GOVERNMENT DESPITE FRAGMENTATION

Despite metropolitan fragmentation urban government in America continues to function, and not ineffectively at that. The divided local governments have not stood still, but have greatly expanded their service capacities regardless of their autonomy from one another. In the period from 1902 to 1956, the annual expenditures for local government in the United States rose from $700 million to $28 billion. By 1970, the figure had climbed to no less than $92 billion. Allowing for inflation and population growth, this increase represents

[15] A detailed summary is to be found in Winston W. Crouch and Beatrice Dinerman, *Southern California Metropolis* (Berkeley and Los Angeles: University of California Press, 1964), pp. 50–63.

[16] The ambitious $3 billion California Water Plan to tap the Sacramento River for the arid South is scheduled for service by 1990, but opponents contend it will dangerously upset the ecological balance of the San Francisco delta.

at least a doubling of service capability from the beginning to the end of each of these two intervals. Still lacking, however, is the ability of local government in the metropolitan areas of the nation—because they are fragmented and competitive—to move toward common goals in education, transportation, housing, and the like on a regional basis. As a result, serious deficiencies remain even though governmental multiplicity has not been entirely incapacitating.

REFORM AND REORGANIZATION

In the maze of American local government, several reorganization trends that are designed to lead to more functional operation are presently discernible. The three types most salient for metropolitan planning, service delivery, and problem solving are: (1) the cooperative approach, including interjurisdictional agreements and coordinated planning; (2) metropolitan consolidation, through annexation or merger; and (3) the two-level approach requiring the creation of the comprehensive urban county, a federation of contiguous municipalities, or special-service districts.[17]

THE COOPERATIVE APPROACH

Interjurisdictional cooperation refers to contractually arranged joint action by otherwise independent local governments. Such cooperation may pertain, say, to standby assistance in the event of large fires, or it may provide for the use of a refuse dump in common. Again, it may take the form of a metropolitan council, like those in Detroit, San Francisco, and Philadelphia, where local contracts and those with state and federal bodies are being systematized. However, quid pro quo agreements alone cannot supply the needs of areas that lack the resources necessary to provide them in the first place.

THE CONSOLIDATION APPROACH

Although compelling in theory, consolidating existing municipalities by adding adjoining territory to them flies in the face of interests to the contrary. Earlier, in the nineteenth century, there was much annexation, Boston growing from 4.5 to 38.5 square miles, and Chicago from 10.5 to 190.[18] The annexation movement declined after 1900, however. Today only a small part of the total amount of municipal territorial expansion is by annexation. Southwestern cities like Houston, Phoenix, and Oklahoma City have been active

[17] See John C. Bollens and Henry J. Schmandt, *The Metropolis* (New York: Harper & Row, 1965), Chs. 10–14.
[18] Ibid., p. 403.

recently in regard to annexation. Statutes making annexation difficult (e. g., forbidding expansion across county lines) are under attack at present. Notwithstanding, vested interests, local pride, and myths (such as the inevitability of higher taxes) suggest dim prospects for annexation as *the* route to more rational local government in the United States.

THE TWO-LEVEL APPROACH

The transfer of some or even all municipal functions to the county to secure a broader tax base and more uniform service denotes the two-level approach to fragmentation. This eliminates multiple structures and gains vital economies through a dual system. Yet only a small number of unions of the two-level variety have occurred in the recent past, four notable ones being between Baton Rouge and East Baton Rouge in 1947; between Nashville and Davidson County in 1962; between Jacksonville and Duvall County in 1969; and between Indianapolis and Marion County in 1970.

The special district is the two-level solution to fragmentation in which a territorially defined area is set up as a governing entity to serve two or more contiguous cities in some respect, such as sewage treatment or highway maintenance. The mushrooming of special districts, from 9000 in 1942 to 23,885 in 1972, conveys the extent of their popularity in the United States in recent years.

A more thoroughgoing version of the two-level approach calls for the county to replace its cities completely by being entrusted with total responsibility for local government within its borders. The creation of a metropolitan county, which may have a federated base, gets away from the antiquated notion that a county is simply a unit of state government by investing county government with the full range of urban functions. The potentialities that the complete urban county has for the implementation of federal programs were recognized recently by the Advisory Commission on Intergovernmental Relations.[19]

Blanketing 27 municipalities, Metropolitan Miami (Dade County), which was initiated in 1957, is a prime example here. Miami Metro was empowered to construct and operate transit systems; back up the local police and fire departments with training and information; administer public health, welfare, and recreation; attend to housing, pollution, and drainage; and also engage in zoning, planning, and metropolitan development.

The problems that work against creating the metropolitan county, like the allocation of representation, also retard development of the metropolitan federation. In 1954, the Municipality of Metropolitan Toronto was established by having powers assigned to it by its 13 constituent cities. During the last 20 years, Toronto has been successful in building physical plants but much

---

[19] *Urban America and the Federal System* (Washington, D.C.: ACIR, 1969), M–47, pp. 95ff.

less so in controversial areas like housing and planning.[20] Political scientist Joseph F. Zimmerman is of the opinion that this two-level approach has little appeal in the United States where "political forces committed to the preservation of the status quo are sufficiently strong to rule out [its] use."[21] On the other hand, Lee Sloan and Robert M. French writing recently on the Jacksonville-Duvall consolidation think that white suburban rings in Southern cities will seek to avert black rule in the central city by engineering transfers of authority from city to county.[22] They cite Atlanta, Richmond, Charleston, Tampa, and Chattanooga as places where some form of metropolitanization is currently being broached.

THE PROSPECTS FOR REFORM AND REORGANIZATION

Experience would suggest that the reform and reorganization of municipal government in the United States will probably proceed along multiple lines depending on local circumstances and leadership. Overcoming metropolitan fragmentation by annexation appears to have little likelihood. But the federated metropolis and the metropolitan county do give promise of gaining acceptance. They have functional value and they allow the retention of locality and the protection of pluralistic interests.

The special district is perhaps the likeliest option in the near future. Since it does not impair existing government and may sucessfully evade state limitations on debt, it offers a welcome opportunity for change. In 1972, two-thirds of all incorporated municipalities in the nation responding to a survey of the Advisory Commission on Inter-governmental Relations reported they had cooperative service districts in force.[23]

In the long run though, these ad hoc arrangements may turn out to be just another uneconomical, unresponsive layer of government added to an already dense thicket of local units.[24] Moreover, resistance to areawide coordination may increase as central city-suburban antagonisms grow out of the widening socioeconomic disparities between their populations.[25] Recent experience with planned development for metropolitan Cleveland, for example,

---

[20] Cf. *A Look to the North: Canadian Regional Experience* (Washington, D.C.: ACIR, 1974), Ch. 3.

[21] Joseph F. Zimmerman, "Substate Regional Government: Designing a New Procedure," *National Civic Review, 61* (June 1972), pp. 286–90.

[22] Lee Sloan and Robert M. French, "Black Rule in the Urban South," in Helen Safa and Gloria Levitas, eds., *Social Problems in Corporate America* (New York: Harper & Row, 1975), pp. 33–39.

[23] *The Challenge of Local Government Reorganization* (Washington, D.C.: ACIR, 1974), p. 147.

[24] *Urban America and the Federal System,* op. cit., gives the breakdown of special districts by type, e.g., 20 percent for fire protection, 18 for natural resources, and 14 for water supply. See Table 13, p. 87.

[25] Cf. Frances Frisken, "The Metropolis and the Central City: Can One Government Unite Them?" *Urban Affairs Quarterly, 8* (June 1973), pp. 395–422.

relates to these tensions although, in 1975, Cleveland did establish a Regional Transit Authority.

RELATIONS WITH STATE AND FEDERAL GOVERNMENT

State-chartered urban government in the United States presupposes that the local community is an independent body supplying needed services without impact beyond the immediate locality. The restrictive nature of a city charter is apparent in the continued application of Dillon's Rule, first enunciated in 1872 as the basic definition of municipal jurisdiction in the United States:

> It is the general and indisputed proposition of law that a municipal corporation possesses, and can exercise, the following powers and no others: First, those granted in express words; second, those necessarily or fairly implied in, or incident to, the powers expressly granted; third, those essential to the declared objects and purposes of the corporation—not simply convenient, but indispensable.[26]

STRENGTHENING CITIES IN RELATION TO STATE GOVERNMENT

So narrow a conception of the functions of municipal government subordinating the city to the state as necessarily had to be broadened, often by means of judicial interpretation to circumvent the Dillon principle, and at other times by action of the state government itself.

Two kinds of municipal powers are commonly recognized today: governmental and proprietary. The first includes public safety, health, land use, education, welfare, and recreation. These are mandated to the cities in their charters. Proprietary powers, on the other hand, are discretionary in the sense that, like transit services and public utilities, they may be exercised by the city simply as a corporation.

Recently, courts have often ruled in favor of the liberal exercise of a municipality's proprietary powers vis-à-vis state government. The operation of utilities is often construed as necessary to health and welfare and not merely discretionary. No fewer than two out of every three cities over 5000 in population in the United States operate municipally owned water systems, and almost a like number, sewage plants.

Similarly, state legislatures have also responded to the added needs of cities by permitting municipalities to qualify for expanded authority. Massachusetts has five options that it offers its cities, the most liberal calling for a home-rule charter drawn up by a local commission and ratified by the

---

[26] John F. Dillon, *Commentaries on the Law of Municipal Corporations* (Boston: Little, Brown, 1911), 5th ed., Section 237.

EXHIBIT 8-2   Activities Which Can and Cannot Be Handled Locally

Activities Which Can and Cannot be Handled Locally

FUNCTIONS	LOCAL ACTIVITIES WHICH CAN BE HANDLED BY A LOCALITY OF		AREAWIDE ACTIVITIES WHICH CANNOT BE HANDLED LOCALLY
	10,000 POPULATION	25,000 OR MORE	
Police	Patrol Routine investigation Traffic control	Same	Crime laboratory Special investigation Training Communications
Fire	Fire company (minimal)	Fire companies (better)	Training Communications Special investigations

Streets
  highways
	Local streets,
	  sidewalks, alleys:
	    Repairs, cleaning,
	    snow removal,
	    lighting, trees
		Same	Expressways
			Major arteries

Transportation			Mass transit Airport Port Terminals
Refuse	Collection	Same	Disposal
Water and sewer	Local mains	Same	Treatment plants Trunk lines

Parks and
  recreation
	Local parks
	Playgrounds
	Recreation centers
	Tot-lots
	Swimming pool
	  (25 m.)
		Same plus
		Community center
		Skating rink
		Swimming pool
		  (50 m.)
			Large parks, zoo
			Museum
			Concert hall
			Stadium
			Golf courses

Libraries	Branch (small)	Branch (larger)	Central reference

Education	Elementary	Elementary
		Secondary
			Community
			  colleges
			Vocational
			  schools

FUNCTIONS	LOCAL ACTIVITIES WHICH CAN BE HANDLED BY A LOCALITY OF		AREAWIDE ACTIVITIES WHICH CANNOT BE HANDLED LOCALLY
	10,000 POPULATION	25,000 OR MORE	
Welfare	Social services	Same	Assistance payments
Health		Public health services Health center	Hospital
Environmental protection		Environmental sanitation	Air pollution control
Land Use and Development	Local planning Zoning Urban renewal	Same plus Housing and building code enforcement	Broad planning Building and housing standards
Housing	Public housing management	Public housing management & construction	Housing subsidy allocation

These listings suggest dividing lines between local and regional or national capabilities regarding a variety of community functions. A further division is shown for localities of 10,000 and 25,000 or more in size.

Source: Advisory Commission on Intergovernmental Relations, *Governmental Functions and Processes: Local and Areawide* (Washington, D.C.: Government Printing Office, 1974), p. 9.

electorate. Somewhat more than one-half of the states now make provision for municipal government under home rule, and two-thirds of all of the nation's cities of more than 200,000 population have taken advantage of the privilege.

Even though local powers have been strengthened with respect to the powers of the state, serious dissatisfactions do remain. One concerns funding, for example, in education. Since the beginning of the twentieth century, all of the states have been aiding local schools financially, because the states have greater sources of revenue than the cities do. Despite increased urban strength in the state legislature that cities have secured recently by overcoming the silent gerrymandering that has worked to the advantage of rural constituencies, "aid formulae have been geared," declares Friedman, "to counties and sometimes town or township needs but seldom to the needs of municipalities."[27] A major reason why the recent antigerrymander-

[27] Robert S. Friedman, "State Politics and Highways," in Herbert Jacobs and Kenneth H. Vines, eds., *Politics in the American States* (Boston: Little, Brown, 1965), p. 431.

ing policy of "one man, one vote" has failed to increase state aid to the cities lies in the fact that the augmented representation for metropolitan areas has gone principally to their suburbs.[28]

Besides financial support, administrative control exercised by the states over municipal government is a second serious source of difficulty for American cities. In the twentieth century, the states have moved toward a parallel development with urban government to raise the quality of local services, insure statewide uniformity, and achieve greater efficiency and economy. Thus the state public utilities commission and the state department of education have been empowered to regulate local utilities and school systems. A general fault that has been found with the states in this regard is that they curb local governments rather than help them. For example, many argue that the states could engage in more training of municipal officials and in expanding municipal facilities instead of regulating them.

RELATIONS BETWEEN THE CITY AND THE FEDERAL GOVERNMENT

Relations between municipal and state government are augmented by federally supplied funds and services, and by controls too. The consequent tripartite system entails severe operational difficulties at the same time that federal resources greatly increase local opportunity.

Five Types of Activity

The multiplex presence of the federal government on the local scene has been lucidly schematized by Morton Grodzins as comprising five types of activity.[29]

1 Federal "direct-to-people" services and programs are exemplified by mail delivery, veterans benefits, and Social Security.

2 Federally organized local governments operating as independent entites provide many things, two among them being environmental protection and the stabilization of the milk market.

3 Certain federally organized governments function in concert with municipal and/or state administrations, such as public-housing authorities and selective-service districts.

4 Large—and numerous—federal grants are funneled through the states. These embrace public assistance, highways, education, and public health.

[28] James Reichley, "The Political Containment of the Cities," in The American Assembly, *The States and the Urban Crisis* (Englewood Cliffs, N.J.: Prentice-Hall, 1970), pp. 169–95.

[29] "Federal and State Impacts," in Daniel J. Elazar, ed., *The American System* (Chicago: Rand McNally, 1966), pp. 190–97.

5 Other federal grants, like those for urban transit, the school lunch program, and technical assistance for law enforcement go directly to the local government itself.

This list is not all-inclusive even though it is extensive. Indeed, actions of the federal government like military procurement and the administration of fair labor standards have substantial consequences for urban areas although they are not, so to speak, carried out locally.

Cooperative Federalism

In the Nixon and Ford Administrations, a more concerted federal program attacked local problems nationally through added resources and uniform standards. Included in this nationwide effort toward "cooperative federalism" was the intention of upgrading the quality of municipal government principally through greater local effort and coordination. Of signal importance has been direct revenue sharing, that is, a federal distribution of some of its income-tax revenues according to population, local tax effort, and local poverty conditions, a program that first materialized in 1972. Between that date and the scheduled expiration of the original revenue-sharing legislation in 1976, 38,000 units of state and local government received $30.2 billion. Although initial results of revenue sharing have been to relieve state and local governments of a part of their fiscal burdens, doubt attaches as to whether revenue sharing is leading to improved government administration, major changes in tax policies, or governmental reform.[30]

Estimates at present differ as to the net effect of cooperative federalism although its need is generally conceded. One particular bone of contention is the sharing of control over highways, housing, and welfare with the local community.[31] Another concerns the impact of direct and indirect federal fiscal policies, such as tax write-offs and investment credits, and how they work to the advantage or detriment of the various segments of the urban locality.[32] In fact, the general policy of Washington in this respect has been widely interpreted as a reduction of federal leadership at the local level in favor of an enlarged role for the states. One clear consequence of the process has been the rapid expansion of special districts stemming from the

[30] David A. Caputo, ed., "General Revenue Sharing and Federalism," special volume of the *Annals of the American Academy of Political and Social Science, 419* (May 1975), pp. 1–142.

[31] Charles J. Goetz, *What Is Revenue Sharing?* (Washington, D.C.: Urban Institute, 1972) is a useful source on issues and prospects.

[32] See Edward W. Meyers and John J. Musial, *Urban Incentive Tax Credits* (New York: Praeger, 1974).

requirement of local coordination to qualify for federal funds.[33]

Both the Conference of Mayors and the League of Cities have called for continued federal support for cities though in a variety of not uncontested ways. Also indicative of stronger interest in—and controversy over—federal intervention in urban affairs has been the rise of organized lobbying by municipalities in Washington. (For federal impact on municipal finance see Chapter 9.)

INTEREST GROUPS AND POLITICAL PARTIES

The exercise of formal government authority in the local area is determined, ultimately, by a complex political process. In its general outline, this is an intricate web of conflict resolution carried on by the electorate, the media, voluntary associations (including political parties), and particular individuals. Throughout the whole scheme of local politics the two most important focal points are interest groups and political parties.

INTEREST GROUPS

Interest, or pressure, groups are issue-centered organized components of the local community competing for governmental power, oftentimes acting through political parties. By lobbying, influencing public opinion, electioneering, screening candidates for public office, keeping officeholders informed, reviewing state and federal legislation affecting the city, and evaluating the performance of officials, interest groups have continuing influence over governmental affairs in their vicinity.

Types of Interest Groups

Understandably, interest groups take many forms, and their net effect is usually difficult to assess. One major study of urban politics defined four types of pressure groups according to kind and degree of concern.[34]

First are the groups having broad interests and a record of continuing intervention in government. These groups emphasize "process," and are concerned with the flow of actions involved in decision making. One example is the group that insists on ongoing publicity being given the city's budget-making process.

---

[33] Comment on this in the context of metropolitan problems is to be found in John C. Bollens and Henry J. Schmandt, *The Metropolis* (New York: Harper & Row, 1975), 3rd ed., pp. 369–71.

[34] Wallace S. Sayre and Herbert Kaufman, *Governing New York City* (New York: Russell Sage Foundation, 1960), pp. 481ff.

A protest group demonstrating in Boston in favor of housing for the elderly.

Second, some groups have narrow interests, say, in the schools, although like the first type they, too, take a continuing interest in government. This second type tends to focus on program, on what the decisions made by officials actually result in accomplishing. Thus a racial group will protest discrimination in hiring teachers.

The third sort of interest group also has a broad range of goals, but is involved only occasionally. Groups falling into this category are inclined to address themselves, for instance, to proposals for establishing new agencies like a civilian review board to oversee the police.

Finally, there are groups that have both a narrow range of interests and a record of only infrequent participation. They are issue-oriented, being concerned over what is happening from time to time. One case in point would be the interest group that becomes active when an expressway is being routed in a particular direction.

In another attempt to summarize the types of urban interest groups, Banfield and Wilson cite one overriding criterion.[35] They refer to the existence of "two mentalities" among pressure groups in the metropolis.

One evidences the middle-class ethos oriented to efficient, impartial, and even restrained administration. This type is encountered most clearly in the more affluent suburbs and among business, Protestant, and the older trade-union groups. In the more well-to-do suburbs, for example, one finds many interest groups advocating public-welfare legislation for the good of the general public. Similarly, the middle-class mentality emphasizes an ethic of self-reliance. However, this orientation is not hostile to privately organized welfare activities or even public programs for that matter because such work is thought to demonstrate responsible leadership, particularly when it is outside the sordidness of professional politics.

The viewpoint of the other category of local interest groups is more akin to the outlook of dependent populations generally, such as immigrants and the poor. This view looks at public decision making in terms of material benefits and narrow favoritism. Such a conception of government condones or at least accepts corruption among officials. Those so persuaded think of their city not as a single, interdependent entity but as a mosaic of different peoples and classes each of which is seeking its own interests, if necessary at the expense of others.

POLITICAL PARTIES

Political parties may be defined as formally organized associations contesting one another for government authority by means of election and appointment to office and, when out of power, by keeping the government in office under surveillance. Political parties involve the activities of interest groups in gaining and exercising power.

Local politics in America has not been a favorite subject of political science. This is due to the complexity of the local political process and possibly the belief that local politics are less important than state and national affairs. At any rate, Duane Lockard's five hypotheses merit use as a framework for the exposition of material in this complex and not wholly clear

[35] Edward C. Banfield and James Q. Wilson, *City Politics* (Cambridge, Mass.: Harvard University Press, 1963), pp. 45–46.

field.[36] These five principles are: (1) one-party dominance, (2) city-suburb polarization, (3) the importance of personalities, (4) diverse party types, and (5) nonpartisanship. These five principles possibly summarize the general features of organized political life in the urban United States at present.

One-Party Dominance

In any given city in America there is a strong tendency for one party to be repeatedly victorious at the polls. This fact relates to the socioeconomic makeup of the community and the continued attachments of its voters to one party or the other. It does not necessarily mean strong one-party rule because, locally, American parties suffer from weak organization. For one thing, local party affiliation does not correspond to the national parties and their stated policies. For another, some 60 percent of all American cities have nonpartisan elections, and their ballots show no party labels. In those municipalities that do retain the partisan system, however, one party or the other remains in office year after year without being replaced by its adversary.

Democratic Cities and Republican Suburbs

America's big cities, especially the nuclei of its metropolitan areas, tend to vote Democratic while their suburbs incline to be Republican. In the 1968 presidential election and despite the Republican victory nationwide, our SMSA's went Democratic more than they did Republican.[37]

There are obvious social and economic concomitants of this pattern of party identification. Trying to explain the Democratic proclivity of America's cities, Sorauf writes that the "very nature of the city" calls for government action. "Crime, unemployment, poverty, traffic snarls, and the other ills of the city, cry out for public solutions, and the Democratic party, more the advocate of positive government, is ideologically better able to advocate them."[38] Banfield and Wilson have described our metropolitan areas as characteristically polarized around the basic cleavages of "haves" and "have-nots," ethnic and racial groups, suburbanites and the central city, and also between Republicans and Democrats corresponding to these interests.[39]

If the inner cities are predominantly Democratic, it does not necessarily follow that all the suburbs surrounding them vote Republican. The wealthiest

[36] *The Politics of State and Local Government* (New York: Macmillan, 1963), pp. 239–52.

[37] Bureau of the Census, *Statistical Abstract of the United States: 1972,* op. cit., pp. 850, 870, and 890.

[38] Frank J. Sorauf, *Party Politics in America* (New York: Little, Brown, 1968), pp. 151–52.

[39] Banfield and Wilson, *op. cit.,* p. 35.

suburbs, of course, do so consistently. In general, the Republican appeal is strong among the new suburbanites who reason that the Republican party "better protects their new interests and status and because it is the political faith of the old-time residents whose friendship is cultivated by the new-comers."[40] This factor, however, does not long override socioeconomic cleavages and a switch back, by many, to the Democratic party. Thus the future appears to augur party competition in our suburban communities if only because they will witness continued growth,[41] and because the existence of racial and ethnic suburbs promises to add strength to the Democrats in suburbia.[42]

Personalities Rather than Issues

In America's local politics, personalities and personal relationships are emphasized and issues played down. Personal popularity, ethnicity, and long-term residence in the local community usually comprise major assets for candidates in local elections. In Boston, for example, neither newspapers, civic associations, nor labor unions count for very much in the election of councilmen. "In the main," says Banfield, "a candidate makes his appeal [in Boston] not as the representative of some organized interest (such as the labor unions or home-owners' associations) but as a 'personality'!"[43] In a like vein, Sayre and Kaufman carefully review the nominating structure of New York politics. They take note of the common belief that personality, a reputation for integrity, actual performance, and membership in an ethnic minority make a man a local vote-getter. They add: "Whether or not any of these factors is as important as the inner core of the parties seem to think, the fact that these considerations enter into the deliberations on the selection of regular nominees indicates how outsiders participate indirectly in the nominating process, at least as far as ticket leaders are concerned."[44]

Four General Party Types

Still another configuration of American city politics is diversity. According to Lockhard, local party activity in the United States falls into four contrasting patterns. (1) There are cities dominated by a political machine. (2) Commu-

---

[40] Robert C. Wood, *Suburbia: Its People and Their Politics* (Boston: Houghton Mifflin, 1958), p. 138.

[41] The view of Richard M. Scammon and Benjamin J. Wattenberg, *The Real Majority* (New York: Coward-McCann, 1970), p. 294.

[42] Consult the studies of suburban voting behavior in Frederick M. Wirt et al., *On the City's Rim: Politics and Policy in Suburbia* (Lexington, Mass.: D. C. Heath, 1972), Pt. 2.

[43] Edward C. Banfield, *Big City Politics* (New York: Random House, 1965), p. 46.

[44] Sayre and Kaufman, op. cit., p. 156.

nities exist in which well organized parties are in competition with each other. (3) Some cities are nominally nonpartisan but in actuality evidence strong factionalism. (4) Not a few of our cities are simply politically disorganized, so that neither parties not stable factions are present in their political life. A few examples can suffice to bring out these different types.

Machine politics had its heyday in the United States during the period of heavy European immigration. Today where conditions permit, the machine continues to exist. In-migration like that of blacks to urban centers definitely favors it. One such case at present is Chicago. There, (the late) Mayor Richard Daley's Cook County Democratic organization must be credited—or charged—with preserving the idea of machine politics.

Black interest in political power, even separatism, has been spurred by the growing realization of two things: that blacks have few policy-making positions in government and private institutions; and that those positions which they do occupy have little power owing to their restriction pretty much to black constituencies. Yet, change has been taking place, and substantial political gains have been made by blacks in America's central cities recently. In Detroit in the period 1967 to 1977, blacks came to occupy the position of mayor, county sheriff, police chief, and school superintendent. They also greatly increased their membership in city council and on the Detroit school board. In 1977 blacks composed 21 percent of the Detroit police force, up from only 5 percent a decade earlier.[45]

Cleveland is similar to Chicago in some respects, but it lacks the machinelike political organization of Cook County for several reasons. One concerns the relative lack of patronage that Chicago's crucial role in national politics provides it with. Another is the lack of anyone with Mayor Daley's astuteness as a power broker. As a result, Cleveland may be described as a community in which relatively well-organized parties are competitive with each other—and where charismatic personalities, notably those of Carl Stokes and Dennis Kucinich recently, make a substantial difference.

Nonpartisan Politics and Class Competition

In two-thirds of America's cities with a population of 25,000 or more, elections are required by law to be nonpartisan. This relates to Lockhard's fifth point, that like manager-council administration, nonpartisan elections are advanced ostensibly "to take municipal affairs out of politics" and on this basis have the support of the higher social classes though they are opposed by those on the lower rungs. Nonpartisanship gives an added advantage to those already established in the community. For example, the news media gain influence because candidates cannot enjoy a party label. Again, nonpartisanship enables superior social groups to reach informal agreement

[45] New York Times (July 24, 1977), p. 1.

through their existing channels of communication: chambers of commerce, service clubs, and the like.

Whether these relative advantages, which have been confirmed in small and medium size cities,[46] are also true of metropolitan communities remains in some doubt today. It may be that we are witnessing a new style of urban politics in our large cities, so that ideology rather than party affiliation based largely on the immediate spoils of office is motivating active participation. To such activitists—usually intellectuals—housing reform, racial integration, ecology, and other liberal causes are to be promoted by means of face-to-face "nonpartisan" canvassing rather than partisan patronage and preference. Additionally, ethnoreligious cleavages have recently come to the fore in the politics of many cities in the United States. Two explanations have been offered for this phenomenon: one, that ethnic and religious solidarity continues, as always, to shape one's political views, and that such ties are simply more manifest today; and two, that enterprising politicians seek a simple way of mobilizing voter support for themselves and, therefore, appeal to such traditional loyalties instead of trying to deal with the complex issues.[47] Doubtlessly, the traditional principle of liberal government, that interest groups may legitimately pressure for the redress of grievances, forms the legal basis of the resurgence of the ethnic factor in our political life.[48]

URBAN POWER STRUCTURES

Discussion of political activity in the city leads to the question that any number of recent investigations into urban life have entertained: Is the decision-making process of a given city in the hands of a centralized structure? In answer it may be concluded that the exercise of power in American society, including its local communities, is presently conceived of in terms of two opposing models of thought, elitism and pluralism.

THE ELITIST INTERPRETATION

The elitist theory derives from European writers, such as Vilfredo Pareto, Gaetano Mosca, and Roberto Michels. The presence of an elitist power

---

[46] Phillips Cutright, "Nonpartisan Electoral Systems in American Cities," in Thomas R. Dye and Brett W. Hawkins, eds., *Politics in the Metropolis* (Columbus, Ohio: Charles E. Merrill, 1967), pp. 298–314.

[47] See Raymond E. Wolfinger, *The Politics of Progress* (Englewood Cliffs, N.J.: Prentice-Hall, 1974).

[48] An analysis covering the last few years is contained in Mark R. Levy and Michael S. Kramer, *The Ethnic Factor: How America's Minorities Decide Elections* (New York: Simon and Schuster, 1973).

structure in America has been studied—and criticized—most forcefully by C. Wright Mills. Elitism holds that any complex society requires centralized coordination. Accordingly, the dominating elites consist of those persons who are in controlling positions of authority in economic, military, and political organizations. Moreover, these elites make use of the media of communication, educational and religious institutions, and also cultural means to persuade, propagandize, threaten, or otherwise influence people and further solidify their hold on the social structure.

In the conclusions of the elitist school, local community power in the cities of the United States today rests principally with businessmen. This contrasts somewhat with the English case, as one study has shown.[49] In the two American cities reviewed, business representation among key influentials was 67 and 75 percent. In English City it was much less, only 25 percent. The difference was said to reflect the higher status accorded professional and trade-union leadership in Britain than in the United States.

While recognizing local differences, Delbert Miller sets down four points for American cities as a whole according to the elitist hypothesis.[50] (1) Businessmen are overrepresented and dominate community policymaking in most cities. (2) Local government is a relatively weak power center, with the city council subordinate to the dominant business forces in the community. (3) The influence of certain persons, groups, and institutions is significantly curtailed and neutralized, among them professionals in education, welfare, religion, and mass communication. (4) Key influentials, the "economic dominants," live outside the city limits but maintain active interest in the central city.

Atlanta

Perhaps more than any other, Floyd Hunter's investigation of Regional City (Atlanta, Georgia) first applied the elitist theory to the study of community power in America. Using the reputational method, that is, having informants identify local figures they deemed to be decision-makers, Hunter found those persons chosen as power-wielders who occupied top positions in Atlanta's business firms.[51]

According to Hunter, influentials operate politically through informal and formal channels, with committees being a favored device because they per-

---

[49] William H. Form and Delbert C. Miller, *Industry, Labor, and Community* (New York: Harper & Brothers, 1960).

[50] Delbert C. Miller, "Democracy and Decision-Making in the Community Power Structure," in William V. D'Antonio and Howard J. Ehrich, eds., *Power and Democracy in America* (South Bend, Ind.: University of Notre Dame Press, 1961), p. 61.

[51] Floyd Hunter, *Community Power Structure* (Chapel Hill, N.C.: University of North Carolina Press, 1953), p. 61.

mit opportune participation for specific purposes. The Regional City power elite, Hunter observed, work through a hierarchy of subordinate leaders. The first level is occupied by the owners and top executives of the large industrial and commercial companies. Below them are second-rate personnel such as the top-ranking public officials and private executives like corporate lawyers. Two still lower strata complete the urban power structure as visualized by Hunter. Third-raters include civic agency executives and media personalities. Finally, there are the fourth-rate ministers, teachers, and small-business managers. In the entire decision-making process of Regional City, wrote Hunter, "The first two ratings are personnel who are said 'to set the line of policy,' while the latter two groups 'hold the line.' "

THE PLURALIST INTERPRETATION

The pluralists argue that despite the appearance of centralized control in any given city, in actual fact decision-making rests in the hands of a broad spectrum of participants. Like their opponents, the pluralists too have impressive forebears, among them Alexis de Tocqueville and James Madison.

Pluralists believe in the existence of a network of influential individuals and groups affecting public policy as well as the decisions of private organizations. These agents may facilitate measures in some instances, and veto them in others. They make those in seemingly very powerful positions responsive to the wishes if not of everyone, then at least of the greater, organized part of the local population. Incremental, step-by-step social change is thus fostered, and this in turn maintains the stability of the whole local system.

New Haven

The pluralistic conception of community power is well represented by Robert Dahl's study *Who Governs?*, based on research done in New Haven, Connecticut.[52] Dahl hypothesized that control calls for organization, and that organization makes it necessary for subleaders and auxiliaries to be recognized and rewarded. Dissension and conflict are thus implied along with unity, and the monolithic pyramid assumed by the elitists is probably an invalid idea.

Dahl determined that New Haven's life had, before 1953, exhibited "a pattern of independent sovereignties with spheres of influence." For a brief period subsequently, there had existed "a coalition of chieftains." Then under Mayor Richard C. Lee the pattern had become one of "a grand coali-

[52] *Who Governs? Power and Democracy in an American City* (New Haven, Conn.: Yale University Press, 1961). See also Nelson W. Polsby, *Community Power and Political Theory* (New Haven, Conn.: Yale University Press, 1963), an outgrowth of the original New Haven research.

tion of coalitions." The political parties of New Haven stood somewhat apart from the decision-making process in action, a process that Dahl chose to refer to as "rival sovereignties fighting it out." He concluded that the pluralistic scene which he described involved economic resources but also political skills of very great importance too, altogether "a widespread consensus on the American creed of democracy and equality," a creed accepted by the professional politicians as well.

ELITISM AND PLURALISM RECONSIDERED

Both elitist and pluralistic theories have their adherents in the study of America's cities. In addition, although these two positions represent opposing schools of thought, there are internal differences within each.

Certain writers profess a monolithic pyramidal conception of the local organization of power. Others recognize the presence of a dual structure, two persistent factions in contention with each other and, for that matter, even a coalitional system of shifting alliances. Still others conclude that in the last analysis greatest validity attaches to the idea of an amorphous system lacking any persistent power organization whatsoever.

Using these four models of community power structure—pyramidal, factional, coalitional, and amorphous, Walton reviewed studies of 55 communities, many of them very large cities, in an attempt to systematize their findings. In his own words, he summed up his findings as follows.

1 The type of power structure identified by studies that rely on a single method may well be an artifact of that method.

2 Social integration and region, variables which reflect something of the political life of the community, show some association with power structure.

3 Economic variables reflecting patterns characteristic of increasing industralization are moderately associated with less concentrated power structures.[53]

To amplify, Walton's conclusions stress that the method of study used would appear to make a difference. For example, subjects asked to designate decision-makers by their reputations may actually endow their designees with illusory power. The demographic characteristics of the community are also important variables. As one case in point, an urban population heterogenous for ethnicity, religion, and occupation inclines to be associated with a diversified authority system rather than a more monolithic structure. Also, a long history endows local business leaders with social status, and this reinforces their influence apart from their place in the community's busi-

[53] John Walton, "Substance and Artifact: The Current Status of Research on Community Power Structure," *American Journal of Sociology, 71* (January 1966), pp. 430–38.

ness life. The type of issue calling for decision is yet another contributory factor.

Finally, there are particular situational factors too. As one recent study of four Wisconsin cities asserts, a given urban community may possess a distinctive civic culture having substantial consequences, such as its tradition of political leadership continually modifying the area's economic base.[54] Another analysis of the "power structure" of New York, Philadelphia, and Cleveland published in 1971 tends to view present-day American cities as having unique mixtures of mechanisms of control and autonomy, so that possibly a taxonomy of constituent elements might best advance our comprehension of them.[55]

The contentions of the elitists and pluralists are thus inconclusive about power in the contemporary American city. However, a number of general observations do seem in order.

First, the two positions probably correspond basically to two divergent politico-philosophical perspectives. Elitists tend to be hypercritical of what they regard as an authoritarian encroachment upon democracy. The pluralists profess to see much more democracy than is possibly actually in existence.

In addition, the elitists tend to think of the entire institutional order of a city, business and politics alike, as being subject to some common form of determination, whereas the pluralists concentrate more exclusively on the political system as separate from the economy. This creates disparities in their findings. For this reason, reviewing a group of community power studies, Colin Bell and Howard Newby of the University of Essex have of late argued for greater comparability of data as essential to progress in community research.[56]

Finally, there is the historical factor. Is it not reasonable to believe that the time makes some difference as to who governs a city? May it not be that as our cities grow that political decision-making would supplant the more centralized control by economic dominants in a more economically-focused period? At least one writer has already reached that conclusion, declaring that "there is a trend in the United States away from centralized forms of power structure in local communities and toward more pluralistic structures."[57]

---

[54] Robert R. Alford, *Bureaucracy and Participation: Political Culture in Four Wisconsin Cities* (Chicago: Rand McNally, 1969).

[55] David Rogers, *The Management of Big Cities: Interest Groups and Social Change Strategies* (Beverly Hills, Calif.: Sage, 1971), Ch. 6.

[56] Colin Bell and Howard Newby, *Community Studies: An Introduction to the Sociology of the Local Community* (New York: Praeger, 1971), Ch. 7.

[57] Claire W. Gilbert, "Community Power and Decision-Making," in Terry N. Clark, ed., *Community Power and Decision-Making* (San Francisco, Calif.: Chandler, 1968), p. 155, the conclusion incorporating 167 studies.

One new empirical study of Woodruff, a fictitiously named midwestern city, makes it plain that this transition may include stages of indeterminacy in which the older, established business leaders of the city are at odds with the younger, more change-minded political leadership, so that for a while at least nothing gets done.[58] Another field study, this in Syracuse, New York, conducted by Linton Freeman, found the city's elitist decision-makers dominant at an earlier time had been succeeded later by a more dispersed set of interest-group leaders.[59] Such findings have led to the earlier concern with "Who governs?" giving way in research into urban power to questions of "What is the decision-making structure?" "In what kinds of cities?" and "With what outcomes?"[60]

CONCLUSION

Urban government and politics are closely related aspects of the exercise of power in the local community. The former denotes the machinery of legitimate control and service, the latter the process of gaining access to that machinery.

The American city embodies the English model of local government, which has promoted not only a high degree of popular participation but also a broad range of local authority that is independent of other municipalities and of the state as well. Despite its common antecedents in English law, municipal government in America today follows three different forms of organization, the mayor, manager, and commission types, each with its own merits and weaknesses.

The multiplication of metropolitan areas at a time of rising expectations with respect to government has revealed the extent to which local government is typically fragmented in the nation. Numerous responses have been forthcoming, none wholly satisfactory in assuring sufficient services or in coping with the regional problems that prevail. Nonetheless, progress toward reform and reorganization, much of it in concert with state and federal government, has not been insubstantial.

As might be expected, the local political process displays no small degree of complexity today. Both interest groups and political parties share in this pattern. One consequence for scholarship on the political conduct of our local communities is uncertainty as to whether power lies, ultimately,

[58] Albert Schaffer and Ruth Connor Shaffer, *Woodruff: A Study of Community Decision Making* (Chapel Hill, N.C.: University of North Carolina Press, 1970).

[59] Linton C. Freeman, *Patterns of Local Community Leadership* (Indianapolis, Ind.: Bobbs-Merrill, 1968).

[60] See Charles M. Bonjean, Terry N. Clark, and Robert L. Lineberry, eds., *Community Politics: A Behavioral Approach* (New York: Free Press, 1971).

with a unified body of elites or is widely diffused among a sizeable number of contentious segments.

FOR FURTHER READING

Joan B. Aron, *The Quest for Regional Cooperation* (Berkeley, Calif.: University of California Press, 1969). The conflicts between the populations of the central city of New York and its suburbs.

Edward C. Banfield, ed., *Urban Government* (New York: Free Press, 1969). On planning, blacks in politics, reapportionment, and other subjects of current importance.

George Frederickson, ed., *Neighborhood Control in the 1970's: Politics, Administration, and Citizen Participation* (New York: Chandler, 1973). Reviews the prospects of decentralization at the local level.

Herbert J. Gans, *The Levittowners* (New York: Pantheon, 1967). Focuses on four questions in suburbia: the origin of the new community, the quality of its life, its effect on behavior, and its system of decision-making.

Ritchie P. Lowry, *Who's Running This Town?* (New York: Harper & Row, 1965). Small-town life in the United States and its community power structure.

Delbert C. Miller, *Leadership and Power in the Bos-Wash Megalopolis* (New York: John Wiley & Sons, 1975). A somewhat coherent community power structure is discerned in this heavily urbanized east coast urban region.

David Rogers and Willis D. Hawley, eds., *Improving the Quality of Urban Management* (Beverly Hills, Calif.: Sage, 1974). The problems facing local officials at present, such as decaying housing, inadequate mass transit, spiraling costs, and falling revenues.

Carol E. Thometz, *The Decision-Makers* (Dallas, Tex.: Southern Methodist University Press, 1963). An attempt to identify the power relationships in Dallas mainly through the reputational approach.

Frederick M. Wirt et al., *On the City's Rim: Politics and Policy in Suburbia* (Lexington, Mass.: D. C. Heath, 1972). Systematic research into the realities of suburban government.

CHAPTER 9

THE
URBAN ECONOMY

An urban economic system consists of the facilities and organization by which the community allocates its scarce resources of labor, land, and materials in order to meet its population's needs and wants. Though a separate entity, a city's economy also ties in with the national economy and the larger social structure. For these reasons this chapter covers five subjects.

First, it examines the economy of the city as a component of the national economy. Second, the large and populous urban area is viewed as an object of economic metropolitanization, in other words, as a largely independent system of local production and distribution. Third, the city is described in light of the political economy and the prevailing sociocultural order. Fourth, the chapter focuses on the adjustive aspects of the economy, particularly on industrial and consumer relations. And, finally, a section on municipal finance is included for insight into the public economy at the local level.

THE CITY AND THE LARGER ECONOMY

Here in modern America, virtually any given city is an element in a single and enormous, interdependent national economic system. Examining the place of cities in the American economy a generation ago, the National Resources Committee observed that our urban centers were even then only quasiindependent economic entities in the national structure. Their participation in the larger economy continues today even more closely, in fact.

During the nineteenth century, America's cities had added an important manufacturing role to their original trading function. During the twentieth century they developed still further from a preoccupation with industry to the creation of a complex commercial and service type of enterprise. This transition was most pronounced in our largest cities. Typically, all of the major cities of the United States serve as integral components of the total national economy. In addition, any sizable community also performs a diversified economic role for its own population.

The relationship of our cities to the total economic system of the United States may be observed in some detail in the study of one illustrative metropolitan area: St. Louis. Important to note are locational factors, the historic development of business and industry, and the linkage of the St. Louis metropolitan economy with that of the nation as a whole.[1]

ST. LOUIS: A REGIONAL DOMINANT

A SMSA of 2.4 million persons in 1970, the tenth largest in the country, and with a territory in excess of 4100 square miles, St. Louis stretches over 40 miles of river flats at the confluence of the Mississippi and Missouri Rivers. Originally a French fur-trading post in 1764, St. Louis became a river port and a center for the westward movement. By 1970, metropolitan St. Louis was second only to Chicago in railroad transport; was an important marketing center for meat, dairy products, and grain; and claimed a sizable share of the nation's production of leather, beer, chemicals, machinery, automobiles, furniture, and nondurable goods such as women's wear and paper. With the passing of time, St. Louis' industry lost its local character and became instead a supplier of a much broader market in machine tools, aircraft, and electrical equipment. In American auto assembly, St. Louis ranks only behind Detroit.

The East Central Upland Region

The St. Louis metropolitan area may be considered a part of the central-eastern upland region of the United States, which stretches from the Shenan-

[1] For historical data on our metropolitan areas, see Donald J. Bogue and Calvin L. Beale, *Economic Areas of the United States* (Glencoe, Ill.: Free Press, 1961).

St. Louis overlooking the Mississippi, in 1855.

doah Valley and the Blue Ridge Mountains of Virginia over 215,000 square miles of high land ending in Missouri's Ozark Plateau. Some 17 million people make up the regional population, many of whom inhabit other metropolitan areas, notably Cincinnati, Nashville, and Little Rock. The border highlands divide the corn belt and industrial North from the Old Cotton Belt of the South. Tobacco, livestock, grain and soybean farming, and forestry comprise the major part of the region's agriculture.

Minerals are plentiful in the highland region. Besides coal, which is now beginning to benefit from competition with oil and gas, the region produces from two-fifths to more than two-thirds of the nation's domestic supply of bauxite, mica, and lead. Both the Tennessee Valley Authority, with its flood-control operations, hydroelectric power, and manufacture of fertilizers, and the location of atomic-energy facilities near Knoxville, Paducah, and Portsmouth have materially benefited the economy of the highland region. Nonetheless, due to mechanization, employment in agriculture is expected to decline, but the rising prices of both food and petroleum may be a retarding factor here and in mining too. Even so, the region's population will probably cluster more around cities of various types, and some people will leave the region entirely.

The St. Louis Area Metropolitan Economy

The St. Louis metropolitan economy has a nonagricultural labor force of about 900,000, as of 1970.[2] Its occupational composition closely resembles that of our other metropolitan areas with the largest numbers employed, successively, in manufacturing; wholesale and retail trade; services; and transportation and public utilities. Heavy industry gives St. Louis a somewhat higher than average proportion of operatives. Yet St. Louis is also one of the nation's top ten wholesale and retail centers.

St. Louis's advantages, which augur economic progress there, are its transportation facilities (e.g., the second largest trucking center in the country); abundant water resources and plenty of fuel (though oil is cheaper in areas closer to its sources); the absence of any very serious waste-disposal problem; an adequate labor supply; and good economic balance and diversification.

Metropolitan St. Louis has certain economic shortcomings at present that need to be balanced against the positive factors in the area's economic life. First, the economic growth of the adjacent territory has been sluggish, and this has hurt St. Louis. The economic weakness of the region has added to another, more immediate problem in the city itself: the shortage of industrial sites, which has raised land prices. Furthermore, the area's integration into the national economy makes it quite sensitive to changes taking place elsewhere. Thus its dependence on military supply results in sudden declines and upturns according to outside circumstances. In 1970–1971, the total work force of metropolitan St. Louis lost 14,000 persons.[3] Though generally growing over the years, St. Louis has been losing ground as a wholesale distribution center to new metropolitan areas, notably Los Angeles and Dallas-Fort Worth. Uniform wages, production requiring inputs from abroad, efficient transportation, and product diversification all tend to pull skill-oriented industries into metropolitan areas. St. Louis is benefiting from this. On the other hand, by creating social and governmental problems, metropolitanization increases certain costs, but these can be offset by rising regional demand. It is here in the comparatively slow economic growth of mid-America that the economic performance of metropolitan St. Louis has suffered recently.

THE METROPOLITAN ECONOMY

Treating a city like St. Louis as a component in the national economy should not obscure the fact that the typical urban agglomeration also constitutes a

---

[2] Bureau of the Census, *Statistical Abstract of the United States: 1972* (Washington, D.C.: Government Printing Office, 1972), p. 884. For the St. Louis economy see also John C. Bollens, ed., *Exploring the Metropolitan Community* (Berkeley and Los Angeles, Calif.: University of California Press, 1964).

[3] Bureau of the Census, *Statistical Abstract of the United States: 1972,* op. cit., p. 884.

distinct metropolitan economy in itself. The immediate metropolitan area makes up a coordinated system of production and distribution for the immediate population which, given today's economic capability, numbers into the hundreds of thousands and even millions. In fact, so decisively has the metropolitanization of our economy occurred that two-thirds of all workers in the United States now reside in metropolitan areas.

The development of St. Louis into an advanced metropolitan market as well as a regional hub has paralleled the recent economic history of the United States in general. Because the consumer has greater impact today than the presence of raw materials does, industry has become more market-oriented. Nationally uniform wage levels and flexible transport and communication have led to the erosion of specialized production by particular cities in favor of all-round output in every metropolitan center itself. This is generally true despite occasional intensely specialized production, Rochester, New York, for instance, for optical equipment.

A progressive homogenization of the American economy has thus been taking place. Accordingly, industrial structures have become more uniform for all regions of the nation since World War II. The South is an exception but that region too is now moving in the same direction. Locational factors continue to be felt though their effect is more selective now. Technological innovation, administrative skills, financial and governmental resources, efficient transportation, quality labor, high income levels giving local populations strength in the market—such factors combine to create the metropolitan-centered economy, which though it has regional and national characteristics, is also decidedly metropolitan.

ITS CHANGING LOCATIONAL PATTERN

The metropolitan economy reveals itself in a dynamic central city-suburban pattern of location. This involves land use, costs, and economies in a concentration into (1) economically significant cores, including commercial precincts of offices, retail stores, parking garages, and storage facilities, and industrial areas of factories, railroads, and docks concentrated in the central city; and (2) an arrangement of other land uses for residential and recreational purposes generally in a pattern of dispersion to the surrounding territory.

The locational pattern of the metropolitan economy is undergoing much change at present. For one thing, the central city is declining in terms of employment opportunities for its own resident work force. In the decade from 1960 to 1970 in our 20 largest SMSAs, the total employment of the central cities dropped from 11.6 million to 11.2, while in their suburban rings employment rose from 10.6 million to 14.9![4] It should be noted though, as

[4] Bureau of Labor Statistics, "Occupational Characteristics of Urban Workers," *Monthly Labor Review* (October 1971), pp. 21–32.

Charlotte Fremon has recently observed, that at the same time central-city population fell at an even faster rate, leaving more jobs proportionately than had existed earlier even if these might not be filled by the inner-city residents themselves owing to their relative lack of education and training.[5]

Responsible for the drift of economic enterprise from the core to the metropolitan periphery are three interrelated factors.

One is technological, namely, motor transport and electronic communication, both of which give business and industry flexibility with respect to location.

Another concerns the replacement of the old "gravity-flow" approach to manufacturing, which used to concentrate production facilities vertically in multistory buildings, by the new "continous-flow" arrangement in sprawling one-story structures that gives not only added efficiency but also the greater amenities that workers desire today. Therefore, the industrial parks that today dot the metropolitan landscape vie for locational space with suburban business offices and shopping plazas—and even residential use.

The third factor motivating the current dispersion of business and industry in our metropolitan areas is the presence in the central city of a tangle of social and environmental pathologies, including crime, intergroup tensions, congestion, noise, air pollution, and ill-suited buildings.

Despite the fact that trade and manufacturing both tend to relocate outside the inner areas of absolescent structures, deteriorated transportation, and increasing crime, certain economic factors continue to work in support of the central city:

The first is the type of industry that needs labor at lower than average wage levels, such as apparel plants employing Puerto Rican and black women in inner-city New York and Philadelphia.

A second is banks, insurance companies, and industrial firms that have large central headquarters. Here, though, peripheral locations well served by expressways are also coming into use. Yet in the ten-year period beginning in 1960, investment in office space in the country's SMSAs increased total space by 44 percent in what has been aptly described as "the most massive downtown office boom in the nation's history."[6] There is reason to believe that as the 28 million Americans employed in office-type jobs in 1965 rise to 59 million in the year 2000

[5] Charlotte Fremon, *Central City and Suburban Employment Growth: 1965–67* (Washington, D.C.: Urban Institute, 1970). Fremon's data may be assumed as representative for the decade as a whole.

[6] R. B. Armstrong, *The Office Industry* (New York: Regional Plan Association, 1972).

that the central business district will continue to share in the expansion to some extent.[7]

Third, the specialty manufacturing plant turning out custom-made products for use in particular assemblies, a business that needs to be close to other sources, is indicative of yet another viable economic function of the central city. The inner city remains the best locational site for these so-called confrontation industries based on much face-to-face contact. They include some fabricating plants and a variety of service industries, especially law, public relations, and consultation.

Fourth, the retailing of nonstandard commodities which can benefit from comparison shopping also appears to offer a prospect for the continued economic life of the core city, particularly its central business district. The fact that cities receive more in taxes from retail stores than they spend on them, as John Weicher has recently argued, indicates added significance for these trends now appearing.[8]

For other reasons too the central business district remains far from dead. It continues to hold on to the "flagship" facilities of department-store chains, to offer the greatest variety of merchandise, and to cater to the large number of white-collar workers there at least on a 9:00 to 5:00, Monday-to-Friday basis. The retention of the latter is aided by the centering of civic facilities like federal and state office buildings and public universities right at the heart of the city in a program of development supported by businessmen, social reformers, and inner-city minorities.

METROPOLITAN DEVELOPMENT

In the metropolitan economy, individual urban areas commonly organize for development, that is, to achieve growth and greater stability. Included are both publicly and privately financed programs and also the activities of development corporations specializing in that type of enterprise.[9]

By Public Agencies

The first category of development contains state as well as local efforts. Basically, states try to provide a legal framework favorable to businesses

---

[7] The projection is from Regina Beltz Armstrong, *The Office Industry: Patterns of Growth and Location* (Cambridge, Mass.: MIT Press, 1972), Ch. 2.

[8] John C. Weicher, "The Effect of Metropolitan Political Fragmentation on Central City Budgets," in David C. Sweet, ed., *Models of Urban Structure* (Lexington, Mass.: Lexington Books, 1973), pp. 177–203.

[9] Much information is available in Area Development Committee, *A Survey of Area Development Programs in the United States* (New York: Committee for Economic Development, 1960).

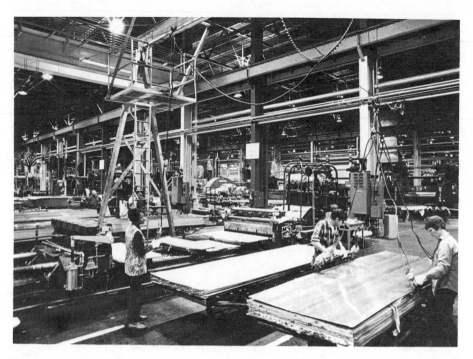

The great concentration of capital investment in modern industrial facilities.

within their borders. They do this by facilitating incorporation and enacting beneficial laws governing contracts, public safety and health, conditions of work, minimum wages, and industrial disability. States also furnish facilities to attract and retain industry, notably highways and bridges, water and sewage plants, and—more indirectly—schools, libraries, recreation areas, and rehabilitation centers. A state's tax structure is of course an additional variable of considerable importance.

Cities too are interested in broadening their manufacturing base; they often have development programs for this purpose, though this does not apply so much to purely residential suburbs and special-purpose communities. Generally, however, cities seek industry because of its tax yield and, more importantly, its employment opportunities. There are, to be sure, unfavorable possibilities that economic agencies try to skirt in attracting industry, such as the ugliness and polluting effects of heavy industry, congestion, the overtaxing of public facilities, and the attraction of "undesirable" minorities. Accordingly, a greater effort is now going into getting preferred industry that will give economic balance as well as environmental and social compatibility.

Urban redevelopment at the local level has been greatly augmented in the United States during the past 25 years. Such endeavors seek mainly to conserve declining sections within a city and to reconstruct those beyond repair. They depend heavily on funds from the federal government. First authorized by the Housing Act of 1949, urban clearance and redevelopment is today being carried on by hundreds of local public agencies, many of them departments of city government. Their purpose is to plan for the clearance of land for subsidized transfer to public or private developers. The land involved is being put to various uses, with possibly somewhat less than half of it committed to residential reuse. A third is serving commercial and industrial purposes, and about one-fourth is being employed for institutional improvement such as community colleges and public centers. From its inception in 1949 to 1971, the federal urban-renewal program had reserved upwards of $10 billion in 3080 separate projects.[10] (See the extended treatment of this subject in Chapter 20.)

By Private Enterprise

Privately financed programs of local urban development include the plans carried out by railroads, gas and electric utility companies, and banks. The railroads, for instance, are interested in the establishment of industrial parks along their lines rather than interstate highways, or at least in the promotion of the "piggy-back" haulage of containerized trucks. Utility companies make use of promotional activities, information services, and financial assistance to other groups for the purpose of attracting industry into their areas, or of inducing established firms to expand there. Banks cooperate a good deal with other organizations. These take in community development agencies, realtors, chambers of commerce, universities, private consulting firms, and various departments of local and state government.

By Community Development Corporations

Community development corporations existing today in more than 2000 municipalities in the United States endeavor to provide private firms with venture capital not available elsewhere. Most commonly, community development corporations sell stock locally to get money, and they invest it chiefly in the construction of plants. Earlier such corporations sought to counteract industrial shutdowns. Nowadays their efforts lean more toward economic expansion even on a regional basis.[11] The community development corporation demonstrates the interdependence of local economic and political

[10] Bureau of the Census, *Statistical Abstract of the United States: 1972,* op. cit., Table 1170, p. 694.

[11] An excellent example is Boston's Research and Development Corporation, organized in 1946, whose first beneficiary was Tracerlab.

institutions, because it often educates the public to the value of industry and leads to changes in zoning and the improvement of public services needed for local economic growth.

BUSINESS AND INDUSTRY

Both the national development of the economy and its metropolitanization refer to a high degree of internal structural uniformity. This is accomplished in business and industry through a common operational pattern: bureaucratic organization and corporate ownership.

BUREAUCRATIC ORGANIZATION

Bureaucracy is social organization distinguished by specialization, coordination, and appropriateness to large-scale enterprise. As bureaucracies the economic enterprises of any given city uphold the broader sociocultural pattern that prevails and, consequently, the values of the men and women taking part in them.

A Coordinated Hierarchy

In theory, a bureaucracy presupposes well defined jurisdictional areas called "offices" or "jobs." These are grouped into a coordinate hierarchy under the direction of superior officers conforming to the rules of the organization. Specialized training is also a prerequisite of bureaucracy, for only persons qualified for their respective positions are normally appointed.

Bureaucratic organization is very efficient because it demands rational, predictable behavior from its incumbents. In this manner, personnel and materials can be provided as needed, work schedules corrected without delay, and accountability reliably determined.

Its Weaknesses

Efficient in general, bureaucratic organization is by no means free of imperfections. What originally are rules intended to expedite the purposes of the organization tend thereby to become ends in themselves, inducing timidity, conservatism, and technicism, so that in time organizations are prone to become rigid and hidebound. Nonetheless, bureaucracy is still conducive to productivity and efficiency in a city's economic life.

THE BUSINESS CORPORATION

Most of the city's bureaucratized economic activity is carried on by means of corporate enterprise. As a legal entity established by action of the state, the

American corporation may own property, possess capital, enter into contracts, sue and be sued, and provide a variety of products and services for the market. This is not to say that the business corporation is the only type of economic endeavor in the urban economy. There are also individual proprietors, like many retailers, and partnerships too, such as one encounters among lawyers. In addition, and performing vital economic functions too are mutual-benefit associations (exemplified by professional societies), service organizations (like legal-aid groups), and commonwealth organizations (for example, the research offices of universities).[12] Yet in total economic significance today, the private-enterprise business corporation dwarfs all others.

That the business corporation has become the major form of enterprise in America's urban economy is attributable to its two unique advantages: its capacity for unified control even over far-flung operations; and its continuity. These figure in the corporation's competitive success as well as its tendencies toward concentration and even monopoly.

Competition

In principle the nation's economy is committed to competition, and a competitive economy commands much ideological support.[13] It is argued that better than any other arrangement competition (1) promotes the flexible allocation of scarce resources; (2) protects the consumer from extortion; (3) is conducive to technological development; and (4) helps raise the level of living generally. In practice though, competition does not lack for drawbacks. One may point to the fact that competition (1) produces the needless diversification of goods and services, wastes resources on advertising and promotion, emphasizes fads and fashions, and cheats the consumer by necessitating the concealment of lower quality in order to cut costs; (2) impairs wages, hours, and the conditions of work when there is surplus labor; (3) militates against the conservation of natural resources and the planned application of improved technology; (4) prevents coordination and also the communication of new ideas; and (5) may result in the vicious circle of failure and loss that imperils not only the individual but also the entire community.

Concentration

Avoidance of the disadvantages of competition shows up in the inclinations toward corporate concentration which business and industry are prone to. In

---

[12] Peter M. Blau and W. Richard Scott, *Formal Organizations: A Comparative Approach* (San Francisco, Calif.: Chandler, 1962), pp. 45–57.

[13] Compare Clair Wilcox, "Competition and Monopoly," in Thomas J. Hailstones, ed., *Readings in Economics* (Cincinnati, Ill.: South-Western, 1969), 2nd ed., pp. 279–88.

1969, the top 100 of the nation's 1.7 million corporations controlled 55.8 percent of America's total corporate assets.[14]

The concentration of economic resources lacks ideological support although it does possess a definite rationale. Monopoly, it is thus asserted (1) serves the public interest in regard to natural resources and the accrual of scale, as in telephone communication, just to give a single case; it (2) protects labor and the consumer, provided proper public regulation exists; and it (3) affords the investor a more secure return, provided again that due controls operate.

The foregoing shows that certain shortcomings are inherent in monopoly, notably the following: (1) the uneconomical allocation of resources; (2) administered prices; (3) the exploitation of labor; (4) inefficiency; (5) stagnation; and (6) governmental authoritarianism. Reflections of this sort explain the large-scale governmental intervention into the economy at present. That intervention provides for regulation and even outright control of production, distribution, industrial relations, money, credit, and banking, all in an effort to achieve the benefits of competition and monopoly while averting their dangers.

GOVERNMENT INTERVENTION

Since the 1930s, the federal government has pursued a fourfold policy with regard to business concentration in the United States.

First, it has provided assistance through research, subsidies, and services.

Second, regulation has been exercised over financing, industrial relations, transportation, and literally a host of other areas.

Third, the government has itself operated business enterprises, at times through the device of public corporations like TVA and the Inland Waterways Corporation.

Fourth, planning and stabilization have been added to the government's economic program most recently. Thus the Council of Economic Advisors helps to coordinate the Federal Reserve System and the Treasury Department.[15]

In all, then, the giant corporation has its counterpart in the consolidated agency of the national government, say, AT&T vis-à-vis the Federal Communications Commission.

[14] Bureau of the Census, *Statistical Abstract of the United States: 1972,* op. cit., Table 764, p. 478.

[15] See Marshall E. Dimick, *Business and Government* (New York: Holt, Rinehart and Winston, 1961), 6th ed.

OCCUPATIONS

Within the bureaucratically organized corporate structure of economic activity in the city, the members of the labor force fill a large variety of occupations. They number in the tens of thousands of kinds of jobs although for convenience they can be classified into three categories: executive, professional, and labor.

Executives

Regardless of the particular firm or the particular rank they occupy in it, executives have six responsibilities. They plan, make decisions, negotiate inside and outside the organization, issue arbitrary orders, serve as the firm's symbolic spokesmen, and, finally, act as a primary target for aggression. In short, the executive is the focal point for making policies and taking responsibility for the employment of human, economic, and technological resources. His is also the crucial function of coordinating the operations of the organization and its relations with the market, government, and the general community.

The executive manner has been undergoing change over the years. Thomas Cochran has shown that the nineteenth-century model of aggressive American industrialist capable of vigorous competiton and capital accumulation has given way to a new concept. In the more recent pattern, whatever the particular industry, broad social responsibility is being stressed. Today the typical executive differs from "the aggressive, often socially irresponsible small competitor who had built capitalism in Europe and America."[16] Certainly in the larger, more professionally staffed businesses and in some smaller ones too, as recent research reveals, the executive relies on a variety of methods by which to achieve stronger employee morale. Among these are job enlargement so as to raise the intrinsic interest of jobs, promote cohesion among workers, raise job prestige, improve compensation, and allow participation in decision-making.[17]

As inferred from expressed beliefs, the contemporary American business ideology represents the adjustment of traditional values to present circumstances.[18] It consists of a conviction in individual responsibility together with an antipathy toward government regulation. Productivity as the source of

---

[16] Thomas C. Cochran, *The American Business System* (Cambridge, Mass.: Harvard University Press, 1965), pp. 11–12.

[17] Consult Dean J. Champion, *The Sociology of Organizations* (New York: McGraw-Hill, 1975), pp. 196–224.

[18] An astute study is Francis X. Sutton et al., *The American Business Creed* (Cambridge, Mass.: Harvard University Press, 1956). See also Richard Eells, *The Meaning of Modern Business* (New York: Columbia University Press, 1960).

material wealth, without which personal autonomy cannot be secured, also stands extolled. Such idealism is seen as absolutely necessary to progress. This is not to say that the business ideology is free from contradictions. As critics insist, the creed reveres the simplistic virtues of small-town America, and lauds the spirit of meliorism without paying sufficient attention to poverty, exploitation, and environmental danger resulting from business practices.

Professionals

If executives administer economic organization, professionals contribute disciplined knowledge to it.[19]

The numbers of professionals in the American labor force has increased with industrial urbanization, and that progression is continuing. In the decade ending in 1970, a further increase in technical and professional workers of fully 50 percent occurred. In the same interval, managers and administrators increased only 17 percent.[20] The sharp upswing in professionals must be attributed, first of all, to the technological development of industry. Another factor has been growth in the size of economic organizations and, hence, the need for adjunct services in planning, communication, and the like. A third reason may also be added: the multiplication of public and private health and welfare services to meet the rising demand.

Labor

Manual, clerical, sales, and service workers make up the largest category of labor in the urban occupational structure. In today's postindustrial, metropolitanized economy, the proportion of workers in communications, trade, and public service far exceeds their presence in the past. The percentage of those in manufacturing, however, has levelled off as industry has matured technologically. In our labor force in 1970, about 47 percent fell into the category of blue-collar and service workers. Operatives made up almost 18 percent of the total employed civilian population that year.[21]

Much of the work performed by industrial labor is minutely specialized and repetitive, calling for neither skill nor special education. Instead of skills and knowledge, the modern industrial worker needs dexterity, speed, precision, and personal adaptability.

[19] Compare Bernard Barber, "Some Problems in the Sociology of the Professions," in Kenneth S. Lynn, ed., *The Professions in America* (Boston: Houghton Mifflin, 1965), pp. 15–34.

[20] Bureau of the Census, *Statistical Abstract of the United States: 1975* (Washington, D.C.: Government Printing Office, 1975), p. 352.

[21] Ibid., pp. 352–56.

EXHIBIT 9-1 Educational Attainment of the Civilian Labor Force 25 Years Old and Over, 1957–59 and 1970–72 Averages and Projected to 1980 and 1990

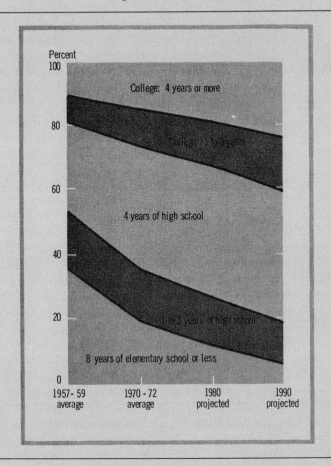

Percent

- College: 4 years or more
- College: 1 to 3 years
- 4 years of high school
- 1 to 3 years of high school
- 8 years of elementary school or less

| 1957-59 average | 1970-72 average | 1980 projected | 1990 projected |

Although the lines do go down from left to right, the spaces between them reveal that in the more than 30-year period covered here the proportion of high-school and college trained workers in the American labor force steadily increases.

Source: Bureau of Labor Statistics, *Education of Workers: Projections to 1990* (Washington, D.C.: Government Printing Office, 1974), Special Labor Force Report 160.

OCCUPATIONAL PROBLEMS

The typical problems that the different occupational groups experience vary from one category to the next. The executive is particularly vulnerable to stress under conditions of uncertainty and conflict with unions and public officials. Professionals suffer from the expansion of knowledge in their fields and the difficulty of keeping up with it, and also from trying to avoid exploiting their clients or failing to serve the public interest. Salaried professionals share an added problem: that of accepting the authority of nonprofessional executives. As for industrial and service workers, any number of dissatisfactions may be pointed to: fatigue, boredom, the lack of opportunity resulting from economic rigidities, and inability to take pride in one's work or to enjoy it in an age when individualism and mobility are valued.[22] All of these tensions have also created an interest in higher wages and shorter hours and, consequently, in both unionization and the consumer-protection movement.

THE PROTECTION OF LABOR AND THE CONSUMER

The diverse, specialized individuals making up the urban labor force share a unity of mutual needs. Yet sheer economic interdependence remains their chief bond, and market relations their main vehicle of expression. The protection of labor and the consumer has thus emerged as an integral part of the modern industrial-labor scene.

UNIONIZATION

Labor unions are not urban phenomena per se, but unionism does occur largely as an urban pattern.[23] The primary function of a union is of course to participate in the exercise of power with respect to wages, hours, and working conditions. Once established though, a labor union tends to evolve into an organization that seeks to broaden its role beyond merely bargaining for the material interests of its membership. It then wants to engage in managerial activities, and to move into political action and a general role in civic life. Similarly, a union may aspire to participation in cultural activities as an outgrowth of its interest in the health, welfare, and recreational needs of its members.[24]

[22] The current social problems of work are reviewed in Lee Braude, *Work and Workers* (New York: Praeger, 1975), especially Ch. 6.

[23] The research on this question is quite clear. See Bernard Berelson and Gary A. Steiner, *Human Behavior: An Inventory of Scientific Findings* (New York: Harcourt Brace & World, 1964), pp. 414–17.

[24] Theories on unionization appear in Eugene V. Schneider, *Industrial Sociology* (New York: McGraw-Hill, 1969), 2nd ed. See also Orme W. Phelps, *Introduction to Labor Economics* (New York: McGraw-Hill, 1967), 4th ed., pp. 214–34.

Types of Unions

Structurally, there are three types of unions.

1 Craft unions enroll their membership from those occupations that require training and skill, like musicians and carpenters. At times, however, skill may amount only to restriction at the job-entry point by virtue of the union's control of an apprentice program.

2 Basing membership on all classes of workers in an industry, the industrial union may be found in the automobile, electrical goods, rubber, and textile fields. Such unionization occurs where an intricate division of labor permits the employment of large numbers of untrained but specialized workers.

3 The federated union, notably the AFL-CIO, affiliates a number of coordinated unions so as to gain greater strength. Each part of a federated union may be a national union itself, having district councils, regional offices, state councils, and other intermediate structures.[25]

Collective Bargaining

Unionization presupposes a conflict situation where the participants struggle, under the rules of collective bargaining, to resolve their differences as a prelude to peaceful, productive collaboration. The bargaining process resulting from large-scale unionism is neither entirely rational nor functional. Kenneth Boulding thinks that "under collective bargaining wage determination steps, as it were, from the marketplace into the football field."[26] Nonetheless, collective bargaining rather than arbitration remains the basic principle of the trade union.

Types of Union Members and Leaders

The rank-and-file membership of the typical American union as well as its leadership bears out the idea that our unions are mainly service organizations operating by means of collective bargaining. In fact, ideological critics condemn the American labor union for its conservatism, especially, relative to the hard-core poor and racism. The validity of this position may be checked by examining the union rank-and-file and their leadership. Few union members subscribe to the social-conflict theory of history and the idea of unions as the forerunner of basic social change. Some union members have even been forced into unions by the law or by racketeers. Labor leaders fall into several types in American unions. The most numerous serve the material interests of their members solely and exclusively. At the other

[25] Consult Jack Barbush, *American Unions* (New York: Random House, 1967).

[26] *The Organizational Revolution* (New York: Harper & Brothers, 1953), pp. 100–01.

extreme is the official who relies on hoodlums to keep himself in power or who engages in collusion with employers for his own personal advantage.[27]

Labor Unions in the Future

The majority of informed opinion about the future of American unionism probably holds that in an era of mass society pragmatic solutions arrived at through the participation of the major organized segments of the economy, all of whom are in substantial agreement on basic values, will continue to dominate. Yet changing conditions are creating new interests, and these are diverting attention from earlier concerns. Commenting on the decade of the 1960s, historian Foster Dulles wrote, "Wage and fringe benefits naturally continued to be of importance in the greatly complicated labor-management contracts of these days, but the protection of union members against arbitrary displacement by machines was invariably a major target in all collective bargaining."[28] This will unquestionably continue. As one new text on organizations points out, a variety of safeguards against loss due to technological change exist, such as attrition, retraining, rules of seniority, and shorter working days, but they call for leadership interested in preserving employee security.[29] This challenge to trade unions can be expected to go on for a long time.

Besides dealing with automation, American unions are presently enmeshed in efforts to organize the new ranks of service employees in hospitals and schools, among retail clerks and office workers, and among technicians in the new light industries. Their success here appears to depend on the acceptability of collective bargaining, a principle unfamiliar to persons who take government responsibility for employee welfare for granted, and who also feel confident in the established channels of mobility.

Certain shortcomings have become apparent in the collective-bargaining approach. One is the far-reaching inflationary impact of major industrial settlements on the economy. Another relates to national emergency disputes and their counterpart locally, that is, the interruption of municipal services: transit, sanitation, education, and safety. Collective bargaining by municipal employees backed by the strike as their ultimate weapon can hardly suffice for the public interest in the metropolitan area. For example, in July 1974, Baltimore was hit by a protracted strike of its sanitation men, who were followed off the job by the city's police. With the safety forces out, hundreds of Baltimore stores were vandalized or looted. Whether arbitration, the only possibly feasible alternative to collective bargaining by public employees,

---

[27] For a class-conscious study of union stewards see Sidney M. Peck, *The Rank and File Leader* (New Haven, Conn.: College and University Press, 1963).

[28] *Labor in America: A History* (New York: Thomas Y. Crowell, 1966), 3rd ed., p. 404.

[29] Compare Champion, op. cit., pp. 265–76.

can in fact be a viable solution remains an unanswered question. Norton Long, a prominent political scientist, holds the view that aggressive city workers incapable of being curbed by the locally elected but intimidated officials have recently boosted expenditures far beyond productivity and thereby intensified our urban problems.[30]

THE CONSUMER

The highly developed division of labor in urban society results in the existence of a large mass of consumers. Using international data, Gibbs and Martin have demonstrated the interdependence of three factors, that is, urbanization, the division of labor, and consumership.[31] Except for noting that some exceptions do exist and that ideologies like liberalism and socialism vary, they concluded that "a high degree of urbanization depends on the division of labor, technology, and organization to requisition dispersed materials."

The consumer is the reciprocal of the urban employee, and has reciprocal interests. The growth of the business corporation and the organization of labor tend, therefore, to lead to two responses by the consumer, one political and the other economic. On the one hand, the consumer seeks government protection over prices and, on the other, he attempts to organize cooperatives that will give him a greater share of power relative to the producer.

Political Protection

In recent years consumer affairs have been receiving governmental protection. Several significant measures are quite new: the creation in 1961 of a consumer advisory council attached to the president's office, and in 1964 the designation of a special assistant for consumer affairs in the White House. The agitation of Ralph Nader was undoubtedly instrumental in this regard.

The American consumer, it would seem, has less representation in government than his opposite number in Britain. After the Labour Party came to power in London in 1945 and undertook to nationalize the economy, consumers were given a substantial voice via consumer councils in the newly nationalized industries. Consumer interests were thus represented nationally, regionally, and locally in such industries as utilities, transportation, and manufacturing, and also in the operation of public facilities too.

[30] Norton Long, *The Unwalled City* (New York: Basic Books, 1972). See also Harry H. Wellington and Ralph K. Winter, Jr., *The Unions and the Cities* (Washington, D.C.: Brookings Institute, 1971).

[31] Jack P. Gibbs and Walter T. Martin, "Urbanization, Technology, and the Division of Labor: International Patterns," *American Sociological Review*, 27 (October 1962), pp. 667–77.

Consumer Coöps

Consumer cooperatives are apt to arise where producers engage in monopolistic practices, provided there are other supporting factors. Favoring the establishment of coöps are the territorial propinquity of people, occupational similarity as the basis of mutual trust, and administrative skill.

By purchasing cooperatively, the members of a cooperative seek low-cost operations from which they can benefit, but stiff competition from chain stores and discount houses has prevented very many organizations here in the United States from flourishing. In fact, farm cooperatives for marketing purposes have proved much more common than the organization of coöps among our urban consumers. By contrast, in Finland, where consumer cooperatives are very popular, being affiliated with industrial unions, nearly the entire population belongs to coöps.[32]

MUNICIPAL FINANCE

Municipal finance is both an administrative problem and an object of political struggle. Hence it needs to be treated as a budgetary matter of fiscal planning as well as a contest over the distribution of the financial burden of government and the allocation of its benefits. In either event, revenues and expenditures are the essential elements of local public finance.

REVENUES

At the local level in America as of 1970, revenues amounted to $60 billion.[33] In any given year at present, about 60 percent of the general funding of local government is derived from local sources, chiefly taxes. Intergovernmental income supplies the remaining 40 percent, as will be seen from Table 9-1. The federal share is somewhat greater than the 7.4 percent shown, because the figure does not include aid-in-kind, such as surplus commodities. Nor does it cover the important factor of state distributions financed by the national government. In 1970 some $30 billion in federal aid went to state and local government.[34]

Municipal revenue obtained from local taxes comes from property, sales, income, use, and special taxes. All are today under much discussion and debate. The first of these, particularly on real estate, has traditionally

---

[32] Heikki Waris, "Finland," in Arnold M. Rose, ed., *The Institutions of Advanced Societies* (Minneapolis, Minn.: University of Minnesota Press, 1959), pp. 193–234.

[33] Bureau of the Census, *Statistical Abstract of the United States: 1972*, op. cit., Table 647, p. 406.

[34] Ibid., Table 656, p. 414.

TABLE 9-1 Sources of General Revenue of U.S. Local Government: 1974–1975

SOURCE	PERCENT DISTRIBUTION	
Intergovernmental revenue	40.7	
From State governments		33.3
From Federal government . .		7.4
From local sources	59.3	
Taxes		43.1
Property		35.2
Other		7.9
Charges and miscellaneous		16.2
Total	100.0	

Source: Adapted from Bureau of the Census, *Local Government Finances in Selected Metropolitan Areas and Large Counties: 1974–1975,* GF 75, No. 6 (Washington, D.C.: U.S. Department of Commerce, January 1976), p. 1.

produced the greatest amount. In 1970, it accounted for more than half of our cities' gross revenues raised locally.[35]

The Property Tax

The property tax on land and buildings is justified by the relationship between the amount that one owns and his ability to pay toward the public welfare. In actual practice, however, the property tax creates numerous problems. For example, the property tax becomes inequitable when it does not correspond to tax-paying ability, say, on the homes of the nonemployed elderly, or when it is underapplied to industrial property (which assessors find very difficult to appraise).[36] Again, real estate values tend to fluctuate less than wages and commodity prices. Accordingly, they will lag behind wage-and-price rises and declines, and the property tax will fail to produce the quick increases in revenue that income and sales taxes do.

The property tax does not meet the major criteria of a tax philosophy of sufficiency, stability, equity, reasonable certainty as to future liability, convenience of collection, and a positive relationship between paying taxes and benefiting from the services paid for. Yet despite its defects the property tax continues to be the basic source of local funds for 66,000 local governments in the United States today.[37] Why? Adrian attributes retention of the property tax to five reasons: (1) tradition and inertia; (2) acceptability—the typical home owner regards his taxes as just another item of maintenance cost; (3)

[35] Ibid., Table 669, p. 426.

[36] Consult Mabel Walker, "Property Tax," *Urban Land,* 31 (December 1972), pp. 18–22.

[37] Dick Netzer, *Economics and Urban Problems* (New York: Basic Books, 1974), 2nd ed., p. 248.

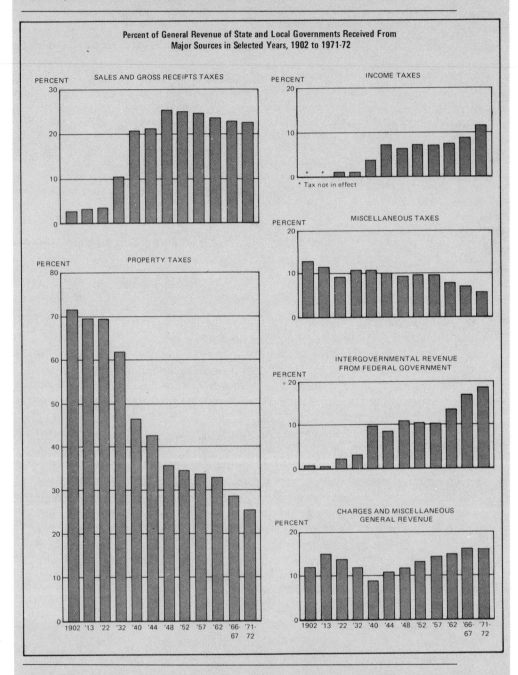

Percent of General Revenue of State and Local Governments Received From Major Sources in Selected Years, 1902 to 1971-72

Percent of general revenue by source reveals property-tax revenues are declining in importance, with local income taxes and the federal government as sources rising.

Source: Bureau of the Census, *Graphic Summary of the 1972 Census of Governments* (Washington, D.C.: Government Printing Office, 1975), p. 48.

the fact that in comparison with income and sales taxes, which can drive people away, the real estate tax probably undermines the tax base less; (4) that it usually produces a high yield; and (5) that no effective substitute has been proposed.[38] Included in the last reason are a number of interesting and ironic observations. For one thing, the property tax has often been poorly administered—by elected assessors who underassess, and by officials with a chronic inability to locate intangibles. Precisely because of its weaknesses, the property tax has retained support!

Other Kinds of Taxes

To improve their fiscal position in the face of mounting needs, cities have been turning to other sources of revenue and also to tax diversification.

Local income taxes (perhaps more properly called payroll taxes because they do not usually apply to interest, rents, or dividends) have become increasingly more common in American cities over the last 30 years. So too though to a lesser extent have corporate income taxes. Typically, a municipal income tax, now levied by more than 4000 municipalities in the United States, calls for a flat amount of from 0.5 to 1.5 percent on wages and salaries withheld by the employer. A local income tax is capable of yielding a large amount of revenue. Nationwide, American local governments collected more than $1.6 billion in individual and corporate income taxes in 1970.[39]

The local income tax is criticized for hurting business by reducing purchasing power. It is also assailed for being regressive, a flat rate without exemptions bearing inequitably upon those of little means. The city income tax also conjures up the evil of taxation without representation because it is levied on the nonresident employee. On the other hand, that may be compensatory justice. Falling on the suburbanites who work in the central city and though nonresidents benefit from its services, a local income tax means that they also pay for them. Among the benefits whose costs they thus defray are the use of the streets, sanitation, and the like. Agreeing to share the tax yield with adjacent communities often helps secure passage of the needed legislation for a municipal income tax.

City sales taxes made their first appearance in America during the Depression. State governments have largely preempted excises on purchases (in 1970, 45 states were using this revenue source). The federal government has tended to rely heavily on income taxes. Both sales and income taxes will probably remain secondary sources of municipal revenue. Yet both of these have already become important elements in the fiscal policy of our cities. In

[38] Charles R. Adrian, *Governing Urban America* (New York: McGraw-Hill, 1961), 2nd ed., p. 359.
[39] Bureau of the Census, *Statistical Abstract of the United States: 1972,* op. cit., Table 654, p. 412.

Illinois alone more than 1000 cities make use of the sales tax. It is very common among California communities too.

Practice has shown the sales tax to be a dependable source of revenue, which the individual pays in small amounts so that it incurs little resentment. Also, a sales tax is particularly effective in reaching a mobile population. Against these arguments one may point to the regressive nature of such a tax. That can of course be softened by exempting the basic necessities. A further shortcoming is administrative: businesses require close supervision in order to maintain the requisite records. Furthermore, a sales tax proves adverse to local business where nearby cities without such a tax are given a competitive advantage in getting the shopper's dollar. One defense against this is to have the urban county levy an add-on sales tax to equalize things.

As seen in Table 9-1, charges for services and miscellaneous fees brought in about a sixth of all local revenues in the United States in 1974–1975. In 1970, they had accounted for $12.6 billion out of the total $89 billion grossed by local government from all sources.[40] Charges and fees cover a broad range: utilities, health and hospital facilities, municipal parking lots and metered street parking, license fees paid by business, sewage disposal charges, and the like. Use taxes and fees are justified as relating to the enjoyment of community benefits. These sources of revenue will in all probability continue to be vigorously pursued in the future. It might be said though that the operation of municipal public utilities, particularly mass transit serving low-income people, seldom yields a profit and cannot be depended on for general revenues.

Tax Reform

The need for careful thought about municipal finance is today being increased by agitation for local reform. The scale of municipal finance has been expanding sharply in recent years. In the decade 1960–1970, the total revenue secured by America's local governments increased 122 percent. Another indication of the rising scale of American local finance is mounting debt. From 1960 to 1970, the net long-term indebtedness of all American local governments doubled, going from $51 billion to $102 billion in that period.[41] Also, as might be expected, controversy over the distribution of the tax burden between the central city and its suburbs has accompanied interest in tax reform at the local level. For the scholar, however, the questions thus raised need to be answered in the light of valid generalizations about municipal finance.

Two things above all are clear. First, public expenditures are positively

[40] Ibid.

[41] Bureau of the Census, *Statistical Abstract of the United States: 1975,* op. cit., Table 398, p. 242.

related to both the aggregate value of commercial, industrial, and residential property and the economic condition of the community's residents. Second, population density affects expenditures by increasing the need for services, chiefly police and fire protection. Unfortunately, many other factors also bear on municipal expenditures, not all of them capable of being quantified nor as definitely established as the two foregoing ones. Included among them are, as one authoritative summary puts it, "type of community, political and ethnic backgrounds of the residents, rate of growth, quality of services, popular attitude toward government, ratio of central city to metropolitan area population, and the property mix."[42]

Reflecting the interdependent character of the variables in municipal finance is the recently formulated prescription put forth by the Advisory Commission on Intergovernmental Relations for a high-quality state-and-local tax system.[43] This can serve at least as an illustration of the multiple factors that need to be considered, not necessarily however with these particular conclusions.

The ACIR asserts that in a sound system reliance will be placed mainly on (1) a state personal income tax, (2) a state sales and use tax, (3) local nonproperty taxes, and (4) a local property tax. The state income tax, says the ACIR, needs to provide at least 20 percent of the amount raised through the federal income tax and also to incorporate exemption and withholding features. Three conditions should govern the state's sales tax, declares the commission: coverage of personal services as well as the retailing of tangibles; exemption of food and drugs; and administrative simplicity. To be effective, moreover, local nonproperty taxes need to apply uniformly to the entire economic area, and also to be implemented by necessary technical assistance. As far as the local property tax goes, it must be regulated by state law to insure uniformity. It also needs, the ACIR continues, to be administered professionally under full disclosure and review proceedings.

The commission opposes *local* income taxes because people are increasingly supplementing their wages and salaries with income from outside sources. A simple payroll tax eliminates some of the inequity, but cities using this device lose some of the benefits of a tax according to ability to pay.

EXPENDITURES

Expenditures of local government in the United States are currently divided into two almost equal parts, one devoted to education and the other to a

[42] John C. Bollens and Henry J. Schmandt, *The Metropolis* (New York: Harper & Row, 1965), p. 366.

[43] Advisory Commission on Intergovernmental Relations, *State and Local Finances—Significant Features: 1967 to 1970* (Washington, D.C.: Government Printing Office, November 1969), pp. 1–5.

TABLE 9-2   Expenditures of U.S. Local Government: 1974–75

FUNCTION	PERCENT DISTRIBUTION	
Education	45.4	
Local Schools		42.6
Institutions of higher education		2.8
Functions other than education	54.6	
Health and hospitals		6.9
Public Welfare		6.8
Highways		5.8
Police protection		4.9
Interest on general debt		3.8
Sewerage		3.7
General Control		2.5
Fire protection		2.4
Parks and recreation		2.4
Sanitation other than sewerage		1.6
Financial administration		1.2
Other and unallocable (includes airports, libraries, parking facilities, and others)		12.6
Total	100.0	

Source: Adapted from Bureau of the Census, *Local Government Finances in Selected Metropolitan Areas and Large Counties: 1974–1975,* GE 75, No. 6 (Washington, D.C.: U.S. Department of Commerce, January 1976), p. 2.

broad spectrum of services. Since most municipalities do not directly operate schools—which are administered by independent school districts—only about one-seventh of their annual expenditures is budgeted for education. In the aggregate, the five functions to which the largest sums are allocated in the area of noneducational services are health and hospitals, welfare, highways, police protection, and interest on the general debt (Table 9-2).

The recent history of expenditures by American local government has been one of sharply rising amounts. In 1960 the operating expenditures of all cities in the United States was $9.8 billion. By 1972 that figure had risen to $29.8 billion.[44] Above-average increases in that period occurred in expenditures for police and fire protection, public welfare, health and hospitals, parks and recreation, airports, and interest on the municipalities' general debt. These trends indicate certain matters in particular concerning local

[44] Bureau of the Census, *Statistical Abstract of the United States: 1975,* op. cit., Table 422, p. 263.

New York City in deep financial trouble as resources fail to keep up with public expenditures. A demonstrator expressing her concern for the Big Apple—and the country.

public finance: the intensification of need in the area of public safety, the growing needs of the indigent, rising expectations concerning health, the pressures of public employees for higher wages, and, finally, the indebtedness of our cities as well as the inflation of the carrying charges on that debt.

The expenditures of the nation's cities do not constitute a single pattern. There are, in fact, important differences between cities according to size. As indicated by data for our SMSA's, America's large cities spend proportionally more for public welfare, health services, and police protection than

EXHIBIT 9-3   What New York City Has Done to Reshape Its Critical Financial Situation

☐ These are some of the economies which the City of New York already has taken to help alleviate its critical fiscal situation:

• Since Jan. 1, 1975, the city has cut the municipal payroll by about 35,000 employees, including 7,000 police officers, firemen, and sanitation workers. (Specifically, 3,000 police officers were dismissed because of the city's fiscal crisis.)

• The city has imposed a hiring freeze to reduce the payroll further by attrition.

• Wage increases for all city employees have either been deferred or frozen.

• All new city construction projects have been halted; those under way have been suspended.

• The transit fare has been raised to 50 cents, making it the highest in the nation, in a city where 70 percent of the work force uses mass transit.

• Eight firehouses, seven schools, and a municipal hospital have been closed.

• The city's libraries have cut their service in half. (Some branches are now operating only one or two days a week.)

• Real estate taxes in the past year have been increased by 10 per cent or $350 million and business taxes totalling $350 million have been added.

• Welfare programs in the city have suffered from cuts in services. One example is the Aid to Dependent Children program, which has discontinued nutrition and consumer education classes.

• The city is committed to a three-year financial plan, by law, that will balance the budget in fiscal year 1977–78 by cutting more than $724 million between now and then.

Places where cuts are probable after further studies include:

• The city cannot afford to underwrite an expansive university system.

• The city can no longer afford to pay for "a large and underutilized hospital system." Other municipal hospitals will be closed.

• The city can no longer afford new housing construction and has ended this program.

• The city's Bicentennial preservation projects for Lower Manhattan are in jeopardy because of a critical need for financial assistance.

• The city can no longer provide present levels of social service funding. This means further closing of day care and senior citizen centers and cutbacks in family planning, manpower training, addiction treatment, and antipoverty programs.

• The city's library system will probably shut down several of its library branches next year. For the next three years, attrition and cuts in quality and quantity of services will most likely continue in the city's libraries.

• The city will increase productivity and eliminate wasteful and costly contract provisions.

• An additional 8,000 employees will be eliminated from the city payroll.   ☐

Eighteen steps taken by New York City's municipal administration to cope with that community's dire fiscal problem.

Source: Andrij Bilyk, "New York City at the Brink," Nation's Cities, 13 (December 1975), pp. 7–10, © 1975 by National League of Cities, 1620 Eye Street, Washington, D.C. 20006.

do those cities smaller in size. In 1970, of the $2.2 billion spent on public welfare by the nation's municipalities, $2 billion of that was expended in our 25 largest cities. New York alone had a public-welfare bill that year of $1.6 billion.[45] In 1970, these same 25 cities appropriated $1.3 billion for health and hospitals and an equal amount for their police.

The Critical Financial Situation

The concentration of need in our metropolitan areas remains a cardinal aspect of local public finance in the United States today. This is especially true of our central cities, because at the very same time that they face a shrinkage in their available resources due to their business, industry, and affluent families moving away, they also confront increased welfare needs and strong pressures from public-service unions. The virtual insolvency of New York City at this writing is doubtlessly the most striking confirmation of the critical financial situation of America's cities at present and in the foreseeable future (Exhibit 9-3). In the words of the Advisory Commission on Intergovernmental Relations, "the financial affairs of cities [will make] them increasingly susceptible to financial emergencies."[46]

CONCLUSION

A city is both a distinct economic entity and a component in the larger economy. This is particularly true of today's metropolitan areas, each of which not only functions as a quasiautonomous economic system but also plays an important role in the national as well as the regional economy.

Internally the local economy adheres to the same bureaucratic and corporate form of organization that characterizes the nation. The system is productive, but it also sets up stresses that have a strong impact on the individuals who staff it together with the community whose needs it serves. The economic structure consists of businesses and industries which though ostensibly competitive tend toward growth and concentration, and as a result bring about government intervention, unionization, and a consumer-protection movement.

The city also possesses a public economy whose financial operations though essential to government are showing signs of increasing distress.

[45] Bureau of the Census, *Statistical Abstract of the United States: 1972,* op. cit., Table 670, p. 427.

[46] Advisory Commission on Intergovernmental Relations, *City Financial Emergencies* (Washington, D.C.: Government Printing Office, July 1973), p. 56.

FOR FURTHER READING

Roger E. Alcaly and David Mermelstein, eds., *The Fiscal Crisis of American Cities* (New York: Vintage Books, 1977). Essays, many of them leftwing, on the financial plight of municipal government today, especially New York's.

Fred Durr, *The Urban Economy* (Scranton, Pa.: Intext Educational Publishers, 1971). The private and public aspects of the economies of the contemporary urban community.

William H. Form and Delbert C. Miller, *Industry, Labor, and Community* (New York: Harper & Row, 1970). The relations between the economic institution and other institutions in an industrial society.

John K. Galbraith, *The New Industrial State* (Boston: Houghton Mifflin, 1967). How the large industrial corporation affects the market, government, and its own staff.

William Gorham and Nathan Glazer, eds., *The Urban Predicament* (Washington, D.C.: Urban Institute, 1976). Dismay over the fiscal problems of our cities.

Robert L. Heilbroner, *Between Capitalism and Socialism* (New York: Random House, 1970). Contemporary economic issues; traces the relationships between government and the economy.

Dick Netzer, *Economics and Urban Problems* (New York: Basic Books, 1974), 2nd ed. Concentrates on poverty, housing, the environment, and transportation.

Harry H. Wellington and Ralph K. Winter, Jr., *The Unions and the Cities* (Washington, D.C.: Brookings Institute, 1971). The growth of public employee unionism and its issues.

CHAPTER 10

SOCIAL STRATIFICATION

Social stratification refers to the structured inequality present in any society or its subunits, including individual cities, and consisting of the pursuit of economic interests and cultural values in a sanctioned system of social control.

These aspects of stratification may be observed historically in the medium-size American city "Middletown" (Muncie, Indiana) studied in 1936 by Robert and Helen Lynd, then of Columbia University.[1] The Lynds wrote perceptively about the Middletown stratification hierarchy whose apex was occupied by a "wealthy family of manufacturers" bestowing "increasingly large public benefactions" and enjoying an "increasing pervasiveness of . . . power."[2] This group the Lynds designated as the "X family."

[1] Robert S. Lynd and Helen M. Lynd, *Middletown in Transition* (New York: Harcourt Brace, 1937).
[2] Ibid., p. 74.

The X family of millionaire manufacturers (originally of glass fruit jars) filled an unostentatious but very influential position in Middletown's life. Though the city's economy was controlled by a business class, the nucleus of that class was clearly the several branches of the X family. Banking, the legal profession, industry, and retailing too, depended on the members of the X family for most major decisions. Moreover, the cultivation of their own interests did not prevent the X family from enjoying great prestige in Middletown. The X's practiced philanthropy, and some member of the family could always be counted on for funds for the hospitalization of tubercular patients, for community gardens, the animal pound, the new Memorial Hospital, and another facility for crippled children located at the state capital. The X's were also politically active. In local Middletown political life, the X's injected "just enough control over the confusion of local politics," wrote the Lynd's, "to enable their central business of money making to go forward without too much interference."[3]

Admitting that it was hazardous to make sweeping generalizations about exactly what a city of 50,000 thought or felt, the Lynd's did conclude that the working class tended to resent the X family, while the business class favored them and coveted their friendship. Yet even the working class of the city subscribed to the same symbols of success and the values of the Middletown business system which the X family were fostering. At the time of the study, the X's were surely regnant in Middletown.

STRATIFICATION IN PRINCIPLE

The brief review of Middletown raises the question of what stratification is in principle. It also suggests the difficulty of gauging stratification in large metropolitan centers and even more so in an entire urban society. In the final analysis, social classes denote a wide range of social reality. In fact, the term social class has five distinctly contrasting meanings.[4]

First, social classes are demographic categories. As such, each is made up of individuals similar in wealth, occupation, and schooling. Second, social classes are emotional groups, consisting of people who feel warm toward those like themselves and indifferent or possibly hostile toward others differing from themselves. Third, social classes are subcultures differentiated from one another by the particular mores and life-styles which they uphold. Fourth, social classes are associations informally organized for recognition and respect in opposition to the efforts of the other social

[3] Ibid., p. 89.

[4] For stratification generally see Harold E. Lasswell, *Class and Stratum* (Boston: Houghton Mifflin, 1965) and Melvin M. Tumin, "Stratification," in Julius Gould and William L. Kolb, eds., *A Dictionary of the Social Sciences* (New York: Free Press, 1964).

classes. Fifth, and finally, social classes are out-and-out interest groups affiliated with political parties, and thus formally organized to contend against other segments of society for material benefits and power.

Although stratification has long been a focal point of social theory, its rationale continues to be disputed. The ideas of Karl Marx, Max Weber, and Thorstein Veblen may be offered in illustration. Marx conceived of society as composed of economic classes engaged in a ceaseless struggle with one another: "freemen and slave, patrician and plebian, lord and serf, guildmaster and journeyman, oppressor and oppressed, bourgeoisie and proletariat." To Weber as to Marx, economic interests were capable of leading to "communal action," in other words, social-class conflict between people having unequal life-chances. Yet Weber also recognized "status groups," which he defined as pluralities varying in degree of honor and finding expression simply in invidiously contrasting honorific positions, such as appointment to government posts and the display of proper conduct. A good example might be the way in which Japan's first generation of industrialists carried on traditional Japanese ceremonial life during the nineteenth century while they also introduced greater socioeconomic mobility than had previously been the case.[5] In a similar vein, Veblen too, laid stress on what he termed "ceremonial differentiation" in establishing status variations in society. Veblen's classic study *The Theory of the Leisure Class,* published in 1899, reveals the extent to which style-of-life competition governs social classes as a whole.

More recent stratification theory centers on the debate between Kingsley Davis and Wilbert E. Moore on the one hand and Melvin Tumin on the other. According to Davis and Moore, some system of stratification is inherent in any but the simplest society, because the problem of motivating individuals to perform social roles and to capitalize on scarce human resources provides the foundation for stratification generally.[6] Thus the differential allocation of money, power, and prestige—the elements of stratification—satisfies an essential social need: of inducing people to supply the necessary services of organized society.

Tumin, however, questions these functionalist premises.[7] Instead he emphasizes the discriminatory and exploitative aspects of stratification. Tumin contends that the functional hypothesis, as the Davis-Moore position is known, is circular reasoning, because dominance creates a tendency for those with power to buttress themselves with authority too. So, Tumin writes,

[5] See R. N. Bellah, *Values and Social Change in Modern Japan* (Tokyo: International Christian University, 1962).

[6] Kingsley Davis and Wilbert E. Moore, "Some Principles of Stratification," *American Sociological Review,* 10 (April 1945), pp. 242–49.

[7] Melvin M. Tumin, "Some Principles of Stratification: A Critical Analysis," *American Sociological Review,* 18 (August 1953), pp. 387–94.

"Social stratification systems function to provide the elite with the political power necessary to produce acceptance and dominance of an ideology which rationalizes the status quo, whatever it may be, as 'logical,' 'natural,' and 'morally right.'"[8]

Present thinking on stratification inclines mainly perhaps to the Davis-Moore reward theory, although conflict thought, stressing relative power as basic to stratification, has been gaining new acceptance.

URBANIZATION AND STRATIFICATION

As a rule, urbanization militates against a simple, static stratification system that divides the community into hereditary strata sustained by religious and legal sanctions. Historically, the growth of cities can be seen to be accompanied by the development of economically differentiated individuals and groups, and to result in a social body of numerous specialized parts arranged in a flexible, shifting hierarchy rather than a set pyramid. Urbanization denotes a massive trend toward the constitutional rights of persons, toward greater access to economic benefits among the members of the population, and toward their greater political participation.[9] Reviewing agrarian and preindustrial urban status systems not only reveals this general principle, but also helps to thrown the stratification processes of the large city and modern urban society into clear focus.

AGRARIAN STRATIFICATION

When an agrarian society like that in Europe during the Middle Ages is surveyed to determine its stratification features, the large peasant class stands out sharply enough. But such an examination discloses other, essentially nonfarming, strata as well. These result from the occupations of government, religion, and military defense as adjunct to agriculture. Thus we may distinguish the governing class, their retainers, the priestly class, artisans, and the pariahlike expendables at the very bottom, all in addition to the peasantry itself.[10] On this basis one may discuss the familiar pyramidal view of agrarian societies as grossly inaccurate. Rather than layers superimposed on one another, as Gerhard Lenski notes, the strata of an agrarian society may perhaps best be described as onion-shaped, with an exceedingly long, narrow neck indicating the great social distance and the small relative size of the governing class.[11]

[8] Ibid., p. 393.

[9] Gerhard E. Lenski, *Power and Privilege* (New York: McGraw-Hill, 1966).

[10] Ibid., pp. 243ff.

[11] Ibid., Figure 1, p. 284.

The preindustrial European city had a class system different from but also related to that of its surrounding agrarian society.[12] The city elite comprised possibly just five percent of the whole population, certainly no more than ten. Except for the merchants the top stratum of the town was not separate from the hereditary landed gentry. The agrarian nobles were themselves present in the towns and visited their estates periodically to collect taxes. They generally chose to stay in town where they could live better and more readily enjoy defense from military attack as well.

The leading merchants also enjoyed superior status. The gentry did more than just tolerate the merchants. They even acceded to them, for the merchants' "wide interpersonal contacts within the lower orders of society, their necessary recourse to manipulation (as occurs in moneylending) as a means of getting ahead, and other factors [resulted in their threatening] the authority structure of the elite."[13] In time the merchants secured a firmly cemented position in the upper echelons of wealth, power, and prestige, as the preindustrial city became a recognized adjunct of the larger agrarian social order.

Nor was this to continue indefinitely. In fact, change in the stratification system was accelerated by preindustrial urbanization. Although the cities were stratified, considerable mobility was now possible, for the standards of social rank, occupation and money, differed from the more inelastic principle of feudal status, the inherited ownership of land. Incidentally, it should be noted that this rural-urban dichotomy, which takes the form of traditionism versus modern values, obtains today in many of the underdeveloped regions of Latin America and Southeast Asia.[14] The rural-urban distinction, however, ought not to be thought simply this, for it also includes status based on resource capital like plantation ownership and the production of rubber or coffee, or factory ownership and the production, say, of textiles.[15]

In premodern Europe the migration of surplus rural population to the centers of trade fed the need for productive labor in the cities. Then as enterprises grew larger, new administrative positions opened up. These were newly occupied by specialists possessing the requisite skills. Hence a threat to the now nascent mercantile patriciate arose. The urban class system that had developed in the preindustrial cities of Europe became the forerunner of the stratification pattern of Western industrial-urban society today.

[12] Gideon Sjoberg, *The Preindustrial City* (Glencoe, Ill.: Free Press, 1960), pp. 108ff.

[13] Ibid., p. 121.

[14] Cf. S. N. Einsenstadt, *Social Differentiation and Stratification* (Glenview, Ill.: Scott, Foresman, 1971), pp. 182–83.

[15] Horace Miner, ed., *The City in Modern Africa* (New York: Praeger, 1966) deals with stratification in transitional societies.

When the still larger members of clerks, artisans, and above all, factory hands required by industry finally become a reality after the Industrial Revolution, two new and dissimilar social strata came into being. These were the ranking industrialists and, at the other extreme, the poor industrial workers. For a time the merchants resisted the encroachments of the industrialists, but the latter's superior power derived from steam production enabled them simply to take over the distribution and investment functions of the merchants themselves. Many of these former businessmen dwindled into petty shopkeepers, and their sons turned toward the white-collar jobs that industry had opened up. The industrialists' power over their factory hands, now deprived of their feudal rights but still lacking trade-union strength, was plain to see. Undoubtedly this gave Marx the outlines for his conception of the modern capitalistic class system: "Accumulation of wealth at one pole [is] at the same time the accumulation of misery, agony of toil, slavery, ignorance, brutality, mental degradation, at the opposite pole."[16]

Marx's prediction notwithstanding, a signal development of urban society since the early period of the Industrial Revolution was the multiplication of white-collar and professional occupations. In the United States in the 80 years following 1860, the some 750,000 new middle-class employees grew to over 12.5 million.[17] By 1970, 48.3 percent of the entire labor force employed in the United States were white-collar workers. In fact, since 1950, the ranks of the professional, technical, managerial, and administrative personnel has almost doubled.[18] These persons were responsible for servicing, distributing, and coordinating the productive part of the economy as well as providing direct services.

The growth of such a new middle class is a leading characteristic of industrial urban society. Also, as the ranks of the middle class expand, the gaps between social classes narrow. That is a second fundamental characteristic. In the presently developing nations, the rate of growth of unskilled workers is slower than it was in the countries that industrialized during the nineteenth century, because the new nations have the advantages of a higher level of technology and productivity. Consequently, administrators, clerks, white-collar persons in general, are conspicuously numerous. That indicates a repetition of the experience of industrial urbanization in the past. No doubt the status systems of the developing nations will also become more indistinct too as their middle-class occupations not only multiply but also diversify.

[16] Karl Marx, *Capital* (New York: Modern Library, 1936), p. 709.

[17] C. Wright Mills, *White Collar: The American Middle Classes* (New York: Oxford University Press, 1953), p. 63.

[18] Bureau of the Census, *Statistical Abstract of the United States: 1972* (Washington, D.C.: Government Printing Office, 1972), Table 366, p. 230.

STRATIFICATION IN CITIES AT PRESENT

Though uniformities such as the foregoing may be imputed generally to stratification in modern urban society, important differences in the stratification pattern of particular cities are apparent too. W. Lloyd Warner has adduced four varieties of stratification structure among America's urban communities, those pertaining to (1) the older city, (2) the growing city, (3) the functionally diverse city, and (4) the suburban community.[19]

THE OLDER CITY: A WELL-ORGANIZED CLASS ORDER

A well-organized class order is more typical of an older, longer established city than it is of a community of more recent origin. In Yankee City (Newburyport, Massachusetts), a long established coastal community, an aristocracy of birth and wealth (and a miniscule 1.4 percent of the city's population of 17,000) continued to dominate (at the time surveyed).[20] The wealthy descendants of earlier merchants, sea captains, and manufacturers were not only socially prominent in Yankee City but also occupied top positions in the city's business concerns and in the elite professions of law and medicine.

The 38 percent of the Yankee City populace who made up its middle classes had their own socioeconomic profile. Occupationally they included proprietors and managers, salaried professionals, white-collar employees, and skilled blue-collar workers. The range among them was quite broad economically.

At the bottom of the Yankee City pyramid were the 59 percent of the city's inhabitants who made up the lower class. Somewhat more than half of the city's lower class were described as "poor but honest workers." Beneath them but still part of the community's lower class were the more severely disadvantaged Riverbrookers, who filled the most menial positions and who experienced the greatest amount of unemployment.

THE GROWING CITY: STATUS CHANGES

Urban growth, especially rapid growth as a result of in-migration or industrial change, tends to create a contrasting stratification system. In the middle west and on the Pacific coast, swift change in one city after another from mining to manufacturing or from transportation to a general-purpose economy has largely wiped out the original "old-family" elites reigning, as in Middletown, over all others. San Francisco may be one surviving example of

[19] See his *Social Class in America* (New York: Harper & Row, 1960), pp. 3–34.

[20] W. Lloyd Warner and Paul S. Lunt, *The Social Life of a Modern Community* (New Haven, Conn.: Yale University Press, 1941).

the older type, but Los Angeles appears typical of the "more amorphous, less well-organized class structure."[21] There, the large and complex economy created only during the last half century results in an indistinct stratification system as a whole and not simply at the upper reaches. One study of the Kansas City metropolitan area early in the 1950s revealed five principal classes (upper, upper-middle, lower-middle, working, and lower class) and 13 substrata (like the "Capital-S Society" segment of the upper class and the disreputable slumdwellers in the lower class).[22]

THE FUNCTIONAL DIVERSITY OF CITIES

The local community need not be representative of the larger society either in the height or the breadth of its status hierarchy. In fact, the occupational structures of cities vary systematically according to their economic functions, that is, whether the cities are predominantly manufacturing or diversified centers, etc. Thus, because the metropolitan area coordinates a regional economy, it has a larger-than-average proportion of high-status persons in its labor force. Conversely, a small industrial town will be overrepresented by manual workers, at the bottom of the social pyramind.

STRATIFICATION IN SUBURBIA

Suburbanization commonly narrows the range of stratification so that a given suburb may be homogeneous as to social class, while the entire metropolitan population of which the suburb is a part will be more broadly stratified. Most suburbs are residential communities by and large, but they do differ by social class. The suburbs inhabited by blue-collar families rank lower on the stratification scale than their typically middle-class counterparts. Other suburbs, like New York's Larchmont and Boston's Chestnut Hills, have a predominantly upper-class population which is not representative of the metropolitan area at all.

THE ELEMENTS OF MODERN URBAN STRATIFICATION

As we have seen, the populations of modern urban communities tend to be stratified, but in complex and indistinct structures defined by factors that are only relatively interdependent. Of primary importance is occupation. Second, style-of-life differences also have status significance. And, third, though technologically and economically dysfunctional, invidious racial, ethnic, and

---

[21] *Social Class in America,* op. cit., p. 18.

[22] Richard P. Coleman and Bernice L. Neugarten, *Social Status in the City* (San Francisco, Calif.: Jossey-Bass, 1971), Table 1, p. 59.

Occupations are a major basis for stratification. Construction workers—"hard hats"—on the job.

religious distinctions continue to be observed in urban centers and continue to affect the status of entire groups of people.

OCCUPATIONAL PRESTIGE

Occupational prestige was measured in the United States in 1947 and again in 1963 by the National Opinion Research Center, originally in cooperation with the President's Scientific Research Board.[23] A cross section of the American public rated 90 occupations as to their relative standing—from excellent to poor. Hodge, Siegel, and Rossi calculated that the ratings had been remarkably stable in the 16-year period, with a positive correlation of 0.99. As a matter of fact, they observed, that no substantial change had taken place in the occupational consensus of the country since 1925![24]

Classifying the 90 rated occupations into eight groups produced a scale showing that government officials had the highest average score, 90.8, followed in order by professional and semi professional workers; proprietors, managers, and non public officials; clerical, sales, and kindred workers; protective-service workers; operatives and kindred workers; service workers

[23] C. C. North and Paul K. Hatt, "Jobs and Occupations: A Popular Evaluation," *Public Opinion News,* 9 (September 1947), pp. 3–13.

[24] Robert W. Hodge, Paul M. Siegal, and Peter H. Rossi, "Occupational Prestige in the United States: 1925–63," *American Journal of Sociology,* 70 (November 1964), pp. 286–302.

TABLE 10-1 Correlations between Prestige Scores or Ranks Given to Comparable Occupations in Six National Studies

	U.S.S.R.	JAPAN	GREAT BRITAIN	NEW ZEALAND	UNITED STATES	GERMANY
U.S.S.R.		.74	.83	.83	.90	.90
Japan			.92	.91	.93	.93
Great Britain				.97	.94	.97
New Zealand					.97	.96
United States						.96
Average correlations	.84	.89	.93	.93	.94	.94

Source: Alex Inkeles and Peter H. Rossi, "National Comparisons of Occupational Prestige," *American Journal of Sociology,* 61 (January 1956), pp. 329–39 © University of Chicago Press.

other than domestic and protective; and, finally, laborers, receiving a composite score of only 45.8.[25]

International Uniformity

The extent to which ratings made by the American public agreed and also the extent to which their ratings remained stable over a long time span have been thought impressive. Perhaps equally noteworthy is the finding, by Inkeles and Rossi, that occupations tend to be ranked uniformly by the people of a number of advanced countries. Reviewing comparable research done in the U.S.S.R., Japan, Great Britain, New Zealand, and Germany in addition to the United States, these sociologists discovered very high correlations among the occupational ratings. (See Table 10-1.)

A more extensive study conducted by Hodge, Treiman, and Rossi not only confirmed the international uniformity of occupational prestige structures. It also indicated that differences "may prove systematically related to patterns of economic development perhaps interwined with diffusion through colonial contacts and the path toward modernization."[26] In all, 24 nations were studied, among them Brazil, Turkey, and the Ivory Coast. The findings lent added support to the so-called structuralist position that occupational prestige fits into a hierarchical arrangement. That arrangement is serviceable for the industrial system, the state, and the secular values associated

[25] Subgroupings of the 90 rated occupations were drawn up to permit the comparison of particular types of jobs making up a category with those in other categories. This revealed that from 1947 to 1963, some categories had appreciated slightly and others had declined a little. See Ibid.

[26] Robert W. Hodge, Donald J. Treinman, and Peter H. Rossi, "A Comparative Study of Occupational Prestige," in Reinhard Bendix and Seymour M. Lipset, eds., *Class, Status, and Power* (New York: Free Press, 1966), 2nd ed., pp. 309–21.

TABLE 10-2 Median Earnings, Employed Males, by Occupational Group: 1950 and 1970

	MEDIAN EARNINGS	
OCCUPATIONAL GROUP	1950	1970
Professional, technical, and kindred	$4,073	$11,577
Proprietors, managers, and officials	3,815	11,292
Craftsmen, foremen, and kindred	3,293	8,833
Sales workers	3,137	8,321
Clerical and kindred	3,103	7,965
Operatives and kindred	2,790	7,017
Service workers	2,303	5,568
Laborers	1,909	4,839

Source: U.S. Bureau of the Census, *Statistical Abstract of the United States: 1972* (Washington, D.C.: Government Printing Office, 1972), Table 536, p. 328.

with both of them, such as health and education. This, said the investigators, is true even when the industrial system "is placed in the context of larger social systems which are otherwise differentiated in important respects," notably ideologically.

Occupation and Income

That occupational prestige is closely linked to income may be seen from the data in Table 10-2 observed in the light of the occupational prestige scores presented earlier. The rank-order distribution of occupational groups by income is quite stable over the 20-year period. Moreover, as Leonard Reissman notes, a job is not just "an index to prestige." A job is also very much "an index of the relative access it typically allows for the exercise of legitimate power in the economic institution."[27] The income derived from a job stands as one sign of the power in that occupation. It also denotes the decision-making scope of the occupational role from which it is derived.

STYLE OF LIFE

Reducing social class to economic and political interests alone ignores the competing modes of living by which people strive to gain deference to themselves and to deny it to others. Max Weber states that, "with some oversimplification, one might say that 'classes' are stratifed according to their relations to the production and acquisition of goods whereas 'status groups' are stratified according to the principles of their consumption of goods rep-

[27] Leonard Reissman, *Class in American Society* (Glencoe, Ill.: Free Press, 1959), p. 208.

resented by special 'styles of life.' "[28] The particular forms of living that people adopt are supposed to reflect the worthiness and breeding of those displaying them. Being thought innate though cultivated, and cultivated with difficulty too, styles of life make mobility more difficult than the mere possession of wealth or occupational achievement does.

The spatial segregation of status groups into distinct residential areas is the major way in which style-of-life differences are given expression in the urban community. The home and its immediate surroundings thus become the site of the family's culturally meaningful possessions, activities, and associations. Alvin Boskoff has generalized that residential segregation is the essential positioning device used in the city.[29] Other criteria of status, especially occupation, are hard to apply in a large, impersonal population. Also, in a culture where the "manipulating" and "nurturing" kinds of class relationships are subordinated to the "circumscribing" and "excluding" type, underscoring social distance by separation and mobility through education and symbol-acquisition (dress, autos, etc.), then "imitation by status objects" becomes a feasible alternative to status claims based on occupation.

A brief description of American social strata as prestige systems can give at least some idea of how power and privilege are buttressed by cultural means.

The Upper Classes

Besides occupying pedigreed space, upper-class people are distinguished in the United States by style-of-life attributes that include membership in exclusive organizations and attendance at private schools. Almost every large city claims at least one high-status club which, E. Digby Baltzell tells us in *Philadelphia Gentlemen,* lies at the very core of access to power and authority.[30] Every city also has a second echelon of clubs frequented by the nouveaux riches and would-be aristocrats. When G. William Domhoff, writing about our ruling circles, says that we have an intermarrying upper class guarded by social secretaries, private schools, and clubs, he seems to be saying that their elite style of life protects their economic and political power.[31]

The Middle Classes

The middle classes generally have little productive property. They are, however, affluent in consumer goods—appliances, automobiles, clothing, and

[28] H. H. Gerth and C. Wright Mills, eds., *From Max Weber* (New York: Oxford University Press, 1946), p. 193.

[29] Alvin Boskoff, *The Sociology of Urban Regions* (New York: Appleton-Century-Crofts, 1970), 2nd ed., pp. 191ff.

[30] (New York: Free Press, 1958).

[31] G. William Domhoff, *The Higher Circles* (New York: Random House, 1970).

The Rolls-Royce, an ultimate symbol of affluence.

appurtenances. These they tend to choose to emphasize their sense of occupational accomplishment, as being "modern," "practical," "well-
engineered," and "well-designed," and to put them and their offspring above
the "common man." W. Lloyd Warner concludes about the middle classes
that, "their feelings about doing the right thing, of being respectable and
rearing their children to do better than they have, coupled with the limitations
of their income, are well reflected in how they select and reject what can be
purchased on the American market."[32]

The Lower Classes

Owing to its inclusion of disparate elements—stable and unstable workers,
certain minorities, and the like—the American lower classes are subject to
varying interpretations. The expenditures of the lower class for furnishings
and clothing, for example, reveal a broad division within the class as a
whole. Some writers have stressed the point that the members of the lower
class regard material possessions as important in their own right apart from
their capacity to symbolize achievement. Others have called attention to
lower-class alienation from work and, correspondingly, to reliance, say, on
bizarre adornment for compensation. Certainly the wounding aspects of low

[32] W. Lloyd Warner, *Social Class in America*, op. cit., p. 15.

status on personality appear real enough even if self-embellishment may not necessarily be the way of salving those injuries.[33]

Life Styles as Change Agents

Patterns of consumption and styles of life are ancillary to socioeconomic position and as such they sustain the status quo. At the same time though, they are also sources of change that impinge on the distribution of wealth and power. As subcultures, social classes are constantly engaged in an interplay of contested claims to deference, challenges to legitimacy, and threats to the established pattern of economic and political control.

Consider as a case in point the deviant life styles that Boskoff has identified in our present-day American urban society.[34] Boskoff contrasts the "consummatory" style of the socially elite with the "striving" style of those near to but not actually at the top. The former exercise power, writes Boskoff, in a "confident, responsible, and self-limited" manner. The latter are the newly rich organization men whose aggressiveness, says Boskoff, amounts to "a civilian form of military strategy." In Boskoff's typology, the new middle class is especially interesting for its ritualistic but also practical valuation of home ownership, formal education, and membership in voluntary organizations to give themselves respectability. This constitutes their leading method in securing honor for themselves and also in solidifying their economic position as well.

ETHNIC STRATIFICATION

As pointed out earlier, in connection with rural-urban types, cities have been thought of as utilitarian systems in which individuals are treated according to their ability to compete in an economy regulated by impersonal law. Urbanization has generally been synonymous with individualistic social mobility based on economic success. Indeed, the ruthlessness of the urban milieu with its heavy cost in human misery has been viewed as the necessary price paid for abandoning the protective guardianship of the master over his ward and of the dominant majority over the ethnic or racial minority.

But individualism apart from subgroup membership has not totally won out in the city. Three decades ago, in Yankee City, Warner and Srole concluded that racial and cultural differences from the majority raised barriers to assimilation, and high barriers at that. They formulated two propositions. One states that "the greater the difference between the host and the immigrant cultures, the greater will be the subordination, the greater the

---

[33] On the self-disparagement resulting from poor status, see Richard Sennett and Jonathon Cobb, *The Hidden Injuries of Class* (New York: Random House, 1972).

[34] Boskoff, op. cit., pp. 201ff.

An impoverished inner-city ethnic neighborhood.

strength of the ethnic social systems, and the longer the period necessary for the assimilation of the ethnic group."[35] The second holds that "the greater the racial difference between the populations of the immigrant and the host societies the greater the subordination of the immigrant group, the greater the strength of the social subsystem, and the longer the period necessary for assimilation."[36] Combining the two, we may infer that where cultural and racial differences coincide, both the cleavage and the time necessary for assimilation will be correspondingly greater.

The continued segregation of ethnic groups in the city has been observed repeatedly. This anomaly of ethnic stratification in the typologically defined impersonally competitive urban milieu warrants extended examination.

New York, Park Forest, and "North City"

In New York City, Caucasians, Negroes, and Mongoloids remain socially identified races, and Germans, Italians, Jews, and Puerto Ricans, ethnic subgroups. "It is striking that in 1963," wrote Nathan Glazer and Daniel

[35] W. Lloyd Warner and Leo Srole, *The Social Systems of American Ethnic Groups* (New Haven, Conn.: Yale University Press, 1945), pp. 285–86.
[36] Ibid.

Moynihan, "almost forty years after mass immigration from Europe to this country ended, the ethnic pattern is still so strong in New York City."[37] Furthermore, the prospect of the ethnic distinction disappearing remains distant.

Even when dispersed, the members of ethnic groups frequently exhibit social preference for one another. Sociability patterns of that sort have been noticed by Gans among the Jewish families of Park Forest, a planned suburb of Chicago.[38] Jews made up less than 10 percent of the Park Forest population of 1800 families. Although similar in appearance and manners to Park Foresters generally, Jewish families there formed a cohesive ingroup that carried on social intimacies among its members. These made possible a deeper feeling of comfort and self-expression than was the rule in associations with non-Jews in the community. The establishment of a Judaic Sunday School in Park Forest helped contribute to a stronger sense of respectability for the Jewish people there.

Studying the Jews of "North City," a metropolitan area in the United States with a Jewish population of 20,000, Judith Kramer and Seymour Leventman learned that the Jewish subcommunity had a complex institutional structure of its own that paralleled the institutional structure of the city.[39] The ethnic ties that North City's Jews had built up after their migration, first in the 1880s from Germany and Austro-Hungary and, after 1900, from Eastern Europe, protected their social and economic interests. Further assimilation of Jews into the life of North City, however, weakened Jewish self-employment and Jewish family enterprise. It also meant that Jews took on the life styles of their host Gentiles. Nonetheless, the third generation North City Jew, Kramer and Leventman discovered, possessed a theological interest in Judaism. This was interpreted as something acceptable to the majority of Americans and also capable of providing spiritual conviction for the Jewish minority. Seemingly, neither organized commitment to synagogue ritual nor the secularism of North City culture was sufficient for the young Jews there.

Racial Subordination

Racial dissimilarities remain a potent source of group formation in urban America today. Racial inequalities are discussed, principally in Chapter 18, "Urban Minorities and Poverty." Here we refer to race only as a basis for social cleavages.

[37] Nathan Glazer and Daniel P. Moynihan, *Beyond the Melting Pot* (Cambridge, Mass.: M.I.T. Press, 1963), p. 291.

[38] Herbert J. Gans, "The Origin and Growth of a Jewish Community in the Suburbs: A Study of the Jews of Park Forest," in Marshall Sklare, ed., *The Jews* (Glencoe, Ill.: Free Press, 1958), pp. 205–48.

[39] Judith R. Kramer and Seymour Leventman, *Children of the Gilded Ghetto* (New Haven, Conn.: Yale University Press, 1961).

In the study of Kansas City mentioned above and done in the 1950s, the isolated position of blacks was found to be very real indeed. "Across the color-caste line," said the report, "there was no socially meaningful equality since no group of whites truly accepted any group of Negroes as worthy of the same intimate interaction or the same respect accorded a white member of the same social class."[40] It should be noted that this judgment antedated the civil-rights militancy of the 1960s and the socioideological change since. Yet the relatively unexpected interest of blacks in separatism beginning in the late 1960s may represent a reactive response to the continuation of castelike separation in the local community no less than it constitutes a movement aimed at creating a political bloc as well.

Assessments of the future do not rule out continued racial distinctions in America's cities. The historian Oscar Handlin has forecast that blacks and Puerto Ricans will probably exhibit the same upward mobility as European immigrants earlier. However, Handlin does not think there will be any "general dispersal" throughout the metropolis. Instead, he anticipates that they, "like the other ethnic groups, will continue to live in cohesive settlements." Gradually, Handlin thinks, "They will be accommodated through the evolution, in the suburbs and in the central city, of numerous neighborhoods at various income levels to which clusters of them will be voluntarily drawn by common interests and tastes."[41]

Professor Handlin's forecast implies the doctrine of pluralism that has recently given legitimacy to the ethnic realities which have continued to exist in our urban communities. Cultural pluralism has replaced the melting-pot theroy of assimilation, that is, acculturating immigrants into the American national character.[42] Pluralism denotes economic and political interaction in common, while at the same time the various racial and ethnic minorities remain residentially, religiously, and endogamously intact. Further, this implies the presence of subsocieties carried on by means of informal relations, cliques, and organization, as Milton Gordon puts it, that "provide the framework for communal existence" among themselves. The recent resurgence of ethnicity in municipal elections in Buffalo, Cleveland, Philadelphia, and Gary, and which have featured black-white tensions, appears to rest on such immediate issues as urban renewal and neighborhood change but, possibly more importantly, on the background significance of ethnic separatism.[43]

Though pluralism and separatism are a part of the stratification system

[40] Coleman and Neugarten, op. cit., p. 66.

[41] Oscar Handlin, The Newcomers: Negroes and Puerto Ricans in a Changing Metropolis (Cambridge, Mass.: Harvard University Press, 1959), p. 119.

[42] For a classical 1909 statement on the melting pot, see Ellwood P. Cubberly as cited in Milton M. Gordon, Assimilation in American Life (New York: Oxford University Press, 1964), p. 98.

[43] Cf. Mark R. Levy and Michael S. Kramer, The Ethnic Factor: How America's Minorities Decide Elections (New York: Simon and Schuster, 1973), especially, pp. 148–50.

of cities, they are not regarded as wholly legitimate, but are often thought of as social problems. In a study of racial residency in metropolitan America, Leonard Reissman looked at the inner city-suburban polarization of blacks and whites as indicating that "some of our most treasured beliefs about the rights of private property, the freedom of entrepreneurial real estate developers, and the immutability of governmental boundaries need to be scrutinized if we believe that the value of equality is worth it."[44] Because racial stratification is a form of cultural deviance and social disorganization, we will again take up the subject in Chapter 18.

SOCIAL MOBILITY

Despite racial and ethnic rigidities in the city, in comparison with both agrarianism and preindustrial urbanism, the industrial-urban order favors social mobility.

SOCIAL MOBILITY AS A CONCOMITANT OF INDUSTRIAL URBANISM

In a major international study, Seymour Lipset and Reinhard Bendix reached the conclusion that social mobility has been a concomitant of industrialization.[45] In fact, they determined that the advanced industrial-urban nations they had surveyed—the United States, Germany, Sweden, Japan, and France—had a high degree of similarity in their mobility rates.

From one generation to the next, between 23 and 31 percent of the non-farm population of these countries moved from working-class to middle-class occupations, or vice versa. Downward mobility varied, but the main finding of Lipset and Bendix remained: that "the countries involved are comparable in their high amounts of total vertical mobility." This had the effect of refuting the common belief that Europe has a closed-class system and the United States an open one. Intead, mobility was interpreted as resulting from the economic expansion accompanying given levels of industrial development. Important cross-cultural differences persist on the availability of higher education to persons with a working-class background, and the like. Yet the conclusion stands, of "relatively little difference in rates of social mobility, as measured by the shift across the nonmanual line, in countries for which sample survey data exist."[46]

---

[44] Leonard Reissman, *Inequality in American Society* (Glenview, Ill.: Scott, Foresman, 1973), p. 123.

[45] Seymour M. Lipset and Reinhard Bendix, *Social Mobility in Industrial Society* (Berkeley and Los Angeles, Calif.: University of Chicago Press, 1959), pp. 25ff.

[46] Ibid., p. 72.

Occupational mobility varies among nations, depending on industrialization. But as S. M. Miller has adduced, upward and downward rates are asymmetrical.[47] That is, high upward rates may be accompanied by either high or low downward rates, and the other way too. Though upward mobility relates to modernization, social structure continues to play a role in either advancing or retarding movement statuswise in modern society.

MOBILITY AND LARGE CITIES

The relative infertility of high-occupation families contributes to social mobility in advanced nations. Furthermore, the concentration of such families in cities, and disproportionately so in large cities, means that the sons of manually-occupied fathers have the opportunity of filling the middle-level positions that economic expansion creates there. In addition, in-migrants to the city can then take up the lower occupations. In this manner, because the urban occupational elite do not monopolize expanding opportunity, a capillary action is characteristic of the centers of population in advanced countries. Indeed, as Lipset and Bendix learned, given democratic systems of education, large cities are centers of mobility.[48]

CLASS CONSCIOUSNESS AND CONFLICT

From the mid-nineteenth century when the Marxian interpretation of history was first expounded—that class struggles are constant in society—the question of class consciousness and conflict has received great attention. No less so perhaps in the sociology of the city.

STABLE PLURALISM OR CLASS CONSCIOUSNESS?

Clark Kerr, formerly Chancellor of the University of California, has contended that industrial-urbanism necessarily produces a pluralistic social system.[49] In it, competing interests agreeing on the common values of suppressing overt conflict and of recognizing the general welfare maintain a regulatory state and also, democratically, submit to its determinations. The Kerr thesis presumes three things: (1) that the middle group, the numerous educated, technical, and managerial white-collar salariat, exercises a good deal of aggregate power; (2) that this segment is affluent and also possesses the

[47] S. M. Miller, "Comparative Social Mobility: A Trend Report," *Current Sociology,* 9 (1960), pp. 1–89.

[48] Lipset and Bendix, op. cit., pp. 218–19.

[49] Clark Kerr et al., *Industrialization and Industrial Man* (Cambridge, Mass.: Harvard University Press, 1960).

common value-attitudes; and (3) that high rates of mobility exist among this meritocracy, thereby keeping the system open to talent. That being the case, say the pluralists, industrially advanced society need anticipate neither totalitarianism nor intense social-class antagonism.

It would be surprising if this roseate analysis went unchallenged. In reviewing Kerr's theory, the English sociologist John Goldthorpe has raised two serious questions. For one thing, Goldthorpe cites the disparity between the manual worker as a producer and the manual worker as a consumer, which prevents his cultural assimilation into the middle class. Second, Goldthorpe views the development of an underclass of people unable, due to lack of education, debilitating forms of socialization, alienation, and discrimination, to benefit from the general leveling up that has taken place in industrial-urban society by and large.[50]

Ralf Dahrendorf, a sociologist and today Director of the London School of Economics, also demures from Kerr's interpretation.[51] Dahrendorf conceives of two trends as being important signs of conflict in advanced society. One is found in the industrial sphere and the other in the political arena. In industry, unions aspire to managerial functions. In government, a service-oriented bureaucracy has come to prevail. Yet even in the democratic countries "purposive rationality" and "managerialism" concentrate on the *how* and not the *what* of authority. Welfare has not been fully achieved. Hence though ostensibly benign the service state, says Dahrendorf, represents an accumulation of power that has only changed, not eliminated, conflict.

THE DISTRIBUTION OF WEALTH

The seeming inelasticity of the national distribution of wealth would suggest that class rigidity is the rule instead of the socioeconomic upgrading Kerr has postulated as typifying industrial urbanism. Contrary to the common belief, those inequalities of wealth that were present two generations ago have not been eliminated or even seriously reduced in spite of tax reforms to do so.

In the United States

The economist Gabriel Kolko has reviewed income distribution movements in the United States over the 25-year period beginning in 1935.[52] He has discerned some minor shifts in the income positions of the major occupational

[50] John H. Goldthorpe, "Social Stratification in Industrial Society," in Melvin M. Tumin, ed., *Readings on Social Stratification* (Englewood Cliffs, N.J.: Prentice-Hall, 1970), pp. 94–112.

[51] Ralf Dahrendorf, *Class and Class Conflict in Industrial Society* (Stanford, Calif.: Stanford University Press, 1959), pp. 299–301.

[52] In *Wealth and Power in America* (New York: Praeger, 1962).

classes. With clerical and sales workers having an income index of 100, there is sharp inequality between the 153 index score of managerial workers and the 57 index-score of unskilled and service workers.[53] Though the income differentials within the ranks of blue-collar workers have continued relatively unchanged, since 1939 their position relative to sales and clerical employees has improved slightly. In fact, the majority of skilled manual workers earn incomes that place them in the wealthier half of the nation. Otherwise, the semiskilled are in the middle range, while the service and unskilled are close to the bottom.

Kolko questions the notion that as a postindustrial country America has moved closer to the ideal of equality. As does Michael Harrington, he stresses economic disparities, poverty, and also insecurity. Although Kolko confirms the leveling up that has recently taken place, he subordinates it to others that he deems more vital: (1) that the relative income shares of the different occupational groups have changed little in the United States since 1910; (2) that white-collar workers are losing ground in their income standing; and (3) that the lack of savings, the prevalence of unemployment, and the incidence of illness among low-income families refute the idea of America as an equalitarian middle-class society.

In Britain

In the period 1911–1913, the top one percent of the British population owned 68 percent of all property in private hands. That one percent were also the recipients of 29 percent of the total British national income. Bottomore reports that though the privileged Britishers now exhibit their wealth more discretely, in toto they retain almost every bit as much as they had before. "In 1946–7, 1 percent of the population still owned 50 percent of all private property, and it is unlikely that the proportion has changed very much since then," Bottomore has written.[54] From 1900 to the present, the distribution of income in Great Britain has, roughly speaking, been so constant that one-tenth of the people has continued to receive about half, and the remaining nine-tenths the other half. This is not to say that no change has taken place at all. In fact, very recent wage and tax policies have eased the British income distribution toward equality about 10 percent in the decade beginning in 1960.[55]

Taxes are alleged to make a real difference in the final allocation of income and wealth in socialist Britain. Yet Bottomore cites Richard Titmuss' able study *Income Distribution and Social Change* as testifying to the "influence of life assurances, superannuation, tax-free payments on retirement,

[53] Ibid., p. 83.

[54] T. B. Bottomore, *Classes in Modern Society* (New York: Pantheon, 1966), p. 38.

[55] M. Nissel, ed., *Social Trends* (London: Her Majesty's Stationery Office, 1970), p. 95.

education covenants, expense accounts and capital gains, in conserving or increasing the wealth and income of the upper class of Great Britain."[56] With regard to the United States, one might recall that expense accounts, sheltered annuities, and tax benefits accruing to capital-gains income serve the same purpose. Thus one study disclosed that in 1968 those with an income of less than $2,000 per year paid 27.2 percent of it in state and local taxes, while the proportion paid by persons with an annual income of $50,000 or more was only 6.7 percent.[57]

A LEVELING UP

Other analysts disagree with such reservations about income distribution in the industrial-urban nations. The economist Simon Kuznets has gathered much data showing that in the United States and in advanced countries generally, a greater distribution of material goods has indeed taken place of late.[58] Though property ownership has not diffused and though the poor have not benefited accordingly, Kuznets asserts that more income is being received and a somewhat greater degree of equality has been realized in the broad middle-income groups. Assessing the same data as Kolko, Kurt Mayer says that "the economic rank order of American society has changed its shape from the traditional pyramid to a diamond bulging at the middle and somewhat flat at the bottom."[59] In constant-value dollars, median family incomes increased by 50 percent in the United States in the 1950s.[60] This occurred despite the fact that in 1959, 20 percent of all families continued to receive less than $3,000. Since 1960, the median income has risen further, by about a third, and the lowest 20 percent have had at least a proportional improvement.

Though disparities in income distribution and wealth continue to be debated, no doubt attaches to the fact that levels of living have risen in the United States. Total national income has grown a great deal. From 1947 to 1972, and measured in constant dollars, the median family income in the nation rose from $5,665 to $11,116, almost doubling in the 25-year interval.[61] This has served to level up the poor in terms of basic needs as well as the

[56] Bottomore, op. cit.

[57] Roger A. Herriot and Herman P. Miller, "Who Paid the Taxes in 1968?" presented at the National Industrial Conference Board Meeting in New York City (March 18, 1971).

[58] Simon Kuznets, *Shares of Upper Income Groups in Income and Savings* (New York: National Bureau of Economic Research, 30 (Winter 1963), pp. 462–68.

[59] Kurt B. Mayer, "The Changing Shape of the American Class Structure," *Social Research,* 30 (Winter 1963), pp. 462–68.

[60] Bureau of the Census, *Statistical Abstract of the United States: 1975* (Washington, D.C.: Government Printing Office, 1975), Table 620, p. 384.

[61] Ibid.

amenities of life, not of course without pockets of poverty remaining. Social services are no doubt more accessible to the less affluent than ever before. The greater average number of years in school—from 10.5 in 1960 to 12.2 in 1970—points in the same direction, that of greater net remuneration.[62] Also, improved working and living conditions have contributed to a sense of economic improvement and social mobility among the general urban populace.[63]

CONTINUED ANTAGONISM

Despite the material betterment of life in America and other advanced nations, dissatisfaction continues to be felt. Using a simple public-opinion method and conceding that it emphasized material rewards, Alex Inkeles found a fairly consistent inverse correlation of felt dissatisfaction with socio-economic standing in 11 countries that he surveyed.[64] Inkeles's data are summarized in Table 10-3. Figures on the middle strata convey some ambiguity. They probably also relate to the difficulty of appraising status in mass society. Status inconsistency (the discrepancy, say, between occupational prestige and income) may perhaps be reflected here.[65]

Many writers insist that the traditional antagonism goes on. They say that the positions of people relative to the political economy are still major variables in the social structure. Consider Joel Montaigne who says, "We may have the most unproletarian proletariat that ever existed, but it is still a proletariat—wage workers and most salaried workers, dependent upon the sale of their labor in the market and propertyless except for the ownership of the hollow symbols of the bourgeoisie."[66] Some of these spokesmen are revisionist Marxists, among them the late C. Wright Mills, who concluded that modern industrial-urban society is not necessarily proceeding toward greater homogeneity and peace under the ideological banner of democratic welfare impelled by a logic of universal industrialism. The political scientist

[62] Bureau of the Census, *Statistical Abstract of the United States: 1972,* op. cit., Table 167, p. 111.

[63] That better working conditions, including debureaucratization, may also induce dissatisfaction over not achieving still more can be observed in Michel Crozier, *The World of the Office Worker,* trans. by David Landau (New York: Schocken, 1971), Ch. 7.

[64] Alex Inkeles, "Industrial Man: The Relation of Status to Experience, Perception, and Value," *American Journal of Sociology,* 66 (July 1960), pp. 13–18.

[65] Mental illness may be related to low status apart from status inconsistency. See Robert E. L. Faris and Y. Warren Dunham, *Mental Disorders in Urban Areas* (Chicago: University of Chicago Press, 1939); A. B. Hollingshead and Leo Srole et al., *Mental Health in the Metropolis* (New York: McGraw-Hill, 1962); and A. B. Hollingshead and F. C. Redlich, *Social Class and Mental Illness* (New York: John Wiley, 1958).

[66] Joel B. Montaigne, Jr., *Class and Nationality* (New Haven, Conn.: College and University Press, 1963), p. 82.

TABLE 10-3   Percentage Satisfied with Progress in Life, by Country and Status[a]

COUNTRY	OCCUPATION: EXECUTIVE, PROFESSIONAL	WHITE COLLAR	WAGE EARNER	SOCIOECONOMIC GROUP: UPPER	MIDDLE	LOWER
Australia	70	64	66	73	70	65
Austria	61	60	47	64	59	60
Belgium	37	36	21	43	41	34
Brazil[b]	74	60	63	81	71	54
Britain	79	66	70	73	68	71
Denmark	77	78	68	81	75	64
Germany	73	71	68	73	72	65
Japan	52	42	33	50	40	13
Netherlands	61	57	59	67	58	66
Norway	89	79	70	87	71	60
Sweden	71	58	67	80	67	60

Source: Alex Inkeles, "Industrial Man: The Relation of Status to Experience, Perception, and Value," *The American Journal of Sociology,* 66 (July 1960), pp. 1–31.

[a] Tabulations from a study conducted by International Research Associates.
[b] Rio de Janeiro and São Paulo only.

Seymour Lipset may infer that class conflict in the democratic industrial nations is limited to disagreement over the distribution of income and does not pertain to the character of the socioeconomic system itself. But the English political scientist T. B. Bottomore, and whom we mentioned earlier, holds, on the other hand, that the ignominy of industrial servitude contrasts disturbingly with the freedom of the workingman's leisure hours. This, says Bottomore, may generate a deep hatred for the industrial order as a whole. Still other commentators see the technocracy of large-scale bureaucracy as stultifying and, as a result, an added source of bitterness.[67]

Calling it perhaps the most underrated class struggle "though one of the more serious and least tractable," Gerhard Lenski cites the conflict between age classes as a persistent well of disturbance.[68] This conflict occurs over rewards in bureaucratized, seniority-prone systems. Concentrating youth in educational institutions just gives them greater opportunity for communication and organization. Though the conflicts actually engendered by the distribution of power may not coincide exactly with the traditionally defined class boundaries, they do give substance to forecasts of continuing struggle eventuating perhaps in hitherto unimagined stratification structures.

[67] See Norman Birnbaum, *The Crisis of Industrial Society* (New York: Oxford University Press, 1969).

[68] Lenski, op. cit., pp. 426–28.

CONCLUSION

Stratification relates to wealth, power, prestige, and style-of-life competition. Understandably, so diffuse a subject has multiple relations with the social process as a whole, and precise generalizations are difficult to substantiate. Urbanization, however, tends not only to make stratification more flexible but also to promote social mobility. Apart from this rule though, a city's stratification profile varies according to the type of community that it functionally is. Also, anomalous forms of ethnic and racial stratification contrary to the generally competitive and individualistic spirit of the city continue to be observed. Finally, despite the overall material improvement and equalitarianism that industrial urbanism has brought about, rigidities in income distribution, interclass culture conflict, and the severe socioeconomic deprivation of some groups raise the question of whether class consciousness and conflict have been largely dispelled from modern urban society.

FOR FURTHER READING

Paul Blumberg, ed., *The Impact of Social Class* (New York: Crowell, 1972). Shows that social class has a strong, determining influence upon human life.

Richard P. Coleman and Bernice L. Neugarten, *Social Status in the City* (San Francisco, Calif.: Jossey-Bass, 1917). Formulates an Index of Urban Status and applies it to metropolitan Kansas City.

Otis Duncan et al., *Socio-Economic Background and Achievement* (New York: Seminar Press, 1972). Accomplishment in American society in the context of occupational mobility and stratification.

A. B. Hollingshead, *Elmtown's Youth and Elmtown Revisited* (New York: John Wiley, 1975). On the persistence of the status structure from 1941 to 1973.

John C. Legget, *Class, Race, and Labor: Working-Class Consciousness in Detroit* (New York: Oxford University Press, 1968). The potential and real class awareness among black and white auto workers.

Joseph Lopreato and Lawrence E. Hazelrigg, *Class Conflict and Mobility* (Scranton, Pa.: Chandles, 1972). The major theorists on social stratification, with considerable reflection on industrial-urban society.

Frank Parkin, *Class Inequality and Political Order* (New York: Praeger, 1971). The stratification systems in capitalist and communist soxieties.

Leonard Reissman, *Inequality in American Society* (Glenview, Ill.: Scott, Foresman, 1973). Emphasizing class and power as primary factors for understanding poverty and racial inequality.

Leo F. Schnore, *Class and Race in Cities and Suburbs* (Chicago: Markham, 1972). The writings of a sociologist known for capable theorizing and careful research.

Holger R. Stub, e.d., *Status Communities in Modern Society* (Hinsdale, Ill.: Dryden Press, 1972). Articles that feature prestige and life style differentiation (status groupings) rather than economic divisions (social classes).

CHAPTER 11

THE
MASS MEDIA

Large-scale communication is an essential component of any industrial or postindustrial urban society. This means, primarily, the activities of the mass media: press, radio and TV, and motion pictures. All of these have in common that from centralized sources they address messages to a broad, heterogeneous, and impersonal audience.[1]

The parallel development of mass communication with modern urban society is clear. Wilbur Schramm, Stanford University professor of international communication, compared the four most highly urbanized and industrial areas in the world with the three most underdeveloped regions—the United States, Western Europe, Japan, and Australia in one group, and

---

[1] A secondary system of communication exists alongside the mass media. This network includes the postal service, telephone lines, and so on. It undergirds the media themselves. The second system, however, differs from the media inasmuch as it tends to be merely technological.

Africa, Asia, and Latin America in the other.[2] The former had, as a whole, for every 100 persons in their population, 6 times as many newspapers, 970 percent more radios, 700 percent more motion-picture theatre seats, and 18 times as many television sets.

Similarly, studying from 54 to 73 nations for which data were available, Daniel Lerner established high correlations between urbanization and literacy (0.64) and literacy and media participation (0.82).[3] "For countries in transition today," observed Lerner, "these high correlations suggest that literacy and media participation may be considered as a supply-and-demand reciprocal in a communication market whose locus, at least in its historical inception, can only be urban."[4] Lerner views the mass media as an inevitable concomitant of modern society, which he defines as "distinctively industrial, urban, literate, and participant." The final attribute designated by Lerner, "participation," refers to psychic mobility evidenced in intense, sustained political and economic behavior. According to Lerner, mass communication contributes to this process of psychic activization in urban areas.

The association between communication and urban life has also been advanced by the urbanist Richard L. Meier.[5] Meier views the growth of urbanization as marked by the continuous appearance of more advanced systems of communication. Meier writes that "the accumulation of knowledge" and "the accumulation of techniques" have gone on in direct relationship to urbanization. In fact, says Meier, "public activity" as distinct from interpersonal and family activities has been inseparable from the development of written languages and the various means of sharing knowledge among people in order to improve their collective life.

The sociologist Scott Greer recently developed the theory of societal scale. Greer sees the expansion of the means of communication and transportation as having paralleled the intense agglomeration of people into large urban communities. Now that both the mass media as well as very efficient high-speed forms of transport are operational, a more widespread and lower-density type of regional urban settlement can take place. Thus Greer concludes, "the classical city is anomalous in large-scale society," and "the revolution in the space-time ratio has made obsolete the older urban community forms."[6]

[2] Wilbur Schramm, *Mass Media and National Development* (Stanford, Calif.: Stanford University Press, 1964).

[3] Daniel Lerner, *The Passing of Traditional Society: Modernizing the Middle East* (New York: Free Press, 1962), pp. 43–44.

[4] Ibid., p. 60.

[5] Richard L. Meier, *A Communications Theory of Urban Growth* (Cambridge, Mass.: M.I.T. Press, 1962), pp. 43–44.

[6] Scott Greer, *Life and Politics in Metropolitan America* (New York: Oxford University Press, 1942), pp. 65–66.

Urbanization and the media show a high correlation. TV antennas, with the Statue of Liberty in the distance at the entrance to New York's harbor.

This chapter takes the point of view that in our urban nation today the media make up an essential but overarching system in which individual urban centers participate in an interdependent but dispersed manner. The magnitude of mass communications in the United States currently may be seen in such facts as the following. In 1973, commercial AM radio stations numbered 4346 and commercial TV stations, 704. Of the latter, the great majority were the outlets of one or another of only three nationwide networks—ABC, CBS, and NBC. The daily net paid circulation of our 1774 daily and Sunday newspapers was 63.1 million.[7] But like TV channels, the American press was undergirded by a single pair of news services and a handful of

[7] Bureau of the Census, *Statistical Abstract of the United States: 1975* (Washington, D.C.: Government Printing Office, 1975), Table 831, p. 503, and Table 841, p. 506.

syndicated feature sources. These facts and figures attest to the vital importance of mass communication to our modern urban life, and also reveal the national patterning of public communication. For these reasons our presentation of the mass media begins with their national organization.

THE ORGANIZATION OF THE MEDIA

Differing social philosophies are evident in the organization of the systems of mass communication serving the advanced nations today. The outstanding authorities in the field—Siebert, Peterson, and Schramm—identify four philosophies: (1) the libertarian; (2) the social-responsibility type; (3) the authoritarian; and (4) the Communist.[8] The American system is basically libertarian.

THE LIBERTARIAN FORM

The libertarian theory first came to fruition in seventeenth century England. At that time the natural-rights conception of a social order inhabited by rational individuals to whom freedom of speech and the media is of vital importance rose to prominence. John Milton, Thomas Jefferson, and John Stuart Mill amplified this position over the years, holding that only the free contest of ideas can produce the knowledge that is essential to the proper conduct of human affairs. Consequently, they could not justify restrictions on communication except possibly such minimal ones as government expediting expression by operating the postal service, affording people remedy for defamation, and curbing obscenity.

Problems inherent in the libertarian theory did arise, however, such as freedom of expression versus national security, and the unequal distribution of wealth barring the underprivileged from having equal acess to the media. The concentration of power is a perennial problem under libertarianism. In America today, communications are largely in the hands of private corporations, but more than 100 newspaper "groups" exist, that is, are associated under common ownership.[9] In fact, about a third of all our daily newspapers have such affiliations. Seven national chains are doing business: the Chicago Tribune, Newhouse, Scripps-Howard, Knight, Hearst, Cowles, and Ridder. As of 1968, the Newhouse group consisted of 23 dailies and 14 Sunday papers; Hearst, 8 dailies and 7 Sundays; and Scripps-Howard, 17 dailies and 7 Sundays. The 12 Chicago Tribune papers had a weekly circulation of 26.3 million. Regional groups, like the 37 papers of the late Frank E. Gannett

[8] Fred S. Siebert, Theodore Peterson, and Wilbur Schramm, *Four Theories of the Press* (Urbana, Ill.: University of Illinois Press, 1963).

[9] Frank Luther Mott, *American Journalism* (New York: Macmillan, 1962), 3rd ed., pp. 813ff.

in medium-sized cities in New York State and New Jersey, also operate here. Concentration of the press is so intense that fully 97 percent of America's cities at present have a local newspaper monopoly.[10]

Still further concentration is evident in the fact that newspapers also own radio and TV outlets. In 1971, 318 of the country's AM stations and 176 of its TV channels were owned by the publishers of newspapers or periodicals.[11] Also, only two wire services gather news in the United States: United Press International for 1656 papers and 1996 radio and TV stations (and also for a total of 1714 abroad), and the Associated Press serving some 7320 institutional clients.

Besides concentration, another major problem of mass communications under the libertarian system concerns its cultural content, notably its tendencies toward salaciousness and violence for entertainment, practices that may have baneful consequences for behavior.[12] This aspect of the media shows up also in other ways as well, like the possibly dysfunctional effects of commercially-geared programming in the developing nations. This refers to the cultivation of consumerism in advance of productive industrialization, which by arousing unsatisfied wants can lead to political instability.[13]

SOCIALLY RESPONSIBLE ORGANIZATION

The contrast between broadcasting in Britain and in the United States illustrates some of the differences between the social-responsibility conception of the media and the libertarian philosophy. Although a recent effort has been made to supply the British public with commercial broadcasting through the Independent Television Authority, the BBC, the British Broadcasting Corporation, has been the cornerstone of the electronic media since 1927. Until ITA began in 1955, the BBC was also a monopoly. Besides disseminating the news, the BBC, headed by an appointed board of governors, has four other aims: (1) to supply a light programme of somewhat frivolous entertainment; (2) the home service for those interested in education and more balanced entertainment; (3) the third program of serious music, talk, and drama; and (4) external broadcasting to keep London a center of international communication.

Although ITA was created for advertising purposes, the commercial

[10] Raymond B. Nixon, "Trends in U.S. Newspaper Ownership: Concentration and Competition," *Gazette*, 14 (1968), pp. 181–93.

[11] Bureau of the Census, *Statistical Abstract of the United States: 1972* (Washington, D.C.: Government Printing Office), Table 808, p. 499.

[12] As a study claiming injurious effects, see Monroe M. Lefkowitz et al., "Television Violence and Child Aggression," in Surgeon General's Scientific Advisory Committee, *Television and Social Behavior* (Washington, D.C.: Government Printing Office, 1972), Vol. 3, pp. 35–135.

[13] See Alan Wells, *Picture Tube Imperialism? The Impact of U.S. Television on Latin America* (Mary Knoll, New York: Orbis Books, 1972).

sponsorship of programs by advertising is not allowed in Britain. This is done to prevent commercialism from having an adverse effect on standards. Whether freed from the profit motive or dedicated to the improvement of mass culture, that BBC has actually been able to achieve greater quality is a debated question. Paulu concludes that British TV standards do not surpass those of the United States.[14] Others detect a preference in BBC programming for the aristocratic but stodgy nineteenth-century Oxford-Cambridge type of culture. They reproach the BBC for neglecting science and other more modern values.

AUTHORITARIAN SYSTEMS

Adopted in modern times by Czarist Russia, Imperial Japan, and by much of Asia and Latin America more recently, the authoritarian rationale of media use was given great appeal by the English social philosopher Thomas Hobbes 300 years ago. Hobbes viewed the needs of the social order as paramount, with freedom of expression necessarily subordinated to the state. Monarchist England followed the Hobbesean teachings by controlling newspapers through the issuance of permits (patents) to their printers, but in time this practice was allowed to lapse and disappear entirely.

A spectrum of authoritarian systems continues to exist around the globe.[15] For example, the censorship of political criticism operates in Arab nations today, and in South Africa editors may be prosecuted for their writings. In Turkey and Indonesia, "unofficial methods" take care of refractory publications.[16] In other countries, still other measures are used to control the media in the interests of national stability.

THE COMMUNIST APPROACH

Communist control of mass communication is even more stringent than the authoritarian type. Soviet Russia's control of its media operates through a pyramid of administrative committees, in the last analysis directed by the communist party.[17] This Russian pattern has evolved in accordance with Marxist-Leninist theory that mass communication has the negative responsibility of minimizing social divisions and the positive duty of fostering unity in behalf of public policy.

Broadcasting in the U.S.S.R. is monopolized by the state, with newspa-

[14] Burton Paulu, *British Broadcasting* (Minneapolis, Minn.: University of Minnesota Press, 1956), p. 380.

[15] Cf. Siebert, Peterson, and Schramm, op. cit., p. 31.

[16] Ibid.

[17] For a thematic analysis see Alex Inkeles, *Public Opinion in Soviet Russia* (Cambridge, Mass.: Harvard University Press, 1951).

pers, radio, and TV controlled by the government, the party, and the military forces. Even word-of-mouth communication is not exempt from efforts at total control in Soviet Russia, for remarks inimical to the regime are subject to punishment. Though itself authoritarian, it is the aim of mobilizing public support through agitation and propaganda that differentiates the communist mass communication system from the simple authoritarian kind. Soviet newspapers, for instance, do not present events as much as they interpret them as part of a larger program of engineering a national consensus. The emphasis in the Russian press is thus on inculcating the attitudes that the party line endorses and on securing greater effort behind official policy.

MEDIA IMPACT

The ideologies according to which communication is organized presuppose functional roles for the media. But to what extent and in what specific ways do the media actually bear out these suppositions?

FOUR FUNCTIONS

The mass media have been observed by Charles Wright to discharge four general functions: (1) surveillance; (2) correlation; (3) cultural transmission; and (4) entertainment.[18]

Surveillance

The surveillance activity of the media refers to the dissemination of news that aids the public in dealing with its environment, its internal activities, and its norms and values. The media inform people about routine events such as sales and deaths, but also about unusual occurrences like epidemics and disasters. Hence surveillance includes a warning function. Also, the fact that newspapers and the other media report extensively on what is going on, and in the process giving publicity to deviant behavior, results in circumstances under which deviance is condemned and more unifying social control achieved. In this manner the surveillance role of the media shades off into the correlation, or editorial, function that they also perform.

Correlation

Through their editorials, signed columns, and published letters, newspapers aim at influencing public opinion. Such correlation helps a community, or an

[18] Charles R. Wright, "Functional Analysis and Mass Communication," in Lewis A. Dexter and David Manning White, eds., *People, Society, and Mass Communications* (New York: Free Press, 1964), pp. 91–109; also Charles R. Wright, *Mass Communication: A Sociological Perspective* (New York: Random House, 1959).

entire society for that matter, to mobilize its resources. For example, an evaluation of a tax policy aids in determining probable business conditions. Similarly, assessing foreign affairs can reduce citizen apathy, anxiety, or hostility.

On the other hand, by merely paying attention to events the media can influence the attitudes of the public. When Nikita Khrushchev, Soviet Premier at the time, visited the United States in 1959, newspapers and broadcasting stations were the targets of thousands of messages urging them to show their disapproval of Russia by ignoring his presence in the country. Yet, according to the Associated Press, not a single American daily failed to give front-page coverage to Mr. Khrushchev's arrival, the minimum amount of space devoted to the event being six paragraphs and the maximum, in the New York *Times,* more than three full pages.[19] No doubt this lent some legitimacy to the Soviet Prime Minister among Americans just as then President Nixon's visits to the U. S. S. R. in 1972 and 1974 occasioned TV broadcasts to the Soviet people in an effort to solidify a policy of detente between the two powers.

Cultural Transmission

Cultural transmission in mass communication is an activity embedded in both the news and editorial functions. The media may cultivate respect for the prevailing political processes, or they may uphold the values of science. At a lower level, they may also propagate beauty hints, the care of pets, the day's horoscope, table decoration, and gardening.

In a study of the Chicago community press—there were no fewer than 94 such local papers in the Windy City at the time—Morris Janowitz found voluntary associations of prominent interest.[20] And in this category, youth and school groups drew the greatest attention. Much space was also devoted to churches, neighborhood councils, and local businesses. Political parties, labor unions, and property-owner groups were mentioned far less frequently, because the community press took a generally apolitical though locally oriented stance. In this way it avoided impairing the popular consensus even if this did not contribute to greater unity in the entire Chicago metropolitan area.

In contrast to local journalism, we also need to take note of cultural transmission at the national level, notably the Baltimore *Sun* with its socially responsible, educated, elitist values; the international humanism of *The Christian Science Monitor;* and the sober liberalism of the St. Louis *Post-Dispatch.*

[19] Clifton Daniel, "Responsibilities of the Reporter and the Editor," in Gerald Gross, ed., *The Responsibility of the Press* (New York: Fleet, 1966), p. 152.

[20] Morris Janowitz, *The Community Press in an Urban Setting* (Chicago: University of Chicago Press, 1967), 2nd ed., pp. 78ff.

Entertainment

Newspaper comics, the popular music of radio, the run-of-the-mill motion picture, and the variety shows and situation comedies of TV are all abundant evidence of the entertainment that the media are capable of and in large measure are engaged in supplying.

Entertainment provides people with a respite from their cares, but it serves social-control functions too. One case is the humor that casts minorities into a bad light and sanctions their already lowly status. In addition, entertainment also socializes people, for example, in acquainting them with particular styles of life. Noting this capacity, Harold Mendelsohn has written, "By its very preoccupation with the middle class . . . mass entertainment reinforces the values and life-ways of the middle class and as a by-product no doubt helps to maintain the middle-class status quo of American society."[21]

DYSFUNCTIONS OF THE MEDIA

The functional treatment of mass communication does not ignore the fact that in each category the media may have deleterious effects on the public. Such dysfunctions include: (1) threatening the stability of the social system by presenting news of superior foreign institutions; (2) undermining public confidence in the established order through the dissemination of information about corruption; (3) increasing blind conformity; (4) strengthening fantasy-prone passivity; and (5) reinforcing antisocial attitudes.[22] One major study of the American uses of television concluded that, "aside from the day's news and weather—which he watches regularly—the average viewer rarely uses the set as a deliberate source of information, and he is extremely unlikely to turn on serious and informative public affairs presentations, even if he is watching while they are on the air."[23] Whether entertainment is dysfunctional remains to be seen. The question itself does indicate the importance of research into the real impact of the media and the specific psychosocial processes involved.

MEDIA INFLUENCE

The ways in which mass communication influences the public include the factors of mediating agencies, reinforcement, canalization, and psychological gratification.[24]

[21] Harold Mendelsohn, *Mass Entertainment* (New Haven, Conn.: College & University Press, 1966), p. 68.

[22] See J. D. Halloran, R. L. Brown, and D. C. Chaney, *Television and Delinquency* (New York: Humanities Press, 1970), which compares the differing interpretations placed on TV program content by matched delinquent and nondelinquent subjects in Britain.

[23] Gary A. Steiner, *The People Look at Television* (New York: Alfred A. Knopf, 1963), pp. 228–29.

[24] Joseph T. Klapper, *The Effects of Mass Communication* (New York: Free Press, 1960).

Through Mediating Agencies

Mass communication operates within a web of mediators. Typically, the media do not have direct impact, as far as influence goes, because the audience is susceptible to a two-step flow of communication. In this process, personal contacts filter the media messages. Numerous so-called opinion leaders function among the public, and in their everyday conduct sanction the credibility of messages, or they impart ideas to their friends and acquaintances that they have themselves picked up from their own selective exposure to the media. Opinion leaders are found within primary groups, and as family members, fellow employees, coreligionists, and precinct committeemen, they engage in face-to-face relationships in their transmission of media content.

Reinforcement

The mediating group, opinion leaders, and interpersonal contacts render the media capable more of reinforcing existing ideas, sentiments, relationships, and tendencies than of significantly changing them. Investigating political opinion formation in Elmira, New York, during the 1948 presidential election, Berelson, Lazarsfeld, and McPhee learned that not only were few citizens converted to the opposite party, but that those who were more exposed to media influence were even less likely to be converted! They tended to select messages in accord with their own views. Hence the conclusion that the media primarily reinforce states of mind already extant.[25]

Canalization

Where the media of communication do effect change, or at least contribute to it, either mediating agents are absent or the persons themselves are already predisposed to change. That is the essence of the media producing change by canalization. More specifically, where the media are responsible for attitude change, it is likely that (1) the issues are not felt to be especially important; (2) the members of the audience are originally uninformed, uncommitted, or neutral; or (3) the persons so affected are not involved in intense interpersonal relationships that bear on the subject. In other words, conversions take place on minor matters, in small degrees, and in minds already entertaining conflicting predispositions.[26]

Some researchers have dissented from the conclusion that the mass media have only a slight effect on opinion. In their view, mass com-

[25] See Paul F. Lazarsfeld, Bernard Berelson, and Hazel Gaudet, *The People's Choice* (New York: Columbia University Press, 1948), which first presented the two-step flow process.

[26] Bernard Berelson and Gary A. Steiner, *Human Behavior: An Inventory of Scientific Findings* (New York: Harcourt Brace & World, 1964), p. 542.

munication has an important cumulative impact over the years, for example, in shaping the political imagery of the public and of people's impressions of events and leaders.[27] Those who hold this position believe that the media structure understanding by limiting the public to certain ways of thinking and no other. One illustration would be the idea of taking free enterprise for granted and possibly regulating it but not doing away with it entirely. Yet, on the contrary, in this respect the media probably only mirror the belief of the general public.

Psychological Gratification

To a limited extent, as in the case of depicting violence or presenting erotic materials, mass communication serves various psychophysical functions.[28] The overall appeal that radio has for its audience furnishes a good example of this in the city. Mendelsohn, who has reviewed the place of radio in seven American cities—New York, Chicago, Boston, Philadelphia, St. Louis, San Francisco, and Los Angeles—calls attention to the "personalization" of radio broadcasting. This highlights the capacity of mass communication to have direct psychological effects on people: by affording companionship; by accommodating the listener's volatile moods (switching from station to station); and by allowing him to share in the experiences of people in his own social category.

It is interesting to note that as TV viewing has preempted time earlier devoted to radio, radio stations have reacted by emphasizing their companionship function. Thus stations now devote themselves in specialized fashion to commuters, night workers, adolescents, foreign-language groups, and invalids.

ADVERTISING AND PUBLIC RELATIONS

In mass communication, influence is also exercised by those persons engaged in the manipulation of symbols who are related to the media but not directly involved in them, such as press agents, advertising men, and market-research consultants. Advertising, mass information and persuasion for commercial purposes, has an important counterpart in public relations. The latter consists of communication aimed at securing public support for an organization or undertaking.

---

[27] Kurt Lang and Gladys Engel Lang, *Politics and Television* (Chicago: Quadrangle Books, 1970), p. 306.

[28] Harold Mendelsohn, "Listening to Radio," in Dexter and White, op. cit., pp. 239–49.

EXHIBIT 11-1 All-News Radio

SAN FRANCISCO.
George McManus, a genial 35-year-old reporter for radio station KCBS, was standing with other news people on a San Francisco street a year ago, waiting for President Ford. Seeing the normal bustle that precedes a President, McManus spoke over his portable transmitter to the 32nd-floor studio in a nearby skyscraper.

"Put me on. Quick, put me on."

An announcer said over the studio microphone:

"We go now to George McManus at the St. Francis Hotel."

The next sounds over San Francisco radios were crowd noises, some applause, a sharp bang, someone screaming and then McManus:

"My God! My God! There's been a shot! There's been a shot! . . . We're being pushed back by the police. . . . Somebody fired a shot here. We don't know if anybody's been hit. My God! Somebody fired a shot. . . . He has a gun in his right hand right in front of me. . . ."

A policeman was heard answering McManus's question:

"No, they didn't get Ford."

"The President has not been hit," McManus said into his microphone. "He has not been hit. . . ."

It was the wild shot fired by Sara Jane Moore from a gun instantly seized by a man near her. McManus's was the only live broadcast of the incident. The recorded sounds were repeated on newscasts all over the country and McManus's words printed in hundreds of newspapers.

All-news radio, a media development that has recently gained great popularity in U.S. cities, seems to appeal to the audience's need to experience other people's troubles or to reassure themselves of their own security.

Source: Ben H. Bagdikian, "Fires, Sex, and Freaks," *New York Times* Magazine (October 10, 1976), pp. 40ff.

ADVERTISING

The mass market of a commercial, industrial society makes up a vast system of product distribution. In it, advertising facilitates the marketing of goods and services both at the wholesale and retail levels.

Advertising first arose in connection with newspapers and magazines selling space for this purpose. Lever's Sunlight soap is an early example of the power of advertising to help sell products. During the 1870s and 1880s, the Englishman W. H. Lever fended off competitors by aggressively promoting his own soap in advertisements and also by packaging his product in a distinctive wrapper. Lever was indeed an advertising pioneer in the Anglo-American world. In the United States, total expenditures for advertising grew

Advertising facilitates the marketing of goods and services, including pizzas and dry cleaning.

from $5 million in 1865 to $2.1 billion by 1940 and $25 billion in 1973.[29]

The rapid expansion of America's advertising budget recently correlates with the swift introduction of other marketing devices, including sophisticated packaging, self-service selling, supermarkets, discount stores, shopping malls, vending machines, and the like. Advertising, however, continues to occupy a strategic place in the nation's mammoth marketing system. In the United States every day some 4.2 billion advertising messages are published in our daily newspapers, and an additional 1.36 billion appear daily in periodicals. Radio stations broadcast 730,000 commercials a day and TV channels another 100,000. In addition, we are confronted by 330,000 outdoor billboards, 2.5 million bus, trolley, and subway train display cards, 51.3 million pieces of direct-mail advertisements, and unknown billions of other promotional materials. It is estimated that the typical American is within reading and hearing range of 1500 advertisements every 24 hours![30]

PUBLIC RELATIONS

A competitive economy and a pluralistic political system both necessitate ramified decision-making, or at least a high degree of coordination. In this

[29] Bureau of the Census, *Statistical Abstract of the United States: 1975,* op. cit., Table 1299, p. 771.

[30] Leo Bogart, *Strategy in Advertising* (New York: Harcourt Brace & World, 1967), p. 2 and p. 11.

setting, public relations has a clear rationale: securing sufficient understanding among a considerable number of individuals to permit enterprise to be carried on.[31] All this creates serious philosophical and political issues as well as cunning strategies in trying to influence the public.

ADVERTISING AND PUBLIC RELATIONS STRATEGY

Advertising and public relations take market considerations and cultural symbolism into account. In other words, socioeconomic interests are exploited at the same time that appeals are made to sentiment.

Market research has recently led to the featuring of the strategy of segmentation, that is, dividing markets in order to conquer them one by one. Segmentation contrasts with the aggregation strategy, say, of Coca Cola selling one standard product everywhere to everyone. Segmentation addresses itself to differences in the geographic or social market, to age and status groups, for instance, and seizing upon them in relation to production, warehousing, transportation, and promotional costs. In this way, different types of cigarettes have been manufactured since World War II—standard size, king, 100s (and even 101s!)—for a variety of consumers.

The proliferation of the mass media has contributed to segmentation because it has made effective communication with distant markets feasible. It becomes simple, therefore, to prepare sales messages for carefully defined publics. The lower middle-class woman, it has been said, wants her living room to be like the "pretty pictures" in medium-level shelter and service magazines, while the upper-lower wife is supposed to be more interested in a full array of white kitchen appliances than in a well-appointed living room. Furthermore, selective advertising can be appropriately reinforced by having specialized sales outlets, special sales-force preparation, aggressive shelf competition, and so on, all perhaps under the umbrella of a distinctive label and a diversified, financially powerful company.

The largest businesses strive for an advertising and public relations program all dovetailed into one coordinated strategy. Howard W. Cutler, long associated with the scientific public relationist Edward L. Bernays, has formulated a model for such an enterprise.[32] In it, a firm's public relations department is charged with maintaining friendly relations with union leaders, giving financial and moral support to "all forward looking movements within the community," with interpreting the public to the company, and, as a consequence, of having the public participate in making the company's policies. The potentially exploitative nature of public relations is perhaps equally apparent in this.

[31] Howard W. Cutler, "Objectives," in Edward L. Bernays, ed., *The Engineering of Consent* (Norman, Okla.: University of Oklahoma Press, 1955), p. 30 is instructive on this point.

[32] Ibid., pp. 45ff.

Advertising has long been challenged on the grounds of social utility and responsibility. It is claimed that the type of advertising which is merely competitive as distinct from the type that is informative wastes money. Conditioning the consumer to be loyal to brand names, it is likewise held, creates monopoly. Again, the charge is made that advertising favors the manufacturer, because advertising claims cannot be easily tested though the costs of advertising can be readily passed on to the consumer. Furthermore, advertising is objectionable to those who view it as inculcating materialistic and hedonistic values. And finally, that since the media are financially dependent on advertising, the evaluative function of mass communication tends to be blunted. In much the same way, public relations practices are condemned for insidiously undermining media credibility, like the drug manufacturer directing a steady flow of information to newspapers to gain public favor and forestall charges of exorbitant pricing.

To these charges, advertisers and publicists have responded with a vigorous defense of their own usefulness and ethics. They have pointed to government curbs against excesses, and the professionalization of the field to guard against false statements, offenses to public decency, and so forth. Yet, probably the greater part of the effectiveness of advertising and public relations results not from literal statements but covert associations. Research even suggests it is possible, say, for TV advertisers "to select programs and places within programs which are most suitable in terms of mood for the advertising of particular products."[33]

Applied social science and the modern technology of the media do combine at present to give public relations and advertising unusual ability to create the background conditions for the kinds of overt behavior their practitioners want from the public. At the same time, public awareness has also been growing about issues such as artificial images, prestige build-ups, the sale of influence, the manipulation of opinion, and the opportunistic claiming of credit for good deeds. To this the thought may be added that the opponents of advertising and public relations have shown a readiness to attribute faults to advertising and public relations that objective research has often failed to verify at all.

THE PUBLIC INTEREST

The preceding sections of this chapter have made it evident that in a pluralistic society adhering to the libertarian doctrine of mass communication

---

[33] Joel N. Axelrod, "Induced Moods and Attitudes toward Products," in Harper W. Boyd and Joseph W. Newman, eds., *Advertising Management* (Homewood, Ill.: Richard D. Irwin, 1965), p. 445.

there is perennial apprehension about preserving the public interest from the presumably powerful media.

FEAR OF MONOPOLISTIC PRACTICES

The churchman Reinhold Niebuhr expressed the fear of monopolistic media practices undermining democracy and debasing the culture by declaring, "The problem of bigness in the field of communication is aggravated even more in the final technical triumph of mass communication, television, because there are only limited air frequencies upon which the words and images can run, so that television is naturally dominated by the big 'chains.' "[34] As early as 1919, in *The Brass Check,* Upton Sinclair was advancing the simplistic thesis of owner-dominated mass communication acting as a manipulative tool of big business. The idea has been fostered since, particularly with regard to the self-interested use of the media by big government as well as by powerful business groups. The dependence of the media on commercial interests, it is held, conditions their political and philosophical outlook. Also, those who administer newspapers, radio stations, and TV channels allow their own interests to intrude on their judgment as to what constitutes the news and how to present it. In addition, it is asserted that public officials resemble business executives in this respect. The cultivation of the media by government agencies has received no little documentation in line with Sinclair's hypothesis of more than 50 years ago.

Consider as an illustration the public information activities of the American military. Beginning in the 1940s, the Defense Department encouraged the formation of semiofficial organizations like the Army Association, Navy League, and the National Security Industrial Association.[35] Each was to have its own aims within the overall mission of the Defense Department and its network of contributing suppliers and professional adjuncts. Thus the Army Association would be expected to foster appreciation of the nation's land forces, and so on. The Defense Department itself would, and actually did, contribute much information for further dissemination in order to cultivate public opinion in line with military interests.[36]

As has been already noted, scholarship on mass communication is inclined to be reserved about just how persuasive the media are. One research scientist surveying the psychological literature concluded that rigorous knowledge about the long-term effects of the media was scanty, to say

[34] Reinhold Niebuhr, "Introduction," in Wilbur Schramm, *Responsibility in Mass Communication* (New York: Harper & Row, 1957), p. xii.

[35] See Joseph Monsen, Jr., and Mark W. Cannon, *The Makers of Public Policy* (New York: McGraw-Hill, 1965), pp. 270ff.

[36] Ibid., pp. 277–78.

the least.[37] Another well-known scholar weighed media impact on political opinion in the United States only to declare that there were few well-established propositions on the subject.[38] He went on to add that these distilled down only to the fact that "the mass audience consists of individuals living within and subject to a variety of group influences."

COMMUNICATION AS A SOCIAL SYSTEM

The simplistic reasoning of Upton Sinclair and others like him has given way to much more complex and usually less fearsome models about the media and how they affect or fail to affect the public. Functionalist sociologists have made a modest beginning toward working out a theory indicating that in mass society communication is itself a differentiated social system. Though related to other institutions, mass communication thus develops partly spontaneously and partly in interaction with its environing systems.[39]

Media Practices: Spontaneous Developments

Many media practices have developed simply with use, and some of them arouse concern for the public interest. For instance, owing to the aim that they have of reaching a wide audience, the media resort, inconsistently, to innocuousness and sensationalism. Unwilling to give offense to the public on which they depend, they practice prudent evasion and blandly try to avert antagonism. A common practice here is for editors to rely on syndicated columnists to make hard judgments on sensitive questions and not to do so themselves. Also, the media avoid making political endorsements, for the same reason. In the 1964 presidential election between Lyndon Johnson and Barry Goldwater, 60 percent of all American dailies were either neutral or failed to support either candidate.[40] At the same time though as they seek to be bland, the media also practice sensationalism. As the Commission on Freedom of the Press put the matter, "To attract the maximum audience, the press emphasizes the exceptional rather than the representative, the sensational rather than the significant."[41] As a result of these two common preoc-

[37] Carl I. Hovland, "Effects of the Mass Media of Communication," in Gardner Lindzey, ed., *Handbook of Social Psychology* (Cambridge, Mass.: Addison-Wesley, 1954), II, pp. 1026–1103.

[38] V. O. Key, Jr., *Public Opinion and American Democracy* (New York: Alfred A. Knopf, 1964), pp. 345ff.

[39] Consult Talcott Parsons and Winston White, "The Mass Media and the Structure of American Society," *Journal of Social Issues*, 16 (1960), pp. 67–77.

[40] Peterson, Jensen, and Rivers, op. cit., p. 231. See also Alfred Balk, "Beyond Agnewism," *Columbia Journalism Review* (Winter 1969–1970), pp. 14–19.

[41] The Commission on Freedom of the Press, *A Free and Responsible Press* (Chicago: University of Chicago Press, 1947), p. 55.

cupations, writers have concluded that the media fail the public interest, specifically, that innocuousness tends to confirm existing attitudes and values, and that sensationalism narcotizes the public concerning inequities in the social structure.

Other journalistic conventions have grown up whose combined effect is to impair media surveillance and evaluation. One might be mentioned in particular, that of attributing information to anonymous sources, such as "a White House spokesman" or "persons close to the governor." This encourages opportunistic leaking of the news by self-interested people. Such leaking, which reached crescendo heights in the Watergate scandal, allows for irresponsible news dissemination. It is true that this practice also permits public opinion to be built up in behalf of constructive measures, but it has great potentiality for the exercise of covert influence as well.

The Media as One Element in the Social Environment

Apart from their own conventional practices that fail to serve the public interest, the media are subject to their social environment, which may compromise their social utility too. Unlike the earlier image which had the agencies of mass communication potentially dominated by the institutions of business and government, the more recent picture of them is that the media function in an indistinct web of multilateral influence. That is, every element involved exerts some influence and also receives some, so that the media are, as it were, mutually implicated instead of simply dominating or being dominated.

One political analyst sees the media as "nodes with individuals and social groupings distant from the centers and from each other."[42] The media are thus both "lateral channels" and "links in other chains." In other words, public officials as well as private executives use the media as a common source of information and try through the media to exert their influence. These persons contribute their own perceptions to the media and have them circulated to others by newsmen who are quasiconfidants of the persons from whom they receive their information.[43] As a result, politicians, officials, and businessmen tend to make their assessment of conditions in common with one another from the same communicated observations. Nationally, for Washington officialdom, the New York *Times,* the Washington *Post,* the St. Louis *Post-Dispatch,* the *Christian Science Monitor,* the *Wall Street Journal,* and a few others from Los Angeles and Chicago currently supply the common discourse in question. In this way, though indistinctly, the media of mass communication create reality for decision makers and the general public as well.

[42] Richard R. Fagen, *Politics and Communication* (Boston: Little, Brown, 1966), p. 45.

[43] See Jeremy Tunstall, *Journalists at Work* (London: Constable and Constable, 1971).

Photographers, movie and television crews swarm over John Dean as he arrives to testify at a Watergate hearing.

Consider the two common tests which the average individual makes of the acceptability of the news he receives from the press or television in connection with the idea of the media supplying its audience a discourse in common. Kurt and Gladys Lang, specialists in the sociology of mass communication, call them the test of effective congruence and the test of consistency.[44] The first, effective congruence, that is, whether the news story agrees with the individual's personal feelings and understanding of such events, is weak, because people usually select the sources they are already predisposed to accept. The second test, consistency, refers to corroboration by other reports. This is also of limited value either due to the unavailability of other reports or of the lack of opportunity to consult them. Consequently, the media may be thought to give the framework within which the members of its audience tend to think.

We may conclude from all of this that the media are not independent of or solely dependent on business and government, but interdependent with their social environment. The media may structure the public's understanding of events, but they do so in conjunction with other institutions and

[44] Lang and Lang, op. cit., pp. 294–95.

with the preexisting sentiments of the general public as well, but not of their own volition or that of any other single source. Perhaps a convincing case of the circular process by which the media operate is the 1973–1974 Watergate scandal whose media coverage consisted of journalistic partisanship, objective reportage, the circulation of self-serving material from various sources, and public-opinion polls, all inextricably bound together in a definition and redefinition of events. This does not dispell anxiety over the social role of mass communication so much as it restates it in a new complex form.

Another and even broader indication of the circular or reinforcing nature of how the media operate has been inferred from detailed research done in metropolitan Detroit by Harold Wilensky.[45] Observing TV habits in conjunction with viewer attitudes, Wilensky concluded that the given individual member of modern "mass" and "urban" society in the United States today participates in the media-fostered mass culture as the "Happy Good-Citizen Consumer": community-attached, enthusiastically consuming goods and services, optimistic about national problems, feeling gratified by his work, and dependent on the media for defining issues for him. Wilensky sums this up by saying, "To be socially integrated in America is to accept propaganda, advertising, and speedy obsolescence in advertising."[46] Such a picture suggests a circumscribed, externally molded personality being helped to remain so by participation in the media, the economy, and political life in a circular manner.

EFFORTS AT REFORM

To cope with the negative value of mass communication for the public interest, many proposals have been made and some adopted, all in the direction of the social-responsibility conception of media organization. The ethic of social responsibility emphasizes the opportunities for public betterment that are open to a conscientiously administered system of mass communication. It also recognizes the dangers of concentrated power, vested interests, and resistance to needed change to protect the public effectively.

Canons of Journalism

The earliest code in the United States, the Canons of Journalism adopted by the American Society of Newspaper Editors in 1923, declared that "the primary function of newspapers is to communicate to the human races what its members do, feel, and think." Untruthful editorial partisanship and the unacknowledged promotion of private interests were prohibited. The canons

---

[45] Harold L. Wilensky, "Mass Society and Mass Culture: Interdependence or Independence?" *American Sociological Review*, 29 (April 1964), pp. 173–96.
[46] Ibid.

also proscribed the dissemination of material that "supplies incentives to base conduct, such as are found in details of crime and vice, publication of which is not demonstrably for the general good."[47]

The Commission on Freedom of the Press

In its 1947 advocacy of still more explicit responsibilities, the Commission on Freedom of the Press went beyond the earlier A.S.N.E. Canons.[48] Behind the commission's concern for the mature ethical management of the media were the dangers of economic concentration, catering to low tastes, sensationalism, and crude materialism. The commission recommended the professional self-regulation of the different media in accordance with five objectives: (1) a truthful and meaningful account of the day's events; (2) the exchange of critical comment on all significant ideas; (3) a fair portrayal of social groups; (4) the clear exposition of general values and goals; and (5) sufficient access to information so that the public can accept leadership in deciding public issues.

Government, the Media, and the Public

Even more adequate responsibility in the conduct of the media has been proposed more recently. Thus, Wilbur Schramm would have government help keep the channels of communication open by fostering conditions favorable to expression and news-gathering.[49] Secondly, says Schramm, the media need to exercise more professional self-regulation. This seems most salient to those members of the public who lack strong interpersonal attachments and who, consequently, depend more on the media for their understanding of events, especially during fluid periods. Finally, asserts Schramm, the public itself needs to become more discriminating and better organized.

CONCLUSION

The media of mass communication constitute a necessary component of urban life. Newspapers, TV, and the other agencies of mass communication not only provide information, they also judge events, transmit the culture, and supply entertainment as well.

Owing to their capacity to influence opinion, the media are also potentially dangerous. Much concern has been aroused over them, and a variety

[47] Mott, op. cit., p. 726.

[48] Commission on Freedom of the Press, op. cit.

[49] Schramm, *Responsibility in Mass Communication,* op. cit., Pt. IV.

of social forms, notably the libertarian, socially responsible, authoritarian, and communist systems, have been instituted to deal with them. Each of these, however, creates derivative issues. In the libertarian structure of the media here in the United States, one of the major problems is that concentrated ownership serves narrow vested interests. Another is the fear that in commercial hands the media are trivializing the public mind.

Research on the actual impact of the media reveals that mass communication operates in a convoluted fashion through interpersonal opinion leaders, and that, for the most part, it only reinforces existing beliefs. In general too, the media are held to function as only one element in the overall social system and to have only a limited capacity to affect the course of events. Some scholars of mass communication, however, are more emphatic on the media creating reality and contributing to public policy. Such thinking no doubt helps stimulate efforts to increase media responsibility, including advertising and public relations too.

FOR FURTHER READING

Alan Casty, ed., *Mass Media and Mass Man* (New York: Holt, 1973), 2nd ed. Articles on the themes of mass media and society, and mass media and culture.

Charles U. Daley, ed., *The Media and the Cities* (Chicago: University of Chicago Center for Policy Study, 1968). Reviews the media material contained in the *Report* of the National Advisory Commission on Civil Disorders.

Edwin Emery, et al., *An Introduction to Mass Communication* (New York: Dodd, 1971), 3rd ed. Current problems and issues in the industrial and professional sides of the media.

Paul Halmos, ed., *The Sociology of Mass Media Communications* (Keele, Eng.: University of Keele, 1969). Case studies on the social context within which the media operate, primarily British television.

W. Sidney Head, *Broadcasting in America* (Boston: Houghton Mifflin, 1972). The electronic media and their problems in the United States.

David L. Lange et al., *Mass Media and Violence* (Washington, D.C.: Government Printing Office, 1969). A report of the Task Force on the subject appointed by the National Commission on the Causes and Prevention of Violence.

Wilbur Schramm and Donald F. Roberts, eds., *The Process and Effects of Mass Communication* (Urbana, Ill.: University of Illinois Press, 1971). Technical studies of the impact of mass communications, for advanced students.

Alan Wells, ed., *Mass Media and Society* (Palo Alto, Calif.: National Press Books, 1972). More than 50 articles on the communications industries and pertinent public issues.

PART FIVE

URBAN SOCIAL AND CULTURAL SYSTEMS

Sculpture, "Family Group" by Henry Moore, completed of Hadene stone in 1954–55 and standing in Harlow New Town, Essex County, England.

Source: Elda Fezzi, *Henry Moore* (London: Hamlyn Publishing Group Limited, 1972), p. 20. Illustrations © SPADEM, Paris, 1971, distributed in the United States by Crown Publishers.

CHAPTER 12

THE
SUBURBAN
COMMUNITY

In earlier chapters, repeated references were made to the suburban community in the history of urbanization, the typological approach to urban life, city politics, and other subjects as well. Having reviewed the power dimension and proceeding now to examine the sociocultural systems of urban society, it appears appropriate to consider the suburban community in depth. The suburban community is so prominent in the United States today that putting suburbia into sharp focus should serve as a useful background to the other four chapters making up this section of the text, which deal with the impact of urbanization on kinship, religion, education, and art and leisure.

THE GROWTH OF SUBURBIA

The shift of population in the United States in recent decades has resulted in a massive buildup of our suburbs. During the period from 1950 to 1970, as shown in Table 12-1, the number of residents in America's Standard Metropolitan Statistical Areas (SMSAs) grew from 94.6 million to 139.4 million. In that same period, however, the aggregate size of the population outside the central cities of the nation's SMSAs rose much more rapidly. It almost doubled, growing from 40.9 million to 75.6 million. So sharply did this segment of the population of the United States expand that in 1970, the number of Americans living adjacent to our central cities made up the largest single component of the total. (See Table 12-1.) The population in proximity to the nation's inner cities substantially exceeded the population in those cities themselves and also exceeded the population in our nonmetropolitan areas. Altogether, the residents of suburbia accounted for fully 37.2 percent of all Americans in 1970 (Table 12-1).

Peripheral settlements, that is, communities no more than a mile from each other and adjoining a large central city (and now also defined by the census as a part of the metropolitan area but outside the inner city), are not new either in the United States or in other countries. Witness the many towns and villages adjacent to Boston and Philadelphia on this side of the Atlantic, and to London and Paris on the other side, even prior to the Industrial Revolution. Difficulties exist in enumerating the inhabitants of such neighboring communities, if only because many of these settlements disappeared as the result of annexation to their central cities during the eighteenth and nineteenth centuries. Generally, however, suburban growth in the United States may be said to be a twentieth-century occurrence, because only in this century have our cities typically stopped expanding by peripheral accretion at

TABLE 12-1 Population by Residence: United States, 1950 to 1970

RESIDENCE	POPULATION (000'S)			PERCENT CHANGE		PERCENT
	1950	1960	1970	1950–1960	1960–1970	1970
SMSA's	94.6	119.6	139.4	26.4	16.6	68.6
Central cities	53.7	60.0	63.8	11.6	6.4	31.4
Outside central cities	40.9	59.6	75.6	45.9	26.8	37.2
Nonmetropolitan areas	56.7	59.7	63.8	5.3	6.8	31.4
Total	151.3	179.3	203.2	18.5	13.5	100.0

Source: Bureau of the Census, Statistical Abstract of the United States, 1972 (Washington, D.C.: Government Printing Office, 1972), Table 15, p. 16.

The ability to construct housing within the means of the public is one factor that has made suburbanization possible.

the same time that the number of their adjoining communities has grown and their size has multiplied. The consequence of this expansion at the edges of the metropolitan area has been to produce settlements possessing relatively new and large homes, sizable amounts of space surrounding them, and a usually well-landscaped, clean, and quiet environment. These suburban communities have also come to possess ample shopping, service, and recreational facilities typically sequestered in zoned precincts.

Twentieth-century suburban development in the United States has been produced by four interdependent variables. First, the basic industries of a given locality have expanded, thereby offering employment opportunities to additional people. Consider the great increases in the fabrication of metals, auto assembly, the production of chemicals, and the building of machinery and appliances that have drawn masses of immigrants and native farm migrants into our centers of population. Second, the presence of that larger population has stimulated further economic opportunity by boosting the non-basic service industries, such as business, government, and education. Third, the availability of the means of transportation and communication, particularly the automobile and telephone, has permitted the growth of a more diffuse and sprawling pattern of settlement. And, fourth, the technological and organizational means of constructing fairly inexpensive housing of a low-density variety—notably, the tract development—have further facilitated the rapid buildup of proximal, suburban settlements. These four factors have combined to create a territorial differentiation of the metropolitan area in which population has shifted outward to nonemploying residential communities, allowing the more central territory to be devoted more fully to commercial and industrial uses.[1]

THE RESIDENTIAL SUBURB AND ITS
DEMOGRAPHIC CHARACTERISTICS

The residential suburb has long been recognized as a major element in the ecology of urban life. Overall, sociologists see the suburb as a specialized area within the larger metropolitan complex, and one which reveals five significant demographic differences between itself and the city beyond which it lies.[2]

1 The suburban labor force has a higher socioeconomic status and a higher median income than the work force of the central city.

2 Suburbs have lower proportions of women in the labor force.

3 In comparison with the central city, the suburbs have a younger population on the average, and ethnically a population tending to be more native white than is the case of the inner city.

4 Both residential mobility and median level of educational attainment favor the suburb over the central city.

5 Professionals, technical and kindred workers, and managers, proprietors, and officials make up a bigger percentage of the gainfully employed in the suburbs than they do in the central city.

Despite the apparent conclusiveness of these generalizations, important qualifications must also be noted. For one thing, the higher socioeconomic status of the suburbs holds true more for those adjacent to the largest urban aggregations than it does for those outside the smaller ones. For another, there are variations for the northern, central, southern, and western regions that reduce the extent of the foregoing five differences between suburb and central city, at least in certain-size metropolitan areas. Also, with the trend toward greater crosscurrents of change in the metropolis, less distinct city-suburb socioeconomic polarization was observed in the 1960–1970 decade

[1] See Leo F. Schnore, "The Growth of Metropolitan Suburbs," *American Sociological Review*, 22 (April 1957), pp. 165–73, and reprinted in his *The Urban Scene* (New York: Free Press, 1965), pp. 152–68. See also John F. Kain, "The Distribution and Movement of Jobs and Industry," in James Q. Wilson, ed., *The Metropolitan Enigma* (Cambridge, Mass.: Harvard University Press, 1968), pp. 1–39.

[2] Otis D. Duncan and Albert J. Reiss, Jr., *Social Characteristics of Urban and Rural Communities* (New York: Wiley, 1956), pp. 131ff.

than in the ten years preceding it.[3] In line with this tendency, researchers like Fine, Glenn, and Monts believe they have demonstrated the existence of very little occupational homogeneity in our suburbs today, perhaps little more than in the central-city neighborhoods themselves.[4] Thus, the Duncan and Reiss study from which we drew our initial generalizations in this section should possibly be best regarded as only a convenient baseline against which ecological and historical dissimilarities can be gauged. Distinguishing between residential suburbs and industrial satellites should also help clarify whatever vagueness arises.

THE ECOLOGY OF SUBURBIA: RESIDENTIAL SUBURBS AND INDUSTRIAL SATELLITES

In their original depiction of the city as a zonal structure at the time of World War I, Robert E. Park and Ernest W. Burgess had called suburbs areas of settlement contiguous to that of the central political administration but not under its jurisdiction. (Park and Burgess' work was reviewed in Chapter 6.) Park and Burgess conceptualized suburbs as residential communities whose inhabitants enjoyed a superior standard of living and commuted to the inner city for employment. In contrast to such dormitory settlements, these two sociologists designated satellite cities as standing outside the administrative city but primarily as industrial, not residential areas. Furthermore, in Park and Burgess' minds a satellite stood generally at a greater distance from the central city than the suburb did, even though like the suburb the satellite was also economically dependent on the city and might, just like the suburb, even be politically incorporated into the city as the metropolitan population spilled outward.

In the 1930s, following Park and Burgess' lead, Roderick McKenzie noted that a more open type of communal pattern was developing in America's metropolitan districts in comparison to cities of the past. McKenzie felt there was a new pattern in this "host of little towns and villages and new residential suburbs that have appeared in recent years around the periphery of every large American city."[5] Eventually, McKenzie concluded that these multitudinous communities occupied specific nuclei within the city's orbit of influence.

The distance of the settlement from the central city and the type of popu-

[3] Consult Norval D. Glenn, "Suburbanization in the United States since World War II," in Louis H. Masotti and Jeffrey K. Hadden, eds., The Urbanization of the Suburbs (Beverly Hills, Calif.: Sage Publications, 1973), pp. 51–78.

[4] John C. Fine, Norval D. Glenn, and J. Kenneth Monts, "The Residential Segregation of Occupational Groups in Central Cities and Suburbs," Demography, 8 (February 1971), pp. 91–101.

[5] Roderick D. McKenzie, The Metropolitan Community (New York: Russell & Russell, 1933), p. 71.

lation inhabiting it, McKenzie discovered, were crucial factors in determining its functional specialization. Adjacent cities no more than 20 miles from the main center of the metropolitan region were much more dependent on the central city for purchases of food, general merchandise, and wearing apparel than were communities 40 to 80 miles off.[6] McKenzie also ascertained that the industrial satellite had a more complete structure of services relative to the needs of the local population than did the residential suburb. The initial distinction between residential and industrial settlements made by Park and Burgess thus came to be associated with the idea of metropolitan regional dominance as a means of understanding the total territory around the large central city.

Pursuing a thought fashioned in 1925 by Harlan Paul Douglass in *The Suburban Trend*,[7] that such outlying but dependent segments of the larger urban center might cogently be viewed as either "suburbs of production" or "suburbs of consumption," Leo F. Schnore sought to define suburbs ecologically in terms of structure and function.[8] Goods and services, Schnore reasoned, flow out of the employing units at the same time that persons come into them for employment. The industrial satellites are therefore, Schnore concluded, the "consumers of labor and suppliers of commodities" in contrast to the residential suburbs, which are "suppliers of labor and consumers of commodities."

Writing a quarter of a century after Park and Burgess had first contrasted residential suburbs with industrial satellites, Schnore testified to the rapid polarization of America's outlying settlements. Residential communities, Schnore observed, were receiving large increments of housing while, contrariwise, industrial places were becoming ever more exclusively committed to conversion from residential purposes to industrial, commercial, and transit functions.[9] Schnore was convinced that these trends stemmed from two things: the undesirability of industrial locations for residential use, and the freedom that flexible automotive transportation was conferring on real-estate developers to open up cheaper and more distant areas for residential construction.

THE SUBURBAN WAY OF LIFE

Establishing the ecological and demographic similarities and differences among suburban communities has been probably of less interest to sociologists than the question of just what is the style and quality of life in subur-

[6] Ibid., Table 32, p. 74.

[7] (New York: Century, 1925).

[8] Leo F. Schnore, "Satellites and Suburbs," *Social Forces,* 36 (December 1957), pp. 121–27.

[9] Schnore, "The Growth of Metropolitan Suburbs," op. cit.

bia and, in fact, whether a specific sociocultural pattern actually prevails there.

Studies of this sort have received impetus from one source in particular. That has been the insistence by Georg Simmel and Louis Wirth and their followers that the urban experience is necessarily impersonal, fragmented, and secondary. (The subject was reviewed in Chapter 5.) Many sociologists have attempted to test if indeed the deterministic theory fits suburbia.

To some extent too, investigation of the sociocultural pattern of the suburban community has been stimulated by dissatisfaction with the alleged shallow, philistine mode of living supposedly characteristic of these settlements Any number of writers, including moralizing essayists, have belabored suburbia for adhering to low personal, family, and community standards. Among the most notable though only impressionistic books to do so are Spectorsky's *The Exurbanites*[10] and Keats' *The Crack in the Picture Window.*[11] Among professional sociologists, however, the impetus to the study of suburban life given by typological theory has been by far the more important consideration.

Resulting from the application of deterministic typological theory to urban life are four contrasting interpretations of the suburban experience. They are the work, respectively, of Herbert Gans, Morris Janowitz, David Riesman, and Claude Fischer. Gans has presented suburban life as having a quasiprimary character; Janowitz, as manifesting limited liability; Riesman, as demonstrating a triballike quality; and Fischer, as evidencing subcultural properties.

GANS: A QUASIPRIMARY CHARACTER

Herbert Gans argues that since Wirth published his paper "Urbanism as a Way of Life" in 1938, the new suburbs of our metropolitan centers have revealed a quasiprimary type of living unforeseen by Wirth. Gans has written that some of Wirth's conclusions do explain the way of life of modern society. Yet, Gans has added, because the theory insists that all of society is now urban, it "does not distinguish ways of life in the city from those in other settlements within modern society."[12] When Wirth studied the city, comparing urban and preurban settlements was very much in order. At present though when urbanization encompasses virtually the entire population, Gans declares, "the primary task for urban (or community) sociology seems to me to

[10] (Philadelphia, Pa.: Lippincott, 1955).

[11] (Boston: Houghton Mifflin, 1956).

[12] Herbert Gans, "Urbanism and Suburbanism as Ways of Life," in Arnold M. Rose, ed., *Human Behavior and Social Processes* (Boston: Houghton Mifflin, 1962), p. 627.

The shopping center, a focal point of residential suburbia.

be the analysis of the similarities and differences between contemporary settlement types."[13]

Gans observes that even now Wirth is essentially correct when his generalizations are applied to the inner city. There the residents can be summed up under five subtypes: the cosmopolites; the unmarried or childless; the ethnic villagers; the deprived; and the "trapped" or downwardly mobile. In the main, these types are detached from neighborhood life and are in accord with Wirth's conception. Their lives, in Wirth's words, do exhibit "anonymity, impersonality, and superficiality."

The residential suburbs have turned out to be different, Gans concludes, for "it is evident that the way of life in these areas bears little resemblance to Wirth's urbanism." In Gans' view, the social relationships of the suburbanite may perhaps best be described as quasiprimary. That is, suburban social ties are more intimate than the formal, segmental transactions of people within large, impersonal organizations. Yet the relationships carried on by the residents of suburbia are also more guarded than the association that goes on within families and between close friends.[14] Suburban social relations are, therefore, neither primary nor secondary but somewhere in between these two poles. In fact, in the final analysis, Gans notes, suburbia suffers from an inability to handle conflict adequately because it cannot

[13] Herbert Gans, *People and Places* (New York: Basic Books, 1968) might also be referred to on this theme.

[14] See Herbert Gans, *The Levittowners: Ways of Life and Politics in a New Suburban Community* (New York: Pantheon, 1967).

establish complete cohesion between the home, the community, and government.

JANOWITZ: LIMITED LIABILITY

Criticism of the model of the urban community of which Simmel and Wirth were exponents has also led to the development of still other concepts designed to capture the exact sociocultural character of suburbanism. One of these is the idea formulated by Morris Janowitz, that the suburb is, so to speak, a community of limited liability.

In studying the local press in its suburban social setting, Janowitz found it necessary to reject the image of the urban metropolis as populated entirely by rootless individuals.[15] Instead, Janowitz discerned innumerable interpersonal contacts, commitments, and involvements in the suburban residential area, with the community newspaper acting as "an extension of real social contacts." Janowitz writes that "these attachments are limited in the amount of social and psychological investment they represent." Still, the fact remains that interpersonal controls do operate in the local community, and that these curb the degree of manipulation that Simmel and Wirth's image of mass society in the urban context conjurs up.

A recent review of the limited-liability community by Gerald Suttles recognizes the potent role in neighborhood communities of such larger, environing forces as the federal government, corporate industry, and nationwide ethnoreligious movements. Suttles declares that "in Chicago and doubtless in other large cities, there are numerous citywide or large-scale organizations which act to create or preserve the reputation and boundaries of some residential areas: the model cities program, the neighborhood phone directories, statistical reports on social problems, and an unknown number of business firms which pitch their advertisements and names in the direction of a local clientele."[16] These factors possibly tend toward some degree of the limited-liability community within the inner city by impinging on the indigenous interests of the residents, and in the suburbs to affect the limited-liability relationship there by organizing and differentiating neighborhoods still further.

RIESMAN: TRIBALLIKE CONFORMITY

Major author of *The Lonely Crowd,* which analyzes the social psychology of contemporary America, David Riesman has also applied himself to achieve

[15] Morris Janowitz, *The Community Press in an Urban Setting* (Glencoe, Ill.: Free Press, 1952).

[16] Gerald D. Suttles, *The Social Construction of Communities* (Chicago: University of Chicago Press, 1972), p. 58.

an understanding of our suburban mode of life.[17] According to Riesman, leisure and complacent privatism describe the generalized social goals of the suburbanite. Suburban people pursue these values in low-keyed, local civic enterprise pertaining to the suburban community as a whole together with much communal association among propinquitous neighbors in the given locale within the suburb. Fellowship and neighboring are both given a high place in the suburbanite's conception of the good life.

As they submerge themselves in a common life, people in the suburbs tend to lose their individuality, Riesman says, but they are not atomized into particles associating with one another simply on a *quid pro quo* basis. On the contrary, they surrender themselves to their community, the idea of which is "an omnipresent dream, carrying overtones of the Bible, peasant life and folk imagery." In sum, despite an undercurrent of "unpleasure" compounded by loss of the Puritan interest in work, Riesman concludes that American suburbia seems to have evolved into—or perhaps reverted to—a secular triballike conformity.

FISCHER: SUBCULTURAL PROPERTIES

The most recent of our four interpreters of suburban life, Claude Fischer reasons that Wirth's deterministic theory simply does not fit the actual character of the inhabitants of urban communities in general and of suburban ones in particular.[18] Fischer maintains that the heterogeneity predicated by Wirth does not have the direct atomizing impact on people imagined for it.

Fischer looks at cities as eventuating in specially composed populations, for example, as having an older median age and containing a greater than average proportion of minorities. In addition, the urban community's division of labor separates the population into socioeconomic interest groups, which then develop into unique subcultures expressing contrasting life styles. Unlike the various areas of the central city, however, where differing social groups are to be found pursuing diverse cultural values, suburbs tend to lack subcultural differentiation. A given suburban population is relatively uniform in culture.

Yet the larger urban condition does divide people into opposing and solidary subgroups by virtue of the more general circumstances such as industrialization and national policies. Hence urban society creates what Fischer calls "critical masses," like political parties, labor unions, and reactive ethnoreligious groups (i.e., responding to the threats posed by other ethnoreligious bodies). These cut across neighborhoods, including those in suburbia, and interfere with the primary ties that link otherwise homogeneous

[17] See his "The Suburban Dislocation," *The Annals of the American Academy of Political and Social Science,* 314 (November 1957), pp. 129–42.

[18] Claude S. Fischer, *The Urban Experience* (New York: Harcourt Brace Jovanovich, 1976).

individuals into solidary associations there. In sum then, according to Fischer, the suburban community evidences a variety of integrative but also divisive tendencies so that to some extent at least, a given suburb is an extension of individual friendships, familism, and noncompetitive values, but at the same time also separatist tendencies as well. The latter may be seen in the antagonisms among suburban age and ethnic groups where they focus on the support of the schools and on minority access to housing.

SUBURBIA—STILL FURTHER DIFFERENTIATION

Each of the foregoing interpreters of the sociocultural pattern of American suburban life, with the possible exception of Fischer, regards the suburban community as approximating one generic type of experience, as expressing a singular character. Others though argue that a generic sociocultural suburbanism is no less a misconception of things than is the notion of a typologically general urbanism.

Historian Scott Donaldson regards William Dobriner's depiction of suburbanism as not only mirroring the popular stereotype but, by being a myth, also poisoning scholarship. Dobriner emphasizes that:

> Suburbs are warrens of young executives on the way up; uniformly middle class; 'homogeneous'; hotbeds of participation; child centered and female dominated; transient wellsprings of outgoing life; arenas of adjustment; Beulah Lands of return to religion; political Jordans from which Democrats emerge Republicans.[19]

In support of his own contrary critical outlook, Donaldson goes on to collate the findings of Whyte's *The Organization Man*[20] and Selley, Sim, and Loosely's *Crestwood Heights*[21] as "professional and thorough investigations" of suburbia. The suburban culture that emerges does show some uniformity, for example, the rise of the nuclear family and the decline of extended kinship.

These books also come up with some significant disparities between Park Forest, the locale of *The Organization Man*, and Crestwood Heights. One is limited civic participation (in Park Forest) versus the almost total involvement in civic affairs in Crestwood Heights. Such differences underscore Donaldson's conclusion that suburbs differ culturally. In these particular cases,

---

[19] William C. Dobriner, *Class in Suburbia* (Englewood Cliffs, N.J.: Prentice-Hall, 1963), p. 6, as cited by Donaldson in his *The Suburban Myth* (New York: Columbia University Press, 1969), p. 5.

[20] William H. Whyte, Jr., *The Organization Man* (New York: Simon and Schuster, 1950).

[21] J. R. Seeley, R. A. Sim, and E. W. Loosley, *Crestwood Heights: A Study of the Culture of Suburban Life* (New York: John Wiley & Sons, 1963).

Crestwood Heights may be thought of as a traditional suburb and Park Forest as a transient one whose population consists of executives who are assigned to absentee-owned firms or are mobile professionals rising socially. Other research reaches similar conclusions.

That suburban residence does not necessarily conform to either of the two divergent, though homologous, types of suburban culture represented by Park Forest and Crestwood Heights, is the import of Bennett Berger's *Working-Class Suburb.*[22] In 1957, Berger surveyed Milpitas, the site of a Ford assembly plant adjacent to San Jose, California. Berger's data argue against "the myth of suburbia." Attitudes of social mobility are almost completely absent from Milpitas, 94 percent of the residents thinking of their jobs with Ford as permanent. Nor is this suburb the melting pot for the new middle class. About half of Berger's sample of Milpitas residents continue to identify themselves as working class, with only five percent seeing themselves as being elevated into the middle class by virtue of their suburban relocation.

Though it differs greatly from both Park Forest and Crestwood Heights, Milpitas contrasts even more sharply with the definitely lower-class and even slumlike suburbs that exist adjacent to a good many of America's large cities. Irwin Deutscher and Elizabeth Thompson describe this so-called other suburbia as mired in poverty and in no few instances, inhabited by disadvantaged minorities.[23] Such enclaves are, in fact, preserved by the resistance to their annexation shown them by the more affluent communities next to them. Usually they originate as industrial locations that attract low-grade laborers who are then fixed there permanently by zoning ordinances. These residents of suburbia have only a loosely organized family structure, as Blumberg and Lalli observe, and show little interest in organized community life.[24]

Such research does cast doubt on the idea of the American suburban mode of life as unitary, especially as being homogeneous, middle class, and conformist.[25] Ironically, the findings of suburban research, which arose from uncertainties concerning Wirth and Simmel's contention about a uniform, atomistic mass society in the entire metropolitan community, only qualify that theory still further. Yet, this area of urban scholarship promises to give us a more valid, if also a more differentiated, picture of the suburban experience than we have to date.

[22] (Berkeley and Los Angeles: University of California Press, 1968).

[23] Irwin Deutscher and Elizabeth Thompson, *Down among the People: Encounters with the Poor* (New York: Basic Books, 1968), pp. 127–54.

[24] See Leonard Blumberg and Michael Lalli, "Little Ghettoes: A Study of Negroes in the Suburbs," *Phylon,* 21 (Summer 1966), pp. 117–31.

[25] Consult Thomas Ktsanes and Leonard Reissman, "Suburbia–*New Homes for Old Values,*" *Social Problems,* 7 (Winter 1959–60), pp. 187–95. Also, John Kramer, ed., *North American Suburbs: Politics, Diversity, and Change* (Berkeley, Calif.: Glendessary Press, 1972).

AMERICA'S SUBURBS: A LOOK AHEAD

Just as our suburban communities arose for historical reasons, it is logical to expect that their future will also be shaped by determining forces and that these are, to an extent, already apparent. The most discernible are the following five.

First, the nation's changing demographic composition will continue to affect the suburbs. Specifically, increases in the proportion of the American population at two intervals on the age scale, among adults under 25 and older persons over 55, will boost apartment living. Such demand for multiple dwelling units is bound to have an impact on the dominant single-home pattern at present. It will most probably encourage building in the open spaces lying between the suburbs and the central city where access to employment and service facilities is maximal.

Second, the declining birth rate will probably weaken suburban family life and also throw the great expense of maintaining separate schools systems into high relief. Consolidations, special districts, and service agreements between neighboring communities will take on higher priority than at present.

Third, and unless checked by an energy crisis, the mobility of individuals and of industry will combine to promote still broader exurban sprawl than that experienced to date. The institutional effects of this trend can hardly be anticipated. They do, however, include higher costs of facilities and unprecedented problems of government leading to more comprehensive planning.

Fourth, increased political power for youth and minority groups at the national level will most likely find expression in federal programs to integrate the suburbs by achieving racial balance in education and also more low- and moderate-income housing outside the central city. Increased political power for these groups at the local level will lead to the levying of more income and payroll taxes on suburban residents at their place of employment outside their own communities.

Fifth, all of these forces, which in a word are urbanizing the suburbs (and creating frustrating crosscurrents too) will probably affect the various facets of the present-day suburban life style. Just how cannot be accurately foretold although in following chapters many of the trends referred to here are treated in some detail.

CONCLUSION

Suburbs—defined as peripheral or proximal settlements adjacent to a large central city—have multiplied greatly in the United States during the twentieth century to the point, in fact, where our suburban population now makes up the largest segment of the total. Responsible for this condition has been a combination of economic and technological factors.

Overall, suburban communities differ demographically from the rest of the American population, owing mainly to the fact that many of these settlements are almost wholly residential. Some suburbs, however, are industrial satellites.

Much sociological research has been devoted to ascertaining the characteristics and dynamics of the suburban way of life. Such study has resulted from tests of the theory that the urban experience has a secondary character. Though investigators do not agree on its nature, the suburban life style appears to challenge that assumption. It is also recognized that a variety of different kinds of suburbs actually exists. Likewise, the common features as well as the dissimilarities among America's suburban communities suggest that the future of suburbia will in all likelihood evidence the continuation of a diverse set of trends. Other chapters of the text, including the ones that make up this section, examine many of these trends in detail.

FOR FURTHER READING

A. B. Callow, Jr., ed., *American Urban History* (New York: Oxford University Press, 1973), 2nd edition. A multiple-authored survey of urbanization, including suburbanization, in the United States.

Charles M. Haar, ed., *The End of Innocence: A Suburban Reader* (Glenview, Ill.: Scott, Foresman, 1972). Edited by the Chairman of President Johnson's Task Force on Suburban Problems, this volume contains selections from its report.

Amos Hawley and V. Rock, eds., *Metropolitan America in Contemporary Perspective* (New York: Halstead Press, 1975). An anthology of writings on our recent urban trends, including the expansion of suburbia.

Louis H. Masotti and Jeffrey K. Hadden, eds., *The Urbanization of the Suburbs* (Beverly Hills, Calif.: Sage Publications, 1973). On the history and future of suburbia as "a new form of urban civilization."

Barry Schwartz, ed., *The Changing Face of the Suburbs* (Chicago: University of Chicago Press, 1976). The social groups in the suburban community and related topics.

CHAPTER 13

KINSHIP
IN THE CITY

The kinship system of any society consists of the cultural norms and social relationships observed by people connected by descent or marriage. This includes patterns of marriage and divorce, the inheritance of property, the obligations of distant relatives to one another, and similar matters. For the most part though, it is the family rather than the kinship system at large that observers are concerned with. That is also generally true of those studying the impact of urbanization on kinship.

URBANIZATION AND THE ATOMIZATION
OF THE FAMILY

The family, which may be defined as the socially effective unit in the total kinship system, has been hypothesized by sociologists in the typological tradition in particular as undergoing change as a result of urbanization. Specifically, in the transition from a rural to an urban mode of life, such scholars perceive three major alterations. (1) Family functions contract, and those that are retained change in character. (2) The extended type of family gives way to the conjugal form. And (3) the familistic scale of values typical of an agrarian society yields to the individualistic viewpoint so characteristic of urban existence generally.

Although qualifications of the typological interpretation will be presented throughout this chapter, the point needs to be stressed at the outset that this "atomistic hypothesis," is doubtlessly an overstatement. Take a single example. Philippe Ariès concludes that long before extensive urbanization in Europe, as early as the thirteenth century in fact, the transition to the atomized nuclear, or conjugal, family was already under way.[1] Hence the atomistic hypothesis oversimplifies the facts of social history, if it does not actually misinterpret many of them. Still, the theory does merit serious review as a baseline for the examination of the family in urban society.

FAMILY FUNCTIONS

How the family serves its members and the community in general constitutes its functional role. Besides making biological, educational, recreational, integrative, and sociopsychological contributions to the social order, the family may also provide economic, military, and religious services exclusive of those of other institutions.

As William F. Ogburn has pointed out, the family's functions may be broad or narrow, but in the city its scope of activities is usually quite restricted.[2] How relatively circumscribed the precinct of the urban family is can be seen, according to Ogburn, in the fact that the family's:

> *Economic function has gone to the factory, store, office, and restaurant, leaving little of economic activity to the family of the city apartment. About half of education has been transferred to the schools, where the teacher is a part-time or substitute parent. Recreation is found in moving pictures, parks, city streets, clubs. . . . The police and social legislation indicate how the protective function has been transferred to the state, as has the educational function. Family status has been lost in marked degree along with these other functions in an age of mobility and large cities. It is the individual that has become more important and the family less so.*[3]

[1] Philip Ariès, *Centuries of Childhood* (New York: Vintage Books, 1962).

[2] In "The Family and Its Functions," in President's Research Committee on Social Trends, *Recent Social Trends in the United States* (New York: McGraw-Hill, 1933), pp. 661–708.

[3] Quoted from William F. Ogburn, "The Changing Family," *The Family*, 19 (July 1938), pp. 139–40.

FAMILY FORMS

As for rural-urban differences in family form, these are believed to be great, and to correspond to the family's diminished functions and its limited role in urban society.

Prior to the Industrial Revolution when Western society was mainly rural, the extended family of two or more nuclear units of the same generation or of successive generations was the typical mode of kinship organization for the most part. Families so compounded were, in general, admirably suited to discharge many if not all of the functions essential to self-sufficiency in a nonurban, agrarian setting. In our own New England colonies, for instance, practically all articles of consumption except salt, spices, and sugar came from the family farm itself. In addition, education, religious training, and even personal safety often devolved primarily on the household unit too.

Conversely, in the highly specialized and organized urban setting today, where the family performs fewer functions, its form, so the atomists insist, must necessarily be simpler and its membership less extensive. And, by and large, it demonstrably is. The family in the city is restricted to the parents and their minor children, that is, the nuclear family. That unit is created at marriage, expands upon the birth of the children, and then contracts with their "emancipation" and marriage. The death of the married couple ends the group altogether.

THE FAMILY'S IDEOLOGICAL SIGNIFICANCE

In rural society not only is the family more extended in form, it is also claimed to be much more prominent ideologically than it typically is in an urban setting.[4] The ethos of the urban family contrasts sharply with that of the rural type. Throughout its life cycle, the atomists contend, the urban family is looked upon not as some corporate body to which one must commit himself, but as a utilitarian arrangement that should effectively serve the interests of its members. The attitude which family members have toward their own family is as though it were a service arrangement to be judged by its adequacy in meeting their needs as individual personalities.

THE FAMILY IN TRANSITION: ATOMIZATION IN THE DEVELOPING COUNTRIES

The typological contrasts in family functions, structure, and ideology between rural and urban systems have been demonstrated to some extent by

[4] Consult Ferdinand Tönnies, *Community and Society: Gemeinschaft und Gesellschaft,* ed. and trans. by Charles P. Loomis (Lansing, Mich.: Michigan State University Press, 1957), pp. 206–07.

the study of the cumulative effects which the transition to urban industrialization has been having on kinship in the developing nations. Examination of the impact of urban industrialization on traditional kinship shows it to be substantial.

In a major study of family changes during the first half of the twentieth century, which included Japan, China, India, the West, Sub-Saharan Africa, and the Arab countries, William J. Goode reached five general conclusions about industrialization and the family.[5] Industrialization, he wrote, is exerting "crucial points of pressure" upon "the traditional family structure" in each of five areas of social life.

> *First,* geographic mobility reduces the contact that people have with one another within their kinship groups. Consequently, as individuals travel more they have less to do with their relatives.
>
> *Second,* industrial opportunities and rewards accelerate social mobility, with the result that estranging discrepancies in income, taste, and style of life arise among blood relatives. This separates kinsfolk still further.
>
> *Third,* industrial conditions lead to the establishment of formal stuctures that replace kinship organization in providing protection, economic security and resources, educational services, and the like.
>
> *Fourth* industrialization facilitates the emergence of a value system emphasizing achievement instead of birth. Accordingly, individualized choice tends to replace the corporate activities of the kinship group.
>
> *Fifth,* an industrial economy leads to specialization so that individuals are more productive, to be sure, but are less able to employ relatives, since they are merely employees themselves.

These crucial points of pressure that an industrial economy exerts upon family relationships establish conditions favorable to personal initiative and individualization. Men find it to their interests to be free of obligations to extended kin, and for women and children to be free from the authority of their husbands and fathers. The reciprocal, so to speak, of having society take over the functions that the family has been traditionally discharging is to free its members of obligations to one another.

Goode concludes from his five generalizations that universally, the forces of industrialization—and the urbanization attendant upon it—have been moving the traditional kinship system to "some type of *conjugal* family pattern—toward fewer kinship ties with distant relatives and a greater emphasis on the 'nuclear' family unit of couple and children."[6]

[5] William J. Goode, *World Revolution and Family Patterns* (New York: Free Press, 1963), pp. 369ff.

[6] Ibid., p. 1.

An extended family lunching in their yard in Minnesota around 1910. This was an important occasion as seen in their formal clothes.

THE ATOMISTIC URBAN FAMILY AND ITS OTHER CORRELATES

Besides those already brought out, there are four other characteristics that the conjugal, or nuclear, family also possesses in an industrial-urban setting:

> *First,* in an urban context, the family inclines to secularism in the conduct of its affairs. Marriage, for example, typically takes place under civil contract not uncommonly without any religious solemnization at all. Similarly, traditional religious barriers to divorce are breached in urban society, as evidenced quite recently in Argentina and Italy after a similar turn of events in many other Western nations earlier. In fact, as one recent analysis concluded, modern nations generally reject the idea of the family as a natural unit and therefore autonomous, and, instead, consider the family as a subunit of the state subject to legal control in the public interest.[7]

[7] Bernard Farber, *Family and Kinship in Modern Society* (Glencoe, Ill.: Scott, Foresman, 1973), p. 155.

Second, the urban family is also typically formed at an earlier age. In other words, industrial urbanization correlates with more youthful marriage. According to the census bureau, in the United States the median age at first marriage for men was 26.1 in 1890 and only 23.5 in 1975.[8] In this three-generation period, the average age at marriage for American women fell from 22.0 to 21.1. Being able to earn an independent living is the factor responsible for the age decline. It should not be supposed, however, that urban marriages necessarily occur at earlier ages. In Lebanon, for instance, generational data show that age at marriage has been rising, and that it is apparently higher for the Lebanese urban population than for the residents of Lebanon's rural areas. Perhaps the major reason is that incipient urbanization affords less opportunity for individuals than industrial urbanization does and hence actually delays marriage. Moreover, postindustrialization requires longer schooling, which may also push up the average age for first marriages.

Third, divorces are definitely more common in urban society than in traditional rural communities. Nimkoff concluded from worldwide evidence that "with few exceptions" (Japan the major one), family disruption increased with advances in industrialization and urbanization.[9] Economic independence and the emphasis in marriage on romantic love and sexual gratification, both associated with individualism, tend to undermine permanent attachments. Also, equality between spouses is more difficult to maintain in marriage than sanctioned authoritarianism is, with the result that termination by divorce is resorted to more frequently. In the United States, the divorce rate for every 1000 married females 15 years and over, which began to rise even before the Civil War, was 4.0 in 1900; 4.7 in 1910; 8.0 in 1920 (a postwar year following hasty wartime marriages); 7.5 in 1930; 8.7 in 1940; 10.3 in 1950; 9.3 in 1959; and 13.4 in 1969. Throughout the decade of the 1960s, the American divorce rate remained consistently higher than it had been prior to World War II.[10]

Fourth, related to the greater prevalence of divorce in urban society is the value of personal happiness in marriage. Satisfaction of the individual personality is an object that characterizes the value-orientation of urban families far more than is probably true of rural families with their more traditional work orientation. Individualism in marriage receives

[8] Bureau of the Census, *Current Population Reports,* Series P-20, No. 287 (Washington, D.C.: Government Printing Office, 1975), Table B, p. 3.

[9] Meyer F. Nimkoff, ed., *Comparative Family Systems* (Boston: Houghton Mifflin, 1965), pp. 354–56.

[10] National Office of Vital Statistics, "Marriage and Divorce Statistics: United States, 1959," *Vital Statistics of the U.S.,* I:2, pp. 2–17, and Public Health Service, *Divorce Statistics, Analysis, United States, 1963* (Washington, D.C.: Government Printing Office, 1967).

social approval in the city because it corresponds to such social standards as status achievement, occupational success, and the demonstration of social skill. Thus, Scott Greer recently described the conjugal family in the suburbs as one engrossed in "community organization and local institutions . . . [with] . . . multifarious voluntary associations. . . ."[11] And Bernard Farber reminds us that the principle of individualism, denoting the "continual, free negotiation of rights and obligations in the family," logically leads to "experimental forms [which] may at times overstep the limits imposed by law," as in the case of "swingers" (the temporary exchange of marriage partners) and the group sexuality of commune life.[12]

Incidentally, greater attention to personal happiness has been held to disprove the contention that the urban family suffers from declining functions, for the family probably has a broader range of aesthetic and leisure-time interests in common than before. Richard Sennett, for one, believes that intense familial interaction is today considered ideal even if this means passivity toward circumstances outside the home. Sennett writes, in fact, that "affluent city life has created a morality of [family] isolationism."[13] Other reasons for qualifying the atomistic interpretation of urban familism have also been brought out, as we shall see, but the emergence of new functions or at least the intensification of some old ones has been thought a challenge to the conception of the city family as simply a fragile, utilitarian nuclear entity.

THE KIN NETWORK

The advantages of the nuclear type of family in an urban setting would appear to dictate its rapid diffusion during industrial urbanization.[14] A conjugal system of kinship does have certain weaknesses though. The unit of parents and minor children is vulnerable to illness, separation, and death. Also, an extended family is better suited to care for the aged, administer property, engage in concerted economic enterprise, and furnish the services of a larger number of people than the atomized nuclear household can. These shortcomings of the conjugal system, however, are responsible for the continued existence of kinship networks, in other words, familistic webs, in urban society.

[11] Scott Greer, "The Family in Suburbia," in Louis H. Masotti and Jeffrey K. Hadden, eds., *The Urbanization of the Suburbs* (Beverly Hills, Calif.: Sage, 1973), p. 1966.

[12] Farber op. cit., p. 148.

[13] Richard Sennett, "The Brutality of Modern Families," *Trans-Action,* 7 (September 1970), pp. 29–37.

[14] See Talcott Parsons, "The Kinship System of the Contemporary United States," *American Anthropologist,* 45 (January 1943), pp. 22–38.

The kinship network of an urban family consists of the relationships that the members of that unit maintain with relatives outside their own group of parents and minor children. Hence while keeping the advantages of its independence, a family connects itself to kinsfolk in order to supply its other needs better. However, propinquity, type of neighborhood (neighborhood stability promoting family ties), alternative institutions (like the availability of credit facilities), and the personal characteristics of the individuals involved all affect the manner in which any kinship network operates.

Some writers think that social class is the single most significant determinant of the formation of urban kin networks, and that these bodies are most commonly found in the lower class. Yet, kin networks are also present in the other social strata as well.[15] In the lower class, the kin network furnishes various kinds of reciprocal aid—emergency services and material goods—for example, among the Italians in Boston's West End district.[16] Similarly, a 1968 study conducted in the Roxbury black ghetto of Boston revealed that not quite half of the families had received aid from their relatives in moving to their present address, and that nearly one-fourth had given or received financial or informational assistance from their kin.[17] The kin network also gives the lower, or working, class individual an appreciable amount of sheer social enjoyment, as Marc Fried's recent review of the west end of Boston prior to its demolition for urban renewal demonstrates.[18]

In the upper class, through property ownership in common and through coordinated social control, the affiliation of nuclear units comprises a strong force for the preservation of both prestige and economic advantage. As in the case of the lower-class family, very similar contributory conditions are needed to encourage upper-class kin networks too, namely, equality of status and geographic immobility, hence opportunity for assistance.

The modified extended family that makes up the kinship network at both ends of the urban social scale is perhaps least apparent in the urban middle class. Yet even there help patterns, one investigator has concluded, "are more integral of family relationships than has been appreciated by students of family behavior."[19] A recent anthropological survey of associations among

[15] Elizabeth Bott, *Family and Social Network: Roles, Norms, and External Relationships in Ordinary Urban Families* (London: Tavistock, 1971), p. 112.

[16] Herbert Gans, *The Urban Villagers* (New York: Free Press, 1962).

[17] Joe R. Feagin, "The Kinship Ties of Negro Urbanites," *Social Science Quarterly, 49 (December 1968), pp. 660–65.*

[18] Marc Fried, *The World of the Urban Working Class* (Cambridge, Mass.: Harvard University Press, 1973), p. 106.

[19] Marvin B. Sussman and Lee Burchinal, "Kin Family Network: Unheralded Structure in Current Conceptualization of Family Functioning," *Marriage and Family Living*, 24 (August 1962), pp. 231–40.

middle-class families in north London made the point that interest in relatives depends on the attitudes of the individuals, and that the personal factor would appear to play the major role in activating any particular kin network at this status level.[20]

The persistence of extended family relationships in the city has not only been verified but has been described in detail by numerous investigators. These have measured the size of the network, the frequency of interaction, and the kinds of activity carried on. In fact, based on several studies of cooperation among relatives in the United States, Eugene Litwak has concluded that "a coalition of nuclear families in a state of partial dependence" is not incompatible with an industrial urban society at all.[21]

THE THREE-GENERATION "STEM"

Within the kin network, the three-generation stem of grandparents, parents, and children has particular importance.

A sample of 312 Minneapolis-St. Paul families linked through three generations revealed what may be the typical pattern of aid-flow between grandparent, parent, and child in the stem type of network. The grandparent generation showed greatest dependency, receiving much more than it gave, especially in regard to illness, household management, and emotional satisfactions. The married-child generation had need of child care and financial assistance although it tended to return as much aid as it received. The intermediate parent generation, however, clearly acted as patron, "giving to both grandparents and married children and receiving markedly less than it gave."[22]

The kin network qualifies, if it does not contradict, the theory of urban atomism. Goode, as we have seen, has brought out the conjugal tendencies of the family under industrial conditions. Yet he himself thinks that allowing for improved transportation and communication in the past, it is not unlikely that extended family interaction, in the form of the kin network, is maintained today at a level perhaps no lower even in metropolitan areas than in the preindustrial, preurban era.[23] This question calls for added research, for it casts serious doubt on urban atomism as a whole.

Goode recognizes, moreover, that cultural distinctions should not be ig-

[20] Raymond Firth, Jane Hubert, and Anthony Forge, *Families and Their Relatives: Kinship in a Middle-Class Sector of London* (New York: Humanities Press, 1970).

[21] Eugene Litwak, "Extended Kin Relations in an Industrial Democratic Society," in Ethel Shanas and Gordon F. Streib, eds., *Social Structure and the Family* (Englewood Cliffs, N.J.: Prentice-Hall, 1965), p. 291. See also Richard Sennett, *Families Against the City* (Cambridge, Mass.: Harvard University Press, 1970), Ch. 4.

[22] Reuben Hill, "Decision Making and the Family Life Cycle," in Shanas and Streib, op. cit., p. 137.

[23] Goode, op. cit., p. 75.

nored either, in asserting a correlation between urbanism and the conjugal family system. In Japan, to cite an important case, the divorce rate fell during the first half of the twentieth century, while in the West it rose. In Japan, the frequency of divorce declined owing to the emancipation of the individual from the family and consequently a drop in the number of arranged—and unhappy—marriages. Conversely, the Western experience was a continuation of an already individualized marriage pattern. In brief, the correspondence between nuclear familism and industrial urbanism has some support, though by no means entirely so.

Harvard University sociologist Gino Germani has recently analyzed the proposition that a close correlation exists between industrial urbanism and the predominance of the nuclear family. Germani asserts that a degree of determinacy is present here, and says, "Perhaps a wider range of family types is compatible with the industrial structure." Still, he goes on, that does not mean complete indeterminacy either. The previous, traditional culture continues to affect family relations under industrial urban conditions, Germani writes, but "the introduction of a normative system of the elective type in relations previously prescriptive," in other words, norms akin to the nuclear family form, do characterize social ties in the modern industrial-urban milieu.[24]

URBAN YOUTH

Urbanization is also associated with a large degree of freedom enjoyed by youth. Urbanization alone is not responsible of course, for ideology also operates here. Thus belief in economic progress has gained precedence over respect for tradition; the individual has been given greater sanction than the preservation of the family has; and sexual equality has become a more widely approved principle than that of male primacy. Values of this type have contributed to the neolocal pattern of family residence, to child-centering, to the provision of a lot of education, to freedom of choice in marriage, and also to the emergence of a largely autonomous youth culture.

INDEPENDENCE, PEER GROUPS, AND SOCIALIZATION

Lacking a productive economic role in the nuclear family, children are apt to believe that parents exist simply to serve them.[25] In this fashion an early basis is laid for independence, and peer-group influences soon add further sanction.

[24] Gino Germani, "Urbanization, Social Change, and the Great Transformation," in the symposium edited by him, *Modernization, Urbanization, and the Urban Crisis* (Boston: Little, Brown, 1973), pp. 40–42.

[25] Dorothy Blitsten, *The World of the Family* (New York: Random House, 1963), pp. 41–42.

Urbanization tends to create greater freedom for youth.

Summarizing the importance of the peer group for the modern American child in his study of teenage social life in 10 high schools (half of them urban), James S. Coleman reasons that not only does the adolescent live more and more in the society of his peers, but that his family is having increasingly less effect on his upbringing.[26] In that peer-oriented community, a fairly distinct youth culture has developed. Featured in it are unique forms of dress, language, aesthetic standards, and social norms. Athletics and diffuse social interaction play very important parts in the youth culture.

Two, and probably three, functions may be ascribed to this peer society, Talcott Parsons, a distinguished social theorist, has inferred.[27] On the one hand, the peer group affords one the emotional security which in the absence of close family ties a young person needs to have supplied from some other quarter. On the other hand, relations with one's age mates impart the social skills that a complex, modern urban society makes essential for effective participation. Parsons even goes on to suggest a third possible role for the peer group: that for those youngsters who are socially immobile, such as lower-class minorities, the peer group, notably the gang, serves as an alternative source of success, sanctioning delinquency in the process.

[26] James S. Coleman, *The Adolescent Society* (New York: Free Press, 1961), Ch. 11.

[27] Talcott Parsons, "The Social Structure of the Family," in Ruth N. Anshen, ed., *The Family: Its Function and Destiny* (New York: Harper & Row, 1949), pp. 173–201.

THE YOUTH CULTURE: CONFLICT, IDENTITY, AND COMMITMENT

As the paragraph above reveals, the peer group can turn into a counterculture directly opposite to the values and norms of the major system controlled by adults. As a matter of fact, a widespread sense of discord between the younger and older segments of the populations of the advanced nations, including the United States, has recently gained great prominence. It is popularly labeled "the generation gap," denoting such values on the part of youth as hedonism, unconventional sexuality, hostility toward bureaucratic administration, and dissatisfaction with government.

One interpretation of the generation gap holds that the values of youth represent the very values that are emerging from the maturation process of industrial-urban and postindustrial-urban society. In *The Lonely Crowd,* David Riesman contends that given a complex social structure, an ideological movement will spring up favoring the individual's submergence in the social group, in place of either simple individualism or conformity to formal authority.[28] In this connection it might also be noted that rising productivity and increasing wealth are conducive not only to hedonism but also to a higher sense of self-regard.

Finally, the major culture itself is committed to the twin ideals of youth and of an evolving society. As a consequence, discontinuity with the past must simply be taken for granted. To be sure, any new life style need not necessarily proceed along the lines of the counter-culture prominent in the 1960s. Yet the premise of a prefigurative outlook in which future progress is confidently expected does at least condition parents to accord their children greater freedom of movement, association, and belief.[29] It also provides sanction for a latitudinarian point of view toward cultural values in general.

Upon further examination, industrial urbanism reveals a number of unresolved conflicts between adults and youth. In fact, the isolated world of youth seems to some to be an unacknowledged strategy of the middle-aged and elderly to keep the young at bay so that they will not gain positions of power, authority, and prestige too soon. Unionization, professionalization, and inflated educational requirements are used, it is claimed, to keep youth out of the economy where demographic progress has enabled men and women to survive longer.[30] True, social adolescence has been lengthened to accommodate the more formal education that is definitely needed in a technolog-

[28] (New Haven, Conn.: Yale University Press, 1950).

[29] For the youth culture *à l 'americaine* in France, see Jesse Pitts, "The Family and Peer Groups," in Norman W. Bell and Ezra F. Vogel, eds., *A Modern Introduction to the Family* (New York: Free Press, 1968) rev. ed., pp. 290–310.

[30] E. Musgrove, *Youth and the Social Order* (Bloomington, Ind.: Indiana University Press, 1965), a study of British society.

ical society. But the kind of schooling given many, it is said, means "the increasing segregation of the young in congregate institutions under the benevolent guardianship of adult wardens and keepers."[31]

Once thought solely American but now possibly characteristic of postindustrialism generally, the youth culture may be regarded as a means of achieving an identity in a complex, impersonal, and even incomprehensible social order—that is, for singling out persons and ideas to trust, for gaining a sense of freedom of the will, and as we proceed further into postindustrialism, for establishing a set of goals other than automatic subordination to the demands of machine technology and to duties handed down from the past.[32] Although many adolescents are estranged and others are hostile, Kenneth Kenniston, noted psychiatrist, writes, most wish to "graduate" into adulthood. Kenniston concludes that those desiring entry into the adult world want to do so after having developed in association with their adolescent cohorts "a viable identity which will provide continuity both within their lives and between their own, their parents' and their future children's generations."[33]

URBAN KINSHIP AND AGING

The urban kin network supplements the conjugal family in the city, but there is reason to doubt whether it appropriately answers the special needs of the elderly today.

"Under the impact of industrialization and urbanization," Ernest W. Burgess, a leading chronicler of urban atomism, has said, "the three-generation family has disintegrated as a household and as a unit of economic production."[34] It is essential not to exaggerate the degree of atomism in urban kinship, and not to ignore the presence of kin networks in urban areas. Still, there is substantial agreement that in modern urban society the elderly have suffered serious loss of authority and status within their families. It is also widely believed that they have sustained economic insecurity by the transfer of economic functions from the home to the industrial market, where their physical disability puts those of advanced years at a competitive disadvantage which they would largely avoid in a familistic agrarian setting. In

[31] Albert K. Cohen, "Forward," ibid., p. xvi.

[32] Erik H. Erikson, *Identity: Youth and Crisis* (New York: Norton, 1968), Ch. 3.

[33] "Social Change and Youth in America," in Erik H. Erikson, ed., *The Challenge of Youth* (Garden City, N.Y.: Doubleday, 1965), pp. 191–222.

[34] "Family Structure and Relationships," in Ernest W. Burgess, ed., *Aging in Western Societies* (Chicago: University of Chicago Press, 1960), p. 297.

1972, an estimated one-fifth of America's elderly were living in poverty in contrast to about 11 percent of the nation's total citizens similarly in need.[35]

THE NEEDS OF THE AGED

Gerontologist Leo Simmons sums up the needs of the aged as falling into five categories:[36]

First, life is precious to the old, and they wish to live as long as the advantages of life outweigh its burdens.

Second, the elderly like to conserve their waning physical and psychic resources, and so they try to avoid hazards.

Third, they desire also to safeguard and strengthen the prerogatives that they have acquired in the course of their lives.

Fourth, the old are interested in taking an active part in the affairs of the various groups, including the family, to which they belong.

Fifth, as Simmons puts it, they wish "to withdraw from life when necessity requires it, as timely, honorably, and comfortably as possible and with maximal prospects for an attractive hereafter."[37]

Although these five wishes were actually drawn from simpler, nonurban societies, they appear, declares Simmons, to be true of aging people everywhere.

MEETING THE NEEDS OF THE ELDERLY IN THE CITY

In what manner then does the shift in the city in the direction of the nuclear family affect the aged?

To start with, one is obliged to dispose of the all too easy assumption that in an industrial-urban milieu the elderly find themselves entirely isolated and neglected. As the World Health Organization report on *Mental Health Problems of the Aging and Aged* observes:

Wherever careful studies have been carried out in the industrialized countries the lasting devotion of children for their parents has been amply demonstrated. The great majority of old people are in regular

[35] Bureau of the Census, *Statistical Abstract of the United States: 1975* (Washington, D.C.: Government Printing Office, 1975), Table 631, p. 389, and Table 637, p. 393.

[36] In "Aging in Pre-Industrial Societies," in Clark Tibbits, ed., *Handbook of Social Gerontology* (Chicago: University of Chicago Press, 1960), pp. 62–91.

[37] Ibid.

EXHIBIT 13-1 Percent of the Elderly Participating in the Labor Force, by Age and Sex, United States: 1940–1975

Percent of the Elderly Participating in the Labor Force by Age and Sex, 1940 through 1975

SEX AND AGE GROUP	1940	1950	1960	1970	1975*
Men:					
65 through 69	59.4	59.7	44.0	39.3	33.3
70 through 74	38.4	38.7	28.7	22.5	14.9
75 and over	18.2	18.7	15.6	12.1	
Women:					
65 through 69	9.5	13.0	16.5	17.2	14.6
70 through 74	5.1	6.4	9.6	9.1	5.2
75 and over	2.3	2.6	4.3	4.7	

*Note: As of May 1975.

Both industrialization and post-industrialization tend to establish a mandatory retirement age. They also encourage the greater participation of women in the labor force. The reduction of labor-force service by elderly men in the United States from 1940 to 1975 may be seen here as accompanied by a general increase in the participation rate for elderly women.

Source: "The Elderly in America," *Population Bulletin*, Vol. 30, No. 3 (Washington, D.C.: Population Reference Bureau, 1975), p. 13.

contact with their children, relatives, or friends. . . . Where distance permits, the generations continue to shoulder their traditional obligations, of elders toward their children, and the children to the aged.[38]

Yet, several caveats do need to be entered in support of the conclusion that in urban society the aged are indeed alienated. One is the fact that, in the United States at least, a fifth of the elderly are childless. A second refers to the lengthening expectation of life, which though beneficial in itself also entails serious ill health in later years. There is yet a third matter too, which results from both familial and industrial causes. That is the combination of mandatory retirement, usually at 65, and the desuetude of parenthood upon the emancipation of children, typically at age 45 to 50. The continuing increase in the proportion of the elderly—in the United States almost 10 percent of the population is now at least 65—only threatens to intensify this state of affairs in the near future.

Also robbing the aged of family influence in an industrial-urban setting,

[38] Technical Report Series, No. 171 (Geneva: World Health Organization, 1959).

Elderly men congregating in the park, north Boston.

is their powerlessness to control the economic opportunities of their children. As Goode generalizes in his excellent study of modernization and the family, upper-class parents can generate opportunities for their children, and they do hang on to authority more successfully. The middle-class elderly and to an even smaller extent the lower-class aged are unable, in the city, to pass on productive property or valuable job openings to their children, hence having little to offer in exchange for youthful independence.[39] In these social classes, which make up the bulk of the population by far, parents often relinquish authority and control out of sheer necessity.

THE AGED IN NONURBAN AND URBAN SOCIETY

The control of economic resources is only one reason why the position of the old person is generally stronger in a primitive or agricultural community than it is in the city.[40] Other factors also come into play.

In the simple nonurban society, the whole framework, including the family, benefits old persons. The elderly are better off because they are proprietors of productive land, the residents of villages or small towns, the members of solidary ethnic groups, and participants in a peasant social

[39] Goode, op. cit., pp. 371–72.

[40] Irving Rosow, "And Then We Were Old," *Trans-Action,* 2 (January–February 1965), pp. 21–26.

class that has a tradition of mutual aid. These conditions are the antitheses of those in an urban setting, especially in the postindustrial metropolitan type of community.

WOMEN IN THE URBAN FAMILY

The impact of industrial urbanization on the family benefits women in a number of ways. It does so by encouraging their gainful employment, by leading to their political emancipation, and also by promoting their educational achievement.

Another manifestation of the positive effects of industrial urbanization for women is the lengthening of the female's average life expectancy, owing principally to the reduction of the birth rate and the availability of medical care during pregnancy and delivery. In the United States the average life expectancy for boys born in 1900 was 46 years, and for girls, 48 years. By 1970, however, the gap in longevity had increased 5 years, with boys born at that time being expected to live 67 years, while girls of that birth year could anticipate an average 74 years.[41]

Still another source of feminine advantage in the urban family lies in the changing character of housekeeping. Given labor-saving devices, the care of the home and family becomes more of an executive rather than a sheer laboring task.

Also, rising expectations regarding the socialization of children can also enhance the woman's role. Such responsibilities call for the exercise of greater decision-making, and hence they confer more personal distinction on the woman than was the case earlier, though this must be weighed against the segregation of sex roles which formerly permitted noncompetitive achievement on the part of the farm woman, for example, in being the mother of productive sons and daughters.

In the industrial urban setting, a tendency for the still further liberation of women can be readily observed. In general though this only continues the preexisting trends benefiting women in the process of urbanization.

The demand for women's liberation aims at two interrelated objectives. On the one hand, moderate exponents seek the eradication of economic and political inequality. For instance, women are disproportionately represented in the less well-paying jobs and even suffer from being paid less than men for equal work. In 1971, the median income of females in the United States with four years or more of college was $6,620 as compared with the male figure of $13,126 that year.[42] Similarly, women fill a much smaller place in political life than do men.

[41] Bureau of the Census, *We the American Women* (Washington, D.C.: Government Printing Office, March 1973), p. 3.

[42] Ibid., p. 8.

On the other hand, the more radical advocates of women's liberation entertain broader objectives. They strive for a fundamental change in the traditional allocation of social roles. That is, such advocates envisage a state in which other institutional arrangements would be created to provide for child care and which would thereby finally free women from what they regard as an arbitrary and essentially exploited social position tending the young. So conceived, feminine liberation is asserted to have the capacity of enlarging the consciousness of women and, as a result, of enabling them to achieve higher levels of self-expression and fulfillment.

It is perhaps safe to conclude that greater equalization of the sexes is a principle universal to advanced industrial urban society. However, whether the abolition of the conjugal family would be functional within that setting remains a matter of acrimonious debate at present. Fundamental to that controversy is the significance of the family to the development of a desirable character structure in children.

THE CONJUGAL FAMILY AND ITS PSYCHOSOCIAL IMPLICATIONS

The atomized conjugal family may be viewed from the standpoint of how it facilitates achievement values—consequently, how appropriate it is to urban society in a psychosocial sense. There is reason to believe that the conjugal unit, especially in the broad middle class, does, in fact, play an important role in sustaining the contemporary urban community in this respect.

The urban middle-class family is projected as consonant with modern urbanism, at least in the United States, due to the family's structural features of small size and isolation from other kin, and also by reason of its cultural configuration. The small size of the institutionalized conjugal unit, Talcott Parsons has theorized, makes for an intensity of socialization which, together with strong reliance on the use of affectual sanctions in controlling children, produces an ambitious personality.[43]

In this regard the mother's role is vital. Arnold Green writes that present-day "scientific child-care means close attention is given to the child and that the parents, especially the mother, are often worrying about the child's diet, behavior, and personal development.[44] Likewise, early psychomotor maturity and peer competition are highly valued, both of which also suggest the need and the desire for achievement.

The correlation between the middle-class family and the achievement drive may be gauged from a comparative study done by Ephraim Mizruchi, who concludes "that symbols of the attainment of success are different for

[43] "The Social Structure of the Family," op. cit.

[44] Arnold W. Green, "The Middle-Class Male Child and Neurosis," *American Sociological Review*, 11 (February 1946), pp. 31–41.

respondents in the several classes."[45] Mizruchi found that two-thirds of the respondents from the lowest social stratum associated home ownership and job security most closely with success. At the same time, 61 percent of those of highest status selected education as most indicative of success, showing their proclivity for "non-material economic symbols" in preference to sheer monetary rewards.

Yet interest in achievement may also be observed in combination with the cultivation of interest in rewards in the socialization of middle-class children. The urban middle-class family socializes its children in the mores of consumership as an accompaniment to the achievement drive that parents seek to instill in their young. In the middle-class family, children are influenced to value formal education, language and social skills, and the protection of their physical health. But they are also encouraged to enjoy fashionable clothing and to acquire a wealth of possessions. Sports gear, electronic equipment, tools, and vehicles occupy a high place in the scale of approval. The consumption standards applicable to adult status have been given especially strong recognition in childhood in recent years.

Training in consumership tends to establish a desire to succeed rather than achieve, in other words, to enjoy rewards in place of accomplished tasks. This may be a historical transition at present. That possibility is suggested by various observations.

Consider Crestwood Heights, an upper middle-class suburb of Toronto as illustrative.[46] In Crestwood Heights, the men believed that to be happy one had to achieve occupationally. The Crestwood Heights women, however, thought just the reverse. For the wives happiness was itself the prerequisite of individual accomplishment. Properly experienced in the home, the Crestwood women thought, happiness would lead on to achievement. To the men though, a happy family life figured as "the standard package of material resources" resulting from occupational accomplishment.[47] Thus for both sexes, the family was inextricably bound up with achievement and happiness—and also the consumer durables of success too.

One critic of the view that the nuclear family produces a personality well equipped to meet the constraints of advanced urban society is Richard Sennett in his monograph *Families Against the City*.[48] Sennett reasons that in the family unit where only one person, typically the father, is gainfully employed, he cannot thoroughly represent the work situation to socialize the children

[45] Ephraim H. Mizruchi, "Success and Opportunity," excerpted from the book (New York: Free Press, 1964), as contained in Celia S. Heller, ed., *Structured Social Inequality* (New York: Macmillan, 1969), p. 299.

[46] John R. Seeley, Alexander Sim, and Elizabeth W. Loosley, *Crestwood Heights: A Study of the Culture of Suburban Life* (New York: Basic Books, 1956).

[47] See also David Riesman and Howard Roseborough, "Careers and Consumer Behavior," in Lincoln H. Clark, ed., *Consumer Behavior* (New York: New York University Press, 1955), pp. 1–18.

[48] (Cambridge, Mass.: Harvard University Press, 1970).

Training for family behavior and consumership: a girl with a Ken and Barbie doll set complete with sports car.

adequately. Goode too, for that matter, wonders if instead of the nuclear household some broader grouping, possibly of the Kibbutz type, might not better serve the personality needs of a modern economy.[49] Such interpretations lend support to those advocating alternatives to the conjugal family. Princeton sociologist Susanne Keller has even gone so far as to consider whether the preconception that monogamy is superior to other forms of marriage or that women naturally make the best mothers are not simply "made-to-order" truths. She reasons that perhaps there lies ahead of us "a world of Unisex, Multi-sex, or Non-sex."[50]

[49] Goode, op. cit., p. 24.

[50] Susanne Keller, "Does the Family Have a Future?" *Journal of Comparative Family Studies* (Spring 1971), pp. 1–14.

OTHER FAMILY FORMS

As we have seen, the presence of the kin network challenges the atomistic interpretation of family life in urban society. So too does the existence in the city of variant family forms traceable to cultural traditions and special historical circumstances apart from urbanization. The families of ethnic and racial minorities found in urban America today illustrate this state of affairs.

THE ETHNIC FACTOR

The ethnic factor in urban kinship relations refers to cultural diversity derived from sources not indigenous to the city itself. These include nationality, religion, and race, the latter not innately but as the expression of a common experience. Ethnicity may be thought of as the totality of cultural attributes that distinguish any population sharing a common biological descent pattern.

Ethnicity affects the family directly, and also indirectly via stratification. Ethnicity does so because not only are there various ethnic norms defining kinship behavior, but also because ethnicity tends to be a basis for the evaluation of people and their assignment to specific status groups. Family, ethnicity, and stratification are usually interwoven, and the factors of race, religion, and national differences relating to the family deserve appropriate attention from urban sociologists.

The Italian Family

Consider Italian kinship in the United States.[51] Mass immigration of Italians to America took place in the period 1890–1910, a time of rapid urbanization here. The bulk of the Italian influx consisted of peasants from southern Italy and Sicily. Their traditional kinship system stressed patriarchal authority, sacred values, strong familism (children living for their parents), fecundity, segregated conjugal relations, puritanical sex mores, an absolute prohibition on divorce, and extreme dependence of the individual on the blood group.

Contact with urban life in America, however, soon induced change in the Italian family. Eventually only slight traces of the traditional type remained, such as weak patriarchal authority, modified role segregation, religious worship, the ban on birth control, adult centering, and sexual modesty for women and sexual aggressiveness for men, at least toward "bad" women.

Yet differences did persist. In a study of working-class Italians in Bos-

---

[51] Paul J. Campisi, "Ethnic Family Patterns: The Italian Family in the United States," *American Journal of Sociology,* 53 (May 1948), pp. 443–49.

ton's inner city, Herbert Gans describes their family type as one between the modern middle-class nuclear family and the extended family typical of peasant society.[52] The Italian family is nuclear in that the conjugal pair occupy a separate domicile, but the family maintains close relations with kin, especially adult brothers and sisters and their spouses. Though interaction across the generations is less, the mother-daughter tie is often close even after the daughter's marriage. Moreover, Gans' study indicates also that the relationship between the sexes and communication across sex lines is generally limited, as contrasted with the American middle class. Finally, in husband-wife relationships, there is segregation because of their differentiation between the tasks of husband and wife, an outlook that divides them. The family that Gans describes is both ethnic and working class. He considers the class dimension the more important, and his comparison of the Italian family in Boston with the working-class family of England testifies to how much of the type is a consequence of social-class standing.

The Jewish Family

Jews in the United States are another illustration of ethnic influence on the urban family. Though immigrant Jews had various European backgrounds— as land owners, village artisans, inhabitants of isolated pariah colonies—in the main they settled in cities upon their arrival in the United States, primarily in metropolitan centers. New York alone contains almost half of all Jews in this country. The institutionalization of marriage as a religious sacrament, the quasisacredness of familism, and great respect for mutual help among extended kin all marked the special traditions of the immigrant Jew in the United States.[53]

These patterns go on today after generations of acculturation. For instance, the intermarriage rate of Jews and gentiles is very low despite the higher-than-average level of higher education among Jews, education generally correlating with intermarriage.[54] Not only in resistance to exogamy but also in fostering cooperation in business among relatives have the values of the traditional Jewish family been preserved. In other respects though, the Jewish family in urban America shows significant sociocultural assimilation: child-centering, middle-class secularism (abandoning the old dietary laws and Sabbath observances), and education for women instead of their past segregation.

[52] The Urban Villagers, op. cit.

[53] Marshall Sklare, ed., The Jews: Social Patterns of an American group (Glencoe, Ill.: Free Press, 1958).

[54] "Cultural Factors in the Selection of Marriage Mates," American Sociological Review, 15 (October 1950), pp. 619–27.

The Black American Family

Black family life in urban America reveals what some observers believe are not patterns systematically at variance with the major conjugal type, but which they think may be normative subcultural features.

During a period of urbanization, from 1865 to 1920, as Jessie Bernard has revealed, the black American family displayed a pattern of development contrary to that otherwise generally evident in the United States.[55] Instead of moving toward a companionate nuclear form, the black family actually developed greater institutionalization during the half century following Emancipation. The overall effect was the achievement of a family structure characterized by Bernard as "external, formal, and authoritarian."

After World War II, especially with large-scale migration of blacks to urban centers in the Northeast, the institutionalization of black families slowed down and, at least as compared with that of whites, came to be reversed. As Reynolds Farley and Albert I. Hermalin report for the period 1940 to 1969, while the proportion of black men associated with family stability remained unchanged and that of black women decreased, "among whites of both sexes, the proportion of married-spouse present has increased."[56] In 1973, more than one out of every three black families was headed by a female.[57] Also, between the years 1940 and 1967, the rate of illegitimate births among nonwhites rose from 35.6 to 89.5, among whites, from 3.6 to 12.5.[58] These deinstitutionalizing tendencies, furthermore, were disproportionately urban.

The "Moynihan Report," so named for its chief author, Daniel P. Moynihan, assistant secretary of labor at the time, attributed the extensive dismemberment, female-headedness, and illegitimacy in the black family to several factors. First was its background in slavery and then exploitation, and more recently, the difficulties of urbanization accompanied by insufficient opportunity. When the black rural family, already weakened by inadequate socialization of the males for institutionalized family life, moved to the city, "poverty, ignorance, and color" compelled it to live in a deteriorated slum. There, further economic adversity and the absence of a strong community life continued to undermine the home, leading to separation and desertion, if not

---

[55] In her *Marriage and Family Among Negroes* (Englewood Cliffs, N.J.: Prentice-Hall, 1966), Ch. 1.

[56] Reynolds Farley and Albert I. Hermalin, "Family Stability: A Comparison of Trends between Blacks and Whites," *American Sociological Review*, 36 (February 1971), pp. 1–17.

[57] Ibid.

[58] Bureau of the Census, *Statistical Abstract of the United States: 1972* (Washington, D.C.: Government Printing Office, 1973), Table 66, p. 51. See also Office of Policy Planning and Research, *The Negro Family: The Case for National Action* (Washington, D.C.: U.S. Department of Labor, 1965).

divorce, and to illegitimacy, a matriarchal form of organization, and to dependence on public assistance.[59]

The Moynihan study aroused much comment and even controversy.[60] Since it was an unflattering portrayal, some simply condemned it as racially inspired. Others questioned whether the deviance that was asserted could validly be ascribed to the black population as possessing a subculture, or whether it was essential to attribute it to the black's general class and income level. Much study followed the appearance of the Moynihan Report. An agenda paper for the White House Conference "To Fulfill These Rights," in 1965, declared that "Negro-white differences in family structure diminish when controlled for income."[61] Again, it was questioned whether the fatherless family does generate ambivalence toward sex roles, including marital ineptitude and passivity on the one hand, and compensatory, violent hypermasculinity on the other.[62]

Certainly there is danger of overgeneralization here on sketchy data. For one thing, Herbert Gans doubts the conclusion that "the tangle of pathology" (Moynihan's phrase) is directly traceable to the matriarchal family. Gans writes that "the absence of the father has not yet been proven pathological, even for the boys who grow up in it."[63] He contends that the black family equilibrates itself by extension on the maternal side, through the mother's sisters, her aunts, and her own mother, and that what may be the source of personality deficiency in black boys is the lack of "emotional strengths and cultural skills in the mothers," rather than the absence of the fathers.[64] Similarly, Joyce Ladner has recently written on the inappropriateness of applying the conventional "moral-immoral dichotomy" to the low-income black American's kinship relations.[65]

Further research will doubtlessly show that ethnicity and social status

---

[59] See *The Social and Economic Status of Negroes in the United States: 1970* (Washington, D.C.: Government Printing Office, 1970), No. 38, p. 23.

[60] For a monograph taking the Moynihan Report into account but seeking to avoid the ideological controversy over it, see John H. Scanzoni, *The Black Family in Modern Society* (Boston: Allyn and Bacon, 1971).

[61] Hylan Lewis, "Agenda Paper V," in Lee Rainwater and William L. Yancey, eds., *The Moynihan Report and the Politics of Controversy* (Cambridge, Mass.: M.I.T. Press, 1967), p. 315.

[62] Consult Thomas F. Pettigrew, *Profile of the Negro American* (Princeton, N.J.: Van Nostrand, 1964), pp. 17ff for a scholarly review.

[63] "The Negro Family: Reflections on the Moynihan Report," in Rainwater and Yancey, op. cit., pp. 445–57.

[64] See John H. Rohrer and Munro S. Edmondson, *The Eighth Generation* (New York: Harper & Row, 1960) and Robert Blood and D. M. Wolfe, *Husbands and Wives* (New York: Free Press, 1960), a study of 116 black families and 595 white families in Detroit.

[65] Joyce A. Ladner, *Tomorrow's Tomorrow: The Black Woman* (Garden City, N.Y.: Doubleday, 1971).

continue to influence families in the city away from the postulated atomistic form, though possibly in directions not fully anticipated as yet.

Conclusion

Urbanization is claimed to produce the nucleated conjugal family, that is, the structured isolation of the immediate unit of parents and their young children. An overview of the effects on the family of modernization in some of the developing regions does largely confirm this generalization. Yet the presence of kin networks among families in an urban setting suggests that the atomistic hypothesis is possibly a typological overstatement in need of some qualification. So too does the existence of variant family forms among the city's different ethnic populations also indicate family forms not entirely congruent with the postulated urban model. However, scant doubt attaches to the existence of certain features of urban kinship atomism: namely, the relative autonomy of the conjugal family, the independence of youth, and the general isolation of the elderly. Appropriate analysis may also succeed in firmly establishing a functional correspondence between the isolated family and the development of the achievement drive that people need to participate effectively in industrial urban life.

FOR FURTHER READING

Bert N. Adams, *Kinship in an Urban Setting* (Chicago: Markham, 1968). The persistence of an informal mutual-aid system among families in contemporary urban America.

Andrew Billingsley, *Black Families in White America* (Englewood Cliffs, N.J.: Prentice-Hall, 1968). Some of the major problems confronting black families.

William J. Goode, *World Revolution and Family Patterns* (New York: Free Press, 1967). On comparative family systems and the social changes which have affected them in recent years.

Michael Gordon, ed., *The American Family in Social-Historical Perspective* (New York: St. Martin's Press, 1973). The social history of the family with special emphasis on modernization.

C. C. Harris, ed., *Readings in Kinship in Urban Society* (New York: Pergamon, 1970). Seventeen articles, with an excellent introduction.

Reuben Hill and Rene Koenig, eds., *Families in East and West* (The Hague: Mouton, 1970). Papers prepared for the International Family Research Seminar, and divided into socialization, relations with extended kin, and research methods.

Edwin M. Schur ed., *The Family and the Sexual Revolution* (Blooming-ton, Ind.: Indiana University Press, 1964). Articles from different fields on the debatable issues of changing sex standards, changing roles of women, and birth control.

Betty Yorburg, *The Changing Family* (New York: Columbia University Press, 1973). On the phenomena of homosexual marriage and residential communes; considers the possible future of the American family.

CHAPTER 14

RELIGION AS AN INSTITUTIONAL SYSTEM

Religion is a body of beliefs about the ultimate meaning of human existence. Religion thus implies a conception of the universe as a coherent, purposeful system governed by absolute though never fully comprehensible spiritual forces. The beliefs that make up any particular religion are articles of faith reinforced by congregate worship.[1]

The motivation to formulate such ultimate beliefs about life lies in the

[1] Emile Durkheim emphasizes the role of collective experience in strengthening religious conviction in *The Elementary Forms of the Religious Life,* trans. by J. W. Swain (Glencoe, Ill.: Free Press, 1947).

tensions which inevitably beset individuals and the communities in which they live: notably, the uncertainties of chance occurrences; the prevalence of evil, that is, unsanctioned behavior; and the eventual termination of human life in death. For the community, the existential difficulties for which no rational solution can entirely suffice are securing adherence to authority and justifying the allocation of wealth, power, and prestige. Both of these types of tensions are susceptible to control through religion. Thus one has the prospect of anticipating postmortem rewards for a frustrating life here and now. Similarly, the community may sanction its system of free elections as, say, congruent with the dignity of people's immortal souls.

Of course, an evangelical movement may also arise, and in the name of the very same God that justifies the existing institutions, challenge the very status quo that the more conservative elements assert is an expression of divine intent. Hence any thorough appraisal of religion as a social force must pay attention not only to the stabilizing role of religious belief but also to the manner in which religion enters into the continuous struggle for power that goes on in any society.

RELIGION IN THE URBAN MILIEU

The religious institution as a whole has a multiplex influence in urban society. Four of its aspects have been well analyzed and documented in sociological literature. They make up the framework of this chapter.

First, insofar as it consists of supernatural ideas supporting an otherworldly outlook, religion is inconsistent with the pragmatic ethos of urbanism. In fact, part of the process of urbanization lies in the very advances people make toward adopting a secular attitude about the world around them. This does not nullify the religious spirit though it does change it considerably, by reducing its miraculous content.

Second, we may note that Protestantism, as Max Weber demonstrated, probably played an instrumental role in the emergence of modern urbanism in Europe, beginning in the sixteenth century. Then, under the impact of the Industrial Revolution 200 years later, the preindustrial European city metamorphosed into the industrial metropolis.

Third, religious conflict has gone hand in hand with the struggle waged between social classes over their competing interests in the cities of Western Europe and the United States since the advent of machine technology. That contest continues today.

Fourth, religion in contemporary urban America can be examined in terms of the adaptation of traditional beliefs, practices, and church organization, to current circumstances and needs. This involves the Americanisation of the customary creed, the development of the "urban church," and also pronounced trends toward ecumenicalism and religious innovation, including political and economic reform.

URBANIZATION AND SECULARISM

As the course of history has moved, in Kingsley Davis's words, from "small isolated societies in the direction of huge, complex, urbanized ones," the process of secularization has been set into motion and has become increasingly more apparent with the passage of time.[2] When we review urbanization from its beginnings onward, we see that not only has the character of religion changed, but the type of influence it is believed to have on people has changed with it.

Davis's trenchant analysis of secularization shows the whole process to consist of five components:

1 The preexisting tribal and village gods lost their identification with their immediate locality after cities arose.

2 Just as the gods were withdrawn from the local scene and made more regional, they were also deprived of their corporeal nature under the influence of urban society. They shed their human characteristics and became abstract entities.

3 As urban society became more complex, religion tended to be removed from everyday, practical affairs. Religious interpretation was withdrawn from technological, economic, and political activities, leaving spiritual reflection confined to the less rational aspects of living.[3]

4 As social diversity became pronounced, religious beliefs and practices became progressively more diversified. Homogeneity disappeared in a multiplication of creeds coexisting in a state of mutual tolerance. The general effect of this process of urban differentiation was a decline in religious belief altogether and the adoption, instead, of naturalistic philosophies.

5 The fifth aspect of secularism was structured fragmentation. Here the separation of church and state ensued, with religion relegated entirely to the private sphere. Thus, when Christianity was finally accepted in Rome, it

[2] *Human Society* (New York: Macmillan, 1949), pp. 542ff.

[3] For additional material on secularization, see Milton Singer, "The Modernization of Religious Beliefs," in Myron Weiner, ed., *Modernization* (New York: Basic Books, 1966), pp. 55–67, and William V. D'Antonio and Frederick B. Pike, eds., *Religion, Revolution, and Reform* (New York: Frederick A. Praeger, 1964).

placed itself, as the French historian Fustel de Coulanges has said, "outside all things purely terrestrial."[4]

In short, as a concomitant of urbanization, secularism has a long history and continues to be evident in modern urban society.

THE PROTESTANT BACKGROUND OF
THE INDUSTRIAL CITY

Though secularization may be thought of as a component of urbanization, like many typological principles this generalization needs to be circumscribed to account for the emergence of the modern industrial urban center originally in Western Europe. Paradoxically, the secular city of today's industrial and postindustrial era may, at least in part, owe its very existence to the religious impulse. One may reason so on the basis of Max Weber's famed hypothesis concerning the Protestant ethic and its influence upon sixteenth-century European economic entrepreneurship and the urban settlement patterns stemming from it.[5]

Weber defined capitalism as sustained profit-making through the utilization of opportunities for exchange. He distinguished capitalism from other forms of acquisition, such as the medieval trading associations (the *commenda*). By comparison, capitalism was both more systematic and larger in scale, and accordingly, Weber deemed capitalism to be a way of life. Earning money was the backbone of an ethic that the Calvinist creed enjoined upon one as a "calling." The nascent capitalist could quote the Bible: "Seest thou a man diligent in his business? He shall stand before kings."[6]

Calvinism taught the predestination of souls, a doctrine that aroused great anxiety in people's minds. However, the resulting emotional insecurity could be eased by accepting successful enterprise on earth as the fruit of earnest toil and disciplined effort, and hence as indicative of one's election to immortal grace. Though he recognized this social psychology of Calvinism, Weber did not attribute capitalism directly to the Protestant ethic. He insisted, rather, that as a religious motive Calvinism legitimized and hence, gave powerful impetus to a whole range of activities, including science, technology, and business.

The Puritan philosophy had two strong effects on personal life. First, by

---

[4] Actually, the separation of political life from religion had been going on for centuries before Christianity succeeded in being adopted in Rome. Christianity only continued the trend of detaching the state from religion.

[5] Max Weber, *The Protestant Ethic and the Spirit of Capitalism,* trans. by Talcott Parsons (New York: Scribner's, 1958).

[6] *Proverbs,* xxii, 29.

austerely condemning consumption it induced thrift and the building up of capital, and by teaching respect for property it also created a strong sense of responsibility and stewardship. Second, despite severe limitations on the enjoyment of material goods, Puritan morality encouraged their production. The overall tendency of these currents, then, was truly cosmic, as Kemper Fullerton said, for it was conducive to "a world dominated by money-making," so much so that its entire organization was subject to this one objective. The industrial cities that arose in Western Europe were arenas for the exercise of this compelling discipline.

EVALUATION OF THE WEBERIAN HYPOTHESIS

The influence of Protestantism upon the origins of industrial capitalism has not been without debate since Weber first published his study in 1905. This whole question has, in fact, been critical in sociological theory because it involves the importance of ideology versus economic interests as the cause of social change.[7]

Though upholding Weber in general, Felix Rachfal, an early critic, disputed several of Weber's ideas. Rachfal questioned the priority Weber assigned to religious motivation over other motivating sources. He also pointed out that rather than differing from each other, the Catholic Benedictines, Franciscans, and Jesuits resembled Calvinism in their attitude toward economic enterprise.

About 10 years after the publication of Weber's research on the beginnings of capitalist business enterprise, Lujo Brentano threw into bold relief the sustained economic activities of the Italian cities of the Renaissance. Brentano argued that when business shifted northward, Catholic entrepreneurs and bankers moved with it to the North Sea—to Breslau, Augsburg, and Amsterdam. In addition, said Brentano, it was the revival of Roman law more than Puritanism that legitimized the growth of business in Europe. Puritanism served merely to reinforce already existing trends.

The English historian R. H. Tawney criticized Weber by asserting that Puritanism only encouraged developments already under way independent of the Protestant religion.[8] The Old Testament view of business life, geographic discoveries, and the existing mercantile houses, like those in medieval Flanders, fed economic enterprise. This affected Calvinistic teachings and not the other way around, although it would be "equally one-sided to say that the religious changes were purely the result of economic movements."[9]

H. M. Robertson is frankly of the view, however, that Weber's hypothesis

---

[7] The position of Weber and of his leading critics is succinctly presented in Robert W. Green, ed., *Protestantism and Capitalism* (Boston: D. C. Heath, 1959).

[8] In *Religion and the Rise of Capitalism* (London: John Murray, 1960).

[9] Ibid., p. 320.

needs to be reversed, and the economist Kurt Samuelson that "almost all the evidence contradicts [it]."[10] Samuelson reasons that it is "over-hasty" to infer that Protestantism established capitalism or, for that matter, that it was even an indispensable ingredient in the spirit of modern business enterprise.

Most writers do agree, however, that inasmuch as Protestantism gave sustained economic activity an ideological weapon, it served to promote capitalism and, with it, industrial urbanization—and that religion, then, did play a role in urbanization despite the process of secularization.

SOCIAL CHANGE AND THE CHURCH

The industrial urbanization of Western Europe beginning in the eighteenth century brought sweeping social changes, including much hardship for the proletarian classes. In this process of unplanned change and later of attempted reform, religion had a conspicuous place. Reviewing that history permits us to further examine the general and continuing influence of religion on the structure of urban society.[11]

SHEFFIELD: A CASE STUDY

For this purpose we may begin with the case of Sheffield, England, an industrial urban center manufacturing cutlery and steel, whose history undoubtedly parallels many others in modern times. Sheffield reveals the significance of organized religion in the class conflict of industrial urban society.

In 1615, a century and a half before the Industrial Revolution, Sheffield had a population of only 2207. The clergy and the leading citizens of Sheffield were Puritan (and parliamentary too) from 1597 to the restoration in 1662. Little is known about the exact religious affiliations of the cutlers and craftsmen although they were probably Dissenters too along with the town's mercantile gentry.

Industrialization and Religious Diversification

With the rapid growth of Sheffield's population as a result of industrialization came a good deal of religious diversification. By 1841 there were 13 churches of the Anglican establishment. "Methodistical" preaching, having begun in 1738, and the building of Independent chapels too—five of them in rapid succession after 1774—bear out the growing religious diversity

[10] See Kurt Samuelson, *Religion and Economic Action,* trans. by E. Geoffrey (New York: Harper & Row, 1961).

[11] See the detailed study of E. R. Wickham, *Church and People in an Industrial City* (London: Lutterworth Press, 1957).

"One beauty of Sheffield," it used to be said, "is that you can see very little of it." Under the screen of "torpid smoke," Sheffield's working classes remained outside the city's religious institutions throughout the nineteenth century.

among the citizens of Sheffield. Methodism spoke not to those of some social height but, rather, to the city's lowly rank and file.[12] Despite such evangelicism, however, the general run of Sheffield's laboring poor were without a tradition of explicit religious belief and practice.

In 1851, the registrar general of the United Kingdom asked the barrister

[12] Ibid., p. 56.

Horace Mann to undertake a religious census of England and Wales. In Sheffield, Mann found that out of the borough population now standing at 135,310, attendance at worship amounted to a total of only 43,421. This was a proportion just slightly more than half of that for the nation as a whole. Mann deplored the "alarming number of non-attendants," and took occasion to note that "especially in cities and large towns it is observable how absolutely insignificant a portion of the congregation is composed of artizans."[13] Continuing, he attributed the alienation of the industrial workers that he had found (and which Frederick Engels had observed even earlier in the 1840s) to the undue attentiveness of the Christian churches to the style of life, if not the interests, of the nonlaboring classes.

Religion as a Conservative Force

At the middle of the nineteenth century, and as evidenced by Sheffield itself, urban England presented a religious picture in which the affluent classes adhered to the churches, and the churches supported the prevailing social morality. These expanding middle classes not only counted on church doctrine for ideological support, they also regarded religious participation as an expression of their own social respectability.

The lower classes alone stood outside the existing religious institutions of Sheffield. Evangelistic approaches were made to the Sheffield poor, and with some small degree of success too. The Salvation Army, Primitive Methodists, and Wesleyan Reformers sought converts among the disadvantaged by "scouring the gutters" and "netting the sewers." Yet by and large, organized religion in Britain was committed to laissez faire and political liberalism, and did not offer the working class any solution to their problems other than eventual salvation. When radical reform finally did take root, it did so in the form of trade unions and new political parties like the Independent Labour Party of 1893 and the Labour Party organized in 1906.

INDUSTRIAL AMERICA AND RELIGIOUS CONSERVATISM

Meanwhile, in the United States, a similar history of religious conservatism was also unfolding. Except for a small sectarian faction, the churches here accepted the misery of the industrial masses as inevitable. In fact, at the outset of modern industrialism in the United States, the churches were interested in industrial conditions only insofar as they sapped traditional religious belief and nothing more.[14] Religious disenchantment had become

---

[13] Ibid., p. 110.

[14] Consult Milton Yinger, *Religion in the Struggle for Power* (New York: Russell & Russell, 1961), pp. 133ff.

pronounced among America's industrial workers as a consequence. Samuel Gompers of the new American Federation of Labor, declared in 1898, "My associates have come to look upon the church and the ministry as apologists and defenders of the wrong committed against the interests of the people." By far, the Protestant churches preached individual morality rather than institutional change as the answer to the problems of an industrial society.

Scarcely any American churchmen were interventionists in the nineteenth century. The nation's religious leaders contented themselves with otherworldliness and expressed concern only for the salvation of souls, not social conditions. The churches eventually came to accept strikes as a means of gaining concessions, notably, the abolition of child labor, workmen's compensation, industrial safety, minimum wages, and the like. But they did not pioneer in these respects.

The Social-Gospel Movement

Despite the ineffectiveness of the churches, it would be shortsighted to ignore the vision of a better social order that was contained in the social-gospel teachings of that part of the Christian pastorate that did come to grips with the problems of modern industrialization.

Some churches sought to combine a social with a spiritual ministry among the urban masses.[15] The American Christian Commission led in this respect. In the 50 years following the Civil War, a large variety of services were administered in our cities under the auspices of religious organizations. There were nonsectarian city missions, guilds, and workingmen's clubs established. Writes Aaron Abell, these "workingmen's clubs helped to counteract the virus of aristocracy in church life by epitomizing the principles of true Christian charity and by pointing the way to the solution of social problems through association."[16] The Y.M.C.A. and Y.W.C.A. were founded and owed their rapid growth to the failure of the churches to deal satisfactorily with the needs of the urban population.

Many similar missionary bodies came into existence in America's cities to advocate temperance, conduct Bible drill, and engage in philanthropy. It was in securing social justice though that even the new religious measures could not suffice. Organized religion was thus for a long time only groping with the dilemma of providing leadership to the new industrial order centered on our cities.[17]

Eventually, however, Protestant bodies, among them the Federal Council of Churches, did propound the social gospel, in which values like equality

---

[15] Aaron I. Abell, *The Urban Impact on American Protestantism: 1865–1900* (London: Hamden and London, 1962).

[16] Ibid., p. 40.

[17] Ibid., p. 254.

The City Mission of Dubuque, Iowa, attempted to bring Christian uplift to the city's non-churched population.

and human integrity long upheld by Christianity were asserted against the prevailing social conditions.[18] This process consisted of spiritually supporting the organized secular effort carried on by labor unions and political parties. It resulted in institutional changes like guaranteed collective bargaining, mediation, and arbitration; public welfare services; and changes in fiscal and monetary policies. In the urban environment specifically, the movement helped bring about zoning and housing codes, public parks, improved sanitation and public health services, and better education.

THE URBAN CHURCH TODAY

Presently three religious patterns are uppermost in urban America, and possibly are true of the other industrial and postindustrial urban nations too, at least in the West. They may be designated as: (1) secularization; (2) the performance of multiple services; and (3) social reform.

SECULARIZATION

First, though any particular religious faith may continue to advance its traditional sacred values in a formal way, in actual practice its ecclesiastical

[18] See Donald B. Meyer, *The Protestant Search for Political Realism: 1919–1941* (Berkeley and Los Angeles, Calif.: University of California Press, 1961).

leadership and its laity subscribe to the contemporary secular standards.

Summarily stated, urban religion tends to be "inclusive, this-worldly, and progressive."[19] The urban church is inclined to dispense with both its supernatural outlook and its adherence to its established beliefs. Instead, the church accommodates itself to the values of the urban milieu, that is, to individualism, economic well-being, civic authority, hedonism, complex mobility patterns, and formal organization. Basing their observations on a national survey, University of California sociologists, Rodney Stark and Charles Y. Glock conclude that "a demythologized modernism is overwhelming the traditional, Christ-centered, mystical faith."[20] Old-time Christianity survives in the fundamentalist Protestant sects and denominations in this country, but otherwise even "to a considerable extent among Roman Catholics," disbelief in traditional theology abounds. Moreover, age differences need to be noted here, so that in all probability, say Stark and Glock, the break with conventional religious commitment is most strongly felt in the minds of the oncoming young.[21] The clergy too subscribe to the new disbelief, but are held back by the older, orthodox laity.[22]

Andrew M. Greeley, a sociologist of religion who has also paid attention to the contemporary religious scene in the United States, asks, however, whether the doubts which Stark and Glock refer to are sufficient to reach the conclusion that orthodoxy has truly been compromised.[23] Greeley debates that inference. Yet even Greeley characterizes religion in America as activist (not contemplative), pragmatic (rather than theoretical), accepting (perhaps more than challenging) of society, pluralistic (not monolithic), fundamentalist (but also flexible), and autonomous (rather than episcopal). In addition, says Greeley, religion here in the United States is also "folksy" and "materialistic."[24]

The American Way of Life

As a result of secularization, humanistic and nationalistic themes tend to be emphasized by urban churches. Will Herberg, in his *Protestant, Catholic, and Jew*,[25] notes that in the United States secularization is occurring together with congregate and symbolic activities in support of the nation's existing values. In fact, declares Herberg, faith in the American way of life is

---

[19] Thomas F. Hoult, *The Sociology of Religion* (New York: Dryden Press, 1958), Ch. 7.

[20] Rodney Stark and Charles Y. Glock, *American Piety* (Berkeley and Los Angeles, Calif.: University of California Press, 1968), p. 205.

[21] Ibid., p. 207.

[22] Ibid., pp. 211–12.

[23] Andrew M. Greeley, *The Denominational Society* (Glenview, Ill.: Scott, Foresman, 1972), Ch. 4.

[24] Ibid.

[25] (Garden City, N.Y.: Doubleday, 1955).

extolled as the essence of religious belief here in America. Our religion, Herberg submits, is simply the idealized American creed. Although this "religion" may be articulated in the different contexts of tabernacle, meetinghouse, cathedral, church, temple, or synagogue, the beliefs making up the creed consist of the same worldly values. Human brotherhood and equality, social justice, sociability, individual self-reliance, fair play for all, and democratic government—these make up the sacred ideology of all three of the major faiths in America today.

Organizational Unity and Religious Disharmony

Besides this ethical unity, interdenominational church organization also attests to the doctrinal convergence of America's religious faiths. In the United States, a process of ecclesiastical cooperation has gone on for a long time. The Federal Council of Churches was organized in 1908, and in 1950 created the National Council of the Churches of Christ. "Conciliar ecumenicity," has, in fact, become sufficiently widespread as to have a thousand councils of churches virtually blanketing every large community in the nation.[26] In addition, especially in the largest metropolitan areas, the National Conference of Christians and Jews has brought together all three faiths in combatting a variety of urban social problems, including discrimination and poverty.

It would be misleading though to give undue emphasis to religious unity in urban America. Among recent issues dividing the churches have been questions of government aid to religiously controlled schools; religious observances in public education (prayer, Bible reading, and teaching belief in God), birth control and abortion, and censorship of the media. In addition to these issues, one may also mention others of a specifically economic nature: the taxation of church property and the regulation of child labor.[27]

True, these conflicts involve value differences, but demographic determinants are not absent here by any means. In the United States, Catholics have a smaller middle-class membership than the population generally, and Protestants a larger one. Occupationally, Catholics are skewed toward the lower end of the national scale, with representation above the national distribution in the service, skilled and semiskilled, and unskilled labor categories. Protestants, particularly Methodists, Presbyterians, Episcopalians, Congregationalists, and Christian Scientists, follow professional occupations to a greater extent than the national frequency. These demographic disparities affect religious issues in various ways. For instance, Catholics are to be

[26] Cf. Claud D. Nelson, *Religion and Society: The Ecumenical Impact* (New York: Sheed and Ward, 1966), pp. 3–21.

[27] David O. Moberg, *The Church as a Social Institution* (Englewood Cliffs, N.J.: Prentice-Hall, 1962), p. 302.

found disproportionately among inner-city whites and, therefore, more immediately affected by the nation's racial policies. The social-class character of church membership thus adds to theological differences in inspiring interreligious antipathy.

Persistence of Traditional Religiosity

In spite of the fact that Protestant, Catholic, and Jew have largely subordinated their own indigenous values to the American way, traditional religious orientations apparently do continue to affect thought and behavior to some extent. Gerhard Lenski's survey of the influence of the religious factor among people in metropolitan Detroit supports some significant generalizations about the persistence of customary religious sentiments in secular urban society.[28]

Lenski divided his sample into four socioreligious groups: white Protestants; Negro Protestants; Catholics; and Jews. Using a questionnaire, his study was concerned with whether religion continues to have a bearing on ordinary conduct in the "secularized, specialized, and compartmentalized modern metropolis." Lenski's research was guided by the assumption that systematic inquiry would show that, in the sense of its being a mode of thought carried on by the members of an interacting group of coreligionists, religion does contribute to the determination of behavior even in the secular urban arena.

The data secured in the Detroit community supported Lenski's overall hypothesis. And Lenski reached the conclusion that "religion in various ways is constantly influencing the daily lives of the masses of men and women in the modern American metropolis."[29] Also, as a set of beliefs about the universe and of man's place in it, religion is effective at the institutional level where it has a causal bearing on people regarding public policy.

Specifically, Lenski found: (1) commitment to the spirit of capitalism was more frequent among white Protestants and Jews than among Catholics and Negro Protestants; (2) Protestant men rose further in the class system than did Catholic men; (3) white Protestants were the strongest supporters of the Republican Party; (4) middle-class Jews thought that government was doing too little in welfare more than did working-class white Protestants and Catholics; (5) white Protestants were most apt to incline toward a literal reading of the Bill of Rights, Negro Protestants the least so; (6) white Protestants were more influenced by friends, Catholics by relatives; and (7) although, surprisingly, educational differences were not great among the various religions, Catholics had a higher school dropout rate than either white Protestants or Jews. Thus the evidence from Detroit showed systematic behavioral effects

[28] *The Religious Factor* (Garden City, N.Y.: Doubleday, 1961).
[29] Ibid., p. 320.

stemming from religious belief and membership in the socioreligious sub-community in the metropolis.

From his study Lenski concluded that "the successor to the ethnic sub-community is the socioreligious subcommunity, a group united by ties of race and religion."[30] This body has replaced simple nationality groups as the basic unit in the larger American community. In fact, Lenski reasoned, the time may be approaching when tensions will crystallize around the socioreligious community. That event will perhaps necessitate some compart-mentalized structure in which groups of people are loyal to their own eth-nicreligious compatriots but not toward other conationals. In that case then, the higher ethical principles of the several religions will have been dis-carded in favor of particular political values. And the national unity that has been achieved by the major religions in the United States will then have given way to a new sectarianism. This possibility could well be latent in the country's socioreligious makeup. For example, one carefully designed study of interpersonal ties in the city done by Edward O. Laumann revealed that religious membership and ethnicity have a decidedly strong influence over interaction, with the inference that the metropolitan community may be said to consist of a mosaic of religious subcommunities.[31] Laumann further rea-soned that homogeneity for ethnoreligion underlies a variety of social net-works in the suburban community, which exist in the first place to compen-sate for the rigors of impersonal competition in the urban economy.[32] Such "localistic pluralism," so to speak, may augur incipient conflict too.

Anticommunism

At the same time, however, an added source of unity among religious groups needs to be kept in view. That is the anticommunist stance which the churches share. In combatting materialistic secularism of the Marxist type, the different religious groups find that they have a great deal in common not only here in the United States but in other countries as well.

The fundamentalism-modernism battle is ages old. One recalls the defen-siveness of Catholicism against Galileo in the seventeenth and later, in the nineteenth century, of both Catholicism and Protestantism against Darwinian evolution. At present, the "scientific" supposition made by Marxists that a godless struggle between classes has created the stupefying illusion of an ultimately purposeful universe (religion as the opiate of the masses) antago-

---

[30] Ibid., p. 363.

[31] Edward O. Laumann, "The Social Structure of Religious and Ethno-Religious Groups in a Met-ropolitan Community," *American Sociological Review*, 34 (April 1969), pp. 182–97.

[32] Edward O. Laumann, *Bonds of Pluralism: The Form and Substance of Urban Social Networks* (New York: Wiley, 1973).

nizes the churches and draws them together against a common enemy.

An aspect of this conflict is whether social progress can result from mere human effort or only through the grace of God. It is this assumption of sacredness that underlies the strong antipathy of the churches to the Marxist conception of history and the communist ideology, which gives the conjunctive organization of the churches possibly its major target.

In another light though, the churches' antipathy to communism is simply the modern version of the common contest between religion and the state, and the protection of their respective spheres of legitimacy. Where statesmen claim obedience on the basis of reason, the ecclesiastic enunciates principles he contends come from intuition or are made clear by revelation. These two kinds of truth, inconsistent in origin, create a tension between them, because both are used to gain credence in the eyes of the same people.

MULTIPLE SERVICES

At present, the urban church tends also to be a community center in which a broad range of services are offered, including recreation, health, education, and welfare. These are often specialized and require professionals to provide them. It is chiefly in the suburbs that the "institutional church," as it is termed, has most notably appeared. Fully developed, the institutional church comprises a staff of educators, recreation specialists, food-service personnel, physicians and psychiatrists, camp counselors, and even vocational testers and placement officers.

In this setting, the minister of an institutional church performs a multifaceted role.[33] First, he plays a communal role toward his congregation, relating himself to them not as communicants but personalities. Second, he is an executive with administrative responsibilities. Third, the minister acts as a business oriented fund-raiser. Fourth, he performs a civic role, interpreting his faith to other agencies and the general public. Fifth, he serves in an ameliorative capacity toward the infirm and needy. Sixth, the institutional minister is an educator. Seventh, the pastor fills a sociospiritual need with respect to interdenominational service organizations. And finally, eighth, he has a liturgical function in which he performs religious rituals and services.

Typically, these multiple duties require that the minister be a capable administrator able to coordinate a sizable staff of subordinate clergymen, professionals and technical staff people, and volunteer laymen. As such, the institutional church closely resembles a corporation understandable more in terms of sheer administration than divine intercession.

[33] Joseph H. Fichter, *Social Relations in the Urban Parish* (Chicago: University of Chicago Press, 1954), pp. 123–37.

In the "institutionalized church" today, the pastor deals with his flock as personalities as well as communicants.

SOCIAL REFORM

The churches that exist in an urban milieu generally also carry on programs of social action aimed at political and economic reform.[34] Here though, the churches are still inclined to follow rather than to lead. That is, they supply strength not to the initiation of policy so much as to its successful implementation.

The Church as an Agency of Social Engineering

Although urbanization results in the recession of religion, further urbanization may actually lead to the intensification of the religious spirit and to activist programs under church auspices. These include the so-called social-engineering approach in which the church is like any secular agency involved in urban renewal, the reduction of racial tensions, the acculturation of the in-migrant, and the administration of civil justice.

In the United States, the urban churches have shown considerable enterprise, not however with substantial success, in combatting inner-city poverty, blight, and social tensions.[35] Much experimentation has resulted as churches have engaged in political action, community organization, and

[34] Sidney E. Ahlstrom, "The Radical Turn in Theology and Ethics," *The Annals of the American Academy of Political and Social Science,* 387 (January 1970), pp. 1–13.

[35] Lyle E. Schaller, *Planning for Protestantism in Urban America* (New York: Abingdon Press, 1965), p. 10.

public-opinion formation in behalf of the deprived ethnic minorities, chiefly those of the inner-city nonwhite. In the process, direct concern for the sacraments and for the doctrine of the incarnation have given way to "the doctrine of the church," in other words, pursuing the beneficence of religious communion through the welfare of the social community.

Theological Reconstruction

Activism also encompasses attempts at theological reconstruction aimed at bringing the concepts of ultimate reality into closer accord with the modern urban consciousness. The philosopher Alfred North Whitehead prophesied that "that religion will conquer which can render clear to popular understanding some eternal greatness incarnate in the passage of temporal fact." Any number of contemporary theologians have been endeavoring to recast religious thinking in a manner more appropriate to modern intellectual standards and hence more engaged with social reality. No little part of their effort requires some erudition to understand.

Both scientific historicism and philosophical humanism have been resorted to in Christian theology in recent years. The first would evaluate religious thought in the light of empirically derived historical processes. The other would judge theology on the basis of its observable effects on society. Often the results have been what Herbert Schneider, a recognized religious scholar, terms complacent radicalism echoing "natural law," "the struggle for existence," and "progress through struggle," and emptily espousing "confidence, progress, and universal brotherhood."[36] Adherents to philosophical humanism, or ethicalism, as Stark and Glock refer to this position, believe that "loving thy neighbor" and "doing good for others" may successfully replace traditional religious orthodoxy and keep the churches from becoming "empty shells awaiting demolition."[37] Yet the evidence that Stark and Glock marshal proves otherwise. "In all cases a concern for ethics tend[s]," they write, "to be incompatible with church attendance and contributions."[38] It appears that the ethical liberals today look on their churches as audiences contemplating theatrical productions, and that they lack a sublime commitment and a mind-gripping rationale.

Following the German Albrecht Ritschl, some Christian leaders have accepted the idea not of God's transcendent essence but, rather, His presence in mankind as evidenced in humaneness and beneficent personality. Theological liberalism has thereby championed the Social Gospel, God

---

[36] Herbert W. Schneider, *Religion in 20th Century America* (Cambridge, Mass.: Harvard University Press, 1952), pp. 121–29.

[37] Stark and Glock, op. cit., p. 214.

[38] Ibid., p. 220.

being thought of not as a powerful sovereign but, in the words of Gerald Birney Smith, as an "immanent co-worker."

Identified with Karl Barth, Paul Tillich, and Karl Jaspers, neoorthodoxy refers to the revival of theology that followed the Great Depression, the failure of the League of Nations, and the frightful success of fascism in the 1930s. Neoorthodoxy is the doctrine of redemption through grace, that is, through "a communion of suffering" instead of through "the resources of human nature or the logic of history."[39]

Still another posture has been existentialism, which is basically concern for subjectivity, in theological terms, the idea that the original Judeo-Christian Scriptures, which conceive of man as a forlorn creature in an alien world, has relevance to modern mass society.

A theological effort along sociological rather than psychological lines is contained in Harvey Cox's *The Secular City,* prepared for the National Student Christian Federation.[40] Following the ecumenicist, Dietrich Bonhoeffer, Cox took up the major themes of religion and contemporary metropolitan society: secularization, urbanization, industrialization, pragmatism, and the fears that have been expressed regarding their danger to human progress. Cox viewed the city positively, and extolled urbanism as man's hope for spiritual fulfillment. He saw secularization as the antithesis of tribalism, because secularism denotes universalism and equal protection before the law. A secular order, Cox declared, entails mobility and self-realization. Its bureaucratic organization means liberating efficiency. Cox claimed to have found Biblical authority for his vision of the metropolis as a phenomenon in conformity with revealed faith. Specifically, since Christ disclosed God's partnership with man in history, Christians are responsible for accepting the problems of the city as their sacred discipline.

Much discussion has taken place regarding Cox's thesis of a secular ethic replacing Christian transcendentalism.[41] Cox has been charged with sociological naiveté, poor biblical scholarship, and theological glibness, although he has not been thought wholly invalid by any means.

CONCLUSION

As a system of ideas about the basic significance of life, religion tends to be supernatural and, consequently, alien to the rational spirit of urbanism. This can be seen in the progressive impact of pragmatic modes of thought on traditional religious beliefs.

Yet religion and urban society are not mutually exclusive. For one thing,

[39] Schneider, op. cit., p. 143.

[40] (New York: Macmillan, 1965).

[41] See Daniel Callahan, ed., *The Secular City Debate* (New York: Macmillan, 1966).

modern European urbanism may stem in some measure, as Weber thought, from the impetus given capitalism by the Protestant ethic. For another, religious controversy has been a long-term concomitant of class conflict in urban society.

In present-day urban America, three religious trends appear quite distinct:

First, secularization has become very pronounced, and the churches have accordingly come to endorse the prevailing secular standards, and also to achieve much organizational unity among the various faiths and denominations.

Second, many of the urban churches have turned into multipurpose community centers. As such they offer a variety of services like recreation and health care that, strictly speaking, lie outside the category of traditional religion entirely.

Third, as exponents of universal values, the churches today engage in a good deal of social-reform agitation. At the same time too, activism is also stimulating attempts to reform theology in order to make it more consistent with contemporary principles of scholarship and thought.

FOR FURTHER READING

Andrew M. Greeley, *Unsecular Man* (New York: Schocken, 1972). A lively book about the place of religion in contemporary society.

Robert Lee, ed., *The Church and the Exploding Metropolis* (Cleveland, Ill.: John Knox Press, 1965). Religion and social conflict at present.

Leo Pfeffer, *Church, State, and Freedom* (Boston: Beacon Press, 1967). Government and religion in America authored by a constitutional lawyer.

Charles Y. Glock, ed., *Religion in Sociological Perspective* (Belmont, Calif.: Wadsworth, 1973). Essays on the empirical approach to religion generally encouraged by the University of California research program on religion and modern life.

Bryan Wilson, *Religion in Secular Society* (Baltimore, Md.: Penguin Books, 1969). A British sociologist explores the effects of secular thought on religious belief.

Gibson Winter, *The Suburban Captivity of the Churches* (Garden City, N.Y.: Doubleday, 1961). The ecological shifts of the city's population mirrored in changes in church location and the composition of their congregations.

J. Milton Yinger, *The Scientific Study of Religion* (New York: Macmillan, 1970). Reviews religion from the standpoint of sociological research.

CHAPTER 15

URBAN EDUCATION

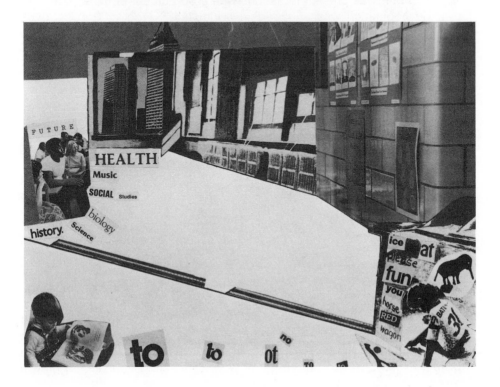

Every society provides for the instruction of its young relative to both the physical world and the social structure. In an advanced industrial or postindustrial nation, however, continuous education conducted on a universal scale is essential. This fact can hardly be overstated, for the preparation of every potentially competent individual for participation in the highly coordinated community and the complex occupational system is absolutely indispensable to the modern urban order.

Take literacy as an illustrative point. Literacy facilitates communication. It also expands the individual's mental powers by broadening his capacity to conceptualize and generalize ideas. Thus literacy strengthens self-interest, but by permitting the more effective accumulation of culture to take place, literacy also strengthens the collective power of the community. In addition, literacy acts to reduce pre-existing in-group loyalties and to replace them, in the words of a UNESCO manual for field workers in underdeveloped regions, with "the increasing belief that economic and social advancement can be obtained through individual competence and effort (rather than through preference based on bribery, political favor, kinship, caste or social status, national origin, race, religion, or sex."[1]

It is hardly surprising to observe that there is a systematic interdependence between urbanization and level of literacy. As Daniel Lerner found, a condition of "high illiteracy" (namely, the majority of adults being unable to read and write) was present in nations where 50 percent or more of the active male population was engaged in agriculture.[2] Algeria, Brazil, Egypt, Haiti, India, Malaya, and Turkey were in this category. By comparison, "low illiteracy" (less than 20 percent of the adult population) characterized countries where fewer than 50 percent of the male population was in farming. These urban nations included Argentina, Belgium, France, Japan, and the United States.

In the United States, according to the 1970 Census, 59.5 million Americans were attending school. This represented 74 percent of the total school-age population (5 to 24), up from 46 percent in 1940. Half of the nation's adult population, 52 percent, in fact, had completed high school in 1970, and slightly more than one-tenth had had four or more years of college.

Not only are the people of the United States receiving more education, consistent with our increasingly greater urbanization, but the disparity between the rural and urban segments, though narrowing, continues in evidence. As Table 15-1 reveals, the median school years completed by farm residents of the United States in 1970 was 10.7, while that of the urban population was 12.2.

The educational development of the United States cannot of course be accounted for simply as an expression of urbanization. Particular cultural tendencies have also been involved, for example, the populist ideology that advanced education is an inherent right of all. Yet urban forces in the form of demands made by the occupational structure, and the opportunities resulting from them, have certainly been at work stimulating educational growth too.

THE PURPOSES OF EDUCATION

Although its specific content and mode of organization vary from one country to another, education has three general purposes. These are: (1) transmitting the cultural values, (2) familiarizing people with the sanctioned modes of behavior, and (3) giving the individual the technical skills necessary to earn a living and help maintain the economy in doing so. Our discussion focuses on the American case.

[1] As cited in I. N. Thut and Don Adams, *Educational Patterns in Contemporary Societies* (New York: McGraw-Hill, 1964), p. 339.

[2] "Communication Systems and Social Systems," *Behavioral Science*, 2 (October 1957), pp. 266–75.

TABLE 15-1 Median School Years Completed in the United States by Rural and Urban Residence, 1970

RESIDENCE	MEDIAN YEARS COMPLETED	
Rural		
Farm	10.7	
Nonfarm	11.2	
Total rural		11.1
Urban		
Central cities	12.0	
Towns of 2500 to 10,000	12.0	
Towns of 10,000 or more	12.1	
Suburbs	12.3	
Total urban		12.2

Source: Bureau of the Census, *We The Americans: Our Education* (Washington, D.C.: Government Printing Office, June 1973), p. 8.

TRANSMITTING CULTURAL VALUES

The school's responsibility for developing appropriate value-orientations in an urban setting pertains to a wide spectrum of cultural standards. Four specific values may perhaps suffice to make the role of the urban school clear. These are: (1) the acceptance of change; (2) the value of science; (3) democratic beliefs; and (4) the achievement ethic. Certainly ideology apart from urbanism figures here, so that it would be more precise to say that these values typify the task of education primarily in the American city though no doubt in the cities of many other industrial and post-industrial nations as well.[3]

First, the citizen of an advanced urban society needs to be imbued with an expectation of change, with the anticipation of continued technological progress, and with sufficient freedom from anxiety to tolerate living in what amounts to a state of ceaseless transition. The modernity of the school, its emphasis on what is contemporary, and its highlighting of "protolearning," that is, thought processes that enhance ability to learn as distinct from content itself, all contribute to this end.

Second, in the urban school, science is advanced as a dominant mode of thought. Science is indispensable to urban life, for it contains the val-

[3] One recent analysis of contemporary education in terms of the crises in industrialized and postindustrialized nations is Don Adams, *Schooling and Social Change in Modern America* (New York: David McKay, 1972), especially Part 2.

Mass education is characteristic of modern urban society. An advanced school in San Juan, Puerto Rico.

ues of universalism (impersonal, objectively arrived at truth); rationality (self-conscious reasoning); skepticism (adherence to evidence); communality (the public nature of knowledge rather than personal gain derived from it); and disinterestedness (placing emphasis on the advancement of knowledge instead of using it for private benefit). Needless to say, science has enormous productive significance too.

Third, the democratic ethos receives close attention from urban educators. As the political scientist Charles E. Merriam reasoned, in a democratic society there are six beliefs whose acceptance is basic: (1) the intrinsic worth of the individual; (2) equality of opportunity; (3) cooperation; (4) the use of reason in solving problems; (5) the improvability of man; and (6) governing by consent.[4] The school imparts cognitive and emotional beliefs regarding such political principles. School texts stress the democratic creed, the citizen's public duty and his ability to discharge it, and also his feelings of patriotism.

It has to be noted that the sought-after democratic principles tend to be added onto the student's kinship, ethnic, religious, and neighborhood loyalties derived mainly from early socialization in the home, not all of which necessarily agree with the democratic creed. Lower-class authori-

[4] See Grace Graham, *The Public School in the American Community* (New York: Harper & Row, 1963), p. 39 and pp. 53–66.

tarianism, ethnic machine politics, and upper-class elitism represent significant discrepancies in urban America at present.

Finally, a city's schools also have the burden laid on them of helping to produce the ambitious personality which is sufficiently motivated to aspire to success in bureaucratic organizations and urban society in general. Admittedly, aspiration may be exhibited in either a collectivist or free-enterprise system, and occupational success pursued within either framework. It is, however, essential to industrial urban society as such, whatever its overall ideology, that a major part of the population be imbued with respect for achievement norms. Otherwise the professional and administrative services necessary for the maintenance of the complex enterprise that makes up the society as a functioning entity cannot be provided.

TEACHING APPROVED BEHAVIOR

Referring to the inculcation of success goals in the individual personality reflects the close connection between value development and the second general purpose of education, that of fostering approved behavior.

The school encourages high success goals in a number of ways, all of which contribute to their realization and hence their acceptability as a value. The school helps to elicit behavior appropriate to success-mindedness by acquainting the individual with success models; by teaching social as well as technical skills; by helping to curb displays of self-defeating aggression; by conditioning the student to accept risk; by assisting in building desirable self-conceptions; and by aiding the student to accept the deferment of gratification.

Besides enhancing the necessary psychosocial states of mind and motor responses that achievement calls for, the schools also aid in placing the given boy or girl—and here family and social-class background are important variables—in a mobile social network. An obvious channel is the one comprised of primary and secondary schools leading up to higher education. Supporting this chain are extracurricular ties, including special-interest clubs, and community resources like libraries and civic associations.

The educational process also orients the individual to the norms governing specific relationships. The occupational setting supplies a good illustration. In school, the child is helped to understand that occupations are specialized; that they are achieved, not ascribed; that they are contracted for between employee and employer; that they are performed in separated work places; and that competition over prestige and remuneration is characteristic of people.[5]

[5] The points are derived from Harry M. Johnson, *Sociology: A Systematic Introduction* (New York: Harcourt Brace & World, 1960), pp. 241–44.

DEVELOPING VOCATIONAL SKILLS

Besides inculcating urban-oriented values and behavioral practices, the schools of the modern city also function in an economic and technological capacity. In doing this they prepare individuals for the myriad of occupational roles that make up the multiplex division of labor typical of the industrial-urban community.

From the lower grades through higher education, vocational training is provided in a process proceeding from the study of the elementary to the advanced as well as from the concrete to the abstract. In this way, mobility is fostered, though it may vary from the British "sponsored" type where the elite choose promising aspirants out of the masses for advanced schooling, or the "contest" type, open to all comers characteristic of the United States.[6] At the same time, however, engineers, accountants, lawyers, industrial designers, metallurgists, bank examiners, and literally thousands of other specialists essential to the urban economy are trained.

In an advanced urban setting, the schools are not alone in affording occupational education. In any large city, proprietary institutions, say, for stationary engineers or computer programmers, give educational services on a fee basis. In addition, business firms engage in education, to train their own staff and to enable other firms to buy equipment from them that require technical ability to use. One might give IBM as a prime example. Its annual educational budget may well exceed that of many large universities.

THE SCHOOLS AND CLEAVAGES IN THE URBAN COMMUNITY

The schools of an urban society serve the system as a whole. They also participate in the divisive processes of the community too. The urban educational system does not train people simply with respect to a common standard of behavior appropriate to the urban setting. In fact, closer analysis reveals that the schools systematically act as agencies of class dominance and subordination. They do so in the following ways: (1) by preventing the socially handicapped from completing the school program either through educational decisions (such as predictions made from IQ tests) or the lack of financial means to permit them to continue; (2) by applying social-class rankings to children that, in the case of those from the higher classes, enhance their reputation and self-conceptions and, conversely, for those in the lower classes, stigmatize them; (3) by assigning children either to advantageous or disadvantageous courses of study by means of "tracking" sys-

---

[6] Compare Ralph H. Turner, "Sponsored and Contest Mobility and the School System," *American Sociological Review*, 25 (December 1960), pp. 855–67.

tems; and (4) by allowing or requiring the school to be a microcosm of the total society, thereby reinforcing the conviction that established social differentials are universals.

All of these conditions demonstrating the pervasive but subtle influence of social class upon education are the products of the interaction of administrators, teachers, students, parents, curricula, and the professions and agencies that are related to the schools themselves. In the words of Howard S. Becker: "in solving such problems as the recruitment and distribution of personnel, the defense of institutional autonomy, etc., the schools, organized in terms of one of the sub-cultures of a heterogeneous society, tend to operate in such a way that members of subordinate groups of differing culture do not get their fair share of educational opportunity, and thus of opportunity for social mobility."[7]

A variety of practices can be cited to show the restrictive social character of the schools. Owing to space limitations, perhaps one might suffice. James S. Coleman successfully tested the hypothesis that in a given American high school the "leading crowd" will be composed of individuals representing the most prevalent social class in that particular student body, thereby reinforcing the existing local discrimination pattern.[8] Despite the plausibility of the idea that the educational system sustains inequality, even strong defenders of this position admit that rigorous research sufficient to fully demonstrate the proposition remains to be done, however.[9]

EDUCATING THE ECONOMICALLY DISADVANTAGED

The fact that many educational injustices have been systematically brought to light in the United States attests to the increasing emphasis being given to the further democratization of education. In the American case the socioeconomic imbalance of the black and Hispanic minority groups is the focal point of much reform—and resistance—in the nation's schools. Particularly affected are the public schools of our metropolitan areas. Yet America is not alone in this respect by any means.

America's cities at present face the problem of educating the economically deprived and culturally disadvantaged as a result of two factors that are indigenous to the urban process:

First, there is a push-pull phenomenon by which changes in agriculture and industry uproot large masses of people in the countryside and lead

[7] Howard S. Becker, "Schools and Systems of Social Status," *Phylon,* 16 (1955), pp. 159–70.

[8] *The Adolescent Society* (New York: Free Press, 1961).

[9] See Christopher Jencks et al., *Inequality: A Reassessment of the Effect of Family and Schooling in America* (New York: Basic Books, 1972).

them to migrate to the city in the hope of finding improvement there. As political scientist Edward C. Banfield has recently expressed it, "The city attracts the poor—especially poor parents with numerous children—by offering better conditions for life—better food, clothing, shelter, health care, schools, and treatment from employers and officials; that is why it has always had so many poor."[10] Furthermore, owing to their rural mores, these people have higher birth rates on the whole than those already inhabiting the city, making the educational problem still more acute.

Second, urbanism denotes social mobility, a sociocultural interest that the leaders of the deprived population, if not the members themselves, exploit. Therefore, the presence of a great many newcomers added to the preexisting lower classes, especially at a time of industrial progress calling for higher levels of preparation, poses a problem (or challenge) for the community's schools as agents of acculturation and mobility.

Although our attention here is on the modern American city and although the disadvantaged are not the same everywhere, they are not confined to the urban United States alone. In the underdeveloped nations generally, modernization is creating educational problems by bringing rural people into the cities and raising their aspiration levels.

The urban disadvantaged are those with the lowest socioeconomic status and who, it is claimed amid much debate to the contrary, cannot live competently in a densely populated, industrial, and democratic society.[11] Characteristically, it is thus argued, the disadvantaged lack occupational, civic, and interpersonal skills. They do not understand urban modes of life. They participate in subcultures differing in various degrees from the generally accepted pattern. In addition, many of the disadvantaged have been traumatized by transciency and minority-group status, a condition that includes discrimination, segregation, and exploitation together with such contributory difficulties as broken homes, unemployment, chronic illness, emotional instability, and crime and delinquency. Consequently, the argument runs, the disadvantaged not only lack opportunity but also lack the knowledge of opportunities that may be open to them. In extreme cases they do not even have the motivation to begin to cope with their problems, because their state of mind may include a strong mistrust of people and institutions and a lack of allegiance to the social order in which they suffer so greatly.[12]

[10] *The Unheavenly City* (Boston: Little, Brown, 1970), p. 115.

[11] Consult Robert J. Havighurst, "Who Are the Culturally Disadvantaged?" in Staten W. Webster ed., *The Disadvantaged Learner* (San Francisco, Calif.: Chandler, 1966), pp. 20–29.

[12] As determined by the Health and Welfare Council of the Baltimore Area, *A Letter to Ourselves: A Master Plan for Human Redevelopment* (Baltimore, Md.: Health and Welfare Council, 1962). See also A. Harry Passow, ed., *Developing Programs for the Educationally Disadvantaged* (New York: Columbia University Press, 1968).

In the United States, such considerations have led to three general approaches being taken toward education for the deprived: (1) compensatory schooling; (2) desegregation and racial balance; and (3) administrative change.

COMPENSATORY EDUCATION

Compensatory education denotes special efforts, including instruction and teacher training, designed to achieve improvement among the disadvantaged. As the Educational Policies Commission of the National Education Association expresses it, the successful compensatory school program assists the disadvantaged by demonstrating "close relationship between school and life;" by providing the remedial services needed for academic progress; and by arousing long-term aspiration.[13] A notable compensatory program has been Project Head Start, originally sponsored in the summer of 1963 by the U.S. Office of Economic Opportunity.

One concrete case of compensatory schooling at the local level, which was undertaken in the early 1960s, was that of Cleveland's Hough Community Project. Conducted by the Cleveland Public Schools and the Ford Foundation in a depressed inner-city community of 72,000 people occupying 2.2 square miles of Cleveland's East Side, the Hough program had as its objective the development of techniques "for increasing the educability of culturally disadvantaged children in the urban setting" by means of curricular modification.[14] Thus one major move was to expand pupil personnel services. Another called for experience-broadening activities, such as field trips to museums, camping excursions, and recreational programs.

In 1967, the Civil Rights Commission reported on its examination of some of the better known compensatory education projects for the purpose of weighing "the measurable results of compensatory programs upon the academic performance of Negro students in majority-Negro schools."[15] The conclusion of the inquiry was that the analysis:

does not suggest that compensatory education is incapable of remedying the effects of poverty on the academic achievement of individual children. There is little question that school programs involving expenditures for cultural enrichment, better teaching, and other needed educational services can be helpful to disadvantaged chil-

[13] Educational Policies Commission, *Education and the Disadvantaged American* (Washington, D.C.: National Education Association, 1962), pp. 15–16.

[14] Lester D. Crow, Walter I. Murray, and Hugh H. Smythe, eds., *Educating the Culturally Disadvantaged Child* (New York: David McKay, 1966), pp. 228–249.

[15] Commission on Civil Rights, *Racial Isolation in the Public Schools* (Washington, D.C.: Government Printing Office, 1967), p. 120. See also Reynolds Farley and Alma F. Tauber, "Racial Segregation in the Public Schools," *American Journal of Sociology,* 79 (January 1974), pp. 888–905.

dren. The fact remains, however, that none of the programs appear to have raised significantly the achievement of participating pupils as a group.[16]

The study panel responsible for the findings that were reported to the commission raised the question of whether the compensatory programs were simply too limited to be able to overcome the depressing effects stemming from racial and social-class isolation. It was also felt that perhaps the very existence of the compensatory projects themselves heightened the sense of inferiority felt by black pupils. More recently, the Carnegie Commission on Higher Education confirmed the modest results of large-scale efforts to improve the cognitive development of disadvantaged youngsters, but urged added attempts be made, utilizing new insights, to improve compensatory education in practice.[17]

DESEGREGATION AND RACIAL BALANCE

Owing to the saliency of the racial factor to the disadvantaged in American cities, desegregation in the sense of achieving racial balance in the schools has been advanced as a second means of securing improved education for this population.

By overcoming the isolation of the races among school-age children, it is claimed that feelings of inadequacy will not develop as readily. Chief Justice Earl Warren wrote in the monumental *Brown* v. *Board of Education* decision (1954), "To separate [Negro children] from others of similar age and qualifications solely because of their race generates a feeling of inferiority as to their status in the community that may affect their hearts and minds in a way unlikely ever to be undone." The benefits of the early inculcation of higher levels of aspiration and of interpersonal skills, taking place in the more affluent and secure white homes during the children's formative years, will be shared by black children lacking such advantages. It is said that these will then be manifested in improved study habits and academic achievement. Further, the proponents of desegregation contend that greater financial support and improved teaching will accrue to the schools enrolling the deprived when they have become racially balanced.

It may be added that this is a complex phenomenon about which recent empirical research has been illuminating, but not always in line with the anticipated consequences. Neither has it been free from controversy. Thus Martin T. Katzman, for one, investigating educational efficiency found in Boston that "students in integrated schools perform, on the average, like those in

[16] Commission on Civil Rights, op. cit., p. 138.

[17] Carnegie Commission on Higher Education *A Chance to Learn* (New York: McGraw-Hill, 1970).

Busing, in Boston, for school desegregation.

white and Negro schools, *ceteris paribus.*"[18] In a much broader review, Christopher Jencks concluded that neither compensatory schooling nor desegregation, where tried, could be shown to have significantly altered cognitive inequalities associated with socioeconomic background.[19] Additional scholarship, however, has called such inferences into question on the grounds of research design or added evidence.[20]

Racial imbalance in the schools may be rectified by a number of specific techniques. Schools in adjacent districts which are residentially segregated may be paired, under the so-called Princeton Plan, with students of both districts enrolling in each school according to grade. Another device, employed in Berkeley, California, is the establishment of a central school serving a large area, but only in a single grade. The enlargement of the attendance area, which the practices above call for too, may also be accomplished by distributing pupils by means of busing. Students can, moreover, be moved without changing attendance areas and simply by instituting

[18] Martin T. Katzman, *The Political Economy of Urban Schools* (Cambridge, Mass.: Harvard University Press, 1971), p. 172. See also David Armor, "The Evidence on Busing," *Public Interest* (Summer 1972), pp. 90–126.

[19] See Jencks, op. cit.

[20] Countering Armor's arguments we have Thomas F. Pettigrew, "Busing: A Review of the Evidence," *Public Interest* (Winter 1973), pp. 88–118; and Jencks', James Guthrie et al., *Schools and Inequality* (Cambridge, Mass.: MIT Press, 1971).

open-enrollment. In 1965, about 600 black pupils, driven by their parents because the city would not furnish transportation, transferred from predominantly black Roxbury in "Operation Exodus." Later, in 1974, compulsory busing between Roxbury and South Boston led to sustained tension there.

De facto segregation in housing and the general ineffectiveness of the uncoordinated actions of parents have led to efforts to secure racial balance in the schools through cooperation between the central city and its surrounding suburbs. In Richmond and Detroit, it was contended that racial balance is constitutionally mandated, and that school officials might be held legally responsible for making busing available to reduce and even avert cultural deprivation. In 1971, the U.S. Supreme Court ruled that busing is in order to reduce segregation resulting from *de jure* actions, but in 1974, in the Detroit case, that busing across jurisdictional lines is not requisite unless racial isolation has been deliberately instituted. Unless amended, this ruling will not permit the nonwhite minority enrollments in our central cities, now at or above the two-thirds' mark in New York, Newark, Detroit, and other core areas, to be reduced by reassignment. In fact, the 1977 *Arlington Heights* decision of the Court that intent to discriminate must be found in order to justify remedial action, and the *Dayton* verdict that the remedy may not exceed the extent of the proven discrimination will probably further impede metropolitan solutions to racial imbalance in the schools.

ADMINISTRATIVE CHANGE

The third approach to the problem of educating the disdavantaged in America's cities focuses on administrative change affecting the basic structure of the school system. In some quarters, it is held that control of the schools within their own residential areas is essential if the disadvantaged are to be brought into the mainstream of the larger society. Therefore, community control of education by the racial or ethnic population in each particular locality of the city is advanced as a necessary step. In other quarters, where such autonomy is rejected, partial decentralization is favored in order to achieve substantial change while retaining the benefits of scale, teacher organization, unified policies, and general standards.[21]

The rationale of both community control and decentralization is that these may be the only means of applying enough pressure to cope with what they believe is inherently inimical in the existing educational system. As Patricia Sexton informs us, most public school boards of education in large cities consist of upper- and middle-class members.[22] Proponents of structural

---

[21] One near current examination of issues is Leonard J. Fein, *The Ecology of the Public Schools: An Inquiry into Community Control* (New York: Pegasus, 1971).

[22] Patricia Cayo Sexton, *The American School* (Englewood Cliffs, N.J.: Prentice-Hall, 1967), pp. 29–30.

change assert that the white middle-class teachers who, accordingly, staff the schools are generally ignorant of the social circumstances of their black, Chicano, or other ethnic pupils and whom, they claim, the teachers victimize through a self-fulfilling prophecy of academic ineptitude.

Restructuring the educational system represents efforts by lower-income and minority groups, with liberal and even radical leadership, to gain added power for themselves and to combat what they view as the self-serving professionalism of educators. Those leaning to community control and decentralization would probably agree with Mario Fantani and Gerald Weinstein who say, "Schools responsive to the needs, aspirations, and cultural style of the communities they serve stand a greater chance of harnessing the energies of professionals, students, parents, and community residents in building a more viable urban social institution."[23]

On the other hand, because community control has become an ideological slogan, significant problems of administration are apt to be overlooked by its proponents. As Morris Janowitz has analyzed the question, these include the inequality of resources (owing to the separation between depressed areas and the affluent suburbs); the problem of determining accountability in the bureaucratic school system; the task of updating managerial processes; and the difficulty of guaranteeing a responsible public presence in the schools.[24] New York City's recent experience with decentralization has been one of considerable tension. In Boston, as a 1971 study discovered, citizen apathy and the lack of cooperation among community groups has led to decentralization having only a "slight impact" on the schools there.[25] Opponents of restructuring deplore what they see in community control as an unnecessary politicization of a problem that is basically technical. Also, they condemn community control because of sectarian disservice to the broader culture.

THE URBAN UNIVERSITY

The urban university, defined as "one located in and serving an urban community," has in the last few years emerged as a distinct type of institution of higher learning.[26] Its appearance represents yet another concomitant of modern urbanism.

Today, more than 200 American campuses have programs of a signifi-

[23] In *Making Public Schools Work* (New York: Holt, Rinehart and Winston, 1968), p. 55.

[24] *Institution Building in Urban Education* (New York: Russell Sage, 1969), pp. 67–76.

[25] Leila Sussman and Gayle Speck, "Community Participation in Schools: The Boston Case," *Urban Education*, 8 (January 1973), pp. 341–56.

[26] Martin Klotsche, *The Urban University: And the Future of Our Cities* (New York: Harper & Row, 1966), p. 3.

cantly urban character. These include technical institutes, community colleges, and municipal colleges and universities. They have in common the fact that they enroll large numbers of students with an urban background and that they also conduct systematic research into urban affairs as well as engage in local public service, such as the formulation of plans to guide urban transportation, housing, and public-health services. Thus, besides providing a channel of upward mobility for youth, particularly those from low-income families, the urban university devotes a good part of its program specifically to the reducation of the various problems of the metropolitan area surrounding it.

Such an institution, with its local orientation, needs to be differentiated from the merely urban-located school, like Harvard (Boston), Chicago University, and Case Western Reserve (Cleveland), with national clienteles. These are not free of local influence but they cannot be regarded as urban universities according to the definition above.

In the United States, the tradition of the practical university, of which the urban university is a modern case, is very long. In fact, the success of higher education relative to farming and industrial technology eventually encouraged ideas about a parallel commitment of universities to the improvement of modern urban life.

Consider the recent report by the Committee on Social and Behavioral Urban Research to HUD. The Committee proposed basic research be undertaken at selected urban university centers in concert with industry, foundations, and municipal development offices. Highest priority, said the report, should be given the "social engineer" in order to facilitate the adoption of technological projects and sociocultural innovations in solving urban housing, transit, and other problems.[27]

A similar point of view is expressed in the idea of having "urban observatories," suggested by Professor Robert Wood of M.I.T. The urban observatory seeks to relate specific research projects, usually carried out by academicians, to master plans for metropolitan advancement, and also to give momentum to the application of successful programs in cities other than those in which they originate. Since 1965 the concept of the urban observatory has been furthered by the use of federal funds in conjunction with the efforts of the National League of Cities and urban universities in such widely scattered localities as Albuquerque, Milwaukee, and Cleveland.

Not only are many urban, and even some urban-located, universities in America involved in urban research and community service at the present time. Often they are also enmeshed in the very difficulties which make up the subject matter of their inquiries. The University of Chicago is a clear example.[28] Located in the deteriorated Hyde Park-Kenwood district, it has at

[27] A Strategic Approach to Urban Research and Development: Social and Behavioral Science Considerations (Washington, D.C.: National Academy of Sciences, 1969).

[28] Klotsche, op. cit., pp. 71–72.

various times since 1952 been engaged in bitterly controversial urban redevelopment. Racial issues, crime and law enforcement, property values, priorities in the city budget, and questions of university interests versus those of the surrounding low-income black community have all figured in the process.

Though not exclusively so, the urban university has at times also been faced by large-scale student unrest. Direct-action tactics calling for mass rallies, marches, strikes, picketing, and even disruption, violence, and terror have not been uncommon. Their objectives have been withdrawal of United States participation in southeast Asia, the admission of minority students, and liberalization of the curriculum. These concerns and their forceful expression by students must be viewed against a background of long-range factors which, according to the American Council on Education, consist of generational conflict; the social irrelevance of youth; possibly obsolete educational practices; the breakdown of legitimate authority; and the prevalence of a widespread social malaise.[29] Of signal importance here, as Martin Trow noted in 1972, has been a collapse of the consensus between the older and younger academics, a majority of the latter approving "the emergence of radical student activism in recent years."[30] That such campus disturbances have diverse roots in the cultural and social institutions of urban society beyond those simply of the United States has become more apparent upon extended reflection since their occurrence.[31]

Urban-located universities have long benefited the socially mobile in the United States, though this function has not been entirely free of strain that has shown up in the problem of combining opportunity with genuine quality, and thus of avoiding the spurious certification of the incapable. As in instruction, so too in its other functions, the same ambivalence about indiscriminately lending itself to various special interests affects the urban university in its research and public-service capacities too. Unquestionably, the community which surrounds the urban university has severe problems. Doubt has been expressed, however, whether it will be advantageous in the long run for the university to lose its identity as a creator and transmitter of knowledge by submerging itself in operations adjunct to the machinery of local government, local voluntary associations, and local institutional interests, and making short-range objectives its primary goals. The more ardent supporters of urban university involvement in practical affairs, it has been said, need to be reminded of the value of philosophic perspective in "giving meaning to urban life and assisting in the creation of a new image of our cities."[32]

[29] Report of the Special Committee on Campus Tensions (Washington, D.C.: American Council on Education, 1970).

[30] Martin Trow, The Expansion and Transformation of Higher Education (New York: General Learning Press, 1972), p. 6.

[31] Cf. Immanuel Wallerstein and Paul Starr, eds., The University Crisis Reader (New York: Random House, 1971), 2 vols.

[32] Klotsche, op. cit., p. 129.

OTHER TRENDS AND PROBLEMS

As revealed in earlier sections of this chapter, a number of trends, problems, and issues have emerged in urban education in the advanced societies, which will probably eventually also affect the developing nations. These are: (1) enrolling enormous numbers of students appropriate to mass mobility and the training of an immense labor force; (2) cultivating sociocultural consensus in an essentially pluralistic, competitive social order; (3) modernizing vocational education; (4) serving the disadvantaged in a context of rising expectations and power struggles; and (5) creating institutions of higher education suitable to the task of research and civic service in communities of unprecedented complexity.

In closing, certain others might be identified as well.

THE CENTRAL-CITY SCHOOL SYSTEM

One problem is the miriad of dire conditions impinging on the school system of the central city. The U.S. Office of Education has summarized these factors as: a shrinking tax base; the deterioration of property; the displacement of people (by urban renewal); population turnover; and the need to replace outmoded school facilities.[33]

Obviously, such circumstances have serious effects. The first of these is financial. In the financing of the public schools of the inner city, it is imperative that new sources of income be tapped, for instance, state aid to supplement local property taxes and economies achieved through the consolidation of school districts. Here the finding by the California Supreme Court in the *Serrano* case (1971) that a child's education ought not to be "a function of the wealth of a pupil's parents and neighbors" may, if sustained, usher in a period of statewide—or even nationwide—financial redistribution that will erase the inequalities of existing local funding.[34]

Second, the organization of the school system of the central city need not be thought permanent even as regards to its basic aspects. Many question the validity of the neighborhood school concept in metropolitan society, some on the basis of its reinforcement of de facto racial segregation, others on the grounds of the support it gives to the present stratification system.

Similarly, much dissatisfaction has been voiced over the performance of the public schools as measured by pupil achievement on standardized national reading examinations. This has given rise to proposals to set up private and competing schools, operating with tuition-grant vouchers from gov-

---

[33] *The Impact of Urbanization on Education* (Washington, D.C.: HEW, 1962). See also Advisory Commission on Intergovernmental Relations, *Financing Schools and Property Tax Relief—A State Responsibility* (Washington, D.C.: Government Printing Office, 1972).

[34] California 3rd, 584, 487 P 2nd (1971).

ernment,[35] or of even "deschooling" completely.[36] Their proponents, like Christopher Jencks, hold that though government may set minimum educational requirements for the public, government is not necessarily capable of operating schools to best advantage. However, the president of the American Federation of Teachers, Albert Shanker, calls funneling money into private schools at the expense of the public system "the height of irresponsibility."[37] That there is potential mass interest in the privatization of education is perhaps indicated by the experience of The Netherlands. When tax money was made available to sectarian schools there, 8 out of 10 students enrolled in the public schools shifted out. Yet, as of 1975, three years after the inception of a federal pilot project in San Jose, California, few parents were using vouchers for their children. Some critics believe teacher opposition responsible for creating a climate adverse to the success of the trial in the United States.[38]

NEW NEEDS IN OCCUPATIONAL EDUCATION

Occupational training in the urban milieu is constantly transitional, though not unpredictably so. At present, two aspects would appear to be of signal importance: (1) the dovetailing of school and industry and (2) the intensification of the continued education of the increasingly larger proportion of technical and service workers in the nation's labor force.

Mechanical occupations have undergone a definite course of development as industrialization has unfolded. At first, the worker confronted machinery that he had to operate himself. In the second phase, that of the semi-automated assembly line, the positions of the two were reversed. Now the worker was governed by the imperious pace of the machinery. Then at last, in the stage of full automation, the worker became responsible for directing, controlling, supervising, and repairing very valuable, complicated devices.[39] An implication of this sequence is that during the third phase work skills tend to be acquired within the industrial organization itself, where selection for personal characteristics, training, and placement can take place more efficiently than it can in the general school.

This being so, then the proper education of the technical workers in the labor force has to include the requisite skills and social aptitudes in the

[35] Compare George R. La Noue, ed., *Educational Vouchers* (New York: Teachers College Press, 1972).

[36] Ivan Illich, "Why We Must Abolish Schooling," *New York Review of Books* (July 2, 1970).

[37] *New York Times* (May 25, 1975), Section 1, p. 38.

[38] Ibid., p. 1.

[39] H. Schelsky, "Technical Change and Educational Consequences," in A. H. Halsey, Jean Floud, and C. Arnold Anderson, eds., *Education, Economy, and Society* (New York: Free Press, 1961), pp. 31–36.

The education of technical workers is a changing process of keeping abreast of new technology and new forms of organization for work. A class in printing.

school-industry setting as a whole. Schelsky has advocated four principles for such occupational preparation.[40]

1 Skill in the traditional sense is becoming meaningless and, therefore, realistic training entails familiarity with the application of technical resources, such as comprehensive milling-machine programs, photocopying, and data-processing.

2 The semiskilled technician will soon predominate in industry. He will be the worker capable of realizing the great productivity of automated machines and electronic devices.

3 The complex service systems being used will necessitate the creation of hierarchies of task combinations calling for the articulation of graded technicians. These technicians will be advanced to higher levels by examination. Clear-cut examples are already present in education and medical services, two developing "industries" where coordinated technicians employing the new technology are multiplying rapidly.

4 Vocational training will have to be concerned not so much with teaching skills as with sharpening working qualities like concentration, quickness of response, and reliability.

[40] Ibid., pp. 35–36.

The vocational prerequisites for the general labor force in the age of full automation will thus affect the personality formation of most citizens.

SOCIOPSYCHOLOGICAL AND ETHICAL PROBLEMS

The sociopsychological and ethical problems created by intense urbanization do pose serious challenges to the schools. As secularization undermines established authority, experimental moral codes gain acceptance, with both threat and opportunity resulting from the process. One observer declares:

> *The threat is of a loss of standards, a tyranny of the peer group in the place of other authority, the subservience of human values to the expediencies of a nationalistic (perhaps militaristic) and technological society. The opportunity is for increasing sensitivity to human needs as formal codes yield to a more imaginative ethic.*[41]

The realization of personal identity becomes more problematic as the organizational complexity of society increases. Concurrently, alienation may deepen as expectations rise and throw social inequalities into sharper relief, and as affluence satiates sensate desires only to lead to anomic boredom even among the young. Concern for student rights and responsibilities and the new provisions being made for student self-expression as well as student participation in school governance at all levels attest to the registry of such tensions on the established institutions.

The restructuring of higher education is now taking place not only in academic decision-making but also in the organization of knowledge. Interdisciplinary studies are a case in point. They combine traditionally separate fields of study in the hopes thereby of achieving deeper understanding. Cluster colleges are a second. Their intent is to develop group-mindedness as well as scholarship. Still another combines affect with cognitive learning, for example, in the various New Schools, sometimes called "universities in dispersion," which seek self-expression, service, and "experience" by students and faculty alike.

Much of the motivation here may, however, be attributable to the limits of intellectualism at present. As a singular weakness in our modern intellectual heritage, we can point to the ignorance that has grown up between advanced science and the humanities as a result of specialization. This is a condition to which the English man of letters C. P. Snow has forcefully called the world's attention. Some of the educational experiments being conducted at present relate to this estrangement between Snow's "two cultures."

[41] Roger L. Shinn, "Human Responsibility in the Emerging Society," in Edgar L. Morphet and Charles O. Ryan, eds., *Designing Education for the Future* (New York: Citation Press, 1967), p. 246.

CONCLUSION

Education is an essential component of the institutional life of urban society. It is probably safe to say that literacy for everyone intellectually competent, and technical and professional training for significant numbers of the population constitute the indispensable goals of education in an industrial or post-industrial urban nation. The general public of such a country also needs to be schooled in the cultural values and modes of behavior that are commonly sanctioned, and adherence to which is required for individual motivation and organizational coordination.

Though urban education has objectives that are functional for the community as a whole, it serves divisive purposes too. Class cleavages show themselves in many aspects of the educational system. One recent consequence, and not just in the United States either, is the effort being made, with opposition, to educate the socioeconomically disadvantaged. This is taking three forms at present: compensatory education, racial balance, and administrative change. The urban university in service to the local community represents yet another educational concomitant of urbanization. Like the schools located in urban areas, the urban university too has been encountering serious problems.

Urban education is a dynamic process subject to continuous change. Among the current manifestations of this developmental character of education are the financial and administrative difficulties of inner-city school systems, new needs in vocational training, and sociopsychological and ethical issues stemming from advanced urbanization.

FOR FURTHER READING

Alan Altschuler, *Community Control: The Black Demand for Participation in Large American Cities* (New York: Pegasus, 1970). Argues that decentralization of schools can lead to racial peace.

Marilyn Gittell, ed., *Educating an Urban Population* (Beverley Hills, Calif.: Sage, 1967). The problems in achieving change in the urban educational system.

Maurie Hillson et al., *Education and the Urban Community* (New York: American Book, 1969). The conflicts in education that exist in American cities.

Doris B. Hollck, *College and the Urban Poor* (Lexington, Mass.: Lexington Books, 1972). How to provide higher educational opportunities for the poor.

Raymond C. Hummel and John M. Nagle, *Urban Education in America* (New York: Oxford University Press, 1973). The trends in education in the 1970s in the nation's 50 largest central cities.

Joseph A. Lanwerys and David G. Scanlon, eds., *Education in Cities* (New York: Harcourt Brace Jovanovich, 1970). Imaginative conjecture on new educational institutions appropriate to developing urban life.

Melvin R. Levin and Alan Shank, eds., *Educational Investment in an Urban Society* (New York: Teachers College Press, 1970). Articles mainly by economists on costs and benefits.

Donald J. McCarty and Charles E. Ramsey, *The School Managers: Power and Conflict in American Public Education* (Westport, Conn.: Greenwood, 1971). Data drawn from a cross section of 51 communities in the Midwest and Northeast and representing several types of power structure.

Herbert J. Walberg and Andrew T. Kopan, eds., *Rethinking Urban Education* (San Francisco, Calif.: Jossey-Bass, 1972). Sections on psychological, sociological, systems analysis, historical, and philosophical approaches to the subject.

CHAPTER 16

ART AND LEISURE

From the very beginning of urbanization cities have been more than mere utilitarian settlements. In the words of Lewis Mumford, the original cities of Mesopotamia and the Indus River valley "built up a great water network for communication and transportation." But these cities also "filled the urban reservoirs with human energy available for other collective enterprises."[1] Among the "other" organized endeavors of cities have been monumental architecture, museums and theatres, and the patronage which assisted the creative and performing artists connected with them. Besides boasting such manifestations of high culture, cities have also been the scene of popular recreation and entertainment. This aspect of urban life has given rise to a centuries-old debate over whether the mass of people are capable of going beyond frivolous diversion, and of achieving undisputed quality in their cultivation of leisure.

[1] *The City in History* (New York: Harcourt Brace & World, 1961), p. 568.

ARCHITECTURAL BEAUTY

In their public and household architecture, in landscaping and monuments, and in their roads and waterways, cities vary from the squalid to the magnificent. Besides abundant ugliness, architectural beauty is often found in cities. The populous places of society have been built, embellished, adorned, scaled, and developed as centers of government, religion, and economic and cultural life—from Ur to Mycenae, classical Athens and Rome, Medici Florence, St. Petersburg, San Francisco, and present-day Brasília.

The town square, the capital city, and special design projects afford evidence of this process.

THE TOWN SQUARE

A perennial architectural device, the town square graces any number of cities in various forms.[2] The square may be "closed," in which case it is a space bounded by balanced structures making up a single entity. The Place Vendôme in Paris is of this type. Conversely, squares may be "dominated," in other words, be visually assimilated to some massive building. This is true of the area in front of St. Peter's in Rome. The impression of a contiguous space created by a central monument or perhaps a fountain is called a "nucleus" square. Barcelona, Spain, has several such squares. Squares may also be "grouped," as in Copenhagen, Denmark, and Rheims, France. In that event, separated but patterned spaces give rise to a feeling of unity. Finally, we have the "amorphous" type of square, which is large but lacking in symmetry, such as New York's Washington Square and Trafalgar Square in London.

Squares should not be thought of as simply functional even if they were so conceived of by their original creators. Architectural historian Paul Zucker makes it clear that each age of city builders has its own conception of space, blending aesthetics, engineering, statecraft, and even piety into one single whole.[3] The Romans surrounded spaces within porticoes and edifices; then axially opened them up through sequences of colonnades carried to some monumental stop in the distance. In medieval Europe the management of space was quite different, for the medieval city was oriented to defense. Only toward the end of the Middle Ages did interest in the use of large aggregates of outside space for aesthetic and symbolic purposes occur, no doubt coinciding with the achievement of economic strength and military security.

[2] Following Paul Zucker's careful study *Town and Square* (New York: Columbia University Press, 1959).

[3] Ibid., p. 96 and pp. 140–42.

Not only do the parts of a city—its administrative structures, monuments, and squares—bear the imprint of aesthetic design, but entire cities have been created as works of art. National capitals are conspicuous in this category.

Such was the case in the planning of St. Petersburg at an unpromising location athwart the sodden, marshy River Neva, beginning in 1703.[4] The Swedish occupation of Russian territory had been broken, giving Russia access to the Baltic Sea and the opportunity of trading with Western Europe. In this economic endeavor supported by Russian mercantile interests, the Emperor Peter the Great set about Westernizing the nation. His projected capital on the Neva was to give concrete expression to that policy.

The city of Peter the Great soon included a magnificent array of buildings, fountains, and formal gardens rivaling the grandeur of Versailles itself, that immense architectural "composition" of Louis XIV just outside Paris. Peterhof, "Mon Plaisir," Tsarskoye Selo (the Great Palace), the Admiralty, the first Winter Palace, Ekaterinenhof (a mansion for Peter's second wife), the residence of Prince Menshikov, the warehouses on Vasilevski Island, and the government offices (known as the Twelve Colleges) were built by forced labor, prisoners, and transported peasants, but they achieved real beauty. In all of this splendor, military defense was not neglected either. A system of canals was dug, and the fortress of SS. Peter and Paul erected to command the quay. By the time Peter died in 1725, the city had a population of 40,000. It grew to five times that size in the next 75 years.

During that period, Peter's successors added substantially to the impressive architectural beginnings. Catherine contributed the Hermitage Theatre and the Academy of Sciences, designed by Giacomo Quarenghi and located on the granite-walled embankment of the Strelka. The Academy came to be the seminal font of Russian science for two centuries. Czar Alexander, the last of the Romanov dynasty, completed the original design of St. Petersburg by building on a grand scale but with the rational simplicity of the original city plan. The great circus wings of the Winter Palace which Alexander commissioned were joined by a monumental archway that terminated the grand vista of the Nevski Prospekt, the main thoroughfare of St. Petersburg.

BUILDING FOR AESTHETICS

Though dazzling, St. Petersburg is perhaps simply representative of much of the history of European urbanization from the late Renaissance to the middle

---

[4] See A. E. Richardson and Hector O. Corfiato, *The Art of Architecture* (London: English Universities Press, 1952), 34d ed., pp. 150ff, and Tamara Talbot Rice, "Eighteenth-Century St. Petersburg," in Arnold Toynbee, ed., Cities of Destiny (New York: McGraw-Hill, 1967), pp. 242–57.

Beau Nash's crescent townhouses near London's Regent's Park are similar to those that he designed for the city of Bath.

of the eighteenth century. In this period, cities and towns other than national capitals were often laid out as the realization of a master plan drawn up by the head of state for the entire country. A provincial capital might be designed in a similar way. Also, large-scale planning schemes might create massive complexes either out in the country or adjacent to some great city. Among these was the landscaped palace of Blenheim at Woodstock outside London, presented to the Duke of Marlborough by a nation grateful to him for his military victory over the French and Bavarians in 1704.

The grandeur of the new architecture appeared during the seventeenth and eighteenth centuries, even in the prosaic parts of existing cities. Market places were transformed into Renaissance piazzas or shielded under colonnades. The fishmarket of London's Billingsgate was formed like a great classic temple! Terraces of identical houses built in long rows arranged in geometric patterns around open spaces and housing the mercantile classes of London and Paris created the impression of royal palaces. John Wood and Beau Nash's crescent development has left a memorable example of this architecture in the city of Bath, England.

MUSEUMS AND THEATRES

Art museums and theatres have long been part of the urban scene. Such places have generally, though not entirely, been an element of urban rather than rural life.

Galleries and playhouses of course provide vehicles for artistic presentation. They give expression to some facet of culture, or they reveal opposition to it. In the earlier preindustrial city, most forms of art bore a close relationship to religion. In the modern industrial city, art is more secular. In its various forms, it refers to man's terrestrial and social life, and gives voice to worldly or subjective values instead of transcendental ones.

There appears to be an analogy between the power that cities possess over their surrounding hinterland and the capacity of these cities to acquire artistic possessions. Cities are not identified with art, however, merely by virtue of their financial and military dominance. What is far more important is the fact that urbanism tends to be inherently associated with the great cultures of history. Hence, at times a notable art collection may be found at a country estate, such as Chatsworth mansion in England's Devonshire County.[5] The occasional rural location of such treasures should not, however, obscure their typical dependence on urban society, owing to the specialization and development of artistic technique without which a high level of art is impossible.

MUSEUMS

The word museum was first used by the Greeks in referring to the place where the Muses made their home. It was later applied to the scientific library at Alexandria, although there were many Greek and Roman public buildings, temples, and villas that contained collections of art. With the deurbanization in the early Middle Ages, both the word museum and the institution itself disappeared from Europe. Later, during the Renaissance, royalty began to assemble works of art in their palaces and the nobility in their homes. Churches were as lavishly adorned as circumstances would permit.

[5] See Douglas Cooper, ed., *Great Family Collections* (New York: Macmillan, 1965), especially pp. 145–68.

The merchant princes of Italy's Renaissance cities emulated their ecclesiastical peers in the construction and appointment of their own town houses. The museumlike Medici Palace (1444–59) in Florence boasted frescoes by Filippo Lippi, paintings on the salon walls executed by Paolo Uccello and Botticelli, bronze and marble statues in the courtyard, and manuscripts of the works of Dante, Petrarch, and Boccaccio. Such collections, including cabinets of scientific and natural objects brought back by Europe's voyagers during the early years of exploration, were private. They were, nonetheless, civic monuments that attracted important visitors and scholars, redounding to the prestige of their local cities. Much later, with the growth of democracy, they were opened to the public, like the Palace of the Louvre in Paris, which after the French Revolution was proclaimed the Museum of the Republic.

The Purposes of the Modern Museum

In the contemporary city, an art museum may be said to have three aims: aesthetic, scientific, and practical.[6]

The first of these refers to the recognition of good art through the application of sound critical principles. Accordingly, a museum may be expected to acquire and exhibit as many good works as it can afford. Civic pride is of great significance in this respect. For example, Jacob Epstein and the Cone sisters, all of Baltimore, made that city's museum world famous. Maxim and Martha Codman Karolik devoted three decades to collecting American furniture of the Colonial and Federalist periods, giving Boston's Museum of Fine Arts the most comprehensive coverage of the work of American artists and artisans to be found anywhere.[7]

The second function of an art museum is to carry on and extend the techniques of authenticating art. Here, purely technical practices are supplemented by scholarship, including history and anthropology. This aim of a museum relates to the art market more characteristic of modern times than earlier periods when artistic production was carried on under direct patronage, although wars and thefts did create a need for authentication in those earlier periods.

Third, a museum exists as an educational center both for children and adults, and as a stimulus for the creation of original art by local artists. Artists and craftsmen can be encouraged when the museum provides them with opportunities to exhibit and, consequently, market their products.

[6] Laurence V. Coleman, *The Museum in America* (Washington, D.C.: American Association of Museums, 1939), Vol. I, pp. 88–90.

[7] Herbert Katz and Marjorie Katz, *Museums, U.S.A.* (Garden City, N.Y.: Doubleday, 1965), pp. 28–110.

Theatrical drama probably originated as a combination of folk dancing, religious observances, and the masked impersonation of spirits, ancestors, and demons. Whatever the beginnings of the stage may have been, drama was raised to the level of art for the first time only with the emergence of the Greek city-states in the sixth and fifth centuries B.C. There, theatrical performances were spiritual celebrations calling for songs, dances, and recitations that encompassed the entire community in a collective effort to experience the common values of the culture.

We need not dwell on the Athenian theatre except to recall Aristotle's *Poetics,* which observes that "both tragedy and comedy originated in a rude and unpremediatated manner, the former from the leaders of the dithyramb, the latter from those who led off the phallic songs." In other words, the ecstatic rhapsodies to Dionysius sung by a leader and a chorus evolved into poetic dramas; and the mummery accompanying the ritualized procession of townspeople together with their stylized chatter was turned into enacted stories.[8] From that time on, theatres were a common feature of urban life in Western civilization.

In the Preindustrial City

Rich, luxurious theatre buildings abounded in the cities of the Roman empire. Instead of using sacred precincts as the Greeks did, the Romans chose desirably located sloping sites, and later even provided walled construction on level places. They erected colonnaded courts and galleries around their open-air structures, which were situated in or near their cities across Asia Minor, North Africa, and Europe, including Britain. Contests between gladiators and wild animals, and bloody games calling for hapless Christians took place in Roman arenas, a notable one being the Colosseum in the capital, which could seat almost 50,000 spectators.

Though the rebirth of cities in Europe during the later Middle Ages brought about a revival of interest in the theatre, the drama that appeared did not in any way rival the major accomplishments in the painting, sculpture, and poetry of the time. Important changes did occur that paved the way for great dramatic triumphs later. Scenery with painted perspectives was introduced. This followed the use of pictorial backgrounds that the priests had been employing to make the church mysteries more understandable to the ignorant peasantry during religious festivals and at country fairs. The procenium arch framing a three-sided stage at one end of a roofed auditorium also came into being. So constructed, the Farnese playhouse at Parma, Italy,

---

[8] Margaret Bieber, *The History of the Greek and Roman Theater* (Princeton, N.J.: Princeton University Press, 1961), pp. 1–17.

which opened in 1628, was the first modern theatre in Europe.

In England, bands of professional actors playing in inns, manor houses, and market places were encouraged by the rise of an educated middle class in London. In fact, many theatrical performances were put on by amateurs who were university students, lawyers of the Inns of Court, and pupils in the lower schools. The upshot of the strong English interest in drama of intellectual value was the construction of several playhouses in London during the last quarter of the sixteenth century—the Swan, Globe, and Fortune—built along Roman lines open to the sky. These theatres were capitalized as the joint-stock ventures of proprietors and players, the latter also organized as a business company to produce plays.[9] They gave the Elizabethan dramatists, Shakespeare among them, a stage for which to write, with the remarkable results we all know.

In England, France, and Italy, the seventeenth and eighteenth century theatre devoted itself to an audience composed of courtiers, in town from the country estates, and the growing mercantile classes. Indeed, the design of the theatres themselves, with a dais in the orchestra and special boxes set aside for titled patrons, showed the concentration of attention on these notables. The theatre was not insulated from outside conflicts either. The closing of the London stage from 1642 to the Restoration reveals the involvement of the English theatre in the century-long struggle between Puritan and Royalist, and the proper place of "amusements" in English social thought.

Nonetheless, as the urban centers of mercantile Europe grew, the theatre usually prospered. Vienna had its spacious Imperial; London, Dorset Garden, Drury Lane, and Royalty; Amsterdam, the baroque Schouwburg; Genoa, the Teatro Falcone; Naples, the San Carlo; Rome, the Argentina; and Milan, the famed Scala. From the beginning of the seventeenth century, musical dramas were presented, as well as spoken plays, and a rapid development of the musical arts ensued from that time.

Theatres in the Industrial City

The industrial city occasioned both a more realistic type of drama and the complete victory of the idea of paid admissions instead of ducal patronage or crown grants supporting the theatre.

Realistic drama, which depicted the familiar problems of ordinary people, had certain inherent difficulties. One was a tendency to be trivial and didactic; another, a proclivity for sordidness and violence; and a third, a preoccupation with the hidden and covert. Consequently, melodrama was common in the nineteenth century theatre, as were vapid bourgeois theatrics and the revelation made in "psychological" dramas of the secret vices of the

---

[9] See Joseph Q. Adams, *Shakespearean Playhouse* (Gloucester, Mass.: Peter Smith, 1960), pp. 234ff.

supposedly respectable. Escapist plays like Victor Hugo's romantic *Hernani* in 1830 proved enormously popular. Buffoonery stemming from the Italian commedia dell' arte turned into vaudevillian shows for the entertainment of the new masses of theatregoers in the larger cities. However, owing to the modern desire to be ordinary, art historian Sheldon Cheney has discerned that, "the theatre that has housed the realistic-intellectual drama has been the least *theatrical* in history."[10]

The architecture of the modern theatre had already been established, and it continued although the content of the drama had changed. In the United States, when the first sizable playhouses were constructed, the Chestnut Street Theatre in Philadelphia (1794) and the Park in New York (1798) were copied from English models. Technical advances in stagecraft were made possible by better lighting and powerdriven machinery for changing scenery. These further contributed to theatrical realism.

PATRONAGE AND THE HIGHER ARTS

Insofar as urbanism is associated with great culture, patronage of the arts may be said to be an urban phenomenon. Some of the record of artistic patronage in European and American cities has been apparent in the preceding sections on architecture, museums, and theatres. More attention to patronage will further explain the role of art in urban life.

Acting on various motives—patriotic, philanthropic, religious, local pride, personal ambition, a love of luxury and power, and the desire to make sound investments, as well as the cultivation of art for its own sake—governments, voluntary associations, the church, and individuals have all at one time or another engaged the services of painters, sculptors, gold- and silversmiths, musicians, and the like. A few patrons have had no further aim than to cultivate art, but more have had other purposes. They have financed art in order to beautify devotional services (*ancilla religionis,* art, the humble handmaiden of religion); to exercise social control by strengthening public attachment to cultural values; to enhance their status, as well as that of their families, and their social class; and to bring renown to their cities.

The bearing that patronage has on the content of art has not been precisely determined.[11] Though the evidence is inconclusive, there does appear to be some correlation between the social situation of the patron and the style of art preferred. One case is the ornate classical style encouraged by royal and aristocratic patrons. The more realistic genres are typical of bourgeois sponsorship. A mixed style appears characteristic of the so-called

[10] Sheldon Cheney, *The Theatre* (New York: David McKay, 1952), 2nd ed., p. 451.

[11] Compare "Patronage" by Francis Haskell in *Encyclopedia of World Art* (New York: McGraw-Hill, 1966), Vol. II, pp. 118–31.

advanced bourgeoisie, such as the merchant dynasts of the Italian Renaissance. Apart from social class, however, individual patrons have exercised much direct influence over the work they themselves have commissioned.

Though urban patronage of the arts is multiplex, it is convenient to divide it into the preindustrial and industrial.

PREINDUSTRIAL PATRONAGE

The quintessence of the preindustrial patron was Gaius Maecenas, Roman benefactor of Virgil and Horace, who was entrusted with budgetary responsibility for the arts by the Emperor Augustus during the first century B.C. Both of these poets proved useful to the empire, for they sought to legitimate the Roman citizen's duty to the state.

Patronage was revived in the cities of north Italy during the Renaissance, particularly by the Medicis.[12] Like Maecenas', Lorenzo's greatest contribution to the arts lay in his support to men of letters. As for painters, Lorenzo chiefly dispatched these to other cities to represent Florentine culture abroad: Leonardo da Vinci to Milan; Bottecelli to Rome; and Verrocchio to Venice.

In Renaissance Italy, Germany, and the Low Countries, the presence of free towns engendered jealous municipal rivalries that at times had important consequences for art. The guilds put up town houses which they furnished as munificently as possible. Merchants endowed local churches, perhaps contributing stained-glass windows with themselves as the figures of patron saints. Or they might supply the capital entirely as Cosimo de' Medici did for the parish church San Lorenzo, built and decorated by Brunelleschi and Donatello.

Commercialism

With the advent of the Reformation when the churches, now Protestant, showed negligible interest in iconography and a new mercantile gentry arose in such cities as Bruges and Amsterdam, a different era dawned for art patronage. Commercialism appeared. Artists entered guilds, contracted with dealers to market their work, and catered to the ambitious merchants who wanted to furnish their dwellings sumptuously.

The vitality of the mercantile communities brought new art into being, especially in Holland. In painting, we have the merchant portraiture of Hans Holbein, the large marketed output of Peter Paul Rubens' studio, Rembrandt's depictions of the Dutch burghers, the paintings done by Frans Hals, and others to portray the civic-guard companies of the Dutch merchants dur-

[12] Cf. Frederick Dorian, *Commitment to Culture* (Pittsburgh, Pa.: University of Pittsburgh Press, 1964), pp. 51–57.

ing the wars of liberation (the greatest of the kind, Rembrandt's *Night Watch*), and Gerard Terborch's pictures of the women of the merchant class washing their hands, taking music lessons, or engaged in other prosaic actions. The urban culture of seventeenth century Holland is nowhere better depicted than in the lucid realism of Jan Vermeer of Delft. Rembrandt, however, and much to his own financial loss, went on to portray deep introspection far beyond the marketable fashions of the time.

Thus established, the art market persisted. More and more there developed a middle-class patronage of arts and letters all over Western Europe. Wealthy urban collectors now vied with the titled landed nobility for the output of superior talent. As corporations, cities were themselves patrons of the arts. Beginning in 1749, the city of Paris sponsored the operas of the Academie Royale. Concurrently, a number of emancipated women, wives of wealthy bourgeoisie, became art patrons from their Paris drawing-room salons. Upon the success of the French Revolution, the feudal privileges of the Royal Academy of Painting and Sculpture were formally rescinded, permitting artists to exhibit freely for the market.

PATRONAGE UNDER INDUSTRIAL URBANISM

In more recent years, as might be expected of a pluralistic society, patronage has been practiced by individuals, private organizations, and government. At the outset though, in the late eighteenth and early nineteenth centuries, industrial urbanism was hostile to art. Patronage declined because the industrialists saw no utility in art. In addition, unlike the preindustrial aristocracy and possibly fearful for their own newly acquired status, they refused to associate with artists.

In the United States during the nineteenth century, the promotion of urban growth helped overcome the pragmatic attitude toward art that industrialized America shared with Europe. It came to be felt in Philadelphia, New York, and Boston that population and business could be attracted by a reputation for "culture." The newer cities to the west followed suit. In this manner the Western Art-Union was organized by subscription in Cincinnati in 1846. Before failing in 1851, the Art-Union regularly exhibited works of art to the citizens of the Queen City of the Ohio.[13] In the east, rich businessmen like R. M. Olyphant and Thomas H. Perkins established an artistic tradition in their respective cities and encouraged native artists. Their private collections were eventually converted into public museums.

In modern times, patronage of the arts in American cities has been used by aspiring men of wealth to gain recognition from the existing preindus-

[13] Lillian B. Miller, *Patrons and Patriotism* (Chicago: University of Chicago Press, 1966), pp. 196–98.

trial aristocracy, as César Graña has recently asserted.[14] Thus industrial leaders have asserted themselves against the socially prominent merchants, possibly so in the founding of New York's Metropolitan Museum of Art endowed by J. P. Morgan.[15] At any rate, the tremendous wealth of American collectors brought treasured art from abroad into galleries here in the United States.[16] New York led in this process and even today, New York City remains the primary center of the American art world. Only there can a serious artist gain the recognition that stamps him a truly critical success.[17]

Municipal Patronage

Municipalities have also been active as art sponsors. In this regard, European cities have a longer and stronger tradition of publicly supporting the arts than is true of local government in America. In Europe, art is assumed to have an affinity with education, and the two to be administered in common. Also, funds earmarked for the arts in particular cities may often originate with the national government in European countries. This is the case of the Arts Council of Great Britain. Even so, municipal government also participates. For example, both the Arts Council and the London County Council help defray the annual deficit of the London Philharmonic. The municipal art program of The Hague subsidizes, among others, the Royal Art Theatre, the Dutch Costume Museum, the Philharmonic, and The Netherlands Opera, the last two jointly with the national government. The policies of London and The Hague express the European tradition of regarding art as a public heritage.

The American Scene

In America, a combination of private, corporate, and foundation support is encouraging art in specific urban locales. To cite several instances: New York City's Metropolitan Opera received $135,000 from the American Export and Isbrandtsen shipping lines to mount a new production of *Aida;* and Dow Chemical contributed to a little theatre in Texas.[18] Allied Stores Corporation is the owner-operator of the Bergen Mall Shopping Center in Paramus, New Jersey. As a promotional venture, Allied underwrote the Playhouse on the Mall, which not only boosted sales but also became self-supporting.[19]

[14] César Graña, *Fact and Symbol: Essays in the Sociology of Art and Literature* (New York: Oxford University Press, 1971), p. viii.

[15] For "creative philanthropy" in the United States see Daniel M. Fox, *Engines of Culture* (Madison, Wis.: State Historical Society of Wisconsin, 1963).

[16] See Aline B. Saarinen, *The Proud Possessors* (New York: Random House, 1958).

[17] See Edward M. Levine, "Chicago's Art World: The Influence of Status Interests on Its Social and Distributive Systems," *Urban Life and Culture,* 1 (October 1972), pp. 293–322.

[18] Alvin Toffler, *The Culture Consumers* (New York: St. Martin's Press, 1964), p. 93.

[19] Ibid., pp. 94–95.

Lincoln Center's two-week outdoor summer festival sponsored by Exxon, the New York State Council on the Arts, and the city's own Parks, Recreation, and Cultural Affairs Administration.

Though unusual, municipal art patronage is not entirely unknown in American cities. Public bond issues have been floated to build museum facilities. St. Paul, Minnesota, has done so. The monumental Lincoln center in New York was organized as a nonprofit corporation from its inception and also received funds from the New York City government. County government in the United States has participated in art patronage too, but uncommonly. For example, the Los Angeles County Music Commission aids the Los Angeles Philharmonic and some smaller nonprofit musical groups.

The chronic financial difficulties of the serious arts in American cities, owing perhaps mainly to rising costs, income and inheritance taxes, and the decline of the single, powerful donor, have given rise to efforts to bring about federal support. This has included pleas for direct aid and for tax incentives to benefit the broad, moderate-income classes as potential patrons.[20]

RECREATION AND ENTERTAINMENT

The high culture of urban society has existed through the centuries alongside popular recreation and entertainment, and in both the preindustrial and industrial eras.

[20] Cf. William J. Baumol and William C. Bowen, *Performing Arts—The Economic Dilemma* (New York: Twentieth Century Fund, 1966) for the case for government support.

THE PREINDUSTRIAL PERIOD

Many pastimes, either growing out of work or calling for daring and competitiveness, were long practiced in urban centers for the sake of the pleasure they gave. The early Sumerians engaged in horse racing and contests with weapons. In Roman cities popular entertainments developed on a large scale, the fourth-century Roman calendar setting aside no fewer than 175 days a year for public games! Roman entertainments were both brutal and licentious. They had already been condemned by the Christian church before being finally discontinued when the northern invaders closed the ampitheatres and circuses in the sixth century.

Bartholomew Fair, made memorable in Ben Johnson's comedy and conducted in London from the twelfth century until last proclaimed in 1855, may be the prototype of the popular entertainment that flourished in the preindustrial cities of medieval Europe.[21] Medieval fairs were occasions for trading in cloth, livestock, utensils, and other merchandise. To this economic purpose entertainment was added. There were acrobats, stilt-walkers, conjurers, and animal-baiters. Recitations, sketches, and open-air plays were performed, their content often salacious. Daniel Pepys recorded in his *Diary* that he had taken his wife to the fair "and there did see a ridiculous obscene little stage-play, called 'Merry Andrey;' a foolish thing, but seen by everybody; and so to Jacob Hall's dancing of the ropes: a thing worth seeing, and mightily followed."[22] The aroma of roast Bartholomew pig and, beginning in the middle of the eighteenth century, of hot sausages too, filled the air.

IN INDUSTRIAL URBAN SOCIETY

Following the Industrial Revolution, the sidewalks and streets of the typical English city were the scene of Punch-and-Judy performances. They also appeared in the popular theatres and inns, or "saloon-theatres," as some called them. Variety music halls, which permitted drinking and smoking but were barred from offering plays, came into existence in the nineteenth century. In them, singers celebrated the humble acts of life, like walking in the zoo on a Sunday or the hawking of the costermonger. There might also be some expression of resentment against the upper classes. For the most part, however, the entertainment in vogue represented lighthearted efforts to be diverted from one's workaday life.

Increased Leisure

More recently, the greater availability of leisure has added incentive to the enjoyment of entertainment. From the middle of the eighteenth century to the

---

[21] Samuel McKechnie, *Popular Entertainments through the Ages* (New York: Benjamin Blom, 1969), Ch. 2.

[22] Recollected, ibid., p. 35.

present, industrial technology has enabled the work week to be reduced from 70 hours or more to about 40, at least in the advanced nations. Correspondingly, the leisure once monopolized by a small segment of the population has been increasingly shared by the other social classes. At present, the average American finds that the time available to him every day beyond that necessary for working, sleeping, eating, and so on has risen from 2.18 hours to 7.48 during the past century alone.[23] Interestingly, early industrialization increased the time one spent at work, so that the present standard represents a return to what the medieval guildsman enjoyed in the thirteenth century![24]

Modern technology has enabled popular entertainment and recreation to be revolutionized, particularly in catering to numbers of people on an unprecedented scale. Movies, record players, radio, and television have added new dimensions to entertainment. Improved transportation, especially the automobile, has had an impact too. More productive industrial processes have also taken effect, for instance, in the output of recreational goods and in building sports facilities. Of the $40 billion Americans spent on recreation in 1970, about one-fourth went for sports equipment; a fifth for radio and TV sets, turntables, records, and musical instruments; and one-tenth for magazines and newspapers.[25] Some 40 million bowlers are active at least once a week in the United States, and possibly 7 million play at least 15 rounds of golf a year.

Active pursuits have not, however, crowded out the more passive forms of recreation. On the average, an American spends 25 percent of his waking hours reading newspapers, attending movies, listening to the radio, and, primarily, watching television. According to the Nielsen audience surveys, "American families spend two-thirds more hours watching TV and listening to the radio than members of those families spend working for a living."[26] Still, in 1972, of $105 billion spent on leisure in the United States, $50 billion went for recreational sports equipment and activities.[27]

LEISURE IN POSTINDUSTRIAL SOCIETY

Moral philosophers have given various meanings to leisure. Aristotle chided the Athenians who worked for the sake of amusing themselves off the job. He

[23] Cited by Harold Wilensky, "The Uneven Distribution of Leisure: The Impact of Economic Growth on 'Free Time,' " *Social Problems*, 9 (Summer 1961), pp. 32–56.

[24] Sebastian de Grazia, *Of Time, Work, and Leisure* (New York: Twentieth Century Fund, 1962), p. 70.

[25] U.S. Bureau of the Census, *Statistical Abstract of the United States: 1972* (Washington, D.C.: Government Printing Office, 1972), Table 330, p. 206.

[26] Arnold W. Green, *Recreation, Leisure, and Politics* (New York: McGraw-Hill, 1964) and Richard Kraus, *Recreation and Leisure in Modern Society* (New York: Appleton-Century-Crofts, 1971).

[27] *U.S. News & World Report* (April 17, 1972).

admitted that relaxation is needed for effective work, but he saw leisure as proper only when it was devoted to aesthetic and intellectual development. Roman thinkers also conceived of leisure as appropriate just for the educated, privileged few. To the Romans, correct leisure meant quiet respite earned as a reward for the successful pursuit of the affairs of state. Yet as a matter of public policy the Romans catered to spectacle and brutality in their entertainments in order to pacify the hoi polloi.

Christian theologians made contemplation of the divine the noblest use of time free from work. In this they agreed with Aristotle, except that they substituted God for wisdom as the valid object of contemplation. Recovering the enterprising spirit of the Romans, Renaissance Europe deemed worldly conquest the supreme good. That is, the north Italian urban patriciate extolled individual feats and outstanding craftsmanship. In England too, Sir Thomas More's *Utopia* envisioned everyone working productively part of the day. The rest of the time all would be free to do whatever they wished without interference from others. A century later, the Italian monk Tomamaso Campanella's *City of the Sun* continued More's philosophy. Sebastian de Grazia has said that such thought marked a turning point, for it tended to regard leisure as unproductive idleness.[28]

Research into leisure and entertainment today appears to confirm the common belief that not only is leisure beneficial for one's work but also that it is to be undertaken for its own sake as well. In this view leisure is: (1) the antithesis of economically motivated work; (2) pleasant; (3) indicative of a minimum of social-role obligations; (4) contributive to a sense of freedom; (5) related to the dominant values of the culture; (6) a variety of behaviors ranging from the trivial to the weighty; and (7) often of a playful nature.[29] In a notable early field study, George A. Lundberg defined leisure in its present-day popular manner as time free from "obligatory occupation" and marked by a "pleasurable adjustment to one's situation."[30]

Not only has leisure been leigitimized in modern urban society, it is even being felt that work and recreation will soon be fused into a new synthesis. The economist John Galbraith sees, in fact, that the New Class now filling professional and administrative occupations already take it for granted that their jobs will be rewarding *and* enjoyable.[31] Margaret Mead heralds a possible cultural shift when she writes that there "must be a revision which will make the members of a society—where delight in high-level proficiency should now replace dogged willingness to work long hours for very limited

[28] de Grazia, op. cit., pp. 11–34.

[29] Max Kaplan, *Leisure in America* (New York: John Wiley & Sons, 1960), p. 22.

[30] George A. Lundberg, Mirra Komarovsky, and Mary Alice McInerny, *Leisure* (New York: Columbia University Press, 1934), p. 2.

[31] John K. Galbraith, *The Affluent Society* (Cambridge, Mass.: Riverside Press, 1958), pp. 334–48.

rewards—able to integrate the shorter hours of work and the new engrossing home rituals [suburban familism] into some kind of a whole in which these outmoded sequences, heritage of an age of scarcity, can be overcome."[32] The French sociologist Joffre Dumazedier also sees the advanced nations on the threshold of a new order of work and leisure. He writes, "This search for a new *joie de vivre,* this new 'rage for life,' is not only part of a *nouvelle vague,* but of a new civilization."[33]

At the same time though, Dumazedier deplores today's mediocre commercial entertainment and calls for planning in order to raise popular taste and realize the cultural potentialities of the greater leisure available now. Similarly, David Riesman declares that, "for many people today, the sudden onrush of leisure is a version of technological unemployment: their education has not prepared them for it and the creation of new wants at their expense moves faster than their ability to order and assimilate these wants."[34] Riesman's critique reflects the humanistic hope that, given ample mass leisure, a high culture can be diffused to virtually everyone.

MASS CULTURE

For centuries intellectuals have been debating whether the rank and file public can enjoy a superior culture if they have the opportunity. The increase in education and leisure sharpens the saliency of this question today.

THE EARLIER CONTROVERSY

The debate got under way in the eighteenth century when the French philosopher Montaigne authored a skeptical view of mankind. Montaigne concluded that for innate reasons human beings are generally simple-minded, frivolous, and ignoble. Religious by temperament and conviction, Pascal, on the other hand, put forth a different conception of human nature. Pascal thought people generally capable of refinement, with the result that society could hope to dispense with escapist, violent, and salacious entertainment completely.

Montaigne and Pascal's views were in accord with the social scene of the eighteenth century. At that time, the landed gentry monopolizing leisure were threatened by the new wealthy class of urban merchants and industrialists—and their increasingly affluent subordinates. This was especially

[32] "The Pattern of Leisure in Contemporary American Culture," *Annals of the American Academy of Political and Social Science,* 313 (September 1957), 11–15.

[33] Joffre Dumazedier, *Toward a Society of Leisure* (New York: Free Press, 1967), p. 234.

[34] David Riesman, *Abundance for What? and Other Essays* (Garden City, N.Y.: Doubleday, 1965), pp. 157–58.

true in England where, Lowenthal writes, "the urbanized members of the emerging middle classes began to find themselves with leisure time, presently to be occupied by those forms of diversion and entertainment which an accommodating market was ready to supply."[35]

The existence of a wide audience for the arts, so different from the patron and the coterie in the preindustrial city, was historically unique. Edward Shils estimates that in fourth century Rome the "life of the intellect" was the province of no more than 5000 altogether! These included writers, politicians and civil servants, and educated landowners. Even Restoration England, two generations after Shakespeare, possessed a relatively small intellectual audience. Shils calculates, there were at that time probably fewer than 70,000 clergymen, teachers, members of the government, writers, lawyers, artists, musicians, scientists, physicians, and other educated persons.[36]

Industrial urbanism greatly expanded the intellectual audience, beginning in the eighteenth century. The question of the quality of the culture of this new mass society was another matter. Lowenthal is informative in tracing the debate between the elitist critics and the democratic defenders of the cultural marketplace in industrial England during the nineteenth century. At the beginning, Wordsworth encouraged popular art for its expressive nature, but he confessed being frightened by the "deluge of idle and extravagant stories." Matthew Arnold deplored the dangers of industrialization to culture, especially emphasis on sports and the popular press, the latter because it was not conducive to personal growth. William Hazlitt flatly condemned the art market of his day.

While Hazlitt defended an elitist conception of high culture, the popular Sir Walter Scott took the position that it was perfectly all right to publish just for money. Scott asserted a moral rather than an aesthetic standard for art. In the pages of The Edinburgh Review, the American press of 1843 was referred to with scathing disrespect for its servility to public taste. Toward the end of the century, however, the Review came to feel that perhaps the masses were being leveled up after all, and that cultural progress had accompanied material prosperity indeed.

THE MASS-CULTURE DEBATE TODAY

Mass culture continues to be debated currently, just as mass culture itself continues to accompany the spread of industrial urbanism around the world. A neutral definition of the term declares mass culture: (1) to be the cultural

[35] The Montaigne-Pascal controversy is summarized in Leo Lowenthal, "An Historical Preface to the Popular Culture Debates," in Norman Jacobs, ed., Culture for the Millions? (Princeton, N.J.: D. Van Nostrand, 1961), pp. 28–42. The sentence quoted is from p. 30.

[36] Edward Shils, "The High Culture of the Age," in Robert N. Wilson, ed., The Arts in Society (Englewood Cliffs, N.J.: Prentice-Hall, 1964), pp. 317–62.

correlate of mass society, especially of the industrial-urban type; (2) to differ in content if not in quality from elite culture; (3) to be diffused by the media; and (4) to be affected by marketability.[37] Included are books, films, TV, radio, phonograph recordings, electronic tapes, paintings, sculpture, furnishings—in short, the whole output of "art" for public consumption. Involved in this cultural consumption here in the United States alone are book expenditures exceeding $3 billion a year (1970); 19 million persons visiting art museums (1971); and 460 million books being borrowed from public libraries (1968).[38]

Three groups of critics, as Bernard Rosenberg has identified them, are participating in the mass-culture controversy in the United States at present.[39] They are (1) those who fear the debasement of high culture; (2) those who believe the public is being crassly manipulated; and (3) those who hope that a significant mass culture is possible.

THE DEBASEMENT OF SERIOUS CULTURE

Ortega y Gasset, T. S. Eliot, and Bernard I. Bell represent the group who condemn mass culture for its debasement of superior values to the level of the commonplace, morally unresponsive, and brutal. Adults are infantilized, and children are overstimulated, for example, by the hyperviolence and glaring pornography of many films and TV programs today.[40] These critics add that for all their effort to the contrary, the avant-garde of serious modern artists, in effect simply discovering the technical potentialities of their media, are overwhelmed by the "spreading ooze" of *kitsch* (mass culture, in German) and cannot reassert superior values any longer.[41]

THE MANIPULATION OF THE PUBLIC

A second group, consisting of Dwight Macdonald, Clement Greenberg, and Irving Howe, has deplored the impersonal manufacture of impersonal commodities. This resembles folk culture, to be sure, except that it is being carried on manipulatively—in the United States for profit and in the U.S.S.R. for political benefit, but in neither case to afford genuine pleasure or to edify the spirit.

[37] Consult "Mass Culture" in Julius Gould and William L. Kolb, eds., *A Dictionary of the Social Sciences* (New York: Free Press, 1964), p. 411.

[38] *Statistical Abstract of the United States: 1972,* op. cit., Table 330, p. 206; Table 332, p. 208; and Table 214, p. 134.

[39] Bernard Rosenberg and David M. White, eds., *Mass Culture: The Popular Arts in America* (New York: Free Press, 1957).

[40] See Russel Nye, *The Unembarrassed Muse: The Popular Arts in America* (New York: Dial Press, 1970).

[41] Clement Greenberg, "Avant-Garde and Kitsch," in Rosenberg and White, op. cit., pp. 98–107.

The historian Oscar Handlin distinguishes between high and popular culture, and finds mass culture unique. In the past the two were functional, one for the aristocracy and the other for the peasants. When the nineteenth-century industrial nabobs began to look on the artifacts of the earlier high culture as property useful for gaining respectability, however, they began the process that has led to mass culture. Concludes Handlin, mass culture is produced by the mass media to sell "artistic" wares to a public without generally accepted standards or individual needs.[42]

THE POSSIBILITY OF A SIGNIFICANT MASS CULTURE

A third group, among them Edward Shils, Gilbert Seldes, and David M. White, has made a more guarded appraisal of mass culture.

Shils feels that there is a public consciousness of a current cultural decline. But he declares that high culture has never been the property of an entire society, and believes, in fact, that today's discriminate minority is "as acutely perceptive as it ever was." The market may accept poor art. Yet there is also a market for superior creations and, besides, tradition calls for profits to be applied to their support, like the publisher who feels obliged to have critically acclaimed books on his list. Still, Shils is afraid that our cultural elite are fragmented and too divorced from the public, and he laments the cultural nullity of America's public schools and "the boorish and complacent ignorance of university graduates."[43]

Similarly, Harold Wilensky's study of TV viewing and newspaper readership in metropolitan Detroit reached an equivocal conclusion about the capacity of mass culture to improve substantially in quality. Behind Wilensky's study was the picture of an industrial population possessed of fluid, homogeneous ideas and, therefore, susceptible to fads and fashions. Standing over them are poorly organized elites, themselves mass-oriented and manipulative, responding to short-run pressures and abdicating to the "sovereignty of the unqualified." Wilensky thinks "the cultural atmosphere is permeated by the mass media." Measured in terms of both TV viewing and exposure to newspapers, the participation in mass culture by the educated differs little from that of the less well educated. In sum, Wilensky's data indicate "that the rising level of education will protect against enervating amounts of the very shoddiest media content but will not cause large populations to break the mediocrity barrier."[44]

Exponent of the popular arts, Seldes believes that mass culture can effectively satisfy public taste (as Robert Burns once did) and also at the same

[42] Oscar Handlin, "Comments on Mass and Popular Culture," in Jacobs, op. cit., p. 69.

[43] Wilson, op. cit.

[44] Harold Wilensky, "Mass Society and Mass Culture," *American Sociological Review*, 29 (April 1964), pp. 173–96.

Can the rising level of education break the TV mediocrity barrier?

time be a valuable adjunct to high culture. Seldes concedes the pernicious consequences of the manipulation of the arts that leads to robotism. Seldes is very conscious of how cynically decisions are made in the mass media, notably in television. In the interests of raising standards though, he favors more governmental presence in the media, possibly of the kind found in the British broadcasting industry.[45] (See Ch. 11.)

White's defense of mass culture is perhaps the most direct. He contrasts present-day taste with that of earlier times—for gladiatorial contests and even public executions! Furthermore, he calls attention to the vast diffusion of the products of high culture, such as the countless phonograph records of the masters being sold and the mass attendance at museums today.[46]

THE CONTINUING CONTROVERSY

Other voices have also been heard evaluating mass culture. David Riesman judges the audio-visual mass media as being psychologically less demand-

[45] "The People and the Arts" in Rosenberg and White, op. cit., pp. 74–97.

[46] David M. White, "Mass Culture Revisited," in Bernard Rosenberg and David M. White, eds., *Mass Culture Revisited* (New York: Van Nostrand Reinhold, 1971), pp. 13–21.

ing than the book.[47] TV and films lack the capacity of the book to induce orderliness in the mind. Riesman, then, finds "men molded as much by the mass media outside their formal education as by their schooling; men who are more public-relations minded than ambitious; men softened for encounters rather than hardened for voyages." He concludes that so great has been the failure of the media to achieve "civic literacy" that one may look on the prospect of human enlightenment as chimerical.

Marshall McLuhan has been most publicly identified with the interpretation of the pictorial media as a new form of communication. He calls them "cool," that they leave much to be filled in or completed by the viewing audience. As a result, they are high in audience participation. The form of the media, according to McLuhan, is thus a significant variable. For example, by virtue of its immediacy, television reinforces group-mindedness and, by ushering in an age of "re-tribalization," TV will ultimately be a source of substantial cultural change.[48]

THE MASS-CULTURE DEBATE AND SOCIOLOGICAL RESEARCH

The continuing controversy over mass culture is evidence of divergent conceptions of human nature and the role played by art in human life. It also stems from the practical problems in convincingly answering the questions that are posed. The concepts are vague. The arguments advanced lack conclusiveness. They bog down in moral relativism—for example, the recent assertion that "pop" culture can bridge the gap between elite and folk culture.[49] Thomas M. Kando, is convinced that the youthful counterculture today, freed of its destructive tendencies, contains within itself the capacity to shape a new sociocultural consciousness appropriate to a "true leisure society" and its necessary life style.[50] Kando does marshal much scholarship in support of his diagnosis of the current trends. In spite of this perhaps, as Lowenthal has aptly written, "it would seem fair to say that the present discussion on popular culture and on the new possibilities of the mass media will continue to turn in circles until a new and systematic effort is made to clear the field from confusions, and to make real discussion possible."[51]

[47] "The Oral Tradition, the Written Word, and the Screen Image," in Riesman, op. cit., pp. 397–421.

[48] Marshall McLuhan, *Understanding Media: The Extension of Men* (New York: McGraw-Hill, 1964).

[49] The theme of George H. Lewis, ed., *Side-Saddle on the Golden Calf* (Pacific Palisades, Calif.: Goodyear, 1971).

[50] Thomas M. Kando, *Leisure and Popular Culture in Transition* (St. Louis, Mo.: C. V. Mosby, 1975), pp. 249–87.

[51] Leo Lowenthal, *Literature, Popular Culture, and Society* (Englewood Cliffs, N.J.: Prentice-Hall, 1961), p. 51.

CONCLUSION

Cities are identified with high cultures. They reveal the fact architecturally as well as in the cultivation of drama and of the fine arts. Imaginatively planned capital cities, museums, and theatres testify to the substantial advancement of the arts in urban communities. Artistic enterprise has not, however, been constant or continuous. Art styles, the importance assigned to art, and the nature of the art market, including the objectives of patronage, vary significantly from one period to the next. Important contrasts can be discerned by comparing the preindustrial and industrial eras of urbanization.

Recreation and entertainment—the elements of low culture—have also been prominently pursued by urban populations. Here too the industrial city has made a great difference, by giving people more leisure time and by multiplying the resources for enjoying it. One effect has been to envisage the assimilation of work to play itself. A second has been to question the quality of mass culture, and acrimoniously too. Still another is the revival of the old question of whether the general public can be sufficiently developed to prefer good art to its debased forms, and sound recreation to frivolous indulgence, or to enjoy a low culture that does not impair the superior culture of the elite, or even to create a new postindustrial culture of leisure-time activities uniting society into a stable, satisfied, and stimulating whole.

FOR FURTHER READING

Frederick Dorian, *Commitment to Culture* (Pittsburgh, Pa.: University of Pittsburgh Press, 1964). Analyzes the nature of European art patronage and what the United States can learn from it.

Joffre Dumazedier, *Toward a Society of Leisure,* trans. by Steward E. McClure (New York: Free Press, 1967). Though French, this is a useful study because the problems of leisure in industrial urban societies are somewhat similar.

James B. Hall and Barry Ulanov, *Modern Culture and the Arts* (New York: McGraw-Hill, 1972). The split between the high arts and popular culture. Illustrated.

William M. Hammel, ed., *The Popular Arts in America* (New York: Harcourt Brace Jovanovich, 1972). On the movies, radio and TV, popular music, and bestsellers.

George H. Lewis, ed., *Side Saddle on the Golden Calf* (Pacific Palisades, Calif.: Goodyear, 1972). On the relationship between the structure of American urban society and the popular culture as expressing a new consciousness.

Roy McMullen, *Art, Affluence, and Alienation* (New York: Frederick A. Praeger, 1968). The present state of the fine arts and the issues arising from it.

Stanley Parker, *The Future of Work and Leisure* (New York: Frederick A. Praeger, 1971). Studies done in England in the late 1960s. Valuable source material.

Bernard Rosenberg and David W. Manning, ed., *Mass Culture Revisited* (New York: Van Nostrand Reinhold, 1971). The pros and cons of mass culture and the mass media.

PART SIX

URBAN SOCIAL PROBLEMS

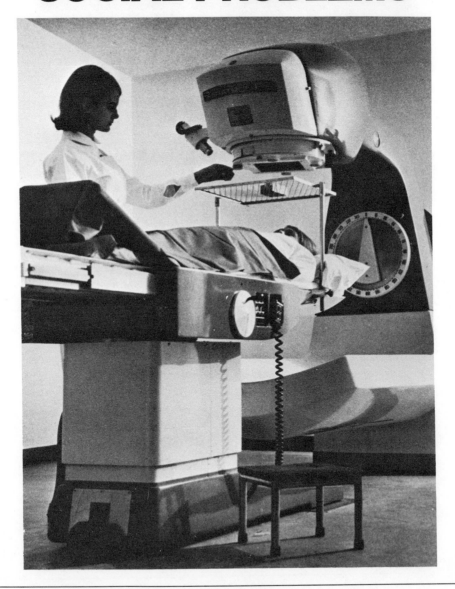

Rising health standards are characteristic of urban society.

Source: Australian News and Information Bureau, *Australia: A Portfolio* (Adelaide: Griffin Press, 1966), p. 52.

CHAPTER 17

DEVIANCE AND LAW ENFORCEMENT

If deviance is regarded as behavior contrary to accepted social standards, particularly the law, then by and large, many types of deviance accompany urban life. This chapter reviews the relationships—frequently very complicated ones—between many of the forms of deviance and the conditions of life in urban society and in large population centers. Proposals being advanced for coping with crime in urban America today are also discussed.

URBANIZATION AND DEVIANCE

Three general distributions of deviance bear out the disproportionate relationship of various kinds of deviance to urbanism:

One is the strikingly greater incidence of crime and delinquency in urban rather than rural populations.

TABLE 17-1 Rates (per 100,000 Population) of Major Criminal Offenses Known to the Police in United States Standard Metropolitan Statistical Areas and Rural Communities: 1974

	RATES	
OFFENSES	SMSA'S	RURAL
Murder and nonnegligent manslaughter	10.8	7.6
Forcible rape	31.2	11.6
Robbery	273.7	20.4
Aggravated assault	242.6	111.5
Burglary	1652.6	693.2
Larceny	2830.9	808.3
Motor vehicle theft	579.6	93.8
Total	5621.6	1746.4

Source: Federal Bureau of Investigation, *Uniform Crime Reports for the United States, 1974* (Washington, D.C.: Government Printing Office, 1975), p. 11.

The second relates to the progressive increase in crime from one stage of modernization to the next.

The third consists of the positive correlation between unlawful behavior and city size.

A good deal of statistical data, authoritative opinion, and impressionistic evidence exists to substantiate all three of these patterns.

RURAL-URBAN COMPARISONS

Differences in the levels of reported crime showing much higher frequencies in urban than rural districts have been observed in any number of foreign countries, including Norway and Denmark, for example. A similar imbalance has been found characteristic of India's cities in contrast with that nation's rural areas. In African countries too, the incidence of breaches of the law has been determined to be greater in towns than in rural sections.

The American experience parallels that of these other regions. As Table 17-1 discloses, in 1970 criminal rates for murder and nonnegligent manslaughter, forcible rape, robbery, aggravated assault, burglary, larceny, and auto theft—the seven actions making up the FBI's criminal index offenses—were all substantially higher in our metropolitan population centers than they were in the nation's rural areas.

For the United States too, as Table 17-2 reveals, crime rates for our population centers over 250,000 in size are consistently higher than rural rates,

TABLE 17-2   Rates (per 100,000 Population) of Criminal Offenses Officially Reported for Cities over 250,000 and Rural Areas, United States: 1974

	RATES	
OFFENSES	CITIES OVER 250,000	RURAL
Murder and nonnegligent manslaughter	21.5	7.6
Forcible rape	55.4	11.6
Robbery	684.4	20.4
Aggravated assault	382.6	111.5
Burglary	2236.7	693.2
Larceny	3171.4	808.3
Motor vehicle theft	982.8	93.8
Total	7498.8	1746.4

Source: Federal Bureau of Investigation, *Uniform Crime Reports for the United States, 1974* (Washington, D.C.: Government Printing Office, 1975), p. 11.

especially for certain property crimes. Traditionally there has been a greater disparity between urban and rural rates of crime against property than there has been in their respective rates of crimes of violence.

Only until the recent and rapid upsurge in crime in the metropolitan areas of the United States, the proportion of homicides in our rural areas usually rivaled our big-city murder rates. Traditions of adult violence are not uncommon in rural communities. Take the Hatfield-McCoy feud along the Kentucky-West Virginia border beginning in 1873, and the 30-year vendetta that went on in Texas after 1869 between the Sutton and Taylor families. Even today, murder is more frequent in rural America than it is in our suburban communities. In 1972, for example, while the murder rate was 6.2 per 100,000 rural population in the United States, the comparable suburban rate was only 4.6. Also, traditionally, criminal assaults on women have been made proportionally more often in rural than suburban communities. Still, in 1969, forcible rape occurred with slightly higher frequency in our suburbs than our rural areas, 13.7 to 10.0, and in 1972, even more so, 17.0 to 11.1.[1]

As Durkheim noted long ago, self-destruction is also apt to be associated with urbanism. Typically, urban areas do have higher suicide rates than rural areas. In 1940 in the United States, the suicide rate for cities of over 100,000 was 16.8 per 100,000 persons. For cities in the 2500–10,000 category, the rate was lower—15.1. And for rural areas it was lower still:

[1] Bureau of the Census, *Statistical Abstract of the United States: 1975* (Washington, D.C.: Government Printing Office, 1975), Table 246, p. 149.

DEVIANCE AND LAW ENFORCEMENT

12.0.[2] Yet rural-urban differences in suicide rates in the United States have been declining. In 1960 the rural rate in the nation was 10.8, as compared with an urban rate of only 10.5! Although the suicide rate for metropolitan counties continued to remain higher than the rural rate, the frequency for nonmetropolitan counties did not.[3]

These figures must remain somewhat ambiguous, as Sanford Labowitz observes, owing to the fact that "rural" and "urban" here are simply demographic and, as he writes, it is "not possible to designate the social or cultural aspects of the two environments that generated the sucide differential."[4] It may not be unlikely though that the increased rural suicide rate stems from the diffusion to the fringe area of the stressful aspects of the urban way of life.

MODERNIZATION, CRIME, AND DELINQUENCY

Deviance differentials for rural and urban populations are paralleled by the steady progression of crime and delinquency rates during the course of modernization, in other words, in the process of industrial urbanization. In fact, so definite is this tendency that the criminologist Marshall B. Clinard has stated categorically that, "increasing urbanization has almost everywhere, whether in the United States, Latin America, Africa, or Asia, been accompanied by a marked increase in various forms of deviant behavior."[5]

Four stages of sociocultural change, each with a bearing on deviance, may be distinguished in the process of modernization. Although each represents a level of development counter-indicative to deviance, each also possesses a degree of potency in motivating misconduct greater than that of the original agrarian stage preceding it. Conducted by the World Federation for Mental Health, the 1964 Topeka Conference reviewed the world situation with significant conclusions about the incidence of juvenile delinquency relative to successive levels of urbanization.[6]

In the first stage, that of tribal culture, delinquency is either totally absent or most infrequent. Continuous family and community control prevents offensive behavior from being committed. Thus there is only a tiny amount of youthful crime among Australia's aborigines.

[2] Andrew F. Henry and James F. Short, Jr., *Suicide and Homicide* (New York: Free Press, 1954), p. 76.

[3] Sanford Labowitz, "Variation in Suicide Rates," in Jack P. Gibbs, ed., *Suicide* (New York: Harper & Row, 1968), pp. 57–73.

[4] Ibid.

[5] Marshall B. Clinard, *Sociology of Deviant Behavior* (New York: Holt, Rinehart, and Winston, 1970), 3rd ed., p. 80. See also Marshall B. Clinard and Daniel J. Abbott, *Crime in Developing Countries* (New York: John Wiley & Sons, 1973), Ch. 3, "Urbanization and Crime," pp. 77–107.

[6] See T. G. N. Gibbens and R. H. Ahrenfeldt, eds., *Cultural Factors in Delinquency* (Philadelphia, Pa.: J. B. Lippincott, 1966).

In the second stage, where rapid modernization takes place, juvenile deliquency becomes virulent "because urbanization is destroying the cohesion of families, and migration towards rapidly growing cities is forcing increasing numbers of juveniles, cut off from their tribal and cultural roots, to fend for themselves."[7] This is the situation today in many African countries and in Asia too.

During the third stage, education, economic security, and social services combine to produce greater conformity among the young. Consequently, delinquency declines from its previous high levels. One may point to the third-generation ethnic groups in American cities whose consolidation into the urban social structure has now been largely completed. At this stage, however, the in-migrants who are experiencing rapid social mobility account for even higher levels of unlawful behavior than before. They are simply at stage two.

Finally, and this stage is still indistinct today, we have yet another possibility. Here "new and unfamiliar forms of adolescent behavior" are exhibited. They relate perhaps to approved precocity, higher need levels, anxiety stemming from formal social controls, tendencies to act out the implications of the principle of personal freedom, and unprecedented opportunities for contact, communication, and deviant group formation to express the particular values of the segregated social category of adolescents. Hence in Canada, for example, despite a declining differential between urban and rural crime there, a rise in the participation of middle-class boys in delinquency is being observed today.

DEVIANCE AND CITY SIZE

Characteristically, there is also a positive correlation between unlawful acts known to the police and city size. In the United States, as shown in Table 17-3, a growth in the number of reported offenses of various types may be noted as city size increases. Homicides are six times as frequent in cities over 250,000 as they are in towns under 10,000. Proportionally, there are 14 times more robberies in the large metropolitan centers than in our smallest cities. Burglaries have a relative frequency two times greater in the most populous places in comparison to the occurrence of such offenses in the least populous ones.

However, the crime level is not proportionally the same for all of the largest cities despite the tendency for unlawfulness to be most common in this category as a whole. Referring to Table 17-4, we see that Chicago had five times the robbery rate in 1965 than was reported for Dallas. In 1972 though, Dallas's rate was only half that of Chicago, while the rate for Wash-

[7] Ibid., p. 22.

TABLE 17-3   Offenses Known (per 100,000 Population) by City Size, United States: 1974

OFFENSES	CITY SIZE					
	UNDER 10,000	10,000–25,000	25,000–50,000	50,000–100,000	100,000–250,000	250,000 OR MORE
Murder and nonnegligent						
manslaughter	3.9	4.9	5.8	6.7	11.7	21.5
Forcible rape	11.3	13.8	17.8	23.1	34.3	55.4
Robbery	47.2	75.9	127.7	167.6	264.9	648.4
Aggravated assault	155.4	155.2	179.4	208.4	289.1	382.6
Burglary	979.7	1138.5	1341.0	1568.3	2078.8	2236.7
Larceny	2406.3	2738.2	3068.5	3255.6	3719.8	3171.4
Motor vehicle theft	214.4	291.4	411.4	517.7	712.4	982.8
Total	3818.2	4417.8	5151.6	5747.4	7111.0	7755.4

Source: Federal Bureau of Investigation, *Uniform Crime Reports for the United States, 1974* (Washington, D.C.: Government Printing Office, 1975), pp. 160–61.

TABLE 17-4   Robbery Rates (per 100,000 Population) for Selected Cities, United States: 1965 and 1972

	1965	1972
New York	114	991
Chicago	421	704
Los Angeles	293	502
Philadelphia	140	498
Detroit	335	1147
Baltimore	229	1070
Houston	135	398
Dallas	79	301
Washington, D.C.	359	1036
Cleveland	213	758
Milwaukee	28	104
San Francisco	278	669

Sources: President's Commission on Law Enforcement and the Administration of Justice, *The Challenge of Crime in a Free Society* (Washington, D.C.: Government Printing Office, 1967), p. 29, and Bureau of the Census, *Statistical Abstract of the United States: 1975* (Washington, D.C.: Government Printing Office, 1975), p. 147.

ington, D.C., which in 1965 had just about equaled that of the "windy city" now exceeded the latter's by more than 147 percent.

Although what produces deviance is discussed later in this chapter, it is useful to point out here that the causal relationship of city size to crime is quite complicated. Some types of crime, such as liquor-law violations and embezzlement, show relative uniformity for cities of all sizes. On the other hand, narcotics offenses, gambling, and certain other kinds of violations conform to the progression pattern according to city size that make up the list of offenses embodied in Table 17-4.

Of course, population concentration itself does not produce crime. "An alternative and more defensible conclusion," as the United Nations Bureau of Social Affairs has said, is that the giant metropolis of today is much more apt than a small rural community to possess the "maladjustments and conflicts and other conditions" that actually lead to increased crime.

URBAN SOURCES OF DEVIANCE

Insofar as urbanism is conducive to criminal deviance, it operates as a complex of causal factors and not as a single determinant. It is the very character of urban society as an entity that, relatively speaking, predisposes its inhabitants to nonconformist conduct.[8]

CAUSAL RELATIONSHIPS

The influence of urban life is such that in comparison with a rural folk society it creates deviant tendencies understandable in terms of six fairly specific principles.

First, because individualism is more intense in the city, wider latitude is allowed for personal choice, and this sets up a tendency towards violations of the law. In other words, by relativizing the norms one is encouraged to overstep the bounds of propriety. Consider the quest today for personal autonomy in areas like the liberalization of the sex mores and the whole movement to decriminalize so-called victimless crimes.

Second, cultural herterogeneity and conflict abound in the city, creating both the need and the opportunity for deviance. No doubt this factor underlies the characteristic increase in crime in neighborhoods undergoing racial and religious transition.

Third, relatively free association permits interaction that not only diffuses deviant behavior patterns but also negates legitimate norms. Consider as one illustration the vandalism of public property by delinquents acting out the counternorms of the lower-class gang.

Fourth, mobility and social change make the continued acceptance of moral and legal change an urban phenomenon, with accompanying moral ambiguity a consequence. Thus a UN consultative group on crime prevention generalized that social changes resulting from a nation's de-

[8] See Harold D. Eastman, "The Process of Urbanization and Criminal Behavior," unpublished Ph.D. dissertation, State University of Iowa (1954), p. 190, as cited in Frank Hartung, ed., *Crime, Law, and Society* (Detroit, Mich.: Wayne State University Press, 1965), p. 97.

velopment, particularly if rapid, raises the risk of "a quantitative increase in deliquency and a qualitative change in its manifestations."

Fifth, the presence of wealth in the city also favors deviance, for it furnishes added opportunity for illicit behavior no less than the drive that necessitates it in the first place. Very simply put: the availability of property motivates criminal conduct. Forty percent of all reported larcenies in the United States are thefts out of automobiles. In another sense, however, affluence takes effect indirectly, most notably by arousing resentment over relative deprivation and blocked mobility.

Sixth—and this point is in some dispute—formal administration in urban areas probably increases awareness of the amount of deviance there. All else equal, the larger the police force and the more efficiently it is organized and equipped, the greater the volume of crime it will be able to detect and therefore establish.

THE SOCIAL CONCEPTION OF DEVIANCE

The forementioned six propositions, as to why urbanism is associated with deviance, embody the social conception of crime, which dominates criminology today. The social conception of deviance has been defined by Albert K. Cohen as "the attempt to understand a society's deviance in terms of the social structure of that society."[9]

The result of such theorizing has been to rivet attention on (1) the general conditions that predispose individuals to deviance; (2) the situations that reinforce those tendencies; and (3) the subsequent states of affairs which finally are responsible for the commission of specific acts of misconduct. As Richard Knudten paraphrases this, "crime results from natural human interaction as persons act within cultural systems, react to social conditions, and respond to existing opportunities."[10] On one side we have the larger social structure, and on the other the more immediate factors that, combined, account for the types of deviance exhibited by the various kinds of individuals.

The social conception of crime includes insights that have been developed over the past half century. W. I. Thomas and Florian Znaniecki's theory of social disorganization propounded around 1920 offers a convenient starting point in reviewing this subject.[11] According to them, society consists of a network of rules calling for obligatory conduct. Hence the social norms such as statutes and customs are objective cultural values that in the case of the

[9] Albert K. Cohen, "Deviant Behavior and Its Control," in Talcott Parsons, ed., *American Sociology: Perspectives, Problems, Methods* (New York: Basic Books, 1968), p. 231.

[10] Richard D. Knudten, *Crime in a Complex Society* (Homewood, Ill.: Dorsey Press, 1970), p. 9.

[11] William I. Thomas and Florian Znaniecki, *The Polish Peasant in Europe and America* (New York: Alfred A. Knopf, 1927).

conforming person correspond to sentiments within his mind. When he is exposed to new values, however, which was the case of the Polish peasant in America and chiefly in the city of Chicago that Thomas and Znaniecki studied, the individual's attitudes no longer conform to established custom, and behavior contrary to legitimate expectation is likely to arise.

Subsequent scholarship has refined the original theory of disorganization. For instance, Thorsten Sellin came to place great weight on conflicting cultural values as responsible for crime.[12] In a pluralistic setting, where sociocultural groups exist each with its own values, the individual will in all probability be exposed to inconsistent obligations. In fact, as Robert Merton established in the 1930s, disparate membership in the social order may be linked to deviance in a crucial manner.[13] Merton observed that the very same social structure that imposes goals on the person also restricts the opportunity to achieve them. In the absence of legitimate opportunity, that is, of making a success of oneself, a tendency is set up to circumvent the culturally prescribed norms of acquiring money and rising socioeconomically. This anomie may be widespread and affect large numbers of people.[14]

Merton's concept of anomie is logically related to the idea of differential association advanced, in 1939, by the criminologist Edwin Sutherland.[15] Sutherland holds that criminal behavior is learned in interaction with others who already possess not only the technical knowledge but also the moral beliefs and attitudes of the criminal. The latter process involves establishing more definitions favorable to violation of the law than unfavorable. In short, the deviant personality is formed in exactly the same manner as the conforming personality.

As an outgrowth of the theory of differential association consider the neutralization process conceptualized by Gresham Sykes and David Matza.[16] For instance, the juvenile delinquent creates a subculture that enables him to overcome, at least for the time being, the moral imperatives of the larger society. Five forms of rationalization are invoked in order to eclipse the anticriminal norms: (1) the denial of responsibility for one's own behavior; (2) the denial of injury to others; (3) the denial of the victim, that is, he deserves the injury done him; (4) condemnation of the accusers, con-

[12] Thorsten Sellin, *Culture Conflict and Crime* (New York: Social Science Research Council, 1938).

[13] Robert K. Merton, "Social Structure and Anomie," *American Sociological Review,* 3 (October 1938), pp. 672–82.

[14] Ibid.

[15] Updated in Edwin H. Sutherland and Donald Cressey, *Criminology* (Philadelphia, Pa.: J. B. Lippincott, 1970), 8th ed., pp. 75–77.

[16] Gresham M. Sykes and David Matza, "Techniques of Neutralization: A Theory of Delinquency," *American Sociological Review,* 22 (December 1957), pp. 664–70.

cealing the criminal act in the imputation of criminality to the condemners and judges; and (5) appeal to higher loyalties, usually the interests of some component of the larger society, say, the family, which takes precedence over conformist demands.

The components of the social conception of deviance have relevancy to urban life as fertile soil for crime. Heterogeneity, individualism, differential interaction, and rapid sociocultural change all foster deviance in various forms in the urban community.

CRIME IN THE CITY

Certain characteristics of deviance in the urban setting are the subject of unusual interest with regard to both social theory and public policy. They include: (1) the ecological patterning of crime in the city; (2) organized crime; (3) institutionalized evasions, notably white-collar offenses; (4) civil disorders; and (5) the present "crime wave" in metropolitan America. They exemplify various combinations of the general and specific factors underlying deviance in the urban milieu.

ECOLOGICAL PATTERNING

As a source of deviance urbanism has received strong support from ecological research. This has revealed that when various types of unlawful behavior are treated according to their geographic distribution within a city, urban forces are responsible for the configurations that are disclosed by the mapping. In other words, the sociocultural traits of urbanism as a way of life, at least as conceived by the classical typologists, tend to be most pronounced in the very areas of the city where deviance rates are highest. Although authorities reject the hypothesis that environmental factors have a direct bearing on criminality, the existence of geographical patterns of deviance in urban communities is generally accepted.

Crime and Delinquency

Clifford Shaw and Henry McKay mapped the spatial distribution of delinquency in Chicago in two successive investigations covering the period 1900 to 1940. Their results showed an uneven distribution of known juvenile offenses. Not only was delinquency most common in the slums adjacent to the central business district, but the delinquency rate generally declined in proportion to the distance from the center.[17] The uneven distribution was

---

[17] Clifford R. Shaw and Henry D. McKay, *Delinquency Areas* (Chicago: University of Chicago Press, 1929) and their *Juvenile Delinquency and Urban Areas* (Chicago: University of Chicago Press, 1942).

taken to indicate the influence of general causal processes characteristic of urbanism. In the "natural areas" of misconduct, Shaw and McKay concluded, were concentrated the conditions, such as weak social controls and severe relative deprivation, which are capable of motivating unlawfulness.[18]

Suicide

Suicide also correlates with the ecology of the urban community. For example, in 1960 suicide occurred in Chicago at a rate of 9.4 per 100,000 population, but only at a rate of 7.8 in all of Cook County, including the city of Chicago itself.[19] Furthermore, the suicide rate tends to decline the further an area is from the city's core.[20]

Following Durkheim three generations ago, Andrew Henry and James Short reason that the city does not provide the individual with as much family and community control as the rural areas do, and hence, urbanism encourages self-destruction. In the skid-row districts of the big city, anonymity is especially intensified. There, "behavior is free from the need for conformity to the demands and expectations of others, because 'others' do not care."[21] Superficially relating to many people, the urban resident, especially in the disorganized central sectors of the city, is most apt to become personally disturbed and commit suicide.

Furthermore, as forms of aggression, suicide and homicide are generally reciprocals. That is, a high rate in one occurs together with a low rate in the other. Yet both suicide and homicide do go together to a great extent in those areas that exhibit the extremes of urbanism, namely, as Henry and Short express it, "the disorganized sectors of cities characterized by high residential mobility [and] anonymity."[22]

ORGANIZED CRIME

In an influential study 30 years ago on the hypothesis that urban mobility and differential association are causally related to property crimes, Clinard

---

[18] The spatial incidence of crime is systematically paralleled by other forms of disorganization some of which act as variables contributing to lawlessness itself. See Ernest R. Mowrer, *Family Disorganization* (Chicago: University of Chicago Press, 1939); Robert E. L. Faris and H. Warren Dunham, *Mental Disorders in Urban Areas* (Chicago: University of Chicago Press, 1939), republished in 1965; and H. Warren Dunham, "Anomie and Mental Disorder," in Marshall B. Clinard, ed., *Anomie and Deviant Behavior* (New York: Free Press, 1964).

[19] Ronald W. Maris, *Social Forces in Urban Suicide* (Homewood, Ill.: Dorsey Press, 1969), p. 71.

[20] Ibid., p. 138.

[21] Henry and Short, op. cit., p. 76.

[22] Ibid., p. 92.

called "definite organized criminal behavior the outstanding characteristic of offenders from more heavily urbanized areas."[23]

Gathering valid, systematic knowledge about organized crime encounters severe difficulties.[24] Speculation must often supplement meager information. Thus estimates of the total clearings of illegal gambling in the nation run as high as $30 billion annually. The gross heroin trade may amount to $350 million a year. The real estate holdings of one single criminal syndicate have been judged to come to $300 million. Labor unions, restaurants, drycleaning establishments, the trucking industry, and waterfront freight handling—all susceptible to strong-arm tactics—are known to be prey to racketeering, although the full extent can only be guessed at.

Two aspects of organized crime are most notable. They are, first, the professional criminal as a personality and as a participant in a subculture, and, second, the conduct of underworld business.

The Professional Criminal

The professional criminal may operate apart from any organization whatsoever. Yet probably more often than not, the professional criminal pursues his illegal career in cooperation with many other people.

The criminal of the professional type can be understood not only as engaged in securing a livelihood but also as expressing his deviant personality. Edwin Schur has observed that much of the attraction to the perpetrator himself of committing a crime "lies in the dynamics and hazards of the sociologically significant forms of activity themselves."[25] It may be added that the total professional criminal element need not be numerically large for its repeated and sustained activity to have serious consequences for the public at large.

Underworld Business

Typically, the professional thief operates within more or less of a network of underworld collaboration involving communication, recruitment, the marketing of illegal goods and services, and even of diplomacy vis-à-vis the legitimate economy and law-enforcement system. For example, the professional auto thief needs a garage or mechanic to change the serial number on the engine or repaint the vehicle he has stolen.

[23] Marshall B. Clinard, "The Process of Urbanization and Criminal Behavior: A Study of Culture Conflicts," *American Journal of Sociology*, 48 (September 1942), pp. 202–13.

[24] Consult President's Commission on Law Enforcement and Administration of Justice, *Task Force Report: Organized Crime* (Washington, D.C.: Government Printing Office, 1967).

[25] Edwin M. Schur, "Sociological Analysis of Confidence Swindling," *Journal of Criminal Law*, 48 (September–October 1957), pp. 296–304. See also Edwin H. Sutherland, *The Professional Thief* (Chicago: University of Chicago Press, 1937).

Wearing a paper bag mask to conceal his identity, a man described as a convicted bootlegger testifies at a special state inquiry into organized cigarette bootlegging to evade the payment of taxes.

According to Thomas Schelling, there are seven broad types of underworld business:[26]

1 Black markets call for the merchandizing of consumer goods and services contrary to law. Usually both parties to the transaction know they are behaving illegally, but they overcome their scruples because the exchange is profitable to them.

2 Racketeering, e.g., extortion, exists where tribute can be exacted or competition forcibly eliminated.

[26] Thomas C. Schelling in President's Commission on Law Enforcement and Administration of Justice, *Task Force Report*, op. cit., pp. 114–26.

3 Black-market monopoly, yet another kind of underworld business, results from the complete elimination of competitors in some line or another, such as prostitution, narcotics, gambling, or pornography, in a given territory.

4 A variant of black-market monopoly, the cartel, also rests on intimidation. However, the cartel uses coercion only to control not to eliminate competition. Collusive pricing and closed-shop labor practices in violation of the law are examples here.

5 Cheating is a broad category that does not differ much from simply dishonest business. Cheating may be part of organized crime, for instance, when an enterprise is operated fraudulently, returning a tax loss in order to conceal illicit profits made elsewhere.

6 Typically too, the underworld requires criminal services, among them legal counsel, accounting, medical care, and transportation. The purveyors of these services must necessarily be both legitimate and illicit at the same time.

7 Finally, organized crime commonly entails the corruption of government. Law-enforcement officials who can mold a political and legal climate favorable to the underworld, if only by not repealing statutes that make certain kinds of organized crime feasible in the first place, need to be helped into office or, if in office, to be bribed. Thus in "Wincanton," an eastern industrial city investigated recently by John Gardner, criminal activity has for decades now been inseparable from the community's political life.[27]

In general, then, the rackets operate in relation to the economy, also with respect to the legal system, and similarly in line with the sociocultural stresses that impinge on the lives of individuals. For one thing, organized crime recruits from among alienated youth who as delinquents have demonstrated their aptitude for illegal behavior. For another, syndicates serve as adjuncts of the legitimate banking institutions when they engage in usurious loan-shark lending among poor credit risks.

La Cosa Nostra

La Cosa Nostra (also known as the Mafia) is possibly the best illustration of the multiplex relationships between underworld business and the urban social structure. Two elements stand out here. One is the fact that organized illegal enterprise caters to covert public demand. The other concerns the importance of illicit activities as a channel of mobility for minorities who are discriminated against, in this case, Italian Americans.

The major underworld cartel in the United States at this writing, La Cosa

[27] John A. Gardner, *The Politics of Corruption: Organized Crime in an American City* (New York: Russell Sage Foundation, 1970).

Nostra was first identified in 1950–1951 by the Kefauver investigation of crime in interstate commerce. J. Edgar Hoover, then director of the F.B.I., described the syndicate as "the largest organization of the criminal underworld in this country, very closely organized and strictly disciplined." La Cosa Nostra, he said, engaged in diverse activities including massive participation in the nation's multibillion dollar gambling industry.

Operating as a pyramid of 24 syndicated groups ("families," so to speak) in cities across the United States, La Cosa Nostra was called by Hoover "a criminal fraternity whose membership is Italian either by birth or national origin, and it has been found to control major racket activities in many of our larger metropolitan areas, often working in concert with criminals representing other ethnic backgrounds." Thus Blacks and Puerto Ricans may be meshed in with the Mafia in our metropolitan ghetto rackets. The F.B.I. head attributed ironlike discipline to La Cosa Nostra which, he declared, adheres to "its own body of 'law' and 'justice' and, in so doing, thwarts and usurps the authority of legally constituted judicial bodies."[28] Some 5000 members are said to comprise the core groups of the Cosa Nostra, who are united by a code of loyalty and mutual aid, submission to the absolute authority of their superiors, and the distribution of material rewards.

In an often cited comment on the Kefauver committee findings, however, Daniel Bell has cautioned that solid evidence for the functioning of the Cosa Nostra syndicate has turned out to be scanty.[29] The prominence of some Italian Americans in politics and business after an earlier period of illegal behavior and the fact that some Italians are convicted mobsters who have continued to enjoy social status in their communities, Bell has said, should not be exaggerated.

INSTITUTIONALIZED EVASIONS

The cumbersome phrase "institutionalized evasions" refers to activities which, though formally contravening the law, are informally condoned. White-collar crime and one of its manifestations, administered prices, are two signal instances.

White-Collar Crime

White-collar crime is conspicuously akin to urbanization. It was originally defined by Edwin H. Sutherland as transgressions of the criminal law com-

---

[28] President's Commission on Law Enforcement and Administration of Justice, *Task Force Report,* op. cit., pp. 6–7.

[29] Daniel Bell, "Crime as an American Way of Life," *Antioch Review,* 13 (Summer 1953), 131–54; also John F. Galliher and James A. Cain, "Citation Support for the Mafia Myth in Criminology Textbooks," *American Sociologist,* 9 (May 1974), pp. 68–74.

mitted during the course of business, usually through the violation of trust.[30] White-collar crime is not only rooted in business. It also is nourished by the urban milieu generally. For example, white-collar crime tends to be countered administratively, by means of consent decrees (agreements to end violations) and cease-and-desist injunctions rather than by punitive sanctions. Sutherland, who studied proceedings against America's top 70 corporations, gives three reasons for this: (1) the businessman is usually respected; (2) as a social instrument, punitive law has been losing ground generally; and (3) the public experiences little moral resentment toward this type of crime, hence its collective opinion is not well organized to combat it.

Administered Prices

One type of white-collar crime is the systematic setting of the prices of goods and services in restraint of trade. Consider as a major case the conspiracy to administer prices in the $2 billion annual electrical-equipment industry exposed in 1961 after almost a decade of existence. Thirty-seven business executives were given prison sentences (23 of them suspended) for violating the Sherman Antitrust Act, and fines totaling $2 million were assessed. Defendants included the aristocracy of American business life: high executives of General Electric, the Carrier Corporation, Allis-Chalmers, Ingersoll-Rand, McGraw-Edison, and the Westinghouse Electric Corporation.[31]

Most of the confessed conspirators later returned to their previous positions. The companies said afterward that they were taking more effective precautions to assure compliance with antitrust law. Yet the conditions favoring "corporate socialism" or "pronounced bureaucracy," as others call it, that motivated the cartels may very well still persist.[32] The circumstances which led to the cartels in the first place are still present, and the industry executives are still under strong pressure to produce bigger gross sales and a wider margin of profit on them. The fact that owing to technical standardization the electrical-equipment industry emphasizes price and not higher quality or improved design creates difficulty for those involved in marketing.

[30] See Edwin H. Sutherland, "White Collar Criminality," *American Sociological Review,* 5 (February 1940), pp. 1–12, and also his *White Collar Crime* (New York: Holt, Rinehart, and Winston, 1961).

[31] See Richard Austin Smith, "The Incredible Electrical Conspiracy," *Fortune* (April 1961), pp. 132–80, and (May 1961), pp. 161–224.

[32] Another review of the case in Gilbert Geis, "White Collar Crime: The Heavy Electrical Equipment Antitrust Cases of 1961," in Marshall B. Clinard and Richard Quinney, eds., *Criminal Behavior Systems: A Typology* (New York: Holt, Rinehart, and Winston, 1967).

Taking the long view that throughout history cities have been "death traps," Richard Meier has recently called violent civil disorders the last remaining mortal threat to urbanism as a way of life.[33] Meier's contention about the earlier tensions of urban life centers on the dolorous health conditions that marked the world's population centers prior to the nineteenth century. Today, according to Meier, expectations are higher and unprecedented numbers of poorly acculturized settlers have converged on cities. Meier is of the opinion that the "problems of disorderly behavior experienced in American cities are still trivial as compared to those yet to come elsewhere in the world." If they can be solved, he concludes, they will constitute the last great plague of urban man.

Earlier Episodes

During the nineteenth century, mass urban violence stemmed chiefly from ethnic differences exacerbated by economic competition. European Catholics and Jewish immigrants encountered opposition in our eastern cities, and Orientals in the west. The 1863 anticonscription riots in New York City had numerous Irish participants, some of whom vented their rage on free blacks in their midst. Also, chronic discord breaking out in overt violence beginning in the 1880s attended the process of unionization in the United States. Strikes especially brought on physical attacks and the loss of life.

The Race Riots of the 1960s

The 1960s saw hundreds of widespread disorders take place in America's cities. In 1963, large-scale mob action occurred in Birmingham, Savannah, Chicago, and Philadelphia. The Watts area of Los Angeles erupted in the spring of 1965, with 4000 persons arrested and $35 million in property damage. Other major disorders followed in rapid succession: 43 riots in 1966 and perhaps as many as 217 disorders, depending on the definition of the term, during the first nine months of 1967. Eight of the latter, including Newark and Detroit, were considered "major" by the National Advisory Commission on Civil Disorders (commonly referred to as the Kerner commission after its chairman, Otto Kerner, then Governor of Illinois).[34]

---

[33] "The Last Urban Epidemic," in Louis H. Masotti and Don R. Bowen, eds., *Riots and Rebellion: Civil Violence in the Urban Community* (Beverly Hills, Calif.: Sage, 1968), pp. 409–18.

[34] See *Report of the National Advisory Commission on Civil Disorders* (New York: Bantam Books, 1968). Also consult Ralph W. Conants, "Rioting, Insurrection, and Civil Disobedience," *American Scholar*, 37 (Summer 1968), pp. 420–33.

National Guardsmen patrolling Newark, New Jersey, following the rioting and looting there in July 1967.

The riots that occurred in American cities in the 1960s were essentially racial but not interracial. That is, violence was committed largely by blacks but almost wholly against property and authority symbols rather than persons. Typically, said the commission, the disorders originated in a chain of "discrimination, prejudice, disadvantaged conditions, intense and pervasive grievances, a series of tension-heightening incidents, all culminating in the eruption of disorder at the hands of youthful, political activists."[35] The commission ascribed the disturbances to deep dissatisfaction with the socioeconomic system as it applied to blacks. Hence the riots were not to be seen as an extension of individual and organized crime but as a violent challenge to the social institutions of American society. The commission termed an "explosive mixture" the "mass tangle of issues and circumstances—social, economic, political, and psychological—which arise out of the historical pattern of Negro-white relations in America."[36]

The Kerner commission inquiry pictured the black American as sharing the general aspirations of American culture: material success and acceptance as a person. But three conditions had arisen that were both threatening the continued pursuit of these goals by blacks, and leading to mass vio-

[35] *Report of the National Advisory Commission on Civil Disorders,* op. cit., pp. 73–74.
[36] Ibid., p. 91.

lence. First, the heightened expectations aroused by the civil rights movement of the 1950s were not being fulfilled. Cynicism and hostility had replaced hope. Second, aggression directed against peaceful demonstrations to achieve reform had legitimized violent protest. Third, the black's sense of powerlessness to alter conditions had alienated him and engendered the counter ideology of Black Power. Accordingly, the mood of many urban blacks had changed to the acceptance of arson, vandalism, and armed conflict as the only means of successfully ameliorating racial injustice, even if this meant nihilistic separatism.

The tensions, grievances, and demands varied, said the commission, from one city to the next. In general though they came down to "white racism." This the commission proceeded to spell out as (1) discrimination and segregation in employment, education, and housing; (2) the concentration of blacks in the deteriorating inner city with an exodus of whites to the suburbs; and (3) dense ghettos breeding dependency, despair, or resentment against society as a whole and white society in particular.[37] Also, the American city needed to be seen in the perspective of historical urbanization to understand why, unlike the European immigrants before him, the black was unable to escape from poverty and the ghetto now. One reason appeared to be America's mature economy, which at this stage of development no longer needed large numbers of unskilled workers. Second, racial discrimination was more intense than the opposition which Americans had shown European newcomers earlier. In fact, the immigration of unskilled European labor to the United States had been preferred over the recruitment into industry of blacks from the South.

Other factors further handicapped the newly urbanized black in the United States. The big-city political machines once administered a spoils system from which European immigrants had benefited. In the present era of reform politics, that was no longer the case. Furthermore, the black lacked the extended family that had been both an incentive and a source of support for the "old world" immigrant. Again, labor unions that had gained economic concessions for the urban in-migrants a generation ago were now being kept closed to blacks. In short, the commission declared, "what the American economy of the late nineteenth and early twentieth century was able to do to help the European immigrants escape from poverty is now largely impossible."[38]

[37] For an analysis that discounts structural features in preference for the idea of the greater the number of disaffected, frustrated blacks possessed of racial solidarity and attuned to the media as responsible for disorder, see Seymour Spilerman, "The Causes of Racial Disturbances: A Comparison of Alternative Explantions," *American Sociological Review,* 35 (August 1970), pp. 627–49.

[38] *Report of the National Advisory Commission on Civil Disorders,* op. cit., p. 145. For perspective on the Commission itself, consult Michael Lipsky and David J. Olson, "Riot Commission Politics," *Trans-Action,* 6 (July–August 1969), pp. 8–21.

In America's urban areas, a steep increase in crime has taken place in recent years. In common parlance this is usually referred to as a "crime wave"
though many object to the terminology. From 1967 to 1972, the rate of violent
crime in the United States rose 59 percent, and that of property crime, 45
percent.[39] During this period, the number of crimes proportional to population remained highest in our metropolitan centers. In fact, the 26 core cities
of more than 500,000 in size in the United States have about 18 percent of
the nation's population. Yet they account for upwards of half of all crimes of
violence and about one-third of the total number of reported property crimes
in the entire country.[40]

Not only has the commission of crimes increased, but far more crime
remains unreported. Probably three times more burglaries, and twice as
many assaults, serious larcenies, and robberies occur as are made known to
the authorities. Probably too, three-fourths of all neighborhood commercial
establishments refrain from notifying the police of offenses committed by
their employees. Of 554 criminal complaints made to the police in Boston,
Chicago, and Washington, D.C., when no suspect was present, the preference of the complainant—for informal handling, say, instead of a formal
follow-up—proved to be decisive regarding the official recognition of
crimes.[41] This, it was concluded, "gives crime rates a peculiarly democratic
character," systematically underrating much crime.

Moreover, even if some authorities believe the increase in reported
crimes to some degree at least denotes more efficient administration in
recording illegal acts,[42] the fear of crime definitely appears to be growing
among the American public. According to one national survey, more than a
third of all Americans keep guns in their homes for defense. In early 1973,
the Gallup poll revealed that only 10 percent of the people questioned in the
nationwide sample said that there was less crime in their neighborhoods
than there had been a year earlier.

Perhaps the most searching analysis of the contemporary crime wave in
America's urban centers was made by the president's commission, though it
was quite inconclusive.[43] Yet it called attention to a number of factors, nota-

[39] Federal Bureau of Investigation, *Uniform Crime Reports for the United States* (Washington,
D.C.: Government Printing Office, 1972), p. 2.

[40] President's Commission on Law Enforcement and Administration of Justice, *Crime and Its Impact* (Washington, D.C.: Government Printing Office, 1967), p. 28.

[41] Donald J. Black, "Production of Crime Rates," *American Sociological Review*, 35 (August
1970), pp. 735–48.

[42] See Albert J. Reiss, Jr., "Assessing the Current Crime Wave," in Barbara N. McLennan, ed.,
Crime in Urban Society (New York: Dunellen, 1970), pp. 23–42. He also considers the likelihood
that official figures give the appearance of a smaller volume of crime than is the case.

[43] President's Commission on Law Enforcement and Administration of Justice, op. cit., p. 26.

EXHIBIT 17-1 Crime Clocks, U.S.: 1975

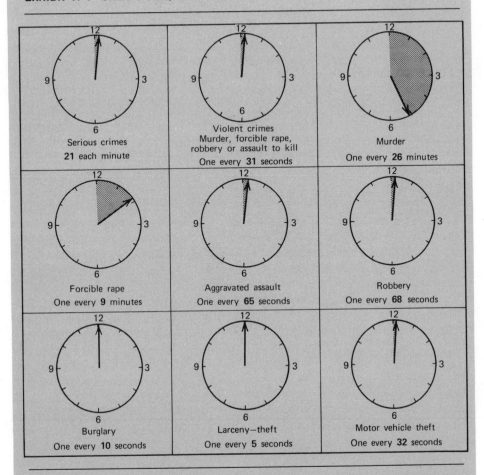

Serious crimes
21 each minute

Violent crimes
Murder, forcible rape,
robbery or assault to kill
One every **31** seconds

Murder
One every **26** minutes

Forcible rape
One every **9** minutes

Aggravated assault
One every **65** seconds

Robbery
One every **68** seconds

Burglary
One every **10** seconds

Larceny—theft
One every **5** seconds

Motor vehicle theft
One every **32** seconds

Crime clocks should be viewed with care. Being the most aggregate representation of uniform crime reports data, they are designed to convey the annual reported crime experience by showing the relative frequency of occurrence of reported offenses. This mode of display should not be taken to imply a regularity in the commission of serious crimes. Rather, it represents the annual ratio of reported crime to fixed time intervals.

Source: Federal Bureau of Investigation, *Law Enforcement Bulletin* (Washington, D.C.: Government Printing Office, December, 1976), p. 10.

bly age, race, and the behavior of the general public. These do not act as causes directly related to the current upswing in unlawfulness, but need to be viewed as expressions of individualization, cultural heterogeneity, differential association, and rapid urbanization.

Youth as a Factor

Youth, especially boys, are disproportionately represented in criminal arrest statistics. For instance, as of 1966 the age group 15 to 17 made up only 5.4 percent of the American population, but it accounted for 2.5 times the number of arrests that might have been expected on the basis of numbers alone.

It has been hypothesized that in industrial-urban societies, relative affluence (an excess of money over what is needed for necessities) seems to be closely tied to delinquency, although it is certainly not at the root of it.[44] According to such reasoning, youthful crime supplements limited resources in the face of rising expectations. Delinquents cluster in segregated peer groups, sometimes structured as gangs rigidly subservient to a delinquent subculture. The less organized engage in outright misdemeanors as a leisure-time activity that shades off into "publicly offensive behavior," including blatant self-assertion and thrill-seeking adventurism.[45]

The actual criminality of youth is of course a significant concern. A changing age composition, such as the United States has been experiencing since 1961 with almost a million *more* youths reaching the age of maximum criminal risk each year, stands as a notable contributing factor to the sharp inflection in the nation's current crime rate.

Racial Considerations

Summarizing much research on crime in urban areas, Clinard has generalized that "even if discrimination in arrests and in the judicial process is allowed for," crime, violence, and arrests are much more prevalent among urban blacks than it is among either rural blacks, the white population, or the general population of the United States.[46] Clinard attributes this unusual incidence of crime and delinquency among urban blacks in America to "a depressing tangle of problems," among them: poverty; broken families; infant mortality; illness; illegitimacy; unemployment; lower education levels; preju-

---

[44] Ruth S. Cavan and Judson T. Cavan, *Delinquency and Crime* (Philadelphia, Pa.: J. B. Lippincott, 1968), p. 232.

[45] From *Juvenile Delinquency: A Problem for the Modern World* (New York: UNESCO, 1964), p. 24.

[46] Marshall B. Clinard, *Sociology of Deviant Behavior,* op. cit., p. 628. See also Thomas F. Pettigrew, *A Profile of the Negro American* (New York: D. Van Nostrand, 1964), p. 21.

dice; discrimination; and fewer organized social controls in the ghetto community.

Noting that low-income urban populations, whether black or white, have a disproportionate incidence of crime, the Kerner Commission observed that crime rates were significantly greater in black than white neighborhoods of economic comparability.[47] It interpreted this as reflecting a "high degree of social disorganization in Negro areas." Most crimes there, the commission remarked, are committed by a small minority of the residents. The greatest part of these acts come to be directed against the residents themselves. For example, in one six-month period, 85 percent of the crimes committed in Chicago by blacks had black victims.

The Behavior of the Public

The conduct of the public may also be shown to contribute to increasing crime in the United States. Two elements are primarily involved.[48]

On the one hand, the public tends to believe crime is the product only of certain deviant groups, and people generally remain oblivious of their own disrespect for the law. For example, the public undermines the administration of justice by challenging court decisions and by weakening the police through noncooperation. It thereby boosts the volume of crime.

On the other hand, the fear of crime acts as a multiplier of crime. Public anxiety about violence in urban areas has mounted rapidly in recent years. In the high crime neighborhoods of two large cities in the United States, it was learned that due to their fear of crime, 43 percent of the respondents said they stay off the streets at night; 35 percent do not talk to strangers any more; 21 percent use cars at night; and 20 percent want to move away.[49] Reducing both pedestrian and vehicular traffic encourages street crimes still further.

COPING WITH CRIME IN URBAN AMERICA

Given the serious nature of crime in the United States today, much thought has been devoted to its control, and two general lines of reasoning have emerged: the ameliorative and repressive philosophies, respectively.

The ameliorative position asserts that as the ranks of the middle class grow, fewer people will commit crimes. Also, more persons will become intolerant of crime, and hence they will report offenses more faithfully. Thus the criminal acts that do occur will be treated more effectively, with the overall

---

[47] *Report of the National Advisory Commission on Civil Disorders,* op. cit., pp. 133–34.

[48] Knudten, op. cit., p. 11.

[49] *President's Commission on Law Enforcement and Administration of Justice,* op. cit., p. v.

result being a still lower level of urban criminality. In order to bring about an expansion of the middle class, it is therefore necessary to upgrade the disadvantaged socioeconomically.

Contrarily, the repressive contention regards urban society as inherently prone to criminal behavior, owing to the decline of familism and informal community controls, greater secularization, and a more egoistic moral code that sanctions personal aggrandizement and unruly behavior in general. Consequently, urban society may at best be expected in the normal course of things to produce an affluent population lacking in personal restraint and civic consciousness. As a result, punitive methods must be employed to redress offenses, and efficient organization and technology used to prevent misconduct in the first place.

THREE STRATEGIES

Regarding law enforcement, corrections, and justice, these two opposing modes of thought have given rise to three policies, or strategies as they are often referred to: punitive; therapeutic; and preventive.[50]

The Punitive Approach

The punitive method regards the offender not only as justifying punishment morally, but as being susceptible to deterrent measures. Punishment is thus to be exercised to incapacitate the criminal for the present and to keep him from engaging in any further criminal acts in the future. The punitive method has lost ground to amelioration, however. Consider that in the United States civil executions which stood at 88 in 1952, 65 in 1957, and 47 in 1962, totaled only 10 in the period 1965–1969.[51] There has been only one to 1977, and the courts have wrestled with the question of abolishing capital punishment entirely. On the other hand, as the Commission on the Cities in the 70s recently noted, the police forces of our municipalities have been investing in special heavy equipment with which to combat violence.[52] This has led some observers to envisage the development of a system of quasimilitary control and repression aimed especially at the inner city. That enclave might, conceivably, even be walled off with traffic monitored at guarded checkpoints.

[50] Elmer H. Johnson, *Crime, Correction, and Society* (Homewood, Ill.: Dorsey Press, 1968), revised ed., pp. 281–358.

[51] Herbert A. Bloch and Gilbert Geis, *Man, Crime, and Society* (New York: Random House, 1970), 2nd ed., p. 444.

[52] Commission on the Cities in the 70s, *The State of the Cities* (New York: Praeger, 1972).

The Therapeutic Solution

The second position for dealing with deviance, the therapeutic response, deems the offender to be malfunctioning and in need of psychological or sociological treatment.

The President's Commission on Law Enforcement and the Administration of Justice found 20 percent of the 21,000 people employed in corrections in the United States having rehabilitation as their primary object. The commission noted too that there were acute shortages in probation and parole officers, educators, social workers, psychologists, and psychiatrists in the field of corrections. This, it decided, made the therapeutic program of the nation as a whole of dubious value, despite the "combination of objective evidence and informed opinion" that convincingly argues for a change in direction against punitive and mere custodial care for violators.[53]

Prevention

Prevention, the third principle of addressing deviance, centers on affecting the interaction of social and individual conditions to forestall offensive behavior. The preventive approach calls for the modification of the sociocultural environment, the strengthening of the social structure, and, accordingly, the development of conforming personalities. Education and recreation can play a part in this respect, as can also a wide range of other practices like vocational placement and community organization.

A COMPOSITE PROGRAM

A blend of punishment, therapy, and prevention theories animated the recent prescriptions of the president's commission for improving law enforcement, the judicial process, and corrections in America's population centers. These are broader than the crime prevention program started by the National Advisory Commission on Criminal Justice Standards and Goals in 1973, and therefore deserve more detailed attention.[54] In fact, the recommendations of the president's commission are noteworthy for their range, since they touch on a broad variety of possible innovations that experience and research appear to favor, at least to many minds.

[53] *The Challenge of Crime in a Free Society* (Washington, D.C.: Government Printing Office, 1967), pp. 159–85.

[54] See *Community Crime Prevention* (Washington, D.C.: Advisory Commission on Criminal Justice Standards and Goals, 1973); also *A National Strategy to Reduce Crime* (Washington, D.C.: Advisory Commission on Criminal Justice Standards and Goals, 1973).

Law Enforcement

Regarding law enforcement, the commission concluded that both police organization and practice could be improved in our large cities. Specialized police roles, some of them performed by paraprofessionals, could prove beneficial. Modern communications, such as the computerized cross-reference handling of offenders, might also help. The proper processing of citizen grievances could improve the efficiency of the police too. In areas with such populations, police could recruit more members from minority groups. Also, police should participate more in community relations and planning. And, finally, in the interests of balancing law enforcement against fairness to the individual, some further restrictions might be placed on the police, though it was recognized that many legal questions, some of perplexing dimensions, remain to be resolved.

The Criminal Courts

Concerning the courts, the commission held it essential for them to come abreast of modern social change. Rapid urbanization, it would appear, has rendered the country's judicial organization archaic if not obsolete. Nor is this all, for in the urban setting the entire judicial process loses much of the definition that it has in the more socioculturally uniform rural community. The commission noted:

> The populations of many cities are made up of groups that have little understanding of each other's ways. The law and court procedures are not understood by, and seem threatening to, many defendants, and many defendants are not understood by, and seem threatening to, the court and its officers. Even such simple matters as dress, speech, and manners can be misinterpreted. A prosecutor or judge with a middle-class background and attitude, confronted with a poor, uneducated defendant, may often have no way of judging how the defendant fits into his own society or culture.[55]

To help achieve the modernization of the judicial process, the commission offered dozens of proposals extending to substantive law, court administration, and proceedings.[56] A sampling of the proposals must suffice. Reasonable standards governing media coverage of court proceedings should be instituted; postconviction remedies for judicial wrongs provided; probation services expanded; and judicial personnel afforded continuing

[55] President's Commission on Law Enforcement and Administration of Justice, *Task Force Report: The Police* (Washington, D.C.: Government Printing Office, 1967), p. 127.

[56] For more details see the President's Commission on Law Enforcement and Administration of Justice, *Task Force Report: The Courts* (Washington, D.C.: Government Printing Office, 1967).

education. It was also urged that the criminal courts dispense with the less threatening offenses that now clog their dockets, like vagrancy and gambling.

Corrections

The Commission's Task Force on Corrections formulated a six point program:[57]

> *First,* it called for reintegration of the offender into the local community, because, "the general underlying premise for the new directions in corrections is that crime and delinquency are symptoms of failures and disorganization of the community as well as of individual offenders."
>
> *Second,* there must be increased use of community treatment, probation and parole, youth services, and employment counseling.
>
> *Third* where institutionalization is resorted to, the distinction between jail and reformatory versus normal life must be blurred by partial release schemes and prerelease centers.
>
> *Fourth,* even custodial care needs the benefits of a "collaborative regime," uniting staff and inmates in joint administration.
>
> *Fifth,* the mass handling of convicts should give way to differential corrections, for example, putting inhibited youngsters in forestry camps and the emotionally disturbed under training-school assignments.
>
> *Sixth*—and paradoxically too—the validity of the criminal law itself was questioned, the task force declaring that "changes in correctional philosophy . . . encourage . . . concern for the rights of offenders."[58]

In its analysis of the administration of criminal justice as a whole, the commission concluded that reform would be "slow and hard and costly," but that it would benefit from local initiative.[59]

RECENT FEDERAL ACTION

Understandably, in view of the foregoing recommendations, the 1968 Federal Omnibus Control bill creating the Law Enforcement Assistance Adminis-

---

[57] President's Commission on Law Enforcement and Administration of Justice, *Task Force Report: Corrections* (Washington, D.C.: Government Printing Office, 1967), pp. 7–13.

[58] Ibid., p. 12.

[59] See also President's Committee on Delinquency and Youth Crime, *Counter-Attack on Delinquency* (Washington, D.C.: Government Printing Office, 1965), and Edwin Powers and Helen Witmer, *An Experiment in the Prevention of Delinquency* (New York: Columbia University Press, 1951).

tration (LEAA) followed a multiple course in coping with crime in the United States. Through annual block grants of as much as $900 million, LEAA funded a broad variety of projects, many of them providing materiel for local police departments. Critics of LEAA have charged the program with "pork barrel" politics that have not alleviated crime and may have actually intensified repression. Defenders, however, argue that despite no ascertainable reduction in the volume of crime, LEAA has produced a differentiated program whose impact remains to be determined over a rather long period of time and should not be judged prematurely.

CONCLUSION

Deviance is associated with urbanization and urbanism, though in a complicated, indirect, and not wholly understood manner. The principal features of urban life that are believed to be causally related to deviance include individualism, culture conflict, permissive association, mobility and social change, affluence and the resulting opportunity for offensive behavior, and possibly increased awareness of the volume of illicit conduct in an urban as compared with a nonurban population. More specific aspects of deviance in the urban community are its ecological patterning, underworld organization, institutionalized evasions, and civil disorders. Of unusual importance at present in the United States is the increased incidence of crime and delinquency in our metropolitan areas.

All of these dimensions of crime in America have contributed to renewed interest in improving law enforcement, the courts, and corrections. The strategies of punishment, therapy, and prevention have their supporters and detractors among authorities and members of the public alike.

Owing to unique cultural, demographic, and ethnic factors, the recent American experience with urban deviance and ways of combatting it may not agree entirely with that of other urban nations. Yet both the deviant-inducing and averting tendencies of urbanization have made themselves quite clear in the cities of the United States.

FOR FURTHER READING

Marshall B. Clinard, *Sociology of Deviant Behavior* (New York: Holt, Rinehart, and Winston, 1968). Chs. 3–5 deal specifically with urbanization.

Marshall B. Clinard and Daniel J. Abbott, *Crime in Developing Countries* (New York: Wiley, 1973). Contrasts the already developed nations with the newly emerging ones as to the incidence of crime and the conditions that foster it.

Federal Bureau of Investigation, *Uniform Crime Reports: Crime in the United States* (Washington, D.C.: Government Printing Office, annually). Provides nationwide coverage of crime based on statistics supplied by local law enforcement agencies.

Daniel Glaser, ed., *Crime in the City* (New York: Harper & Row, 1970). On metropolitan lawlessness, 23 articles attempt a cohesive presentation of urban crime and delinquency.

Daniel Glaser, ed., *Handbood of Criminology* (Chicago: Rand McNally, 1974). Comprehensive treatment of the whole field; useful for reference.

Elmer H. Johnson, *Social Problems of Urban Man* (Homewood, Ill.: Dorsey Press, 1973). Chs. 16–17 are devoted to crime in the urban milieu.

Edwin M. Schur, *Our Criminal Society* (Englewood Cliffs, N.J.: Prentice-Hall, 1969).Emphasizes the gradual shift of criminology from individual-centered studies to the sociolegal sources of crime.

Harwin L. Voss and David M. Peterson, ed., *Ecology, Crime, and Delinquency* (New York: Appleton-Century-Crofts, 1971). Brings out the disproportionate concentration of deviance in certain areas of the city.

CHAPTER 18

URBAN MINORITIES AND POVERTY

As the physical and cultural heritage possessed in common by the members of a minority group, ethnicity has been frequently referred to here due to its bearing on urban life. We have seen repeatedly that ethnic differences are perpetuated in the city despite the modifying influence of urbanism to the contrary.

In this chapter, we wish to treat America's urban life primarily from the standpoint of current concerns about (1) reducing poverty stemming from systematic discrimination against minorities, and (2) achieving greater equality with respect to the application of civil rights to minorities. These two questions are among the most acrimonious issues facing the nation at present. Harvard sociologist Lee Rainwater is not alone in speaking of this with apocalyptic emphasis. "In the long run," he has declared, "the destructiveness of American poverty (and its twin, racial prejudice and exploitation of the Negro and other minority groups) will eventually place it high on the national agenda, not only on humanitarian grounds, but also because without a solution to these problems it seems likely that the American city as we know it today will itself be destroyed."[1]

First, however, a word about the surprising persistence of ethnicity in our urban society in spite of the supposed presence of forces in opposition to it.

THE ETHNIC FACTOR IN URBAN LIFE

In Chapter 5, where rural and urban were presented as contrasting types of human settlement and as differing forms of social organization and modal personality, urban life was shown to be typologically alien to ethnicity. We saw one social theorist after another declare urbanism to be synonymous with self-interest rather than community interests; with specific and not diffuse social responsibilities; and with rational, contractual relationships as distinct from sentimental and traditional ones. Though differing in the terms they employed, Tönnies, Durkheim, Redfield, Simmel, Wirth, and others agreed on the proposition that urban people evidence individualism, segmentalism, atomism, and universalism. In other words, according to typological analysis, urban existence represents the antithesis of the communal, unified, homogeneous, and primary kind of life present in ethnically grounded communities.

It is true that the typological conception of urbanism did not go unchallenged in Chapter 5. Both logically and factually the typological interpretation was shown to have serious shortcomings. Logically, the urban concept lacks preciseness and other qualities as well. Empirically, primary associations, kinship, neighboring, tradition, and social solidarities expressive of a consciousness of kind all appear in urban environments such as New York, San Francisco, Detroit, and Chicago. In the studies of Gans, Janowitz, Whyte, and Selley, Sim, and Loosley, suburbanism in America reveals a quasiprimary mode of association, interpersonal attachments, indigenousness, localism, and even, in Riesman's mind, a tribal-like conformity in the pursuit of generalized social goals.

In cities outside the United States, especially those in developing regions, the atomistic hypothesis demonstrates even greater weaknesses. Preindustrial patterns survive today in the urban settlements of Asia, Africa, Latin America, and the Middle East. Frequently the rabbit-warren "old towns," cut up into ethnic wards, continue to exist alongside the newly built

[1] Lee Rainwater, "Poverty in the United States," in Daniel P. Moynihan, ed., *Toward a National Urban Policy* (New York: Basic Books, 1970), p. 205.

sections devoted to the modernization of the economy and the introduction of bureaucratic individualism. Village enclaves spring up in these cities as transplanted countrymen pursue their local ways in the otherwise up-to-date national capitals or primate centers. Value orientations incommensurate with the Western urban experience, which underlies the typological tradition in sociology, are widely in evidence in the developing and urbanizing nations at present. In fact, these cultural configurations may even produce an urban social order that, we said in Chapter 5, "the typological tradition has not prepared us to anticipate."[2] Central to the emergent urban culture in Asia and other contemporary cities is a substantial emphasis on ethnicity in the form of tribal loyalties and sectarian solidarities.

America's national experience with urbanization can be seen as opposed to ethnic differentiation. Witness the following phenomena all of them combatting traditional ethnic expression and all of them focusing on our urban communities: free public education; the increasing democratization of our political institutions; secularism; the achievement ethic; and a high level of geographic mobility, much of it cityward. Ideologically, the people of the United States have opposed continued ethnic identification through the doctrine of the "melting pot" whereby immigrants coming to our shores have been expected, through the schooling, citizenship, and economic competition available to them here, to acculturate into American society as individuals devoid of specific ties to their own countrymen. Nonetheless, the ethnic factor remains very prominent in our urban centers.

THE PERSISTENCE OF ETHNICITY

In *Beyond the Melting Pot,* published early in the 1960s, Glazer and Moynihan discovered unmistakable signs of deep ethnicity among New York City's major nationality groups.[3] Each of New York's Italian, Jewish, and Irish minorities not only had a consciousness of being set apart from one another by differences in ancestry and history, but had developed separate social structures based on separated neighborhoods, church bodies, and voluntary associations to secure themselves economically and to gain political influence for themselves. In each case, the ethnic groups took an interest in foreign affairs, in good measure, according to the welfare of the national homelands with which they identified. New York's large Puerto Rican and black minorities possessed strong feelings about themselves also, the latter in particular a conviction of being unjustly underprivileged. In brief, *Beyond the Melting Pot* refuted the ideology of Americans as a homogeneous blend—and in the nation's largest and presumably most modern metropolis no less!

[2] Supra, p. 110.

[3] Nathan Glazer and Daniel Patrick Moynihan, *Beyond the Melting Pot* (Cambridge, Mass.: M.I.T. Press, 1963).

EXHIBIT 18-1 Population in Metropolitan Areas by Race, United States: 1900–1970

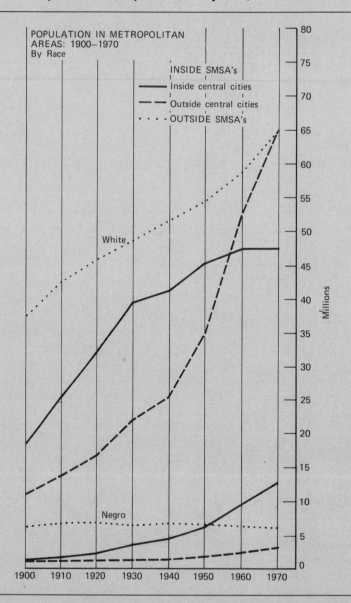

POPULATION IN METROPOLITAN
AREAS: 1900–1970
By Race

INSIDE SMSA's
——— Inside central cities
– – – Outside central cities
· · · · OUTSIDE SMSA's

White

Negro

Millions

Seventy years of change are shown here in the distribution of population by race in the Standard Metropolitan Statistical Areas of the United States. In that time the proportion of white population in SMSA districts outside the central cities rose from about 13 to 65 percent, while Negro population inside the central cities increased from approximately 3 percent to 13 percent.

Source: Executive Office of the President, Office of Management and Budget, *Social Indicators, 1973* (Washington, D.C.: Government Printing Office, 1973), p. 243.

If the discovery of ethnic communities among third and subsequent generation immigrants bore witness to the persistence of ethnicity in our urban areas, the extent of racial segregation then and now underscores it unquestionably. In 1973, blacks had settled in metropolitan areas to a greater degree than whites. In that year, 76 percent of the nation's 23 million black citizens were residents of SMSAs as compared to only 67 percent of the 180 million whites.[4] The residential segregation of the two races at that time could easily be read from the fact that while six out of every ten blacks in metropolitan areas lived inside the central cities, only one-fourth of the white SMSA population did. By contrast, 41 percent of the SMSA whites inhabited suburbia but only 16 percent of the blacks. It should be noted that owing to the relatively small proportion of blacks in the total American population—approximately 11 percent—only a few of the SMSAs had very large black concentrations, and these for the most part were in the east and north. Still, where black Americans did inhabit metropolitan areas, their residential cleavage from whites stood out with stark clarity. Nor should this fact obscure two other important observations: one, that because of the presence of disadvantaged nonwhites on the periphery, southern cities failed to show the segregation pattern of those in the east, north, and west;[5] and, two, that the socioeconomic improvement of black Americans in the 1960s and 1970s was probably producing novel migration trends that would eventually modify the racial separation now present in urban America.

The reason behind the segregation of the races were analogous to those responsible for the cleavages among the country's urban ethnics. These were cultural on the one hand and economic as well as political on the other. The European nationalities in the United States had long sought to express their native ways, speak their own languages, and follow their particular religious persuasions. American institutions, such as the separation of church and state, legitimized cultural pluralism so that the country's ethnic minorities found themselves free at least of formal opposition to their traditional forms of expression. Politically and economically our immigrant peoples encountered a system of dominance and subordination in which against their will they were alien groups. Thus, and especially the southern European Catholic, Eastern European Jew, and the Oriental here in the United States, owing to cultural, religious, and racial differences, found themselves exploited and discriminated against. As a result, their ethnicity became a stigma used to justify their confinement into subcommunities. One response that these minorities made was counter-exclusion, in other words, preventing others from entering their ghettoes and by practicing endogamy preserving their stock. The conflict that ethnics experienced reinforced their ethnicity

[4] Bureau of the Census, *The Social and Economic Status of the Black Population in the United States: 1973* (Washington, D.C.: Government Printing Office, 1974), Table 4, p. 11.

[5] See Leo F. Schnore, "Social Class Segregation among Non-Whites in Metropolitan Areas," *Demography*, 2 (1965).

and hence contributed to a stronger cultural pluralism. Note, for example, the recent resurgence of ethnic identity in the Black Power movement and, among whites such as Poles, Hungarians, and Italians, in Michael Novak's phrase, the "unmeltable ethnics," who have defensively reacted against gains made by nonwhites, they believe, at their expense.[6]

THE FUTURE OF ETHNICITY

Ethnic differentiation, despite the countervailing forces present in urban society, has produced no little speculation about its future persistence. What is the outlook for the ethnic factor in urban America? This question can be answered with some degree of assurance if we look at history and the observable present trends, and if we limit the question to the near-term foreseeable future.

On balance, ethnicity will probably continue manifesting itself in the United States, if we follow Milton Gordon's view, in a context of structural pluralism.[7] That is to say, four forces work today toward the reduction of segregation, prejudice, and discrimination in American society. They are: (1) industrialization, which raises the standard of living and makes possible greater achievement for all; (2) the service state, which confers political and economic rights on a broader and broader scale; (3) internationalism, which challenges ethnic and racial discrimination as national policy; and (4) urbanization, which raises the level of education and rationality. All of these tendencies combine to make cultural pluralism more legitimate at the same time that the functional integration of people into effective social, political, and economic structures can also advance. Therefore, the differential association of ethnic, religious, and racial minorities in voluntary associations and residential enclaves can coincide with the harmonious interaction of their populations in industry, the marketplace, and government.

In the longer run, extensive minority accommodation and assimilation can be reliably anticipated in the United States as a further stage beyond the structural pluralism of the near future. The former refers to the acceptance of a stable mode of association on an agreed-upon basis, and the latter to the behavioral absorption of people into a general, common culture. This represents the continuation of our history with regard to the many varieties of immigrants we have received. But this is not to say that antagonism, hostility, and conflict will disappear. The latitude open to minorities to preserve their sociocultural distinctiveness will itself guarantee ideological friction. Also, advantages secured by one minority to redress inequality will create new imbalances. But a none too pessimistic answer to the question What is the

[6] Michael Novak, *The Rise of the Unmeltable Ethnics* (New York: Macmillan, 1971).

[7] See Milton M. Gordon, *Assimilation in American Life* (New York: Oxford University Press, 1964).

Garbage and other waste accumulate along railroad tracks and paths in this very crowded and extremely poor *kampung* (neighborhood) in Jakarta, Indonesia.

future of ethnicity? appears warranted. The present gains and difficulties with urban poverty and civil rights supply evidence for that conclusion.

THE URBAN POOR

There are few places in the world where poverty is unknown. Though unevenly distributed, poverty may be found in every region of the globe. Consider a few figures. As of 1968, 22 nations averaged individual incomes of less than $79 per year. The three major countries of southern Asia—India, Indonesia, and Pakistan—had annual per capita incomes that fell in the range of only $80 to $99. Mainland China was in the next higher class, having between $100 and $199 per person per year. Brazil, Turkey, Ghana, and the Philippines stood in the $200–$299 category, while countries like Cuba, Portugal, and Yugoslavia had per capita figures between $300 and $399 annually. In all, 1.9 billion people subsisted in 1968 on average incomes below $200. And about 2.1 billion, two-thirds of the entire world population, had no more than $300 each per year![8]

Though poverty is present worldwide, industrial urban populations tend to have higher average incomes than do those of the nonurban, agricultural nations. This six most highly developed and urbanized countries selected for comparative study by the United Nations Secretariat had the following (1968) per capita incomes: United Kingdom, $1,451; Australia, $1,620; The Netherlands, $1,265; Sweden, $2,046; Finland, $1,399; and the United States, $2,893. In comparison, selected countries and territories with a less than 10 percent urban population in 1960 had much lower per capita incomes: Thailand, $105; the Congo, $90; Ivory Coast, $188; Liberia, $148; Kenya, $77; Sudan, $90; Guinea, $83; Ethiopia, $42; Chad, $60; and Uganda, $77. They were among the very lowest in the world.[9]

POVERTY IN AMERICAN CITIES

Urbanization is certainly no complete bar to indigence, for even among the most urbanized—and most affluent—nations poverty is to be found both absolutely and relatively. The United States in general and its largest cities in particular bear this out. Table 18-1 shows that, in 1972, more than 5 million American families lived below the poverty line (according to the price index then, $4,275 for a four-person nonfarm family).

The term "above the poverty line" or simply "above the low-income group" refers to the purchasing power necessary for a basically decent standard of living during a given year. As an illustration, the 1967 poverty income developed by the Federal Interagency Committee allowed a four-member family $3,410. This was budgeted on a monthly total of $285, with $122 of that going for food; $91, rent; $57, clothing and personal care; $9, recreation, education, tobacco, and other items of consumption; and $6 for transportation. The food plan on which the budget was based was, in the

[8] David Simpson, "The Dimensions of World Poverty," *Scientific American,* 219 (November 1968), pp. 3–11.

[9] Ibid. Also J. R. Kasun, "U. S. Poverty in World Perspective," *Current History,* 64 (June 1973), pp. 247–75.

TABLE 18-1 Families below the Low-Income Level in 1972, by Type of Residence and Race of Head (in 000's)

| | ALL RACES BELOW LOW-INCOME LEVEL | | | WHITE BELOW LOW-INCOME LEVEL | | | BLACK BELOW LOW-INCOME LEVEL | | |
	TOTAL	NUMBER	PERCENT	TOTAL	NUMBER	PERCENT	TOTAL	NUMBER	PERCENT
Nonfarm	51,860	4,753	9.2	46,093	3,171	6.9	5,152	1,481	28.7
Farm	2,513	323	12.8	2,384	270	11.3	113	48	42.6
Metropolitan Areas	36,941	2,938	8.0	32,303	1,819	5.6	4,117	1,059	25.7
inside central cities	16,159	1,828	11.3	12,595	901	7.2	3,263	892	27.3
outside central cities	20,782	1,110	5.2	19,708	918	4.7	854	167	19.5
Nonmetropolitan Areas	17,433	2,137	12.3	16,174	1,622	10.0	1,148	471	41.0
United States	54,373	5,075	9.3	48,477	3,441	7.1	5,265	1,529	29.0

Source: Bureau of the Census, *Characteristics of the Low-Income Population, 1972* (Washington, D.C.: Government Printing Office, June, 1973), *Current Population Reports*, Series P-60, No. 88, Table 5, p. 7.

words of the department of agriculture, "nutritionally adequate," giving somewhat less than four ounces of meat per person per day, but calling for beans, cereals, and potatoes instead of the more meat, dairy products, and fruits and vegetables found in the diet of the average American. The 1976 low-income threshold for a nonfarm family of four was $5,500, with consumption needs budgeted proportionally to the price index current at the time.

Such facts would argue that subsistence at the poverty level in the United States is not entirely relative to our high standards, but borders on malnutrition, unhealthful housing, and insufficient clothing conducive to physical morbidity and mortality. Economic distress to this degree is also often associated with sociocultural deprivation, including alienation and counterproductive work habits.[10]

According to Table 18-1, 9.3 percent of all families in the United States live in poverty. America's poor families are found one-half again as frequently in our metropolitan areas as in our nonmetropolitan communities. However, the inner cities of our metropolitan areas have proportionally twice as many of their families in poverty as do their suburban rings. Though nonmetropolitan areas account for two-thirds the number of poor families that the metropolitan districts do, the former have a greater share of their family units in poverty, 12.3 percent to 8.0 percent, owing to the more stringent economic conditions in our small and medium-size cities.

POVERTY AND MINORITIES

Minority ethnic groups, especially blacks, make up a substantial part of the problem of urban poverty in the United States at present. As Table 18-1 reveals, proportionally more blacks live in poverty than do whites, with 25.7 percent of black families in metropolitan areas and 41.0 percent in nonmetropolitan areas below the low-income level. These figures are greater than even the poverty rate for the aged past 65 in the United States, 15 percent of whom were below the poverty threshold in 1972.[11] In addition to blacks, the other nonwhite groups, Chicanos, Puerto Ricans, and Indians, make up concentrated poverty populations. However, whites comprise the majority of the poor: in 1972, 17.5 million of them to 7.9 million nonwhites, including 7.5 million blacks.

According to the comparative data secured by the Commission on Income Maintenance more than a decade ago, in 1960, black (two-thirds of them urban) sustained an overall poverty rate of almost 50 percent. Mexican Americans (79.1 percent urban) had 34.8 percent of their families below the

[10] Compare Jerome Cohen and Arthur Pearl, eds., *Mental Health of the Poor* (New York: Free Press, 1964).

[11] Bureau of the Census, *Characteristics of the Low-Income Population: 1972*, (Washington, D.C.: Government Printing Office, 1973), *Current Population Reports*, Series P–60, No. 91, Figure 3, p. 2.

poverty line. Puerto Ricans (96.3 percent of whom were urban) experienced a 32.0 percent family rate of poverty. American Indians had the lowest percentage urban, only 30.4, though a very high degree of impoverished families, 53.8 percent. By contrast, the other nonwhite minorities, Japanese and Chinese Americans, constituted less than 1 million persons (74.0 to 95.8 percent urban) and experienced poverty with far less frequency than the American people as a whole.[12]

By 1972, however, as Table 18-1 shows, significant gains had been made in reducing poverty among these minorities. Though 1.5 million disadvantaged black families continued to be below the poverty line, they comprised only 29 percent of the nation's total number of black families. Progress was possibly made by all of the other non-white groups during this interval too. In 1972, only 27.2 percent of all families of Mexican origin in the United States were below the low-income level. Also, by 1972, the rate for Puerto Rican families had dropped to 30.2 percent.[13]

THE CULTURE OF POVERTY

Female-headed families (in 1972, 64 percent of all black families in poverty in the United States were headed by women), continued indigence, and dependence on public assistance—these three factors occurring in combination have led some scholars to postulate the existence of a culture of poverty as being typical of a large segment of the poor. These writers have asserted that once established, the mode of life of such poor people is learned, shared, and transmitted from old to young like any other cultural pattern.

Characteristics of the Poor

Evidence, says Elizabeth Herzog, supports the following psychological and sociocultural traits as characteristic of the poor in America.[14] The poor have a low level of formal-group membership. Apart from mere attendance in school, their educational achievement is low. They harbor a low sense of efficacy. They are prone to concrete rather than abstract thinking, and to fatalism and resignation instead of optimism and hope. The poor have a localistic orientation: their world view is narrow. Politically, they lean toward economic liberalism and noneconomic conservatism. In addition, in comparison with the more affluent, the poor appear to experience greater tension

---

[12] President's Commission on Income Maintenance, *Background Papers* (Washington, D.C.: Government Printing Office, 1961), pp. 131–60.

[13] Bureau of the Census, *Characteristics of the Low-Income Population: 1972*, op. cit., Table 3, p. 25.

[14] Elizabeth Herzog, "Some Assumptions about the Poor," *Social Science Review*, 37 (December 1963), pp. 391–400.

and hostility, while at the same time, also in comparison with the more prosperous, to have less a sense of personal autonomy and less trust in government authority. This catalogue of traits suggests the makeup of the culture of poverty.[15]

Scholarly Uncertainty

The culture of poverty has been challenged in two ways. The first regards clarity, that is, whether it denotes a distinctive, morally-based life style or merely a practical adaptation to circumstances. Second, the idea of a culture of poverty has raised the question of whether, in effect, it blames the poor themselves for their plight and thus, unwittingly, justifies only a gradualist reform approach to the elimination of poverty instead of a more immediate restructuring of the economy.

Oscar Lewis, who more than anyone else gave the notion of the culture of poverty its start in recent thought, has sought to document it in *La Vida* and other books.[16] Lewis concludes that the culture of poverty has four cardinal aspects: (1) the hiatus that separates its members from the larger society and culture; (2) the gregariousness of the slum community but its lack of organization and serviceability; (3) the haplessness of the poverty-embedded family sustained only by authoritarian mother-centering; and (4) the individual personality who grows up embued with "a strong feeling of fatalism, helplessness, dependence, and inferiority."[17]

Similarly, the political scientist Edward Banfield has written of the need to give serious thought to the improvident present-mindedness that he is convinced typifies many of our urban ghetto dwellers.[18]

Peter Rossi and Barbara Blum, however, reject the notion of a culture of poverty as empirically invalid. They say that "our review of the literature does not support the idea of a culture of poverty in which the poor are distinctively different from other layers of society."[19] A recent study of mothers in poverty done in Syracuse by Louis Kriegsberg leans more toward the situational interpretation of poverty. Yet it does not wholly dismiss continued indigence as a source of behavioral values either.[20] Not unlike Kriegsberg, Herzog herself recognizes a certain "unincorporated" quality of life in the slum, a condition

---

[15] Walter Miller, "Lower Class Culture as a Generating Milieu of Gang Delinquency," *Journal of Social Issues,* 14 (1958), pp. 5–19, are appropriate here.

[16] (New York: Random House, 1966). See also his *Five Families* (New York: Basic Books, 1959).

[17] For a brief presentation, see Oscar Lewis, "The Culture of Poverty," *Scientific American,* 215 (October 1966), pp. 3–9.

[18] In *The Unheavenly City Revisited* (Boston: Little, Brown, 1974).

[19] Peter H. Rossi and Zahava D. Blum, "Class, Status, and Poverty," in Daniel P. Moynihan, ed., *On Understanding Poverty* (New York: Basic Books, 1969), pp. 36–63.

[20] Louis Kriegsberg, *Mothers in Poverty: A Study of Fatherless Families* (Chicago: Aldine, 1970).

implying the absence of a strong sense of social cohesion among slum residents. This is something less than a culture of poverty. But on balance, Herzog thinks that the poverty-culture idea is "a very useful concept, if and only if it is used with discrimination."[21]

Lee Rainwater, who has advocated income equalization as the most practical solution of the poverty problem, questions not only the poverty-culture concept but also the feasibility of intervention to modify it.[22] He does so on the grounds that since culture is an adaptive mechanism, deep social change can come about only "through a change in the social and ecological situation to which lower-class people must adapt." Along with Herbert Gans, Rainwater asserts that the disciminatory culture of the majority will have to be modified in order to remedy the environment in which the poor are forced to adjust themselves. As a result, Rainwater urgers far greater public assistance than any to date. Finally, perhaps only to show the manifold implications of the culture-of-poverty idea, in a logical though not an entirely serious manner, the late Leonard Reissman raised the question whether, if a culture of poverty does prevail, it might not legitimately sanction poverty as a policy in preference to the very ideal of equality itself![23]

Heterogeneity of the Poor

Generalizing about the culture of poverty fails to do justice to the psychosocial differentiation that many observers have reported within the ranks of the poor.

S. M. Miller prefers combining economic and style-of-life criteria in delineating America's poor.[24] Miller's resulting typology consists of four identifiable groups: (1) the stable poor (principally rural but also many of the elderly); (2) the strained (economically secure but familially unstable); (3) the copers (effective socially even if deprived); and (4) the unstable poor (mainly the new black in-migrants, the slum-trapped ethnics, the physically handicapped, and the destitute aged).

William McCord and his coworkers distinguish a spectrum of six individual like styles in the ghetto.[25] They are: (1) the stoic, like the religious ones who believe, to cite one case, that violence is never justified and that the

---

[21] Herzog, op. cit.

[22] Lee Rainwater, "The Problem of Lower-Class Culture and Poverty-War Strategy," in Moynihan, *On Understanding Poverty,* op. cit., pp. 229–59.

[23] Leonard Reissman, *Inequality in American Society* (Glenview, Ill.: Scott, Foresman, 1973), p. 65.

[24] S. M. Miller, "The American Lower Classes: A Typological Approach," *Social Research,* 31 (Spring 1964), pp. 1–22.

[25] William McCord, John Howard, Bernard Friedberg, and Edwin Harwood, *Life Styles in the Black Ghetto* (New York: W. W. Norton, 1969), pp. 105ff.

Watts riot hurt rather than helped the black cause; (2) the defeated, who desperately use alcohol, drugs, and even suicide; (3) the achiever, with a relatively high level of aspiration—and perhaps success too; (4) the exploiter, in predatory politics, the rackets, and ghetto business; (5) the "rebel without a cause," who lashes out in blind aggression against accessible targets; and (6) the activist, either reformist or revolutionary.

In their research on 373 subjects at the Community Co-op Center in New York's Bedford-Stuyvesant ghetto (a 2-square-mile area of 430,000 residents, 98 percent of them black), Henry Etzkowitz and Gerald Schaflander portrayed three psychocultural style-of-life postures.[26] First, they identified the "lower economic, lower social class, emanating from gang and criminal patterns." Second, they contrasted the "black college intellectuals coming from both lower- and lower-middle-class upwardly mobile parents." The third group, they found, consists of the upwardly mobile though psychologically rigid individuals. Etzkowitz and Schaflander describe the first group as nervous, suspicious, and preoccupied with material possessions and sexuality. The second type values being cool, appearing very relaxed, moving slowly, and demonstrating aplomb at all times. Finally, the third type are hostile toward type one and jealous of type two. Also, politically sensitive, they appear to be "planting rumors and maneuvering for position all the time."

Such descriptive classifications of the poor weaken the idea that a single broad culture of poverty envelopes our economically deprived urban population. They do, however, point up hampering values and attitudes that the concept of a culture of poverty denotes as working against a simple economic solution to the poverty problem.

COMBATTING POVERTY

Government intervention against poverty began in the United States on a large scale decades before the rediscovery of the poor in America's cities around 1960 by observers like Michael Harrington, in *The Other America,*[27] and Herman P. Miller, in *Rich Man, Poor Man.*[28] Modern antipoverty efforts originated under the New Deal, whose Social Security Act of 1935 provided old-age and survivors' benefits, unemployment insurance, and aid for several categories of the needy: the blind, the elderly, the disabled, and dependent children. Later, wages-and-hours legislation was added, and public-housing and health services similarly.

Those New Deal programs assisted large number of the poor. But they

[26] Henry Etzkowitz and Gerald M. Schaflander, *Ghetto Crisis: Riots or Reconciliation?* (Boston: Little, Brown, 1969).

[27] (New York: Macmillan, 1962).

[28] (New York: Crowell, 1964).

failed to relieve the so-called hard-core poor, those persons who did not have steady jobs or if they did, worked at very low paying ones. The hard-core poor are largely synonymous with poverty in the urban areas of the United States today.

THE WAR ON POVERTY

To ameliorate hard-core poverty, that is, indigence resulting from severely limited employability rather than weaknesses in the economy, the federal government undertook a forcefully proclaimed—some would say over-proclaimed—"war on poverty" in 1964.

The Economic Opportunity Act

Possibly the most innovative part of the war on poverty was the Economic Opportunity Act (EOA). Title I of the EOA pertained to youth programs. It included a "job corps," work training, and a work-study program. Under this title of the act, education, work experience, and vocational training were made available. "Head start" schooling for those of preschool age was initiated in order to help overcome some of the handicaps of socialization under great adversity. Furthermore, agreements with state and local governments, nonprofit corporations, and educational institutions to permit youths to continue their schooling or to increase their employability were negotiated by the Departments of Labor and Health, Education, and Welfare.

Title II of the EOA authorized community-action with "maximum feasible participation" of the poor themselves to combat poverty through local service centers, neighborhood coordination, and local action groups to improve the capacity of the poor to cope with present-day social conditions on a permanent basis.

Three strategies of community action were possible within Title II.[29] One capitalized on existing institutions and the expectation that the schools and local government, for example, would be improved through better coordination. The second strategy was essentially one of research and planning. Finally, the third (identified with the radical organizer Saul Alinsky) sought to mobilize the poor to communicate their own interests to such institutions. Yet these three strategies were neither carefully spelled out in the legislation nor even acknowledged for that matter. The rationale of the title itself was clear enough, however: that of rehabilitation through education, self-help, and local betterment, thereby enhancing the ability of the poor to benefit from the opportunity of earning a living and being an active citizen.

[29] Compare James L. Sundquist, "Origins of the War on Poverty," in the volume published under his editorial supervision, *On Fighting Poverty* (New York: Basic Books, 1969), pp. 6–33.

EXHIBIT 18-2 Percentage of Illiterates in the U.S. Population, by Total and by Race: 1870–1969

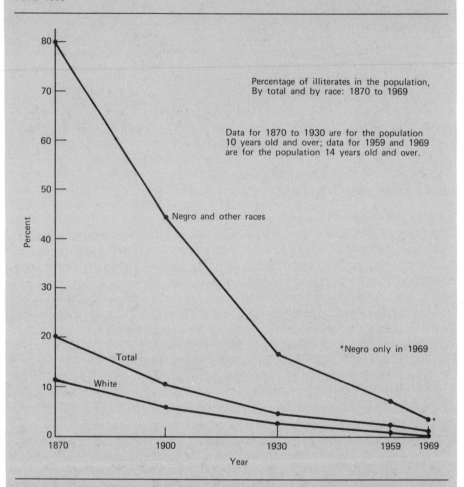

Percentage of illiterates in the population, By total and by race: 1870 to 1969

Data for 1870 to 1930 are for the population 10 years old and over; data for 1959 and 1969 are for the population 14 years old and over.

The dramatic downturn in illiteracy rates in the United States over the 100-year period shown here occurred during a time of virtually continuous urbanization. This helped spur the civil rights movement and anti-poverty measures.

Source: Bureau of the Census, *Current Population Reports: Population Characteristics* (Washington, D.C.: Government Printing Office, 1971), Series P-20, No. 217.

VISTA volunteers working as architects under this war-on-poverty program to obtain vacant lots in Harlem (a New York City black ghetto) and turn them into low-cost housing projects.

Origins of the EOA

Behind the enactment of the EOA, as James Sundquist has summarized it, lay four streams of thought.[30]

> *First,* the discovery during the Eisenhower administration that a "sick" urban community was spawning a rising tide of juvenile crime. Diagnosed by Cloward and Ohlin, the deviance being recorded came from a social setting denying many of the poor legitimate opportunities.[31] Consequently, a program of antidiscrimination activities, vocational training, and guidance appeared called for. This Congress authorized in 1963 in the form of local projects like New York City's Mobilization for Youth.
>
> *Second,* urban renewal administrators reached the conclusion that more attention needed to be given the people displaced in the process of raz-

[30] Ibid.

[31] Richard A. Cloward and Lloyd E. Ohlin, *Delinquency and Opportunity* (New York: Free Press, 1960).

ing and reconstructing blighted districts. Moved by Edward Logue and Paul N. Ylvisaker, the Ford Foundation contributed more than $12 million for community development in the "grey areas" of New Haven, Oakland, Boston, Philadelphia, and all the cities in North Carolina.

Third, the interest of of the Kennedy administration in making the children of ablebodied but unemployed parents eligible for public aid while at the same time alleviating local welfare costs led to federal action in 1962. The newly established Bureau of Family Services undertook to stimulate community work to broaden socioeconomic opportunities and prevent future dependency by caring for needy children immediately.

The *fourth* contributory element was added to this redirection of the nation's welfare program in 1961, when the Manpower Act passed Congress. This legislation sought to educate the jobless for productive employment. However, it soon became apparent that the depth of the problems of training had not been correctly diagnosed. A fifth of the unemployed lacked even a grade-school education. Among unemployed blacks almost a half had not finished the eighth grade. As a result, the 1963 amendments to the manpower statute added basic education. Thus the background for the Economic Opportunity Act was completed.

EOA's Accomplishments and Failures

Evaluating EOA as an antipoverty program is difficult for several reasons. For example, are short-term or ultimate criteria to be used? Similarly, how is social change envisoned through community action to be measured?[32]

Gauged in term of employment, it would seem that EOA and its related programs were relatively successful. In the three-year period following EOA's inception, the nation's poor were reduced by 4.5 million.[33] But this cannot be ascribed to the war on poverty alone. Most of the gains resulted from sheer economic growth, much of that brought about by a tax cut in 1964.[34] Some must also be credited to the vigorous civil-rights movement carried on at the time.

Yet a balanced judgment on the war on poverty would no doubt contain four essential points:

First, the EOA sensitized communities to the poor and made institutions like welfare departments more responsive to them.

Second, community action proved a source of discord, discouraging to further social restructuring. This "revolutionary change," as some called

[32] See Robert A. Lavine, "Evaluating the War on Poverty," in Sundquist, op. cit., pp. 188–216.

[33] Reynold Farleys and Albert Hermalin, "The 1960s: A Decade of Progress for Blacks?" *Demography,* 9 (1972), pp. 353–70.

[34] Robert Lampman, *Poverty: Four Solutions* (Eugene, Ore.: University of Oregon Press, 1966).

it, financed from public sources dismayed and angered many. The whole thing was evidence to the nonpoor, declared Daniel Moynihan, "that the community was sicker than ever."[35]

Third, the government's performance did not equal its rhetoric against poverty. In fact, this discrepancy may have contributed to the disorders in many cities beginning in 1965. Urban historian Zane Miller reasons that throughout the 1960s, the federal government actually did far more, by means of highway construction, FHA financing, and favorable business taxes, to help America's more affluent population disperse toward the metropolitan fringe than it provided "to bring the poor into the mainstrem of the economy."[36] In an assessment not unlike Miller's, George Sternlieb has labeled the typical city of our metropolitan areas as "sandboxes."[37] In these sandboxes, Sternlieb claims, a public bureaucracy has been established to sustain the poor who are piled up there in minimal fashion and, periodically, to ward off their possible insurrection—and thereby pacify them, like children in a sandbox, without materially changing their conditions of life.

Fourth, the war on poverty probably also promoted black participation in politics. Moynihan has said, "Very possibly the most important long run impact of the community action programs of the 1960s will prove to have been the formation of an urban Negro leadership echelon at just the time when the Negro masses and other minorities were verging towards extensive commitments to urban politics."[38] Moreover, the abortive War on Poverty probably also stimulated organization among our other nonwhite minorities like the Chicano Black Berets in Los Angeles and the Puerto Rican Young Lords of New York.

OTHER MEASURES

Even as the war on poverty was being implemented, proposals for more financial aid for the poor were being pressed energetically. These included a guaranteed annual income and a negative income tax.

A Guaranteed Annual Income

In 1968, some 200 economists declared that it was the duty of government to assure everyone "an income no less than the officially recognized definition

[35] Daniel P. Moynihan, *Maximum Feasible Misunderstanding: Community Action in the War on Poverty* (New York: Free Press, 1969), p. 129.

[36] Zane A. Miller, *The Urbanization of Modern America* (New York: Harcourt Brace Jovanovich, 1973), p. 210.

[37] George Sternlieb, "The City as Sandbox," *Public Interest,* 25 (Fall 1971), pp. 14–21.

[38] Moynihan, *Maximum Feasible Misunderstanding,* op. cit.

of poverty." Today a guaranteed annual income above the poverty line has many endorsers as the solution to poverty in the United States, but far more opponents. Social theorist Alvin Schorr has called the guaranteed income a "comparatively radical idea" in that it would presume work is not required of everyone in order to subsist, and he thinks the notion fantastic at present.[39] Schorr does, however, regard a partial "demogrant" made to specific populations, such as children and the elderly, as quite feasible. A measure of this sort would not seriously affect work and probably have no substantial influence on the birth rate.

A Negative Income Tax

A negative income tax has also been proposed. Under it people would be subsidized to the degree their income failed to exceed the officially set poverty standard. For example, if every person were entitled to $750 a year, only one's income above that figure would be taxed. If he were below $750, he would receive a cash supplement to bring him up to it.

The major problem anticipated in connection with a negative income-tax scheme concerns work incentives, just as it does a guaranteed annual income too. Helen Nicol has written on this crucial point that:

> There are millions of workers whose earning are below or near the poverty line and who therefore might face the choice of working or not working. How many of them would prefer subsidized leisure— even though at a minimum guaranteed income—to work at perhaps a physically exhausting and demanding job, or a tedious and monotonous job, or an outdoor job in all kinds of weather, or a job that requires long and expensive commuting from their own neighborhood? Little is known about how different people would react to a guaranteed annual income or to different monetary work-incentives. But it can be assumed that older people, physically frail people, working mothers, and less-motivated people in general might prefer to give up all or a part of the jobs they are holding. For these reasons it is believed that any broad noncategorical plan would raise major administrative and enforcement problems quite aside from problems of equity.[40]

To cope with the incentive problem, many advocates of income maintenance accept the idea of a subminimum. They believe that only half the gap ought to be closed between the poor person's income and the poverty stan-

[39] Alvin L. Schorr, *Explorations in Social Policy* (New York: Basic Books, 1968), pp. 296–98.

[40] Quoted from Helen O. Nicol, "Guaranteed Income Maintenance: Another Look at the Debate," *Welfare in Review*, 5 (June–July 1967), pp. 1–13.

dard. That way initiative would be rewarded and at the same time assistance be given the indigent. Yet need would not be entirely met. If on the contrary the poverty line were raised in order to furnish more help, another problem would be encountered besides that of sapping the inclination to work: the cost of assistance would simply mount. That of course could be reduced by a means test, but doing so would have the effect of restoring public assistance with its present shortcomings, including overhead expense, degradation of the client, and an inability to eliminate poverty except by offering palliatives.

Family Aid

Citing inequities in the public assistance system, President Nixon urged a family assistance program in 1969 and again in 1972. In a public message he called for a basic federal payment of $1,600 a year for a family of four now on welfare and with no outside income. He went on to link the income guarantee with work, for under the proposal he made, assistance would require employment or availability for it. No action was taken on the Nixon proposal, however. Opponents like the National Welfare Rights Organization branded it a subterfuge for perpetuating minimal security by supporting a low level of subsistence and expediently denying aid on the basis of the "work ethic." Daniel Moynihan defended the President's plan, saying that unreasoning anti-Nixon partisanship misconstrued the measure.

For the Future

As the Nixon plan suggests, some combination of monetary and other measures probably will materialize in the United States in the not too distant future in dealing with poverty. Schorr, whom we referred to earlier, would improve social security for the elderly, provide medical care and decent housing for all, adopt a program of financial allowances for children, and also finally add a "modest" negative income tax for the indigent generally.[41] Many hold similar views though differing on the particular mix of items. Thus as an antirecession measure, the 1975 Ford administration tax reform act included a rebate for those who had paid no income tax at all during the year.

One's confidence in the speed and ease with which poverty can be overcome in the United States probably depends on one's judgment of the willingness of the affluent segments of the population to make the necessary resources available. Herbert Gans' analysis of the positive functions of poverty is suggestive here.[42] Gans argues that among other things, the poor do

[41] Schorr, op. cit., pp. 298ff.

[42] Herbert Gans, "The Positive Functions of Poverty," *American Journal of Sociology*, 78 (September 1972), pp. 275–89.

the dirty work, facilitate savings by others, provide work for the police, and buy shoddy goods. Yet poverty's dysfunctions—notably crime, public assistance, and disruptions—may come to be seen as outweighing the benefits of tolerating economic deprivation in our midst. That would be conducive to a more concerted attack on it.

Such a program might well encompass an imaginative array of experimental methods, like use taxes for central-city services (because that is where poverty remains most acute); public expenditures calculated to create employment; the allocation of urban land predicated on employing the hard-core poor; and even perhaps public ownership of industry operated in accordance with a service ethic of affording jobs to the needy.[43] Measures of this sort gain credence when viewed against the recent findings of micro-data analysis (computation from systematic, comparative figures) showing existing limitations on the availability of employment for the ghetto-dwelling poor.[44]

In the final analysis, as most impartial authorities would probably agree, specific measures to combat poverty require certain general conditions to succeed. These are: continued economic growth; improved educational opportunities; a more adequate social-security system (see Ch. 19); and suppression of discrimination against minorities.

CIVIL RIGHTS AND THE DISADVANTAGED

Poverty among our urban minorities has been interwoven with restrictions on their civil rights. Segregated housing patterns, discrimination in employment, and unequal education evidence a social system which, contrary to formal ideology, simply has not guaranteed equal protection of the laws and civil rights for all.

Civil rights mean that neither race, color, nor religion justifies infringements on (1) the exercise of speech and religion and also appeals for the redress of grievances; (2) procedural protections in judicial actions; (3) eligibility to vote; and (4) the allocation of government services and facilities. Civil rights also extend to the protection of minorities from discrimination by private individuals or groups like business firms and labor unions. This bears on the public interest, particularly in housing, employment, and the use of accommodations.

[43] Consult Bennett Harrison, *Urban Economic Development* (Washington, D.C.: The Urban Institute, 1974), pp. 191–95.

[44] See Bennett Harrison, "Education and Underemployment in the Urban Ghetto," *American Economic Review*, 62 (December 1972), pp. 796–812.

URBANIZATION AND THE CIVIL RIGHTS MOVEMENT

Minority interest in civil rights has been strong enough in recent decades to amount to a mass movement. That movement needs to be viewed against the background of the further urbanization of the United States, especially the rural blacks confined for the most part to the South who have now migrated to metropolitan areas, many of them in other regions of the country. An important aspect of the process has been the added political power gained by blacks through migration to cities where political participation already received legal sanction. Politically too, the urbanization of blacks has meant the closer proximity of persons, improved communication between them, speedier issue formation, and more effective organization into interest groups.

Besides politicization, urbanization acts to modernize consciousness. As Hyland Lewis says, urban life generally gives the black "an automatic increment" in his effort to improve his life. Writes Lewis, "The urban premium on freedom, impersonality, efficiency and profits, voluntary associations, and participation by representation provides for Negroes and whites a new frontier for the shaping of a common destiny."[45] As the nonwhite American has urbanized, he has acquired higher aspirations and has increased his organizational skills to effect social reform.

ACTIVE PROTEST

Recent civil rights gains for America's minorities have also come about as a result of intensely active protest carried on mainly by blacks themselves. A variety of direct-action techniques have been used. Sit-ins conducted by black college students under the auspices of the Southern Christian Leadership Conference and the Congress of Racial Equality proved effective in ending racial discrimination in public eating places. Boycotts by black patrons and their white sympathizers helped to get established discrimination in retail business brought to an end. Sit-ins and other demonstrations spread to parks, swimming pools, libraries, churches, and stations. Besides accommodations, direct protest was also designed to affect voting, employment, education, and union membership.

CIVIL RIGHTS LEGISLATION

A civil rights act had passed Congress in 1960 after an eight-week filibuster by southern senators. It was a weak measure, one that Thurgood Marshall,

[45]Hyland Lewis, "Innovations in the Contemporary Southern Negro Community," *Journal of Social Issues,* 10 (1954), pp. 19–27.

Martin Luther King in the Selma, Alabama, civil-rights march.

who had presented the *Brown* case in court, said was not "worth the paper it's written on."[46] Title VI, the heart of the 1960 statute, permitted the attorney general to determine if a pattern of discrimination with regard to voting existed in a jurisdiction and to have referees register those who were being disfranchised. It was a procedure infrequently resorted to.

The 1964 Act

In contrast, the Civil Rights Act of 1964 was comprehensive. No doubt the 1963 Freedom March on Washington, coming on the heels of protest confrontations in Birmingham, Alabama, had created a climate of purpose and urgency that was reflected in the legislation that President Kennedy had proposed and his successor successfully supported.

[46] Daniel M. Berman, *A Bill Becomes Law* (New York: Macmillan, 1962), p. 117.

The 1964 legislation, benefiting from Republican Senator Everett Dirksen's endorsement (1) presumed a sixth-grade education evidence of literacy; (2) prohibited disservice on account of race in public accommodations, such as hotels, restaurants, theatres, and gas stations; (3) gave blacks equal access to public facilities like parks and swimming pools, with Justice Department suit to compel compliance; (4) empowered the attorney general to sue for school desegregation; (5) provided federal funds be withheld from discriminatory state and local agencies; (6) prohibited discrimination by employers and unions; and (7) established a community relations service to assist in the settlement of racial controversies. The act thus covered many aspects of public life, and except for the omission of open housing, seemed to respond to practically every demand made by the civil-rights movement.

The Voting Rights Act of 1965

Impressive as such civil-rights legislation appears, serious obstacles to enforcement were encountered. In the case-to-case approach followed prior to 1965 to remedy exclusion of blacks from the polls, refractory officials had required a long, drawn-out judicial procedure. Consequently, the 1965 Voting Rights Act was designed to authorize federal examiners to register persons qualified under state law but where fewer than half the voting-age population were registered or voted and some test or device was being employed on prospective voters. Penalties were also strengthened against intimidation of those seeking to vote. How effective the 1965 act was may be gauged from the fact that from 1965 to 1969, more than 800,000 additional blacks became registered voters. In 1972, 65 percent of black Americans of voting age were registered in comparison with 73 percent of whites.[47] The extension of the voting rights measure in 1975 added a proviso for ballots in other languages to aid principally Chicanos and Puerto Ricans.

Open Housing

The momentum of the legislative current to enact civil rights guarantees continued even after 1965. To combat overcrowded ghetto schools, health hazards, and rising crime rates, as well as the failure of costly social programs, President Johnson proposed a legal attack on discrimination in the sale, rental, and financing of homes and other residential units. The National Association of Real Estate Boards lobbied to prevent restrictions being placed on brokers. In Chicago, black open-housing marchers were stoned in a white neighborhood. Out in California, a referendum overturning the state's non-discrimination housing law passed with a large majority, but that action was

[47]Bureau of the Census, *The Social and Economic Status of the Black Population of the United States, 1972* (Washington, D.C.: Government Printing Office, 1973), Table 75, p. 97.

nullified by the California Supreme Court as contrary to the 14th Amendment. Finally, after a cloture move in the Senate, a national open-housing statute was enacted in 1968, going fully into effect in 1970 and applying to 80 percent of the country's dwelling units. That measure was accompanied by antiriot penalties on the transportation and employment of explosive or incendiary devices in the furtherance of civil disorders. (For further material on housing, see Ch. 20.)

JUDICIAL ACTION

Supreme Court decisions have accompanied legislative progress on civil rights.[48] In fact, the Court was for years the most active of the three branches of government in supporting the civil-rights movement. After the 1954 *Brown* decision on school desegregation, the Court often showed its impatience over the tardiness of compliance in many districts. Important judicial decisions were also entered in the fields of housing, voting rights, and antimiscegenation laws.

In 1969, during the initial period of the Nixon Adminstration and the decline of White House support for civil-rights legislation, the Court continued to exercise leadership. For example, the tribunal rejected the administration's strategy of delay with regard to further school desegregation. At the same time though the Nixon Adminstration insisted on benign quotas of minority-group workers, the "Philadelphia Plan," on construction projects receiving federal funds. Declared the then Attorney General, John Mitchell, in responding to the question of whether the 1964 Civil Rights Act outlawed race as a factor in hiring, "The legal definition of discrimination is an evolving one, but it is now well recognized in judicial opinions that the obligation of nondiscrimination, whether imposed by statute or by the Constitution, does not require, and, in some circumstances, may not permit obliviousness or indifference to the racial consequences of alternative courses of action which involve the application of outwardly neutral criteria."[49] The problem of benign quotas or affirmative action having specific substantive goals remains a current issue even after the *Bakke* decision in 1978.

THE WHITE HOUSE CONFERENCE: "TO FULFILL THESE RIGHTS"

During the most productive legislative period of the civil-rights movement, the White House Conference "To Fulfill These Rights" convened in Washing-

[48]See *Congress and the Nation* (Washington, D.C.: Congressional Quarterly Service, 1969), Vol. II, pp. 351–54.

[49]*Congressional Quarterly Almanac—1969* (Washington, D.C.: Congressional Quarterly Service, 1970), Vol. XXV, p. 418.

ton, in June, 1965, upon the invitation of President Johnson. As projected by Mr. Johnson, the theme of the 2600 conferees representing a broad spectrum of American society was how better to bring our nonwhite minorities fully into the social structure of the United States. The multiplex recommendations made by the conference reveal the depths to which civil-rights groups now believed the problem of economic deprivation and cultural disadvantage extended, and the solutions they felt were called for.[50] They also show conviction as to the key role of the federal government in ameliorating conditions. The scores of measures advanced by the conferees fell into eight general categories: administration of justice; community institutions and social action; education; the family; health and welfare; housing; jobs, job training, and economic security; and voting. In short, a many-sided attack was held to be in order.[51] In that way, by compensatory efforts now the inherited disabilities and disqualifications of the past might be overcome.

CONTINUED CONTROVERSY

Historian Foster Dulles may well have had the White House conference citations in mind when he observed that the issues over the horizon were perhaps more pressing than those already disposed of. Dulles wrote, "If a legal foundation for upholding the equal protection of the laws guaranteed by the Fourteenth Amendment was finally secure after a century of indifference, the economic and social challenge which the Negroes were raising with their militant demands and the divisive, provocative slogan of Black Power still remained."[52]

That the 14th Amendment extends to state activity abetting private discrimination would appear to be incontestable at present. Yet as the legal scholar Henry Abraham has put it, a judgment of proper balance is necessitated: "Where does the Constitution draw the line between the right to legal equality and to equality of opportunity and the rights of liberty, property, privacy, and voluntary association?"[53] The evolutionary nature of civil rights has led to the point where positive duties are being urged upon both government and private individuals not only to avoid discrimination and denial of equal opportunity, but also to provide employment, health care, security, the amenities of life, and even more respect for all. The question of equal results instead of merely equal opportunity which is thus implied would appear to presage continued controversy.

[50] See *Congress and the Nation,* op. cit., pp. 392ff.

[51] Report of the White House Conference, *To Fulfill These Rights* (Washington, D.C.: Government Printing Office, 1966).

[52] Foster Rhea Dulles, *The Civil Rights Commission: 1957–1965* (East Lansing, Mich.: Michigan State University Press, 1968), p. 260.

[53] Henry J. Abraham, *Freedom and the Court* (New York: Oxford University Press, 1967), p. 303.

So apprehensive a view may be invalidated by the racial trends observable in the labor market since the mid-1960s. Thus black participation in the professions is rising at an unprecedented rate, particularly among younger workers. At least in some minds, facts such as this argue that discrimination differentials are "disappearing in reality."[54]

CONCLUSION

Although industrial urbanization is a force for the reduction of ethnicity, ethnicity continues to exist even in the modern metropolitan center. It does so owing to positive and negative factors. These are legitimate pluralism, on the one hand, and intergroup competition and conflict on the other, expressed in terms of prejudice, discrimination, and segregation. Similarly, industrial urbanization is also a force for the reduction of poverty. Yet poverty too continues to exist even in the midst of urban affluence.

Despite the millions of deprived whites in America's cities, the poor tend to be concentrated among our nonwhite minority groups. Their economic distress stems from discrimination, but the two operate in a circular manner, with poverty reinforcing discrimination and racism as an expression of ethnicity contributing to further deprivation.

People living in poverty are often thought to possess a culture of poverty which helps them adjust to deprivation, but also perpetuates their poverty. Yet many scholars dispute the validity of the culture-of-poverty concept. They conclude that changing the socioeconomic structure would ameliorate poverty, or that the poor are a varied rather than homogeneous population.

Economic and welfare programs have been resorted to in attacking poverty in the United States, and some progress has been made, but poverty continues to remain a problem. The most concerted drive against economic distress in America in recent years was that of the Johnson administration's war on poverty. Its results are ambiguous at best and in certain respects counterproductive. At present, thinking centers on welfare measures but also extends to possibly a guaranteed income, a negative income tax, or a family-aid plan.

The moves against poverty have not been unrelated to efforts aimed at achieving civil rights for our disadvantaged minorities. Here too, owing to its modernizing effects, urbanization has been influential. The cityward migration of nonwhites, their acquisition of political power in our urban centers, vigorous protest strategies, and considerable judicial support have all combined to result in substantial institutional reform favorable to desegregation and the curtailment of racial discrimination. Impressive gains toward legal

[54] See Stuart H. Garfinkle, "Occupation of Women and Black Workers, 1962–74," *Monthly Labor Review,* 98 (November 1975), p. 29.

equality have been made. Yet future controversy over demands for socio-economic parity between the races, particularly if that is to be accomplished by compensatory means, seems probable despite some impressive gains to date.

FOR FURTHER READING

Warren Bloomberg, Jr. and Henry J. Schmandt, eds., *Urban Poverty: Its Social and Political Dimensions* (Beverly Hills, Calif.: Sage, 1970). The war on poverty is viewed as a failure.

Kenneth E. Boulding, Martin Pfaff, and Anita Pfaff, eds., *Transfers in an Urbanized Economy* (Belmont, Calif.: Wadsworth, 1973). Technical papers dealing with urban poverty by means of grant payments according to various strategies.

Edwin Eames and Judith Granick Goode, *Urban Poverty in a Cross-Cultural Context* (New York: Free Press, 1973). Concentrates on the differences between the American view of the "poor" and perspectives elsewhere.

Eleanor B. Leacock, ed., *The Culture of Poverty: A Critique* (New York: Simon and Schuster, 1971). A symposium offering different viewpoints in the culture-of-poverty controversy.

Frances F. Piven and Richard A. Cloward, *Regulating the Poor* (New York: Pantheon, 1971). How American welfare programs control the poor politically and economically.

Leonard Reissman, *Inequality in American Society* (Glenview, Ill.: Scott, Foresman, 1973). The difficulties of changing the socioeconomic system to achieve the ideal of equality more closely.

Richard B. Sherman, ed., *The Negro and the City* (Englewood Cliffs, N.J.: Prentice-Hall, 1970). Deals both historically and analytically with the urban life of American blacks.

Karl E. Taeuber and Alma F. Taeuber, *Negroes in Cities: Residential Segregation and Neighborhood Change* (Chicago: Aldine, 1965). A detailed study which examines patterns of residential separation and mobility.

CHAPTER 19

SOCIAL WELFARE AND THE ADMINISTRATION OF HEALTH

Modern welfare services, notably social insurance and public assistance, and the administration of health, including family planning, the subjects of this chapter, are not restricted to urban areas. Yet they are unmistakably an essential component of modern urban society. In fact, early industrial urbanism provided the major impetus to the welfare-and-health movement of recent years. This can be traced here in the United States and also in Western Europe.

THE DEVELOPMENT OF WELFARE

During the middle and final decades of the nineteenth century, American society was converted from an agricultural to an industrial economy. Especially after the Civil War, industrial urbanism in America resulted in distressing conditions that were beyond the capacity of the existing institutions of kinship, religon, and the state to remedy. The new money economy experienced periodic shocks, with the business cycle repeatedly marked by joblessness, bankruptcies, and foreclosures. Interludes of bitter industrial disputes—strikes, lock-outs, boycotts, and even violence—added new strains to what was already a harshly insecure environment. Besides health problems, industrial accidents, the exploitation of both women and children, abysmal housing, and inadequate sanitation also wracked the cities of industrial America. Nor was the industrial city of Europe significantly different at the time.

ORGANIZED CHARITY

The distress of the industrial city in the United States and Europe gave rise to much private charity to supplement the miniscule aid grudgingly given by the county almshouses dating back in principle to the Elizabethan poor laws of the sixteenth century.[1] By 1882, 22 charitable societies were operating in American cities having a combined population of over six million. Ten years later, 92 socieites served an aggregate urban community of upwards of 11 million.[2]

These early charities were administered in a spirit of religious altruism. At the same time however, stern disapproval was shown the recipient. The scientific theory of the time held that personal character was the crucial variable in combatting indigence. Therefore, an ameliorative relationship between patron and client was necessary. Toward this end of helping the poor to help themselves, elaborate case investigations were undertaken, and aid administered in a coldly benevolent manner.

GOVERNMENTAL INTERVENTION

In spite of all this, the conviction steadily grew that certain hazards were not only inherent in the social structure, but were such that an individual's character simply could not surmount them, and that social reform under government auspices was called for. By 1912, Theodore Roosevelt's "Bull Moose" Progressive Party advocated a ban on child labor and the enactment of a national workmen's compensation law. The party platform that year called for

[1] See Roy Lubove, *The Professional Altruist* (Cambridge, Mass.: Harvard University Press, 1965).
[2] Ibid., p. 2.

In its 1912 platform, ex-President Theodore Roosevelt's Progressive Republican Party advocated the abolition of child labor such as that performed by these youthful coal miners.

unemployment, health, and retirement insurance and "such legislation as is demanded by the modern industrial revolution and which will secure a better and more equitable diffusion of property."

Welfare in Britain

At this time in England, Charles Booth, a businessman by profession, published his monumental 17-volume study, *Life and Labour of the People of London,* after years of painstaking investigation beginning in 1886.[3] This statistical picture of the pauperizing consequences of industrialization on the inhabitants of East London brought to light the persistent conditions associated with poverty in a laissez-faire economy: joblessness and underemployment, chronic ill health, a debilitating struggle for existence, large families, the lack of education, and insecure old age. From Booth one learned that London's poverty extended to 30 percent of the whole population and was not confined to the sweatshops and waterfront alone.

This expose led to a series of legislative acts in the United Kingdom

[3] (London: Longman's, 1900–1911).

providing relief, employment services, workmen's compensation, unemployment and health insurance, and, eventually, old-age insurance too. Although a far broader program of welfare would be achieved in Britain in the future, mere concern for the destitute had given way there to the idea that systematic aid was a necessary activity of government.

Early American Measures

By 1920, a long series of accomplishments in social welfare had also materialized here in the United States under public as well as private sponsorship. Philanthropic foundations had been established in the fields of health and social services. Public parks, playgrounds, neighborhood centers, and recreational agencies appeared or grew in number. State and local departments of public health came into being. The new general hospitals that had been erected to serve those able to pay now created out-patient dispensaries for the indigent. At the same time too, social work was being professionalized, with welfare services delivered by trained specialists instead of volunteers.

State programs for the rehabilitation of the handicapped were undertaken too, but in the administration of local public assistance, little progress was made. Few states furnished careful supervision in this area, although a small number of cities, among them Detroit, Cleveland, and Kansas City, did take steps to improve their handling of relief. Not until the Great Depression was there a major turn of events here. At that time both the welfare ideal and the social-service system as it continues to exist today in the United States were established.

THE WELFARE IDEAL

Implicit in the emergence of the welfare ideal have been two ideas. One concerns building appropriate institutions to cope with the exigencies of life at present resulting from the operations of the economy and the settlement of people in large population centers. The other refers to a rising level of expectations concerning the quality of life in general.

THE WELFARE STATE

Both of these concepts are embodied in the modern welfare, or service, state as it is otherwise known. Basically, the welfare state denotes government-supported standards of consumption and the provision of opportunity for individual development assured people as part of their rights as citizens.[4] In

[4] Compare Harold L. Wilensky and Charles N. Lebeaux, *Industrial Society and Social Welfare* (New York: Free Press, 1965), p. xii. See also P. Streeten, "Welfare," in Julius Gould and William L. Kolb, eds., *A Dictionary of the Social Sciences* (New York: Free Press, 1964), pp. 756–57.

TABLE 19-1 U.S. Public Welfare Expenditures, by Type of Program and Percentage of Gross National Product, at Five-Year Intervals from 1935 to 1970 ($ millions)

TYPE OF PROGRAM	EXPENDITURES								
	1935	1940	1945	1950	1955	1960	1965	1970
Social Insurance	$ 406	$1,272	$1,409	$ 4,947	$ 9,835	$19,307	$28,123	$ 54,653
Public Aid	2,998	3,597	1,031	2,496	3,003	4,101	6,283	16,476
Health Programs	427	616	2,354	2,064	3,103	4,464	6,246	9,568
Veterans	597	629	1,126	6,866	4,834	5,479	6,031	9,018
Education	2,008	2,561	3,076	6,674	11,157	17,626	28,108	50,332
Housing	13	4	11	15	89	177	318	697
Other Programs	99	116	198	448	619	1,139	2,066	4,606
Total (in millions)	$6,548	$8,795	$9,205	$23,508	$32,640	$52,293	$77,175	$145,350
Total (as percent of gross national product)	9.5	9.2	4.4	8.9	8.6	10.6	11.8	15.2

Source: U.S. Bureau of the Census, *Statistical Abstract of the United States: 1972* (Washington, D.C.: Government Printing Office, 1972), Table 451, p. 278.

The Health and Welfare Department of Tucson, Arizona.

the welfare state, an acceptable level of goods and services is made available to the individual or the local community as a matter of course without payment or the establishment of a special need. Such a state of affairs supplements the market place as well as the other distributive mechanisms that exist, like the family and the church, in achieving a high plateau of human fulfillment.

Table 19-1 reveals the size and internal composition of the national welfare budget in the United States during the period from 1935 to 1970. In 1935, 9.5 percent of the country's gross national product was budgeted for welfare. By 1970, the figure had risen to 15.2 percent.

THE RESIDUAL CONCEPTION OF WELFARE

The welfare state is the product of the shift that has taken place from the residual to the institutional conceptions of social service.[5] Under the residual philosophy, welfare services have only an emergency and remedial function. Family, friends, and the normal economy are presumed to be able to meet people's needs except in unusual circumstances, when added services have to be employed. These are thus available on a back-up basis, so to speak.

[5] Wilensky and Lebeaux, op. cit., pp. 138ff.

THE INSTITUTIONAL CONCEPTION

The residual interpretation does not, however, fit in well with the exigencies of life resulting from industrial urbanization. This became glaringly apparent here during the 1930s when the Depression caused the residual interpretation to be subordinated to the institutional conception for the first time. Since then the institutional definition of welfare has gained more ground.

Institutionalists now assert that individuals require systematic help to achieve personal fulfillment. Thus universal education is called for, as are medical care for all and the provision for decent retirement for people following their productive years. The proponents of institutional social welfare claim that in the last analysis such effort is essential not only for the individual but also for society as a whole. By adequately developing its human resources, the institutionalists assert, a nation benefits its economic stability and growth, which, in fact, are otherwise unattainable.

SOCIAL SECURITY

The Social Security Act of 1935, consisting of social insurance and public assistance, signaled the change from the residual to the institutional philosophy of the service state here in America.

SOCIAL INSURANCE

The Social Security Act levied a tax on employees and employers for old-age and survivors insurance. The statute also established a cooperative federal-state unemployment compensation system, with a national levy on payrolls supporting state administered unemployment-insurance plans. In addition to social security, two other programs antedating 1935 were continued in operation: civil-service retirement and railroad retirement. As of 1970, 95 percent of all Americans turning 65 were protected under one or another of these three plans. And 80 percent of the nation's wage and salary workers were covered against short-term involuntary joblessness by the unemployment compensation feature of the Social Security Act. Beginning in 1965, the Social Security System also established a medical care program for the elderly, covering hospitalization. A supplementary program providing voluntary health insurance to cover 80 percent of doctor bills was added soon afterward.

Contemporary Issues

Although universal social-security protection has been almost completely achieved in the United States, serious issues remain. One is the level of benefits. These tend to be low, particularly in connection with continuing inflation. Social insurance does not effect a redistribution of wealth. Indeed, as Wilensky and Lebeaux declare (following Richard Titmuss, the noted English social administrator), our nonstatutory "social-security" devices like pensions, expense accounts, and other fringe benefits outweigh public social security by far.[6] Thus there is an inherent antiegalitarian tendency in our present social-security system—which keeps benefits low.

Nonetheless, rising benefits stimulated by inflation as well as underfunding due to low contributory rates and a high level of unemployment have recently combined to create a major fiscal problem for the social-security system. As of mid-1977, the Carter Administration was advocating the use of general government funds to augment social-security resources. In view of the expected increase in the proportion of retirees and the decline in the proportion of Americans of productive age later in the century, an improved funding pattern definitely needs to be developed.

Another question concerns bureaucratic regimentation and inflated costs. Medicare, as the medical services added to social security in 1965 were soon known, had been opposed by the American Medical Association on the grounds that it would impair service and also raise costs. The latter soon proved to be true. According the HEW, hospital expenses per patient day doubled in the period from 1965 to 1975.[7] They have climbed still more since. However, even though the evidence for bureaucratic abuse remains ambiguous, much public resentment of how the program is being administered appears to exist.

PUBLIC ASSISTANCE

The Social Security Act also involved the federal government, indirectly through state administration, in providing assistance to the indigent. Under the act, financial grants were authorized via the states to pay pensions to the indigent aged, stipends to the destitute blind and to dependent children, and funds too for public-health, vocational rehabilitation, and children's services.

Despite the careful scrutiny of applicants and improvements in the economy, the costs of welfare mounted, particularly for dependent children. (See Table 19-2.) Recipients of Aid to Families with Dependent Children (AFDC) rose from 2.2 million in 1950 to 4.4 million in 1965, and total AFDC expenditures from $554 million to $1.6 billion in the same period.[8] The ex-

[6] Ibid., pp. xvff.

[7] Health, Education, and Welfare Department, *Social Security Bulletin* (Washington, D.C.: Government Printing Office, March, 1976), Vol. 39, No. 3, p. 69.

[8] Social Security Administration, *Social Security Programs in the United States* (Washington, D.C.: Health, Education, and Welfare Department, 1966), Table 13, p. 97.

TABLE 19-2 U.S. Public Assistance Recipients and Payments, by Program, Selected Years, 1940–1972

PROGRAM	1940	1950	1965	1970	1972
Number of recipients (thousands)					
OAA	2,070	2,786	2,087	2,082	1,934
AB	73	97	85	81	80
AFDC	1,222	2,233	4,396	9,659	11,065
APTD	—	69	557	935	1,168
GA	3,618	866	677	1,056	864
Total payments for year (millions)					
OAA	$473	$1,454	$1,594	$1,862	$1,877
AB	22	53	77	98	106
AFDC	133	547	1,644	4,853	6,908
APTD	—	8	417	1,000	1,390
GA	392	293	261	618	741

Note: OAA (Old-Age Assistance); AB (Aid to the Blind); AFDC (Aid to Families with Dependent Children); APTD (Aid to Permanently and Totally Disabled); GA (General Assistance)

Source: Social Security Administration, *Social Security Programs in the United States* (Washington, D.C.: Government Printing Office, January, 1973), Table 15, p. 109.

pansion in aid for dependent children occurred despite the fact that, it has been estimated, only a fraction of the poor received public assistance. In 1963, the nation's AFDC bill was $1.5 billion, although merely 23 percent of the poor were aid recipients that year.[9] By 1972, as Table 19-2 shows, AFDC recipients totaled II million and received almost $7 billion in payments. Of that number, almost 8 million were children.

Added Emphasis?

Contrary to the concern apparent in public opinion over AFDC expenditures, the proponents of public assistance, such as the HEW Advisory Council on Public Welfare, have called in fact for added government emphasis on the program as essential.[10] These advocates say that a galaxy of children's services should augment financial aid, and these should include "protective and social service for children in a vulnerable situation, foster care place-

[9] See also Helen M. Crampton and Kenneth K. Keiser, *Social Welfare* (New York: Random House, 1970), pp. 218–21.

[10] Advisory Council on Public Welfare, *Having the Power We Have the Duty* (Washington, D.C.: Government Printing Office, 1966), p. xii.

ment in homes and institutions at reasonable rates of reimbursement, adoptive placement services, services to unmarried mothers, homemaker services, day care, other types of group services, provisions for specialized institutional care, probation and school social service (where not otherwise available), special programs for young people, and services related to the licensing of nongovernmental programs."[11]

Recent Revisions

In 1968, PL 90-248 amended the public-assistance sections of the Social Security Act. That measure did not conform to the broader dimensions envisaged by the supporters of greater aid. What it did was require every state to participate in a work-training-and-incentive program administered by the Labor Department for all recipients under AFDC except children, the incapacitated, and those needed at home. Incentive payments of $30 a month were provided for everyone accepted for training. Those who refused jobs or training were to be denied assistance. It was anticipated that public-service jobs would be made available to those who had completed training but could not find private employment. Day-care centers for recipient mothers with children were set up to facilitate the program.

Further Proposals

Liberal critics have scored the public-assistance system for its commitment to socioeconomic mobility without providing the necessary means of making the program truly effective.[12] Thus the American Public Welfare Association advocates welfare standards much higher than those existing at present. It urges aid be given persons who because of their own background or because of poor economic conditions are working but are underemployed. The APWA also encourages administrative simplification in order to reduce needless documentation and record keeping.[13]

Another type of criticism concerns the desirability of approaching welfare by means of structural change rather than services to individuals. One recent exponent of rearranging social systems to get at problematic behaviour is Robert R. Mayer, who argues for at least experimental programs, perhaps interracial housing and social integration of the aged, to combat individual disability.[14] Thinking in the health services, discussed below, has of late been turning in that direction too.

[11] Ibid., p. xv.

[12] Consult Richard M. Elman, *The Poorhouse State* (New York: Pantheon, 1966), p. 281, and Martin Rein, *Social Policy: Issues of Choice and Change* (New York: Random House, 1970), p. 98.

[13] Note the APWA's Statement to the Advisory Council on Public Welfare (August 12, 1965).

[14] See Robert L. Mayer, *Social Planning and Social Change* (Englewood Cliffs, N.J.: Prentice-Hall, 1972).

HEALTH SERVICES

The solution of public-health problems is inseparable from stable urbanization, and has been so from the very earliest cities in history.

PUBLIC-HEALTH SERVICES

Contemporary public-health services in America's urban areas consist of six interrelated activities:[15]

> *First,* environmental control denotes the purification of water by means of filtration and chlorination, the pasteurization of milk, the elimination of architectural hazards, and the minimization of air, soil, and water pollution as well as the exposure of living things to injurious radiation.
>
> *Second,* improving human resistance to disease related to vaccination and inoculation, the enrichment of foods (e.g., iodized salt), and the fluoridation of water.
>
> *Third,* is curbing transmittable disease through isolation and quarantine, including the sterilization of germ-carrying material and the elimination of disease-bearing animals and insects.
>
> *Fourth,* education, is particularly instrumental in reducing infant mortality and possibly the incidence of untreated communicable disease.
>
> *Fifth,* municipal health departments cooperate with state and national agencies in exercising public leadership in the establishment of health standards, the construction and operation of hospitals and other facilities, and the coordination of medical and health services.[16]
>
> *Sixth* is the coordination of public-health activity, that of maximizing complementary services such as dentistry, nursing, and medical social work.

The pursuit of these municipal public-health goals, which accounted for 11 percent of all expenditures by local government in the United States in fiscal 1971, has contributed to the very rapid growth of medical personnel and facilities during the past several decades. In 1940, the health-service industries of the United States employed a little more than 1 million persons. By 1960, that figure stood around 2.5 million, and by 1970, 4.4 million. From

[15] Berwyn F. Mattison, "Public Health," in Harry L. Lurie, ed., *Encyclopedia of Social Work* (New York: National Association of Social Workers, 1965), pp. 606–14.

[16] Consult Walter Guzzardi, Jr., "What the Doctor Can't Order—But You Can," in W. Richard Scott and Edmund H. Volkart, eds., *Medical Care: Readings in the Sociology of Medical Institutions* (New York: John Wiley & Sons, 1966), pp. 528–43.

Maternal and children's health services in the out-patient department of a large municipal hospital.

a 1940 ratio of 7.8 practitioners per 1,000 population, the health-service industries reached a ratio of 13.9 in 1960 and 22.2 in 1970.[17]

THE COMMUNITY HEALTH CONCEPT

The leadership and coordination functions of urban public-health agencies underscore the reason why authorities have lately taken to using the term "community health" rather than public health in discussing services aimed at promoting the optimal physical and emotional functioning of a population. Community health denotes the complementary practices of public-health offices, private practitioners, and voluntary health and welfare agencies as well.

For all of its breadth, even community health seems a limited concept, at least in the United States at present. As Smillie and Kilbourne note, since 1925 health has been "nationalized" here.[18] From being a "community affair, administered under local self-government with some slight degree of state government supervision," concern for health has become "a subject of na-

[17] For background see Monroe Lerner and Odin W. Anderson, *Health Progress in the United States: 1900–1960* (Chicago: University of Chicago Press, 1963).

[18] Wilson G. Smillie and Edwin D. Kilbourne, *Preventive Medicine and Public Health* (N.Y.: Macmillan, 1963), 3rd ed., pp. 11–13.

tion-wide interest and importance." Accordingly, an indirect attack has been made on ill health involving social security, education, housing, recreational facilities, and the like. In addition, innovations keep appearing too, like neighborhood health centers for the poor and group practice on an insurance basis. Medical insurance was itself developed only recently although its progress since has been rapid. By 1970, 74.5 percent of the American civilian population was covered by voluntary health insurance, with the urban Northeast having the largest proportion insured.[19]

THE IMPROVEMENT OF HEALTH IN URBAN AREAS

As a consequence of much effort, much progress has been made in the improvement of health in our urban areas.

Rural-Urban Differences

It is true that the incidence of heart disease, tuberculosis, and cancer is today higher for the American urban population than it is for our rural residents. On the other hand, pneumonia, influenza, typhoid, and malaria have higher rates in rural districts. Allowing for differences in the age and sex composition of the two populations, diagnostic practices, and the two differing modes of life, all of which account for much of the discrepancy, Ralph Thomlinson declares that "urban-dominant [principally degenerative] diseases tend to be those that medical science cannot control effectively, whereas the [communicable] afflictions most common in rural areas are conquerable by modern medicine."[20] As the benefits of urbanization diffuse further in the United States, differences in the level of health between city and country can be expected to shrink still more. In fact, regional mortality differences now over-shadow rural-urban differentials in the nation.

The improvement of health that has been observed in our cities shows the extent to which urbanization has been accompanied by ameliorated health care in the United States. But morbidity and mortality differences are attributable not only to the availability of sanitary and medical services but also to income differentials, the composition of the populations, the level of education, and the aggregate impact of a population's entire mode of life.[21] Thus the prevalence of poverty, intergroup tensions, and less effective social organization in certain segments of our urban population continues to create a serious health problem in our cities, particularly as regards infant mortality and psychiatric disorders.

[19] Bureau of the Census, *Statistical Abstract of the United States: 1972* (Washington, D.C.: Government Printing Office, 1972), Table 740, p. 464.

[20] Ralph Thomlinson, *Population Dynamics* (New York: Random House, 1965), p. 132.

[21] Lerner and Anderson, op. cit., pp. 105–6.

EXHIBIT 19-1   Ten Leading Causes of Death, United States: 1900, 1940, and 1970

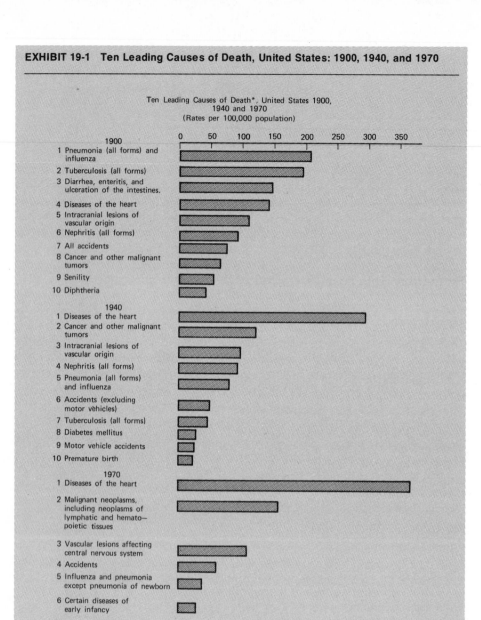

Ten Leading Causes of Death*, United States 1900,
1940 and 1970
(Rates per 100,000 population)

*Terminology is that used in the edition of International List of Causes of Death in effect at the time

From 1900 to 1970, the chief causes of death for Americans changed from the infectious to the degenerative diseases. Compare the degree of urbanization in the United States for the years given.

Source: Leon F. Bouvier and Everett S. Lee, "The Health of Americans: Trends in Illness and Mortality," *Population Profiles* (Washington, D.C.: Center for Information on America, 1973), Chart No. 5, p. 5.

Infant Mortality

Infant mortality rates, which earlier were relatively high in America's urban areas, have declined, as have also our cities' maternal death rates. These rates are inversely correlated with the availability and use of appropriate medical facilities, but the relationship between urbanization and health, including infant mortality, is by no means simple. Lerner and Anderson offer an authoritative summary on the subject, claiming that socioeconomic influences are now cutting across the rural-urban differential, and also that extensive mobility is doing the same thing, with the result that, they write, "it is difficult to determine to what extent the mortality experience of an area at any given moment reflects the entire life experience of its inhabitants."[22]

Biostatisticians have rarely questioned the assumption that infant mortality is the single most sensitive index of the level of well-being of an industrial urban population. Studies of infant deaths in Syracuse and Providence done around 1950 cast doubt on this belief in favor, instead, of the significance of biological factors unrelated to social and economic conditions. Monroe Lerner, however, has observed the "substantial" differences in infant mortality between inner-city populations and other residents of metropolitan areas that have been recorded recently, and also the high rates of infant mortality among Southern and Mountain migrants in our large cities.[23] Hence he has cautioned against disuse of infant mortality as a prime measure of the general level of life of a population. In Chicago, for example, the 1964 infant mortality rate of 38.5 per 1000 in the city's poverty areas was 75 percent higher than the nonpoverty area rate of 22.2. For nonwhites living in poverty areas in Chicago, the infant mortality rate was almost twice that of the city's population as a whole.[24]

Further Health Goals

As postindustrial urbanization continues, our levels of acceptability concerning health will no doubt be raised still further. Mortality and morbidity are already outmoded as the sole measures of health achievement. Alchoholism and drug abuse will probably be added as indexes of community health. True, such problems pose difficulties of measurement and treatment—and perhaps even of philosophical validity. Yet their eradication is consistent with the long-held goal of public health: of establishing the necessary conditions of well-being "primarily in the physical environment, but also in the

[22] Ibid., p. 113.

[23] Monroe Lerner, "Social Differences in Physical Health," in John Kosa, Aaron Antonovsky, and Irving Kenneth Zola, eds., *Poverty and Health* (Cambridge, Mass.: Harvard University Press, 1969), pp. 69–112.

[24] Ibid.

structure of society and of the individual personality."[25] However, as the Carter administration indicated in 1977, curbing the high cost of medical care referred to above and of removing barriers limiting access to medical services are possibly the most universal goals in the field of health in the United States today. Here, national insurance and prepaid group practice each have their supporters as solutions to the problem.

MENTAL HEALTH

Apart from physical health, the improvement of mental health represents still another objective of urban welfare.[26]

Correlation Between Urbanism and Mental Illness

The probable association of psychiatric disorders with the particular circumstances of urban life makes mental illness a genuine objective of organized effort aimed at its alleviation. Indeed, urbanization may be regarded as a causative factor in the etiology of mental illness. This is true in the sense of imposing greater psychic stress on people and also in facilitating the recognition and treatment of their emotional disorders.

Early studies of the incidence of mental disorders in urban and rural populations of the United States definitely established their disproportionate occurence in urban areas. For the United States generally from 1910 to 1922, urban rates of psychiatric illness ranging from 78.8 to 86.0 per 100,000 were found in comparison to a rural rate range of only 41.1–41.4.[27] Moreover, it was learned that the larger the city, the higher was the incidence of mental disorders, though the rural rate did exceed that for small cities. Thus a 40-year survey of schizophrenia among Norwegian-born immigrants in Minnesota from 1889 to 1929 revealed a relative percentage frequency of 61.0 for Minneapolis, 5.8 for minor cities, and 33.2 for the rural part of the Rochester State Hospital District.[28] Also, for the first 50 years of the twentieth cen-

[25] Sir Geoffrey Vickers, "What Sets the Goals of Public Health?" in Alfred Katz and Jean S. Felton, eds., *Health and the Community* (New York: Free Press, 1965), pp. 852–66.

[26] Mental illness manifests itself in a disturbed emotional and reasoning process and in aberrant forms of overt behavior. Three major categories are commonly recognized, though not without overlapping and vagueness of distinction: organic mental illness; psychoneurotic states; and the psychoses. Compare P. V. Lemkau, *Mental Hygiene in Public Health* (New York: McGraw-Hill, 1955), 2nd ed.; and American Public Health Association, *Mental Disorders* (New York: APHA, 1962).

[27] Pitirim A. Sorokin and Carle C. Zimmerman, *Principles of Rural-Urban Sociology* (New York: Henry Holt, 1929) in Arnold M. Rose, ed., *Mental Health and Mental Disorders* (New York: W. W. Norton, 1955).

[28] Studies cited ibid.

tury, a period of continuing urbanization in the United States, both the number of patients in American mental hospitals and their ratio to the population rose without interruption. After 1955, at which time there were 631,000 resident patients in the nation, the trend was reversed slightly, but this was due to the newer policy of early release and not a drop in admissions.[29]

Currently, the rural-urban imbalance in the United States continues to be present. For example, according to the biometry branch of the National Institute of Mental Health, the hospital admission rate for schizophrena is twice as high for the residents of Baltimore as it is for the population of the rest of Maryland.

Who Are the Mentally Ill in the City?

Summarizing 34 studies of the relationship between social-class position and severe psychic disorder, Marc Fried learned that 85 percent of the total number of studies showed the highest rate of illness or hospitalization among the lowest status groups.[30] In fact, 71 percent of the inquiries even confirmed a "linear trend with inverse relationship between social class and severe disorder." Fried also concluded that the data showed overwhelmingly higher rates of severe disorders among blacks than whites.

Extrinsic factors, such as readier hospitalization due to less accessible out-patient services, would account for some of the difference in the rates of mental illness for class and race. More to the point regarding etiology among blacks, however, would be particularly severe situational stress. This would include unemployment, family disruption, community exclusion, and migration. Fried writes that the studies of social class and mental illness "suggest that the minority status of newcomers to a community (as newcomers, as foreigners, as less urbane, as preindustrial, and as Negroes) may be the central factor in the relationship between migration and mental illness."[31]

This may account for the high mental illness rates of southern rural blacks who move into northern metropolitan centers. Specifically, the cumulative-stress hypothesis refers to the relative absence of supportive external resources together with less than average personal efficacy, the latter of great significance in a situation of unusual deprivation and disruption. Hence the greater incidence of severe malfunctioning among lower-class urban blacks. Noting studies done in New York, California, and Ohio, which encountered higher rates of hospitalization among migrants than non-

[29] Lerner and Anderson, op. cit., p. 162.

[30] Marc Fried, "Social Differences in Mental Health," in Kosa, Antonovsky, and Zola, op. cit., pp. 113–67.

[31] Ibid., p. 139.

Rockland State Mental Hospital. Patients who cannot help themselves are voluntarily served by other patients.

migrants, the National Institute of Mental Health further substantiated the psychic vulnerability of blacks who had migrated to urban areas.[32]

Coping with Mental Illness

The plight of the inner-city resident has stimulated new thought regarding provisions for the mental health of urban America. This is not to say that recent progress has been great. It has not. But a good deal of planning has been going on.[33]

To relieve pressures on hospitals, increase their therapeutic effectiveness, and make out-of-hospital services available, the following policies are currently receiving wide support: (1) a variety of mental hospitals, including open-door arrangements and scattered-site facilities; (2) psychiatric services in general hospitals, especially diagnosis and referral; (3) strategic services by related professions like teachers, lawyers, and social workers; (4) family care, nursing homes, foster homes, and golden-age centers; (5) re-

[32] Public Health Service, *The Mental Health of Urban America* (Washington, D.C.: Government Printing Office, 1969), p. 21.

[33] Kosa, Antonovsky, and Zola, op. cit., p. 320.

habilitation for released patients extending to vocational counseling and placement; and (6) the community health center offering readily accessible teams of specialists oriented to the patient as a member of a family, church, neighborhood, and other social structures.[34]

The Community Mental Health Center

Of special promise recently has been the development of the community mental health center. Community mental health centers were first funded in the United States under federal legislation in 1963 that provided the states with money on a matching basis for the construction of facilities each serving a population of from 75,000 to 200,000 people. Priority was to be assigned by the states according to their judgment of relative need within their own borders.

The 1963 Mental Health Act combined two perspectives. One was the social conception of a community with its public supporting the operation of a local mental health center. The other was administrative, which envisioned a geographic catchment area served by a central professional facility. The two ideas were joined by the notion of the community as a therapeutic milieu for the mentally ill out-patient. Yet the ideas were also contradictory. In point of fact, the viable urban community is apt to be small, local, and particularistic, and perhaps not even residentially contiguous. On the other hand, administrative imperatives would require the service of a large, geographically intact but socially diverse area. Sadly, it has been said that the " 'bold new approach' of 1963 shows great promise of becoming merely an expensive expansion of decentralized facilities closely resembling the out-patient clinics predating its adoption."[35]

Alternative Approaches

Such a cautious estimate of the community mental health center would indicate that stress needs to be placed also on alternative approaches to the problem of mental health in the city. Three proposals appear worth serious consideration. First, manpower development and better housing could make city life less stressful for the disadvantaged. Second, the disadvantaged themselves might be encouraged by their own leadership to view with forebearance the progress that has been made, while those better situated renew their constructive efforts. Admittedly, that is a conservative position. And, third, programs to reduce the volume of in-migration to the cities might

[34] See Nina Ridenour, *Mental Health in the United States* (Cambridge, Mass.: Harvard University Press, 1961), pp. 133ff.

[35] Consult Robert H. Connery et al., *The Politics of Mental Health* (New York: Columbia University Press, 1968), p. 501.

be strengthened and thereby reduce the number vulnerable to breaking down. Such programs would include area economic development and social services in the communities where the migrants oiginate so as to forestall their movement out.

FAMILY PLANNING

Family planning, that is, the deliberate control of reproduction, is still essentially a private practice in the United States although government family-planning programs have recently gotten underway on a small scale. Continued urbanization has been a major factor in realizing that this nation has a population problem despite its relatively low rate of growth and its generations' old belief in the economic advantages of unchecked expansion, which since 1965 has been about one percent a year, a rate sufficient to double our numbers in 50 years.

THE AMERICAN POPULATION PROBLEM

Most Americans today probably believe that the rate of our population growth constitutes a problem to some degree. As the director of the Center for Population Planning at the University of Michigan, Leslie Corsa, says, "more and more Americans are recognizing that population size, distribution, and density are critical underlying causes of many present American problems, such as air and water pollution, urban decay, and inadequacies of transportation, higher education, health services, and recreation space."[36] Perhaps three aspects of the general population problem in the United States have received major attention from the public." They are (1) the fertility of the indigent; (2) population fluctuations; and (3) population growth and concentration.

Fertility of the Indigent

A high rate of population growth amounting to as much as 3.5 percent annually is of great significance for the cities of the developing nations of the world today.[37] The same resulting social pattern may be observed in American urban areas although on a smaller scale. The process begins in the rural countryside where the declining death rate leads first to population growth

---

[36] "United States: New Efforts, but Still Not Enough," in Bernard Berelson, ed., *Family-Planning Programs: An International Survey* (New York: Basic Books, 1969), pp. 146–54.

[37] See Amos Hawley, "Population and Society: An Essay on Growth," in S. J. Behrman, Leslie Corsa, Jr., and Ronald Freedman, eds., *Fertility and Family Planning* (Ann Arbor, Mich.: University of Michigan Press, 1970), pp. 189–209.

and then to increased poverty. The excess population, particularly young adults, migrate to the beckoning metropolitan areas. There the migrants obtain unskilled, service jobs or, failing that, fall back on public assistance. Utilities, education, and civic institutions find themselves burdened and overtaxed, and due to the lack of capital, housing is inadequate. Furthermore, due to their marginal existence, the newcomers to the city are prey to rapacious businessmen and loan sharks.

In the United States as a whole, the great numbers of European immigrants from 1860 to 1920 were relatively successfully drawn into the dynamic institutional system of the nation though by no means without hardship and strain. Of late, the urban migration of blacks, Puerto Ricans, and Chicanos has posed added problems of racial differences on top of demographic ones. The need for public assistance in our cities is doubtlessly related to the higher than average birth rates of our indigent, and frequently nonwhite, populations. Thus in 1970, while the general fertility rate (births per 1000 females 15 to 44) of whites was 83.9, for nonwhites it was 114.3.[38]

Population Fluctuations

Besides the difficulty of assimilating rural overpopulation, an urban society like the United States has still another problem, that of population fluctuations. As demographer Ronald Freedman and his associates have observed, "The fluctuations in the birth rate have affected capital investment, housing, recreation, education, manpower recruitment, and many other aspects of society that depend not only on the size of the population but also on the relative number of people in each age group."[39] In turn, each age group depends for its size on the size of the parent generation as well as the relative fertility which that generation has exhibited. Thus both the bulges and hollows are carried forward in successive population cycles. For example, the crisis in schools in the 1950s was the result of the postwar surge in marriages and births, and the drop in school-age population in the 1970s the result of a reduced birth rate the decade before.

Growth and Concentration

The third population problem in the United States, that of growth and concentration, has taken on awesome proportions. Given recent rates of net increase, by the year 2000 another 100 million persons will have been added to the present population of the country. Moreover, if we extrapolate past distribution trends, by the turn of the century perhaps 75 percent of that

[38] Bureau of the Census, *Statistical Abstract of the United States: 1972,* op. cit., Table 26, p. 25.

[39] Ronald Freedman, Pascal K. Whelpton, and Arthur A. Campbell, "Family Planning in the U.S.," *Scientific American,* 200 (April 1959), pp. 50–55.

larger number will be occupying only about 10 percent of the nation's land area, and the whole population will be crowded into our metropolitan areas even more densely than it is today. In anticipation the National Commission on Urban Growth Policy has recommended the creation of 100 new cities accommodating 100,000 each, and another 10 supercities with populations of one million. The added 100 million Americans by 2000 could well present even greater difficulties in terms of congestion, transportation problems, blight, water supply, fuel shortages, and ecological pollution.

VOLUNTARY FAMILY PLANNING

In the United States at present, voluntary fertility limitation is widely practiced, in fact, almost universally so. Only two to three percent of fecund white couples have never used or expect to use some form of family planning.[40] Yet after 15 years of marriage, about a quarter of the couples studied in the Growth of American Family 1960 sample reported that they had more children than they wanted.

Our experience with voluntary fertility restriction underlies the continued apprehension of some authorities. Demographer Judith Blake, for one, believes far too many Americans create a growth rate exceeding what is needed for population stability. Some experts go so far as to assert that coordinated measures are in order for the entire population, including those above average socioeconomically. Indeed, since the affluent consume more and also create greater ecological stresses, Jean Mayer has declared, "it is even more urgent to control the numbers of the rich than it is to control the numbers of the poor." Nor, of course, can voluntary fertility control solve the problems of population distribution, density, and fluctuations.

TOWARDS A NATIONAL POLICY

The United States has been slowly moving toward the institution of a national population policy centering on rational planning for optimum size, composition, and distribution. By a large majority the American public supports birth-control information for married people today. As many as 50 percent might possibly also approve having information supplied to those who are single. Two-thirds may feel the federal government should aid the states and cities with regard to family planning, even furnishing birth-control supplies to achieve greater fertility control. Probably a small majority condone early abortion for nonclinical purposes, but according to a May, 1975, Harris poll, Americans oppose abortion after the third month of pregnancy by a margin of 68 to 20 percent. Possibly too, sentiment favorable to elective sterilization

[40] Charles F. Westoff, "Fertility Control in the United States," *World Population Conference* (New York: United Nations, 1965), pp. 245–52.

has been gaining ground of late. Needless to say then, no definite resolution of the many issues involved has as yet been achieved, but a national policy of some comprehensiveness may be expected in the foreseeable future.

Many proposals have been made for governmental coordination of population measures on the assumption that "the principal unmet need for family planning in the United States is among the poor and is a specific aspect of the lack of adequate health services for the poor," Planned Parenthood's vice president Frederick S. Jaffee has proposed a strategic process of eight points, including numerous local family-planning clinics offering free educational and medical services.[41] As remarked earlier, not all agree that educating the poor to practice contraception will solve the nation's population problems. Hence they stress a broader approach.

William Moran of the Population Reference Bureau has proposed to cut the expected American growth of 100 million by the end of the century in half. That would, he believes, necessitate concerted if not drastic steps, such as the following: (1) fertility restriction by all available means; (2) the relocation of population in new centers; and (3) an extensive program of economic development that would raise the level of life for a hopefully stable population and also assure it a favorable ecological balance.[42] Each of these paths possesses serious problems of technology and social organization.

THE FUTURE OF WELFARE IN AMERICA

As a system public welfare in the United States has been the product of the existing socioeconomic order, and no doubt its future will also be so determined.[43]

Certain circumstances can be viewed as unfavorable to the further implementation of the welfare ideal in the United States, certainly at a rapid pace. Notable are the denunciations of the welfare state as un-American and socialistic. Such utterances continue to have polemical value although the drift of events continually proves them anachronistic. The "trying and degrading conditions" that observers often see in our legislation governing public assistance attest to the foregoing sentiment, however.[44] These condi-

[41] In "The United States: A Strategy for Implementing Family Planning Services," *Studies in Family Planning*, 17 (February 1967), pp. 5–12.

[42] See the debate in "Population Trends in 1969: The U.S. Scene," *Population Bulletin*, 25 (December 1969), pp. 121–33.

[43] For this rationale see Evelyn M. Burns, *Social Security and Public Policy* (New York: McGraw-Hill, 1956), pp. 269–75.

[44] Richard A. Cloward and Richard M. Elman, "Poverty, Injustice, and the Welfare State," in Philip Ehrensaft and Amitai Etzioni, eds., *Anatomies of America* (London: Macmillan, 1969), pp. 129–42.

tions include restrictive residence rules; suitable-home laws; night raids to establish the presence of able-bodied men in the homes of AFDC recipients; and elaborate and byzantine bureaucracies through which the poorly educated indigent are expected to receive aid. The result, then, is that the social restructuring which the welfare ideal calls for remains distant.

Projected shortages of trained social-welfare manpower further demonstrate the tentativeness of the welfare ideal in the United States. Acute manpower needs exist in the group-service, correctional, and health fields. Less acute, but still severe, are the staff shortages in public assistance, family, and child welfare agencies. Not uncommonly, incentives to pursue a career in some welfare occupation remain unattractive. Salaries tend to be low and conditions of work poor. Caseloads often exceed reasonable limits, and by preventing occupational satisfactions from being achieved, they further reduce incentives for recruitment.

Failure to advance more rapidly toward the welfare ideal is traceable also to political cleavages in the American public. The perceptive Swedish economist Gunnar Myrdal has stressed the political factor in the causal chain by which an impoverished American underclass has grown.[45] The American poor, says Myrdal, are unorganized and mute. They give little voice to the severity of their plight. "They are the least revolutionary proletariat in the world," he says. Even their participation in conventional political action is halting and sporadic. No doubt ethnic differences, governmental fragmentation at the local level, and the unwieldiness of the federal system contribute to the political apathy of the poor in the United States. Probably too the absence of national leadership is an important element.

In Great Britain by contrast, the welfare state was greatly advanced by the common national consciousness that a patrician leadership and a wartime beleaguerement from 1939 to 1945 created. As Maurice Bruce has written, the war "stirred consciences already uneasily aware" of the inadequacies of welfare services in the United Kingdom.[46] Accordingly, national health insurance, child care, family allowances paid out of general revenue, a full-employment standard, the democratization of education, New Towns, and other welfare measures enabled the British people to round off "the system of social security that they had sketched and to maintain in peace the consideration for all which had so impressively marked the war period."[47]

CONCLUSION

Social insurance, public assistance, health administration, and family planning, the aspects of social welfare reviewed in this chapter, all pertain to the

---

[45] Gunnar Myrdal, *Challenge to Affluence* (New York: Pantheon, 1963), pp. 41–43.

[46] Maurice Bruce, *The Coming of the Welfare State* (London: B. T. Batsford, 1966), pp. 259–91.

[47] Ibid., p. 291.

welfare ideal. That principle declares that the greater the degree to which the material and psychic needs of its individual members are met, the greater the advantage to the community as a whole. The development of that ideal received strong impetus from industrial urbanization, particularly in the nineteenth century when the new economy and the new mode of settlement had produced serious dislocations for a large part of the population. However, owing to its indefinite objectives and its tendency to redistribute wealth and opportunity, the welfare ideal arouses resistance as well as support.

Here in the United States, the welfare programs that have been adopted, most of them dating back only to the New Deal's effort to stem the Depression during the 1930s, continue to encounter widespread opposition. Yet they can be expected to expand in the future as the result of continued popular interest in reducing the vicissitudes of life and improving its quality, two goals that certainly in the case of public health have remained constant since the earliest urban settlements arose. At present, the vast technological and organizational resources of urban society increase the means available for achieving the welfare ideal.

FOR FURTHER READING

Joseph S. Berliner, *Economy, Society, and Welfare* (New York: Praeger, 1972). Combines economics and sociology to create a socioeconomic model for the analysis of welfare policy.

Amasa B. Ford, *Urban Health in America* (New York: Oxford University Press, 1976). On humanizing health care in mass society.

Herbert H. Hyman, ed., *The Politics of Health Care* (New York: Praeger, 1973). Reviews programs ranging from medicaid to the extermination of rats in New York City.

Carol H. Meyer, *Social Work Practice: A Response to the Urban Crisis* (New York: Free Press, 1970). The practice of social work relative to urban problems.

Daniel P. Moynihan, *The Politics of a Guaranteed Income* (New York: Random House, 1973). On social policy in the United States, particularly useful for the problem of dependency and the family assistance plans of the Nixon Administration vis-à-vis Congress.

Social Security Administration, *Social Security Programs in the United States* (Washington, D.C.: Government Printing Office, annually). Explains the welfare statutes and agencies making up the national system.

Walter I. Trattner, *From Poor Law to Welfare State* (New York: Free Press, 1974). An historical review appraising the role of social workers in the development of our welfare policies.

Harleigh B. Trecker, ed., *Goals for Social Welfare: 1973–1993* (New York: Association Press, 1973). Objectives in casework, group work, community organization, welfare planning, and social-work education and research for the near future.

Louis A. Zurcher, Jr., and Charles N. Bonjean, eds., *Planned Social Intervention* (West Trenton, N.J.: Chandler-Davis, 1970). A collection of articles on social science and social policy.

CHAPTER 20

HOUSING, TRANSPORTATION, AND THE ENVIRONMENT

Men, said Aristotle, establish cities in order to live. They continue there, he went on, in order to pursue the good life. Yet the good life remains elusive even in today's modern urban environment. In a typical city, America's included, together with progress and riches, we are apt to find overcrowding, dwellings in disrepair, deteriorating public services, increasing congestion, and the poisoning of the environment. Housing and slums, transportation, and ecological impairment, the three subjects of this chapter, are recognized social problems of high priority. They have provoked a great deal of inquiry and no little ameliorative action.

HOUSING, SLUMS, AND URBAN RENEWAL

HOUSING

Any consideration of a housing problem in America's urban areas must, like the question of poverty, recognize both its absolute and relative aspects. Housing is a necessity of life. It is also a luxury, and the standard of housing adequacy varies with the prevailing level of living.[1]

The 1960 census definitions of unfit dwellings steered a reasonable middle course between the idea of housing as an absolute necessity and the idea of it as an elected luxury depending on one's purchasing power. In 1960 the census recognized three categories of inadequate housing, namely, the dilapidated, the substandard, and the deteriorated.

Census enumerators saw a dilapidated house as one that does not provide "safe and adequate shelter" because:

> it has one or more critical defects; or has a combination of interme-
> diate defects in sufficient number to require extensive repair or
> rebuilding; or is of inadequate original construction. Critical defects
> result from continued neglect or lack of repair or indicate serious
> damage to the structure. Examples of critical defects include: holes,
> open cracks or missing materials over a large area of the floors,
> walls, roof, or other parts of the structure; sagging floors, wall or
> roof; damage by storm or fire. Inadequate original construction in-
> cludes structures built of makeshift materials and inadequately con-
> verted cellars, sheds, or garages not originally intended as living
> quarters.[2]

Substandard housing includes dilapidated buildings as defined above but also dwellings lacking separate sanitary facilities, that is, a washbowl, a bathtub or shower, and a toilet all set aside from the other rooms of the residence.

Finally, deteriorated housing consists of those units that possess defects which require repairs greater than those of normal maintenance. If not properly remedied, deterioration leads to dilapidation.

These criteria pertain only to the structures themselves and not their surroundings or their manner of use. To the physical defects of dilapidated, substandard, and deteriorated structures must be added other deficiencies in order to arrive at a more comprehensive conception of really inadequate

---

[1] See Margaret G. Reid, *Housing and Income* (Chicago: University of Chicago Press, 1962, pp. 378ff.

[2] Bureau of the Census, *U. S. Census of Housing: 1960* (Washington, D.C.: Government Printing Office, 1961), Vol. I, p. 111.

housing. The additional shortcomings are overcrowding; neighborhood blight in the form of heavy vehicular traffic, noise, fumes, and excessive building so that there is too little outdoor space for the population; and also insufficient public services resulting in unmet safety, health, educational, and recreational needs.

America's Urban Housing Picture

Though definite improvement in housing was made in the urban areas of the United States during the decades from 1950 to 1960 and also from 1960 to 1970, notable deficiencies still exist.

According to the 1960 housing census, 15.9 percent of the nation's total stock of 53 million occupied dwelling units were substandard. However, fully 27.7 percent of all housing outside Standard Metropolitan Statistical Areas (SMSA's) were substandard.[3] Assuming more than one person per room as the standard of overcrowding, 10 percent of all households in SMSA's were overcrowded in 1960. This compared with 14 percent outside SMSA's.

Overcrowding among nonwhites was materially higher than for white households. In fact, it was four times more: 28 percent in contrast to 7 percent. Inner-city location, as one might expect, bore a close relationship to the incidence of substandard housing. Thus for 1960, while 52 percent of United States SMSA population lived in the nation's central cities, some 57 percent of the millions of occupied substandard housing units were located in the central cities.[4]

Between 1950 and 1960, not only did the nation's housing picture brighten considerably, it improved more in our urban areas than it did in our rural regions. In that interval, occupied substandard units dropped from 36 to 16 percent of the total stock. Though deficiencies in urban housing, particularly units occupied by non-white renters, were not uncommon even in 1960 (750,000 units having been downgraded in the decade), substandardness was much more apparent in rural nonfarm housing than it was in our metropolitan communities. Many metropolitan areas showed dramatic upgrading in that 10-year interval: St. Louis from 34.9 percent of its dwellings substandard in 1950 to only 15.6 percent in 1959; Philadelphia, 14.3 to 7.3; Los Angeles, 9.1 to 2.6; Baltimore, 22.1 to 5.8; and Pittsburgh, 32.2 to 14.2.[5]

Moreover, progress toward the national goal of "decent housing for all" has continued in America's SMSAs in the decade since 1960. In 1970, while 6.0 percent of all occupied households in the country lacked some or all

[3] *Report of the President's Committee on Urban Housing* (Washington, D.C.: Government Printing Office, 1967), Vol. I, Table 1, p. 9, and Table 2, p. 10.

[4] Ibid., Tables 6 and 23, p. 12 and p. 26.

[5] *U. S. Census of Housing: 1960*, op. cit., Vol. IV, IA, Table 1.

TABLE 20-1 Total Occupied Housing Units, With and Without Plumbing Facilities, for SMSAs and Areas Outside SMSAs: 1960 and 1970

	UNITED STATES	NUMBER		PERCENT	
		INSIDE SMSAs	OUTSIDE SMSAs	INSIDE SMSAs	OUTSIDE SMSAs
1960					
Occupied Units	53,024	34,000	19,024	100.0	100.0
Lacking some or all plumbing	9,778	3,521	6,257	10.3	32.9
1970					
Occupied Units	63,417	44,064	19,353	100.0	100.0
lacking some or all plumbing	4,678	1,628	3,050	3.7	15.8

Source: Bureau of the Census, *Census of Population and Housing: 1970* (Washington, D.C.: Government Printing Office), Series PHC (2)-1.

plumbing, the corresponding figure for all SMSAs of 200,000 or more population stood at only 3.0 percent. Overcrowding was also less severe in our SMSAs than in the United States as a whole, 7.7 percent as compared to 8.2 percent.[6] Table 20-1 presents the housing characteristics of the United States, contrasting SMSAs with areas outside SMSAs for 1960 and 1970, with plumbing as the criterion of condition. The superiority of housing in our metropolitan areas is no less apparent than the progress made in housing from 1960 to 1970 in the nation generally. As Nathan Glazer has summaried America's housing state, despite some limitations "the United States offers a degree of housing plenty that is not to be matched in most other countries, whether rich or poor."[7]

Yet an urban housing problem of some dimensions continues to exist in the United States. According to one recent study, possibly six million American households are physically substandard.[8] The nation's housing deficiencies are especially concentrated in our central cities, where out of 20.1 million dwellings in 1970, 4.1 percent lacked some or all plumbing, and 8.6 percent (a figure slightly higher than that for the country by and large) were overcrowded. The American urban housing problem is also concentrated among nonwhites. Even though in 1970 black-occupied units in the central cities of our SMSAs included proportionally fewer substandard ones than those that were black-occupied in the country generally, inner-city blacks had a rate of substandard or dilapidated housing half again as high as the

[6] Bureau of the Census, *Statistical Abstract of the United States: 1972* (Washington, D.C.: Government Printing Office, 1972), p. 846.

[7] Nathan Glazer, "Dilemmas of Housing Policy," in Daniel P. Moynihan, ed., *Toward a National Urban Policy* (New York: Basic Books, 1970), pp. 50–65.

[8] Morton B. Schussheim, "Housing in Perspective," *Public Interest* (Spring 1970), pp. 18–30.

Puerto Ricans in the Chelsea district of New York City. The Spanish sign says, "Mister landlord, we are living here, where shall we move to?" The owner is trying to evict the tenants and then renovate the building for higher rent.

United States as a whole.[9] Finally, when in addition to unsound construction and overcrowding one also evaluates housing as to its excessive expense relative to income, then perhaps as many as 13 million families in the nation, not all urban by any means, remain inadequately housed at present.[10]

[9] Bureau of the Census, *Statistical Abstract of the United States: 1972,* op. cit., p. 847.

[10] *America's Housing Needs: 1970–1980* (Cambridge, Mass.: MIT-Harvard Joint Center for Urban Studies, 1973).

In comparison with such prosperous countries as the United Kingdom, Soviet Russia, West Germany, France, and Sweden, the housing problem of the United States today is not general but specific. It is specific, as Glazer recognizes, with regard to "problems of poverty, problems of neighborhood, and problems of segregation and ghettoization."[11] In brief, America's poor housing is tied to significant social problems in some interdependent causal fashion, with a myriad of undesirable social concomitants in the urban slum.

Physically, slums consist of dilapidated, grossly substandard housing located in congested areas having poor public facilities and services.[12] In addition, slums are socially identifiable by virtue of the fact that their resident population exhibits a higher-than-average disease rate and also consistently higher levels of crime. According to David Hunter's rule-of-thumb estimate, slums containing one-fifth of a given city's residential area will have perhaps half of all its disease.[13] Hunter also lists, as typically identifiable features of any slum: crime, broken families, isolation, and alienation. In New York City in 1960, 27 percent of the population concentrated in the city's run-down areas were responsible for slightly more than half of the juvenile delinquency in the whole metropolis and a substantial incidence of economic dependency, infant mortality, and venereal disease as well.[14]

Several explanations have been advanced to account for the continued presence of urban slums. These hypotheses not only emphasize poor housing but also relate the slum areas to the economy and social structure of the entire surrounding urban community.[15]

Slums of Despair.

One theory holds that slums signify an essential aspect of the urban social process. That is, they are residential areas where the community's failures settle and live. In Charles Stokes's term, we thus have slums of despair.[16]

These house the city's rejects, its social skidders who for constitutional or circumstantial reasons are unable to secure steady work or engage in normal social relationships. They are the ones who have sustained defeat in society and who seek the oblivion of skid row or hobohemia. Careful analysis

[11] Glazer, op. cit.

[12] Compare David R. Hunter, *The Slums: Challenge and Response* (New York: Free Press, 1962).

[13] Ibid., pp. 71–73.

[14] Ibid.

[15] John R. Seeley, "The Slum: Its Nature, Use, and Users," *Journal of the American* Institute of Planners, 25 (February 1959), pp. 7–14, asserts that slums display a logic of necessity and also of opportunity.

[16] Charles Stokes, "A Theory of Slums," *Land Economics,* 48 (August 1962), pp. 187–97.

shows four main reasons for skid-row residence: economic hardship, poor mental health, poor social adjustment, and poor physical health or disability. The death rate of these solitary men living in poor hotels or dormitories is more than six times that of white males in general.[17]

More common today than the problem of the derelict is the trauma of the racially segregated slum. The victims of severe discrimination often find themselves forced into the confines of this despairing habitat. There, in vermin-ridden dwellings, with foul odors, buildings in disrepair, and signs of demoralization all around, society's outcasts congregate. Studies of urban segregation patterns reveal the large scale on which racial separation has recently contributed to the building up of slums in American cities. Indexes of racial residential segregation in our cities have shown general increases. From the early 1950s to the present, the in-migration and natural increase of our urban nonwhite population, mainly in the central cities, together with white out-migration to the suburbs, have combined to divide the total population of a given metropolitan area along racial lines. This fact, as Farley and Taeuber express it, "has greatly intensified the magnitude of the problems of segregation and desegregation of neighborhoods, local institutions, and schools."[18] It has also added to the problem of improving housing.

Slums of Hope

The second type of slum houses that part of the city's population which has newly arrived, typically an ethnic composition whose cultural background is not too strongly disfavored by the host community. They are potentially mobile.

In the slum of hope, again borrowing from Stokes' terminology, the low-income newcomers perfect their social skills to gain entry into the larger society. By and large, events show these people educable, employable, and reasonably capable of success. New York's Lower East Side, long the site of the massive influx of European Jews into the metropolitan economy, is probably *the* type case of the slum of hope. Participating in mutual-aid organizations, sustained by religious tradition, benefiting from the public schools, and gaining an economic toehold through small-business enterprise and family sacrifice, the Jews of Manhattan were eventually able to move into middle-class Bronx neighborhoods and even far beyond. In fact, as Moses Rischin has observed, because it was a subcultural center the Lower East Side even attracted some Jews from other sections of New York as permanent residents.[19]

[17] Hunter, op. cit., p. 86.

[18] Reynolds Farley and Karl E. Taeuber, "Population Trends and Residential Segregation since 1960," *Science,* 159 (March 1, 1968), pp. 953–56.

[19] Moses Rischin, *The Promised City: New York's Jews, 1870–1914* (Cambridge, Mass.: Harvard University Press, 1962).

To an extent, our present urban newcomers, black, Chicano, and Puerto Rican, are now probably engaged in much the same process of mobility through the development of social organization and competence in the slum. The greater difficulties they face, Warner and Burke explain, result from the addition of color barriers to the "socioreligious identifications" already present in the urban stratification system.[20]

Functional Slums

Another interpretation of the slums also views them as blighted physical environments inhabited by a particular population. However, in this perspective the slum is seen as a functional adjunct of the city's economy and land-use pattern.

Adjacent to an area of high land values centrally located and suitable for business development, the slum contains housing that its absentee owners allow to deteriorate. These "slumlords" do so because the dwellings there no longer attract affluent residents, and long-term maintenance and investment are counterindicated. Land in this zone in transition, as Park and Burgess called it, is usually held for speculative purposes. Unable to afford better housing, the inhabitants cannot bargain for improvements or, for that matter, even normal upkeep. A good deal of organized community life exists in the slums, but political organization there is weak. It is especially weak in comparison with the articulate, resourceful power wielded by property interests. Consequently, the enforcement of the housing code suffers, and both the public and private amenities decline. Constituting a weak and vulnerable environment populated by the underprivileged, the slum, whose most tangible asset is its poor housing, comes to supply the city with a variety of illegal services. notably prostitution, drugs, gambling, the black market, pornography, and stolen goods.

A More Positive Conception

Nonetheless, we need also to emphasize a fourth, and more positive, view of the dense, low-income urban neighborhood. This conception of it as an urban village, as Herbert Gans has called it, has become particularly prominent in connection with opposition to business-oriented programs of urban renewal to eliminate blighted areas without due regard to the interests of the local inhabitants themselves.

Boston College's Marc Fried together with Peggy Gleicher surveyed Boston's West End to secure more knowledge of the sociocultural aspects of stable, working-class slums for the guidance of city planners.[21] Their ul-

[20] Sam B. Warner and Colin B. Burke, "Cultural Change and the Ghetto," *Journal of Contemporary History,* 4 (October 1969), pp. 173–87.

[21] Marc Fried and Peggy Gleicher, "Some Sources of Residential Satisfaction in an Urban Slum," *Journal of the American Institute of Planners,* 27 (November 1961), pp. 305–15.

timate objective was to avoid doing slum residents harm while at the same time making available to them "some of the advantages of modern urban facilities, ranging from better plumbing and decreased fire hazards to improved utilization of local space and better neighborhood resources." It became apparent to these investigators that there was a good deal of sentimental attachment to the West End, and that social relationships there made up a network blanketing practically the whole neighborhood. In fact, interpersonal commitments correlated with strong localist feeling among West Enders. The West End streets served as annexes of the homes, showing, Fried and Gleicher wrote, "the high degree of permeability of the boundary between the dwelling unit and the immediate environing area." In a more recent summary of the high degree of satisfaction of these Bostonians with their modest surroundings, Fried explained it by saying that "it is both the compensatory significance of social relationships and of local participation and their intrinsic value for lower status people that is important."[22] (For a related study of community solidarity done by Gerald D. Suttles in Chicago's Near West Side slum, see Ch. 5.)

In the final analysis, then, whether a given slum is deleterious or beneficial requires rather careful observation.

URBAN REHOUSING AND DEVELOPMENT

The relationship of poor housing to other indexes of social pathology is by no means clear, but the diminution of unacceptable housing in order to alleviate many social problems, as well as physical distress, has long been a major public policy in the United States. Inadequate housing has had any number of social deficiencies ascribed to it, including failure in school, family disorganization, poor health, crime, and antisocial behavior in general.[23] Yet David Wilner's study of Baltimore shows that except for communicable diseases and accidents, improved housing has little effect on diminishing ill health.[24] In like manner, the west coast studies of Nathan Glazer and his colleagues suggest that not only is good housing unlikely to generate beneficial social change but, indeed, that unstable family organization and social alienation can even prevent the sustained utilization of standard housing.[25] Nevertheless, considerable effort has been expended in the United States to develop the nation's housing for social as well as mere physical purposes.

[22] Marc Fried, *The World of the Urban Working Class* (Cambridge, Mass.: Harvard University Press, 1973), p. 93.

[23] See Alvin Schorr, *Slums and Social Insecurity,* Research Report No. 1, Social Security Administration (Washington, D.C.: Government Printing Office, 1963), pp. 31–32.

[24] David M. Wilner et al., *The Housing Environment and Family Life* (Baltimore, Md.: Johns Hopkins Press, 1962).

[25] Nathan Glazer and Davis McEntire, eds., *Studies in Housing and Minority Groups* (Berkeley, Calif.: University of California Press, 1960).

The Federal Rehousing and Urban Renewal Program

A latecomer among nations subsidizing housing for the urban poor, the United States first furnished federal housing assistance with the passage of the National Housing Act of 1934. Since then 35 national housing programs have been legislated, with possibly the acts of 1937, 1949, and 1965 the most significant.

By encouraging construction the Federal Housing Act of 1937 was intended to alleviate unemployment. But it had another aim too, "to remedy the unsafe and insanitary housing conditions and the acute shortage of decent, safe, and sanitary dwellings for families of low income, in rural and urban communities, that are injurious to the health, safety, and morals of the citizens of the Nation." To implement this goal, the U.S. Housing Authority was created. In addition, the principle of slum clearance was worked into the Housing Act of 1937 with the proviso that construction of any public housing project could be undertaken only on condition that at least an equal number of substandard units were demolished at the same time, in other words, in blighted areas suffering from social pathology and disorganization, which new construction often simply could not surmount!

The 1949 Housing Act supplemented the earlier legislation. It authorized speedier construction in keeping with the newly enunciated national policy of achieving "a decent home and a suitable living environment for every American family." Originally the federal housing program sought to assist only the marginal working poor. Said New York's Senator Robert Wagner, sponsor of the 1937 Housing Act, when the question arose of helping the severely impoverished: "there are some people whom we cannot possibly reach. . . . Obviously this bill cannot provide housing for those who cannot pay the rent minus the subsidy allowed."[26] Slowly the 1949 housing effort came to be directed toward the very poor, especially the nonwhite minorities of our large central cities. By the end of the 1960s, about one-half of all public-housing units in the nation were occupied by black tenants. Another third housed the elderly. Yet by 1968, the public housing program included only 673,000 dwelling units housing 2.5 million persons as compared to 3 million poverty-income renter households in substandard housing, to give some idea as to the overall scope of this enterprise.

Beginning in 1965, Congress reorganized the administration of public housing by establishing the Housing and Urban Development Department (HUD). It also instituted a variety of alternatives to public projects. Thus rent supplements, the funding of voluntary nonprofit corporations, scatter-site housing instead of massive high-rise buildings in the midst of blight, rehabilitative social services, and others as well. They were designed to broaden and diversify the federal effort in behalf of housing the urban poor. Many of

[26] Quoted in Lawrence M. Friedman, *Government and Slum Housing* (Chicago: Rand McNally, 1968), p. 109.

---

these ventures remain issues today, since they entail considerable public expense, no little administrative ineptitude and waste, and direct influence on nonpoverty neighborhoods.

Weaknesses of the Federal Program

The federal presence in housing and urban development has been neither simple, consistent, nor wholly effective. Two aspects stand out prominently.

First, the national housing effort has had three income-group beneficiaries: (1) low-income families below the poverty line; (2) moderate-income families above the poverty line but who, unaided, would have to spend more than one-quarter of their income for standard housing; and (3) middle-income families in need of insurance-like guarantees to secure mortgage loans. Of these three groups, our middle-income families have been the major factor in America's national housing program with the Federal Housing Administration (FHA) securing the mortgages on about one-fourth of all new nonfarm housing construction.

Yet those most in need, the slum dwellers, have benefited in the long run. Since loans guaranteed by FHA and also the Veterans Administration have been predicated on the governmentally defined amenities, construction standards have been generally upgraded. By a filtration process FHA is responsible for releasing homes for the benefit of people too poor to qualify for direct FHA support. FHA, however, has not brought new housing substantially within the reach of our very low-income population. In fact, as some contend, it may also have inflated building costs.[27]

Second, urban renewal has evoked no little criticism—and much of it bitter too. Calling urban renewal a program so complex that "few people have more than a skewed random image of it," Scott Greer has declared that at an expenditure of billions, it has actually reduced the supply of low-cost housing in our cities.[28] Greer concedes that "patches of new construction" have appeared, but he argues that urban renewal has not only failed to rehouse the disadvantaged, but that it has also played havoc with the neighborhoods of many of America's urban poor. Bearing this out are the results of a careful study recently published of the aftermath of urban renewal in Boston's West End, beginning in the late 1950s: an eradication of social relationships that even 10 years later many of the earlier inhabitants found "irreplaceable."[29]

Much of Greer's critique is based on published case studies of urban

[27] Consult Sam B. Warner, Jr., *The Urban Wilderness: A History of the American City* (New York: Harper, 1972), pp. 230–66.

[28] Scott Geer, *Urban Renewal and American Cities* (Indianapolis, Ind.: Bobbs-Merrill, 1965), Ch. 1.

[29] Described in Fried, op. cit., pp. 81–87.

renewal in big cities like Chicago, and field observations in Little Rock, Miami, Tacoma, and other cities as well. Greer points to the lack of definition in urban-renewal legislation of crucial terms like "inadequate housing" and "a suitable living environment for all." This vagueness is compounded by the variability of municipal housing-code standards. For example, among 56 cities reviewed, minimum dwelling space per occupant varied by a factor of 100 percent.

Almost everywhere the major emphasis of urban renewal grants has come to be placed on revitalizing the central business district, improving public institutions, and fostering the trickle-down process of building expensive high-rise housing so as to release cheaper units to the less well-to-do. As a result, urban renewal has separated itself from the public-housing program. Also, viable neighborhoods have been uprooted to make way for industrial and institutional clients. And, finally, the relocation of low-income, aged, and nonwhite persons has actually suffered. In the words of Herbert Gans, the urban renewal program "has cleared slums to make room for many luxury-housing and a few middle-income projects, and it has also provided inexpensive land for the expansion of colleges, hospitals, libraries, shopping areas, and such other institutions located in slum areas."[30] Still another major critic, Martin Anderson, has also scored the program equally for its economic wastefulness and its unfortunate social consequences.[31]

THE FUTURE OF THE URBAN HOUSING PROBLEM

The history of urban renewal may well illustrate the probable logic of any long-term solution to the housing problem of America's urban poor: the need for a broader based approach. As Lawrence Friedman has expressed the matter, "laws for the poor . . . are unlikely to be generated unless (a) the poor are a majority and have fair and adequate political representatives, or (b) on balance, proposed legislation serves the interests of some class larger and broader than the poor."[32] In keeping with this conclusion, a recent analysis of 20 rent strikes in the Harlem ghetto of New York City shows some improved services being brought about and some rent reductions, but apart from organization-building for long-range political purposes, "it cannot be said that the pay-offs for rent strike participants were commensurate with the effort involved."[33] Hence it would appear that effective strategies to secure better housing for our urban poor—mainly inner-city nonwhites—call

[30] Herbert J. Gans, "The Failure of Urban Renewal," *Commentary*, 39 (April 1965), pp. 29–37.

[31] Martin Anderson, *The Federal Bulldozer: A Critical Analysis of Urban Renewal: 1949–1962* (Cambridge, Mass.: MIT Press, 1964).

[32] Friedman, op. cit., p. 191.

[33] Michael Lipsky, *Protest in City Politics: Rent Strikes, Housing, and the Power of the Poor* (Chicago: Rand McNally, 1970), p. 156.

for the service of the interests of other groups as well. Among these other groups are the aged, the working-class poor, and the moderately situated lower-middle class.

Many authorities feel that the poor will continue to seek political allies from the groups mentioned. They also believe that a high order of political statecraft disposing of large public expenditures benefiting other interests will be indispensable if America's urban housing problem is to be successfully resolved. Not a few critics think that the Model Cities program, which includes social-welfare services, manpower development, and community organization as well as construction, and which more than 150 cities were participating in by the end of 1970 has great potential.[34] Others, like Anthony Downs, emphasize strategies of nonwhite dispersion from the central city into the suburbs, making sure first that the whites will not leave the suburbs affected.[35] Careful programming is vital here. Dispersion programs to date, as Murray Schumach observes in New York City at least, may actually be eroding middle-class and lower-middle-class neighborhoods by placing even drug addicts or mentally disturbed patients in neglected apartment buildings or hotels.[36] Such facts suggest caution with respect to the appraisal of ongoing development programs apart from prospective ones.

TRANSPORTATION

The cities of any advanced urban nation and certainly those of the United States are all linked together by one vast circulatory system moving people and goods through space. This vital transit pattern consists of autos, buses, and trucks travelling over roads and highways; fixed-track vehicles like trains and trolleys; aircraft of various kinds; and rivertine as well as maritime vessels operating between port cities. Within any urban community there is a corresponding internal system of transportation, one essential to the immediate locality. In fact, the largest cities today have exceedingly complex structures made up of surface, underground, and overhead railways; paved streets and expressways; bridges, viaducts, and underpasses; different kinds of terminal installations—airports, piers, marshalling yards, and the like; and a very technical system of communication joining them together into an operational entity.

[34] Department of Housing and Urban Development, *1970 HUD Yearbook* (Washington, D.C.: Government Printing Office, 1971), p. 19.

[35] Anthony Downs, *Opening Up the Suburbs: An Urban Strategy for America* (New Haven, Conn.: Yale University Press, 1973), pp. 87–102.

[36] Murray Schumach, "Middle-Class Areas Called Victims of Poverty Pockets," *New York Times* (July 8, 1973), p. 1.

THE URBAN TRANSPORTATION PROBLEM

Modern urban transport represents a singular combination of technology and human organization, but one that exhibits such serious weaknesses that the typical American city is commonly described as burdened by a transportation problem. Depending on the particular writer, that problem may even be described as critical, certainly severe. In the words of a member of the Brookings Institution staff, "Every metropolitan area in the United States is confronted by a transportation problem that seems destined to become more aggravated in the years ahead."[37] Lyle C. Fitch and his associates have analyzed this urban transportation problem in terms of three interrelated types of difficulty: (1) the physical; (2) the institutional; and (3) the conceptual.[38] This division offers much insight.

Physical Deficiencies

Physical deficiencies relate to traffic congestion and costly, inconvenient delays, like airliners circling over airports waiting to land. Also, much space needs to be devoted to transportation in the form of roads, parking lots, loading zones, and service facilities. In downtown Los Angeles, for instance, two-thirds of the whole area serves the automobile exclusively—by means of streets, parking lots, and the like. (Lest it be misconstrued, it should be noted that expressways alone occupy less than two percent of the whole Los Angeles land area.) Finally, there are physical health hazards stemming from the common transportation pattern. According to the Air Pollution Control District, which administers the 1630-square-mile Los Angeles basin, autos discharging 700 tons of noxious chemicals daily are responsible for 80 percent of the air-borne contaminants and particulates in the atmosphere there.

Institutional Deficiencies

The second kind of transportation problem, institutional deficiencies, concerns organizational and financial weaknesses. Organization for transportation purposes is typically fragmented in the urban communities of the United States. The difficulties created by the lack of organizational unity in our cities are further augmented by the shortages of financial resources that this leads to.[39] And the lack of financial support means that not only service

[37] Wilfred Owen, *The Metropolitan Transportation Problem* (Washington, D.C.: The Brookings Institution, 1966), p. 2.

[38] Lyle C. Fitch et al., *Urban Transportation and Public Policy* (San Francisco, Calif.: Chandler, 1964), pp. 9–24.

[39] See *Urban Mass Transportation: 1961*, Hearings before Subcommittee No. 3 of the House Committee on Banking and Currency, June 27–28 (Washington, D.C.: Government Printing Office, 1961), p. 165.

but also research and development for future economies also tends to be handicapped. As a result, many American cities have been left without mass transit service at all. In fact, between 1950 and 1970, 606 transit companies ended their operations in the United States.[40]

Furthermore, the financing of urban transportation in America has evolved largely in a laissez-faire manner. Each mode of transportation has been funded independently, the principle being that its users should bear the cost themselves. Our roads have been financed primarily by gasoline taxes, but their collection is not related to the type of road used or the time or even the individual's ability to pay. For example, the suburban driver who uses the central city's streets regularly may not contribute to their upkeep. The consequence has been an uncoordinated transportation system with a good deal of haphazard change

Conceptual Deficiencies

As the third general aspect of the urban transportation problem, we have a set of conceptual shortcomings, in other words, a lack of valid knowledge. "Many of the areas of dispute with respect to urban-transportation policy today," Fitch asserts, "reflect inadequate understanding of the functioning of urban-transportation systems and failure to consider the alternatives of urban development."[41]

One case of conceptual weakness concerns the question of whether to conserve the present land-use pattern, with one central business district as the nucleus of the entire metropolitan community, or to hasten the dispersion of the population around a plurality of centers separated by a good deal of space. John R. Meyer concludes that since urban property values are less dependent today on public transit than they formerly were, it is uncertain whether improved transit will actually benefit businesses that are centrally located.[42]

Determining the optimal roles of motor-vehicle traffic versus mass transit in the urban transportation system is still another conceptual defect. The cost-benefit value of each of these modes of transportation is not entirely understood, owing to their relationship to various significant factors. The factors themselves have been recognized and are reasonably clear: the existence of corridors, tracks, density, and the like.[43] But their interrelationships are another matter. Consider the case of the automobile. The diffusion of

[40] Bureau of the Census, *Statistical Abstract of the United States: 1972,* op. cit., Tables 887, 888, and 910.

[41] Fitch, op. cit., p. 20.

[42] John R. Meyer, "Urban Transportation," in James Q. Wilson, ed., *The Metropolitan Enigma* (Garden City, N.Y.: Doubleday, 1970), pp. 44–75.

[43] Cf. John R. Meyer, "Urban Transportation," in Moynihan, op cit.

jobs in the typical metropolitan area means that peak densities are not apt to reach the rail mass-transit threshold economy in the foreseeable future in any city in the United States except New York, Chicago, Philadelphia, and Boston. Therefore, a rail system cannot generally be expected to achieve competitive economy against the automobile. On the other hand, certain additional costs of the automobile need to be weighed in the balance. Heavy reliance on auto transportation results in freeway construction that uproots neighborhoods and disrupts businesses. Avoiding putting routes through built-up districts necessitates the destruction of park and recreation land. These circumstances together with air pollution indicate that the social costs imposed by the automobile need to be reckoned with too.

COPING WITH THE TRANSPORTATION PROBLEM

In line with the physical, institutional, and conceptual aspects of our urban transportation problem, a variety of responses have been forthcoming from local and national agencies and from private interests as well. These may perhaps best be examined as efforts directed at (1) accommodating automobile traffic or (2) instituting or improving mass transit.

Accommodating Automobile Traffic

The continually increasing volume of auto travel accounts for three-fourths of total American consumer transportation expenditures today in comparison with just 30 percent in 1929. This confirms the willingness of America's urban public to accept the private car as the basis of its local transportation system. (For the growing popularity of the automobile and the decline of other modes of transportation in the United States since 1950, see Table 20-2.) Moreover, though not usually appreciated, careful research into automobile use shows that economic and other advantages are actually realizable here.[44]

Low-density residential development definitely favors the automobile. Such a condition is widespread in urban America and has, in fact, benefited from federal support for more than 30 years now. The Highway Act of 1944 included measures to facilitate the local distribution of traffic carried by the national highways. Similarly, the Highway Act of 1956, which created the interstate expressways, allowed inner- and outer-belt urban circulation roads to be built. Six years later, highway grants came to be predicated on comprehensive transportation planning by major cities. The result has been a proliferation of arterial motorways that have greatly facilitated automotive traffic in our cities and metropolitan regions. They have not, however, solved

---

[44] J. R. Meyer, J. F. Kain, and M. Wohl, *The Urban Transportation Problem* (Cambridge, Mass.: Harvard University Press, 1965), p. 249.

TABLE 20-2   Motor Vehicle Registration and Mileage Driven, Rural-Urban, as Compared with Operating Transit Systems, United States: 1950, 1960, and 1970

	1950	1960	1970
Motor vehicle registration, (millions)	49.2	73.9	108.4
Mileage, passenger cars (billions)			
Rural	181.1	303.3	406.4
Urban	182.5	284.8	494.5
Operating transit systems	1,406	1,251	1,079
Motorbus systems	1,354	1,236	1,075
Revenue passengers carried (millions)	17,246	9,395	7,332

Source: Adapted from Bureau of the Census, *Statistical Abstract of the United States, 1972* (Washington, D.C.: Government Printing Office, 1972), Tables 887, 888, and 910.

the transportation problem, witness air contamination, congestion, the division of communities, and the plight of the dependent poor deprived of mass transit.

These limitations of the automobile and expressway indicate that other approaches are also needed. Moderately large cities of medium residential and work-place densities would appear to require some combination of methods in order to succeed. Perhaps here a highway-oriented solution of cars and buses will have to be resorted to. In that case though, there will need to be careful development, with inner-belt motorways to relieve downtown congestion; scheduling to relieve peaking; and economic practices (subsidizes for mass transit, for instance) as part of every particular solution to improve urban transportation further.

In the large Eastern coastal cities, established rail lines do offer inexpensive solutions, provided they are coordinated with feeder bus lines and distribution subway systems.

In short, though popular, the automobile cannot entirely dispense with the various forms of mass transit in any serious effort to resolve our urban transportation problem on a comprehensive scale.

Instituting or Improving Mass Transit

A number of our metropolitan areas have undertaken the construction of large-scale modern transit lines. The greatest single project of this type is the one in the San Francisco Bay Area Rapid Transit District. There, a $1.5 billion, 75-mile system, running 80-mile-an-hour trains opened for regular operation in 1972. It was designed to connect the counties of San Francisco,

Bumper-to-bumper traffic jam. The popularity of the automobile and truck for moving people and freight.

Alameda, and Contra Costa. A good idea of the engineering accomplishments of the project may be obtained by noting that it includes 4 miles of tunneling under the Bay waters, 24 miles of surface track, and 20 miles of undersurface track. The 30-mile trip from Daly City to Concord, the two terminals of the system, is designed to take 45 minutes in comparison with the 75-minute rush-hour trip by car. This complex computerized system, however, has been plagued by safety problems and disappointing patronage.

To aid their financially troubled transit systems, burdened as they are by urban sprawl, declining ridership lost to the automobile, and mounting overhead costs, city governments have been exempting their common carriers from both franchise fees and taxes. Local subsidies have also been given to private companies, as in Philadelphia and Boston, to keep them going. Even the outright purchase of private transit firms as a means of maintaining service has been resorted to. Attempts to save or improve downtown transit facilities, especially at public expense, receive strong support from business interests located at the core and from disadvantaged groups largely dependent on mass transit in the inner city. At the same time though, suburbs and the metropolitan fringes oppose public aid to mass transit.

Urban mass transportation has not received the federal support that automotive transportation has, but some national aid has been provided recently. It was the Housing Act of 1961 that first brought the federal government into the area of urban mass transit. The Housing and Home Finance administrator was authorized to make grants not exceeding $25 million for "the improvement of mass transportation service, and the contribution of such service toward meeting total urban transportation needs at minimum cost." Building on this, the 1962 Federal-Aid Highway Act declared that it was in the national interest to coordinate urban transportation into an overall plan. The federal transportation program gained still further momentum in 1964 and 1966 when under the Urban Mass Transportation Act, capital funds were authorized for local transit facilities and equipment and, in 1974, also for operating expenses.

In 1970, about $175 million was supplied for capital and demonstration grants, up from $110 million in 1968. Alternating current as a means of propulsion has been tested in San Francisco. Automated fare collection systems have been evaluated on New York's Long Island Railroad. Other demonstration grants have permitted Pittsburgh to try out a medium-capacity rapid transit line, and also research teams at Kansas State and West Virginia Universities to inquire into the computerization of bus scheduling. Service improvement trials have also been conducted on the Grand River Avenue bus route in Detroit, on Seattle's monorail, and on the whole mass-transit area of Boston, Worcester, Pittsfield, and Fitchburg. One main research finding is that frequency and quality of service are usually more important than reduced fares in increasing mass-transit patronage.

LOOKING TO THE FUTURE

Even with the support of the Department of Transportation created in 1966, the proponents of mass transportation express only guarded optimism as to the eventual success of such modes of travel in our urban areas.[45] Lewis Schneider, for one, has advised urban planners to reserve judgment on the competitive ability of mass transit to divert people from their cars "until at least one modern route is built embodying [current] standards of speed and comfort."[46] Most persons, he says, have simply never experienced a *modern* rapid-transit system. A setup of this sort provides air conditioning; tailored commuter service appealing to the special needs of patrons; shuttle buses terminating at automobile parking lots; nonstop express service like Los Angeles' Freeway Flyer; expressway lanes reserved exclusively for buses; a

[45] George M. Smerk, "The Urban Mass Transportation Act of 1964: New Hope for American Cities," *Transportation Journal* (Winter 1965), pp. 35–39.

[46] Lewis M. Schneider, *Marketing Urban Mass Transit* (Boston: Graduate School of Business Administration, Harvard University, 1965), p. 182.

EXHIBIT 20-1 Percent of Workers Using Public Transportation, by Size of Place, United States: 1970

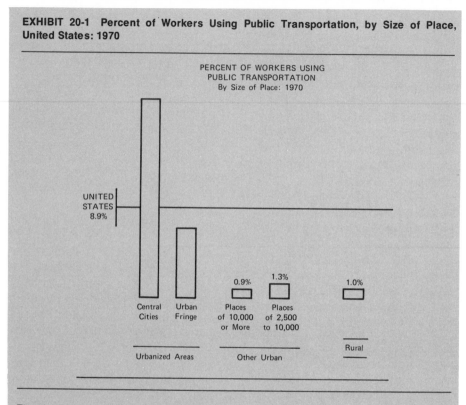

The significance of mass transit for urban workers and especially those living in central cities is apparent from these data compiled by the U.S. Census Bureau.

Source: Executive Office of the President, Office of Management and Budget, *Social Indicators, 1973* (Washington, D.C.: Government Printing Office, 1973), p. 354.

seats-for-all policy; spartan (low-fare) service for school children; the elimination of disagreeable surcharges like transfer fares; lightweight trains; quality loading and unloading facilities; automated and computerized controls producing higher speeds; security guards; and still other features too.

Such futuristic solutions to urban transportation ills, and even more so the visionary ones that call, say, for the pneumatic-tube distribution of goods, personally owned land-and-air hovercraft, and overhead high-speed cable systems, in all probability offer little promise in the near future. A mundane, evolutionary process seems to be inevitable. The Chicago Area Transportation Study of 1960 predicted that over the next two decades total trips to and from the central business district would increase only a few percentage points, but that trips elsewhere in metropolitan Chicago, territory not amenable to mass transit, would rise as much as 77 percent.

In like manner confirming the continued versatility of the private automobile for urban transportation, a RAND study anticipated that in the 1970s the automobile would be lighter and smaller, more comfortable, and more economical of fuel, but otherwise essentially the same as now.[47] Note that the 1977 deadline for a pollution-free auto engine mandated under the Federal Clean Air Act has been under fire from both auto manufacturers and the car-buying public alarmed by the prospect of added expense and lower operational efficiency. The action beginning in 1973 of the oil-exporting nations of the Middle East to regulate their production and drastically raise petroleum prices has dealt a further blow to antipollution efforts that require greater automobile fuel consumption.

The manifold political, organizational, and technological steps entailed in achieving solutions to the problems of urban transportation will doubtlessly remain with us for some time to come. It will continue to be necessary for various interest groups—transit companies, banks, suburbanites, and downtown businesses—to clarify their common needs and then secure local support for legislation. Realistic engineering and economic planning cannot be ignored any more than obtaining the requisite financial resources can be. In 1977, for example, despite massive federal subsidies the nation's urban transit systems had a collective deficit of $1.8 billion.

Lest it be concluded that only a massive, long-range systems approach to the urban transportation problem can work, economist Dick Netzer recently pointed out that simple solutions may be at hand. One is the jitney bus, owned by ghetto residents, furnishing cheap, flexible service while augmenting the income of the poor. Netzer offers this not as a panacea but as an easily adopted device and with, as he says, "promising near-term rather than remote payoffs."[48]

ECOLOGICAL IMPAIRMENT

John W. Gardner, then Secretary of HEW and now head of Common Cause, provided the keynote address to the third National Conference on Air Pollution in 1966. Gardner pointed out that ecological contamination, once thought the price of progress, had become so bad in the nation that it was turning into a brake on further advancement. He added that the problem centered chiefly on our cities.[49]

Gardner then reminded his audience of scientists and officials that only three weeks earlier, New York City had put out a warning for persons with heart or respiratory diseases to stay indoors and avoid the very heavy pall of

[47] Cited in A. Scheffer Lang and Richard M. Soberman, *Urban Rail Transit: Its Economies and Technology* (Cambridge, Mass.: MIT Press, 1964), p. 107.

[48] Dick Netzer, *Economics and Urban Problems* (New York: Basic Books, 1974), 2nd ed., pp. 218–19.

[49] HEW, *Proceedings: 3rd National Conference on Air Pollution,* December 12–14, 1966 (Washington, D.C.: Government Printing Office, 1967), p. 12.

fumes then hanging over the city. An "ugly shroud of pollution," Gardner went on to say, covers the eastern seaboard from Boston to Norfolk, Virginia. He continued:

> *Nor is the rest of the country free of the threat. In Pittsburgh, the Golden Triangle is tarnished again by an air pollution problem that is both less obvious and more complex than the old smoke problem under whose pall Pittsburgh almost disappeared three decades ago. The new stainless steel arch towering 630 feet into the air above St. Louis was virtually obscured last October (ironically during Cleaner Air Week) by air pollution, arising from both Missouri and Illinois, despite sunny skies and clear weather.*[50]

Even Texas, Gardner judged, is no longer big enough to adequately accommodate the pollutants being poured into the sky by that state's many metropolitan centers. Similarly, Denver and Phoenix are despoiling the big sky of the Rockies and the Great American Desert. Gardner saw the air pollution problem as one growing in intensity and becoming more troublesome to comfort, safety, and health.[51]

INDUSTRIAL URBANIZATION AND TYPES OF POLLUTION

The concentration of population in compact areas together with the industrial growth characteristic of advanced urbanism is basically responsible for our various forms of environmental pollution. Urbanization increasingly burdens the natural assimilative capacity of the finite environment surrounding a city. Industrialization tends to have a similar adverse effect by withdrawing materials from nature and also by setting deleterious consequences into effect, such as the discharge of toxic chemicals into waterways.

It needs to be pointed out though that pollution is not altogether simply attributable to industrialization and urbanization per se. Otherwise, its abatement would be impossible without *de*industrialization and *de*urbanization. An individualistic laissez-faire policy emphasizing the exploitation of the environment without due regard for the viability of the ecosystem has, in fact, been the critical element. It is then the adoption of conservation and protection consistent with the benefits of industrial-urban life that is needed, and which will make our environmental problems remediable.

Ecological impairment takes seven forms: (1) air pollution, mainly from internal-combustion engines and furnaces utilizing hydrocarbon fuels; (2) contamination of surface water by domestic sewage, industrial emissions,

[50] Ibid.
[51] Ibid., p. 13.

The individualistic policy of exploiting the environment. Heavy industry along Cleveland's Cuyahoga River, a waterway so contaminated with oil and combustible chemicals that it was declared a fire hazard!

and siltation; (3) the pollution, through on-site disposal, of both the soil and the ground water which contains it; (4) thermal pollution originating, say, in the cooling water of nuclear reactors; (5) radioactive pollution stemming from the careless introduction of such wastes into the soil, air, and water; (6) solid waste accumulation; and (7) insecticides, pesticides, and organic nitrates for fertilization (prevalent in agriculture, to be sure, although intensive commercial farming is carried on principally for the high-consumption urban market).[52]

These different kinds of pollution and contamination may be grouped together, as we do below, insofar as they affect either the (1) atmosphere, (2) water, or (3) soil.

Atmospheric Contamination

Three types of pollutants are mainly responsible for contaminating the atmosphere: inorganic gases, organic gases, and particulate matter. They arise as

[52] Norman Day, "The Dimensions, Issues, and Determinants of Urban Development," in Billy Ray Wilson, ed., *Environmental Problems* (Philadelphia, Pa.: J. B. Lippincott, 1968), pp. 30–53.

TABLE 20-3 Relative Severity of Air Pollution among the 20 Most Severely Affected Standard Metropolitan Statistical Areas of the United States: 1967 (as Measured for Particulates, Sulfur Oxides, Hydrocarbons, and Carbon Monoxides)

SMSA	RANK SUM OF AIR POLLUTION
1. New York	457.5
2. Chicago	422.0
3. Philadelphia	404.5
4. Los Angeles–Long Beach	393.5
5. Cleveland	390.5
6. Pittsburgh	390.0
7. Boston	389.0
8. Newark	376.5
9. Detroit	370.0
10. St. Louis	369.0
11. Gary–Hammond–East Chicago	368.5
12. Akron	367.5
13. Baltimore	355.0
14. Indianapolis	351.0
15. Wilmington	342.0
16. Louisville	338.0
17. Jersey City	333.5
18. Washington, D.C.	327.5
19. Cincinnati	326.5
20. Milwaukee	301.5

Source: Health, Education, and Welfare Department, *Relative Severity of Air Pollution in SMSA's With Industrial Populations of 40,000 or More* (Washington, D.C.: Government Printing Office, 1967).

byproducts of the conversion of energy that takes place under human direction. Annually some 150 million tons of gaseous and particulate "garbage" are spewed into the blanket of air covering the United States. The Public Health Service found in the late 1960s that every year motor vehicles alone were responsible for 66 million tons of carbon monoxide, 12 million tons of hydrocarbons, 6 million tons of nitrogen oxides, and 1 million tons each of sulfur dioxides and particulates.[53] Typically, a single automobile discharges 1,600 pounds of carbon monoxide, 230 pounds of hydrocarbons, and 77 pounds of oxides of nitrogen every year.

Although air pollution may be thought of generally with respect to the nation as a whole, it is important to keep population concentration clearly in

[53] Paul R. Ehrlich and Anne H. Ehrlich, *Population, Resources, Environment: Issues in Human Ecology* (San Francisco, Calif.: W. H. Freeman, 1970), p. 118.

mind. This relates to the size of a given city, its emission sources, and the special features of the city's location. Table 20-3 lists the 20 SMSAs suffering the greatest severity of air pollution in the United States, as measured in 1967. Understandably, the rank sums are relatively imprecise, and the conditions described quite inconstant.

As Table 20-3 shows, the condition of New York City was especially acute at the time. New York discharges 1.5 million tons of carbon monoxide, 600,000 tons each of hydrocarbons and sulfur dioxide, and upwards of 200,000 tons of particulate matter every year. Responsible for this atmospheric fog are the manifold generating, manufacturing, transportation, heating, and incinerating activities of the giant metropolis. New York is also being constantly invaded by streams of air pollution carried in by currents from other states, notably New Jersey.[54]

The unhealthful consequences of air pollution generally, but not exclusively in the urban atmosphere alone, can be read in the results of clinical and experimental studies. Carbon monoxide denies the blood oxygen and hence causes suffocation. Low levels of carbon monoxide cause the heart to work harder, and this can prove lethal to one with chronic heart strain. Nitrogen oxide has a like potentiality. In persons with normal hearts, exposure to carbon monoxide or nitrogen oxide may induce discoordination, pain, and impaired vision. Air-borne sulfur oxides create respiratory difficulties, and their deposit of sulfuric acid in the lungs can prove dangerous. Finally, sulfur dioxide intensifies asthma, bronchitis, and emphysema, while the hydrocarbon pollutants and certain particulates, like asbestos fibres, are probably cancer-producing.

Establishing the hazards of actual air pollution involves all of the well-known problems of research, such as isolating individual factors and subjecting them to systematic study; precisely determining the degree of exposure to them by the subjects being studied; and considering the harmful aspects of pollutants singly and also in combination with other factors.[55] At present little is definitely known about the respiratory effects of the prolonged breathing of air having only low levels of contamination. Nonetheless, progressive atmospheric pollution may indeed have dire cumulative consequences.[56]

On several occasions unusual concentrations of acid oxides in the atmosphere have contributed to sizable increases in the death rates of the elderly and of persons already ill with heart and lung disease. In 1948 in Donora, Pennsylvania, 18 such deaths and thousands of respiratory problems—aggravated shortness of breath, coughing, and nausea—were charged to severe air contamination. There at Donora, some 30 miles south

[54] Melvin A. Benarde, *Our Precious Habitat* (New York: W. W. Norton, 1970), pp. 174–75.

[55] These are amplified in Ehrlich and Ehrlich, op. cit., Box 6–2, p. 123.

[56] *Proceedings: 3rd National Conference on Air Pollution*, op. cit., pp. 23–26.

of Pittsburgh in the narrow Monongahela Valley, a zinc reduction plant roasting sulfur ores, a steel mill, and coal furnaces being used to generate electricity had built up a heavy cloud of pollutants. More recently, during the Thanksgiving weekend of 1966, perhaps as many as 80 persons succumbed to the high levels of sulfur dioxide that had accumulated in New York City at that time. Even more disastrous events have befallen areas elsewhere in the world. Sixty-three lives were lost to a dense blanket of gaseous contamination that gripped the industrial Meuse Valley of Belgium for several days in December, 1930. Similarly, a week's saturation of aerial wastes, fog, and smoke cost London as many as 4000 premature deaths in 1952.

Los Angeles is very vulnerable to temperature inversion, a phenomenon that adds to the dangers of air pollutants. Temperature inversion occurs when the layer of air nearest the earth is cooled by its contact with the ground, and the warm air higher up comes to be trapped by a still more elevated layer that has happened to be cooled, perhaps by incoming ocean winds. Consequently, normal air circulation slows down.

In Los Angeles, situated between the Pacific Ocean and the San Gabriel Mountains, about three days out of four during the year are marked by temperature inversion. For temperature to be rendered perilous, however, large amounts of aerial contaminants need to be present. Fortunately as yet this has seldom been the case. Although the early Spanish explorers knew Los Angeles as the Valley of the Smokes, it is the ubiquitous presence of the automobile and motor truck in the twentieth century that has given the Los Angeles basin its characteristic massive smogs. In addition, sunlight, which is so common in southern California, contributes to a photochemical processing of the air-borne pollutants that increases their irritability if not health-injurious potency.

Authoritative opinion differs on the extent to which air pollution is an imperative problem in urban America today. Paul and Anne Ehrlich, who have written extensively on the subject, think that if present trends toward an intensification of the problem continues, the deadly significance of air pollution will become truly obtrusive.[57] More conservatively, Glenn Hilst generalizes that "in the complex mix of factors which affect human health there is a strong suspicion that prolonged exposure to gases and particulates common to our atmosphere has a deleterious effect on health."[58] Still more conservatively yet, the director of the San Marino Air Pollution Foundation, W. L. Faith, has recognized air pollution as annoying to the senses and as interferring with production and services (like the loss of tourist trade), but he says that its effects on health have not been conclusively ascertained.[59]

---

[57] Ehrlich and Ehrlich, op. cit., p. 122.

[58] Glenn R. Hilst, "Pollution: Another Dimension of Urbanization," in Moynihan, op. cit., pp. 94–106.

[59] W. L. Faith, *Air Pollution Control* (New York: John Wiley & Sons, 1959), p. 27.

Water Problems

Turning now to water pollution, we have a state of affairs involving water-borne and viral diseases, toxic chemicals, heat, and radioactivity. As a result of improved water treatment, water-borne diseases like typhoid tend to be very rare nowadays. Yet viral diseases such as infectious hepatitis and polio remain a more continuous problem.

More than 400 different kinds of chemical substances are created every year. Many of them find industrial use and are finally discharged as effluent materials into the water system. Best-selling author Rachel Carson referred to the present period in history as an "age of poisons."[60] Toxic chemicals introduced into the water supply, for instance, nitrates, fluorides, and phosphates originating in industrial processes, interfere with the natural animal and plant life there. They also constitute a danger to humans. Thus the communities of the central valley of California have been experiencing a severe nitrate problem (nitrate in the human body impairs the oxygen-carrying ability of the red blood cells). Elgin, Minnesota, has been forced by the same difficulty to find a new water supply.[61]

Industrial processes commonly generate great heat that requires water cooling. The water that absorbs the heat and is then returned to the place from which it was taken raises the temperature of the entire body of water. Many marine animals and plants cannot tolerate a temperature even a few degrees higher than normal. Thermal pollution also reduces the oxygen-carrying capacity of water. This has further deleterious consequences, for instance, in the absence of oxygen iron compounds become more soluble. Thus, eutrophication (akin to over-enrichment) sets in, with huge blooms of algae appearing and as they die stepping up the bacterial consumption of the oxygen remaining in the water. The magnitude of thermal pollution in the waters adjacent to specific urban areas may be judged from a report of the Northeastern Illinois Planning Commission.[62] In Chicago, it said, 15 times as much water is employed for cooling as for domestic consumption!

The Federal Power Commission has estimated that by 1980 the electrical energy requirements of the nation will impose a total heat load on our rivers of 3.5 million billion Btu annually. By the turn of the century this may rise to 20 million billion. The Mahoning River of western Pennsylvania is already 20 to 30 degrees Fahrenheit warmer than air temperatures. Large nuclear reactors will mean still greater thermal pollution. A 2000 megawatt nuclear generator will heat about 3 billion gallons of water 10 degrees Fahr-

---

[60] In her *Silent Spring* (Boston: Houghton Mifflin, 1962). See also R. L. Rudd, *Pesticides and the Living Landscape* (Madison, Wisc.: University of Wisconsin Press, 1964).

[61] Ehrlich and Ehrlich, op. cit., p. 127.

[62] Cf. J. Carroll Morris, "The Problem of Thermal Pollution," in Wilson, op. cit., pp. 123–30.

enheit daily. This is about one-eighth the flow of the whole Hudson River! [63]

Besides thermal pollution, water is also susceptible to radioactivity. Water may become radioactive from nuclear weapons tests, the atomic wastes of industry, and from radioactive materials used in scientific research and medicine. Also, nuclear reactors may induce radioactivity into their cooling waters.

Organisms acquire radioelements by ingestion at one or another point in the food chain. Their effects can be debilitating and lethal. Strontium, for example, is a bone-seeking substance. In general, radiation has been linked to genetic mutations, abortion, and cancer. Hence radioactivity in water constitutes a public hazard which, all agree, should be minimized—and it can be done. According to Clark and Viessman, controlling radioactive discharges is "no different in principle" from that of any other industrial discharge. [64]

Soil Pollution

The contamination of the soil by the addition of solid wastes represents still another pollution problem of urban America. [65] Solid wastes refer to a variety of different types of materials. Rubbish (discarded goods), garbage (food waste), dead animals, demolition waste (the remains of buildings and houses), and sewage make up what in general may be called solid waste material. [66] By 1980, an American population of more than 235 million will be producing upwards of 8 pounds of such wastes per person per day, that is, more than 340 million tons per year. These figures pertain merely to those wastes that it is expected will be gathered up by collection agencies. Even now, at least 360 million tons all told are being generated in household, commercial, and industrial operations, though not all of it is being collected. Moreover, seven million passenger cars, trucks, and buses are junked every year.

Solid waste has certain implications for public health, particularly in regard to air and water pollution. The burning of waste materials discharges volatile chemicals and particulates into the air. Besides creating unsightly and rodent-breeding nuisances, disposing of decomposing materials by dumping may result in water contamination.

Solid waste entails serious problems of disposal, which cost money but which also offer a technological challenge that, properly dealt with, may through reclamation and recycling create vast new economies. For instance, in the mid-1970s, the treatment of municipal sewage has become a business of more than $2 billion per year. Typically, a city's sewage effluents are re-

[63] Ibid., p. 126.

[64] John W. Clark and Warren Viessman, Jr., *Water Supply and Pollution Control* (Scranton, Pa.: International Textbook, 1965), p. 369.

[65] See Mitchell Gordon, *Sick Cities* (Baltimore, Md.: Penguin, 1965), pp. 282ff.

[66] See American Public Works Association classification in Benarde, op. cit., pp. 153–54.

moved through a network of drains and conduits. The gross solids are first screened out at a sewage-disposal plant. Then primary sedimentation removes many of the suspended organic solids. Following this step, aerobic biological treatment is undertaken in order to get out both the dissolved and suspended materials that remain. Here, filtration and the action of bacterial organisms in the presence of a great deal of oxygen are employed before the sewage effluent is then pumped out into the area's waterways. Chlorination may also be used to destroy the pathogenic microorganisms that inhabit the discharge. The sludge that has accumulated is removed for oxidation and, finally, conversion into soil additives.

RESOLVING THE POLLUTION PROBLEM

Serious as it is, the urban pollution problem is by no means insurmountable. To deal effectively with ecological contamination requies scientific research, economic analysis, public education, and concerted political action, all in a spirit of enlightened determination.[67] Certainly the achievement of systematic sewage disposal, without which the modern city would be nonexistent, supplies an encouraging model for a successful attack on our current ecological difficulties.

The Need for a Broad but Feasible Program

The multiplex nature of an effective antipollution system was recently underscored by a 10-point program drawn up by an HEW task force on environmental health and related problems.[68] The 10 points included air-quality restoration; water-quality testing; a grant-in-aid water-disposal program; determination of the effects of population trends on environmental protectional goals; the reduction of crowding, congestion, and noise; a chemicals-control effort; consumer protection; radiation control; protection against occupational hazards; and the clarification of standards in federally assisted services. The solutions adopted, the Task Force concluded, would have to be such as to be compatible with the present general direction of urban life and not cripple it. The task force declared:

> As the facts become clear, the public will be shocked at the price it is paying for its affluence. But, if it is obvious that one way to halt the contamination of the environment is to prohibit automobiles, stop the generation of electricity and shut down industry, it is just as obvious that this way is impossible. What is possible is to find ways to eliminate contamination at its source. Or, next best, to capture a pollutant and use it in a non-harmful way; or, finally, to bring the

[67] Day, op. cit., p. 45.

[68] A Strategy for a Livable Environment (Washington, D.C.: Government Printing Office, 1967).

EXHIBIT 20-2 An Environmental Matrix

	CAUSATIVE FACTORS 1. size of population 2. concentration of population 3. per capita income level 4. consumption pattern 5. technology	CHARACTER OF INSULT 1. temporary insult 2. cumulative insult 3. reversible damage 4. permanent damage (human time scale) 5. synergistic potential	PROBLEM THRESHOLD 1. continuing 2. now or soon 3. one generation 4. more than one generation	AREA AFFECTED 1. local 2. regional 3. national 4. international 5. global
ENVIRONMENTAL PROBLEMS BY ORDER OF GRAVITY				
Amenity considerations				
Litter	4,3	1,2	1	1,2
Noise	2,5	1	1	1
Odor	5	1	1	1
Air, visibility aspects	2,5,4	1	1	1,2
Water quality, recreational aspects	5,2,1	1,2,3,5	1	1,2,4
City, aesthetic aspects	4,5	N	1	1
City, convenience and efficiency aspects	2,4	3	1,2	1
Country, aesthetic aspects	5,4,1	2,4	1,2	1,2,3
Access to country and nature	4	2,3	1,2	1,2
Human health effects				
Air pollution—combustion products	5,4,2,3	1,3,5	1,2,3	1,2
Water pollution:				
Pathogens	2,5	1,3	2,3	1,2,4
Nitrates	5	2,3	2,3	1,2
Industrial chemicals	5	All	2,3	1,2,4
Pesticides (via food chain)	5,1,3	2,3	3	2,4,5
Radioactivity	5,3	2,4	3	1,2
Heavy metals	5	2,4	All	1,2,4
Human genetic and reproductive effects				
Radioactivity	5,3	4	3,4	3,5
Pesticides	5,1,3	4	N	3
Industrial chemicals	5	4	2,3,4	1,2,5

APPROPRIATE MANAGEMENT LEVEL[a] 1. local 2. regional authority 3. national 4. multinational agreement or authority 5. global	POSSIBLE ECONOMIC APPROACHES 1. environmental charge 2. tax on material 3. subsidy	POSSIBLE INSTITUTIONAL APPROACHES 1. laws and regulations 2. enlarged systems management or planning 3. court actions	POSSIBLE TECHNOLOGICAL APPROACHES 1. containment at source 2. neutralization of objectionable discharges 3. reduction in discharge volume via process and material changes 4. increased recycling	EFFICACY OF POSSIBLE VALUE CHANGE BRINGING: 1. reduced population growth 2. slower income and more equal distribution 3. less burdensome consumption patterns 4. curtailment of property rights
1,2	1,3	1,2	4,3	3,2
1	N[b]	1	3,1	N
1	N	1	2	N
1,2	1,3	1,2	3,2	2,3
1,2,4	All	All	All	2,1
1	2,3	1,2	N	4,3
1,2	All	2	N	4,3,2
2,3	3	All	N	4,2,3,1
1,2,3	2,3	2	N	3,1
2,3,4	All	1,2	All	3,2
1,2,4	3	1,2	2	1
1,2	2,3	1	3,1	3,4
1,2,4	1,2	1,2	All	2,1
3,4	2	1	3,1	3
3	N	1	3,1	2,1
2,3,4	N	1	3,1	N
3,5	N	1	3,1	2,1
3	2	1	3,1	N
3,4	1,2	1,2	All	2,3

EXHIBIT 20-2 An Environmental Matrix *(Continued)*

ENVIRONMENTAL PROBLEMS BY ORDER OF GRAVITY	CAUSATIVE FACTORS 1. size of population 2. concentration of population 3. per capita income level 4. consumption pattern 5. technology	CHARACTER OF INSULT 1. temporary insult 2. cumulative insult 3. reversible damage 4. permanent damage (human time scale) 5. synergistic potential	PROBLEM THRESHOLD 1. continuing 2. now or soon 3. one generation 4. more than one generation	AREA AFFECTED 1. local 2. regional 3. national 4. international 5. global
Effects on ecological system and the earth's life-supportive capacity				
Human occupancy of biospace	5,1,3,4	2,4,5	All	3,5
Ocean threats:				
Pesticides	5	2,4,5	3	5
Oil	3,4	3,5	3	5
Other chemicals	5	2,4	3,4	5
Erosion	5,1,3	2,4	1,4	1,2,5
Fertilizers and damage to mineral cycling	5	3	4	1,5
CO_2, albedo, and climate	5,1,3	2,5	4	5
Heat rejection:				
Local aspect	5,2	1,5	2,3	2,4
Global aspect	3,1	3,5	4	5

[a] Irrespective of source of financing.   [b] N =none, unknown, uncertain, not applicable, negligible.

The table spanning pp. 506–509 shows the causes, effects, and possible remedial measures that can be taken toward various environmental problems that beset most large population centers at the present time.

Source: Resources for the Future, *Annual Report: 1972* (Washington, D.C.: Resources for the Future, 1972), pp. 84–85.

APPROPRIATE MANAGEMENT LEVEL[a] 1. local 2. regional authority 3. national 4. multinational agreement or authority 5. global	POSSIBLE ECONOMIC APPROACHES 1. environmental charge 2. tax on material 3. subsidy	POSSIBLE INSTITUTIONAL APPROACHES 1. laws and regulations 2. enlarged systems management or planning 3. court actions	POSSIBLE TECHNOLOGICAL APPROACHES 1. containment at source 2. neutralization of objectionable discharges 3. reduction in discharge volume via process and material changes 4. increased recycling	EFFICACY OF POSSIBLE VALUE CHANGE BRINGING: 1. reduced population growth 2. slower income and more equal distribution 3. less burdensome consumption patterns 4. curtailment of property rights
3,5	All	All	1	2,3,1
5	2	1	3	N
5	1	1	3,2,1	2,3
5	1,2	1,2	All	2,3
1,3	3	1	3	4,2,1
1,3	2	1	N	2,1
3,5	N	1,2	3	2,1
2,3,4	1,3	All	2	3
5	N	1	3	2,3,1

level of pollution down to a point compatible with the requirements of human health and welfare.[69]

Local Leadership Essential

The participation of local urban leadership remains an obvious necessity in curbing ecological pollution. In fact, such participation is called for under present federal programs. They tend to refer the determination of standards, deterence, and assistance to state and local government.

[69] Ibid., pp. ix–x.

In some respects environmental pollution is a problem common to the United States as an industrial urban society. Thus research as to exposure tolerances may be made applicable to all persons everywhere, and the necessary standards can be established nationally. On the other hand, local conditions and needs must not be ignored. For example, in some localities where wind movement is typically vigorous and temperature inversion rare, the emission of wastes into the air may be an acceptable solution. In others not. Similarly, the availability of land may indicate the feasibility of the landfill disposal of solids in one city but not in the next. For such reasons local leadership has a vital role in antipollution strategies.[70]

Governmental Fragmentation and Vested Interests

Yet local government in America (as shown in Ch. 8) suffers from fragmentation. In addition, strong resistance from local special interests continually weakens efforts aimed at curbing pollution.[71]

The fragmentation of government in the United States is a handicap that must be overcome if material progress is to be made against environmental difficulties. Successful measures will often require cooperation between wider and wider jurisdictions. One case is that of levying effluent charges on industry—and municipalities too—to the extent to which each discharges objectionable wastes into the common waterways of an entire region.

Political implementation to improve the environment often sustains injury from the opposition of vested interests in given localities. About two-thirds of the states now have central agencies to contend with pollution, but only a fourth of them make financial provision to help local communities with their air, ground, and water problems. Again, public-utility corporations arouse public opinion against further antipollution measures or higher standards by playing upon fears of added taxes, increased rates, and the loss of jobs. In fact, projections of long-term gains in productivity are often used to justify the adverse environmental effects of proposed projects, as a survey of 76 statements on highway projects in cities of over 500,000 in size recently revealed.[72] Industrial interests generally oppose legislation that they deem to be inequitably at their own expense. Today industry discharges into our lakes and rivers a volume of effluents twice as great as the total of all municipal sewage. Yet industry spends only half as much on processing as the cities do on sewage treatment, and it usually objects to be being required to do

[70] Compare Azriel Teller, "Air-Pollution Abatement: Economic Rationality and Reality," in Roger Revelle and Hans H. Landberg, eds., *America's Changing Environment* (Boston: Houghton Mifflin, 1970), pp. 39–55, who argues for a selective approach to the problem.

[71] For political rivalries in environmental issues, see Lynton K. Caldwell, *Environment: A Challenge to Modern Society* (Garden City, N.Y.: Natural History Press, 1970), pp. 206ff.

[72] James B. Sullivan and Paul A. Montgomery, "Surveying Highway Impact," *Environment*, 14 (November 1972), pp. 12–20.

more. Indeed, writes Roger Revelle, the five cents municipalities spend on treating 1000 gallons of sewage compares with the mere one cent expended per 1000 gallons of discharge by industry.[73]

Such resistance notwithstanding, the HEW task force cited earlier reached the conclusion "that the environmental contamination man creates man can correct, and that the nation's industrial and technological genius needs to be brought to bear on this problem."

CONCLUSION

Environmental problems have long accompanied urbanization. In recent decades though, industrialization has complicated and intensified some of these, notably the pollution of air, water, and soil. At the same time too industrial capability has also made available the technological resources by which, given appropriate social and political organization, the problems of housing and transportation as well as ecological contamination can be resolved. However, all of these aspects of urban life at present involve serious conflicts between interest groups, among them producers and consumers, minorities, social classes, and levels of government. Added to our as yet incomplete knowledge about the problems themselves, these clashes of interest would appear to suggest that at least some of the environmental dfficulties treated in the present chapter will continue to exist well into the future, and possibly even become worse before getting better.

FOR FURTHER READING

The American Assembly, *The Future of American Transportation* (Englewood Cliffs, N.J.: Prentice-Hall, 1971). The weaknesses of our national transportation system and some possible solutions.

Lynton K. Caldwell, *Environment: A Challenge for Modern Society* (Garden City, N.Y.: Natural History Press, 1970). The historical basis of our attitudes towards the environment; explains what new attitudes need to be developed.

Rex R. Campbell and Jerry L. Wade, eds., *Society and Environment* (Boston: Allyn and Bacon, 1972). Articles that the editors say "provide the breadth of perspective a concerned person needs for a good understanding of the current environmental situation."

Anthony Downs, *Federal Housing Subsidies: How Are They Working?* (Lexington, Mass.: Heath, 1973). The federal programs and recommendations for alternatives.

[73] Roger Revelle, "Pollution and Cities," in Wilson, op. cit., p. 119.

Frank S. Kristof, *Urban Housing Needs Through the 1980's* (Washington, D.C.: National Commission on Urban Problems, 1968). An anticipation of the housing deficit through the next decade.

John R. Meyer et al., *The Urban Transportation Problem* (Cambridge, Mass.: Harvard University Press, 1965). Changes in the technology of urban transport; the changing pattern of land use; trip-making behavior; and government policies.

William W. Murdock, ed., *Environment: Resources, Pollution, and Society* (Stanford, Conn.: Sinauer, 1971). Environmental degradation and how to deal with it.

Philip Nobile and John Deedy, eds., *The Complete Ecology Fact Book* (Garden City, N.Y.: Doubleday, 1972). A wealth of data on the different kinds of pollutants and their effects.

Jon Pynoos, Robert Schafer, and Chester W. Hartman, eds., *Housing Urban America* (Chicago: Aldine, 1973). Readings on almost every facet of housing problems.

PART SEVEN

TOWARD TOMORROW'S CITY

Building for tommorow.

Source: Australian News and Information Bureau, *Australia: A Portfolio* (Adelaide: Griffin Press, 1966), p. 133.

CHAPTER 21

URBAN DESIGN AND PLANNING

Both design and planning refer to guided, structured urbanization. Design denotes the architectural and engineering aspects of this process, while planning encompasses it altogether. Planning thus means deliberately and systematically providing not only for the safety and convenience of a population but also for its economic, organizational, and cultural advancement. Planning features three components: (1) the formulation of a coherent scheme for the attainment of general goals like community well being, economic progress, and beautiful surroundings; (2) the selection of the major elements in the physical makeup of the city: its streets, public buildings, transit lines, and parks; and (3) the adoption of the legal, financial, and political means by which to construct the physical facilities and reach the goals that have been set.

Urban planning has acquired new importance in recent years as a result of the severe problems commonly associated with rapid urban growth. At present, urban planning commands much attention in the United States and abroad, and much more so than ever before. This is attributable to five sets of converging interests; (1) the concern of the engineering sciences for precise, quantiative, and functional solutions to the problems of sanitation, transportation, and public services; (2) the aesthetic interests of architects, stylists, and decorators; (3) the objectives of political and institutional administrators; (4) business and industrial leadership; and (5) the aims of social-welfare practitioners to achieve a quality of urban life commensurate with progressive standards.[1]

Although until quite recently urban design and planning were employed only occasionally, they are of ancient origin and were practiced both in the era of preindustrial urbanism and in the early industrial age as well.

PLANNING THE PREINDUSTRIAL CITY

CITY PLANNING IN ANTIQUITY

Perhaps the earliest case of a city laid out according to a definite plan was Kahun, which existed in the Nile Valley between 3000 and 2500 B.C. A small acropolis overlooked the town and served as the center of government and religious rites. Other ancient cities were also chiefly oriented to their lofty and towering palaces, notably the palace of Sennacherib at Nineveh; Solomon's in Jerusalem; and of course the Parthenon in Athens.[2]

The design of imperial Rome differed in motif from the cities of classical Greece. The Greek model was modest, a city relatively small and focused on the agora adjacent to the acropolis. Rome, however, strove to exercise power over a vast empire. Roman architects, engineers, statesmen, and planners cooperated in trying to create in Rome itself an urban center manifesting an overpowering dominion. Triumphal arches, baths envelopng great reaches of space, stadia and circuses, and orchestrated vistas all combined to enhance the capital city's magnificence. In addition, the center of the empire was also the nucleus of a visible network of aquaducts and highways that not only provisioned the city, but also enabled its legions to subdue and garrison the entire Mediterranean world.[3]

THE RENAISSANCE

City planning on a scale comparable to that of the ancient civilizations did not arise again in Europe until the Renaissance at the end of the fifteenth

[1] Amplified in William I. Goodman and Eric C. Freund, eds., *Principles and Practice of Urban Planning* (Washington, D.C.: Internation City Manager's Association, 1968).

[2] See Carl B. Lohmann, *Principles of City Planning* (New York: McGraw-Hill, 1931), Ch. 3.

[3] Robert C. Fried, *Planning the Eternal City* (New Haven, Conn.: Yale University Press, 1973).

century. The principles of Renaissance urban design and planning have been summarized by the British architectural historian Sir Patrick Abercrombie under five headings: (1) the primary straight road; (2) fortification; (3) garden design; (4) the place (church, guildhall, or palace); and (5) the squared, or checkerboard, plan.[4] So imaginative and yet unified are these premises that, understandably, the legacy of Renaissance urban planning has been one of great weight and scope.

The Rebuilding of Rome

Of signal importance to Renaissance planning was the reconstruction of Rome late in the sixteenth century by Pope Sixtus V. Under him, a star-shaped network of roads was conceived of as a means of linking together all of the seven main churches and shrines of the city. Privately, Domenico Fontana, chief architect of the project, confided that "at a truly incredible cost" the Pope had extended the streets completely across town, levelling the hills and filling in the valleys, and had thereby sustained the devotions of the populace and charmed "the senses of the body."[5]

EIGHTEENTH CENTURY EUROPE: THE BAROQUE AGE

In the eighteenth century, when monarchy strengthened its hold on the nations of Europe, the Baroque period of city planning began to evolve. During the Baroque era, "the desire for unconfined space gripped the city's rulers and their designers."[6] This represented a distinct ethos, in Siegfried Giedion's words, "the development of a specific kind of universality."[7] Roads, buildings, plazas, and the entire landscape were to be engulfed in a single design. France was a notable case of Baroque planning, indeed the most outstanding one. In France, the landscapist Andrew Le Notre was commissioned by Louis XIV to create the gardens of Versailles and to focus them on the magnificent royal palace that was going up just outside Paris, and in the process created a masterpiece still unrivaled.

London

In London, Baroque city planning was "naturalized," so to speak, by the land developers of eighteenth century England. At that time many of the city's now

[4] Sir Patrick Abercrombie, ed., *Town and Country Planning* (London: Oxford University Press, 1965).

[5] Cited in Sigfried Giedion, *Space, Time, and Architecture* (Cambridge, Mass.: Harvard University Press, 1965).

[6] Arthur B. Gallion, *The Urban Pattern: City Planning and Design* (New York: D. Van Nostrand, 1950), p. 47.

[7] Ibid., p. 109.

famous squares were laid out by landowners like the Duke of Bedford, allotting their estates for homesites. Instead of providing land behind the houses, they opened up space in front in the form of a large common available to all. Thomas Adams contrasts the London square with the forum, *piazza,* and *platz* of the cities on the continent. The English common garden, he writes, gave the adjoining property more lasting value, because private deed restrictions resulted in a kind of zoning. Adams goes on to add that "simple, homelike, visible, sunny and eventually beautiful, it made for community instead of individualistic privacy."[8]

COLONIAL AMERICA AND THE UNITED STATES

Urban planning was evident in colonial America and in the early history of the United States too. Any number of urban settlements in the British seaboard colonies bore the imprint of deliberate design from the very outset. New Haven was laid out as a large square at an angle to the harbor. That square was further divided into nine equal parts, each 858 feet on a side, the center square reserved for public use.[9] The original plan for Detroit was that of a startling spider's web. However, little of that unusual design materialized. Yet present-day Broadway, Woodward, Madison, Bagley, and Adams Roads, and Cadillac Square too, all harken back to the weblike plan proposed for Detroit at the outset.

Washington, D.C.

The design of Washington, D.C., the capital of the new United States, bears the distinct imprint of Renaissance city planning ideas. The plan for the nation's capital, drawn up in 1791 for a malarial swamp on which land speculators had profited handsomely, placed important public buildings at the intersection of rectangular and diagonal streets. Parks and monuments were established at focal points not set aside for buildings. The main feature of the whole design, the 400-foot-wide Mall, linked the Capitol and the White House, the two principal buildings of the new government. The Capitol was set atop an eminence 80 feet above the Potomac as a structure that would give inspiration to all.

THE INDUSTRIAL CITY AND THE URBAN PLANNER

Affected by the Industrial Revolution, urban planning in nineteenth century Europe revealed two major trends: (1) the Baroque carried over from the past, and (2) industrial anarchy, in other words, the absence of planning.

[8] Thomas Adams, *Outline of Town and City Planning* (New York: Russell Sage Foundation 1935), p. 110.

[9] Anthony N. B. Garvan, *Architecture and Town Planning in Colonial Connecticut* (New Haven, Conn.: Yale University Press, 1951), pp. 45–49.

Washington, D.C., a planned city, with the Capitol Building as its centerpiece.

THE BAROQUE

Some attempts were made to renew old cities along monumental lines largely derived from the aristocratic past. The best example is the reconstruction of Paris by Baron George-Eugène Haussmann under Napoleon III, beginning in 1853. Expenditures of some 50 million livres enabled spacious boulevards to be carved out, plazas and parks boldly situated, and public buildings exposed to panoramic view. Paris was thus turned into the stately world capital which it remains today.

INDUSTRIAL ANARCHY

What Abercrombie calls the "industrial town production" of England bespeaks the other tendency of town planning (or its absence) in the nineteenth century. That was the spirit of individualism which commanded that building and demolition be guided only by private expediency. The result has been described as industrial anarchy, and may be observed in the history of both Great Britain and the United States.

During the first decades of the nineteenth century, rapid construction unfettered by considerations of either design or future need prevailed in urban Britain. Houses there were thrown together as near to factories as possible, regardless of health or future consequences.[10] A parliamentary committee found in 1833, for instance, that "narrow courts and confined streets" abounded in the country's cities. Liverpool had 2400 tiny courts each closed on all four sides and entered only by a tiny archway. Nearly 90,000 people of the working class inhabited them. Liverpool also had more than 7800 cellar units housing 39,000 persons. The gutters were literally choked with filth.[11]

REFORM MOVEMENTS

In Britain

Parliamentary inquiries led to a series of British Sanitary and Public Health Acts following 1840, and gradually restrictions for sanitary control led to broader and broader urban planning in Britain.

The urban historian Thomas Adams has claimed that the "negative influences" of overcrowding, squalor, and lack of sanitation did play a part in stimulating the modern city-planning movement in Britain.[12] The rise of democratic government with its concern for greater public welfare also contributed to this movement. The motivation afforded city planning in the United Kingdom at this time by utopian thinkers must be acknowledged too. In his 1884 lecture on "Art and Socialism," William Morris described London as a "spreading sore . . . swallowing up with its loathsomeness field and wood and heath without mercy and without hope, mocking our feeble efforts to deal even with its minor evils of smoke-laden sky and befouled river."[13]

Without a doubt, the foremost exponent of visionary urban planning in Britain was Ebenezer Howard, most prominently identified with the garden-city type of modern city design. Howard disliked bourgeois urban society intensely, and he anticipated that the lure of garden cities around London would be catastrophic to land values in the inner areas and would bring about a financial crisis that would empty the city almost completely. Events turned out otherwise. A year after the 1898 publication of Howard's booklet *Tomorrow: A Peaceful Path to Real Reform,* a corporation organized for the purpose had bought a 4500-acre site some 35 miles from London, but even three decades later the resulting community of Letchworth had a population of only 13,500 as compared with the 35,000 originally projected. Christopher Tunnard remarks that Howard's idea of a town-and-country fusion has had its greatest impact in changing the character of existing cities rather than in

[10] Abercrombie, op. cit., pp. 77–82.

[11] William Ashworth, *The Genesis of Modern British Town Planning* (London: Routledge & Kegan Paul, 1954), p. 17.

[12] Adams, op. cit., p. 160.

[13] Cited by Ashworth, op. cit., p. 171.

ushering in their antitheses.[14] In such developments inside London itself as the Hampstead Garden Suburb, Howard's influence can be traced even today.

In Other European Countries

The British were not alone in the field of urban design and planning early in the twentieth century. By the time of World War I, city planning had scored some substantial gains in Europe, and also contributed to serious weaknesses too.[15] Sweden's town-planning law of 1874 led to clean, serviceable layouts, though of a dull gridiron pattern. German cities were practicing zoning against tenements, converting the old fortifications around the central areas into circumferential avenues, and preserving their medieval landmarks. In Italy, local authorities received the power of eminent domain and even expropriation, which permitted them, conveniently, to recover the cost of public works.

In the United States

American urban planning at the beginning of the twentieth century resembled its European counterparts with respect to monumental civic architecture and humanistic reform oftentimes against resistance by vested interests.

Modern city planning in the United States received grat impetus from Daniel Burnham's design of the Chicago World's Fair of 1893. Burnham's classical style, basically Greek ornament applied to modern construction, came to dominate the entire plan of the exposition. The White City, which Burnham and his associates designed to house the Fair, commanded attention not only among architects and builders but also civic leaders and public officials. In fact, the large buildings arranged around a lagoon were destined to set off a wave of city planning that spread to Washington, D.C., San Francisco, Chicago, Detroit, Los Angles, Minneapolis, St. Louis, and Cleveland.

As John Reps summarizes it, Burnham's "City Beautiful" movement—which it came to be called—gave rise to six guiding principles of urban design and planning.[16] (1) Stress was laid on monumental groupings in conjunction with the civic life of the large city. (2) Attention was given to harbors, railroads, and utilities as well as to parks and public buildings. (3) Public sponsorship was invited. (4) Zoning, that is, the regulation of land use, was thought to be very important. (5) Housing took on new significance. And (6) city planning was seen as more a matter of redeveloping already existing

[14] Christopher Tunnard, *The City of Man* (New York: Charles Scribner's Sons, 1952), p. 238.

[15] See Harold M. Lewis, *Planning and the Modern City* (New York: Wiley, 1949), pp. 8–11.

[16] John W. Reps, *The Making of Urban America: A History of City Planning in the United States* (Princeton: Princeton University Press, 1965), pp. 524–25.

cities instead of establishing new ones in uninhabited locations.

Although the city beautiful movement popularized urban planning in the United States, two major shortcomings soon became apparent.[17] One was that beautification had to be weighed against cost, and practicality could overrule adornment. The other concerned the problem of subordinating private interests to public control, something that required unavailable authority at the local level. For example, at the same time that Chicago's civic leadership was pledging $100,000 to aid in beautifying the center of that city by adopting Burnham's design, $75 *million* was being invested by U. S. Steel in laying out a new town, including its gigantic mill, in adjacent Gary. Reform-minded city planners experienced great frustration in bucking vested interests.[18]

Still, urban planners did make some headway in the 1920s. Specifically: (1) planning was recognized as legitimate; (2) engineers and lawyers came to be involved as well as architects; and (3) emphasis was placed on zoning as the key to rational city development. By 1931, five years after the Supreme Court had sanctioned comprehensive zoning, 800 American cities had enacted enabling legislation.

CONTEMPORARY URBAN DESIGN AND PLANNING

Today, city planning in the United States, a function carried on by 90 percent of all our cities over 10,000, combines an instrumentalist mentality and a reformist ideology. That is, the urban planner is concerned not only with the technical efficiency of the city, but also with its ability to satisfy humanistic needs in housing, education, recreation, family life, and other areas as well.[19] Given these multiple objectives, it is understandable why the efforts of planners at the present time fall into no fewer than three major categories: (1) redevelopment, in other words, correction; (2) relocation, that is, the creation of New Towns; and (3) coordinated regional strategy.

REDEVELOPMENT

Redevelopment is to be understood as the replacement of old structures with new ones, and the reutilization of land, including but not necessarily restricted to slum clearance and housing. Since World War II, probably the strongest tendency in the United States and in many other countries too has

---

[17] James G. Coke, "Antecedents of Local Planning," in Goodman and Freund, op. cit., pp. 19–25.

[18] See ibid, p. 22.

[19] Donald H. Webster, *Urban Planning and Municipal Public Policy* (New York: Harper & Row, 1958), pp. 77–133; and Harvey S. Perloff, *Education for Planning* (Baltimore, Md.: The Johns Hopkins Press, 1957), pp. 11–12.

been the improvement of existing cities rather than the establishment of entirely new ones.[20] In Europe, overcoming the ravages of war has been an added objective, particularly in London, Berlin, Warsaw, Rotterdam, and Leningrad.[21]

Redevelopment is apt to be stimulated by the urgency of problems like substandard dwellings, obsolete transportation, declining property values, and the need for new industry. A search for short-range solutions—and therefore redevelopment—appears imperative, especially in the context of the typical confusion of opposing and conflicting interests among business, ethnic, labor, and residential segments of the large city. Often political fragmentation limits authority only to relatively small undertakings that are compatible with the existing patterns of land-use, transit, and social organization. Even the swift pace of metropolitanization itself requires a redevelopment role for planning, because private investments, decisions to relocate, the multiplication of cars, and the like all press in as accomplished facts without centralized control.

Empirical Research

Fact-finding occupies an important place in urban development planning. One of the basic features of such planning is the avoidance of dogmatic assumptions about what a city's population wants and needs.[22] Hence planners rely on empirical research to determine how people feel about mass transit, say, or what actually happens to be the composition of a neighborhood, or the true distances people have to travel to work or to visit their friends. This trend toward prolonged consultation with the various interest groups affected by proposed innovations or contemplated ones is being increasingly accepted by planners as part of their professional role.[23] Yet it would be an error to neglect to add that the technical sophistication achieved by planners has probably become a barrier to communication with laymen and even officials. As Garry Brewer has recently written, "communication or immediate human management problems are seen as far from trivial and warrant serious consideration in future undertakings" like model-building and computer simulation.[24]

[20] D. Rigby Childs, "The First Half-Century of Planning," in Abercrombie, op. cit., pp. 249–79.

[21] See Leo Grebler, *Urban Renewal in European Countries* (Philadelphia, Pa.: University of Pennsylvania Press, 1964).

[22] See Donald L. Foley, "An Approach to Metropolitan Spatial Structure," in Melvin M. Webber et al., *Explorations into Urban Structure* (Philadelphia, Pa.: University of Pennsylvania Press, 1964), pp. 21–78.

[23] Consult Melvin L. Mannheim, "Reaching Decisions about Technological Projects with Social Consequences: A Normative Model," *Transportation*, 2 (April 1973), pp. 1–24.

[24] Garry D. Brewer, *Politicians, Bureaucrats, and the Consultant: A Critique of Urban Problem Solving* (New York: Basic Books, 1973), p. 218.

Flexibility

Flexibility is another characteristic of urban redevelopment planning today. Instead of trying to impose preconceived ideas on existing cities, the urban planner now exhibits a sense of adaptation. For instance, planners are discarding the older practice of zoning land into strictly single-use categories. What formerly were industrial or commercial areas are now being redeveloped for plural use, with housing, shopping, and industry, at least light industry, all intermingled. According to Donald Foley, the adaptive planner regards the city as dynamic process rather than the static structure which the unitary planners of the past thought it to be. The adaptive planner sees the city as a functioning, evolving entity and, therefore, he "would seek to influence various of the development forces at work rather than aiming for a future metropolitan form as a goal."[25]

Yet flexibility should not be equated with the absence of any comprehensive design whatsoever. In fact, redevelopment is frequently oriented to some general plan. T. J. Kent, Jr., an exponent of the idea of a general plan has described it as a statement to provide for the total physical improvement of a city consistent with its socioeconomic goals.[26]

The Planning Process

As Kent has indicated, redevelopment is usually not only guided by an overall plan, it also requires a well-defined process or series of steps to be taken. The process itself may be divided into three successive stages: (1) goal specification; (2) decision-making; and (3) execution.[27]

1. In the American city, redevelopment goals tend to be set in accordance with the interests of significant segments of the community. At present these include big-city officialdom, downtown business, and the economically deprived in the inner city. Alvin Boskoff writes, "The astonishing fact is that comparatively little corrective planning serves the needs of middle class families, who constitute not only a large segment of the urban region, but also seem to be the typical carriers of urban culture and social organization."[28] The goal-setting aspect of redevelopment in our major cities is possibly best examined with regard to the politics of urban renewal. Indeed, where corporate headquarters have created strong demands for central of-

[25] Foley, op. cit., p. 57.

[26] In his *The Urban General Plan* (San Francisco, Calif.: Chandler, 1964), pp. 90ff.

[27] F. Stuart Chapin, Jr., "Foundations of Urban Planning," in Werner Z. Hirsch, ed., *Urban Life and Form* (New York: Holt, Rinehart and Winston, 1963), pp. 217–45.

[28] Alvin Boskoff, *The Sociology of Urban Regions* (New York: Appleton-Century-Crofts, 1970), 2nd ed., p. 358.

Redevelopment. A residential street is closed and the space turned into a mall and tot-lot.

fice space, as in New York, Boston, Atlanta, and Philadelphia, large downtown renewal projects have had unusual success in the past few years.[29]

2. Decision-making means the selection of alternatives. Thus, either the demolition or reconstruction of an area may be chosen. Also major or minor changes may be elected.

Three degrees of change are illustrative of the tactics of decision-making. The hold-the-line approach may be utilized in urging owners to refurbish their property or in having the city institute some small-scale street engineering, like one-way traffic for better vehicle flow. Rehabilitation is more intense. It may call for a downtown business plaza for pedestrians only. The multifunctional center is another form of rehabilitation. It combines retail shopping, office, entertainment, and apartment units in a single framework, such as Montreal's Place Bonaventure, Rochester's Midtown Plaza, and Cleveland's Park Center. This sort of thing has been much favored of late.[30] Finally, full development requires the redesign of the whole central business district along with the reorganization of land use in outlying areas. One illus-

[29] A vigorous defense of downtown revitalization is Jonathan Bartlett, *Urban Design as Public Policy* (New York: Architectural Record and McGraw-Hill, 1974), Ch. 5.

[30] Cf. Victor Gruen, *Centers for the Urban Environment* (New York: Van Nostrand Reinhold, 1973), pp. 95–155.

tration is the construction of Wayne State University near downtown Detroit and the miles-long Woodward Corridor stretching down to the renovated waterfront.

3. After the plan has been decided on, the planning process enters its final stage, that of execution, requiring legislation and construction. Here, unintended consequences often arise and require accommodation. A major planning campaign in Minneapolis, for example, resulted in only one important project directly traceable to the plan itself, the Nicollet Avenue transit axis.

Advocacy Planning

The tentativeness of redevelopment planning as well as the many issues of poverty, race, housing, and education in our cities have recently given rise to a somewhat different interpretation of the planner's function, that of his being an advocate of the objectives of certain disadvantaged groups on the assumption that their goals are conducive to the best interests of the whole community.[31] Hence planning takes on a frankly partisan character, even a radical one, as Robert Goodman of the M.I.T. Department of Architecture has expressed it, "where professionals plead the cause of the poor and the disenfranchised before government forums."[32] Also, a form of advocacy is being practiced covertly today by "underground administrative guerrillas," who secretly instigate public pressures and demonstrations to guide development along paths they favor despite official policies to the contrary.[33]

Recent federal legislation has contributed a good deal to the emergence of advocacy planning in urban America, for urban redevelopment has come to denote omnibus change. Thus in the Demonstration Cities and Metropolitan Development Act of 1966, Congress declared that "improving the quality of urban life is the most critical domestic problem facing the United States."[34] Advocacy planners today reveal a strong interest in such innovations as the maximum utilization of federal power and resources; direct access to the mayor as the prime mover in the whole urban process; reform of the municipal budgeting process to speed up welfare measures; and the decentralization of planning to permit the participation of clients in allocating funds, appointing staff, and programming. One good example of such redevelopment planning is the strategy of dispersed economic integra-

---

[31] Alan A. Altshuler, "The Goals of Comprehensive Planning," *Journal of the American Institute of Planners,* 31 (August 1965).

[32] Robert Goodman, *After the Planners* (New York: Simon and Schuster, 1971), p. 171.

[33] Consult Martin L. Needleman and Carolyn E. Needleman, *Guerrillas in the Bureaucracy: The Community Planning Experiment in the United States* (New York: Wiley, 1974).

[34] United States Statutes, Public Law 89–754 (1966).

tion currently advocated by economist Anthony Downs.[35] Downs believes it imperative to reunite the suburbs and the central city by means of national incentives for housing that will mix socioeconomic classes, curb crime, and provide for the economic health of the metropolitan community as a whole.

Formerly Deputy Administrator of the New York City Human Resources Administration, Henry Cohen is one who endorses the concept of advocacy planning. But he also argues that this be done "only within a framework of carefully defined powers, rights, and responsibilities, and with systems of consultation, review, and appeal."[36]

RELOCATION

The second type of urban planning at present is the establishment of "New Towns" and the relocation of people in them.

The British New Towns

The prominence of British thinkers like Ebenezer Howard and Sir Patrick Geddes in the "New Towns" movement shows that Britain has been a world leader in the design and construction of new urban centers. The British have been motivated by real and very practical considerations in this regard. In Britain, the expense of building roads and of expanding public utilities in already crowded areas has made open land away from them attractive for new construction. The fear of military attack from the air has also contributed to a decline of interest in adding to already dense concentrations when settlements limited in size but containing a balance of commercial and industrial resources and the amenities of urban life as well offer a feasible alternative.

In Britain the Barlow Commission took 26 volumes of testimony before it issued its report in 1940 condemning unplanned urbanization in the United Kingdom as injurious to the nation's health and welfare, and proposing decentralization instead. World War II was being fought at the time, but immediately after victory Parliament passed the New Towns Act of 1946, authorizing the creation of public town-development corporations endowed with governmental powers. Soon, 14 communities were started, 12 in England and Wales, and 2 in Scotland. Plans for a third Scottish town were given approval in 1956.

Eight of the New Towns were meant to relieve population pressure in London. These were Basildon, Bracknell, Crawley, Harlow, Hatfield, Hemel

[35] Anthony Downs, *Opening Up the Suburbs: An Urban Strategy for America* (New Haven, Conn.: Yale University Press, 1973), pp. 131–51. See also Edward M. Katz and Herbert H. Hyman, *Urban Planning for Social Welfare: A Model Cities Approach* (New York: Praeger, 1971).

[36] Henry Cohen, "The Changing Role of the Planner in the Decision-Making Process," in Ernest Erber, ed., *Urban Planning in Transition* (N.Y.: Grossman, 1970), p. 181.

MAP 21-1 New Towns of Great Britain.

Source: Office of International Affairs, U. S. Department of Housing and Urban Development, *General Observations on British New Town Planning* (Washington, D.C.: Government Printing Office, 1973), p. 1.

Housing in Crawley New Town, one of England's relocation projects built since World War II.

Hempstead, Stevenage, and Welwyn Garden City. (See Map 21-1.) Similarly, Cumbernauld and East Kilbride were designed to alleviate congestion in Glasgow. Of the others, Peterlee and Glenrothes were planned to bring about better population distribution than was possible in certain mining districts; and Corby Cwnbran and Newton Aycliffe to achieve more feasible housing. By 1968, 8 more New Towns had been started, 6 in England (Skelmersdale, Telford, Redditch, Runcorn, Washington, and Milton Keynes), and 2 in Scotland (Livingston and Irvine). (See Map 21-1.) Half of these were not really New Towns for they were intended to expand present cities into regional centers. Several, however, were meant to decant population from metropolitan Birmingham.

In spite of its accomplishments, the British new town movement has not been without opposition. In a judicious discussion of the subject, Osborn and Whittick have presented no fewer than seven serious reservations that have been raised.[37]

First, there is the question of wasting land. Yet, say Osborn and Whittick, given normal population growth, 90 percent of the British Isles can be left as attractive open space.

Second, the output of food should not suffer, provided care is taken to avoid using up the most productive acreage.

Third, there must be action to prevent exurban dormitories masquerading as New Towns from destroying the metropolitan greenbelts.

Fourth, the so-called urban fetishists, say Osborn and Whittick, mistakenly think architectural diversity and compactness are innately urban, and object to the low silhouettes, parklike spaces, structural uniformity of the New Towns.

Fifth, a community's business interests are usually afraid that the erection of New Towns in their vicinity will lose them business. However, the expenditures for new streets and services as well as the high-density housing required by additions to an existing city offset the economic gains that they bring in, particularly without the government subsidies that have been relied on to absorb the costs.

Sixth, the relocation of people from the London, Birmingham, and Glasgow conurbations to the New Towns is not without social difficulty. Surveys conducted in the Liverpool, Coventry, Sheffield, and Bethnal Green areas on the effects of moving in connection with redevelopment disclosed a number of ill effects. Some lower-class people who had relocated lacked an interest in "respectability," in other words, in cleanliness and in having well-mannered children, and they were resented by their neighbors. The elderly could not make friends in their new locations. Also, mixing persons of different status aspirations led to severe tensions too. Yet effective voluntary associations, cultural facilities, garden plots, a variety of housing, and suitable employment can avert much of the distress that may otherwise be experienced as a result of being relocated.

Seventh, and finally, there is political resistance to new towns from officials and party leaders who fear losing power. Nonetheless, experi-

[37] Frederick J. Osborn and Arnold Whittick, *The New Towns: The Answer to Megalopolis* (London: Leonard Hill, 1969), Ch. 10. See also Frederick J. Osborn, *Green-Belt Cities* (New York: Schocken Books, 1969), pp. 167–80.

EXHIBIT 21-1 Heating Cities by Geothermal Energy

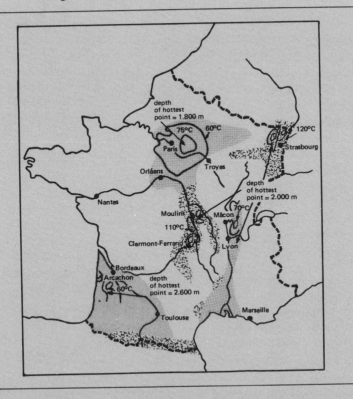

The French government is currently active in attempting to tap heat trapped in the earth to augment other sources of energy available to that country's industrial-urban centers.

Source: France (N.Y.: French Embassy, Press and Information Division, May, 1976), p. 3.

ence in Britain has tended to minimize new towns as a source of political disturbance even though individual incumbents have at times been hurt by the new social ecology.

Despite Osborn and Whitick's defense of the new town movement, M.I.T.'s Lloyd Rodwin has pointed out two fundamental weaknesses in Britain's new towns.[38] On the one hand, he says, they have not actually relieved the pressures of population in London, Birmingham, and Glasgow. And on the other, owing to inadequate planning, the new towns have not achieved a balanced national economy in the United Kingdom.

These judgments of Osborn and Whittick and of Rodwin would suggest

[38] Lloyd Rodwin, *The British New Towns Policy: Problems and Implications* (Cambridge, Mass.: Harvard University Press, 1956), pp. 162–83.

that some reservations are now tempering the earlier approval given new towns by the British public and urban planners alike.

New Towns in Other Countries

Besides Britain, new towns development has taken place recently in Canada, Czechoslovakia, Poland, Yugoslavia, and Hungary. Also, France and Germany have created new settlements adjacent to natural gas and oil fields (Exhibit 21-1). Soviet planners too have concerned themselves with new towns. Among the Soviets, ideological arguments about the curse of urban bigness in the capitalistic West have spurred the conception of satellite cities 20 to 30 miles from the metropolitan centers. Though having their own distinctive regional functions, when completed these satellites would depend on the metropolis for both employment and sociocultural services. New towns are to be set up farther away from metropolitan areas, 60 to 150 miles away, to bring Soviet agriculture and industry into a single, unified system.[39] They are to be located on a transportation grid developed with respect to the nation's natural resources. Owing to consolidated industrial planning which favors the expansion of existing facilities in the big cities, however, population dispersal has not been successfully accomplished in the Soviet Union as of this writing.

New Towns in the United States

In America, new towns have been the product mainly of private developers, not government. New towns in the United States also differ from their British analogues in other ways as well. New towns in the United States have been located near metropolitan centers and not away from them. Ours lack protective greenbelts around them. And being without government authority except for local housekeeping, our new towns can only attract, not mandate, the establishment of industry within their precincts.

The first new town in the United States, Radburn, New Jersey, 16 miles from New York, was designed in 1929 by Clarence Stein and Henry Wright as a garden city without a protective greenbelt.[40] Stein and Wright drew up neighborhood superblocks, surrounding parks and serviced by cul-de-sacs rather than vehicular roads. The homes faced gardens not streets, and passovers allowed roadways to carry traffic overhead. Here was a design to make life safe from the automobile!

Despite the attempt by the Radburn City Housing Corporation to build a

---

[39] D. G. Khodzhayev and B. S. Khorev, "The Conception of a Unified System of Settlement and the Planned Regulation of City Growth in the USSR," *Ekistics*, 34 (December 1972), 410–13.

[40] Cf. Edward P. Eichler and Bernard Norwitch, "New Towns," in Daniel P. Moynihan, ed., *Toward a National Urban Policy* (New York: Basic Books, 1970), pp. 302–12.

The Bryant Woods neighborhood in Columbia, Maryland. The streets are laid out in cul-de-sac fashion.

balanced community of industry and residences, Radburn was hampered by the collapse of the economy in 1929. The company finally went bankrupt, and the receiving corporation eventually completed two superblocks, nothing more.[41] Several other new towns were authorized as public-service demonstration projects under the New Deal but were soon converted into private holdings divested of all government involvement.

Recently private interests have brought quite a few new town communities into being in the United States. The two outstanding ones are Columbia and Reston. Located on 14,000 acres along Route 29 and within 25 miles of the nation's capital, Columbia is to build up to a population of 110,000 by 1981. The promoters have secured a $50 million mortgage principally from the Connecticut General Insurance Corporation. They have also added several hundred row houses and apartment units built with federal subsidies for low- and middle-income families. An authentic new town, Columbia is to have not only residential and business facilities but also industry. A 1000-acre assembly plant of General Electric has already gone into operation there.

Reston stands on 7000 acres around an artificial lake 23 miles northwest

---

[41] Clarence S. Stein, *Towards New Towns for America* (Cambridge, Mass.: M.I.T. Press, 1957).

of Washington. It has one high-rise residential building and a number of apartment houses. In addition, it also provides sites for single-family homes, many of them around a golf course, and scattered town-houses as well. By 1966, Reston had more than 6000 residents, mainly upper-middle class, and also several industrial plants making some local employment possible. By 1973, its population numbered 22,000 with a median family income of $25,000. When it is completed in 1982, Reston is expected to have 25,000 dwellings, and at a ratio of 1 to every 3 persons there provide about 25,000 jobs.

Other large-scale exurban projects in different degrees of completion are also to be found in the United States today. They include Franklin Town, a $400 million, 50-acre development in metropolitan Philadelphia; Litchfield, Arizona; Hamilton, near San Francisco; Valencia, in southern California; and a $500 million enterprise, Cedar-Riverside, Minnesota, whose population may reach 30,000 by 1992. Inside Minneapolis itself, Cedar-Riverside is being financed by the Northwest Mutual Life Insurance Company under a $24 million HUD guarantee. Leisure-oriented communities are also springing up in the United States mainly in response to interest from retirees. Several are in California and others on the East Coast.

The Future of the New Towns Movement in America

Their mixed results have dimmed many of the high hopes entertained for new towns by earlier enthusiasts here in the United States. Though the 1968 Housing and Urban Development Act and the 1970 Urban Growth and New-Communities Act have authorized funds for new towns, "the social hopes of our legislators," writes architectural historian Mel Scott, "may be irreconcilable with the unvarnished facts of the market place."[42] Scott believes that most of our urban population increase will continue to be absorbed into the metropolitan areas rather than by New Towns designed for guided social change. In fact, most of the so-called planned communities which have arisen in the United States, though they have made provision for stores, have been essentially dormitory tracts. They have not represented a new turn of events at all, these New Town Levittowns, Park Forests, and San Lorenzo Villages.

Notwithstanding, William Levitt, operative builder of three Levittowns in New York, New Jersey, and Pennsylvania, has declared that the New Town idea may be a feasible model for future growth. Levitt has said that land close to our metropolitan centers has been almost completely used up, and that what remains is both tightly restricted and very expensive. Consequently, Levitt reasons that "the only solution is to create jobs where there

---

[42] Mel Scott, *American City Planning since 1890* (Berkeley and Los Angeles, Calif.: University of California Press, 1969), pp. 647–48.

is open land and to provide housing close to those jobs."[43] Others argue that by emulating its herculean World War II production program, the federal government could step in and build settlements at least near the metropolitan fringe for employment, residential, racial-integration, education, and health purposes all together.[44]

Such views, however, do not squarely face the problem of securing mandatory power to exercise eminent domain, locate industry, and determine transportation routes. That New Towns too are not a ready solution to the problems of urban poverty and race relations has also been advanced.[45] Finally, many Americans, and possibly most, prefer the suburban mode of life to the quasipastoral, self-contained alternative of the New Town, so that some type of suburban development rather than the New Town per se may prove to be the only viable course to pursue here in the United States.

REGIONAL PLANNING

Regional planning, the third type of contemporary urban design and planning, originates in the fact that any large city is the focal point of a broad geographic area beyond its immediate vicinity. Accordingly, regional planning consists of coordinated efforts to cope systematically with urban problems on a territorial basis beyond the given metropolitan area. Regional planning in the United States has had three stages since it first began in the Depression. Originally, in the 1930s, regional planning centered on natural resources, the TVA being doubtlessly the best single example. The second phase was the regionalism seen in the attempts to aid depressed areas like Appalachia. And, third, we have the present urban-metropolitan focus on major cities as the key to their respective hinterlands.

The Elements of Regional Planning

At present, regional planning combines metropolitan planning with long-term economic development for the surrounding geographic territory. Six elements are involved here.[46] (1) Regional planning goes beyond architecture and engineering to include social, economic, and cultural objectives. (2) Community and human resources planning calls for the anticipation of ways and means to alleviate poverty, develop manpower, and sustain constructive

---

[43] John B. Willmann, *The Department of Housing and Urban Development* (New York: Praeger, 1967), p. 162.

[44] Sam B. Warner, Jr., *The Urban Wilderness* (New York: Harper, 1972), pp. 113–49.

[45] See Harvey Perloff and Neil Sandberg, *New Towns: Why and for Whom* (New York: Praeger, 1973).

[46] Maynard M. Hufschmidt, "A New Look at Regional Planning," in his edited volume *Regional Planning: Challenge and Prospect* (New York: Praeger, 1969), pp. 28–42.

community action. (3) Environmental planning entails measures to insure public health and aesthetic well-being. (4) Natural-resources planning is conducted in concert with these other modes of planning. (5) Regional science and operations research embracing quantitative methods such as computer simulation, systems analysis, and cost-benefit study is conducted. And, finally (6) economic development is planned on a broad basis, including public-private and intergovernmental consultation and coordination.

Two Current Regional Plans in the United States

Two present-day regional plans in the United States illustrate the application of the regional planning concept. They are (1) the Washington Year 2000 Plan and (2) the long-standing effort of regional planners in the New York metropolitan area.

1 Regional planning for Washington began in 1950 when in order to insure government continuity in the event of nuclear attack the Regional Planning Commission undertook to decentralize federal offices throughout a four-county area.[47] Today about one out of three federal employees assigned to Washington works at least 20 miles from the District of Columbia. Further decentralization of federal employment, up to the two-thirds mark in fact, by means of mass transit over a constellation of radial corridors to the outlying communities is anticipated by the Year 2000 Plan, as are also two other goals. These are the renewal of the central city, where more than 60 percent are black, many of them inhabiting substandard housing, and the preservation of 300,000 acres of open land surrounding Washington and lying between the corridors.

Coherent as the Washington regional plan may be, it has its critics. Some object to the satellites of from 25,000 to 50,000 in size and assert the need for regional centers ranging between 250,000 and 400,000. It is also feared that the radial corridors will perpetuate racial segregation by making commuting easy. Finally, whether the radials will keep the interstitial areas unoccupied and green has also been raised as a debatable point. The plan has also encountered a lack of legal and administrative means. True, the National Transportation Agency has been set up to aid the development of mass transit. But how can the corridor cities be built unless there is government authority with sufficient power to mandate construction? For political and financial reasons, federal policy makers have continued to prefer short-term instead of innovative, long-range planning and implementation.

2 Regional planning in the New York City area exhibits not only the need for it but the typical obstacles standing in its way too, and emphatically so.

---

[47] Cf. National Capital Planning Commission, *1965–1985 Proposed Physical Development Policies for Washington, D.C.* (Washington, D.C.: Government Printing Office, 1965).

Since the publication, in 1929, of the *Regional Plan of New York and Its Environs* by the Regional Plan Association, New York City has often been defined as simply the focus of a vast geographic, economic, and sociocultural entity extending across three states. The fact that 1500 political units exist in that area, many of them with severe financial problems, has only emphasized the critical need for comprehensive action despite Byzantine multiplicity.[48] Yet regional coordination there has been hampered by numerous difficulties. Among these are a lack of financial support for cooperation between governments; the absence of statutory authority to implement recommendations; and the fear by home-rule advocates of pernicious "supergovernment." As a matter of fact, the Metropolitan Regional Council of New York saved itself from extinction by becoming a non-profit technical-assistance corporation so as to qualify for funds under the 1965 Housing and Urban Development Act!

The Future of Regional Planning in the United States

Prospects for more effective regional planning in the United States are generally favorable though not entirely so. The federal government now offers financial aid for areawide intergovernmental coordination. Moreover, the creation of HUD can be expected to expedite joint planning at both state and local levels. Examples of statewide planning agencies are the New York State Urban Development Corporation and that state's Office of Planning Coordination; the Connecticut Department of Community Affairs; the Tri-State Transportation Commission; and the Southeast Michigan Council of Government.[49]

The future of regional planning councils in the United States is not altogether assured, however. Though committed only to planning, these agencies tend also to become administrative units, because as they channel federal grants to local areas they take on a decision-making character themselves. Consequently, regional planning councils become involved in contested political questions. Furthermore, though the Supreme Court has enunciated the one-man, one-vote doctrine, it has not seen fit to preclude unequal representation on "the structure of public bodies, equipped with new capacities and motivations," perhaps adding additional tensions.[50]

Regional Planning in Britain and France

In both Britain and France regional planning benefits from the direct imposition of central powers less hampered by the local autonomy and federalism

---

[48] See Joan B. Aron, *The Quest for Regional Cooperation: A Study of the New York Metropolitan Regional Council* (Berkeley and Los Angeles, Calif.: University of California Press, 1969).

[49] Willmann, op. cit., p. 159.

[50] Avery v. Midland County, 390 U.S. 474 (1968).

characteristic of the American system of government.

The British government has prepared eight regional studies covering most of the country. These were undertaken because urgent problems, particularly the growth of population, land shortages, and a maldistribution of labor, were affecting the entire national economy far beyond the specific regions themselves. Thus the south-east study of London and its environs advocated a dispersal strategy, while a second strategy called for a second major national-international center in the north.

In France, regional planning distinguishes between congested, intermediate, and lagging regions.[51] French planning has aimed at both decongesting Paris and also building up cities in the provincial desert of the Massif central, the west, and the southwest. Industrialization is being stimulated in the West around Nantes, Bordeaux, and Toulouse. There, the government is investing funds in higher education and research institutes, modernizing farming, and building up recreational facilities. At the same time, by restricting building permits and the growth of public institutions in Paris, some success is being realized in slowing down the growth of the capital. Also, five new towns are being planned around Paris, and four others adjacent to other French cities. Incidentally, in this manner, French regional planning turns into comprehensive national planning, the subject to which we turn in the final chapter of this text.

CONCLUSION

The deliberate, systematic provision of resources for the achievement of community goals, urban design and planning have taken on new significance recently. True, they achieved distinct success in the preindustrial city, but such efforts occurred rather rarely. It was the rapid growth of the industrial city in Europe and America that ushered in a new era of design and planning, calling for their application in a continuous, large-scale, concerted manner. Since the nineteenth century, this has taken three major forms: the redevelopment of existing cities; the creation of New Towns; and the adoption of regional strategies covering the metropolitan area and its surrounding territory. Also, urban design and planning have been moving from a concentration on physical engineering and economic variables to greater interest in social and cultural matters. Finally, while the whole planning function has by now been firmly established as essential to sound urban administration, it continues to be handicapped by a general unavailability of financial and governmental resources as well as by a lack of clear goals.

[51] See Niles M. Hansen, *French Regional Planning* (Bloomington, Ind.: Indiana University Press, 1968).

FOR FURTHER READING

Don T. Allensworth, *The Political Realities of Urban Planning* (New York: Prager, 1974). The planning process as an integral part of the political system.

James Bailey, ed., *New Towns in America* (New York: Wiley, 1973). Relocation, from basic physical design to social planning, economic factors, transit planning, and development problems.

Earl Blecher, *Advocacy Planning for Urban Development* (New York: Praeger, 1971). Advocacy planning evaluated in six demonstration projects.

Marion Clawson and Peter Hall, *Planning and Urban Growth* (New York: Russell Sage Foundation, 1974). Contrasts the centralized British attempt to avert urban sprawl with American planning for optimal land use.

Anthony J. Ctanese, *Planners and Local Politics* Beverly Hills, Calif.: Sage Publications, 1974). The complex relationships between planners and politicians, and how the two may work together better.

Ernest Erber, ed., *Urban Planning in Transition* (New York: Grossman, 1970). The framework of urban planning, the state of the art, and the professional planner's role.

Bernard J. Frieden and Robert Morris, eds., *Urban Planning and Social Policy* (New York: Basic Books, 1968). Planning for redevelopment, including housing, race relations, and the reduction of poverty.

Constance Perin, *With Man in Mind* (Cambridge, Mass.: M.I.T. Press, 1970). How to bridge the gap between planning objectives and human wants.

Arnold Whittick, ed., *Encyclopedia of Urban Planning* (New York: McGraw-Hill, 1974). A compilation of informative material and technical data on planning; liberally illustrated.

CHAPTER 22

URBANIZATION AND URBAN PLANNING IN UNDERDEVELOPED AREAS

Urbanization in the underdeveloped nations of Asia, the Middle East, Africa, and Latin America today is exerting great influence over life within these countries themselves and over international affairs as well. It is also generating significant modes of planning. Urbanization in these underdeveloped but modernizing regions will doubtlessly continue to have such an impact for years to come. John Palen, who has written extensively on the subject, believes that this process "is not gradually transforming traditional societies throughout the world; rather, it is bursting them asunder and upsetting traditional attitudes, beliefs, customs, and behaviors."[1] Palen's view may be somewhat an overstatement although the consequences he envisages can be readily observed in many instances.

URBANIZATION IN THE NEWLY DEVELOPING COUNTRIES

Little uncertainty exists about either the extent or the speed with which urban settlement is proceeding in the underdeveloped areas. In 1975, the less well developed regions, specifically East and South Asia, Latin America, and Africa, had 22 percent of their population in places of 20,000 or more.[2] This compared with a figure of 52 percent for the more developed regions (Europe, North America, the U.S.S.R., and Oceania). However, in the 55-year period from 1920 to 1975, the former group of nations increased their degree of urbanization 220 percent in contrast to the latter's 75 percent rate of growth. The rapidity of urbanization in the developing nations is of course affected by the relatively low level of urban concentration in the world's traditional, unmodernized areas in 1920. Yet the very large population of Asia and to a lesser extent of Latin America has led to massive concentrations in the settled areas there. In 1974, Asia already had 50 cities of 1 million and over, and 641 cities of at least 100,000, a figure that almost equaled the total for Europe and North America combined.[3]

Continued population growth in the developing regions will further add to their urbanization to such an extent, according to United Nations demographers, that by the year 2000, while the more advanced regions will have about 784 million persons in agglomerated settlements (20,000-plus), the less developed major areas will probably have 1553 millions, almost exactly twice as many.[4]

THE EFFECTS OF URBANIZATION IN UNDERDEVELOPED AREAS

The consequences of urbanization in the world's less well developed regions may be seen to be of three types. These are: (1) the impact of city-

[1] J. John Palen, *The Urban World* (New York: McGraw-Hill, 1975), Table 4B, p. 332.

[2] W. Parker Frisbie, "The Scale and Growth of World Urbanization," in John Walton and Donald E. Carns, eds., *Cities in Change* (Boston: Allyn & Bacon, 1977), 2nd ed., p. 49.

[3] United Nations, *Demographic Yearbook, 1974* (New York: United Nations, 1975).

[4] United Nations, *Growth of the World's Urban and Rural Population, 1920–2000* (New York: United Nations, 1969), Table 32, p. 59.

building on traditional societies; (2) tendencies toward over-urbanization; and (3) the emergence of possibly new forms of social organization resulting from urban life.

CHANGING TRADITIONAL SOCIETIES

Urbanization affects traditional societies in many ways, three of which are perhaps most noteworthy.

> *First,* economic opportunity expands, but it expands unevenly. Employment typically grows most quickly in government service, public utilities, personal services, and trade, but it lags behind in health, education, and welfare.

> *Second,* small-scale home industries multiply, generally when artisans move from the villages to the towns and cities. But large-scale industrial development moves ahead with uncertainty due to the lack of capital and strong consumer purchasing power. The result is that parasitic urbanization occurs, parasitic because population concentration goes on faster than the development of industrial resources to sustain it properly.

> *Third,* these processes of uneven development in employment and of sluggish industrialization transpire in the presence of masses of uprooted peasant families transplanted to makeshift encampments usually at the edges of the more permanent urban districts.

Overall, then, a mélange of new and old cultures comes about following the onset of urbanization in an underdeveloped region. Traditional and modern social structures intertwine. For example, hitherto unachievable caste expectations, particularly in symbolic activities in the home and between householders and their servants, are realized by many who now have the monetary means for doing so for the first time in their lives. Simultaneously, preexisting ideals of *machismo* or tribal hegemony fed by the pressures of poverty and by rising hopes find expression in mass political movements outwardly proclaiming nationalist or Marxian objectives which are said to be on the threshold of attainment. In these ways, traditionalism and modernization come together not in a fusion but in a mixture of dissimilar elements.

OVER-URBANIZATION

Many of the nations of Latin America, Africa, the Middle East, and Asia are not yet fully industrialized. Yet a sizable proportion of their people inhabit places of high density and are engaged in nonagricultural occupations. This is the case in spite of the fact that in terms of such indices as iron-and-steel production and the consumption of electricity, industrial development has not proceeded very far. Hence the term over-urbanization has come into use to designate the condition in which "larger proportions of [a nation's] population live in urban places than their degree of economic development justifies."[5]

This does not mean that over-urbanization occurs uniformly in the underdeveloped regions. Far from it. The urban centers of the developing nations have their own particular histories.[6] In certain of the new nations, cities resulted from colonization by an imperial power, for instance, by the French in Vietnam. Or urbanization has been the consequence of the termination of foreign exploitation, such as the demonstrative expansion of Jakarta by Indonesian nationalists after Indonesia became independent. In both of these cases, nonintrinsic forces were responsible for the establishment and growth of particular cities.

There is considerable agreement that on account of the pressure of numbers on capital resources, rapid population growth now impedes economic progress in many of the less well developed nations. One recent Ford Foundation report concluded that "urban dilemmas [are becoming] evident throughout the developing countries."[7]

Consider several specific cases.

In Latin America

The *barriadas* of Lima are an example of over-urbanization. Lima is the capital of Peru and an expanding population center. In 1940, Lima's population stood at 533,645. In 1972, it was estimated as 3.8 million, with much of the growth attributable to in-migrants coming from the hinterlands of the Andes where they were being pushed out by population pressure and a decline in the market for hand-crafted goods. Inhabited by possibly 1 million persons, the *barriadas* of Lima are the settlements of the most recent newcomers to the city.[8]

Sprawling areas of makeshift shanties constructed of waste materials and situated all around the capital, Lima's *barriadas* exemplify the socioeconomic inadequacies of Peru. The *barriadas* are strikingly unstable. Nutrition is poor and the level of health miserably low although, paradoxically, it has

[5] Philip M. Hauser, "The Social, Economic, and Technical Problems of Rapid Urbanization," in Bert F. Hoselitz and Wilbert E. Moore, eds., *Industrialization and Society* (Paris: UNESCO and Mouton, 1963), p. 203.

[6] See Gerald Breese, *Urbanization in Newly Developing Countries* (Englewood Cliffs, N.J.: Prentice-Hall, 1966).

[7] Frederick C. Terzo, *Urbanization in the Developing Countries: International Survey* (New York: Ford Foundation, 1973), p. 126.

[8] William Mangin, "Squatter Settlements," *Scientific American*, 217 (October 1961), pp. 21–29. See also John P. Robin and Frederick C. Terzo, *Urbanization in Peru* (New York: Ford Foundation, 1971).

An open-air laundry site in one of Lima, Peru's, *barriadas*.

been the declining death rate in Peru's rural regions that has brought about population pressure in that country.

Transferred to the cities, the displaced peasants have simply depressed wages and further arrested Peru's economic development. The United Nations *Report on the World Social Situation* concludes:

> *There is reluctance on the part of employers to adopt labour-saving devices in view of the supply of cheap labour, and on the part of the workers themselves, who fear unemployment as a consequence. . . . Underemployment and unemployment in the labour force, along with instability, are thus not only wasteful but also slow down the development of industry, which is concurrently slowed down by the lack of qualified and skilled manpower.*[9]

In Africa

Africa's over-urbanization is perhaps equally notable. In underdeveloped Africa, the economic demands made by World War II, the capital subsequently invested in Africa, and the multiplication of secondary administra-

[9] United Nations, *Report on the World Social Situation* (New York: United Nations, 1957), p. 175.

tive services have recently combined with population pressure in the countryside to induce considerable urbanization south of the Sahara.[10] Bamako, Bangui, and Pointe Noire in the formerly French territories, Kampala in West Africa, and Beira in Mozambique are only a few of the African cities that have grown rapidly in the past few years. The result though is that "in the whole of Africa, what has been called the growth of new towns . . . is first and foremost the conglomeration of uprooted human masses, who are camping in the expectation of remunerated labour, but who maintain ties, sometimes at a very long distance, with the native bush and for whom a true adaptation to urban life is not facilitated since it can be guaranteed only by adequate wages, lodging, and security provisions."[11]

As in Latin America, urbanization in Africa appears to be having a generally unfavorable impact. Wages are low for the urban Africans, and labor turnover runs at a high rate, even 100 percent a year. Housing is clearly inadequate, with severe over-crowding, primitive sanitation, and outright squalor. Disease, including dietary deficiencies, parasitic worms, salmonellosis, malaria, yaws, amoebic dysentery, and venereal infections, continues to be widespread.

THE CASE AGAINST OVER-URBANIZATION

Not all observers agree on the judgment that most of the underdeveloped countries are over-urbanized. And there is reason to believe that cities in the nonmodernized nations act as sanctuaries for peasants fleeing even more dire conditions in the farming areas. Although meagre, the amenities of the city and its welfare services are magnets, and it is not the prospects of steady employment but rather the "push" of the countryside that is mainly responsible for sending these refugees to the urban centers. The cities are preferable to outright destitution back home.

In this light, think again about the *barriadas* of Lima. As José Mar shows, many of their inhabitants have migrated to the city in the hope of acquiring education for their children and of advancing themselves occupationally.[12] The economically active population of the *barriadas,* of whom surprisingly perhaps not more than 10 percent are literate, work principally as laborers, domestics, and street peddlars. Most of them have some "stable" employment, and only a scattering of the able-bodied declare themselves unemployed. The people of the *barriadas* are not only better educated than their

[10] International African Institute, *Social Implications of Industrialization and Urbanization in Africa South of the Sahara* (Paris: UNESCO, 1956).

[11] Quoted from Pierre Naville, "Données statistiques sur la structure de la main-d'oeuvre salariee et de l'industrie en Afrique noire," *Le travail en Afrique noire* (Paris: Aux Editions du Seuil, 1952), ibid., p. 147.

[12] José M. Mar, "The Barriadas of Lima," in Philip M. Hauser, ed., *Urbanization in Latin America* (New York: Columbia University Press and UNESCO, 1961), pp. 170–90.

rural countrymen. They may even have greater economic security than the farmers of Peru.[13]

Nor should the *barriadas* be thought of as lacking social organization entirely. Dozens of residents' associations negotiate for services for their propertyless members, as can be seen from the fact that a majority of the *barriadas* have drinking water, electric service, schools, and even some sewers. The associations also seek to work out arrangements with the authorities so that the inhabitants of the *barriadas* can eventually secure title to the land on which they live. The resident associations thus supplement the family organization which the migrants bring with them from the rural areas.

A BALANCED VIEW ON OVER-URBANIZATION

We might say that urbanization in the underdeveloped countries has not one but two faces, much as the earlier period of industrial urbanization in Europe and America did. Its total effect on any society must therefore probably be ambiguous or at least of a dual character.

The roles which a city in a given developing country plays shows this in greater detail. Five aspects appear germane here.[14]

1. The cities of the emerging nations are points of contact with the outer, modernized world. These cities are sources of change that the traditionalist elements resist and the modernists welcome.

2. The cities of the underdeveloped countries serve as seats of political and economic power. Whatever central banks, business and government headquarters, and major professional services are available are typically located in the midst of these population centers.

3. These cities are the places where the media of mass communication are located. In this way too they bring about cultural diffusion. They also broaden economic opportunity and administrative efficiency.

4. Although it does furnish what little opportunity is available, the central, or primate, city in an emergent country draws talent away from the more backward areas of the interior, and in the process it speeds up social decay there.

5. The primate city in an underdeveloped nation is the recipient of investment captial. This has two sides to it. The funds can be used for the long-range basic expansion of raw materials and productive facilities or, as is often the case, the primate city may prefer to use its resources for immediately marketable consumer goods, and therefore slow its economic development and that of the country as a whole.

[13] Ibid. See also John F. C. Turner, *Housing Policy for a Developing Latin Economy* (Rio Piedras, P.R.: University of Puerto Rico, 1966).

[14] Following Breese, op. cit., pp. 40–43.

As these observations suggest, there is much debate over the value of urbanization in the industrially underdeveloped lands. The controversy over urbanization is affected, of course, by the existence of different points of view regarding the relative desirability of rural and urban ways of life and by interpretations of the course of industrial urban development.

NEW URBAN PATTERNS

There is another type of debate over urbanization now taking place in the modernizing countries that centers on the question of whether the new wave of urbanization will ultimately follow the course already taken by the growth of urban society in the West.

The urban sociologist Gideon Sjoberg views modernization as a process consisting of four concurrent subprocesses: the continuity, modification, and disappearance of traditional forms, and the emergence of new forms.[15] This outlook is valuable because it assumes that the past will, in part at least, survive into the future despite urbanization. Few definite conclusions have been reached, however, by research that has been done on this hypothesis.

Some generalizations though do appear reasonably valid. For one thing, the mass media socialize the urban newcomers enabling them to observe some of the conventional modes of urban life as they are known in the West. In the cities of Latin America, the rural migrants soon share a common culture with the earlier urban population and are readily acclimated to the wage economy. By and large, these newcomers strive to take on the symbols of modern Western ways in dress and speech in order to rid themselves of the *caboclo* (hayseed) stigma.

Other tendencies may also be noted. Wage labor strengthens the emancipation of women. Land use becomes more rational. In these and other ways too, the Western model of industrial urbanization is being spontaneously reproduced, and this lends credence to the conclusion that a universal process of urbanization is now going on among the developing nations.

Yet, indigenous sociocultural forces are apparently also affecting urbanization in the modernizing lands and giving the process a potentially different character. For instance, urban growth in Africa resembles that of Latin America's with respect to the continued presence of earlier colonial centers and lagging industrialization. It differs from the latter, however, in that African cities are much more socially heterogeneous; tribal loyalties are strong in their populations, with much two-way traffic between country and city; and racial tensions in these population centers complicate the other strains of cultural adaptation and modernization already present.

[15] Gideon Sjoberg, "Cities in Developing and in Industrial Societies: A Cross-Cultural Analysis," in Philip M. Hauser and Leo F. Schnore, eds., *The Study of Urbanization* (New York: Wiley & Sons, 1965), pp. 213–63.

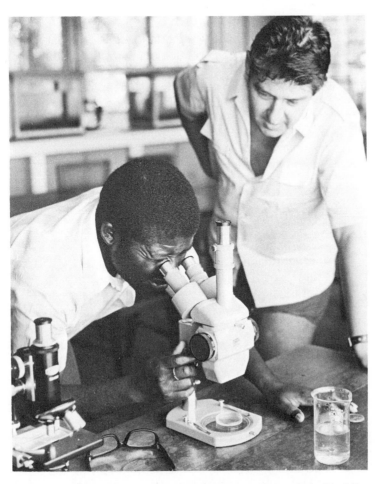

Fishery training center in the Central African Republic near the capital city of Bangui where fishermen are taught modern techniques of fish-rearing. The project is aided by the UN.

Though many of the urban elites in Africa possess an orientation to the West—with its market economy, professional standards, bourgeois lifestyles, and nuclear family structure—others proclaim more indigenous goals for the future development of their own nations if not the entire continent.[16] As yet, these are not especially clear, but often they focus on a collectivist economy, communal solidarity, a high level of political mobilization, and tribal art forms. Such an ideology makes up still another yardstick for measuring the relative merits of urbanization in the emerging nations.

So considered, the cities of the underdeveloped nations also offer us

[16] See UNESCO, *International Social Science Bulletin,* 8 (1956), No. 3.

reason for thinking that the process now unfolding among them may be no mere duplication of the early history of the industrialized West, but rather the makings of a new and unique type of sociocultural configuration. One who thinks so is Brian Blouet. He argues that having access to modern transportation makes it unnecessary to locate industries near fuel and the sources of other raw materials. This can help produce metropolitanization from the outset.[17] In fact, whether future urbanization elsewhere in the world will duplicate the earlier Western experience raises the question which the so-called new urban history has been posing of late: whether we ourselves actually know our own urban past or merely have an incorrect idea of it.[18]

URBAN PLANNING IN THE NEWLY DEVELOPING COUNTRIES

Various kinds of urban planning are being pursued today in the developing nations undergoing urbanization. In general, however, planning is hampered by a lack of resources, such as capital and professional manpower, although in many of the modernizing lands ideological doctrines favorable to planning receive strong support.

Take as examples four southeast Asian countries attempting modernization now: India, Ceylon, Burma, and Indonesia. In all of them socialism is the official government creed. Yet as a doctrine socialism has not been rigorously defined in any of the four, and the socialism followed by them is being adapted to their native values.[19] As a case in point, in India the predominant general objective is to attain balanced industrialization with all the necessary supporting utilities, human accommodations and services, and a political organization sufficient to integrate rural and urban areas into one single coordinated system. Toward this general objective, four policy directives have been formulated by Indian national planners: (1) the establishment of new industries away from the large and congested cities; (2) the adoption of the regional concept in economic planning; (3) the consolidation of rural and urban components within regional plans; and (4) the achievement of a diversified, semiurban occupational pattern even in the areas remaining substantially rural.[20]

---

[17] Brian W. Blouet, "Factors Influencing the Evolution of Settlement Patterns," in Peter J. Ucko, Ruth Tringham, and G. W. Dimbleby, eds., *Man, Settlement and Urbanism* (London: Gerald Duckworth, 1972), pp. 3–15.

[18] Compare Stephan Thernstrom and Richard Sennett, eds., *Nineteenth-Century Cities: Essays in the New Urban History* (New Haven, Conn.: Yale University Press, 1969).

[19] Gunnar Myrdal, *Asian Drama* (New York: Pantheon Books, 1968), Vol. 2, p. 801.

[20] C. P. Malik, "Housing and Urban Development in India," in *Report of the Ad Hoc Group of Experts on Housing and Urban Development* (New York: United Nations, 1962), p. 63.

The planning that has thus emerged not only in India but in the rest of South Asia calls for much community development, including the establishment of local credit unions and coops, and reaches directly into the individual family. Strengthening local self-government to become more effective assumes great significance in this so-called Third World planning for continued urbanization. But educational, health, and social services require sophisticated, centralized direction, much capital, and sound social organization if modernization is to be achieved rapidly, and these are all in short supply, creating serious tensions.

The pace of urbanization in the developing lands should not be thought the product of deliberate planning. Nationalist regimes like those in Indonesia, Senegal, and other countries may favor systematic development ideologically, but the lack of professional staff, adequate theory, money, and effective organization hampers efforts when coordinated schemes do get underway, and frequently the leadership ends up in merely paying lip service to the planning ideal.[21] One generally unanswered question among urban planners in these regions concerns whether adding to the primate city, like Dakar, is preferable to a more distributed pattern of city building. Another question, mainly in areas like Albania where Communist Chinese influence has been very heavy, relates to the relative value of ideological fervor versus technical means as regards the development of industry, transport, communication, and health services without which successful urbanization cannot be achieved. Consequently, urbanization in such regions is coming about not as the result of coordinated development but rather as the product of spontaneous change, including population growth, foreign trade, and war, together with the client-patron relationship between the developing nations and the world's superpowers, the United States and Soviet Union. Nonetheless, the urbanization of the developing lands is presumably having lasting effects internally within the preexisting traditional societies and possibly equally important consequences in the outer world.

The mixture of dissimilar elements, traditional and modern, resulting from urbanization in the developing countries appeals to academic scholars interested in social theory. This mixture is also of concern to planners charged with working out designs that can meet demographic, industrial, and administrative problems and also guide the development of their countries toward greater stability, strength, and prosperity. For instance, of 102 developing nations, 24 have family-planning programs and an additional 23 have official antinatalist policies. But fully 55 of the entire 102 make no concerted effort in this respect at all.[22] It does not need to be pointed out that the 24 activist nations here govern four times the number of people in the other

[21] Breese, op. cit., pp. 128–32.

[22] Dorothy Nortman, *Population and Family Planning Programmes* (New York: Population Council, 1971), Table 10.

55. Yet the lack of population planning in more than half of the developing nations shows a good deal about the practical problems in trying to modernize "by blueprint," as it were.

URBAN PLANNING IN COMMUNIST COUNTRIES

Planning to direct urbanization into preconceived forms is very much in evidence in the Communist world. Examine the Soviet Union, Poland, Yugoslavia, and China in this regard. Note too that in these Communist countries urbanization is being subjected to comprehensive national planning that goes far beyond the redevelopment, New Towns, and regional types of planning discussed earlier in Chapter 21.

THE U. S. S. R.

The Soviet Union has long thought of urban development as a fundamental object of state planning.[23] Accordingly, population in the U.S.S.R. is being redistributed to the more thinly settled eastern provinces, with the result that above-average population growth has been experienced in the Urals, Siberia, the Far East, and Kazakhstan. This is being accomplished by constructing factories away from the large cities and assigning workers by fiat when propagandizing relocation as patriotic fails. In the U.S.S.R., 976 New Towns and 1941 workers' settlements came into being in the 35-year period following the inception of the program in 1926. The rigid bureaucratic control and the absence of local participation in directing urban programs, however, contrasts with the lofty humanistic goals proclaimed by Soviet national planners.

POLAND

In theory, Polish national urban planning calls for the calculation of costs relative to total national economic effect.[24] Since 1964, the central Ministry of Building assisted by provincial and county planning offices has had responsibility for physical design; industrial, service, and residential construction; transportation; sewerage; power lines; and land use. Over the ministry stands the State Planning Commission handling general social planning, defined as "the long-range reshaping and development of the national econ-

[23] Compare Maurice F. Parkins, *City Planning in Soviet Russia* (Chicago: University of Chicago Press, 1953).

[24] See Jack C. Fisher, ed., *City and Regional Planning in Poland* (Ithaca, N.Y.: Cornell University Press, 1965).

omy in terms of adapting to the planned division of labor within the international framework of socialism."[25]

Five trends in Polish national urban planning since World War II are noteworthy. (1) Land-use patterns show much industrialization. (2) The nationalization of land has given planning greater freedom to work toward balance, decentralization, and zoning. (3) Incomplete plans, suggesting indecision and scarcity of resources, have been produced for Poland's transportation system. The mix there of private automobiles, bus lines, and railroads appears subject to further clarification. (4) Despite the reconstruction of war-damaged places, service centers inconveniently located at long distances from the salvaged midtown centers have been built. And (5) considerable attention has been devoted to the restoration of historical structures destroyed or wrecked during the war.

YUGOSLAVIA

In Yugoslavia too, national intervention into urban planning has been instituted.[26] Reception centers to assist in orienting rural newcomers to the city have been set up, and minimum housing standards have been adopted. However, in spite of the acceptance of the neighborhood as the basic unit of city planning, Yugoslavia's failure to provide adequate services on a neighborhood basis has led to the bureaucratic concentration of such amenities at the urban core.

Yugoslav doctrine adheres to a 10:1 population ratio between a region and its major city as the optimum. Yet the absence of regional as distinct from national planning in Yugoslavia and the rapidity of urban growth there have prevented this goal from being reached. On the other hand, even if prefabrication gives a dull uniformity to housing, the level of household facilities has been definitely raised. Finally, though the country's town-planning and economic-expansion programs are not being fully implemented, Yugoslavian Marxist principles do contain some vague but decidely ideal visions of the city of the future.

CHINA

Though still overwhelmingly agrarian, China has more than a tenth of its enormous population concentrated in towns and cities.[27] China is indus-

[25] Boleslaw Malisz, "Urban Planning Theory: Methods and Results," ibid., p. 70.

[26] Consult Zygmunt Pióro, Milos Savić, and Jack Fisher, "Socialist City Planning: A Reexamination," *Journal of the American Institute of Planners,* 31 (February 1965), pp. 31–42.

[27] Leo A. Orleans, "The Recent Growth of China's Urban Population," *Geographic Review,* 49 (January 1959), pp. 43–57. See also Morris B. Ullman, "Cities of Mainland China," in Gerald Breese, ed., *The City in Newly Developing Countries* (Englewood Cliffs, N.J.: Prentice-Hall, 1969), pp. 81–103.

trializing relatively rapidly today. Traditional administrative cities, such as Peking, Kaifeng, Loyang, and Soochow, have been overtaken in size by factory, rail, and shipping points like Shanghai, Dairen, Canton, and Tientsin. An exodus from the overpopulated countryside has long been taking place in China, and it is now encouraged by Communist policy in order to hasten industrialization. Nevertheless, rural China remains very densely settled, Shantung Province, for instance, having possibly upwards of 3000 persons per square mile. Much denser still, China's cities are chronically congested. Chengtu's walled 12-square-mile core may have a density twice as great as New York's.[28]

As far as urbanization synchronized with industrialization goes, China is handicapped not only by population pressure but also by inadequate numbers of trained specialists and the maintenance of a large standing army. In addition, since fertilization with "night soil" has traditionally been relied on in Chinese agriculture, the most highly advanced farming goes on immediately adjacent to the large cities, so that urban expansion in China threatens to encroach upon the nation's most productive farmland.

Chinese urbanization is being accomplished today though not without much hardship. A detente with the United States would probably bring technological benefits to China and ease the transition to urbanism there.

INTERNATIONAL ORGANIZATION AND URBAN PLANNING

In addition to planning for urbanization by individual governments in the underdeveloped regions, urbanization today is also a subject to which international organization is devoting close, though perhaps insufficient, attention. Planning from these quarters takes two forms: (1) programs by particular countries assisting their neighbors or allies on a bilateral or multilateral basis; and (2) action under the auspices of the United Nations and that body's constituent agencies.

BILATERAL AND MULTILATERAL PLANNING

Bilateral and multilateral aid for urban development is being extended by a number of countries on their own initiative. Four governments, especially, have fostered the establishment of industry in the developing regions and in the process have underwritten the construction of new cities. These are the United States, the U.S.S.R., Great Britain, and the Federal Republic of West

---

[28] Urban densities are treated in Y. F. Yuan, "A Preface to Chinese Cities," in R. P. Beckinsale and J. M. Houston, eds., *Urbanization and Its Problems* (Oxford: Blackwell, 1968).

EXHIBIT 22-1 Projects in Urbanization Approved for Assistance by the World Bank and the International Development Association in Fiscal 1974

BOTSWANA: IDA—$3 million. This credit will help improve the social environment and public health conditions for Francistown's low-income population. Included in the project are community facilities, sites and services and traditional housing plots for 1,800 households, and improvements to existing low-income areas affecting more than 1,000 households. Total cost: $4.36 million.

INDIA: IDA—$35 million. Forty-four schemes covering water supply, sewerage and drainage, roads and traffic improvement, environmental hygiene, garbage disposal, and housing and area development comprise this project in support of the Calcutta Metropolitan Development Authority's program for rehabilitation and improvement of basic urban facilities. Total cost: $96.9 million.

IRAN: Bank—$42 million. This project will help meet Tehran's most urgent needs for improved bus transportation, relieve traffic congestion in the city, and guide future growth of the Tehran urban region. The bus fleet will be increased, two bus depots will be built, old buses rehabilitated, and bus company management improved. Total cost: $65.9 million.

JAMAICA: Bank—$15 million. About 6,000 low-income families will be provided low-cost housing under this comprehensive sites and services project in four cities. Most of the lots will be located in Kingston; all will be provided with related infrastructure and community facilities. Small- and medium-sized industries, to be located in or near the sites and services areas, will also be financed. Total cost: $30 million.

TUNISIA: Bank—$11 million: IDA—$7 million. Planning of urban growth and an improvement in public transportation in the Tunis metropolitan area will be aided by this project, which will principally benefit low- and middle-income earners. Total cost: $28.6 million.

Note the scope of the urban development efforts underwritten by these central funding sources in the underdeveloped nations listed.

Source: World Bank, *Annual Report 1974* (Washington, D.C.: World Bank, 1974), p. 52.

Germany. Still others, among them Belgium, Czechoslovakia, Denmark, Poland, and The Netherlands, have also provided technical services to developing nations for the administration of their urban affairs. Our own Agency for International Development (AID) is a source of technical assistance and funds but, considering the extent of demonstrated need, these are of rather limited scope. In addition, multilateral urban planning and development are also taking place currently, again though on a restricted basis. Since the 1940s the World Bank has been making long-term capital available for development. And since 1973, the United States and the Soviet Union have joined forces in trying to deal with solid-waste management and urban trans-

Teheran, the expanding primate city of Iran, which the Iranian government is trying to prevent from growing too fast.

portation and, at the behest of the U.S. delegation, also with housing management and recreation.[29]

A major consequence of urbanization in the developing lands lies in the potential clientship to the great powers that is thus created. A variant is the monopolistic manipulation of international trade to obtain capital. Take Iran—ironically, one of the scenes of the original urban revolution six millennia ago. Iran is experiencing rapid population concentration at present. Teheran, the Iranian capital, had three million inhabitants in 1970. At an expected growth rate of 5.6 percent annually, Teheran will be 12 to 16 million in size by 1991. That would mean an imbalance for a nation of perhaps 60 million then. The Iranian government wants to prevent Teheran from going beyond the 5.5 million mark. To keep the capital so confined requires controlling in-migration by setting up "alternative attractive locations" elsewhere.[30]

[29] See Office of International Affairs, *Report on the U.S./U.S.S.R. Working Group on the Enhancement of the Urban Environment* (Washington, D.C.: Department of Housing and Urban Development, 1974).

[30] See Office of International Affairs, *Brief: Program Report No. 8* (Washington, D.C.: Housing and Urban Development Department, June 1971), pp. 16–23.

A leading petroleum producer, Iran joined OPEC in 1973 in raising crude oil prices and limiting output, thereby gaining a stronger trade position for itself in order to carry out its development plans for building housing in existing cities, creating industrially oriented new towns, and constructing buildings in rural areas to relieve Teheran. Iran has also been the recipient of major American arms shipments in recent years. In part, this policy of the United States has been to build up a barrier to Soviet influence southward; in part, possibly to weaken the OPEC cartel; and, in part, probably to furnish the Shah's government with the means of suppressing internal unrest occasioned by poverty and rising expectations among Iran's modernizing masses.

Without wishing to prejudge the success of Iran's urban policy relative to international affairs, one may still validly feel a sense of uncertainty about the outcome. As Wilbert E. Moore and Neil J. Smelser, noted sociologists, have concluded, "the convulsive emergence of the colonies into independence and their subsequent struggle to join the ranks of the prosperous, powerful, and peaceful is the most remarkable revolution of our time."[31] One quite probable trend among the urbanizing underdeveloped lands will be the eclipse of liberal-democratic institutions by differing forms of communitarian management stressing equalitarian distribution instead of productive achievement.[32] The international effects of such social change can only be guessed at. One guess would be that the strongest powers other than the United States and Soviet Russia will have opportunities for trade and influence greater than they do at present. West Germany, France, Italy, Britain, Brazil, and Japan will be in this category. At any rate, the urbanization of the developing world will remain a permanent international force expressing itself in a variety of ways.

THE UNITED NATIONS

United Nations efforts have generally encouraged national planning for orderly and effective urbanization in the developing regions. As an illustrative case, in 1976, the UN's Center for Housing, Building, and Planning scored the dire insufficiencies in industrial development, food, agriculture, housing, health services, education, professional training, finance, and meteorological forecasting in these areas.[33] For the period beginning in 1976, the Center gave priority to three "global projects" in regard to urbanization in the modernizing countries: research into low-cost, labor-intensive housing construction; inquiry into population trends and environmental quality; and pilot

[31] "Editorial Forward" to Breese, 1966, op. cit., p. iii.

[32] See John Friedman, "The Future of Urbanization in Latin America," *Studies in Comparative International Development,* 5 (1969–1970), 193ff.

[33] United Nations, *Human Settlements: Special Habitat Issue* (New York: United Nations, May 1976), pp. 61–90.

demonstration projects to improve slums and squatter quarters. Obviously these needs outstrip the capacity of the underdeveloped countries to supply them themselves.

Take, for example, the detailed urban-development plans drawn up for Kampala by the department of economic and social affairs of the UN.[34] Greater Kampala consists of the capital of Uganda, the capital of Buganda, and certain other territories, all totaling some 200,000 people. A large volume of immigration led to the Ugandan request for the UN planning mission that when fielded worked together with the East African Institute of Social Research in drawing up a master plan for a multi-million dollar renewal project to be financed by land-secured funds. A total of 99 recommendations were eventually made in the master plan, ranging from postgraduate education through the levying of punitive taxes on land being used improperly, to the reconditioning of sludge-drying beds for the treatment of sewage.

Many other programs have also been initiated by the UN. Technical assistance in construction is being supplied to as many as 48 countries in a single year. Regional housing centers have been set up in New Delhi and Bandung, and physical planning institutes in Indonesia, Peru, Turkey, and Ghana. Economic commissions organized for Asia, Africa, Latin America, and Europe have stimulated regional concern for orderly urbanization. The recent creation of the Center for Housing, Building, and Planning indicates still further UN activity in national urban planning.

ILO, WHO, and UNESCO.

UN-related agencies are similarly involved in national urban development. The International Labour Organisation (ILO) provides vocational training, while the World Health Organization (WHO) operates in the field of public health and environmental sanitation, where its work has special importance for urbanization, particularly in connection with rapid population expansion.

The Educational, Scientific, and Cultural Organization of the UN (UNESCO) has been singularly active in planning designed to solve contemporary urban problems. Five international conferences have been called under UNESCO auspices to assess urban trends and prescribe measures for coping with over-urbanization. Dealing separately with Africa, the Far East, Latin America, and the Mediterranean, these meetings have confirmed the view that many of the difficulties of underdevelopment need to be thought of as the product of accelerated urbanization, including the need for "adequate housing and urban amenities, adjustment and acculturation of immigrants, accommodation to rapid social change, effective economic organization and

---

[34] See Alvin H. Scaff et al., *Recommendations for Urban Development in Kampala and Mengo* (New York: United Nations, 1964).

growth, and efficient local government."[35] It was also made apparent that data are at present generally insufficient for sound planning in these regions.

PRIVATE AGENCIES

Private agencies, too, have been active in supplying nonfinancial, chiefly consultative assistance concerning national planning for urban affairs in the developing regions. Besides certain universities and the Ford Foundation, one might mention the International Co-operative Alliance, the World's Veterans Federation, and the International Conference of Free Trade Unions. Their efforts have been quite meagre. And like internationalism in urban development as a whole, they too have been handicapped by a lack of coordination, limited technical capacity, insufficient information, and inadequate political support.[36]

CONCLUSION

Urbanization in the underdeveloped areas of the world is an ongoing process today. As such, it is having myriad effects besides accomplishing the redistribution of population. Urbanization can be seen undermining traditional social structures, perhaps parasitically over-urbanizing regions, and bringing about new but unclear forms of social and cultural organization.

Urban planning is also quite evident in the developing nations at present. Oftentimes this activity has a Marxist character, but it generally suffers from insufficient material resources. In the communist world, urban planning tends to be of national scope, yet there too inadequate support is proving to be frustrating.

The urbanization of the modernizing countries is also having an impact on international relations and world organization. In this respect, urbanization contributes to the rivalries between the superpowers and the economic tensions that exist among nations.

FOR FURTHER READING

Wayne A. Cornelius and Felecity M. Trueblood, eds., *Latin American Urban Research* (Beverly Hills, Calif.: Sage Publications, 1975). Views South American urbanization as a colonializing process that is making inequalities still worse.

[35] Philip M. Hauser, ed., *Handbook for Social Research in Urban Areas* (Paris: UNESCO, 1965), p. 13.

[36] Frederick C. Terzo, *Urbanization in the DevelopinghCountries* (New York: International Urbanization Survey of the Ford Foundation, 1972).

Kevin Cox, ed., *Urbanization and Conflict in Market Societies* (Chicago: Maaroufa Press, 1978). Articles by geographers, economists, and city planners showing the tensions resulting from the urbanization process.

Gino Germani, ed., *Modernization, Urbanization, and the World Crisis* (Boston: Little, Brown, 1973). Argues that the problems of industrialization need to be seen independently of the difficulties inherent in urbanization.

Leo Jakobson and Ved Prakash, eds., *Urbanization and National Development* (Beverly Hills, Calif.: Sage Publications, 1971). Attempts to apply social-science knowledge derived from Western urban experience to conditions prevailing in south Asia.

Jack A. Underhill, *Soviet New Towns* (Washington, D.C.: Department of Housing and Urban Development, July 1976). A balanced appraisal of Soviet planned satellites designed to supplement existing cities.

CHAPTER 23

NATIONAL PLANNING
AND
THE FUTURE OF
URBAN SOCIETY

In Chapter 21 we examined urban planning in terms of redevelopment, new towns, and regionalism. Following our excursion, in Chapter 22, into urbanization and planning in the underdeveloped areas of the world today, we turn now to national urban planning in the advanced countries. In this chapter we also attempt a modest projection into the urban future that may lie ahead for many of us.

Given the degree of urbanization today, it is understandable why planning for an entire country as a single system and under the auspices of the national government would be a logical undertaking. In this type of activity, individual urban areas are treated merely as subunits within the larger .network in which they function. National planning embraces the physical pattern, highways, factories, housing, airports, transmission lines, and the like, of the country as a whole, and it seeks to facilitate their more effective provision and utilization. National planning also endeavors to supply services in ways best calculated to realize the nation's economic, political, social, cultural, and defense capabilities as well.[1] As Chapter 22 demonstrated, urbanization in the modernizing regions and in the Communist world has in certain instances led to national planning, but the lack of resources there has generally prevented national planning from being successfully implemented. In the more advanced countries currently, it is not straitened circumstances but ideological resistance that has been impeding national urban planning. Nonetheless, the need for national planning is being acted on with varying degrees of achievement in many of the highly urbanized countries, including the United States.

NATIONAL URBAN PLANNING IN THE UNITED STATES

A movement toward national urban planning is observable in recent American history, although its objectives and policies have changed in the course of time. Before World War II, national planning in the United States was concerned principally with promoting the physical and economic base as deemed essential to urban growth. Highway construction, the improvement of rivers and harbors, subsidies for air transport, and housing for slum-clearance purposes illustrate the range of federal effort in the 1930s.

Since then, our conduct of national urban planning has involved a great diversity of specific projects, programs, and administrative agencies.[2] Beginning in 1955, the Metropolitan Planning Program established planning offices in three-fourths of the nation's SMSAs. In the interim the program also assisted more than 400 projects for regional planning, 77 statewide plans, and upwards of 1300 projects in small urban areas. From 1965 to 1974, federal grants to our cities and states went from $11 billion to more than $48 billion.[3]

National planning in America has also leaned toward greater coordination under direction from Washington. Planning as a precondition for receiv-

[1] Cf. John W. Dyckman, "Social Planning in the American Democracy," in Ernest Erber, ed., *Urban Planning in Transition* (New York: Grossman, 1970), pp. 27–44.

[2] Norman Beckman, "Changing Governmental Roles in Urban Development," in Bernard J. Frieden and William W. Nash, Jr., eds., *Shaping an Urban Future* (Cambridge, Mass.: M.I.T. Press, 1969), pp. 147–77.

[3] Bureau of the Census, *Statistical Abstract of the United States: 1975* (Washington, D.C.: Government Printing Office, 1975), Table 406, p. 249.

An elevated monorail, a project under consideration by HUD planners.

ing assistance at the local level is mandated in many federal grant-in-aid laws. In this regard, Norman Beckman found that only three years after the enactment of the Housing and Urban Development Act in 1965, 80 metropolitan planning councils had been set up for "the study of metropolitan-wide legal, governmental, and administrative problems."[4] In addition, Congress has established urban-centered regional planning commissions for Appalachia, New England, the Upper Great Lakes, Alaska, the Ozarks, and the Four-Corners Indian country of the arid Southwest. It has done so, in the words of the Public Works and Economic Development Act, where there are potential growth points having "sufficient population, resources, public facilities, industry, and commercial services to ensure that [in each case] its development [will] become relatively self-sustaining and that . . . its growth [will] help alleviate distress in the redevelopment area."[5]

[4] Beckman, op. cit., p. 155.

[5] Lloyd Rodwin, *Nations and Cities* (Boston: Houghton Mifflin, 1970), p. 229.

National planning has its technical difficulties, but its major problem, per-haps, is not technical but ideological. Disagreement over planning can be acrimonious because in many minds planning equates with socialistic inter-ference with the free market or at least with sheer government expansion. Most American authorities would possibly concur in the thought that national planning to solve urban problems can be accomplished democratically. Still, just how much more centralized decision-making is imperative remains debatable though testimony before a Congressional committee recently em-phasized the need "to orchestrate" local-state-and-federal systems in carry-ing out "strategies for shaping the future growth and development of the na-tion."[6] Hesitancy in doing so is deepened further today by the weakening national consensus following Watergate and Vietnam.

Resistance to coordinated, centralized planning may be read in some of the policies formulated by the government under our existing legislation. For example, the economic development administration's program of scattering aid instead of concentrating it continues to remain in effect. Such a diffuse approach stems, of course, from the need to gain Congressional support at the national level for government action at the local level.

Proponents of democratic national planning in America often look to Britain as a model. The British program for urban management affords a clear example of national planning that is based on democracy and local determination. The means employed by British planners have been varied and many: financial incentives to lure businesses away from London: restric-tion and selective taxes to guide investment; a department of economic af-fairs advised by regional councils; and district development concentrated around growth points. Public representation is mandated throughout. Lloyd Rodwin calls British national planning "an experiment with mixed results," but adds that "there is almost no disposition in Britain to give up the quest."[7]

ANTIURBAN BIAS

The concerns that libertarians have over national planning undoubtedly also involve an ages-old antiurban bias—an antipathy toward cities and every-

---

[6] Cf. Office of International Affairs, *Urban Growth Policies in Six European Countries* (Washington, D.C.: Department of Housing and Urban Development, 1973).

[7] Rodwin's brief statement on the subject is "British and French Urban Growth Strategies" in Daniel P. Moynihan, ed., *Toward a National Urban Policy* (New York: Basic Books, 1970), pp. 273–91. For more extended treatment consult Rodwin, *Nations and Cities*, op. cit., pp. 107–55; and Donald L. Foley, *Controlling London's Growth* (Berkeley and Los Angeles, Calif.: University of California Press, 1963); and for background material, William Ashworth, *The Genesis of Modern British Town Planning* (London: Routledge and Kegan Paul, 1954), Ch. 8.

thing they stand for. From the Old Testament's celebration of pastoral life over the iniquities of Sodom and Gomorrah through Plato's agrarian utopia in *The Republic* to Rousseau's primal Eden in *The Social Contract,* major contributions to the history of social thought have feared and dreaded urbanization. The American mind has been definitely shaped by this tradition.

AMERICAN ANTIURBANISM

Here in the United States at least until quite recently, enmity toward urban life amounted to a virtual ideology. As the historians Charles Glaab and Theodore Brown judge our past, "a formal doctrine of political antiurbanism, to which successful candidates had to pay a greater or lesser measure of homage, persisted long after we had become an urbanized nation."[8]

Jeffersonian Agrarianism

Thomas Jefferson was unquestionably the fountainhead of this aversion to the city, although he borrowed his ideas from Europe. According to Jefferson, agriculture not only was close to nature and therefore morally sound, but agriculture alone was truly productive. Urban merchants and artisans might add value to what the farmer, fisherman, and lumberer produced. Yet that value could hardly match the importance of the original product. Even worse, mercantilism led to luxury and avarice, and this was particularly dangerous in view of the propertyless urban mobs swarming in the large, densely populated places. To Jefferson and his physiocratic (agrarianist) followers, cities were centers of depravity dangerous alike to personal morality and republican government.

Philosopher, pragmatist, humanitarian, and idealist, Jefferson approved of the landed yeoman only as much as he denigrated the urban rabble. Jefferson wrote of these two classes of people in sharply etched prose: "Those who labor in the earth are the chosen people of God [while] the mobs of great cities add just so much to the support of pure government, as sores do to the strength of the human body."[9]

Other American Antiurbanists

Following the War of 1812, Jefferson did reconcile himself to the necessity of tolerating cities here on this side of the Atlantic if only as a matter of national expediency. Later, however, Andrew Jackson and William Jennings Bryan

[8] Charles N. Glaab and Theodore Brown, *A History of Urban America* (New York: Macmillan, 1967), p. 53.

[9] Jefferson as cited in Vernon Louis Parrington, *Main Currents in American Thought* (New York: Harcourt, Brace, 1927), Vol. I, p. 347.

resurrected Jeffersonian antiurban agrarianism, adapting it to their own times.

What Jefferson, Jackson, and Bryan expressed politically, other Americans stated intuitively, metaphysically, historically, and even as economic theory.[10] Thus, Thorstein Veblen condemned the city as the principal arena of conspicuous waste. Ralph Waldo Emerson not only deprecated the city for being "artificial and curtailed." He also harbored a deep distrust of science—the ally of industry—when science was being praised as the true basis for human thought. Thoreau was still more antipathetic to urbanism. In his mind, the city stood as the direct opposite of benign Nature and the naturally autonomous individual.

In the 1830s, in *Democracy in America,* the French political philosopher Alexis de Tocqueville had lauded the United States for its lack of any commanding metropolitan center. Yet the possibility of unruly urban masses in America's future did make Tocqueville apprehensive. He regarded some of the inhabitants of our then largest cities "as a real danger" to democracy. And he went so far as to predict that American society would be destroyed by this tyrannical mass "unless the government succeeds in creating an armed force which, while it remains under the control of the majority of the nation, will be independent of the town population and able to repress its excesses."

Historical Pressures Creating Urban Enmity in America

Two forces in particular have been responsible for the apprehension Americans have felt toward cities and urban civilization. First, we had the conservative rural reaction to urbanization that, defensively, overstated urban defects. Second, the emergence of urban communities in the United States especially after the Civil War was attended by any number of social problems peculiar to that period apart from the cities, notably, industrial disputes, child labor, poor housing, and the business cycle. Unfortunately, these were thought to be intrinsic to urbanization rather than possibly incidental to it.

Though there might be bitter disillusionment with farming in the United States, the American metropolis would continue to be pictured as embodying man's inhumanity to man. A realistic novelist like Hamlin Garland could deal harshly with the actual conditions of rural life in the 1890s, where the road "is long and wearyful and has a dull town at one end and a home of toil at the other."[11] But powerful voices with telling effect, in *The Bread-Winners,*

[10] Cf. Morton White and Lucia White, "Intellectual Versus the City," *Daedalus,* 90 (Winter 1961), pp. 166–78.

[11] Consult Arthur M. Schlesinger, *The Rise of the City: 1878–1898* (New York: Macmillan, 1933), pp. 259–62.

The Mammon of Unrighteousness, and *Maggie: A Girl of the Streets,* were all too ready to damn the sordidness and misery of urban life as inescapable. In fact, even those early twentieth-century realists Frank Norris and Theodore Dreiser, whose novels depicted the fascinations of San Francisco, Chicago, and New York, saw the city as a malignant organism that just overwhelmed everyone.

As noted, considerations of national power led Americans, including Jefferson, to condone urbanization. Two factors, however, came to be seriously inimical to whatever respect cities were paid here in the United States: the rapidity with which the nation urbanized, and the change in scale that overtook our cities. Gigantic commercial enterprises, swiftly expanding industry, and the arrival of waves of culturally heterogeneous immigrants precipitated grave social ills in America. These included the exploitation of labor, intergroup conflict, crime, and, as many claimed, the degradation of the culture. Even so sociologically astute a scholar as Robert E. Park, possibly the leading urban sociologist of his age, remained unimpressed with what he considered as inalienably urban life. "One is tempted to say," the cultural historians Morton and Lucia White reason, "that Park's published statements on the city reveal more the admiration of the scientist investigating a fascinating phenomenon than the delight of a person who finds that phenomenon intrinsically pleasing."[12]

A NEW PROURBANISM IN AMERICA?

Not all earlier American scholars condemned the urban mode of society by any means. Walt Whitman and William James both approved of cities for the opportunities they afforded people to engage in human association. The philosopher John Dewey reconciled himself to urbanization as inescapable, although he urged the reestablishment in the urban milieu of the localism which the metropolis was everywhere destroying.

Given such intellectual forebears, can it be said that the further urbanization of the United States since then has weakened antiurbanism on the part of the nation's intellectual leadership at present? In other words, is there a new mood in America favorable to urban life today?

William F. Whyte typifies the point of view that antipathy to urban institutions continues to be strong. The author of *The Organization Man,* Whyte is of the opinion that the very people planning and rebuilding our cities simply do not like cities, and that they reject "the values that since the beginning of civilization have always been at the heart of great cities."[13] In 1975, when

[12] White and White, "Intellectual Versus the City," *Daedalus,* op. cit., p. 167.

[13] William H. Whyte, Introduction to Editors of *Fortune, The Exploding Metropolis* (Garden City, N.Y.: Doubleday, 1958), p. vii.

New York City's municipal government appealed to Congress for emergency aid, the antiurban bias of the national legislature quickly came to the surface. Delaware's senator Joseph Biden said in a public interview, "Cities are viewed as the seed of corruption and duplicity, and New York is the biggest city."[14] Beneath that attitude lay concern about New York's political liberalism and the ethnic composition of its population, but the traditional antipathy to urbanism also contributed to it.

Affirmative urban voices are, however, making themselves heard today. As we noted in Chapter 4, geographer Jean Gottmann equates the megalopolis with both affluence and an advanced degree of social organization. Whether such a viewpoint can counteract the strong tradition of intellectual opposition to the idea that, even if not innately perverse, urbanism in America has failed to realize its potentialities remains an unanswered question. In fact, many of our city planners take it for granted that America's communities simply must be remodeled to give them the rural qualities of neighborliness, personal relationships, and a sentimental sense of location. They even think that solving the urban crime problem, the urban culture of poverty, and the urban ghetto awaits the restoration of earlier, essentially rural sociocultural phenomena.

Northwestern University's Scott Greer recently advanced the idea that in general the public's thinking about the urban community is at variance with the normtive model of what he calls "the intellectuals of local government."[15] These planners, Greer said, admire the centralized metropolitan system more or less as an unexamined outgrowth of the nineteenth-century city. Time and again, by voting against metropolitan government, by opposing annexation, and by trimming bond issues devoted to consolidation, the public has shown its implicit preference for, in Greer's words, "a scattered, variegated set of low-density neighborhoods, looped together by freeways, which bind them also to the centers of production and distribution." In short, according to Greer, one normative image stands now in competition with another one as regards the metropolitan community.

Urban geographers and city planners are not, so to speak, the only "urban evangelists" today. The theologian-historian Havey Cox submits that modern secularism is opening up new possibilities to men and women. In the modern metropolis, Cox asserts, there are unprecedented opportunities for human self-fulfillment, such as deliverance from drudgery and the achievement of new modes of spirtual association.[16]

Similarly sensing new realities, urban architects and designers point to undeveloped aesthetic potentialities in the large city. Kevin Lynch contends

[14] New York Times (May 25, 1975), Section 1, p. 1.

[15] Scott Greer, The Urbane View (New York: Oxford University Press, 1972), pp. 230–43.

[16] The Secular City: Secularization and Urbanization in Theological Perspective (New York: Macmillan, 1965).

that city design is an art which, practiced astutely, can make the large city "a romantic place, rich in symbolic detail" and a "source of daily enjoyment to millions of their inhabitants."[17] "True enough," Lynch writes, "we need an environment [so poetic and symbolic that it can] speak of the individuals and their complex society, of their aspirations and their historical tradition, of the natural setting, and of the complicated functions and movements of the city world."[18] In a like manner, Americanists Alan Trachtenberg, Peter Neill, and Peter C. Bunnel have urged us to become aware, and positively so, of the values of urban culture, and to move forward to a higher plane of aesthetic and emotional life.[19] Until these spiritual achievements are realized though, and despite the recognition of the city's role in fostering socioeconomic advancement, as Bayard Still reasons, "To many Americans, the large city . . . still seems alien to the national tradition."[20]

THE FUTURE OF NATIONAL PLANNING

In spite of our antiurban background, national planning in the United States is regarded by many capable observers as not only necessary but also probable. Norman Beckman, for one, gives specific reasons why the separate states can be expected to move into the urban area more and more.[21] The increasing size of the urban population will give it greater political power. The one-man, one-vote doctrine will erode rural gerrymandering. Federal inducements will elicit coordination. And the cities themselves will want to move out of the impasse of governmental fragmentation. Altogether, Beckman contends, these factors presage more planning and more planning of a centralized, national character too.[22]

OBJECTIVES OF NATIONAL PLANNING

It is possible to identify certain general objectives that may presently claim the attention of planners in the United States. In MIT's Lloyd Rodwin's judgment, the following are discernible: (1) the strengthening of local government, but within a national framework; (2) the involvement of the local citizenry in community decision-making; (3) the enlargement of national efforts to cope with metropolitan tendencies to coalesce into either nucleated or rib-

[17] Kevin Lynch, *The Image of the City* (Cambridge, Mass.: M.I.T. Press, 1960).

[18] Ibid., p. 119.

[19] Alan Trachtenberg, Peter Neill, and Peter C. Bunnell, eds., *The City: American Experience* (New York: Oxford University Press, 1971).

[20] In "The History of the City in American Life," *American Review*, 2 (May 1962), p. 33.

[21] Beckman, op. cit., p. 147.

[22] Ibid.

Staff members of the Pittsburgh Architects' Workshop checking on neighborhood projects with community people and businessmen.

bonlike complexes; and (4) the provision of greater resources in order to make it more possible for cities to satisfy the higher aspiration of their people.[23]

Similarly, Daniel Moynihan, for two years urban counsellor to the White House, has formulated a ten-point national urban policy for America. It includes reducing the isolation of minorities in our central cities; restoring fiscal vitality to local government; achieving greater state participation in urban affairs; and also sharpening the nation's awareness of "the finite resources of the natural environment, and the fundamental importance of aesthetics in successful urban growth."[24]

Scott Greer whom we referred to earlier also recently formulated a set of prescriptions for a national urban policy in the United States.[25] Assuming that the forces of both centralization and dispersion will continue to be exerted in urban America in the foreseeable future. Greer has concentrated on (1) determining the optimal population concentration capable of being serviced by efficient transportation; (2) achieving the proper balance between

[23] Rodwin, "British and French Urban Growth Strategies," op. cit., pp. 280–86.

[24] Daniel P. Moynihan in his edited volume, op. cit., pp. 3–25.

[25] Scott Greer, *The Urbane View* (New York: Oxford University Press, 1972), pp. 322–37.

homogeneity and heterogeneity in the economic, social, and cultural spheres; and (3) reordering our political instruments so as to realize an appropriate blend of local and national government. Greer admits the speculative nature of his propositions but insists that there already are "many signs of such a movement" toward the national policy he envisages.

THE PROCESS OF NATIONAL PLANNING

The national planning process refers to the variables which need to be considered in devising suitable methods of reaching postulated goals. These include a whole battery of specific measures. They are federal revenue sharing; housing supplements; subsidized mass transit; economic development; public information services; income strategies such as family allowances and negative income-tax payments; intergovernmental coordination; environmental protection measures; incentives to encourage the poor to become more constructively competitive; user bureaucracies, for example, tenant-managed public housing; and others as well. All of these have their supporters, and their detractors too. The political significance of the variables of national planning clearly implies that as elsewhere the process of national planning in the United States is bound, ultimately, to be ironed out in the political arena. Many sharp clashes of interest will occur.

A PLURALISTIC RESOLUTION

Democratic national planning in the United States would appear to make a pluralistic resolution virtually certain. Such a method is merely a continuation of present trends. Peter Lewis, at the time he wrote it an assistant director of the budget bureau, has outlined a model for the planner's art under American conditions patterned after the bureau itself.[26] Lewis speaks of the budget bureau not so much as having a master plan, but as being a gadfly stimulating action and also attempting to reconcile competing interests. Lewis thinks that national planning will need to encompass analysis, synthesis, collaboration, education, mediation, and advocacy, instead of seeking imperative grand designs locking all elements into one rigid blueprint. In all probability, future national planning in the United States is apt to be in accord with the asymmetrical, individualistic American system, so that consistency will have to be grafted onto diversity in resolving our national urban problems.[27]

[26] Peter A. Lewis, "The Uncertain Future of the Planning Profession," in Erber, op. cit., pp. 142–46.

[27] Beckman, op. cit., p. 176.

UNIVERSITY, PRIVATE, AND PUBLIC
URBAN RESEARCH

Planning for urban America has led to a proliferation of organizations engaged in research to furnish planners the necessary knowledge with which to work. The most notable research bodies are: (1) university institutes; (2) private and nonprofit associations; and (3) government agencies.

UNIVERSITY INSTITUTES

By the early 1960s there were about 25 urban research centers attached to American universities. These conducted studies as part of their programs to qualify students for advanced degrees in various disciplines. They also staffed local government with interns seeking careers in public administration if not in research and development. Moreover, these centers did contract research for public and, at times, private concerns like banks and utility companies. In this respect, they made budget, demographic, land-use, transportation, and other kinds of surveys, analyses, and projections. By 1967, the same two dozen university research centers in the country had grown to 80, and by 1969 to almost 200.[28] Just about every state had at least one research or community-service center as part of its system of higher education by then.

Illustrative of the specific research projects carried out by university centers are the following. The Harvard-MIT Center for Urban Studies has dealt with basic theory in urban politics, city planning, demography, law, economics, and public health. A group of research institutes at Berkeley has concerned itself with regional urban planning, land economics and investment analysis, and public administration. At the University of North Carolina, the center for urban and regional studies has been stimulating predevelopment land transactions on the city's rim, and has also attempted the evaluation of recent experience with New Towns.

PRIVATE URBAN RESEARCH CENTERS

Nonprofit and private organizations often work in cooperation with university research offices. At times they perform the same type of activity, such as providing consultation for local officials. In general, the better known nonprofit and private urban research agencies make publication on a regular basis more an integral part of their operations than do their university counterparts. Thus, the Center for Urban Education puts out *The Urban Review;* the Tax Foundation, *Tax Review;* Urban America, *City;* Urban Land Institute,

---

[28] See *A Directory of University Urban Research Centers* (Washington, D.C.: The Urban Institute, 1969); also Scott Keyes, ed., *Urban and Regional Studies at U. S. Universities* (Baltimore, Md.: The Johns Hopkins Press, 1964).

Land-Use Digest; National Planning Association, *Looking Ahead;* and the American Society for Public Administration, *Public Administration Review.*

Among the largest of the nonprofit, private urban research organizations are the Center for Urban Education, the Institute for Community Studies, the Institute of Public Administration, Midwest Research Institute, National Planning Association, Public Administration Service, and Urban America. These organizations maintain libraries housing special collections on urban affairs, consisting of tens of thousands of books, pamphlets, and periodicals. Access to the public is made partially available.

GOVERNMENT CONDUCTED URBAN RESEARCH

Government sponsored and affiliated urban research agencies include the Building Research Advisory Board (gives unbiased guidance in building science and technology); the Research Department of the Council of State Governments (makes studies of governmental processes); the National Association of Counties (acts as a reference service for county officials); National League of Cities (offers information and consultation on municipal problems, and also represents cities in federal circles); National Municipal League (provides legislative reference services to its members); U. S. Advisory Commission on Intergovernmental Relations (directs studies on the modernization of government); and the Urban Institute (was set up by the federal government to do research on varied subjects, including urban unrest, safety, and public finance).

Since its inception in 1968 and with Ford Foundation support added, the Urban Institute has worked on family assistance programs, public housing management, and unemployment and inflation studies. Its staff has also devised a system to enable a federal agency to measure the impact of the programs which it administers. Lately the institute has been advocating full states rights and powers for cities, to allow municipalities to bypass state government and deal with Washington directly. Needless to say, this political issue is a sensitive one and its resolution hardly imminent.

The federal government has encouraged planning for the solution of urban problems. Seven vehicles are especially significant.[29] (1) The 1964 Housing Act authorized graduate fellowships in city and regional planning, public administration, urban sociology, and urban law. (2) The Public Health Service Act makes funds available for health planning studies. (3) Housing and environmental research grants are provided under the several public health service acts. (4) The 1966 Demonstration Cities and Metropolitan Development Act channels funds directly to city demonstration agencies who, in turn, may contract with universities for planning services. (5) Comprehen-

[29] Compare Committee on Urban Affairs, *A Guide to Federal Funds for Urban Programs* (Washington, D.C.: American Association of State Colleges and Universities, 1969).

sive urban planning may be financed under the 1954 Housing Act, including inquiry into the improvement of planning itself. (6) The Housing Act also funds projects capable of ameliorating slum conditions. (7) The Housing and Development Act of 1974, which consolidated certain earlier authorizations, underwrites community improvement activities. A variety of other statutes allows federal efforts—including planning—to be aimed at crime prevention, manpower training, public assistance, environmental control, and transportation. The most notable recent effort here is the Comprehensive Employment and Training Act of 1977 (CETA), which makes funds available for local government to put the long-term jobless to work on public-service projects added to existing efforts.

THE FUTURE OF URBAN RESEARCH

HUD has become the major urban planning instrument in the entire federal establishment. Where HUD will probably move in the future may perhaps be gauged from synchronized reports made to it several years ago by two bodies of the National Research Council These were the Committees on Social and Behavioral Research and on Urban Technology. Appointed to advise HUD on long-range urban research strategies, the two groups recommended that the Department rely on a network of resources: university, industry, nonprofit, municipal, and HUD's own in-house capabilities. Such a structure, it was claimed, would be able to plan effectively on an extended footing. It would also make possible the employment of technology in accord with social and behavioral knowledge.[30]

One also surmises from these reports that the whole field of urban theory and practice reveals serious difficulties. The need for HUD to show results in a hurry was said to be unfortunate, because this leads to the neglect of future planning. Moreover, the ambiguity of public goals, such as the reduction of poverty, makes it hard for HUD to operationalize its efforts. Not only is HUD faced by chronic problems, but some of them arise from the very remedies applied as solutions. Notice that rent supplements attract exploitative landlords. Policy-making participation by the poor may divide the community. And urban renewal often hurts people of low income by erasing one slum and creating another.

There are many problems of methodology and theory too. Take just one example. Transposing the systems approach, even with computor-aided simulation, from the aerospace industry to society and the urban community with their "disorderly and extremely ramified" collective life, is short-sighted

[30] Committee on Social and Behavioral Urban Research, *A Strategic Approach to Urban Research and Development: Social and Behavorial Science Considerations* (Washington, D.C.: National Academy of Sciences, 1969); and Committee on Urban Technology, *Long-Term Planning for Urban Research and Development: Technological Considerations* (Washington, D.C.: National Academy of Sciences, 1969).

and naive—though it is popular. Nevertheless, both committees agreed that "systematic research, using already established methods and concepts of the social and behavioral sciences, can play a much larger role than it has in influencing the actions of administrators and legislators with respect to the support, abandoment, or modification of programs addressed to urban problems." Tough-minded analysis may not suffice to insure the survival of modern urban society. Yet, the committees agreed, it can contribute to sound policy, and they urged HUD to act accordingly.

URBAN PHILOSOPHERS: THE CONTEMPORARY UTOPIANS

At the other extreme from empirical urban research stands the "grand theorizer," the philosophical designer of the ideal city and the ideal urban society. Lewis Mumford called such urban planners "the contemporary utopians." Grand theorists formulate grandiose conceptions. Their sweeping proposals may even be arbitrary in content and visionary in method. Any conception of the ideal community may also raise false hopes by thinking away real problems and putting forth unrealizable goals. Still, the ideal is often the stimulus for real innovation. Certainly at the present time, when responsible leadership frequently describes urban problems as critical, notions of the ideal can inspire us to renewed effort, if not assured success.

APPREHENSIONS OVER SCIENTIFIC PLANNING

In spite of present-day urban problems and recognition of the need for planning if we are to resolve them, fears are being voiced concerning the ultimate effects that scientific planning may have. This apprehension increases interest in philosophical conjecture and judgment about the urban future as a matter of moral values and not merely technology. Architectural scholar Melvin Charney has written that "It is now a commonplace idea that planning has become imperative for our times, and what used to be for the most part a diverting excursion into the future is now part of the decision-making apparatus of the technologically advanced nations."[31] While acknowledging the formal, scientific role of what sociologist Daniel Bell refers to as "intellectual technology," Charney deplores the loss of wonder and of fantasy from modern prediction, for he senses that there is afoot "a lingering fear of the future . . . a latent paranoia."

The increasing industrialization of the environment, Charney adds, fills many people with dread. Interchangeable mobile homes occupying con-

---

[31] Melvin Charney, "Environmental Conjecture: In the Jungle of the Grand Prediction," in Stanford Anderson, ed., *Planning for Diversity and Choice* (Cambridge, Mass.: M.I.T. Press, 1968), p. 314.

crete pigeonholes! Plastic service modules! Microcircuitry linking innumerable operational units into trunkline networks! Inflated, nylon-vinyl envelopes serving as lightweight, instantly installed architecture! All of this denotes not so much the use of technology, Charney declares, but "inherent technological evocations."

Charney is far from alone in his concern over the dangers of over-planning. Gunnar Myrdal, famed Swedish economist, advocates planning as the very means of avoiding control, but Myrdal scorns "false scientism," which confines planning to the few and which fails the test of all great scholarship, namely, of informing the layman of the problems, methods, and goals for which planning is being done.[32] The architectural critic of the *Washington Post,* Wolf Von Eckardt, is dismayed by what he calls "computerized crystal-gazing," in other words, the statistical projection of present tendencies into the future without critical thought as to the desirability of more expressways, more public housing, and more tract development.[33] Considerations of efficiency crowd out the far more important question of whether, when completed, the city will actually be a suitable human habitat.

Enemy of conventional city planning, Jane Jacobs also enphasizes the need to bear in mind the multiplex, spontaneous human particulars that give security, pleasure, and meaning to the citizens of any successful urban center.[34] City planners, Jacobs writes, cannot progress as long as they "cling to the unexamined assumptions that they are dealing with a problem in the physical sciences" and as long as they ignore the philosophy of urban life.

MODERN UTOPIAS

Faced by the dilemma of the need for planning and of the dangers in it, we may draw guidance from the many urban utopias that have been created since the Industrial Revolution gave the city its present form. These ideal communities, which spell out the locational features of the good city as their authors conceive them to be, are valuable as general models for projected change. We need to take note specifically of the creations of Theodor Fritsch, Edgar Chambless, Le Corbusier (Charles Edourd Jeanneret-Gris), Clarence Perry, Frank Lloyd Wright, Paul and Percival Goodman, Eliel Saarinen, Buckminster Fuller, Paolo Soleri, and Constantinos Doxiadis.

[32] Gunnar Myrdal, "The Necessity and Difficulty of Planning the Future Society," in William R. Ewald, Jr., ed., *Environment and Change: The Next 50 Years* (Bloomington, Ind.: Indiana University Press, 1968), pp. 250–63.

[33] Wolf Von Eckardt, "Urban Design," in Moynihan, op. cit., pp. 107–18.

[34] Jane Jacobs, *The Life and Death of Great American Cities* (New York: Random House, 1961).

Fritsch's City of the Future

The "city of the future" was first imagined by Fritsch in 1896 as a means of combatting the weakness of industrial urbanization.[35] The central feature of Fritsch's ideal city is a set of concentric bands in each of which is located one particular type of activity: industrial, civic, commerical, and residential. Fritsch had the high-income residential areas near the center of town, where he also located the main institutions, all in the manner of the preindustrial city. Conversely, the low-income neighborhoods were placed farther out. In keeping with the needs of such high-density settlements, they were situated adjacent to the broad wedges of open pastoral space on the city's circumference.

In the Fritsch design, transportation is supplied in two ways, radially and circumferentially, for Fritsch had industry placed in strategic outlying sites serviced by waterways and a mass-transit ring around the circumference of the proletarian quarters. Fritsch thus combined the industrial and preindustrial cities by anticipating greenbelt environs for the working classes on the perimeter rather than affluent suburbs there.

Chambless' Roadtown

In 1910, Edgar Chambless proposed Roadtown, a long, indeterminate, ribbony architectural arrangement built over a monorail.[36] Running through the basements of 21-by-20-foot row houses, this transit system would also serve the industrial, public, and commercial buildings constructed at intervals between the residential units. Alongside the indefinite stretches of Roadtown were to be gardens, agricultural fields, and recreational areas. Hence the rural and urban spheres would be brought together into one unified and apparently pleasing entity.

Chambless thought Roadtown the ideal solution to the chronic urban problems of congestion, waste, estrangement, and demoralization, for he imagined small Roadtowns of only 100 families running for just a half a mile, and also a whole continent tied together into one vast network of ganglia. So single-mindedly did Chambless advance the concept of Roadtown that he failed to see its defects. Factory and commercial sites naturally attract complementary activities around themselves, for they cannot remain independent of intense land use. Second, a household economy and a modern rail system are inconsistent with each other. Third, locating everything in one linear form deprives the consumer of the choice that clustering does. It also increases the expense of transportation. In spite of these shortcomings, as

---

[35] Theodor Fritsch, *Die Stadt der Zukunft* (Leipzig, Germany: Hammer, 1896).

[36] In his *Roadtown* (New York: Roadtown Press, 1910).

Thomas Reiner points out, Roadtown represents "a relatively well-thought-out extreme solution of some aspects of the relation between circulation and modern life."[37]

Le Corbusier: "The city is man's grip on nature"

The Swiss-born architect and planner Le Corbusier, long an exponent of the thorough-going reconstruction of the present-day urban pattern, first conceptualized his city of tomorrow in the early 1920s.[38] Le Corbusier condemned the city as we know it for its preservation of obsolete circulation plans suitable to the draft animals of the past but not the vehicles of today. The placing of urban functions, he felt, was equally outmoded and inefficient. Narrow corridor streets lined by tall buildings that shut out the sunshine humble and beggar the spirit. New York City Le Corbusier called "a spectacular catastrophe." Even our homes remain only large, uncomfortable, cluttered relics of the age of the cottage and of handicrafts carried on by the isolated family.

What is needed, Le Corbusier submitted in 1945 after France had been liberated from the Nazis and was ripe for reconstruction, is for us to take full advantage of science and technology and bend them to human purposes.[39] As "a machine to live in," one's home must be set inside an overarching rural-urban establishment. In this single structure, according to Le Corbusier, are (1) the radioconcentric city having administrative and business functions; (2) the linear industrial city, that is, the stretched out transportation system knitting the region's many manufacturing units into an efficient flow of components and finished products; and (3) the agricultural district, in which raw materials are turned out for further processing. A nation, then, consists of an integrated combination of radio-concentric cities, linear industrial cities, and urban-centered agricultural districts.

Each of these subcomplexes of Le Corbusier's urban nation has its own natural structure. First, the radioconcentric city combines mass and proximity. As a result, it needs to be built vertically in the form of tall, concrete-and-glass skyscrapers that free the land beneath for use as parks. The towering buildings themselves must be free of idle decoration, for their geometric functionalism is aesthetic. "The city," Le Corbusier writes, "is man's grip on nature," and what we build has to complement, not imitate, natural forms. Second, the linear city has parallel belts on both sides of the expressways, screening the factories from the residential sections. Finally, the third es-

[37] Thomas A. Reiner, *The Place of the Ideal Community in Urban Planning* (Philadelphia, Pa.: University of Pennsylvania Press, 1963), whose systematic exposition we have followed closely, subjects twenty modern ideal communities to a uniform and searching analysis. The quotation appears on p. 34.

[38] See Le Corbusier, *The City of Tomorrow and Its Planning* (New York: Payson and Clarke, 1929).

[39] Le Corbusier, *The Three Human Establishments* (Paris: Denoel, 1945).

The reflecting pool of the new Christian Science Center in Boston and the towers surrounding it bear the influence of Le Corbusier's idea of the radio concentric city.

tablishment, the one for the farming countryside, is made up of villages built around cooperative structures housing stores, repair shops, the community center, and other agencies designed to provide the farmers with the amenities of modern life.

Oddly, considering the far-reaching character of his thinking, Le Corbusier underestimated the heavy investment in transit facilities necessary for the core concentration that is at the heart of his ideal community. He also ignored the tendency inherent in auto transportation to disperse population over a continually widening territory.

Perry's Neighborhood Unit

An approach to the shortcomings of the modern city from still another quarter is Clarence Perry's concept of the neighborhood unit, which came out of his participation, in 1929, in drawing up the New York Regional Plan.[40] Essentially, Perry's neighborhood unit was formulated as a social and administrative entity sequestered from the disintegrative forces of the metropolis. A neighborhood unit consisted of homes and the immediate facilities and services needed by their families: a school not more than half a mile away, local stores, and the like. Whatever had to be on a larger scale, such as a department store or an apartment house, would be located on the boundary between two or more neighborhood units. By all means, however, the neighborhood unit would be protected from the eroding impact of the arterial highway and the commercial use of land that breaks down community solidarity, family life, and property maintenance, and that brings the slum and social disorganization in its wake. The 5000 to 9000 persons Perry saw as making up a neighborhood unit would by virtue of their planned surroundings constitute a social group within the larger, but potentially harmful, urban environment.

In a recent critique, Princeton sociologist Susanne Keller reviewed the weaknesses of the neighborhood unit: whether the school alone is a sufficient nucleus; whether the conception of the neighborhood arbitrarily assumes the family with young children as typical; and so on.[41] She also examined the alternatives of the "neighborhood circle" (the families immediately adjacent to one's own); the "social network" (interaction among not necessarily spatially proximate persons); the "roving neighborhood" (identification through common symbols like the local shopping mall); the "service neighborhood" (for example, the clientele of a clinic); and the "neighborhood of collective responsibility" (the organized, socially constructive antithesis of the natural area of crime and delinquency). Clearly then, debate over Perry's neighborhood unit persists 50 years later.

Wright's Broadacre City

Architect and urban derogator, Frank Lloyd Wright has been described as "the last of the true Americans." To Wright are ascribed the sentiments of freedom of the individual, social equality, opportunity for all, daring innovation, and, over everything else, belief in the desirability of people "living as

---

[40] Clarence A. Perry, "The Neighborhood Unit," *Regional Survey of New York and Its Environs* (New York: Committee on the Regional Plan of New York, 1929), Vol. 7, pp. 22–140.

[41] Susanne Keller, *The Urban Neighborhood* (New York: Random House, 1968).

individuals in individual settlements—not a society of masses living in giant cities." Wright's Broadacre City, a creation of his formed in the 1920s and 1930s, fits into this frame of mind, for it smacks of the Midwestern prairie town of an earlier, basically agrarian America.[42]

Dramatically, Broadacre City provides each family with a homesite of at least one acre of land! True, St. Marks Towers—romantic Romeo-and-Juliet windmills of four projecting walls cradling interlocked two-story apartments cantilevered out from the core—are there for those who love apartment life. By and large though, Broadacre City is projected for the agrarian urbanite, for low-density, open residential land use prevails against all else. Other uses, industrial, commercial, and civic alike, are interspersed, but scattered around the periphery.

While the various forms of transportation are anticipated in Wright's design for Broadacre City, the superhighway for automobile use remains the most important. In fact, Wright saw modern transportation as the key to a new and overdue urban ecology.[43] Wright erred though in combining decentralization with great reliance on the automotive expressway. Both of these necessitate far greater organization than his scheme would allow. Nonetheless, Wright conceived of an updated prairie town auguring the present automobile-fed suburbanization of the United States. Broadacre City is diametrically opposite the European model of the city as an entity with a definite form, a boundary, and a determinate size.

Wright's proposal embodies the democratic ethic, but otherwise it posits an amorphous exurbia. Wright did not have in mind what the English geographer Peter Hall has called "the most characteristic single feature of the American landscape": "this civilization of the gas station and the hamburger bar—apparently endless, formless, sprawling, tasteless, exuberant."[44] Still, as Wright himself wrote, "The new city will be nowhere, yet everywhere." In Broadacre City, Wright, the champion of inspired architecture, mixes airplane factories with cinemas and clinics. His plan is without any discernible centering except on the dispersed residential areas and their many supporting facilities: the arboretum, aquarium, sanitarium, forest cabins, educational plots, vineyards and orchards, music garden, and stables and paddock. Not only are there the columbarium and cemetary, but even nine sectarian temples surrounding the central edifice devoted to universal worship. Thus in effect, Wright prophetically realized America's postindustrial urban age in his projected ideal community of Broadacre City.

[42] Peter Blake, *The Master Builders: Le Corbusier, Mies Van Der Rohe, Frank Lloyd Wright* (New York: Alfred A. Knopf, 1966).

[43] Frank Lloyd Wright, *The Living City* (New York: Horizon Press, 1958), p. 81.

[44] Peter Hall, "Urban Culture and the Suburban Culture," in Richard Eells and Clarence Walton, eds., *Man in the City of the Future* (London: Macmillan, 1968), p. 105.

The Goodmans: Pluralistic Urbanism

The Goodman brothers, Paul and Percival, planners with a humanistic background, have advanced a set of three city proposals embodying a rationale similar to Frank Lloyd Wright's Broadacre City.[45] Like Wright, the Goodmans take postindustrial wealth for granted as something that makes a desirable level of living possible in the first place. Like Wright too, they project their standard of living on a somewhat less than maximum scale. They also agree with Wright that quasirural values can be effectively preserved in the city of the future at the same time that productive technology continues to be cultivated.

In the first of their three models, this one patterned after New York and having perhaps eight million people, the Goodmans conceive of a dense urban core devoted to economic life, containing warehouses, offices, department stores, and financial institutions. This they surround with civic agencies, and beyond them they place highly built up residential neighborhoods, each containing some 4000 inhabitants. Then on the outskirts are industry and farms. This first proposal of the Goodmans embodies the culture of consumption, and is thus closest to the city as we know it today.

The second ideal community of the Goodmans features not an elevated material scale of living, but the values of workmanship and creativity. Hence they plan for a half dozen medium-sized cities, each with a population of a third of a million, all located within a single urban region. At the core of each of these, serviced by intersecting highways, stands the whole complex of civic, industrial, and commercial facilities. Such a layout combined with the modest size of the community, in fact one out of three inhabitants lives in a semirural state, allows for much productive endeavor. Since considerable ease of movement between home and workshop is anticipated, and also between these and the institutional life of the city, the full social participation that many utopists have idealized is here made possible.

In their third plan, the Goodmans postulate a subsistence economy, and for only a small- to moderate-size population, from 5000 to 75,000. Work and residential structures are so arranged here that they should produce sufficient output, under government regulation, to avoid uncertainty and create security. In this third model, we have still another cultural contrast to the values of consumption and production of the first two.

The three Goodman paradigms are not related to each other in any larger structure. Whether their contrasting philosophies could indeed coexist in a single society is itself problematical. Moreover, each of the three proposals has its own serious shortcomings. The first makes no provision for growth or for decentralization. Despite its importance for distribution, little thought is given to transportation, and the question of the centrifugal potenti-

---

[45] Paul Goodman and Percival Goodman, *Communitas* (New York: Random House, 1960), originally published in 1947.

alities of the automobile is not taken up either. This is also true of the Good-mans' second model. There, the composition of the neighborhood remains unexamined. Finally, with respect to their third venture in idealization, neither its regional importance nor its internal structure is given searching thought. Yet as Reiner concludes, "this group of plans remains among the most significant contributions to the field's efforts of ideal building."[46]

Saarinen: Functional Decentralization

Finnish architect, designer, and urban planner, Eliel Saarinen has emphasized decentralization as the basic motif of the city of the future.[47] The concentrated medieval town, Saarinen observes, was built to protect itself from armed attack, but then improved industry and trade allowed the late-medieval city to expand beyond its walls. Nonetheless, the absence of good communication necessitated continued concentration even after military circumstances no longer required it. With the facilities available now though, decentralization is not only possible but imperative.

To be successful, decentralization must be combined with functional groupings. So, as Saarinen writes, we have "concentration of the individual's living and working conditions, and decentralization of the city's various activity groups."[48] Traveling for everyday activities needs to be minimized, and at the same time a friendly, relaxed home atmosphere made a cultural necessity. Applying his theory to the "stony desert" of New York City, as he calls it, Saarinen proposes moving the Manhattan docks to other sites; relocating industry on better transportation lines; replacing many present residential arrangements with suitable dwellings around new sources of livelihood; and consequently freeing the innermost slum center of the metropolis for "green lands and playgrounds."

In spite of his optimism about the practicality of his decentralization scheme, Saarinen recognizes the economic and legal obstacles standing in its way.[49]

Fuller's Tetrahedron City

R. Buckminster Fuller first gained renown for his invention of the geodesic dome. That is the light-weight aluminum or steel frame resembling an egg, which may be topped with a filmy plastic cover or have an enveloping cap-

[46] Reiner, op. cit., p. 106.

[47] Eliel Saarinen, *The City: Its Growth, Its Decay, Its Future* (Cambridge: M.I.T. Press, 1966), originally 1943.

[48] Ibid., p. 207.

[49] Ibid., p. 241.

sule hung under it.[50] It has the advantages of low cost and heavy weight-bearing capacity as well as the ability to enclose large spaces. In fact, Fuller has gone so far as to propose enveloping whole cities in domes of polarized glass to control their environment, including the extraction of solar energy.

As a designing engineer, Fuller has also developed an imaginative solution to what he considers the impending needs of an advanced urban society like our own. The scattered, sprawling pattern today, Fuller believes, demonstrates our ability to harness entire regions without centralizing partic-ular habitats for economic purposes. The modern means of transportation and communication suffice for long-distance control. Fuller concludes that "cities, as we know them, are obsolete with respect to all of yesterday's func-tions."[51] Consequently, he says that cities should be reconstructed to serve sociocultural purposes. As such, they ought to resemble ocean liners! The very best design, Fuller is convinced, is the tetrahedron structure rising high in the air, with extended legs like an Eiffel Tower, but floating on water so as to permit economical cargo transfers and also mobility for redeployment.

At sea, the tetrahedronal city, even with a million inhabitants, will utilize atomic energy for power, including the desalinization of its water supply. A byproduct of this maritime mode of settlement will be the penetration of the ocean bottoms for their rich marine life and chemical resources.

Fuller's imagination carries him even further than this startling innova-tion. He visualizes the construction of a miniaturized, computerized "little black box" of about 20 cubic feet in size, weighing no more than 500 pounds, and built at a cost of possibly $1000 that will enable a family any-where on earth, however remote or barren, to recycle all the elements needed to live comfortably. Only small annual additions to the recirculating chemistry of the little black box would be necessary to make it effective in-definitely. With these boxes, people would then also be able to live in sky-floating cities made up of large geodesic spheres deployed in the atmo-sphere like clouds, or tethered to mountain tops![52]

Paolo Soleri: Arcology

Italian-born architect Paolo Soleri apprenticed himself to Frank Lloyd Wright, but the two eventually separated in disagreement. Soleri continued though to work in Scottsdale, Arizona, in the vicinity of Wright's studio, Talliesin West, near Phoenix. There, Soleri pursued original studies in arcology (the synthe-sis of architecture and ecology, and originally spelled archology) in order to

---

[50] See R. Buckminster Fuller and Robert Marks, *The Dymaxion World of Buckminster Fuller* (Gar-den City, N.Y.: Anchor Press/Doubleday, 1973), pp. 57–68.

[51] R. Buckminster Fuller, *Utopia or Oblivion: The Prospects for Humanity* (New York: Overlook Press, 1969), p. 346.

[52] Cf. Fuller and Marks, op. cit., Illustration 489.

Model of a floating tetrahedron city designed for maneuverability.

design structures he believed necessarily based on organic principles.

Like Fuller, Soleri is convinced that modern technology must be incorporated into urban planning, particularly the miniaturization of programming and controlling electronic instruments to overcome what Soleri calls "the time-space straight jacket."[53] Through technological development, man will free himself of dependence on the presently inhabited spaces of the earth and on the earth itself. Orbital colonies interacting with earthly ecologies will thus become possible. Mechanistic as his projected settlements appear to be, Soleri anticipates them in a humanistic spirit dramatically opposed to the materialism he feels is currently making our cities uninhabitable. The communities Soleri envisages would allow for both the public metropolitan functions and for noninstitutionalized, private lives of their citizens. To the "plumbing system" of the city today, Soleri proposes adding, through electronic communication and cybernation, large increments of social, cultural, and aesthetic opportunities. Again, like Fuller, Soleri also conceives of his city of the future in the manner of an ocean liner but so planned and organized as to achieve the ultimate human goal: the "aesthetacompassionate universe."

What will Arcology look like? There will not be a single type but a considerable variety of arcological communities—30 no less—yet all resem-

[53] Paolo Soleri, *Arcology: The City in the Image of Man* (Cambridge: M.I.T. Press, 1969), p. 2.

bling space ships, that is, engineered capsules containing a combination of location-uses: industrial, residential, and the like. The smallest as well as the largest of the arcologies (some with populations into the millions) will be either land-based or floating islands embodying mounded, circular, or podlike structures as well as immense flared, cylindrical, or pyramidal towers built around service cores, and in no few cases massive towers a mile high! In the names he gives his arcological colonies, one recognizes Soleri's philosophical leanings toward the communal mode. Consider Archibuz, Babel, Novanoah, Arcvillage, and Arcosanti. Essentially, Soleri's utopian urbanism is intended to reverse the suburban sprawl that he contends is straining our natural resources at the same time that it is also estranging people from one another. In opposition to this, he proposes an implosion of humanity into a high-density, three-dimensional, energetic bundle capable, he believes, of evolving into a true "super-organism."[54]

Doxiadis's Ecumenopolistic Age

Constantinos Doxiadis, Greek city planner and until his death in 1975 head of a consulting firm that had participated in urban planning efforts affecting tens of millions of people in Greece, Iraq, Lebanon, Libya, Pakistan, Brazil, Ghana, France, Zambia, and in the United States, treated the city of today and tomorrow as more than a settlement, rather as "a dynamic growing organism."[55] Today, asserted Doxiadis, however we consider it, politically, financially, culturally, or socially, the city is in crisis. Not only in the United States but elsewhere, urban centers are devouring land, polluting the environment, endangering their citizens, offending people's sensibilities, wasting their time, and frustrating their ambitions. And still, urban growth continues, because cities do provide needed services and opportunities in spite of all their shortcomings. Moreover, the population explosion continues to fuel the urban fire, and gigantic growth is taking place, as here in the United States between Boston and Washington, D.C., in truly "ecumenopolistic" fashion.

Doxiadis envisioned 28 billion urban inhabitants when the world's population finally levels off, almost 30 times as many as at present! This means that the average city will be 30 times larger; that its area may be 60 to 100 times larger; and that its problems will possibly increase disproportionately to its expansion in size and area. Consequently, the entire globe will comprise one enormous, interconnected ecumenopolistic urban system.

The separate components of the universal city, declared Doxiadis, must

---

[54] See also Donald Wall, *Visionary Cities: The Arcology of Paolo Soleri* (New York: Praeger, 1971).

[55] Constantinos A. Doxiadis, "How to Build the City of the Future," in Eells and Walton, *op. cit.*, pp. 163–88.

each serve as centers of primary production, providing employment, shelter, and the support of human values, which even now are often lost sight of in big cities. The smaller population centers in the whole gigantic mass need to be preserved absolutely, and that will necessitate economic specialization and also efficient transportation and communication. The very largest concentrations in the entire complex will have to be rescued from simply more sprawl, because suburbanization and exurbanization continue to bring added pressures on the core. The best way to do this, Doxiadis thought, is to engineer the establishment of new metropolitan areas at only a moderate distance away as nodes in a hierarchical pattern suitable to the ecumenopolitan phase of human history. Then, in an oracular manner looking even beyond the "world-spanning city," Doxiadis saw mankind of the future even moving in the direction of an extraterrestrial Cosmopolis, "the city of the Cosmos."[56]

CONCLUSION

National planning treats an entire country holistically, as an entity whose urban settlements are merely subunits of a single system. Much national planning is being conducted today in the United States, and despite fears, nurtured by a lingering antiurbanism, that it may presage collectivism, more national planning will probably occur here in the future. The British experience with national planning would seem to indicate that democratic principles need not be sacrificed.

No small volume of research is being conducted at present in order to facilitate national as well as regional and local urban planning in the United States. A good deal of it is the work of university institutes. However, concern over the possibly illiberal tendencies of scientific planning for the future of urban society has sharpened inquiry into the ultimate value of urban life. Accordingly, urban philosophers, some of them architects and industrial designers, have formulated grand theories about the desirable ways in which the cities of the future should be built. In doing so, thinkers like Le Corbusier, Frank Lloyd Wright, and Buckminster Fuller are again working in the tradition of the ancient utopists who centuries ago tried to design the ideal city.

FOR FURTHER READING

F. Stuart Chapin, Jr., *Urban Land Use Planning* (Urbana: University of Illinois Press, 1965). On the techniques of analyzing land use, measuring trends, and estimating future requirements.

[56] Constantinos A. Doxiadis, *Urban Renewal and the Future of the American City* (Chicago: Public Administration Service, 1966), pp. 125–26.

John Cook and Heinrich Klotz, eds., *Conversations with Architects* (New York: Praeger, 1973). Nine American architects discuss their work and the problems of building a humane environment.

Albert N. Cousins and Hans Nagpaul, eds., *Urban Man and Society* (New York: Alfred A. Knopf, 1970). Especially the selections in the section "Urban Sociology in Transition."

Peter Cowan, ed., *The Future of Planning* (Beverly Hills, Calif.: Sage Publications, 1973). Planners appraise foreseeable urban planning difficulties and policies for tackling them.

J. B. Cullingworth, *Problems of an Urban Society* (Toronto: University of Toronto Press, 1973), 3 volumes. A review of the major urban conditions in Britain today.

Robert Fishman, *Urban Utopias in the 20th Century* (New York: Basic Books, 1977). The greenbelt, Jeffersonian, and high-rise visions of Ebenezer Howard, Frank Lloyd Wright, and Le Corbusier reviewed in the light of the more recent but actual planning that has occurred.

Bernard J. Friedan and Robert Morris, eds., *Urban Planning and Social Policy* (New York: Basic Books, 1968). Planners and social scientists recommending particular measures and procedures.

C. W. Griffin, *Taming the Last Frontier* (New York: Pitman, 1974). On the economic impracticability of urban sprawl and the need to defend the "historic city."

Robert A. Levine, *Public Planning* (New York: Basic Books, 1972). The thesis that public programs in the United States have not worked well and that new approaches are needed.

Anselm Straus, *The American City* (Chicago: Aldine, 1968). Significant and entertaining glimpses of our urban communities.

Max Weber, *The City,* ed. and trans. by Don Martindale and Gertrude Neuwirth (New York: Free Press, 1958). Written before World War I but published after the great German sociologist's death, a classic on the quality of urban life.

PHOTO CREDIT LIST

Chapter 1
Opener: *The City, 1919* by Fernand Leger. Philadelphia Museum of Art, Photograph by A. J. Wyatt, Staff Photographer.
8: James R. Holland/Stock, Boston.
15: National Park Service Photo. Courtesy D.C. Redevelopment Land Agency. Photograph by Fred Fizell.
17: Owen Franken/Stock, Boston.

Chapter 2
Opener: *The Professor's Dream* by C. R. Cockerell (detail) Royal Academy of Arts, London.
29: Courtesy Oriental Institute, University of Chicago.
38: George Holton/Photo Researchers.
40: Alison Frantz.

Chapter 3
Opener: Engraving by S. Beudet. New York Public Library, Picture Collection.
49: German Information Center.
55: New York Public Library, Picture Collection.
57: French Press and Information Service.

Chapter 4
Opener: *River Rouge Plant* by Charles Sheeler, 1932. Oil on canvas. 20 x 24 inches. Collection of Whitney Museum of American Art. Photo by Geoffrey Clements Photography.
63: Photo by Walter Steinkopf.
70: New York Public Library, Picture Collection.
73: New York Public Library, I. N. Phelps Stokes Collection.
77: Culver Pictures.
81: Photograph by Jacob A. Riis. The Jacob A. Riis Collection, Museum of the City of New York.
84: Courtesy Port Authority of New York.

Chapter 5
Opener: *The Harvesters* by Pieter Bruegel the Elder. The Metropolitan Museum of Art, Rogers Fund, 1919.
93: Smithsonian Institution National Anthropological Archives. Photo by W. H. Jackson.
97: Georg Gerster/Photo Researchers.
103: Bill Owens/Magnum.

Chapter 6
Opener: *The Brooklyn Bridge* by Samuel Halpert, 1913. Oil on canvas. 34 x 42 inches. Collection of Whitney Museum of American Art. Gift of Mr. and Mrs. Benjamin Halpert. Photo by Geoffrey Clements Photography.
115: New Orleans District of U.S. Army Corp of Engineers.
118: Courtesy Greater Boston Convention and Tourist Bureau.
121: Courtesy Houston Chamber of Commerce.
133: George W. Gardner.

Chapter 7
Opener: *Harlem* by Jacob Lawrence, 1943. Hirshhorn Museum and Sculpture Garden, Smithsonian Institution.
149: WHO, photo by D. Henrioud.
161: Elizabeth Hamlin/Stock, Boston.

Chapter 8

Opener: *The Opposition* by William Gropper. Memorial Art Gallery of the University of Rochester, Marion Stratton Gould Fund.
176: H.U.D.
191: James R. Holland/Stock, Boston.

Chapter 9

Opener: *Waterfront Mill* by Niles Spencer. The Metropolitan Museum of Art, Arthur H. Hearn Fund, 1942.
205: Courtesy Chicago Historical Society.
210: Nikoley Zurek.
229: Tim Eagan/Woodfin Camp.

Chapter 10

Opener: *Cocktails* by Guy Pène du Bois. The Metropolitan Museum of Art, George A. Hearn Fund, 1946.
241: Harry Wilks/Stock, Boston.
245: Sepp Seitz/Woodfin Camp.
247: Charles Gatewood.

Chapter 11

Opener: *Radios* by Robert Cottingham, 1977. Oil on canvas. 78 x 78 inches. Collection of Whitney Museum of American Art. Gift of Frances and Sydney Lewis. Photo by Geoffrey Clements Photography.
261: Bruce Davidson/Magnum.
271: James R. Holland/Stock, Boston.
277: Marc Godfrey/Magnum.

Chapter 12

Opener: *The City* by Charles Burchfield. Collection, The Museum of Modern Art, New York. Gift of Abby Aldrich Rockefeller.
285: Peter Vandermark/Stock, Boston.
290: Charles Harbutt/Magnum.

Chapter 13

Opener: *The Untilled Field* by Peggy Bacon. Collection of the Whitney Museum of Art, New York. Gift of Mr. and Mrs. Albert Hackett.
301: Albert Munson/Minnesota Historical Society.
307: Owen Franken/Stock, Boston.
312: Jeff Albertson/Stock, Boston.
316: Bill Owens/Magnum.

Chapter 14

Opener: *Ave* by Ben Shahn. Courtesy Wadsworth Atheneum, Hartford.
329: Culver Pictures.
332: F.S.A. Farm Security Administration.
338: James R. Holland/Stock, Boston.

Chapter 15

Opener: Lei Stratford
346: Peter Menzel/Stock, Boston.
353: Owen Franken/Stock, Boston.
360: James R. Smith.

Chapter 16

Opener: *Theatre Francais in the Rain* by Camille Pissarro, 1898. The Minneapolis Institute of Arts.
368: British Tourist Authority.

377: Susanne Faulkner Stevens.
385: Cary Wolinsky/Stock, Boston.

Chapter 17
Opener: *Tattoo and Haircut* by Reginald Marsh. Courtesy of the Art Institute of Chicago. Gift of Mr. and Mrs. Earle Ludgin.
403: U.P.I.
408: U.P.I.

Chapter 18
Opener: *Employment Agency* by Isaac Soyer. Collection of the Whitney Museum of Art, New York.
427: Jacques Danois/UNICEF.
437: VISTA.
444: Bruce Davidson/Magnum.

Chapter 19
Opener: *Prenatal Clinic* by Ben Shahn. New Jersey State Museum Collection, Trenton. Gift of the Association for the Arts of the New Jersey State Museum.
453: Lewis Hine/Library of Congress.
456: Mimi Forsyth/Monkmeyer.
462: Barbara Pfeffer/Photo Researchers.
468: Paul Fusco/Magnum.

Chapter 20
Opener: *Approaching a City* by Edward Hopper. The Phillips Collection, Washington, D.C.
481: Jason Lauré/Woodfin Camp.
494: Courtesy Port Authority of New York.
499: Charles E. Rotkin/P.F.I.

Chapter 21
Opener: *The Paris Bit* by Stuart Davis, 1959. Oil on canvas, 46 x 60 inches. Collection of Whitney Museum of American Art. Gift of the Friends of the Whitney Museum of American Art. Photo by Geoffrey Clements Photography.
519: Library of Congress.
525: Bedford Stuyvesant Restoration Corp.
529: Ian Berry/Magnum.

Chapter 22
Opener: *North Wall: Part production and assembly of motor* by Diego Rivera. Courtesy of the Detroit Institute of Arts.
545: Peter Menzel/Stock, Boston.
549: United Nations.
556: Iranian National Tourist Association.

Chapter 23
Opener: *Business* by Charles Demuth. Courtesy of the Art Institute of Chicago. Gift of Alfred Stieglitz.
563: H.U.D.
570: VISTA.
579: Massachusetts Department of Commerce.
585: Courtesy Buckminster Fuller Archives.

AUTHOR INDEX

Abbott, Daniel J., 394n, 418
Abell, Aaron I., 331
Abercrombie, Sir Patrick, 517, 519
Abraham, Henry J., 447
Abrams, Charles, 170n
Abu-Lughod, Janet 108
Acton, Harold, 54
Adams, Bert N., 321
Adams, Don, 344n, 345n
Adams, Joseph Q., 372n
Adams, Thomas, 518, 520
Adrian, Charles R., 176, 223
Ahlstrom, Sidney E., 338n
Ahrenfeldt, R. H., 394n
Alcady, Roger E., 232
Alderfer, Harold F., 170n
Alford, Robert R., 200n
Alihan, Milla, 117
Alinsky, Saul, 435
Allensworth, Don T., 539
Altschuler, Alan A., 362, 526n
Amato, Peter W., 125n
Anderson, C. Arnold, 359n
Anderson, Gallatin, 106n
Anderson, Martin, 488
Anderson, Nels, 87, 115
Anderson, Robert T., 106n
Antonovsky, Aaron, 465n
Arensberg, Conrad, 19
Aries, Philippe, 298
Aristotle, 371, 379, 477
Armor, David, 353n
Armstrong, R. B., 208n
Arnold, Matthew, 382
Aron, Joan B., 202, 537n
Ashton, T. S., 87
Ashworth, William, 564n
Avila, Manuel, 102n
Axelrod, Joel N., 273n

Babchuk, Nicholas, 107n
Bacon, Roger, 56
Bagdikian, Ben H., 270n
Bailey, James, 539
Balk, Alfred, 275n
Baltzell, E. Digby, 244
Banfield, Edward C., 177-178, 192, 194, 202, 350, 432
Barber, Bernard, 216n
Barbush, Jack, 219n
Barth, Karl, 340
Bartlett, Jonathan, 525n
Baumol, William J., 377n
Beale, Calvin L., 204n
Becker, Howard S., 349
Beckinsale, R. P., 554n

Beckman, Norman, 562n, 569
Behrman, S. J., 470n
Bell, Bernard I., 383
Bell, Colin, 200
Bell, Daniel, 12n, 405, 575
Bell, Norman W., 308n
Bell, Wendell, 104, 162, 164
Bellah, R. N., 235n
Benarde, Melvin A., 501n
Bendix, Reinhard, 250, 251n
Benson, Edwin, 59
Bentham, Jeremy, 67
Berelson, Bernard, 218n, 268
Berger, Bennett, 294
Berliner, Joseph S., 475
Berman, Daniel M., 444n
Bernard, Jessie, 319
Bernays, Edward L., 272
Berry, Brian, 125n
Beshers, James M., 136
Biden, Joseph, 568
Bieber, Margaret, 371n
Billingsley, Andrew, 321
Birnbaum, Norman, 256n
Black, Donald J., 410n
Blake, Peter, 581n
Blake, Judith, 472
Blau, Peter M., 213n
Blecher, Earl, 539
Blitsten, Dorothy, 306n
Bloch, Herbert A., 414n
Blood, Robert, 320n
Bloomberg, Jr., Warren, 449
Blouet, Brian W., 550
Blum, Barbara, 432
Blum, Zahava D., 432n
Blumberg, Leonard, 294n
Blumberg, Paul, 257
Boat, Marion D., 104
Boccaccio, 370
Bogart, Leo, 271n
Bogue, Donald, 76n, 129, 147n, 156, 204n
Bollens, John C., 182n, 190n, 206n, 227n
Bonhoeffer, Dietrich, 340
Bonjean, Charles M., 201n, 476
Booth, Alan, 107n, 111
Booth, Charles, 79, 453
Boskoff, Alvin, 20, 129, 130n, 244, 246, 524
Bott, Elizabeth, 304n
Bottomore, T. B., 253, 256
Boulding, Kenneth E., 449
Bowden, Witt, 69n
Bowen, Don R., 407n
Bowen, William C., 377n
Bowra, Sir Maurice, 54n
Boyce, A. J., 165

Boyd, Harper W., 273n
Boyden, Stephen, 151n
Braude, Lee, 218n
Breese, Gerald, 127n, 544n, 551n, 553n
Brentano, Lujo, 327
Brewer, Garry D., 523
Bridenbaugh, Carl, 73n
Brody, Eugene B., 165
Brown, L. Carl, 51n
Brown, R. L., 267n
Brown, Theodore, 73n, 87, 565
Bruce, Maurice, 474
Buckley, T. A. W., 59
Buddha, 35
Bunnel, Peter C., 569
Burchinal, Lee, 304n
Burckhart, Jacob, 59
Burgess, Ernest W., 114, 116, 119n, 135n, 287, 309
Burke, Colin B., 484
Burnham, Daniel, 521-522
Burns, Evelyn M., 473n
Burns, Robert, 384
Butts, R. Freeman, 53n

Cain, James A., 405n
Caldwell, Lynton K., 510n
Callahan, Daniel, 340n
Callow, Alexander B., 87
Callow, Jr., A. B., 296
Camilleri, Santo F., 163
Campanella, Tomamaso, 380
Campbell, Arthur A., 471n
Campbell, Rex R., 511
Campisi, Paul J., 317n
Cannon, Mark W., 274n
Caputo, David A., 189n
Carson, Rachel, 503
Casty, Alan, 280
Cather, Willa, 75
Cavan, Ruth S., 412n
Cavan, Judson T., 412n
Chambless, Edgar, 576-578
Champion, Dean J., 215n
Chaney, D. C., 267n
Chapin, Jr., F. Stuart, 524n, 587
Charney, Melvin, 575-576
Cheney, Sheldon, 373
Childe, V. Gordon, 26, 42n, 43
Childs, D. Rigby, 523n
Chudacoff, Howard P., 78n, 87
Clark, Colin, 12n
Clark, John W., 504
Clark, Terry N., 200n, 201n
Clawson, Marion, 539
Clinard, Marshall, 394, 401-402, 406n, 412-413, 418
Cloward, Richard A., 437, 449, 473

Clough, Shepard B., 30, 43
Cobb, Jonathon, 246n
Cochran, Thomas C., 215n
Cohen, Albert K., 309n, 398
Cohen, Henry, 527
Cohen, Jerome, 430n
Cohen, Yehoshua S., 125n
Coke, James G., 522n
Coleman, James S., 307, 349
Coleman, Laurence V., 370n
Coleman, Richard P., 240n, 257
Columbus, Christopher, 58
Confucius, 36
Connolly, Howard X., 134n
Connery, Robert H., 469n
Cooper, Douglas, 369n
Cook, John, 588
Corfiato, Hector O., 367n
Cornelius, Wayne A., 559
Corsa, Jr., Leslie, 470
de Coulanges, Fustel, 326
Coulborn, Rushton, 43
Cousins, Albert N., 588
Cowan, Peter, 588
Cowgill, Donald O., 134n
Cox, Harvey, 340, 568
Cox, Kevin, 560
Crampton, Helen M., 459n
Cressey, Donald, 399n
Cressy, Paul F., 135
Crouch, Winston W., 181n
Crow, Lester D., 351n
Crump, C. G., 52n
Ctanese, Anthony J., 539
Cullingworth, J. B., 588
Cunningham, W., 70n
Curtis, James, 107n
Cutler, Howard W., 272
Cutright, Phillips, 196n

Dahl, Robert, 198
Dahrendorf, Ralf, 252
Daley, Charles U., 280
Daley, Richard, 195
Daniel, Clifton, 266n
D'Antonio, William V., 325n
Davidson, Basil, 51
Davie, Maurice, 116-117
Davis, Kingsley, 6n, 165, 235, 525-526
Day, Norman, 499n
Deedy, John, 512
de Grazia, Sebastian, 379n, 380
DeJong, Gordon F., 165
Deutscher, Irwin, 294
Dewey, John, 567
Dewey, Richard, 101-102
Dexter, Lewis A., 265n
Dickinson, Robert, 59

Dillon, John F., 185n
Dilworth, Richardson, 175
Dimbleby, G. W., 4, 550n
Dinerman, Beatrice, 181n
Dirkson, Everett, 445
Dobriner, William, 293
Domhoff, G. William, 244
Donaldson, Scott, 293
Dorian, Frederick, 374n, 387
Douglass, Harlan Paul, 288
Downs, Anthony, 489, 511, 527
Doxiadis, Constantinos, 17, 576, 586-587
Dreiser, Theodore, 75, 567
Dulles, Foster Rhea, 220, 447
Dumazedier, Joffre, 381, 387
Duncan, Beverly, 104n, 129n
Duncan, Otis D., 104n, 129, 142n, 257, 286
Dunham, H. Warren, 255n, 401n
Durkheim, Emile, 92, 94, 323n, 393, 401, 422
Durr, Fred, 232
Dyckman, John C., 562n
Dyckman, John W., 19n

Eames, Edwin, 449
Eastman, Harold D., 397n
Eberhard, Wolfram, 36n
Edmondson, Munro S., 320n
Edwards, J. N., 111
Eells, Richard, 581n
Ehrlich, Anne H., 500n, 502
Ehrlich, Paul H., 500n, 502
Eichler, Edward P., 532n
Eisenstadt, S. N., 237n
Elazar, Daniel J., 188n
Eldredge, H. Wentworth, 21
Eldridge, Hope Tisdale, 139n
Eliot, T. S., 383
Elman, Richard M., 460n, 473n
Ely, Richard T., 173n
Emery, Edwin, 280
Engels, Frederick, 330
Epstein, Jacob, 370
Erber, Ernest, 527n, 539, 562n
Erikson, Erik H., 309n
Etzkowitz, Henry, 434
Ewald, William R., 576n

Fagen, Richard R., 276n
Faith, W. L., 502
Fantani, Mario, 355
Farber, Bernard, 301n
Faris, Robert E. L., 108n, 255n, 401n
Farley, Reynolds, 134n, 319, 351n, 438n, 483
Fava, Sylvia, 21
Feagin, Joe R., 304n
Felton, Jean S., 466n
Fichter, Joseph H., 337n
Fine, John C., 287

Firey, Walter, 117-118
Firth, Raymond, 305n
Fischer, Claude, 292-293
Fisher, Jack C., 552n, 553n
Fishman, Robert, 588
Fitch, Lyle C., 490-491
Floud, Jean, 359n
Foley, Donald L., 523n, 524, 564n
Fontana, Domenico, 517
Ford, Amasa B., 475
Ford, Gerald, 270
Ford, Thomas R., 165
Forge, Anthony, 305n
Form, William H., 197n, 232
Frankfort, Henri, 32n
Frederickson, George, 202
Freedman, Ronald, 470n, 471
Freeman, Linton, 201
Fremon, Charlotte, 208
French, Robert M., 184
Freund, Eric C., 516n
Fried, Marc, 304, 467, 484-485
Fried, Robert C., 516n
Friedberg, Bernard, 433n
Frieden, Bernard J., 539, 562n, 588
Friedman, John, 557n
Friedman, Lawrence M., 486n, 488
Friedman, Robert S., 187
Frisbie, W. Parker, 542n
Frisken, Frances, 184n
Fritsch, Theodor, 576, 577
Fuller, R. Buckminster, 576, 583-584, 585

Galbraith, John K., 232, 380
Galileo, 336
Galliher, John F., 405n
Gallion, Arthur B., 517n
Gama, Vasco da, 58
Gans, Herbert J., 111, 202, 248, 289, 289-291,
    304n, 318, 320, 422, 433, 441, 488
Gaudet, Hazel, 268n
Gardner, John A., 404
Gardner, John W., 487-498
Garfinkle, Stuart H., 448n
Garvan, Anthony N. B., 518n
Gasset, Ortega y, 383
Geddes, Sir Patrick, 527
Geis, Gilbert, 406n, 414n
Germani, Gino, 306, 560
Gibbens, T. G. N., 394n
Gibbs, Jack P., 221
Giedion, Siegfried, 517
Gilbert, Claire W., 200n
Gittell, Marilyn, 362
Ginzberg, Eli, 21
Glaab, Charles, 72n, 73n, 87, 173n, 565
Glaser, Daniel, 419
Glasgow, Ellen, 75

Glass, David V., 153
Glazer, Nathan, 232, 247, 423, 480, 485
Gleicher, Peggy, 484-485
Glenn, Norval D., 287
Glob, G., 39n
Glock, Charles Y., 333, 339, 341
Goetz, Charles J., 189n
Goldwater, Barry, 275
Goldthorpe, John H., 252
Gompers, Samuel, 331
Goode, Judith G., 449
Goode, William J., 300, 305-306, 321
Goodman, Paul, 576, 582-583
Goodman, Percival, 576, 582-583
Goodman, Robert, 526
Goodman, William I., 516n
Gordon, Michael, 321
Gordon, Milton M., 249, 426
Gordon, Mitchell, 504n
Gorham, William, 232
Gottmann, Jean, 82n, 82-83, 568
Gould, Julius, 383n
Graham, Grace, 346n
Graña, Cesar, 376n
Grebler, Leo, 523
Greeley, Andrew M., 333, 341
Green, Arnold W., 314, 379n
Green, Robert W., 327n
Greenberg, Clement, 383n
Greer, Scott, 164, 180, 260, 303, 487, 568,
    570-571
Griffin, C. W., 588
Griffin, Ernest S., 172n
Grodzins, Morton, 134n, 188
Grosseteste, Robert, 56
Gruen, Victor, 525n
Guest, Avery M., 122n, 133n
Gulick, Luther H., 180n
Guthrie, James, 353n
Guzzardi, Jr., Walter, 461n

Haar, Charles M., 296
Hadden, Jeffrey K., 18n, 296
Hall, James B., 387
Hall, Melvin G., 82n
Hall, Peter, 539, 581
Halloran, J. D., 267n
Halmos, Paul, 280
Halsey, A. H., 359n
Hammel, William M., 387
Hammond, Barbara, 67n
Hammond, L., 67n
Hammond, Mason, 43
Handlin, Oscar, 249, 384
Hansen, Niles M., 538n
Hardoy, Jorge E., 43
Harrington, Michael, 434
Harris, C. C., 321
Harris, Chauncey D., 125n, 125-127

Harrison, Bennett, 442n
Harrison, G. A., 165
Hartman, Chester W., 512
Hartung, Frank, 397n
Harwood, Edwin, 433n
Haskell, Francis, 373n
Hatt, Paul K., 241n
Hauser, Philip M., 86, 101n, 110, 111, 544n,
    546, 548n, 559n
Havighurst, Robert J., 350n
Hawley, Amos, 470n
Hawley, Amos H., 116n, 116-117, 137, 202, 296
Hazelrigg, Lawrence E., 257
Hazlitt, William, 382
Hazzard, Samuel, 72n
Head, W. Sidney, 280
Heilbroner, Robert L., 232
Heller, Celia S., 315n
Henry, Andrew F., 394n, 401
Herberg, Will, 333-334
Hermalin, Albert I., 319, 438n
Herrick, Neal G., 16n
Hertz, Hilda, 6n
Herzog, Elizabeth, 431-433
Hill, Reuben, 305n, 321
Hillery, Jr., George A., 105
Hillson, Maurie, 362
Hilst, Glenn, 502
Hodge, Patricia L., 86
Hodge, Robert W., 241, 242n
Hollck, Doris B., 362
Hollingshead, A. B., 118-119, 257
Hoover, J. Edgar, 405
Hoselitz, Bert, 110, 544n
Hoult, Thomas F., 333n
Houston, J. M., 554n
Hovland, Carl I., 275n
Howard, Ebenezer, 520, 527
Howard, John, 433n
Howe, Irving, 383
Hoyt, Homer, 6n, 122-125, 124n
Hubert, Jane, 305n
Hufschmidt, Maynard M., 535n
Hummel, Raymond C., 362
Hunter, David R., 482
Hunter, Floyd, 197-198
Hurd, Richard M., 119n
Hyman, Herbert H., 475, 527n

Illich, Ivan, 359n
Inkeles, Alex, 242, 255, 264n

Jacob, E. F., 52n
Jacobs, Jane, 576
Jacobs, Norman, 382n
Jaffee, Frederick S., 473
Jahn, Julius, 134n
Jakobson, Leo, 560
James, William, 567

Janowitz, Morris, 266, 289, 291, 355, 422
Jaspers, Karl, 340
Jencks, Christopher, 349n, 353, 359
Johnson, Elmer H., 414n, 419
Johnson, Harry M., 447n
Johnson, Lyndon B., 275, 445
Johnson, Tom L., 175
Jones, A. R., 111
Jones, H. Stuart, 41n

Kain, John F., 286n, 492n
Kando, Thomas M., 386
Kaplan, Max, 380n
Karp, David A., 111
Kasun, J. R., 428n
Katz, Alfred, 466n
Katz, Edward M., 527
Katz, Herbert, 370n
Katz, Marjorie, 370n
Katzman, Martin T., 352
Kaufman, Herbert, 190n
Keiser, Kenneth K., 459n
Keller, Susanne, 316, 580
Kenniston, Kenneth, 309
Kent, Jr., T. J., 524
Kerner, Otto, 407
Kerr, Clark, 251
Key, Jr., V. O., 275n
Keyes, Scott, 572n
Khodzhayev, D. G., 532n
Khorev, B. S., 532n
Kilbourne, Edwin D., 462
Klapper, Joseph T., 267n
Klotsche, Martin, 355n
Klotz, Heinrich, 588
Koenig, Rene, 321
Kolb, William L., 383n
Kocko, Gabriel, 254
Komarovsky, Mirra, 103, 380n
Kopan, Andrew T., 363
Kosa, John, 465n
Kramer, John, 294n
Kramer, Judith R., 248
Kramer, Michael S., 196n 249n
Kriegsberg, Lowis, 432
Kristof, Frank S., 512
Kroeber, Alfred, 95
Ktsanes, Thomas, 294n
Kuroda, Toshio, 159n
Kurtz, Richard A., 104
Kuudten, Richard D., 398
Kuznets, Simon, 254

Labowitz, Sanford, 394
Ladner, Joyce A., 320
Lalli, Michael, 294n
Lamberg-Karlovsky, C. C., 33n
Lamberg-Karlovsky, Martha, 33n
Lampman, Robert, 438n

Landberg, Hans H., 510n
Lang, A. Scheffer, 497n
Lang, Gladys Eugel, 269n, 277
Lang, Kurt, 269n, 277
Lange, David L., 280
LaNowe, George R., 359n
Lanwerys, Joseph A., 363
Lanmann, Edward O., 336
Lasswell, Harold E., 234n
Laurenti, Luigi, 135-136
Lavine, Robert A., 438n
Lazarsfeld, Paul F., 268
Leacock, Eleanor B., 449
Lebeaux, Charles N., 454n, 458
Lee, Robert, 341
Lefkowitz, Monroe M., 263n
Legget, John C., 257
Lemkau, P. V., 466n
Lenski, Gerhard E., 236, 256, 335-336
Lerner, Daniel, 160, 260, 344
Lerner, Monroe, 462n, 465
Leventman, Seymour, 248
Levin, Melvin R., 363
Levine, Edward M., 376n
Levine, Robert A., 588
Levy, Mark R., 196n, 249n
Lewis, David T., 143n
Lewis, George H., 386n, 387
Lewis, Harold M., 521n
Lewis, Hylan, 320n, 443
Lewis, Oscar, 101, 111, 432
Lewis, Peter A., 571
Leiberson, Stanley, 129n
Lineberry, Robert L., 201n
Lipset, Seymour M., 250, 251n, 256
Lipsky, Michael, 409n, 488n
Litwak, Eugene, 305
Lockard, Duane, 192-193
Lohrmann, Carl B., 516n
Long, Norton, 221n
Loomis, Charles P., 92n
Lopreato, Joseph, 257
Loosley, Elizabeth W., 293, 315n, 422
Lowenthal, Leo, 382, 386n
Lowry, Ritchie P., 202
Loyd, Anne, 22
Lubove, Roy, 452n
Lundberg, George A., 380
Lunt, Paul S., 239n
Lurie, Harry L., 461n
Lynch, Kevin, 568-569
Lynd, Helen, 233
Lynd, Robert, 233

McCarty, Donald J., 363
Maccoby, Michael, 16n
McCord, William, 433-434
MacDonald, Austin F., 177n
Macdonald, Dwight, 383

McEntire, Davis, 485n
McHennan, Barbara N., 410n
McInerny, Mary Alice, 380n
Maclaglen, Michael, 59
McLuhan, Marshall, 386
McKay, Henry, 400
McKechnie, Samuel, 378n
McKelvey, Blake, 74n, 76n, 87
McKenzie, Roderick D., 78n, 114, 115, 119n, 287-288
McKinney, John C., 92n
McMullen Roy, 388
Madison, James, 198
Maine, Henry Sumner, 95
Malik, C. P., 550n
Malisz, Boleslaw, 553n
Manzin, William, 544n
Mannheim, Melvin L., 523n
Manning, David W., 388
Mantoux, Paul, 67n
Mar, José, 546
Maris, Ronald W., 401n
Marks, Robert, 584n
Martin, Walter T., 221
Masotti, Louis H., 18n, 296, 407n
Matre, Marc, 128
Matras, Judah, 165
Mattison, Berwyer F., 461n
Matza, David, 399-400
Mayer, Jean, 472
Mayer, Kurt B., 254
Mayer, Robert L., 460
Mayer, Robert R., 460n
Marx, Karl, 68, 235, 238
Mead, Margaret, 380-381
Meadows, Paul, 111
Meier, Richard L., 260, 407
Mellart, James, 26n
Mendelsohn, Harold, 267, 269
Mermelstein, David, 232
Merriam, Charles E., 346
Merton, Robert K., 399
Meyer, Carol H., 475
Meyer, Donald B., 332n
Meyer, John R., 491, 492n, 512
Meyers, Edward W., 189n
Michels, Roberto, 196
Miller, Delbert C., 197, 202, 232
Miller, Herman P., 434
Miller, Lillian B., 375n
Miller, S. M., 251, 433
Miller, Walter, 432n
Miller, Zane L. 18, 88, 429
Mills, C. Wright, 197, 238n, 255
Minter, Horace, 100-101
Mizruchi, Ephraim, 111, 315
Moberg, David O., 334n
Moffit, Louis W., 63n

Monsen, Jr., Joseph, 274n
Montagne, Joel, 255
Montgomery, Paul A., 510n
Monts, J. Kenneth, 287
Moore, Harry E., 129
Moore, Wilbert E., 235n, 544n, 557
Moran, William, 473
Morphet, Edgar L., 361n
Morris, J. Carroll, 503n
Morris, R. N., 102
Morris, Robert, 539, 588
Morris, William, 520
Mosca, Gaetano, 196
Mott, Frank Luther, 262n
Mowrer, Ernest R., 115, 401n
Moynihan, Daniel P., 247-248, 319-320, 423, 439, 475, 480n, 532n, 564n, 570
Mumford, Lewis, 28n, 59, 365, 575
Mundy, John H., 59
Murdock, William, W., 512
Murray, Walter I., 351
Musgrove, E., 308n
Musial, John J., 189n
Myrdal, Gunnar, 474, 550n, 576

Nader, Ralph, 221
Nagle, John M., 362
Nagpaul, Hans, 588
Nash, Jr., William W., 562n
Nam, Charles B., 159n
Naville, Pierre, 546n
Needleman, Carolyn E., 526n
Needleman, Martin L., 526n
Neill, Peter, 569
Nelson, Claud D., 334n
Netzer, Dick, 223n, 232, 497
Neugarten, Bernice L., 240n, 257
Newby, Howard, 200
Newman, Joseph W., 273n
Nicol, Helen O., 440
Niebuhr, Reinhold, 274
Nimkoff, Meyer F., 302n
Nisbet, Robert, 5
Nixon, Raymond B., 263n
Nobile, Philip, 512
Norris, Frank, 567
North, C. C., 241n
Nortman, Dorothy, 551n
Norwitch, Bernard, 532n
Novak, Michael, 426
Nye, Russel, 383n

Odum, Howard W., 129
Ogburn, William F., 298
Oglethorpe, James, 72
Ohlin, Lloyd E., 437
Olson, David J., 409n
Orleans, Leo A., 553n

Osborn, Frederick J., 530-532
Owen, Wilfred, 490n

Palen, J. John, 541-542
Pareto, Vilfredo, 141-142, 196
Park, Robert E., 79, 114, 116, 119n, 135n, 287, 567
Parker, Stanley, 388
Parkin, Frank, 257
Parkins, Maurice F., 552n
Parrington, Vernon Louis, 565
Parsons, Talcott, 275n, 303n, 307, 314
Passow, A. Harry, 350n
Paulu, Burton, 264
Pearl, Arthur, 430n
Peck, Sidney M., 220n
Penn, William, 72
Pepys, Daniel, 378
Perin, Constance, 539
Perloff, Harvey S., 522n, 535n
Perry, Clarence A., 576, 580
Peterson, David M., 419
Peterson, Theodore, 262
Peterson, William, 142n
Pettigrew, Thomas F., 320n, 353n
Pfaff, Anita, 449
Pfaff, Martin, 449
Pfeffer, Leo, 341
Piggott, Scott, 26n
Pike, Frederick B., 325n
Piono, Zygmunt, 553n
Pirenne, Henri, 59
Pitts, Jesse, 308n
Piven, Francis F., 449
Plato, 565
Poland, F., 41n
Polanyi, Karl, 43
Polsby, Nelson W., 198n
Poplin, Dennis E., 111
Powicke, F. M. 54n
Prakash, Ved, 560
Price, Don K., 175
Pusalker, A. D., 34n
Pynoos, Jon, 512

Quant, Jean B., 91
Quinn, James A., 116-117, 121n, 133n
Quinney, Richard, 406n

Rachfal, Felix, 327
Radcliffe-Brown, A. R., 95
Rainwater, Lee, 421-422, 433
Ramsey, Charles E., 363
Rashdall, Hastings, 54
Reichly, James, 188n
Redfield, Robert, 37, 92, 95, 422
Regan, D. E., 22
Redi, Margaret G., 478n

Rein, Martin, 460n
Reiner, Thomas A., 578
Reisinger, E., 41n
Reiss, Jr., Albert J., 12n, 98n, 142n, 286, 410n
Reissman, Leonard, 163-164, 243, 250, 257, 294n, 433n, 449
Reps John, 521
Revelle, Roger, 510n, 511
Richardson, A. E., 367n
Richardson, Harry W., 142n
Rice, Tamara Talbot, 367n
Ridenour, Nira, 469n
Rider, Norman B., 7n
Riemer, Svend, 50n
Riesenberg, Peter, 59
Riesman, David, 191-292, 308, 315n, 381, 385-386, 422
Rischin, Moses, 483n
Ritschl, Albrecht, 338, 340
Rivet, Paul, 37
Roberts, Donald F., 280
Robertson, H. M., 327-328
Robin, John P., 544n
Robson, William A., 22
Rock, V., 296
Rodwin, Lloyd, 531-532, 563n, 564, 569-570
Roebuck, Janet, 88
Rogers, David, 200n, 202
Rohrer, John H., 320n
Rose, Arnold M., 222n, 466n
Roseborough, Howard, 315n
Rosenberg, Bernard, 38n, 383n, 388
Rosow, Irving, 312n
Rossi, Peter H., 241, 242, 432
Rousseau, Jean Jacques, 565
Rudd, R. L., 503n
Russell, Josiah C., 59
Ryan, Charles O., 361n

Saarinen, Alice B., 376n
Saarinen, Eliel, 576, 583
Samuelson, Kurt, 328
Sandberg, Neil, 535n
Savic, Niclos, 553n
Sayre, Wallace S., 190n
Scaff, Alvin H., 558n
Scammon, Richard M., 194n
Scanlon, David G., 363
Scanzoni, John H., 320n
Schafer, Robert, 512
Schaffer, Albert, 201n
Schaffer, Ruth Connor, 201n
Schaflander, Gerald M., 434
Schaller, Lyle E., 338n
Schelling, Thomas C., 403
Schelsky, H., 360
Schlesinger, Arthur M., 75n
Schmandt, Henry J., 182n, 190n, 227n, 449

Schmid, Calvin F., 134n, 163
Schneider, Eugene V., 218n
Schneider, Herbert W., 339
Schneider, Lewis M., 495
Schnore, Leo F., 101n, 111, 122n, 134n, 137, 258, 286n, 288, 425n, 548
Schorr, Alvin L., 440, 485n
Schrag, Clarence, 134n
Schramm, Wilbur, 259, 262, 279, 280
Schumach, Murray, 489
Schuman, Howard, 104n
Schur, Edwin M., 322, 403n, 419
Schussheim, Morton B., 480n
Schwartz, Barry, 296
Schwirian, Kurt P., 128, 137
Scott, Mel, 534
Scott, Sir Walter, 382
Scott, W. Richard, 213n, 461n
Scullard, H. H., 41n
Seeley, John R., 293, 315n 422, 482n
Seldes, Gilbert, 384, 384-385
Sellin, Thorsten, 399
Sennett, Richard, 88, 246n, 303, 550n
Sexton, Patricia, Cayo, 354
Shank, Alan, 363
Shanker, Albert, 359
Sharp, Harry, 134n
Shaw, Clifford R., 115, 400
Sherman, Richard B., 449
Shevky, Eshref, 162
Shils, Edward, 382, 384
Shinn, Roger L., 361n
Short, Jr., James F., 394n, 401
Siebert, Fred S., 262
Siegal, Paul M., 241n
Sim, R. A., 293, 315n, 422
Simmel, Georg, 92, 96-98, 289, 294, 422
Simmons, Leo, 310
Simpson, David, 428n
Sinclair, Upton, 274, 275
Singer, Milton, 325n
Sjoberg, Gideon, 46, 59, 108, 237n, 548
Sklare, Marshall, 318n
Sloan, Lee, 184
Smelser, Neil J., 557
Smerk, George M., 495n
Smillie, Wilson G., 462
Smith, Adam, 66
Smith, Joel, 104
Smith, Richard Austin, 406n
Sundquist, James L., 435n, 437
Smythe, Hugh H., 351n
Snow, C. P., 361
Soberman, Richard M., 497n
Soleri, Paolo, 576, 584-586
Sorauf, Frank J., 193n
Sorokin, Pitirim A., 92, 94-95, 94n, 466n
Speck, Gayle, 355n

Spectorsky, A. C., 289
Spilerman, Seymour, 409n
Srole, Leo, 246
Stanford, Quentin H., 165
Stark, Rodney, 333, 339
Starr, Paul, 357n
Steffens, Lincoln, 80
Stein, Clarence 532, 533n
Steiner, Gary A., 218n, 267n, 268n
Sternlieb, George, 439
Still, Bayard, 569
Stokes, Charles, 482
Stone, Gregory P., 111
Straus, Anselm, 588
Stub, Holger R., 258
Sullivan, James B., 510n
Sumner, William Graham, 95
Sussman, Leila, 355n
Sussman, Marvin B., 304n
Sutherland, Edwin H., 399, 405-406
Suttles, Gerald D., 106, 291, 485
Sutton, Francis X., 215n
Sweet, David C., 209n
Sweetser, Frank, 128
Sykes, Gresham M., 399-400

Taeuber, Karl E., 134n, 157n, 449, 483
Taeuber, Aliva F., 156n, 351n
Tawney, R. H., 327
Taylor, Miller Lee, 111
Teller, Azriel, 510n
Terzo, Frederick C., 544n, 559n
Theodorson, George, 116n, 137
Thernstrom, Stephan, 88, 550n
Thomas, W. I., 398-399
Thometz, Carol E., 202
Thomlinson, Ralph, 119n, 137, 463
Thompson, Edgar T., 129
Thompson, Elizabeth, 294
Thompson, Eric S., 38n
Thompson, James W., 58n
Thompson, Warren S., 143n
Thrasher, Frederick M., 114
Thut, I. N., 344n
Tibbits, Clark, 310n
Tillich, Paul, 340
Tisdale, Hope, 11
Titmuss, Richard, 253, 458
Tocqueville, Alexis De, 198, 566
Toffler, Alvin, 376n
Tönnies, Ferdinand, 92, 92-93, 299n, 422
Toynbee, Arnold, 17n, 367n
Trachtenberg, Alan, 569
Trattner, Walter I., 475
Trecher, Harleigh B., 476
Treinman, Donald J., 242n
Tringham, Ruth, 4, 550n
Trow, Martin, 357

Trueblood, Felecity M., 559
Tumin, Melvin M., 234n, 235
Tunnard, Christopher, 520-521
Tunstall, Jeremy, 276n
Turner, John F. C., 547
Turner, Ralph, 32n, 43, 348n

Uccello, Paolo, 370
Ucko, Peter J., 4, 550n
Ulanov, Barry, 387
Ullman, Edward L., 125-127, 125n, 127n
Ullman, Morris B., 553n
Underhill, Jack A., 560

Van Arsdol, Maurice D., 163
Vance, Rupert B., 129
Veblen, Thorstein, 235
Vickers, Sir Geoffrey, 466n
Viessman, Jr., Warren, 504
Vogel, Ezra F., 308n
Volkart, Edmund H., 461n
Von Eckardt, Wolf, 576
Voss, Harvin L., 419

Wade, Jerry L., 511
Wagner, Robert, 41n, 486
Walberg, Herbert J., 363
Walker, Mabel, 223n
Wall, Donald, 586
Wallerstein, Immanuel, 357n
Walton, Clarence, 581n
Walton, John, 199
Waris, Heikki, 222n
Warner, Jr., Sam B., 487n
Warren, Earl, 352
Warner, Sam B., 484, 535n
Warner, W. Lloyd, 239, 245, 246
Wattenberg, Benjamin J., 194n
Weber, Adna, 68n
Weber, Max, 59, 235, 243, 324, 326-328, 588
Weber, Michael P., 22
Webster, Donald H., 522n
Weicher, John, 209
Weinstein, Gerald, 355
Wellington, Harry H., 221n, 232
Wells, Alan, 263n, 280
Westoff, Charles F., 7, 472n
Wheatley, Paul, 4
Wheeler, Mortimer, 44

Whelpton, Pascal K., 471n
White, David Manning, 265n, 383n, 384
White, Lucia, 566n, 567
White, Morton, 566n, 567
White, Winston, 275n
Whitehead, Alfred North, 339
Whitman, Walt, 567
Whittick, 530-532, 539
Whyte, Jr., William F., 293, 422, 567
Whyte, William H., 567
Wickham, E. R., 328n
Wilcox, Clair, 213n
Wilensky, Harold L., 278, 379n, 384, 454n, 458
Willhelm, Sidney M., 137
Williams, Marilyn, 162
Willman, John B., 535n, 537n
Wilner, David M., 485
Wilson, Bryan, 341
Wilson, James G., 192, 286n, 491n
Winter, Gibson, 341
Winter, Jr., Ralph K., 221n, 232
Wirt, Frederick M., 202
Wirth, Louis, 92, 98-99, 114, 115, 289, 294, 422
Wohl, M., 492n
Wolf, Eleanor, 136n
Wolfe, D. M., 320n
Wolfinger, Raymond E., 196n
Wood, Robert C., 19, 180n, 194n, 356
Woytinsky, E. S., 154n
Woytinsky, W. S., 154n
Wright, Charles R., 265
Wright, Frank Lloyd, 576, 580-581
Wright, Henry, 532
Wrong, Dennis, 154n
Wycherley, R. E., 39, 44

Yinger, J. Milton, 330n, 341
Ylvisaker, Paul N., 438
Yoels, Wlilliam C., 111
Yorburg, Betty, 322
Yuan, Y. F., 554n

Zimmerman, Carle C., 92, 94-95, 129, 466n
Zimmerman, Joseph F., 184
Znaniecki, Florian, 398-399
Zola, Irving K., 465n
Zorbaugh, Harvey W., 115
Zucker, Paul, 366
Zurcher, Jr., Louis A., 476

SUBJECT INDEX

Advertising and public relations, 270-273
  social utility of, 273
  strategy of, 272
Advisory Commission on Intergovernmental Relations, 227
Advocacy planning, 526-527
Aged, 312-313
Aging, 309
Agrarian stratification, 236
Air pollution, 499-502
Antiurban bias, 564-567
  in United States, 565-567
Aoudaghast, 51
Architecture, 366-369
Arcology, 584-586
Art and leisure, 365-388
Arts, patronage of, 373-377
Associations, voluntary, 102-107
Atomistic family, correlates of, 301-303
Automobile traffic, 492-493

Bakke decision, 446
Barlow Commission, 527
Bedford, Duke of, 518
Beyond the Melting Pot (Moynihan and Glazer), 423
Birth rates, 151-153
Botticelli, 370
Brass Check, The (Sinclair), 274
British urban planning, 520-521
Brown v. Board of Education, 352
Bryan, William Jennings, 565-566
Bureaucratic organization, 212
Business and industry, 212-218

Cairo, 108-109
Capitalism, industrial, 69-71
Carolingians, 47
Carter Administration, 466
Cathedral cities, 52-53
Central business district, 119
  future prospects, 208-209
Centralization, 131-132
Charity, organized, 452
Chichén Itzá, 37
China, early urbanization, 25, 35-36
Church and social change, 328-332
Church, today's, 323-340. See also Religion
Cities, large, 8-9
Cities, rise of, 31ff
City, 572
City and federal government, 188-190
City-manager, 174
City of the Sun (Campanella)

City, The (Park and Burgess)
City planning, 516-522
  in antiquity, 516
  in Baroque Age, 517-519
  in industrial era, 518-522
  in Renaissance, 516-517
Civil disorders, 407-409
Civilization and urbanism, 25-44
Civil Rights Act of 1964, 444-445
Civil rights movement, 442-448
Class consciousness, 251-256. See also Stratification
Commission type of local government, 174
Communication and urban life, 259-280
Communist mass media, 264-265
Concentric-zone theory, 119-122
Consumer, 221-222
Cooperative federalism, 189-190
Corporation, business, 212-214
Crack in the Picture Window, The (Keats), 289
Crestwood Heights (Seeley, Sim, Loosely), 293-294
Crime, 400ff
  in city, 400-413
  coping with, 413-418
  "crime wave" today, 410-413
  white-collar, 405-406
  and youth, 412
Criminal offenses, 392ff
  by city size, 396
  rural and urban, 393
  in SMSAs, 392
Culture;
  mass, 381-386
  of poverty, 431-433

Delinquency Areas (Shaw), 115
de'Medici, Cosimo, 374
Democracy in America (Tocqueville), 566
Democratic Party, 193-194
Demographic transition, 150
Demographic perspective, 139-165
Demography, urban, socio-cultural characteristics, 159-162
Demonstration Cities Act of 1966, 526
Dependency ratio, 143-144
Developing nations:
  migration, 159
  urbanization of, 541-559
Deviance, 391-419
  and city size, 395-397
  and law enforcement, 413-418
  and urbanization, 391-397
  social conception of, 398-400
  sources of, 397-400
Dillon's rule, 185
Dispersion, 132-133

Division of Labor in Society (Durkheim), 94
Divorce, 302

Ecological impairment, 497-511
Ecological processes and structures, 128-136
Ecological perspective, 114ff
    classical school, 114-115
    neoclassical, 116-117
Ecology, urban, 113-137
Economic affairs, 212-222
    and consumer protection, 221-222
    and labor unions, 218-221
    see also municipal finance
Economic competition, 213
Economic concentration, 77-78
Economic development, 209-212
    by community development corporations, 211-212
    by private enterprise, 211
    by public agencies, 209-211
Economic Opportunity Act of 1964, 435-439
Economic organization, 212-222
    and business corporation, 212-213
    and government intervention, 214
    and occupations, 215-218
Economy and the city, 204
Economy, urban, 203-232
    changing locational pattern, 207-209. *See also*
        Central business district
    components of, 203
    historical change, 204
    metropolitan character, 206-207
    regional character, 204-206
Education:
    of economically disadvantaged, 349-355
        and administrative change, 354-355
        and compensatory education, 351-352
        and desegregation, 352-354
    purposes of, 344-348
        and approved behavior, 347
        and cultural values, 345-347
        and vocational skills, 348
    urban, 343-363
        and central-city school system, 358-359
        and cleavages in community, 348-349
        ethical problems of, 361
        objectives, 344-348
        and occupations, 359-361
        and urban university, 355-357
Egyptian urbanization, 25, 26n
Elderly, participation in labor force, 311
Elitism and pluralism, 199-201
Environment, 497-511. *See also* Ecology
Environmental pollution, 498-505
Erech, 26
Essay on Population (Malthus), 68
Ethnicity in urban life, 422-427
    and family forms, 317-321
    future of, 426-427

persistence of, 423-426
and racial subordination, 248-250
and stratification, 246-250
Exurbanites, The (Spectorsky), 289

Families Against the City (Sennett), 315
Family Disorganization (Mowrer), 115
Family:
    in developing countries, 299-300
    forms, 299, 317-321
    functions, 298
    ideological significance of, 299
        and American population problem, 470-472
        and national policy, 472-473
        and voluntary efforts, 472-473
    psychosocial implications, 314-316
    "stem" type, 305-306
    in transition, 299-300
    and urbanization, 297-303
Fertile Crescent, 31
Fertility:
    and community size, 152
    rural-urban differentials, 151-152
Finance, municipal, 222-231
    current crisis in, 231
    expenditures, 227-231
    revenues, 222-227
        and property tax, 223-225
        and other taxes, 225-226
    tax reform, 226-227
    and New York City's current program, 230
Florence, medieval, 54-55
Fragmentation, metropolitan, 177-182
    consequences of, 180-181
    sources of, 177-180
Families Against the City (Sennett), 315

The Gang (Thrasher), 115
Gemeinschaft, 92-93
Gesellschaft, 92
Ghana, medieval urbanization, 51
Ghetto, The (Wirth)
Gold Coast and the Slum, The (Zorbaugh)
Government: local:
    reform of, 182-185
        by consolidation, 182-183
        via cooperative approach, 182
        by two-level approach, 183-184
    relations with state and federal government, 185-190
    systems of, 170-171
        English model, 170
        French form, 170-171
        Soviet variety, 171
Governmental intervention, 214-215
Government and politics, urban, 169-202
    American background of, 171-173
    and home rule, 171-172

Government and politics (*continued*)
   promotion of trade in, 172
   and populism, 172
  municipal forms of, 173-174
   commission variety, 174, 176-177
   city-manager type of, 174-176
   mayoral type of, 173-175
Greek city-states, 39-40
Guaranteed annual income, 439-440

Hammurabi, 30
Harappa, and early urbanization, 26, 34
Haussmann, Baron George-Eugène, 519
Health, 461-466
  administration of, 461-469
  and disease and death, 464
  and further goals, 465-466
  improvement of in urban areas, 463-466
  and infant mortality
   see also Mental illness
  rural-urban differences, 463
Hobbes, Thomas, 264
Horace, 374
Housing, 478-481
  and America's housing picture, 479-481
  and FHA, 487
  future of, in urban areas, 488-489
  and rehousing, 485-488. *See also* Urban renewal
  substandard, 478-479
Hugo, Victor, 373

Income Distribution and Social Change (Titmuss), 253
Income and stratification, 243, 254-255
Indus Valley, ancient cities of, 25, 33-35
Infant mortality, 155
International Development Association, 555
Introduction to the Science of Sociology (Park and Burgess), 114
Industrial urbanization, 61-88
  agricultural progress, 63-64
  and capitalism, 69-70
  in England, 66-71
  legal changes in, 65-66
  and preindustrial city, 62-66
  and railroads, 68-69
  technological innovation, 64-65
  in United States, 74-76
Interest groups, 190-192
  and political parties, 190-196
International organization and urban planning, 554-559
  via bilaterial and multilateral agencies, 554-555
  and United Nations, 557-559
   Center for Housing, Building, and Planning, 557-558
   International Labour Organization, 558-559
   and UNESCO, 558
  World Bank in, 555

Jackson, Andrew, and antiurbanism, 565-566
Jefferson, Thomas, and antiurbanism, 262, 565-566

Jericho, 26n
Jewish family, 318
Jobs, *see* Occupations
Jonson, Ben, 378
Justice, administration of, 413-418
  criminal courts in, 416-417
Juvenile delinquency, *see* Crime; Deviance

Kefauver, Estes, 405
Khruschev, Nikita, 266
Kin network, 303-306
  and atomistic theory, 305-306
  functions of, 304-305
  and social class, 304-305
Kinship in city, 297-323
  and aging, 309-313
  and women, 313-314
  and youth, 306-309
  see also Family
Kucinich, Dennis, J.

Labor and consumer, 218-222
Labor unions, 218-221
La Cosa Nostra, 404-405
LaGuardia, Fiorello, 175
Lancashire County, industrial revolution in, 64-65
Land Use in Central Boston (Firey), 117
Land-Use Digest, 573
Lao-tze, 36
La Vida (Lewis), 432
Law Enforcement Assistance Administration, 417-418
Le Corbusier (Charles Edouard Jeanneret-Gris), 578-579
Lee, Richard C., 198-199
Leisure in postindustrial society, 379-381
Le Notre, Andrew, 517
Lever, W. H., 270
Levitt, William, 534-535
Life and Labour of the People of London (Booth), 453
Lippi, Filippo, 370
Literacy and urbanization, 160-161, 343
Local government, U.S., merits and shortcomings of, 174-177
Logue, Edward, 438
Lonely Crowd, The (Riesman), 308
Looking Ahead (573)
Los Angeles water system, 180-181

Mafia, 404-405
Maecenas, Gaius, 374
Maggie: A Girl of the Streets (Crane), 567
Malthus, Thomas, 68
Managerial plan of city government, 175-176
Man, Mind, and Land (Firey), 117-118
Mann, Horace, 330
Marshall, Thurgood, 443-444
Mass media, *see* Media, mass
Mass transit, 493-495. *See also* Transportation
Mayas, ancient cities of, 25, 37-39

Mayoral plan of city government, 173-175
Media, mass, 259-280
  efforts at reform, 278-279
  impact of, 265-269
  organization of, 262-265
  and public interest, 273-279
  as social system, 275-278
Medieval city, Europe, 49-51
Megalopolitan America, 82-85
Mental health, 466-470
Mental illness, coping with, 468-470
"Metropolis and Mental Life, The" (Simmel), 96-98
Metropolitan dominance, 131. See also Regionalism
Metropolitan development, 209-212
Metropolitan regionalism, 76-77. See also Metropolitan
  dominance
Michelangelo, 55
Middle class, rise of, 70-71. See also Stratification
Middletown (Lynd and Lynd), 233-234
Migration, U.S., 155-159
Mill, John Stuart, 262
Milton, John, 262
Minorities and poverty, 430-431. See also Ethnicity in
  urban life
Mitchell, John, 446
Mobility, social, 250-251
Modernization, 61ff, 107-110. See also Developing na-
  tions, urbanization of
Modern urban stratification, see stratification
Mohenjo-Daro, 26, 34
Montaigne, Michel De, 381
Morgan, J. P., 376
More, Sir Thomas, 380
Mortality, 153-155
Motor-vehicle registration, rural-urban differences, 493
Multiple-nuclei theory, 125-127. See also Ecology, urban
Museums, 369-370

Napoleon III, 519
Nash, Beau, 369
National Advisory Commission on Civil Disorders,
  407-409
National Advisory Commission on Criminal Justice Stan-
  dards and Goals, 415
National Housing Act of 1934, 486
National Housing and Development Act of 1974, 574
National League of Cities, 573
National planning, 561-588
  objectives of, 569-570
  opposition to, 564
National Planning Association, 573
National planning, U.S., 562-564
National Research Council, 574
Negative income tax, 440-441
Neighborhood, The (McKenzie), 115
New Towns, British, 527-532
  reservations about, 530-531
New Towns, U.S., 532-535
Nixon, Richard M., 266, 441

Occupational education, 359-361
Occupational prestige and stratification, 241-243
  international uniformity of, 242-243
Occupational problems, 217-218
Occupations:
  and income, 243
  urban, 215-218
    executives, 215-216
    labor, 216
    professionals, 216
Old Testament, 565
Organization Man, The (Whyte), 293-294, 567
Other America, The (Harrington), 434
Over-urbanization, 543, 546-548
  in Africa, 545-546
  in Latin America, 544-545

Pascal, Blaise, 381
Peer groups and youth, 306-307
Peter the Great, 367
Petrarch, 370
Philadelphia Gentlemen (Baltzell), 244
Pittsburgh, social problems of, 79-81
Pluralistic power structure, 198-199
Poetics, The (Aristotle), 370
Political party types, 194-196
Politics and class competition, 195-196
Population, 139-165
  and age, 142-143
  composition of, 142-148
  distribution of, 140-142
  and fertility, 151-152
  growth of, 148-149. See also Demographic transition
  and levels of living, 161-162
  life expectation of, 154
Population problems, U.S., 470-472
Population, urban, world areas, 7
Poverty:
  in American cities, 428-434
  programs, 434-442
Power:
  organization of, 167-280
  structures, 196-201
Preindustrial stratification, 237
Preindustrial urbanization, 56-58, 62-66, 72-74
President's Commission on Law Enforcement and Ad-
  ministration of Justice, 415
Property tax, 223-225
Protestant, Catholic, and Jew (Herberg), 333-334
Protestantism and industrial city, 326-328
Prourbanism in America, 567-569
Public Administration Review, 573
Public assistance, 458-460
Public Health Service Act, 573
Public Relations, see Advertising

Race, see Ethnicity
Race relations cycle, 135
Railroads, 68-69

Recreation and entertainment, 377-381
Redevelopment, 522-527
    and empirical research, 523
    flexibility of, 524
    and planning process, 524-526
Regionalism, metropolitan, 129-130. *See also* Metropolitan dominance
Regional planning, 535-538
Regional Plan of New York and Its Environs, 536-537
Rehousing and development, 484-488
Religion:
    conservatism in, 330-332
    institutional system, 323-341
    in urban milieu, 324-325
Relocation planning, 527-535
Rembrandt, 375
Republic, The (Plato), 565
Republican Party, 193-194
Research, urban, 572-575
Riots, *see* Civil disorders
Retirement, 311
Rich Man, Poor Man (Miller), 434
Robbery rates, for selected cities, 396
Role structure of family, 299-300
Roman cities, 40-42
Roosevelt, Theodore, 452

St. Louis, regional dominant, 204-206
Savonarola, 55
Schools:
    and cleavages in urban community, 348-349
    desegregation of, 352-353
    years in, rural and urban, 345
Sector theory, 122-125
Secular City, The (Cox)
Secularism, 57-58, 332-333
Segregation, 133-134
Sex ratio, 144-147
Shakespeare, William, 372
Sixtus V, Pope, 517
Slums, 482-485
Social-area analysis, 162-164
Social gospel movement, 331-332
Social security, 457-460
Social welfare, 451-476
    development, 452-454
    expenditures for, U.S., 455
    philosophy of, 454-457
Sociocultural urbanism, U.S., 79
Sociological Tradition, The (Nisbet), 5
Solidarity, mechanical and organic, 94
Standard consolidated area (SCA), 10-11
Standard metropolitan statistical area (SMSA), 9-10
Stephenson, George, 69
Stokes, Carl, 195
Stratification, social, 233-258
    in cities at present, 239-240

in industrial city, 238
and style of life, 243-246
Suburbanization, U.S., 78, 284-286
Suburban community, 283-296
Suburban style of life, 107, 288-293
    and limited liability, 291
    quasiprimary character, 289-291
    subcultural properties, 292-293
    and triballike conformity, 291-292
Suburban Trend, The (Douglass), 288
Suburbia, growth of, 284-286
Suburbs:
    demographic characteristics, U.S., 286-287
    future of, 295
Succession, 135-136
Sumerian cities, 31-33

Tax Review, 572
Theatres, 371-373
Theological reconstruction, 339-340
Theory of the Leisure Class, The (Veblen), 235
Tigris-Euphrates Rivers, early urbanization, 25
Timbuktu, 51
"To Fulfill These Rights" (White House Conference), 320
Tomorrow: A Peaceful Path to Real Reform (Howard), 520-521
Trade, underworld, 402-404
Transportation, 489-497. *See also* Mass transit
Transportation problem, urban, 490-492
Typology, rural-urban, 91-111

Unionization, 218-221
Urban agglomerations, 8-9
Urban concept, 9-12
Urban diffusion, medieval Europe, 48-49
Urban fringe, 130
Urban Institute, 573
"Urbanism as a Way of Life" (Wirth), 98-99, 289
Urbanism, constructive, 19-20
Urbanism, detrimental effects of, 17-19, 31
Urbanization, contemporary, 5ff
    and economic development, 14
    and individual enhancement, 16-17
    in newly developing areas, 548-552
    preindustrial, 45-59
    and rational organization, 14-16
    renewal in Europe, 47-51
    and stratification, 236-238
    in U.S., 7, 71-76
Urbanized area, 9
Urban place, 9
Urban planning, 522-538
    in colonial America, 518
    in Communist countries, 552-554
    preindustrial, 516-518
    in under-developed areas, 541-560
    in Washington, D.C., 518
Urban planning reform, 520-522

Urban reform, U.S., 81-82
Urban renewal, 485-488
  legislation of, 486-487
  weaknesses of, 487-488
Urban Review, The, 572
Urban revolution, 26-28
Urban Social Structure (Beshers), 136
Urban university, 355-357
Urban way of life, 12-17
U.S. Agency for International Development (AID), 555
Utopia (More), 380
Utopias, modern, 576-587
Urban trend, modern, 5-8

Vermeer, Jan, 375
Village enclaves in city, 108-109
Virgil, 374
Voting Rights Act of 1965, 445

War on Poverty, 435-439
Washington Year 2000 Plan, 536
Water problems, 503-504
Watt, James, 62

Wealth, distribution of, 252-256
  in Britain, 253-254
  and levelling up, 254-255
  in United States, 252-253
Wealth of Nations (Smith), 66
Weberian hypothesis, 327-328
Welfare expenditures, U.S., 455
Welfare ideal, 454-457
Welfare state, 454-456
Who Governs? (Dahl), 198-199
Women:
  elderly, 147-148
  in labor force, 147
Wood, John, 369
Working-Class Suburb (Berger), 294
World Bank, 555

Youth, urban, 306-309
  and independence, 306-307
  and migration, 156
  and youth culture, 308-309
Yugoslavian New Towns, 532

Zone in transition, 119-120